Lugosi

LUGOSI

*His Life in Films, on Stage,
and in the Hearts of Horror Lovers*

GARY DON RHODES

with a foreword by
F. Richard Sheffield

McFarland & Company, Inc., Publishers
Jefferson, North Carolina, and London

Frontispiece: Portrait of Lugosi from Universal Studios' Edgar Allan Poe chiller, *The Black Cat* (1934).

The present work is a reprint of the illustrated case bound edition of Lugosi: His Life in Films, on Stage, and in the Hearts of Horror Lovers, *first published in 1997 by McFarland.*

LIBRARY OF CONGRESS CATALOGUING-IN-PUBLICATION DATA

Rhodes, Gary Don, 1972–
    Lugosi : his life in films, on stage, and in the hearts of horror lovers / Gary Don Rhodes with a foreword by F. Richard Sheffield.
       p. cm.
    Includes bibliographical references and index.

    ISBN 0-7864-2765-5 (softcover binding : 50# alkaline paper) ∞

    1. Lugosi, Bela, 1882–1956.   2. Actors — Hungary — Biography.
3. Motion picture actors and actresses — United States — Biography.
I. Title.
PN2859.H86L836   2006
791.43'028'092 — dc20   96-46131
[B]

British Library cataloguing data are available

©1997 Gary Don Rhodes. All rights reserved

No part of this book may be reproduced or transmitted in any form or by any means, electronic or mechanical, including photocopying or recording, or by any information storage and retrieval system, without permission in writing from the publisher.

On the cover: Bela Lugosi, circa 1930s *(Photofest)*

Manufactured in the United States of America

McFarland & Company, Inc., Publishers
  Box 611, Jefferson, North Carolina 28640
    www.mcfarlandpub.com

For Mom and Pop

Table of Contents

Foreword by F. Richard Sheffield — ix
Preface and Acknowledgments — xi

I. Lugosi, the Man — 1
  1. A Biography — 3
  2. Personal Data — 39
      Imperial-Cameo Pictures Corporation
         Biographical Information (1935) — 39
      Residences — 42
  3. Lugosi in Court — 47
  4. Lugosi in Politics *by Frank J. Dello Stritto* — 57

II. Lugosi, the Performer — 65
  5. Feature-Length Films — 67
      Hungary — 67
      Germany — 70
      United States and United Kingdom — 74
  6. Serials — 146
  7. Stage Appearances — 152
      Hungary — 153
      United States, United Kingdom and Canada — 165
  8. Vaudeville and Live Appearances — 188
  9. Radio Performances — 201
  10. Television Appearances — 208
  11. Other Celluloid Appearances — 212
  12. Newsreels and Short Subjects — 215
  13. Unfinished Projects and Canceled Roles — 217

III. Works By or About Lugosi — 227
  14. Reviews, Articles, and Pamphlets — 229
  15. Books — 278
      Biographies — 278
      Film and Stage Histories — 279
      Novels and Film Novelizations — 282
      Published Scripts — 286
  16. Quotations from Lugosi — 288

17. Quotations About Lugosi ... 300
18. Quotations About Lugosi and Karloff ... 309
19. Sources and References ... 321
    Audio Sources ... 321
    Visual Sources ... 324
    Documentary Sources ... 327
    Multimedia Sources ... 332
    Theatrical References ... 332
    Animation References ... 332
    Visual References ... 333
    Verbal References ... 336
    Television Sources ... 336
    Archival Sources ... 337

IV. Critique and Appreciation ... 339
20. Image, Apparition, and Icon ... 341
21. Authority Survey ... 354
22. Advertising Lugosi ... 359
23. Collecting and Merchandising Lugosi ... 363
24. Unmasking the Mysteries ... 370

V. Index ... 385

Foreword

I must have been about 11 on one Saturday afternoon in 1948 when my usual matinee gang — Brian, his little tagalong brother Mike, his sister Sue, and a few others — were off again. This time it was to the Ritz at Wilshire and La Brea, to see *Abbott and Costello Meet Frankenstein*. We loved them. But this particular Saturday resulted in much more than I had ever bargained for. We went for the first time to see Lugosi, and boy, was I hooked. I longed to see more. I was fascinated, enthralled ... his hands, his voice, his gestures.

In the early 1950s, Bela's career was practically finished. There were few of his films on the limited television programming of the time, and next to nothing at the theaters. By the time we got into junior high, a small knot of other kids who had also been zapped — Dave Katzman, Norman Fist, Tony Kemp, and Mike Spencer — and I got together to see everything we could get our eyes on. So, since we could not see enough of him on the screen, we started a project to meet him in person.

Kemp had an uncle working on *The Hollywood Reporter*, and through him we were able to get a phone number that was supposed to have been Bela's. After gathering much courage, and following a lot of "You make the call" ... "No way, you do it" ... "What am I gonna say?" ... the call was made, only for us to be totally deflated. It was Lugosi's nephew's home. But, he was totally cooperative and gave us his uncle's correct phone number. We couldn't go through all that torment again, so we consulted with my grandmother, who wrote for *The Pasadena Star*. To her, it was no problem to call and ask Mr. Lugosi for an interview for her newspaper. But ... deflated again. Lugosi advised her that he had recently been ill and was not giving interviews (this was at the time his fourth wife, Lillian, had just left him).

More time ... more gathering together of nerves ... and Dave called, and I took the phone and said that we were a small group of fans. Lugosi quickly invited all of us to come on over to the apartment the following Saturday ... a seemingly endless wait for the day that finally came. We put together our collections of stills and organized a million questions. We were all about 14 by then, and Norm's indulgent mother drove us to the Baldwin Hills. In the hallway: "There it is, the door on the left" ... "You knock" ... "Hell no, you" ... "Okay, we'll knock together." When the door opened, we were staring upward, mouths agape, and there he was ... Lugosi.

This initiated a three-year glory trail that took us on undreamed-of adventures: lifting Bela's water bottles into his dispenser, lunching on stale toast and goulash, visiting Lake Elsinore and the set of *You Asked for It*, taking a midnight tour of former residences, instituting a new and official fan club, campaigning for Universal to refilm *Dracula* in 3-D, getting coached in Lugosi's acting techniques, watching his films with him on television, organizing his desk and being paid for it with articles of clothing from his films, transcribing his "true story," viewing *Moby Dick* at the Pantages.

Through Bela I met Tor Johnson, John Carradine, Lon Chaney, Jr., Basil Rathbone, Mack Sennett, Jack Oakie, and many others. I ditched classes to visit the set of *The Black Sleep*, spent hours admiring Lugosi's pipe collection, the summer cape, the winter cape, the Dracula ring, and the scrapbooks. I remember so well the unmade Ed Wood projects like *The Vampire's Tomb*, reciting and recording scenes from *Dracula*, and visiting the Tarbox Theatre. There was Paul Marco and Eddie Wood and Forrest Ackerman and Hope Lugosi. There was scotch and beer and the unemployment office. And finally, there was his funeral. In addition to acting as a pallbearer, I tucked some of his "El-Stinko, El-Ropo" cigars into his pocket. We laughed and cried for three years. What adventures we had. What excitement. What a rare privilege.

Forty years have passed since our friendship took place, and I try to recall and share those precious moments. It saddens me that so many details are gone, as I see what would have given Bela unbounded joy: a resurgence of interest in his work. Though I knew him as a close friend, I have read the Lugosi writings from a myriad of perhaps well-meaning critics, experts, and intellects who analyze and dissect Bela's personal and public life. I have found some of their opinions annoying, and others quite interesting and thought-provoking. But to me, as an adolescent, he was an icon. Lugosi definitely remains one of a kind.

I thought I knew so much about my friend through my own experiences and the things I've read, ranging from Lugosi's own scrapbooks to magazines like *Famous Monsters* and all prior biographies. Yet in reading Rhodes's work, I couldn't put it down. There's so much here that hasn't been told yet. It even accompanied me to the bathtub. It's a must for any Lugosi fan and also for any serious student of cinema history.

F. Richard Sheffield
León, Guanajuato, Mexico
1995

Preface and Acknowledgments

Henry Miller once likened memories to images that have lost their vividness, "like time-bitten mummies caught in a quagmire." Yet some of my early cinema memories, while fragmented, retain their strength. Three women, dressed in white and swaying at the command of a figure dressed in evening clothes and cape, illuminated on a small kitchen television as glowing jack-o'lanterns lit the neighborhood streets. Pudgy Lou Costello, shivering as the same actor arose from a coffin in McDougall's House of Horrors into a Saturday morning television. Sunday afternoon with barbecue and Mom and Dad and *The Wolf Man* (1941). Images like this remain not merely as extensions of old nightmares, but they also spark the same intense curiosity that sends characters in such films through secret doors no one in his or her right mind would ever open.

My oldest sister, Lee, once purchased a children's paperback on horror films at a grade school book sale. Even though I could not yet understand the text, the photos etched themselves into my mind. Later, as I began to read, I discovered a slim volume on *Dracula*, replete with stills of Bela Lugosi. The name struck me as unforgettable, and my library card soon obtained for me not Dr. Seuss but volumes on vampire legends and horror stories. And, even if I became addicted to flashy science fiction films at the local theater, the black-and-white character of Universal's horror films danced on in my dreams, strengthening their grasp.

Scenes from *White Zombie* (1932) affected me the most, particularly the closing sequence when Lugosi introduced actor John Harron and me to the "angels of death." Fortunately, after smuggling a copy of a Warren publication called *Vampirella* into the house, I discovered *Famous Monsters of Filmland*. The magazine's mail-order outfit, Captain Company, allowed me to purchase various Lugosi materials thanks to Mom turning my coins into money orders. Yet, a culminating point in my move toward Lugosi research came through meeting the man behind *Famous Monsters*, Forrest J Ackerman.

Just barely a teen, I once noticed a man and woman walk by my family in a Sheraton Hotel lobby. Though I knew of no reason why it would be him, I recognized the man as Ackerman. Seeing them again moments later convinced me; I literally chased after the duo, though an elevator door closed before I could board. Taking the next one up, I scanned several hallways, but to no avail. At the front desk, I managed to ask if "my friend Forry Ackerman" had arrived. Amazingly, Forry was soon on the house phone saying hello, and moments later he returned to the lobby to meet me. He really did become my friend after that evening, always encouraging me to do this kind of book.

My enthusiasm for Lugosi then became not a kind of idolatry or even a fascination with the mythology of horror, but rather an embodiment of my interests in film history. If Francis Ford Coppola once likened Bram Stoker's novel *Dracula* (1897) to the history of cinema, I believe much the same could be said of Lugosi. An investigation into his career yields insight into early narrative film, Germany's Weimar period, and the transition the cinema made from the stage. Lugosi represents the genre-specific nature of the classical Hollywood paradigm, as well as the fickle qualities of the public that consumes it. The tragic aspects of his life and career highlight the inevitability of the star system: the dark spaces of silence between the frames.

After meeting Ackerman, I began publishing a newsletter called *The World of Bela Lugosi*. Within a short time, subscriptions increased to something like 1,000, with such persons as Richard Sheffield, Carroll Borland, and others on the mailing list. Lugosi's son endorsed the newsletter, which soon featured authors like Robert Bloch (of *Psycho* fame) and Gregory Mank. Important work in uncovering Lugosi films and unpublished photographs brought in subscribers from over eight countries, including numerous archives. When the newsletter ceased, I was somewhat saddened. After many address changes, I find it amazing to receive so much mail inquiring about the newsletter, though it's unfortunate that several such letters have probably been returned to their writers.

Even before the newsletter, I planned to write a book on Lugosi, receiving encouragement from many of his costars and acquaintances. The earliest incarnation would have been *The Bela Lugosi Scrapbook*, a place to deposit much rare information and photographs. Multiple ideas followed, until, years later, this volume became a reality. Various problems have blocked many planned Lugosi books from reaching print, ranging from stolen manuscripts, uninterested publishers, and tales as grisly as any horror story.

My intentions for this volume, however, are clear. Rather than write a personal biography or narrative critical study, I hope to catalogue as much information on Lugosi's career and life as feasible in one text. A biographical chapter and an essay on Lugosi's image act as a foundation for the remaining empirical data. Furthermore, the chapters have been arranged so that the reader can dip into a specific area of interest without being encumbered by the entire work. Arrangement of information is chronological whenever possible to place the film, performance or written work within the context of his life. Just as I believe researchers will profit from the existence of such a text, I hope Lugosi collectors and students will find a book that compiles much needed information in one place, as well as previously unavailable data. From this can come not only a deeper empirical understanding of Lugosi, but also the ability better to analyze his life and career.

The alert reader will note the spelling of Bela appears sometimes as "Béla." Lugosi himself used the diacritical marking until the midforties, at which time he seemingly dropped it. This book adopts the same preferences. However, references to works are intended to reflect the spelling use in original titles, as are quotations from period publications.

To avoid the plague of mistakes and misinformation that have marred many works in the horror genre, primary sources have been used to the greatest extent possible. Trade papers, magazines, newspapers, letters, fliers, posters, court records, films, radio shows, and every conceivable kind of original period source have been put to use. Furthermore, the memories of many who knew the actor professionally and privately also have become important to this work. The compilation of such data was possible only due to the great many wonderful people who freely gave of their time, their research, and their photos to help. Perhaps my only regret is that footnotes for every fact become nearly impossible, as they would double the length of an already massive volume.

I must thank the following persons for their important assistance: Jason Asenap, the late Robert Bloch, the late Carroll Borland, Tom Brannan, Conrad Brooks, Bart Bush, Dr. Juan Jose Camacho Romo, Mario Chacon, Spencer Christian, Cinema Collectors, Michael Copner, Lee and Tray Cox, Marc Cramer, Bill Crawshaw, Brad Crouch, Louise Currie, *Cult Movies* magazine, Rick Daub, Michael J. David, Marta Dobrovitz, Harald Dolezal, Geraldine Duclow, Rajnai Edit, Philip R. Evans, the late William K. Everson, Don Fellman, *Filmfax* magazine, Phillip Fortune, Alex Gordon, Richard Gordon, JoAnne Graham, Rudolph Grey, Gordon Guy, Jon Hand, Don Harrell, Dr. Tibor Herczeg, Roger Hurlburt, Ronnie L. James, the late Steve Jochsberger, John Johnson, John Jones, Bill Kaffenberger, Eugene Kirschenbaum, Dr. Andor C. Klay, Patric Knowles, Howard W. Koch, Leonard Kohl, the late Reginald Le Borg, Frank Liquori, Jim Lowder, the late Arthur Lubin, Bela G. Lugosi, Jim McNeely, Bob Madison, David Manners, Paul Marco, Shirley Michael, Peter Michaels, Nancy Moore, Barry Moreno, Dr. Michael Morrison, Dottie Nielsen, Gerard Noel, John Norris, Maila Nurmi, Jim Nye, Bill Obbaggy, Ted Okuda, László Ottovay, Sam Peeples, Bill Pirola, Wendy Michele Pugh, Joanna Rapf, Robert Rees, Lana Rhodes, Elizabeth Russell, Linda Ryan, Don G. Smith, Dr. John Springer, Billy C. Stagner, Bob Stovall, Vera Surányi, László Tábori, David Tambo, Brian Taves, Maurice Terenzio, Chris Todd, Johanne L. Tournier, Leonard A. Weisbeck, Sr., Mike Wilson, and Robert Wise.

Also thanks must go to the following organizations and archives: The Hungarian Film Institute of Budapest, the Orságos Széchényi Könyvtár in Budapest, the Országos Színháztörténeti Múzeum és Intézet in Budapest, the Somogyi Könyvtár in Szeged, Hungary, the Bundesarchiv in Koblenz, Germany, the Alden Public Library of New York, the Ardmore Public Library of Oklahoma, the Bizzell Library at the University of Oklahoma, the Department of Special Collections/Davidson Library at the University of California in Santa Barbara, the Fayetteville Free Library of New York, the Free Library Theatre Collection of Philadelphia, the Lobero Theater of Santa Barbara, the Margaret Herrick Library in Los Angeles, the National Park Service at Ellis Island, the New Rochelle Public Library of New York, the New York City Public Library, the Norwich Public Library of New York, the Saratoga Springs Public Library of New York, the Trenton Public Library of New Jersey, the United States Department of the Interior, the University of California in Los Angeles, and the Yonkers Public Library of New York.

I must also express tremendous gratitude to the following individuals who so freely gave of their time, friendship, and encouragement: Forrest J Ackerman, Buddy Barnett, Richard Bojarski, Robert Cremer, Michael Ferguson, Charles

Heard, Gregory W. Mank, Jean-Claude Michel, Lynn Naron, Dennis Payne, Victor Pierce, David Skal, Mario Toland, Beth Waldrop, Tom Weaver, Glenn P. White, John Wooley, and Gregory Zatirka.

In terms of numerous suggestions, proofreading, valuable clippings, and the contribution of an entire chapter ("Lugosi in Politics"), I sincerely thank Dr. Frank J. Dello Stritto. Few researchers or friends could ever surpass him or his work.

For his unending encouragement, camaraderie, and the contribution of the foreword, I owe an enormous debt of gratitude to Richard Sheffield. He is one of the most unique individuals I have ever met, and I am particularly proud to call him my friend of over ten years. His confidence counted very strongly in the completion of this text.

Finally, to Don and Phyllis Rhodes, my parents, I owe tremendous thanks, far beyond the mere dedication of this book.

With regard to everyone who helped on the project, I sincerely hope the long struggle has proved worthwhile. "'Twas a good game, Hjalmar."

Gary Don Rhodes
Norman, Oklahoma
August 1995

Lugosi. Horror. Box office. Fine. And I am horror.
— Bela Lugosi, 1939

I. Lugosi, the Man

1. A Biography

During his Hollywood heyday, Bela Lugosi once asked, "Is it mad to tell deliberate lies to serve a purpose? Lies that do not harm anyone...? If so, then chalk this down on the ledger under 'mad.'" Throughout the thirties and forties, studio publicists, fan magazines, and the actor himself certainly fabricated outlandish stories to reinvent his past. The cinema's Dracula transformed himself into one of Hollywood's most mysterious actors. Even after his death, many sources skewed the realities of his life and emphasized only his work in the horror film genre.

Lugosi's career itself spanned over 50 years, however, and represents a large body of work covering stage, vaudeville, screen, radio, and television. His personal life charted an adventure of several disparate episodes, canvassing some six countries, five marriages, and two world wars. The result provides a biography equal to that of any of the bizarre characters he portrayed. And, just as every film was bettered by his participation, so are audiences by experiencing them. Although a large number remain essentially poor cinema, the entire career presents a legacy of considerable worth that—like his own life—deserves further study.

Béla Ferenc Dezsö Blaskó was born on October 20, 1882, in Hungary, and he remained profoundly Hungarian until his death. His hometown of Lugos, located in southern Hungary, was then part of the Austro-Hungarian Empire. The town dates back to the fourteenth century, with a population of fewer that 16,000 during the actor's youth. By the late nineteenth century, Lugos featured an active wine trade and was itself the territory of Greek and Latin bishops. The beautiful Olt River flowed nearby, and some 50-odd miles away stood the ruins of Vlad Tepes's castle, the historic "Dracula" on whom Bram Stoker based his 1897 novel.

Béla's proud Magyar ancestors survived as farmers, with the name "Blaskó" recorded as early as 1627. His father, István, broke tradition to become a baker and later a banker. The family, in which Béla was the youngest son, held a respectable place in the small community. His three older siblings, László, Lajos, and sister Vilma, moved from childhood to respectable positions in life. Young Béla attended grammar school before entering the Hungarian State Superior Gymnasium in 1893. Just as István's strictly run household disagreed with Béla, so did the strain of formal education. He trudged away from home one morning, never again returning to Lugos.

"I was very unruly as a boy, very out of control," Béla once confessed. "Like Jekyll and Hyde, except that I changed according to sex. I mean, with boys I was tough and brutal. But the minute I came into company with girls and women, I kissed their hands. I kissed their hands again. With boys, I say, I was a brute. With girls, I was a lamb. Not madness, that, I submit. Rather, I like to think, the warrior and lover which are in every man ... for men, the kill; for women, the kiss."

Three hundred miles south, the mining town of Resita became Béla's destination. He traveled much of the way on foot. To make ends meet, Lugosi labored in the mines, later commenting on the horror he felt deep beneath the earth's surface. He also labored as a riveter and as a machinist's apprentice, but he quickly desired work in the theater. To the touring groups that came to Resita, however, he seemed embarrassingly uneducated. "They tried to give me little parts in their plays, but I was so uneducated, so stupid, people just laughed at me," Lugosi later recalled. "But I got the taste of the stage. I got, also, the rancid taste of humiliation."

In 1897 Lugosi again searched for something better. Traveling to Szabadka, he discovered his sister Vilma and his mother. They broke the news that István had died in 1894, shortly after losing the family savings in a financial venture. Feelings of renewed motivation caused Lugosi to enter school again in 1898, but he quit after just four months. Manual labor remained the only possibility, and for a time he sweated on a railroad. Vilma had married, and her husband eventually found work for Béla in the back of a theater chorus. Even though his lack of education remained a detriment, the 18-year-old departed with the theater company.

At Szeged — their next stop — audiences enthusiastically received Lugosi's performances. Soon, the Academy of Performing Arts accepted him, which led to a role in *Brigadier General Ocskay* in August 1902. One day later, in a play called *We're Married*, he billed himself with the last name "Lugosi," referring to his town of origin. Subsequent appearances saw him use a variety of pseudonyms, from first names like "Géza" or "Dezsö" to last names such as "Lugossy." Many plays followed in areas like Temesvar, Sibiu, and Kolozsvar. One of his more interesting roles came in 1903 with his interpretation of Gecko, Svengali's servant, in *Trilby*.

Lugosi's steps become harder to trace from 1904 to 1909, though most likely he toured provincial areas in the Austro-Hungarian Empire. By 1910, the Szeged theater employed Lugosi in a variety of roles. Critics particularly noted his unusual approach to Shakespeare, as in his interpretation of Romeo, and Béla most certainly appealed to the area's females. Among the other notable plays he appeared in during this period were *Richard III*, *Hamlet*, and *The Taming of the Shrew*. This led to work in Budapest's Hungarian Theater during late 1911 and 1912. By January 1913 Lugosi performed as a member of Budapest's National Theater, the most prestigious in Hungary.

The National Theatre had no real stars, with its members doing everything from lead parts to off-stage voices. *Cyrano de Bergerac*, Goethe's *Faust*, and more Shakespeare added to the actor's résumé. Moreover, he appeared in the plays of Hungarian masters like Szigligeti and Jókai. Yet for reasons unknown Béla bowed out in June 1914 to enlist in the army. Fighting the Russians near the border in the Forty-third Division, Lugosi showed patriotism but also a dislike for military life.

"There was a moment I could never forget," he mentioned years later. "We were protecting a forest from the Russians. All of us were cowering beneath huge trees, each man beneath a tree. A young officer, incautious, went a little way out

Lugosi appears here during his tenure at the National Theatre in Hungary.

of cover and a bullet struck his breast. I forgot the Russians were firing from their line with machine guns. Not a selfless man, I had one selfless moment ... I ran to him and gave him first aid. I came back to my tree and found that it had been blown to the heavens in heavy, crushing pieces. I became hysterical. I wept there on the forest floor, like a child ... not from fear, not even from relief ... from gratitude at how God had paid me back for having that good heart."

By 1916 Lugosi had been discharged, supposedly convincing army physicians

Lugosi (third from right) engages in conversation with friends during his latter days in Hungary.

that he was mentally unstable. The National Theatre again welcomed him, though perhaps his most important role of the era became Jesus Christ in *The Passion*, which he created on the stages of Debrecen. Surviving photographs from the play reveal Lugosi as sympathetic, benevolent, and somewhat sad, resembling the solace and pathos of a religious icon. The role differed from the suave, aristocratic look he developed in Hungary, and certainly contrasts with his later Hollywood image.

Perhaps it was those suave characteristics that attracted his first wife. On June 25, 1917, Béla married Ilona Szmik, the beautiful member of an upper-class Budapest family. Along with providing the wedding, Szmik's father very possibly funded the couple's honeymoon. Lugosi's meager postmilitary salary also forced the duo to move into an apartment directly above the Szmiks, as well as to spend time at the family's summer home. The extent of Lugosi's affections for Ilona is unknown; when the time came, however, his own career and political beliefs proved more important.

Also following the Great War, Béla's friend Alfréd Deésy persuaded him to give movies a try. The Hungarian film industry was forging ahead, despite the fact that stage actors still looked down on the cinema. Receiving only minor roles at the National Theatre possibly convinced Lugosi to make the transition. In his films directed by Deésy, Béla chose the pseudonym Arisztid Olt, the last name derived from the Hungarian river. Milhály Kertész — later known in the United

During his brief encounter with the German cinema, Lugosi (right) appeared as a hypnotist in 1919's *Slaven Fremdes Willens (Slave of a Foreign Will).*

States as Michael Curtiz, the director of *Casablanca* (1943) — helmed Lugosi's other films, for which he used the name Béla Lugosi. Budapest's Star Company — whose logo featured an ominous bat — released the Kertész-Lugosi films.

Béla continued acting with the National Theatre into 1918 but became involved heavily with the status of Hungary's cinema. Lugosi helped combine the Free Organization of Theater Employees and members of the film industry into the National Trade Union of Actors, and acted as its secretary; the group itself is generally considered the first film actors' union. Lugosi not only made it a point to give speeches in favor of actors, he also wrote politically oriented articles for such theater journals as the *Szinészek Lapja.*

Hungary itself was mired in major political problems following the end of World War I. A Communist regime headed by Béla Kun took control and received much support from Hungarian artists. Along with Kertész, László Vajda, and Sándor Korda, Lugosi was instrumental in Kun's Hungarian Council's Republic, which nationalized the country's film industry. Romanians under Miklós Horthy soon deposed the Kun government, however, leaving its supporters to be purged or jailed. Lugosi, Kertész, Korda, Pal Lukács (Paul Lukas), and others appeared on the arrest list.

"After the war, I participated in the revolution," Béla said in 1932. "Later, I found myself on the wrong side." He fled to Vienna in 1919, supposedly buried

Enjoying a meal at the Royal Hawaiian Hotel during the filming of *The Black Camel* (1931).

under a mound of straw in a cart. He then went to Germany, but, at the behest of her parents, his wife, Ilona, soon abandoned him. After she returned to Hungary, a telegram detailing her divorce proceedings arrived in Béla's hands. Quickly, however, his romantic attentions diverted to German actress Violette Napierska, with whom he had a short-lived love affair.

Still marked by its defeat in the war, Germany's artistic community strode ahead fervently. The German film industry rose in status to one of the best in the world. Expressionism influenced Weimar art, and — with *The Cabinet of Dr. Caligari* (1919) — the style took hold of the German cinema. Lugosi rapidly found work in Berlin, and even portrayed an eerie, Svengali-like hypnotist in *Slave of a Foreign Will* (1919).

Lugosi also nabbed a part in F.W. Murnau's unauthorized version of Robert Louis Stevenson's *Dr. Jekyll and Mr. Hyde*. Titled *The Head of Janus* (1920), the film also featured Conrad Veidt of *Caligari* fame. The subject matter and collaboration with the director foreshadowed Lugosi's future ties to the horror genre. Murnau later gained immortality with *Nosferatu* (1922), his pirated, cinematic version of Bram Stoker's *Dracula*.

Also curious was a two-part film based on James Fenimore Cooper's *Leatherstocking* tales, in which Lugosi played the Native American Chingachgook. Had the actor decided to remain in Germany, he could possibly have become an important

Top: Having fun in the thirties with two of his close friends, composer/musician Duci Kerekjarto (with violin) and possibly Manly P. Hall. Bottom: Lugosi on the MGM lot in 1935 with Jean Hersholt, Binnie Barnes, and (standing) Lee Tracy.

player in the film community there. Yet his relative success at finding work did not dissuade him from emigrating to the United States. From Germany Lugosi trekked to Italy. At Trieste he became third assistant engineer on a ship bound for New Orleans. Bad storms and a crew not in favor of Béla's politics plagued the five-week voyage. The result found him greatly at odds with his fellow shipmates.

"In a very heavy sea and storm, the cargo of the boat was floating in a terribly slanting position, which resulted in a delay in our scheduled arrival to New Orleans before Christmas," Lugosi once recalled. "You can imagine spending unprepared, a Christmas Eve on a slanting, floating cargo boat. I locked myself in my cabin, and the rest is too personal to me to be given to the public."

Thanks to a sympathetic engineer who apparently helped fend off the actor's newfound enemies, Béla arrived on American soil with his life. The *Graf Tisza Istvan* docked at New Orleans on December 4, 1920. He quickly disappeared from Louisiana, making his way to New York City. Hungarian Americans in the city helped prevent his possible deportation, and the United States lawfully admitted Lugosi the following March. This was early 1921, and Lugosi's feelings about the United States strengthened to the extent that ten years later he officially became a citizen.

The Hungarian theatrical community welcomed Lugosi to New York, and Béla soon organized several actors into a repertory company. He often both directed and acted in such efforts, which were staged in Hungarian. In addition, he quickly fell in love with another Ilona, this time an actress named von Montágh. Again, the marriage would not hold, lasting only a few years. Despite their shared profession, Lugosi's growing success as an actor seemingly moved him away from her affections; few details are known of their relationship. By October 1924, however, Ilona's attorney appeared before the court to enter her complaint, with the divorce finalized in February of the following year.

Béla's career definitely progressed in a more positive direction than his love life. In 1922 producer Henry Baron saw Lugosi in a Hungarian version of Madách's *The Tragedy of Man* and decided the actor was perfect for a role in *The Red Poppy*, with Estelle Winwood. Although he basically could not speak English at the time, Béla learned his lines phonetically. A young Arthur Lubin, who later directed the Lugosi film *Black Friday* (1940), assisted the actor in this regard. Allegedly, at one point the Hungarian also enrolled in an English course at Columbia University.

Though the play itself closed to poor notices, the exposure opened the door for Lugosi to his first American film, *The Silent Command* (1923). As would be the case with his later horror films, the spy tale used extreme closeups of Lugosi's eyes for effect. With the silent film still in vogue, the actor's lack of English skills was not a major handicap. After the production, the actor made several other film appearances at New York studios. Generally the parts were minor, but he took a sizable role in a drama titled *The Midnight Girl* (1925), with Lila Lee.

During the twenties, Lugosi stayed very close to the Hungarian community in a section of New York City known as Yorkville. In addition to offering a living, breathing memory of his homeland, such camaraderie perhaps added a comfort lacking in his marriage. For example, he often frequented a Hungarian men's club

The camera captures an image with a fellow actor and friend, cowboy star Buck Jones.

on Southern Boulevard and Prospect to play cards. Also, when he had nowhere specifically to go, Lugosi visited Nicholas Adler, occasionally even sleeping in the spare room at his friend's shoe repair store. And, while publicity generally dropped European diacritical markings, the actor's signature still bore the acute accent over the *e* in his given name.

The stage quickly offered more roles, such as a brief appearance in a Chicago production of *The Werewolf*, a farcical sex comedy. A year later Lugosi became the Apache for torrid love scenes in the lavish *Arabesque*. Newspapers sometimes

Though posed by an automobile, Lugosi neither drove nor held a driver's license.

referred to him as the "Hungarian Barrymore," and — despite the poor reviews thrown at such plays — critics usually singled out Lugosi's unique qualities. To an extent, Lugosi's publicity resembled the image he fashioned of his Hungarian career: suave and romantic parts in important productions.

In 1926 Hungary itself offered a general amnesty to exiled citizens, allowing Lugosi to return at will. However, he apparently did not consider the option, later even taking a special course to help pass the citizenship exam. Lugosi submitted a Declaration of Intent to become a U.S. citizen in 1928 and became officially naturalized on June 26, 1931. Apparently, he did not even consider returning to his homeland; America, on the other hand, soon extended even greater career possibilities.

By 1927 a producer named Horace Liveright considered the potential profits from an American theatrical run of the vampire play *Dracula*. A version starring Raymond Huntley as the vampire proved strong box office in Great Britain. As preparations were made for a Broadway run, however, Huntley decided against taking the role because of its small salary. By chance, Liveright heard of the dark, handsome Hungarian and, convinced of his possibilities, cast Lugosi as Dracula. The actor almost turned down the role due to the vampire's lack of dialogue.

Rehearsals began, and Lugosi soon etched his way forever into history, culture, and nightmares. Unlike the prior depictions of Stoker's novel or the London stage, Lugosi became a handsome, alluring, and sexually charged vampire. His

With an available mike to provide some audio commentary, Lugosi appears at one of his beloved soccer games. This one is presumably from the midthirties.

slicked hair, aristocratic features, and thick accent created an indelible image. After 33 weeks on Broadway, *Dracula* toured the West Coast with success in 1928 and 1929. Audiences lined up in both Los Angeles and San Francisco to experience the well-touted thriller.

"It is a marvelous play. We keep nurses and physicians in the theatre every night ... for the people in the audience who faint," Lugosi told the *Los Angeles Times*. "Only one thing I fear, that after I play this Dracula some more, I become too like him in myself. But, you understand, I am not really bad character in this role. It is a curse upon me. I am to be pitied, not condemned. I am vampire because I must...."

Movie studios took notice of *Dracula*'s stage success, with Universal considering it a potential vehicle for their cameras. Meanwhile, Lugosi became better known and attracted as many female spectators as he frightened. The Hamilton Deane and John Balderston stage adaptation itself did not feature a predominantly large part for the vampire. However, Lugosi's dark and unique personality generally moved the spotlight to his role.

Dracula's appearance in Los Angeles also opened other opportunities at film studios for the Hungarian. If not yet a star to the entire nation, he certainly attracted the attentions of actress Clara Bow. The "It Girl" became a fan after seeing *Dracula* in 1928, inviting Lugosi home after briefly meeting him backstage with Jack Oakie.

He later stayed a weekend at her Malibu cottage, and the two developed a passionate yet brief love affair. Bow apparently left a strong impression on the Hungarian, as for years he kept a large, nude painting of her.

"Women wrote me letters. Ah, what letters they wrote me," Lugosi recalled. "Young girls. Women from seventeen to thirty. Letters of a horrible hunger. Asking me if I cared only for maiden's blood. Asking me if I had done the play because I was in reality that sort of Thing. The women of America are unsatisfied, famished, craving sensation, even though it be death draining the red blood of life. It is women who love horror. Shudder and cling and cry — and always willing to come back for more."

On another occasion, Lugosi defined the fan letters that came from masculine members of the audience. "Most of the men who write are either astrologers or spiritualists," he explained. "They try to catch me up on theories." No doubt many of the men at theaters witnessed and admired in Lugosi a unique presence.

While touring the West Coast, Lugosi found company with various Hungarians of note in the film community. During the 1928 *Dracula* in Los Angeles, for example, he spent his spare time with such Hungarians as Lya de Putti, Vilma Banky, Victor Varconi, Alexander Korda, and Michael Curtiz. Movie studios also took notice, and Lugosi appeared in several films, including *Prisoners*, a part-talkie based on Ferenc Molnár's novel.

In 1929 Lugosi appeared in a sound mystery film called *The Thirteenth Chair*. Tod Browning, whose flair for atmosphere and the unusual had led him to collaborate with Lon Chaney on a series of classic silents, directed the film. The movie marked a starting place for Lugosi in the Hollywood mystery genre and also his first meeting with Browning, who later directed the cinematic version of *Dracula* (1931). The director claimed Lugosi as a major discovery for the screen.

"Would you like to know what I have found is the best way for my work toward perfecting a characterization since I have been in this country?" Lugosi asked a reporter in the late twenties. "I first get a part in my own Hungarian, thinking it out as though I were going to act it in my native tongue ... you see? I study it and seek to perfect it as though I were going to act it in Budapest for Hungarian audiences. Then, when I begin to feel quite at home in it, I begin to concentrate on the English diction, so that I may speak the part as it should be spoken for the American audiences."

Also in 1929, Lugosi married for a third time. The year before he confessed to a reporter that, as a bachelor, he was "open for business." His new bride, Beatrice Woodruff Weeks of San Francisco, came from an upper-class background, as had Ilona Szmik. "It is a true romance," Lugosi told a reporter from the *San Francisco Examiner*. "I fell in love with Beatrice Weeks at first sight." His infatuation with her took place initially in San Francisco during 1928. Though it was not a completely spur-of-the-moment romance and wedding, the two were certainly ill-acquainted when they married.

Weeks, age 32, fit the mold of a liberated flapper with a taste for bootleg liquor. If Ilona Szmik's actions had been ruled by her parents, it was the Roaring Twenties that set the stage for Weeks. The actor, on the other hand, was obviously not used to such strong individuality in his mates. The entire marriage, which began on July 27, 1929, lasted only three days. Weeks obtained an official divorce in Reno later that year, claiming to a scandal sheet that her husband maintained barbaric habits and once even slapped her in the face with a lamb chop. She also blamed Clara Bow for the breakup of the marriage. Lugosi himself believed Weeks to be too much the modern woman for his tastes; he did, however, maintain limited contact with her following the divorce.

Shortly after the couple's breakup, the stock market crashed and America's economy crumbled. The Great Depression also hit the film studios hard, and Universal was no exception. Like the other movie manufacturers, the studio needed box office success more than ever. The sound era had already been ushered into theaters with *The Jazz Singer* (1927), thus making the possibilities of turning *Dracula* into celluloid more feasible. While scandal sheets wrote of his divorce, one movie magazine claimed Béla was already being considered for the Universal's "Super-Production" of the Bram Stoker novel.

Lugosi himself told reporters that *Dracula* would make a great film, just as he saw "talking pictures" to be a great opportunity for stage actors. He lauded the technical progress of American cinema and spoke of the doom awaiting many silent screen stars. "I like your California," he told reporters in 1928, "and who knows—I may go into pictures here."

Conversely, Lugosi told reporter Fred Johnson the following year that the future held no hope for the "audibles." Taking the same stand as Charlie Chaplin, he now claimed talkies were merely a novelty. "There won't be a permanent compromise between the stage and screen," he said. "The stage will not only survive, but will increase its appeal. The flesh and blood actor will become more popular— the talking pictures already have whetted the desire to see and hear him on the stage. We will continue to have pictures—silent ones, likely—and the radio will carry the dialogue of the world's best actors in broadcasting of plays. If this doesn't satisfy, those who are within reach of legitimate theaters will have the enjoyment of the best of drama."

Even more confusing is an interview printed the day after Johnson's. "The screen will learn to draw on the vast fund of stage technique perfected through the centuries, and when it has learned this, talking pictures will become as great a medium as the stage," the actor proclaimed. Either some of Lugosi's interviewers misinterpreted his feelings on the monumental subject, or the actor was simply mired in the same confusion as much of the industry.

Dracula (1931) itself proved to be something entirely new to the American cinemagoers. Most of the U.S. horror movies of the twenties centered around deformities rather than incarnates of evil. The famed Lon Chaney, Sr., was the standard-bearer of this cinema, portraying the unfortunate *Hunchback of Notre Dame* (1923), *The Phantom of the Opera* (1925), and many others. A film of *Dracula* for American cinemagoers, with its European setting, sexual undercurrents, and the sheer, bloodthirsty terror embodied in a suave aristocrat made for not just a powerful idea but an indelible image.

Universal certainly considered Lon Chaney, Sr., for the lead, though he died in 1930 from throat cancer. Others, like William Courtenay, Ian Keith, Conrad Veidt, and Paul Muni, were also strong possibilities. Lugosi was in the group as well, but not at all the foremost choice. At one point, Universal telegrammed the actor's representatives that they simply were not interested. Lugosi actively lobbied for the part, however, even to the extent of acting as a liaison between Universal and Stoker's widow in negotiating the rights for the story. Eventually, the studio offered the actor a contract.

Universal released the finished film to several key cities in February 1931 as "The Strangest Passion the World Has Ever Known." Reviews were generally good, and — with the exception of a few audience members finding it *too* chilling — the public loved it. Lugosi's name suddenly appeared almost everywhere, with fan letters coming in far greater numbers than ever before. He arose as Hollywood's mystery man ... a masculine version of Garbo, only darker in personality. Many journalists made comparisons to the late Lon Chaney and often hyped Lugosi's birthplace, which had been so close to Transylvania.

When asked if he was a vampire himself, or if he believed in them, Lugosi responded, "I answer them both in the same way. I say I have never met a vampire personally, but I don't know what might happen tomorrow; this saves me from lying and it does not give away my trade secrets."

On another occasion, he recalled for columnist Hedda Hopper the shooting of *Dracula* through an anecdote. "This may sound like a publicity story," Lugosi began, "but during the making of *Dracula*, I had an infected finger and when the doctor cut it and it bled a little, I fainted and couldn't go back to being Dracula for two days."

Film publications definitely capitalized on Lugosi's persona as a horror star. One author, Gladys Hall, wrote a series of articles on Lugosi, building an image of him that was at least as bizarre as the cinema vampire. Such writings presented fascinating stories, but were on the whole biographically inaccurate. Yet in retrospect these tales give an important clue as to how the public must have perceived Lugosi at the height of his fame.

Lugosi's sleek, handsome look embodied audiences' image of the Count, with his aristocratic manners and evening dress. Important also was the accent Lugosi brought to the part. In 1929 he said of his voice, "Some tell me in Hollywood, 'you lose your accent, you have many parts.' Others say to me, 'you lose your accent and you will be without a part.' I do not know what to do. Then I meet my fiancée [Beatrice Weeks]. She love the accent. So I will keep it!" Long after Weeks became part of Lugosi's past, the accent remained. Years later, during a theatrical appearance in *Tovarich*, Gregory Ratoff even hopped into an orchestra pit to instruct Lugosi on controlling an accent. While the accent in his voice never disappeared, the actor's custom of placing an acute accent over the *e* in his first name ceased by the forties.

Even before the film version of *Dracula*, Lugosi understood Hollywood's habit of typing actors. "On the continent," he explained in the late twenties, "an actor gets no encouragement to proceed with his career unless he is really talented. There he is not chosen as a particular type and doomed to continue as that for all his professional career. He gains attention because he can *create* types instead of merely *being* types. Therefore he is versatile, and almost equally artistic in a variety of dramatic expressions. American acting would be better if it submitted to some such requirements. I don't speak, of course, of the John Barrymores and the Holbrook Blinns and others of the really foremost actors. They are not merely national. Like all great artists, they belong to the world."

Universal Studios made a fortune as a result of *Dracula*, though of course Lugosi never received more than his initial $3,500 salary. With its success, they grew anxious to place their new "Chaney" into more horror film productions. Universal considered a remake of *The Hunchback of Notre Dame* (1923), but instead chose Mary Shelley's novel *Frankenstein* as the next chiller. The French director Robert Florey received the project, with Lugosi slated to portray the monster. Florey did much important work on the script and even shot test footage of the Hungarian. However, Lugosi disliked the heavy makeup and the character's lack of dialogue. Historians often view the actor's reluctance to portray the monster as the greatest mistake of his Hollywood career. As a result of his decision, Lugosi soon became adrift within the same cinema genre he helped spark.

Universal later handed *Frankenstein* to director James Whale and transferred Florey to a film version of Poe's *Murders in the Rue Morgue*. The studio soon transferred Lugosi to the *Rue Morgue* set as well. An unknown William Henry Pratt— under the pseudonym Boris Karloff— essayed the role of the monster as a sympathetic but terrifying creature. Released in December 1931, Whale's film became an enormous success and created Lugosi's greatest rival. Karloff's box office appeal rapidly eclipsed Lugosi's, much to the latter's chagrin. "You see," Lugosi reminisced in his later years, "I created a Frankenstein monster for myself."

His business decisions after the success of *Dracula* also proved less fortunate. The habit of becoming involved in secondary roles or headlining B movies eventually took its toll on Lugosi's luminary status. Curiously, the trade publication *Variety* actually lauded him in May 1933, claiming, "In the past four years and two months, Bela Lugosi has landed fifteen parts as a freelance agent."

Even so, Lugosi's business sense developed into the enemy of his earnings. By October 1932, he filed for bankruptcy. The mounting debts included old rent, a year's salary for his maid, and hundreds of dollars owed to various stores. Legally, it took Lugosi some two years to finalize the paperwork. The problem, however, remained. Lugosi's tendency to spend large sums of money rapidly — embracing the belief that tomorrow would "take care of itself"— continually problematized his finances. The cause of such difficulties was not outright foolishness, however. If Lugosi enjoyed living extravagantly, it merely helped make him happy. Good times with the best of everything gnawed at his earnings and paved the way for perpetual financial troubles.

Despite his lack of formal education, he also read voraciously, placing tremendous emphasis on knowledge. Cinema newsreels and travelogues fascinated Lugosi, and he found time to peruse several newspapers each day, his favorite being the liberal *Los Angeles Daily News*. The actor devoured a multitude of magazines as well, subscribing to *Reader's Digest*, *The Nation*, *The New Republic*, *The New Masses*, *In*

Fact, Forum, and some 12 Hungarian publications. Among others, he occasionally even wrote articles for the *Magyar Jovó.*

"Knowledge is a never-ending fount," he maintained. "I have mastered many interesting courses of progress ... spiritually, economically, physically. There isn't a city or hamlet in any country in the world that I cannot immediately place its environs, its people, its habit, industries, and policies. When there is an outbreak in China," he continued, "I can readily trace the source through my researches. There is no fascination like that. To keep one's fingers on the many threads of life like a great harp and follow their many vibrations ... that is my greatest joy."

In 1932 Universal released Florey's *Murders in the Rue Morgue* after much cutting. The end product became inferior to both *Dracula* and *Frankenstein.* Yet, in this instance, Florey cannot necessarily be blamed. He successfully fought for period costumes and Expressionist sets. As with *Dracula* (1931) and many of Lugosi's "classics," however, *Rue Morgue* remains flawed. Despite such problems, his characterization of the mad Dr. Mirakle retains much strength.

More important to the Lugosi canon is *White Zombie* (1932), a low-budget film made by the Halperin brothers. Though Lugosi later regretted accepting a tiny salary for what became a hit film, *White Zombie* offers one of the finest playgrounds for his acting style. Lugosi's strong presence, combined with what occasionally bordered on overacting, needed freedom in dreamlike settings that allowed villains to dress in black, represent complete evil, and thus act as the antithesis of all that is "normal." A stark, fairy-tale mood still surrounds this minor classic of the cinema. *White Zombie* is thus one of his best films, containing scenes allegedly directed by Lugosi himself.

In addition to film work in 1932, he also appeared in a stage production of *Murdered Alive.* The tale gave Lugosi the opportunity not only to act, but also to exploit his talent as a sculptor. The plot called for a clay likeness of his head, so producer Arthur Collins commissioned Lugosi to sculpt it himself. At that time, the actor's sculptures attracted interest at various exhibitions. "I have seriously studied sculpture, not only for its own sake, but because it teaches many things about posture and line when applied to stage technique," Lugosi explained to a journalist. "With a knowledge of sculpture an actor can put his personality across the footlights without saying a word."

Lugosi also attested to the importance of the arts in his acting: "Dancing is another art which helps the actor to acquire ease and the grace of manner which is so essential upon the stage. Speech should be musical, and the more an actor knows about singing, the better will he be able to apply its principles to the speaking voice. Of course a knowledge of painting helps an actor in many ways, as proper color schemes for costumes and makeup are so essential in adding a touch of reality to his interpretation."

The following year, on January 31, Béla wed 20-year-old Lillian Arch, a bookkeeper. The duo eloped to Las Vegas, where they were married by Judge William E. Orr. Lugosi gave his residence as San Bernardino and attempted to conceal his identity; Lillian claimed to be 21. Despite three decades separating their ages,

Lillian endured as his bride for some 20 years; the marriage became the most successful marriage of the actor's life. Lugosi's intense love for her seems clear, even if he persisted with his dominating, Old World attitudes toward women. His jealousy aggravated other difficulties and slowly caused the marriage to disintegrate.

Lugosi discussed her by mentioning, "I pick out everything my wife wears. I like to see her in simple things. I don't like exotic things on women. When we were first married, I stopped my wife from using makeup. I did it, she will tell you, very gradually and very delicately."

His film releases of 1933 included Paramount's *Island of Lost Souls*, a gruesome story based on an H.G. Wells novel. In it, Lugosi wore heavy makeup and spoke few lines, playing a Frankenstein-style monster with even less screen time. The film remains one of the most grisly movies produced in Depression-era Hollywood. No doubt Lugosi preferred *International House* (1933), a comedy featuring W.C. Fields, George Burns, Gracie Allen, and Rudy Vallee. Yet he wasted much talent on childish serials and lampooning his own image with Betty Boop, helping decrease his credibility as a serious, versatile actor.

At the same time, Universal Studios planned various films for Lugosi, many to costar Boris Karloff. The first of these became *The Black Cat* (1934), which had little to do with Edgar Allan Poe or black cats. Lugosi's character was essentially a "good guy" juxtaposed against Karloff's devil-worshipping villain. The sadistic tale came to life in an ultramodern setting; the overt Bauhaus style complements the odd but classic horror film.

On June 5, 1934, *Variety* announced that Lugosi had signed with Universal for an additional film, as well as an option for three more. While preparing for more "KARLOFF and Bela LUGOSI" films (as the screen billing read), Lugosi worked in numerous movies at several other studios. More B films like Monogram's *The Mysterious Mr. Wong* (1935) soon made their way into the Lugosi filmography. If such movies were themselves inconsequential, together they slowly helped build an image of an essentially B actor.

In 1935 Lugosi also reunited with director Tod Browning for a remake of Browning's *London After Midnight* (1927). The exotic Carroll Borland — a young friend of Lugosi's — played his vampire daughter in the new version. The two had very limited dialogue, and a "cheat" ending exposed them for fake children of the night. Additionally, fear of censorship caused an incestuous relationship between the two characters to fall onto the cutting room floor. Nevertheless, Lugosi's last film under Browning's direction teems with an atmosphere equal to that in their earlier collaboration on *Dracula* (1931).

The same year Lugosi accepted a special honor from Los Angeles: a commission as reserve captain in the Los Angeles Police. Department Mayor Shaw commended Lugosi's "splendid leadership of Los Angeles' colony of Hungarians." The actor also received a badge that represented his "civic mindedness." His overall commitment to the Hungarian community of California proved very strong, with the actor not just an "easy touch" for a friend in need, but also a standard-bearer for the culture and rights of his fellow Hungarians.

Lugosi also believed strongly in the opinions and rights of lower-echelon crew members. He often cited the "working men" as his friends, overcoming racial barriers to befriend African American actors like Clarence Muse. In 1933 his dedication to the craft of acting even swept him into the struggle for a Hollywood film union. Along with Boris Karloff, James Gleason, Ralph Morgan, and several others, he founded the Screen Actor's Guild. For the most part, however, his work remained anonymous; perhaps experiences in Hungary with the National Trade Union of Actors and the Horthy regime plagued his memories to the extent that he kept a low profile.

However, Lugosi's unexpected interest in a dude ranch did not go unnoticed by the press. As well as mentioning the idea on a personal information form in 1935, Lugosi purchased some property near Hangtown for that purpose. His friend and fellow actor Buck Jones, who also owned land in that area, helped select the site. Though the idea of a "Lugosi ranch" never came to fruition, it seemed a far cry from the usual "haunt" of a screen menace.

Universal soon unleashed the villain to pair with Karloff again in *The Raven* (1935), and, though it had little resemblance to Poe, the film captures a number of Lugosi's most overt emotions and gestures. While less stylish than *The Black Cat* (1934), *The Raven* genuinely becomes a tour de force for the Hungarian. However, Karloff still received top billing on the credits, and *Variety* offered his name that year as a Universal "contract star." The studio considered Lugosi a mere "featured player," with his Hollywood status showing further disintegration.

Following Poe, Lugosi sailed on July 5, 1935, for England and *The Mystery of the Mary Celeste*. Lugosi's first British film offered the part of a haggard seaman, a great departure from his average Hollywood roles. Lugosi believed it to be a "wonderful story" and enjoyed his stay in England. "They pay all the money in the world in London," he exclaimed. "I don't get half as much in Hollywood."

Despite his glowing comments, Lugosi rejected a contract for additional work in the country. Staying in Britain meant his four beloved dogs faced a six-month quarantine; he refused to be parted from them. The actor and wife Lillian also planned to visit Hungary during their stay overseas. However, studio commitments in Hollywood forced him to cancel the trip. Though he definitely had other opportunities to visit his homeland, Lugosi never did. Perhaps he feared that too many changes had occurred. Budapest remained important in his memories; he did not want to ruin it by seeing the city's and country's changes.

After returning to American soil, he rushed to the West Coast for the next "KARLOFF and Bela LUGOSI" film. *The Invisible Ray* (1936), however, resulted in more of a Karloff film than a team effort. The story created a sympathetic but decidedly supporting part for Lugosi. This juxtaposition of status is most obvious in movie posters for the film in which the Karloff name towers greatly over the "...and Bela Lugosi." While trying to capitalize financially on Lugosi's association with horror, Universal considered Karloff the true star.

The same year also brought sequels to both *Dracula* (1931) and *White Zombie* (1936), but neither included Lugosi. Instead, a wax bust and dummy took his place for *Dracula's Daughter* (1936). Lugosi was a headstrong, multitalented individual who wanted to branch into areas other than tales of terror. Yet as he found himself unable to escape the clutches of horror, he must also have realized what situations like *The Invisible Ray* and *Dracula's Daughter* meant. His status within the genre eroded, while other roles outside horror seemed almost impossible to obtain.

"I am definitely typed, doomed to be an exponent of evil, but I want sympathetic roles," Béla once said. "Then perhaps parents would tell their offspring, 'Eat your spinach and you'll grow up to be a nice man like Béla Lugosi.' As it is, they threaten the children with me instead of the bogey-man." He mentioned on another occasion, "This typing is overdone. I can play varied roles, but whenever some nasty man is wanted to romp through a picture with a wicked expression and numerous lethal devices, Lugosi is suggested. Why, they even wanted to cast me as the Big Bad Wolf in *The Three Little Pigs*!"

As with his days in the Hungarian community of New York when he produced plays out of his own tenacity, Béla hoped to form his own production company. While common years later, the practice was almost unknown in the thirties. Lugosi planned *Cagliostro* as the first venture of the fledgling operation, hoping with each project to establish roles better suited to his talents. But, a lack of financing caused this idea eventually to fall apart. Another opportunity to escape typecasting evaporated.

Meanwhile, pressbooks for *The Invisible Ray* and other films referred to Lugosi as "the only star in Hollywood who does not own an automobile." Though somewhat inaccurate (he owned a car, but only Lillian drove), such publicity attempted to set him apart from the average cinema actor. "I take no part in the so-called night life of Hollywood," Lugosi proclaimed. "Life is too grim and cruel to permit such frittering away of time that might be better spent in its rebuffs."

Lugosi automatically distanced himself from others with such comments as these: "I am a stern taskmaster over myself, disciplining my mind no less than my body. Often I take long hikes through the hills before dawn, and each day I walk between five and ten miles. My only meal of the day that is worthy of the name is evening dinner, at which I eat one pound of meat, either boiled or broiled, green vegetables and fruit. My morning and noon meals consist only of fruit and vegetable juices, and I eat no starchy food whatsoever."

Greater career problems arose when Universal Studios and others halted production of horror movies following Great Britain's ban on such films. The United States had often seen various moral and religious groups cry out against the sinister cinema of Lugosi, Karloff, and others, but studio revenue had never been hurt by such minor protests. The British government's involvement posed a more frightening threat to Hollywood than any role Lugosi ever portrayed.

By May 1936 horror films found themselves disappearing from Universal's production schedule, with the London representative for the studio warning executives to avoid potential conflict with the British censors. England's prohibition meant the loss of important overseas ticket sales, with Universal believing that profits within the United States alone would not make such films worthwhile. Actors like Karloff moved to character roles in other genres, but Lugosi was left with almost no work. Universal brought an end to his option with *Postal Inspector* (1936), a relatively uninteresting crime story that praised the U.S. Postal system.

A West Coast stage version of *Tovarich* in 1937 encouraged the actor, who received strong reviews in his nonhorror part. The Tanforan racetrack even named one horse race after Lugosi while he was appearing in San Francisco, with the Hungarian consul and "distinguished members of the colony" honoring Lugosi in the same city. The Federation of American-Hungarian Societies turned out en masse when *Tovarich* played Los Angeles, with the actor no doubt pleased by the attention from his fellow countrymen.

To help stave off unemployment, Lugosi's agency published advertisements informing producers who thought Lugosi's name meant horror that they were in "*error*." And, as far as his popularity went, the program for *Tovarich* claimed that Lugosi held the "distinguished reputation of having one of the largest fan followings of most actors ... he receives from four to eight and twelve dozen fan letters two and three times a day...." Unfortunately, the fan mail numbered less than claimed; what little did arrive at studios apparently did not impress them.

"I wouldn't expect them to remember I played a Spanish lover in *The Red Poppy* in New York fifteen years ago, or everything from *Hamlet* to *Lilliom* in Budapest ... comedy, tragedy, tragi-comedy ... everything old Polonius named," Lugosi told the *San Francisco Call-Bulletin*. "But perhaps after *Tovarich*, they'll call me for something half-way civilized ... no Draculas, White Zombies, Chandus, or 'Mysterious Mr. Wongs' I hope."

The phone, however, stopped ringing entirely. Horror remained taboo, and *Tovarich* inspired no real succession of offers. "Why is Bela Lugosi jobless?" movie columnists asked, as Lugosi himself certainly must have. Except for a Ralph Byrd serial, no work came as the calendar moved toward 1938. Financial strain haunted him even more when Lillian gave birth to their son, Bela G. Lugosi, on January 5, 1938. Actor's Relief helped pay for the birth, further shattering the Hungarian's pride.

Columnist Louella Parsons mentioned that "one of the largest auto service concerns in Hollywood and one to whom the industry has paid thousands threatened to take the unpaid tires from [Lugosi's] car ... he was in a state of near collapse expecting the child to be born and no way to get the expectant mother to the hospital." Parsons, however, heightened the drama; even with tires, Lugosi did not have a license to drive. Ironically, 1938 also became the first year *The World Almanac* listed him as a film star.

"Horror, to me, is sitting, as I sat, night and day, day and night, by the telephone, thinking, 'Now comes the call ... now ... now ... now!' Horror, to me, is knowing that if the call did not come, there would not be food in the ice-box, nor light nor heat nor a place for my unborn baby to lay his head, nor a roof over the head of his mother. There is no agony like it," Lugosi commented after his period of unemployment lifted.

Yet Béla's career resumed life not due to a new and groundbreaking role but rather because of a prior performance. An autumn 1938 rerelease of *Dracula* and *Frankenstein* caused long lines and crowded theaters. The inspired reissue began at Beverly Hills' Regina Theatre in August. Packed crowds watched the films until 6:00 A.M. the following morning, with audience members driving from as far as San Diego, Fresno, and Stockton to experience the chills.

In the early forties, Lugosi and his fourth wife, Lillian, look to see some unknown scenery.

Lugosi soon made live appearances at the Regina, and Universal began sending innumerable prints to other theaters. New York's Rialto experienced its best business in a year with *Dracula* and *Frankenstein*, which also resulted in the second-best opening in that theater's history. Sensational ticket sales occurred across the country, with several thousand would-be patrons in Salt Lake City breaking through police lines, smashing a box office, and bending the front doors in order to witness the horror.

"One day, I drive past and see my name and big lines of people all around," Lugosi happily proclaimed. "I wonder what [it] is [they are] giving away to people ... maybe bacon or vegetables. But it is the comeback of horror, and I come back."

Universal Studios finally realized how much money could be mined from horror in the United States alone. Trades in October 1938 announced that the studio whisked *Son of Frankenstein* into production with Basil Rathbone, Boris Karloff, and Lugosi. Despite the success Lugosi achieved through the revival of *Dracula*, however, the studio took advantage of the actor's situation and signed him to a meager salary, intending to keep him on the lot as little as possible.

He took a relatively small part as the broken-necked Ygor, an evil associate of the Frankenstein Monster. Director Rowland V. Lee allowed Lugosi to develop the character on his own, with the part gradually becoming larger and larger. Very unlike his usual aristocratic and sophisticated appearance, Lugosi's Ygor remains a testament to the versatility many critics claim he lacked. For once, Lugosi successfully moved away from his Dracula image. By January 18, 1939, Universal signed him to a new, five-year contract.

Less than three hours after inking the document, Béla bought back his six beloved dogs. He had been forced to sell the malamutes during his dry period. Furthermore, as a show of his goodwill, Lugosi deposited $1,000 during July into a bank fund to repay an anonymous donor of that same sum. This came after Lugosi attempted for two months to find his temporary benefactor.

"It all happens, you see, when the baby comes," Béla explained to inquirers about his comeback. "It is like the proverb the peasants have in Hungary ... God makes a place in the pasture for the new lamb. Now we have a small house. I do not have to telephone from room to room to find out where's my wife. Not if I had millions would I go back to the old way."

With demand for him rising, Lugosi replaced Peter Lorre as a foil for the zany Ritz Brothers in *The Gorilla*, and sailed for England in late March 1939 for a grisly dual role in *The Dark Eyes of London*. Returning to the United States at the end of April sent him quickly back to Universal, where he tried to destroy the world in *The Phantom Creeps* serial. He also happily accepted a dramatic part opposite Greta Garbo in MGM's *Ninotchka*. Though Lugosi's part as a Russian was minor, it pleased him to appear in a romantic comedy.

"It took Mr. Lubitsch just ten minutes to change the whole course of my screen existence," the actor said of his film with Garbo. "I think *Ninotchka* will show producers that I can play straight characters acceptably and thus take me out of the rut of horror into which I've been typed. Not that I'm ungrateful to *Dracula* and the rest. But the trouble is that horror pictures go in waves and the actor in them has a couple of years of idleness between the waves. Right now they are in the ascendant and I'm in demand. But when producers decide it's time to stop horror for awhile, nobody ever thinks of poor Lugosi as a business man, a lawyer, or even a janitor in a picture."

During 1939 Lugosi also stayed for a time in New York to guest star on a couple of radio broadcasts, with reporters chasing after him for interviews. "I go back to Hollywood," he told the journalists. "Here is too dear to stay. I live at this hotel for bluff's sake ... to impress you boys from the press. But, God, how it costs! Every time I drink a glass of water, there goes another quarter!"

The forties started with Lugosi climbing further back into the spotlight. Although nabbing more and more film roles, however, he usually found himself playing either supporting parts at the majors or leads at poverty row studios like Monogram. Moreover, despite his enthusiasm over *Ninotchka*, Lugosi remained in horror films. The genre refused to release its grip on his career. The decade began with the last Karloff-Lugosi teaming at Universal, *Black Friday*, but casting changes left Lugosi with a minor part. Béla was ill-suited for his part as a gangster, but he received much attention in newspapers and fan magazines for supposedly being hypnotized to act out a death scene more effectively.

Lugosi in a snapshot with Sterling Holloway and Paulette Goddard. Presumably this photograph is from their coinciding appearance on a 1944 episode of radio's *Command Performance*.

The actor's impatience for work generally meant he frequently changed agents. Though he may have received poor advice from some, the flux in representation itself caused problems. In 1938, for example, the William Stephens, Inc., Agency represented Lugosi; for 1939 the Hollam Cooley Agency handled him; and by 1942 the William Morris Agency assumed the responsibility. The following year he again moved, this time to the Kline-Howard Agency.

Béla hoped to play the lead in 1941's *The Wolf Man*, but instead Universal gave the actor a token role as a gypsy. Lon Chaney, Jr.— bearing the name of his famed father—took the title role and quickly arose as the new horror sensation of World War II cinema. Lugosi shared screen time with him again in *Ghost of Frankenstein* (1942), as well as *Frankenstein Meets the Wolf Man* (1943). In the former, Bela reprised his role as Ygor; in the latter, he portrayed the role he had turned down 12 years earlier: the Frankenstein Monster. Shadows of Mary Shelley's creature no doubt haunted Lugosi's ego as he mechanically stalked and terrified villagers on Universal's back lot.

While portraying the monster, Lugosi collapsed on the set under Jack Pierce's 35-pound makeup. Physicians ordered him home to recover, though they noted the cause as merely "exhaustion." In addition to such outward incidents, Lugosi's age itself began to show more and more in his appearance. The years of struggle subtly emerged in his face, with the battles of life and career far from complete.

Some of his most commonly viewed films of the early forties remain the low-budget efforts he made for the B studios of Hollywood. Lugosi the mad scientist created *The Devil Bat* (1941) at PRC for instance, though the nocturnal flyer looked more Sears and Roebuck than hell spawned. Regardless, Lugosi's performance in the film won a gold medal from the "Chicago Horror Club." The organization included experts and authorities studying fear psychology and suggestive effects on the mind. Lugosi had previously received three other commendations from them, setting a new record for the group.

Also, a production unit under Sam Katzman at Monogram Studios churned out nine Lugosi films, all bearing a distinctly B appearance. For better or worse, Béla met the East Side Kids in *Spooks Run Wild* (1941) and *Ghosts on the Loose* (1943). Furthermore, he was *The Invisible Ghost* (1941), one of the diabolical *Black Dragons* (1942), the unfortunate *Ape Man* (1943), and the diabolical *Voodoo Man* (1944).

For the premiere of *The Invisible Ghost* (1941), Lugosi took part in a live spook show at a Chicago theater. A cast of 33 performed on the stage, with Lugosi shrugging his shoulders to a reporter later that year and moaning, "It's a living." The Monogram films usually themselves offered Lugosi in mad scientist roles, with occasional overtones of Dracula. In addition to continuing his horror image, they associated him more and more with B productions. However, if critics and adults generally labeled these movies as juvenile, the youth population embraced the call. A stage tour in 1944, for example, found children rushing en masse to see the actor perform live.

During World War II, Lugosi also spent much time selling war bonds, rallying for the safety of his homeland, and even giving blood to help in the war effort. On one occasion, he organized 10,000 Hungarians in the Los Angeles area at the American-Hungarian Defense Federation. With his assistance, the event raised $65,000 in war bonds, $1,600 for the Red Cross, and enough donations to purchase and equip an ambulance for the U.S. forces. Lugosi also became a figurehead president for the Hungarian-American Council for Democracy, though critics of the group later exposed its Communist affiliations.

The actor with his son, Bela Jr., and his wife, Lillian, in the mid to late forties.

Like other horror film stars, Lugosi also took to the road for numerous vaudeville tours, usually excerpting scenes from *Dracula*. Wife Lillian often portrayed the female victim in order to save money. In a more legitimate setting, Lugosi donned the cape for a revival of the full-length play *Dracula* in 1943, though the actor heard few gasps. Critics noticed that some patrons tittered at scenes that years before caused shudders. Despite a few successful performances, the tour of Eastern cities proved an overall disappointment.

Furthermore, Lon Chaney, Jr., received the lead role in *Son of Dracula* (1943), playing the vampire that Lugosi popularized over a decade before. As with *Dracula's Daughter* (1936), Universal Studios denied the actor a chance to perform what was in many ways his own creation. Lugosi did take top billing at Columbia in *Return of the Vampire* (1943). Although not the bona fide Bram Stoker creation, the part of Armand Tesla became a near–Dracula characterization.

Lugosi achieved greater success on the stage in *Arsenic and Old Lace*. He portrayed the murderous Jonathan Brewster, a part that Boris Karloff created in the highly successful Broadway run. After assuming the role for a 1943 West Coast version, Lugosi took to the road for a successful tour through the Midwest and East. Many reviewers believed his interpretation of the role to be highly original and even superior to Karloff's.

Various radio shows also kept the actor's horror image in place. Lugosi made guest appearances on dramas such as *Suspense*, comedies like *The Fred Allen Show*,

Lillian and Bela at an unknown event during the latter stage of their marriage.

and *Mail Call*–style programs dedicated to the armed forces. Among these was an attempt at his own radio series in 1944, *Mystery House*. While radio waves carried his unique and often spellbinding voice into the homes of America, Lugosi sometimes performed his parts in a stilted, uninspired manner. Reading a script cold did not suit his talents, nor did the ad-libbing of comedians.

Yet Lugosi didn't particularly enjoy doing radio shows, signing autographs, or posing for photographs. He was much more content to support his beloved Hungarian soccer teams. The Magyar Athletic Club soccer team found great

Bela and an unknown acquaintance during the fifties.

assistance from the actor, and the Bela Lugosi Trophy held a high place on their mantel. Lugosi also served for a time as honorary president of the Los Angeles Soccer League, occasionally kicking out the first balls at Loyola Stadium.

Lugosi also greatly loved music, with his favorite songs including "Rhapsody in Blue" and "The Girl with the Blue Eyes." A lover of many kinds of music, Bela was particularly fond of Hungarian melodies. His affinity for music led him to close friendships with pianist Ervin Nyiregyhazi and violinist and composer Duci Kerekjarto, as well as to haunting Hollywood-area restaurants like the Little Gypsy to hear the music.

His stamp collection, beginning as a result of his wife's saving them from postmarked envelopes, also occupied his free time. At one point, his collection supposedly numbered over 150,000. Lillian mentioned to reporters that Béla once frantically rushed to finish a set of Hungarian stamps, after friend Manly Hall had already beaten him. While visiting Boston in 1944, Lugosi told reporters he intended to visit all 18 stamp dealers in the city. He also mentioned that whenever he got some unexpected money, half of it went to war bonds, with the remainder going to the "soundest investment" he knew of: philately.

"Stamp collecting is a hobby which may cost you as much as ten percent of your investment," Lugosi explained. "You can always sell your stamps with not more than a ten percent loss. Sometimes you can even make money." Unfortunately, when he finally sold his collection, he lost much more than 10 percent.

Béla's great love of Hungarian food and imported sulphur water also remained fixed in the memories of his friends. Along with food, he appreciated fine tobacco. His pipe smoking resulted in a large collection, though if he couldn't fit his thumb into the bowl of a pipe it usually became a gift for someone else. The actor also adored good cigars, though when money became scarce he resorted to a cheap brand he called "El-Stinko, El-Ropos."

The company of fellow Hungarians meant a great deal to Lugosi as well. Along with the Hungarian musicians and actors he knew, friends like Willi Szittja, Joe Pasternak, and others helped revive fond memories of his homeland. The wine, Hungarian food, music, dancing, and talk often lasted late into the night. Lugosi's parties generally included those from the Hungarian community rather than the usual big-name stars. Friends remember Lugosi at such gatherings with fellow countrymen like Louis Sass and writers László Bus and László Fodor. Occasionally, Michael Curtiz and the Korda brothers also became guests. The typical Hollywood parties, however, still held no appeal for him.

"No, life is too short for that," he would say. "I wouldn't waste my time. There's so many interesting and wonderful things in the world that a man could achieve and experience. Besides, I don't even know how to play the ... what do you call it? ... the ukelele. I guess I'm pretty much of a lone wolf."

At any rate, Lugosi's relationship with Lillian had clearly declined by this point, as newspapers featured such headlines as WIFE SUES THE MONSTER. She even left him, temporarily moving with Bela Jr. to her sister's home in Los Angeles. The separation occurred in August 1944, though by the second week of March 1945 Lillian asked for a dismissal of her divorce charges. The couple reunited, though the separation certainly reflects her complaints that he was too jealous and controlling.

"The Monster," meanwhile, continued to frighten theatergoers. In fact, the overall popularity of horror films during World War II surprised many studios. Crowds lined up for such entertainment, though a war-torn England cast a critical eye on the genre. Many Lugosi films received "H" certificates in England, limiting the viewings of such films to persons aged 16 and above. *Son of Frankenstein, The Gorilla, Ghost of Frankenstein, Frankenstein Meets the Wolf Man, The Ape Man, Voodoo Man*, and *The Corpse Vanishes* fell into this category. Moreover, films like *Bowery at Midnight* met severe trimming at the hands of British censors.

Béla's comments in regard to this phenomenon remained much the same as they had always been. "I'd like to be liked," he confessed in 1944. But, horror remained the dragon on his doorstep, never loosening its hold on his career. More than many other performers of his day, he faced extreme typecasting and was essentially stranded within a genre that itself had ups and downs.

When asked if he scared Bela Jr. with his screen tactics, Lugosi responded, "How could I? He sees me in my underwear, and how can a man have any dignity in his underwear?" For his son, Béla did hope he would choose a career other than entertainment. "Acting is too hazardous a career. The income is uncertain and it is one field in which very few succeed. I would prefer to see Bela Jr. in chemistry or electrical engineering." As a child, the younger Lugosi spent much of his time in military schools before becoming a strong student and an important member of the swimming team at a Hollywood-area high school in the fifties.

By the end of World War II, the entertainment business sagged and studios produced fewer horror films. In 1945 Lugosi starred with Ian Keith in an ill-fated play called *No Traveler Returns*, which found trouble with critics and audiences in both San Francisco and Seattle. Essentially for name value RKO added the Hungarian to the cast of *The Body Snatcher* (1945), which headlined Boris Karloff. Their last film together could be more accurately described as a Karloff film that only incidentally included the Lugosi. The screen domination of his British counterpart became more complete than ever before. Those on the set later cited Béla's poor health, which forced him to spend much of his time on a dressing room daybed.

In 1947 Lugosi appeared on theater screens in only one film release, *Scared to Death*, a wretched effort notable for being the only chiller he made in color. Its incoherent plot still leaves viewers mystified. Director Christy Cabanne earlier achieved fame during the silent film era; he and star Lugosi shared a sole commonality. Both seemed to be period pieces, the fading remains of prior successes.

Lugosi did find himself among *Three Indelicate Ladies* in the brief Off Broadway effort, portraying an Irish-flavored character, Francis O'Rourke (aka "Turk the Jerk"). Though the play carved out little success, Lugosi's stay in Massachusetts gave him the opportunity to lecture college students at Boston University on abnormal psychology and criminology.

As an attempt to better his waning career, Lugosi signed a contract with Don Marlowe, based on the latter's promise of several important projects. These included a British stage tour of *Dracula*, a CBS program called *The Bela Lugosi Show*, a role in MGM's *Inner Sanctum*, and a proposed Invisible Man film at Universal. None of these finally became Lugosi projects, though Marlowe did engineer a short roadshow version of Poe's *The Tell-Tale Heart*. The actor spent much time in the latter part of the decade at minor theaters, either performing in second-rate "spook shows" or appearing in quick, summer stock versions of *Dracula* and *Arsenic and Old Lace*. Trade publications generally ignored such efforts. Bela no longer stirred the same excitement or ignited coverage in fan magazines. Though the residue of horror remained, widespread attention slipped through his fingers.

Perhaps the most memorable work Marlowe arranged for Lugosi resulted in his second and final appearance as Count Dracula in a feature-length film. *Abbott and Costello Meet Frankenstein* (1948) found him again at Universal Studios, this time in a spoof of the horror genre. Although showing his years more than he had 17 years before in the original *Dracula* (1931), Lugosi remained a suave and aristocratic vampire. And — despite the comedy — the monsters played their parts straight, with Bela's Dracula even making some impressively animated man-to-bat transformations.

The film received good reviews, as did Lugosi. While searching the floor for a missing shirt stud, Lugosi looked up to a reporter long enough to express his gratitude to Universal. A certain sadness hovers over such comments, however, as the studio that built Lugosi into a star in 1931 spent the following years of his life taking advantage of him or outright forgetting his existence.

Unfortunately, Lugosi's career continued to decline even after the fun with Bud and Lou. Vaudeville still opened its arms occasionally, with Bela hitting such spots as Detroit, Miami, and Atlantic City. During 1950 Bela did many live appearances in small theaters along the eastern seaboard, with screenings of his earlier Monogram films accompanying the act. Though this generated badly needed revenue, the circumstances themselves were miserable. Disrespectful audiences occasionally heckled the actor, who certainly understood firsthand the deteriorating nature of his career.

Despite harder times and combating what he termed the "Dracula curse," Lugosi remained true to his old interests and friends. In 1949, for example, he spent a week in Syracuse with actor Paul Lukas. The same year, Bela contemplated a vacation to Hungary, but for reasons unknown it didn't materialize. He still maintained contact with his sister, and enjoyed dining at Hungarian restaurants and visiting such hotels as New York's Gotham and Drake with fellow countrymen. Lugosi's charm and personality even took him to a 1947 cocktail party aboard a Chinese junk to swap "believe it or not" stories with Robert L. Ripley.

Bela also continued to watch photographers to correct their angles of him, as well as to keep them from snapping pictures while he wore his glasses. One of his favorites in the profession was Gabriel D. Hackett, whom he said always caught his best side. Hackett and Lugosi met as early as 1928 and remained friends for many years. The two often spoke of a mutual interest: photography.

His sporadic television guest appearances began in the late forties as well. For instance, he appeared with cape in hand opposite Milton Berle, and had a dramatic role on *Suspense*, which had made the move from radio to television. In the fifties, Bela was also a guest on a few more programs, such as *The Red Skelton Show* and *You Asked for It*. As with his radio work, however, the popular medium gave him few opportunities and showed him to be less than adept at dealing with unexpected diversions from the written script.

In the summer of 1950, he nabbed an important role in Fritz Rotter's play *The Devil Also Dreams*, which made only a handful of performances before folding. The comedy gave Lugosi the chance to play an ex-actor turned butler, whose big scene allowed him to discuss his days as a great actor who believes Shakespeare to be much richer in its Hungarian translation. His character proceeded to quote a short passage in his native language, which echoed the real-life tragedies of Lugosi's own career and virtually put them on display before a live audience.

Though certainly aware of whatever parallels existed between himself and the character, Bela was simply overjoyed to appear in a comedy. "Having threatened people for the last 23 years," Lugosi smiled, "I'm having the best time of my life making people laugh." Unfortunately, the play's run ended abruptly and the laughs ceased.

Bela's career continued to sink, but a young Richard Gordon began a sincere effort to assist him as an official manager. Gordon arranged a 1951 British tour of the stage *Dracula*, with Lugosi and his wife sailing on the *Mauritania* in April. Bela performed a modernized version of the play, with Dracula now traveling by plane instead of ship to London. Many newspapers rushed to interview Lugosi, with several of them commenting on Lillian's nickname for him, "Bel." Yet, despite some encouraging reviews, the tour became financially unsuccessful.

"I look in the mirror and say to myself, 'Can it be that you once played Romeo?' Always it is the same," he explained to author Harry Ludlam before one of the British performances. "When a film company is in the red they come to me and say, 'Okay, so we make a horror film.' And so that is what we do. It is what I always do."

The same strategy was employed to raise money for the broke actor. The result, *Mother Riley Meets the Vampire*, covered the cost of the Lugosis' return voyage to the United States, but the film itself found no real audience. In it, the actor appeared opposite Arthur Lucan, a female impersonator. *Mother Riley* has moments of true comedy, but — even under several title changes — it never received any lengthy American distribution. By December 12, 1951, the Lugosis finally arrived back in New York City.

Journalists did herald a reissue of the 1931 *Dracula*, with newspaper interviewers finding time to ask the aging horror star if anyone scared him. The response brought Margaret O'Brien's name at the top of the list. "Child actors!" Bela continued, "No actor can compete with them. Put down Zsa Zsa Gabor, too. She's a publicity stealer from the rest of us Hungarian actors." The list further included wife Lillian ("She's not afraid of me ... I do what she says"), Hopalong Cassidy ("He's trying to get me to ride a horse"), newspaper interviewers, and Mae West.

As the Red Scare and McCarthyism cast a dark shadow over the fifties, several persons called into question Lugosi's patriotism. He certainly donated to various Hungarian causes during World War II, some of which were actually fronts for Communist organizations. Moreover, the young Lugosi had supported a Communist regime under Béla Kun in Hungary following World War I. Newspapers like the *New York Daily News* strongly accused Lugosi of Communist sympathies; the result of these few inquiries made the actor voice his love of democracy and the United States in Hungarian publications. Lugosi also requested that his friend Andor C. Klay facilitate an appearance for him before the House Committee on Un-American Activities. Though he never finally spoke before the congressional group, his printed statements — along with the fact that his career simply did not merit much of a spotlight at the time — kept this from becoming a more heated issue.

"I herewith emphatically state that I am not now, nor have I ever been, a member of the Communist Party," Lugosi wrote. "I have never attended any Communist meetings — I have never entertained at a Communist gathering — I have never donated one cent to any Communist cause."

Though he loudly proclaimed his patriotism, the status of his film career caused little noise. Titles like *Bela Lugosi Meets a Brooklyn Gorilla* (1952) exemplify the C and D grade films in which he appeared. Lugosi also became acquainted with Edward D. Wood, Jr., a hopeful but hopelessly untalented filmmaker who employed him for the very bizarre *Glen or Glenda* (1953).

Wood had long been a fan of Lugosi's and genuinely wished to help his career. The other side of the coin was that Lugosi knew Wood might get him film work and was thus amicable. *Glen or Glenda* itself dealt with transvestism and medical sex changes, with Lugosi appearing as a sort of omniscient narrator who spouted bits of odd dialogue. A live appearance at the premiere of *The House of Wax* (1953) with an "ape" on a leash added to the perception of Lugosi as a mere caricature of his former persona.

Besides financial problems, Bela again faced divorce in 1953 from his fourth wife, Lillian, who took with her Bela Jr. Lugosi was devastated by the loss, though there is little doubt that his jealous, domineering nature slowly ruined the 20-year marriage. Profoundly hurt by the divorce, he tried to convince her to return. His suicide attempt reportedly occurred that year as well, though Lugosi later laughed it off to the press as a publicity stunt. Photographs of the actor with a police officer from the alleged event remain.

"I had a very young wife ... she was thirty years younger than I," he later mentioned, "and she felt that perhaps she had a right to be happy and not be chained to an old man." He offered such words for public consumption; his letters to Lillian expressed a deep sense of pain.

The actor's alcoholism was also a factor in the decline of his marriage to Lillian, though he in fact became a member of Alcoholics Anonymous. Lugosi sincerely appreciated their help, and even friends who did not drink recall his prompting them to attend the meetings with him. Despite his attempts to control the habit, he continued to drink heavily, usually keeping a bottle of scotch on his nightstand.

In late October 1953 Lugosi moved to an apartment and sold many of his possessions at a public auction. When asked by a reporter what he intended to do for Halloween that year, he responded, "I have no plans. I told my agent to find me a TV job, but I haven't heard from him. I'm open to suggestions ... if there's money involved." Bela was on the stage again in January 1954 in St. Louis, appearing in yet another version of *Arsenic and Old Lace*. The next month, he went to Las Vegas's Silver Slipper for *The Bela Lugosi Revue*. Getting favorable notices, the show lampooned Lugosi's horror image. Large crowds appeared, with the *Las Vegas Sun* printing many of the actor's words of wisdom. The attention and success must have placed a glimmer of hope in Lugosi's eyes. Many have suggested, however, that the show placed more strain on the actor's health than he could bear.

Ed Wood, wholeheartedly attempting to find work for the actor, arranged the Las Vegas appearance. His other ideas included a radio show called *The Terror*, another roadshow version of *Dracula*, a Lugosi comic book, and numerous film plans. As with Don Marlowe's failed attempts, none of these projects materialized.

In April 1955 Lugosi came forward with another serious personal problem. He shocked many with headlines telling of his plea for drug rehabilitation. Lugosi's move in this direction was voluntary, coming after a private sanitarium advised him to obtain help. Friend Manly Hall accompanied him to the Los Angeles County General Hospital where he requested assistance.

"I don't have a dime left," Lugosi said at the hospital. "I am dependent on my friends for food and a small old-age pension. I am anxious to rehabilitate myself and decided this was the only way to do it."

Judge Ware, after ordering the terms of Lugosi's rehabilitation on April 22, commended the actor for his courageous effort. The hearing itself took place at the hospital, necessitated by Lugosi's poor health. Newspapers quickly printed innumerable stories referring to "Dracula" as a narcotics fiend. The real story, however, was far different. Lugosi actually had become addicted to prescribed painkillers.

"Shooting pains in my legs back in the days when I was making horror films made a medical addict out of me," he told the press. "I started using morphine under doctor's care. I knew after a time it was getting out of control." He also spoke of other painkillers like Demerol and methadone. In one interview, Lugosi made clear that he "didn't buy it on the black market."

"There was one period, a few years ago, when I quit," he continued. "My wife, Lillian, who divorced me in 1953, got me to quit. She gave me the shots. And she weaned me. Finally, I got only the bare needle. A fake shot, that's all. I was done with it. Then she left me. She took our son. He was my flesh. I went back on the drugs. My heart was broken."

He stayed for three months of rehabilitation at the Metropolitan State Hospital in Norwalk under the care of Dr. Nicholas Langer. On August 3, 1955, the board of directors released the actor, claiming he passed a staff examination "with flying colors." The hospital also mentioned that Lugosi would remain under the jurisdiction and supervision of the Department of Mental Health for one year.

"It's a terrible ordeal to go through withdrawal," Lugosi told an interviewer. "It's the greatest pain in the world. I became a new man ... a new lease on life. I'm cured. I feel like a million dollars." When another reporter asked about his age, Lugosi fudged, with a twinkle in his eye. "Well, let's say 63. After all, Jack Benny is only 39."

While in the hospital, Lugosi heard from friends and fans across the globe. Fellow Hungarians like Joe Pasternak and Paul Lukas offered their support. Frank Sinatra also a sent a word of encouragement, even including a monetary gift. During this period, Ed Wood helped put together a benefit premiere of Lugosi's film *Bride of the Atom* at the Paramount Hollywood Theater, with part of the proceeds going to the actor. The box office brought in poor ticket sales, and Universal Studios reportedly balked when asked to buy a block of seats.

One fan in particular, Hope Lininger, wrote the actor letters almost every day. At the time, she was a 39-year-old employee of RKO Studios. This "dash of Hope" had admired Lugosi since she was a little girl in Johnstown, Pennsylvania, watching the actor's films at her local theater.

Upon his release, the two wed on August 24 at a small L.A. ceremony, with 17-year-old Bela Jr. acting as the best man. Manly Hall, Lugosi's friend who supposedly hypnotized him for his role in *Black Friday* (1940), married the couple in his home. Hall, an ordained minister, also headed the Philosophical Research Society. Mrs. Pat Delaney, a police department employee, acted as matron of honor, and Phyllis Holmes Buffington signed the marriage certificate as the witness. Gilbert Olson, Jo Wiley, Paul Marco, and Dale Buffington attended the small ceremony.

Newspapers mentioned that Hall had to help Lugosi through the vows, adding that the actor "muffed" his lines at the section "with all my worldly goods, I thee endow." Despite that, Lugosi "stood tall and gray in a blue double-breasted suit and white carnation." The two planned a honeymoon to New York, though they instead vacationed at Big Bear Lake with Ed Wood.

"If I fail in my attempt to love, honor, and obey this wonderful woman," Bela told the press, "I hope you'll write the worst stories you can about me." Their short marriage encountered numerous difficulties, not the least of which was Lugosi's tremendous jealousy. His new wife also spent much time finding and disposing of his hidden liquor bottles.

Bride of the Atom, even after transforming into *Bride of the Monster*, did not find major release. Rather, it found only a few poor reviews. The film gave Lugosi his last speaking role on the screen, though overall it remains an implausible and particularly low budget production. Perhaps film buffs most fondly remember a lengthy speech Lugosi gave within the film, in which his character expressed troubles that in some ways mirrored the actor's own difficulties. Though most of Ed Wood's plans for Lugosi, such as costarring him with Gene Autry in a film called *The Ghoul Goes West*, didn't materialize, United Artists inked the actor to a mute role in *The Black Sleep* (1955). The film featured Basil Rathbone, Lon Chaney, Jr., John Carradine, and Akim Tamiroff as well. But, this minor part certainly did not spark any hoped-for comeback, and in June 1956 Lugosi even collapsed on stage during a promotional tour for the film. "Horror is not what it used to be," the actor groaned to a reporter.

During these years important support came from a small group of teenage fans in the Hollywood area who idolized Lugosi. One of these, Richard Sheffield, started a fan club and even petitioned Universal Studios for a color, three-dimensional remake of *Dracula* with Lugosi. Nothing came of this, but these admirers provided much moral support for the aging actor. Sheffield became one of the closest and truest friends of Lugosi's last years, once even writing down a firsthand account of the Hungarian's life. Others in the group included Michael Spencer, Jimmy Haines, Norman Fist, and David Katzman.

His last few years also gave him the opportunity to spend time with a few old friends, particularly Willi Szittja and his nephew Béla Loosz. Moreover, Lugosi crossed paths with such acquaintances as Edward Van Sloan and Jack Oakie at a Hollywood tribute to Mack Sennett; on the whole, however, he lived quietly and waited for work that never came.

One of Bela's last acting jobs was at small Hollywood theater in *The Devil's Paradise*, an exposé on the evils of drug use. Though the show was produced very cheaply, Lugosi genuinely wished to help others avoid drug addiction. Even in interviews he urged youngsters to understand the problems that drugs posed.

With many loyal friends and various projects in the works, Lugosi still believed he would return to the cinema spotlight. This was not to be, however, as his fifth wife found him dead in their apartment on August 16, 1956. An oft-told but untrue story claims he was clutching a script for *The Final Curtain* when Hope discovered him.

Along with being disheartened by the death of friends like Louis Calhern,

With his fifth and final wife, Hope Lininger, in 1955.

Lugosi once openly declared, "I am afraid of dying. I am very much afraid of dying. But not of death itself. No ... because now, in this concentrated time, with all of the changes going in the world, I would suffer to miss any of it." On another occasion, he spoke of death by saying, "That is the only thing that really is frightening to me. The calendar turns, and eventually you have to go."

Lugosi's funeral was a rather small affair, attracting only a few notables like Zoltán Korda. Ed Wood and several of his cohorts attended; Forrest J Ackerman and Don Marlowe were also among the hundred or so friends. Such close companions as Michael Spencer and Richard Sheffield acted as pallbearers. The Catholic Lugosi was laid to rest at Holy Cross Cemetery in Culver City, California, near the grave of Bing Crosby.

One tale claims that as the hearse left the Utter-McKinley Mortuary, the car was mysteriously and unexpectedly diverted from its usual route and turned down to the Hollywood and Vine area where Lugosi had so often walked to buy his newspapers and cigars. Another story insists that as Boris Karloff and Peter Lorre passed Lugosi's body at the funeral, the latter joked, "Come now, Bela, you're putting us on." Though a colorful story, it is also untrue. Neither attended the services.

Unfortunately, the actor never witnessed the revived popularity of his films and died virtually forgotten by Hollywood. Just as the shroud of Dracula consumed his career in life, Lugosi wore the vampire's cape to the grave. "I became Dracula's puppet," Lugosi once reflected. "The shadowy figure of Dracula—more than any casting office—dictated the kind of parts I played."

2. Personal Data

The following represents a form Lugosi completed for Imperial-Cameo, a studio that produced *Murder by Television*, with Lugosi's answers in italics. Interestingly, Lugosi wrote incorrect answers to some questions, particularly his date of birth (actually October 20, 1882), his first stage role (more likely it was Count Königsegg in 1902's *Brigadier General Ocskay*), his first film role (actually 1917's *The Leopard*), his checkmark by "college." Following this form are listings of the various addresses at which Lugosi lived in the United States and of the numerous talent agencies that handled him.

Imperial-Cameo Pictures Corporation Biographical Information (1935)

This is to insure accuracy in our publicity, and to provide complete and accurate material necessary for newspaper and magazine stories.

1. Screen name *Bela Lugosi*
   Real name in full was *Bela Blasko — legally changed to Bela Lugosi.*
2. Height *6'1"*   Nickname *None*
3. Nationality *Hungarian*   Color of hair *Brown*   Weight *170 lbs.*   Color of eyes *Blue*
4. Birthplace *Lugos, Hungary*   Date *October 20, 1888*
5. Education *High School*   College [checkmarked here]
6. Parents' names *Stephan Blasko — Paula von Vojnics*   Both living *no*
   Where Buried *at Lugos, Hungary*
   Father's Business *was Bank President*
   Famous Ancestors or relatives *None*
   Brothers or sisters names *Vilma — Lajos — Laszlo*
   Earliest childhood ambition *Highway Bandit*
7. Present ambition *Dude Ranch*
8. First Occupation *Actor*   Where? *Travelling Repertoire*
   Past and present business interests apart from the screen *— None*
9. How did your career begin? (Amateur shows, college dramatics, beauty contests, started by famous actor or director, for a lark) *College Dramatics*
10. Stage debut in *Romeo*   Year *1906*   Place *Lugos, Hungary*
    Broadway debut *Red Poppy*
    Year *1923* co-starred with Estelle Wynnwood [sic]
    Last play *Murder in the Vanities*   Year *1933*
    Place *New York City*
    Other important plays *In America — "Dracula"*

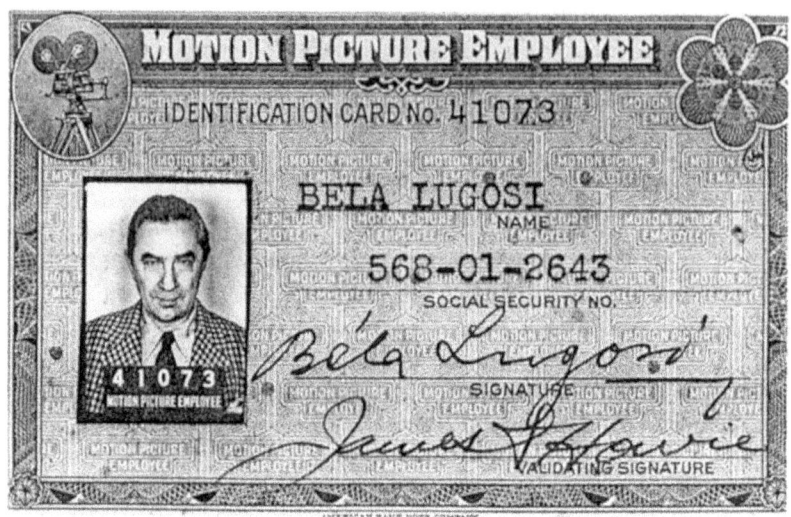

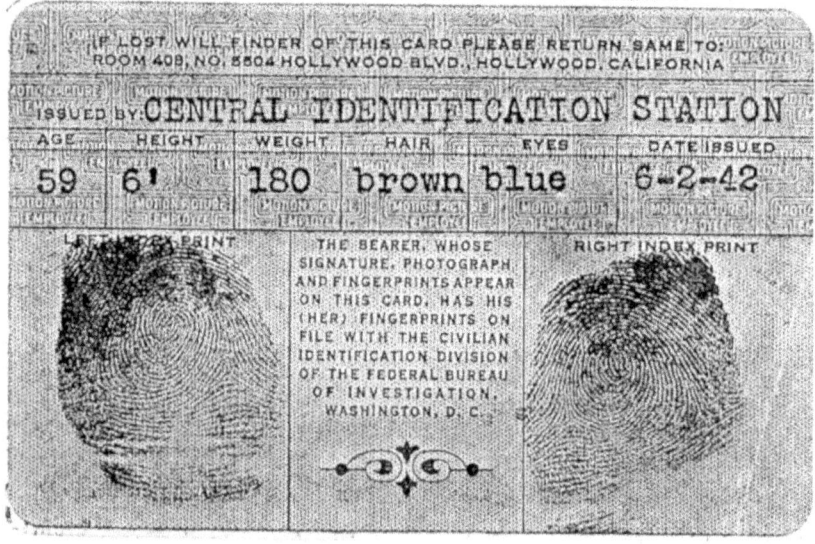

Lugosi's Motion Picture Employee card from 1942, offering not just his Social Security number and signature but even fingerprints. (Courtesy of the Charles Heard collection.)

    In Hungary — *All the great parts in literature*
    Stock in what cities *None*
11. Film debut in *"The Silent Command"* Year *1923*
    Star — *Heavy with all-star cast*
    First large part in *same* Year — Star —
    First Talkie *"Prisoners"* Year *1929* Star — *Corinne Griffith*

Last Picture *"Mark of the Vampire"*   Year *1935*
Star —*All Star*
Other pictures (next to last, etc.). *"Mysterious Mr. Wong"*
"Return of Chandu"   "Black Cat"
12. Favorite screen role *"Count Dracula" in "Dracula"*
13. Favorite stage role *"Cyrano de Bergerac" in "Cyrano de Bergerac"*
14. Prefer screen to stage? *Yes*   Why? *Variety*
15. What type of role have you played most? *Great characters*
16. What type do you prefer *Human interest*
17. Favorite stage players *None*
18. Favorite screen play [after marking out *None*, Lugosi penciled in *Mickey Mouse*]
19. Favorite playwrights —
20. Favorite books *Social Science and Economy*
21. Favorite authors *None*
22. Favorite sports to watch *Soccer*
23. Favorite sports to play *Golf*
24. HIGHSPOTS of your life (in chronological order)
    1 to 10 years
    10 to 20 years   *It is no one's business*
    20 to 30 years
    Ad infinitum
25. CLOTHES prefer conservative or modest *Conservative tailored*
                    ready made or tailored
    Favor sports or formal wear? *Sports*
    Favorite colors *Bright*
    Favorite materials *Flannels*
26. Have you any beauty secrets such as methods of make-up, care of hair, eyes, hands, skin, facials, massages, oils, creams? *None*
27. How do you keep in condition (Health institute, *daily* or weekly *massages, sun-baths, setting-up exercises*, sports?)
28. FOOD favorite dish *Stuffed Cabbage*   Like to cook? —
    Between meal snacks *No*   Bedtime snack? *No*
    Favorite recipe: Dish: —
29. Married *Yes*   Or want to be?   To whom?
    Date *Jan 31, 1933*   Children?
    Favorite type of man or woman *Reserved and Honest*
30. What do you do for diversion and recreation aside from sports?
    (Dance, sing, write, paint, compose music, *sculpt, read*, games)
31. Where do you prefer to live permanently? (Seashore, *mountains*, city, abroad)
32. Where do you live now? (Apartment, *house*, seashore, city, *mountains*)
33. Where have you traveled? *All over the world*
34. Who are your closest friends? *Stage Hands*
35. What makes you angry? *Talk*
36. What pets have you? *3 dogs*
37. What do you do on the set? *Smoke*
38. Where do you go on weekends? *Outing*
39. Do you have any cars, airplanes, yachts, horses? *Car*
40. Interested in politics? *Yes*
41. Pet peeves *Aggravation*   Live with parents? *No*
42. Pet economy *Matches and Corks*

Pet extravagance *Old Wines and Good Cigars*
43. Favorite dress— Favorite perfume *Eau de cologne*
44. Do you smoke? *Yes* Speak any foreign language *Hungarian and others*
45. Your greatest thrill *When I got abroad [sic] ship to come to America*
46. Do you like

Rain? *No*	To travel alone? *Yes*	To pose for stills? *No*
Autographs *No*	To write letters? *No*	To carry umbrellas *No*
Night clubs? *No*	Animals *Yes*	Showers or bathtubs *both*
Streetcars? *No*	Children *Yes*	Modern architecture *Yes*
Prohibition? *No*	Sun baths *Yes*	Fan mail *Yes*
To entertain *Yes*	Holidays *?*	Personal appearances *No*
To sleep late *Yes*	Premiers *No*	To drive your car *No*
Silk underwear *No*	To dine at home *Yes*	Open cars *No*
Radio Programs *No*	Airplanes *No*	Read before sleeping *Yes*
To go shopping? *Yes*	Bathsalts *No*	Letters of intro. *No*
Ice cream cones *No*	Hollywood *Yes*	Bright or subdued colors [Lugosi crossedout the word *subdued*]

Residences

1. New York City, New York.

According to the U.S. Immigration Service, Lugosi lived at a boardinghouse on 109 West 93d Street when he first came to New York in late 1920. Lugosi remained at this address when he underwent primary alien inspection on March 23, 1921.

2. New York City, New York.

According to the May and October editions of the 1923 New York City phone book, Lugosi had moved to 30 Fairview Avenue, phone number BILlings 0718.

3. New York City, New York.

The May and October editions of the 1924 phone book offer the following address for Lugosi: 54 West 55th Street, phone number CIRcle 8418.

4. New York City, New York.

The May and Winter editions of the 1925 New York City phone book give Lugosi's address as 225 East 79th Street, phone number BUTterfield 0119.

5. New York City, New York.

Summer and Winter editions of the 1927 phone book print Lugosi's address as 48 West 49th Street, phone number BRYant 4811. Lugosi stayed at this address through the summer of 1928.

6. Los Angeles, California.

Lugosi stayed at the Ambassador Hotel during his 1928 stage version of *Dracula*, reveling in the tennis courts, golf course, and swimming pool.

7. Hollywood, California.

Lugosi lived at the Hollywood Athletic Club on Sunset Boulevard during the late twenties, which featured a bar, restaurant, swimming pool, and gymnasium. Lugosi lived here again briefly between his stays at North Hudson and at Creston Drive.

8. San Francisco, California.

While briefly married to Beatrice Woodruff Weeks, Lugosi stayed with her at the Huntington Arms Apartments. Weeks's former husband, architect Charles Peter Weeks, had designed the apartment building. Prior to his marriage to Weeks, Lugosi's 1928 appearance as *Dracula* in San Francisco found him at the Mark Hopkins Hotel.

9. Hollywood, California.

The 1930 casting directory listed Lugosi's

Posed comfortably with a plant during his Hollywood heyday in the thirties.

number as GLAdstone 8092. Between early 1929 and his move to Creston Drive, Lugosi lived at 1146 North Hudson.

10. Hollywood, California.
Lugosi lived at 2643 Creston Drive after signing a one-year lease on October 21, 1931. The owners canceled the lease before the 12 months expired, yet Lugosi remained a resident at least until the end of May 1932.

11. Hollywood, California.
The August 1932 phone book lists Lugosi at 6381 Hollywood Boulevard, phone number HOllywood 0111.

12. Los Angeles, California.
The May 1933 phone book gave 6521 Sunset Boulevard as the Hungarian's address, with HEmpstead 1161 as the phone number.

13. Los Angeles, California.
Béla and Lillian moved into a home at 2829 Westshire early in their marriage, leaving it for a several month's stay in New York in late 1933.

14. Hollywood, California.
Lugosi and Lillian purchased a brick and stone home at 2835 Westshire after he appeared in 1934's *The Black Cat.*

15. Los Angeles, California.
The June 1935 phone book listed Lillian Lugosi at 3515 South LaBrea, phone number WE-9-3970. By late 1935, however, the couple lived at 2227 Outpost Drive, located in the Hollywood Hills. The grounds included a guest house, wine cellar, and a waterfall. The home also had a secret panel under its stairwell.

16. North Hollywood, California.
Due to his financial troubles in 1937, Lugosi lost his home at Outpost Drive, moving to a house at 3714 Lankershim Drive.

17. New York City, New York.
During his New York stay in 1939, Lugosi lived in room 3601 of the Essex House.

18. North Hollywood, California.
Beginning in 1941, the Lugosis lived at 10841 Whipple Street. This home, often referred to as the "Dracula House," became Bela's favorite residence during the decades he lived in California. Lugosi allegedly said of the house, "It will be called Castle Dracula. It is rustic, odd with iron grille work within and strange birds mounted on the roof." A piano, a study lined with books, and many paintings on the walls helped the house reflect Lugosi's interests.

19. Hollywood, California.
The tenth edition of *Who's Who in the Theatre* (1947) offered Lugosi's address as 3714 Lankershim Drive. The twelfth edition of the same text, printed in 1952, still listed that address for Lugosi. The house on Whipple Street and the subsequent apartment at Rodeo Lane were actually his residences during the period these books were printed.

20. New York City, New York.
While Lugosi lived in New York City during 1950, he first stayed at a hotel on West 64th Street. Later, he and wife Lillian rented an apartment on 55th Street between 7th Avenue and Broadway.

21. Baldwin Hills, California.
Lugosi's address shortly before and for some six months following his 1953 divorce from Lillian Arch was 4601 Rodeo Lane, Apartment 2. The phone number was AX-3-6609.

22. Los Angeles, California.
In 1954 Lugosi stayed for a time at 1427 North Laurel Avenue, Apartment 2. The phone number remained AX-3-6609.

23. Norwalk, California.
Lugosi stayed for three months during the summer of 1955 in the Metropolitan State Hospital at 11400 Norwalk Boulevard. The hospital released him in August.

24. Hollywood, California.
Upon his release from the Metropolitan State Hospital, Bela moved in with his nephew, Béla Loosz, at 1534 North Serrano, HO-5-2241.

25. Hollywood, California.
Shortly after his marriage in 1955 to Hope Lininger, Lugosi lived at an apartment on 5620 Harold Way, with the phone number HO-9-5911. Until the time of his death, this remained his residence.

Agent Listings

1. Harry Weber

After first nabbing him a role in *Oh, for a Man*, Weber's offices placed both Lugosi and Virginia Sales in *Fifty Million Frenchmen* in August 1930. Presumably, Weber placed Lugosi in other films of this era.

2. Collier and Flinn, Ltd.

After his success in *Dracula* and *Murders in the Rue Morgue*, this agency handled Lugosi for a time. The phone number given in one listing for this agency (HO-0111) is curious in that it was listed in phone books as Lugosi's home number at the time.

3. John Zanft Agency

The January 1937 edition of the Academy of Motion Picture Arts and Sciences' *Players Directory Bulletin* listed Lugosi with this agency. Along with the phone number CR-4181, the agency included the following note: "*Dracula* led producers to consider Lugosi preeminent solely in the horror field. *This is an error*. His greatest European successes were accomplished in character roles." The June 1937 listing gave a new phone number: HE-1893.

4. William Stephens, Inc., Agency

By September 1937, the Stephens agency handled Lugosi. The *Players Directory Bulletin* listed the phone number HO-2231.

5. Robert Knowlden Agency

With the phone number CR-11103, this agency represented Lugosi as of March 1938.

6. Hollam Cooley Agency and S. George Ullman

During most of 1939, this agency claimed to handle Lugosi from phone number CR-5-6161. May, July, September, October and December editions from 1939 list Béla with this agency.

7. William Morris Agency, Inc.

This prestigious agency handled Lugosi during 1940, as mentioned in the March and May editions of the *Players Directory Bulletin*. The same agency represented Lugosi throughout 1941 and the first half of 1942. The agency could be reached at phone number CR-1-6161.

8. Salkow Agency

From phone number CR-1-9134, the Salkow Agency managed to find multiple film projects for Lugosi. The *Players Directory* first lists Lugosi with this agency in August 1942.

9. Kline-Howard Agency

The September and December *Players Directory* gives this agency (phone number CR-6-7055) as Bela's representative. The same agency handled Lugosi throughout 1944 and most of 1945.

10. Management, Harry E. Edington, Gerard B. Cloutman, Associate

From November 1945 until mid-1946, Lugosi let this outfit represent him from phone number CR-1-6239.

11. Virginia Doak Agency, Inc.

During mid-1946 through Lugosi's signing a contract with Don Marlowe in October 1947, Doak marketed Lugosi's talents, though with no real benefit. Apparently few calls rang at her HI-0714 phone number. Upon signing with Marlowe, however, Lugosi encouraged Doak to continue trying to get work for him.

12. Don Marlowe Agency

After Lugosi signed a contract with Marlowe in October 1947, listings soon appeared in the *Players Directory Bulletin*. In January 1948, Marlowe's phone number was HO-8422, though for the rest of 1948 the number became CR-4-6211. By January 1949, the phone number again had changed, with its newest incarnation as GR-8367.

13. Bertha Klausner

While staying in New York, Lugosi

allowed Klausner to represent his talent from 130 East 40th Street, phone number Murray Hill 5-2642. The August 1950 *Players Directory* offered her name as handling him.

14. Herdan-Sherrill Agency

This agency, with Lou Sherrill in particular pushing Lugosi, turned up in the November 1953 *Players Directory* as representing the actor. The 1954 *Players Directory Bulletin* also gave this agency's name, with the phone number CR-1-5236.

15. Ed Wood

Though never appearing in any official listings as representing Lugosi, Wood attempted to find work for the actor as early as 1954. Initially, the young transvestite filmmaker ran into a few skirmishes with Bela's agent Lou Sherrill. By the time Lugosi went into the Metropolitan State Hospital, as well as upon his release, Wood acted alone as Lugosi's manager.

3. Lugosi in Court

1. Divorce from Ilona Szmik. Budapest, Hungary. July 17, 1920.

While in Berlin, Lugosi received a telegram informing him of divorce proceedings between him and his first wife. The hearings were held on July 17, 1920, at the Fifth District Court of Budapest, 14 Alkotmany Street, Second Floor, Room Seven, at 9:00 A.M. Judge Medwezcwesky presided over the proceedings, which Lugosi did not attend. The court ruled in favor of plaintiff Ilona Szmik.

2. *Inspector's Interrogation During Primary Alien Inspection.* Immigration Services, Ellis Island, New York. March 23, 1921.

The following represents questions asked of Lugosi and the answers he verbally offered. These answers would have been translated, and, given the active nature of the Immigration Service at that time, the errors that follow could be the translator's or the result of the speed at which Lugosi was processed. The spelling and grammar are duplicated from the original, and Lugosi's answers are given in italics.

Name? — *Bela Lugosi*
Age? — *Thirty-eight*
Marital Status? — *Single*
Calling or Occupation? — *Sailor*
Able to —
    Read? — *Yes*
    What Language? — *Roumanian*
    Write? — *Yes*
Race or People? — *Roumanian*
Last Permanent Residence —
    Country? — *Italy*
    City or Town — *Trieste*
Nearest Relative or Friend in Country from whence Alien Came? — *No one*
Final Destination — *New York City, New York*
By Whom was Passage Paid? — *Member of Crew* (meaning Lugosi was a crew member of the *Graf Tisza Istvan*)
How Much Money in Possession? — *$100.00*
Whether ever in United States before? — *No*
Will Alien Ever Return to Country from Whence He Came? — *No*
Length of Stay in U.S.? — *Permanent*
Intends to Become a U.S. Citizen? — *Yes*
Ever in Prison or Almshouse, Insane asylum, or supported by Charity — *No*
Polygamist? — *No*
Anarchist? — *No*
Believes in or Advocates the overthrow by Force of U.S. Gov't? — *No*
Coming by Solicitation or Offer of Employment? — *No*
Whether Alien was previously Deported this Year? — *No*
Condition of Health, Mental & Physical? — *Good*
Deformed or Crippled? — *No*
Height? — *Five feet, ten inches*
Complexion? — *Dark*
Colour of Hair? — *Brown*
Colour of Eyes? — *Black*
Country of Birth? — *Roumania*
Town of Birth? — *Lugos*

3. *Lugosi vs. Hubert Henry Davis.* Municipal Court of the City of New York, Borough of Manhattan, Third District. New York City, New York. May 21, 1924.

Producer Irving Davis (real name Hubert Henry Davis) contracted Lugosi to direct *The Right to Dream*, a stage play. Davis quickly fired the Hungarian, claiming he was unable to function in that capacity. Plaintiff Lugosi's breech of contract lawsuit called for a jury trial. Yet after the defendant mentioned the actor's fabricated connections and misrepresentation of his talent, the jury members cast their votes in favor of Davis.

4. *Notice of Levy Against Personal Property of Bela Lugosi.* New York City Marshal. New York City, New York. October 1, 1924.

Due to the $65.16 in court costs from his unsuccessful suit against Hubert Henry Davis, Lugosi eventually had to sell some of his belongings to free himself from debt.

5. Divorce from Ilona von Montágh. New York City, New York. November 11, 1924.

Plaintiff Ilona Lugosi brought action against defendant Béla Lugosi before Judge William P. Burr on October 24, 1924. Ilona Lugosi's attorney appeared to present her verified complaint. The proceedings were tried under "Cat. No 1936/1924," with the County Clerk's Index Number being 28365/1924. The interlocutory judgment on default included the charge of adultery against the defendant with the stipulation that he could not remarry "any other person during the lifetime of the plaintiff except by express permission of the Court."

The charge and stipulation were a standard part of the form, filed on February 13, 1925, the first action since the entry of the interlocutory judgment. The only changes made on the paperwork were the deletions of the decrees for the custody of the children (since there were none) and for the monetary compensation of the plaintiff by the defendant.

6. Divorce from Beatrice Woodruff Weeks. Reno. December 9, 1929.

The Associated Press picked up the story of Weeks's divorce plea from Reno, alleging Lugosi was temperamental to the extreme. "Mrs. Lugosi indicated he had a violent temper which he displayed toward her and the servants," the *San Francisco Chronicle* claimed. Furthermore, he was "sullen and morose," and "unable to cast aside his irascible part of the role [Dracula] when he entered his home." While staying at Reno's Riverside Hotel, Weeks testified to the divorce court on December 9, 1929. She mentioned she was in no need of money and expected none from Lugosi.

Shortly thereafter, Lugosi commented, "I cannot see what use a Reno decree would do us." The actor also mentioned he was entitled to part of her fortune but simply did not want it.

Along with a front-page announcement in the *Chronicle* (titled "Wife of 'Dracula' Star Says Role Carried Too Far"), the *New York Daily Mirror* featured a cover story on November 5, 1929. The less-than-reputable paper entitled its exposé, "Lugosi Wins Heart of Clara Bow, Says Second Wife, Seeking Divorce: Film Star's Secret Love Is Revealed." The *Daily Mirror* claimed its story was an exclusive, coming to the paper when Weeks filed for the divorce on November 4.

The article itself called Lugosi a "Hungarian Count," and quoted Weeks as having said, "He slapped me in the face because I ate a lamb chop which he had hidden in the icebox for his after-theatre, midnight lunch. 'If you want lamb chops—buy your own,' my husband said." Weeks also claimed Lugosi demanded her checkbook and keys to her safe deposit vaults. She also spoke of his poor manners, with the *Mirror* adding that the "actual breaking point came where her husband elaborately furnished his own bedroom, afterward informing her that if she didn't care to equip her own, she could sleep on the floor." She supposedly "fled" the apartment at that point.

Topping off the *Mirror*'s exclusive was the "news" of Lugosi's impending wedding to Clara Bow, who was then involved in a divorce from entertainer Harry Richman. "I don't know when they will be married," Weeks said. "But before I left my husband he told me he and Clara had been engaged; that they had agreed to remain away from each other a year to test their love."

Though the *Daily Mirror*'s story should not necessarily be taken as the complete truth, Weeks did obtain her divorce. After the first few articles, however, the press devoted almost no attention to the matter.

Weeks died at age 34 on May 20, 1931, having been plagued by pulmonary disease and a drinking problem. Her last days were spent in Colón, Panama, to seek relief in the warm climate. The estate she left behind, valued then at some $50,000, became divided through a will filed on May 26, 1931, in the superior court. Milton J. Ferguson, a former California state librarian, received $6,000, with the remainder placed in trust. One-fourth of the net income went to Ida F. Searles of Columbus, Ohio, one-fourth to Claire Weeks Roberts of San Jose, California, and one-fourth to Marian P. Woodruff of Atlantic Highlands, New Jersey. The Regents of the University of California and the Board of Trustees at Stanford received the remaining quarter of the trust income.

7. Naturalization as a Citizen. Los Angeles, California. June 26, 1931.

Lugosi originally submitted a Declaration of Intent to become a U.S. Citizen in 1928, claiming his last foreign address to be Berlin and that he had emigrated aboard the *Graf Tisza Istwan* (more accurately the *Istvan*) from Trieste, Austria, a port city that was declared part of Italy after World War I. Mentioning Austria is not necessarily a mistake, however, because although Trieste was traditionally Italian, Austria had laid claim to it for some time, using it as an outlet to the Mediterranean. Furthermore, he claimed to have arrived at New Orleans on December 4, 1920, though in reality the *Tisza* docked on October 27.

Agent O.A. Pixley completed Lugosi's later petition, dated June 11, 1931. Witnesses testifying on his behalf included Joseph Diskay (a singer living at 672 Lafayette Park, Los Angeles), Bertalan Rakasi (of 545 South Coronado Street, Los Angeles), and Irving Adler (an optometrist of 807 Boston Street, Los Angeles). Lugosi claimed friendship with the three since March 1926.

Lugosi enrolled in a special course to pass the citizenship exam and no doubt felt pride in his success. This issue did arise again in January 1933, however, as Murray W. Garsson, special assistant secretary of labor, conducted an investigation to determine the status of foreign actors in U.S. films. On January 24, Lugosi declared his status, with the press noting "Actor Shows Citizenship."

8. Bankruptcy Petition and Financial Difficulties. Los Angeles, California. 1932.

On October 14, 1932, Lugosi appeared in court and filed for bankruptcy three days later (#19,639 H) to the Honorable Rupert B. Turnbull. In addition to Lugosi's signature as the Petitioner, attorney Frank H. Love, a notary public, signed the paperwork. Among Lugosi's possessions were four suits of clothing and "miscellaneous haberdashery, etc." located at 4534 North McCadden Place, Los Angeles, as well as $500 equity in furniture purchased under lease contract from Barker Brothers at Seventh and Figueroa in Los Angeles.

His initial liabilities, totaling $2,965.50, were made up of the following: $1,000 to Alexander and Oviatt for merchandise purchased between September 1931 and August 1932; $318 to the Dow Limousine Service for transportation during 1931 and 1932; $175 to Fred Bergman at the Union Oil Building for "goods and wares"; $165 to *The Cast*; $143.81 for various merchandise to the Central Hardware Company; $80 to the General Directory; $59.67 to the Bonded Tobacco Company; $235 to tailor Eddie Schmidt; $60 to dentist Raymond Beebe; $35 to E.T. Remmen; and $140 to Dr. Maxwell Fields. Additionally, he owed the Roth Furniture Company $34.15; Wolf's Market $99.77; Mildred Shneider $115 for services rendered in May and June 1932; $150 to Mrs. Karl Biehl for unpaid rent from 1926; $150 to Mrs. Charles Rowland for a personal loan dating from 1926; and $5 to the Pacific Patrol.

His debts to the Wolf Brothers grocery,

to Raymond Beebe, and to Bonded Tobacco of New York were initially greater than the aforementioned amounts. Partial payments had lowered them to their above figures, with all three bills settled on January 30, 1933, by the court. In addition to these claims, his former maid Lulu Schubert demanded $700 in unpaid salary. The IRS was knocking on his door for $65.56 as well. Another $700 suit came for rent on his apartment at 2643 Creston Drive. Each of these three was added to his petition.

The latter action, entitled *W.W.F. Cavanaugh, Plaintiff, vs. Bela Lugosi, Defendant*, was numbered as case 301253 in the Municipal Court of Los Angeles. Frank Love signed another amendment to Lugosi's bankruptcy papers on February 10, 1933, for the $3,731.06 alleged liability. In regard to the additional amount given by the plaintiff, Lugosi admitted having signed a one-year lease with M.T. and Sadie Willard on October 21, 1931. Yet, he went on to point out that the lease at Creston Drive (officially Lot 13, Block 5, Tract 7, 011, Sheets 1 to 6 inclusive of Maps, in the County Recorder's Office of Los Angeles) had been mutually canceled between the two parties and that he had surrendered the property to the owners. Thus, Lugosi claimed he didn't actually owe the additional amount.

Following the October 17 filing and additional petitions officially of the twentieth and twenty-second, the first meeting of creditors was announced for November 7. As of October 28, Lugosi had been notified to appear at the meeting, and the court filed an affidavit of the mailing notice to him. At the meeting itself, William I. Heffron became the trustee. The following day Heffron's $100 fee was filed, as was his own report of Lugosi's exempted property. On January 12, 1933, Heffron's "Return of No Assets" form was filed, and shortly thereafter he fixed January 30 as the final meeting of the creditors. The meeting continued on March 1, after which Lugosi's exempt property was confirmed and Heffron was discharged.

Lugosi signed the "Petition for Discharge and Order Thereon" on November 9, 1933, with the line he added under his name striking vigorously through the printed word *Bankrupt*. This paperwork led to a January 2, 1934, hearing at 10:00 A.M. in the Los Angeles Federal Building. Judge Harry A. Hollzer formally discharged Lugosi for his debts and claims at the time of his October 17, 1932, filing, inclusive of the later amendments.

9. Divorce Proceedings Filed by Lillian Arch Lugosi. Los Angeles, California. August 1944.

The Los Angeles County Clerk's Office filed Lillian Lugosi's suit on August 17, 1944, as D264947. The complaint was extreme cruelty (a standard term used in California divorce paperwork at the time), and the form mentioned the case as *Lillian Arch Lugosi vs. Bela George Lugosi*. The Americanized "George" is inaccurate, as well as a reflection of Bela Lugosi, Jr.'s middle name. The two had separated the previous day, with the paperwork claiming that the cruelty had occurred for more than one year prior to the filing. Attorney Delvy T. Walton acted as Lillian's legal adviser.

The Lugosis' property was listed as a house (10841 Whipple Street, North Hollywood), furniture, "fixtures and equipment," two Buick automobiles, life insurance, war savings bonds, funds in a joint bank account, and "other personal property." Lillian asked $500 a month support, breaking it down to $330 for herself and $170 for her son. To offer reasons of her need for alimony, she mentioned she had not worked since 1932 and that Lugosi's monthly salary was in excess of $2,000. An estimate of his 1943 earnings exceeded $24,000.

Lillian and Bela Jr. moved to her sister's home in Los Angeles, and the court ordered Lugosi to appear on August 28, 1944. His lawyer, Philip L. Wilson, Jr., asked for a postponement until October 3. The court placed a restraining order on Lugosi, apparently due to the paperwork, mentioning,

The actor with a portrait of his fourth wife, Lillian. After almost divorcing in 1944, the two finally ended their marriage in 1953.

"If not restrained, defendant threatens to and will dispose of certain personal property of the parties." Meanwhile, newspapers announced the separation of the couple after their 11 years of marriage with headlines like WIFE SUES THE MONSTER.

By November 1, 1944, however, William S. Baird dissolved the restraining order. Lillian herself moved for a dismissal of the suit on March 8, 1945. The marriage survived, but only for another eight years.

10. Divorce from Lillian Arch Lugosi. Superior Court of and for the State of California and County of Los Angeles. Los Angeles, California. July 17, 1953.

On June 3, 1953, several newspapers ran articles mentioning that Lillian Lugosi had filed a divorce suit the prior day. Cruel and inhuman treatment were the charges, though the complaint filed gave no details. The *Los Angeles Times* commented that the couple was negotiating a property settlement, but Lillian asked the court to award her all community property if no agreement could be reached. Lillian also asked for $50 a month child support and $1 a month token alimony for herself. The document prepared by attorney Algerdas N. Cheledan, claimed Lugosi was not a "fit and proper person" to have custody of their son.

The two signed the property settlement agreement on May 28, 1953, thus making the *Times*'s remark regarding Lillian's request for all property if "no settlement is reached" out of date. Lillian received the 1947 Buick Roadmaster, and Lugosi agreed to continue payment on two Continental Casualty Company life insurance policies without changing the beneficiary on either. Lugosi also agreed not to use either policy as collateral or to take further loans against them after $2,000 then owed was paid. Face values on the policies were $5,000 and $10,000.

Stephen Arch became the exclusive agent for both in regard to the lots owned at Lake Elsinore, California. Any sale of the lots required the written consent of Bela and Lillian, with the proceeds to be split equally between them. The lots were as follows: 10, 11, 15, 16, 17, 18, 19, 3, 4, 5, 1, 2, 21, 22, 23, 24, 25, 26, and 27, Block D, Rancho La Laguna, Lake Elsinore, County of Riverside. Lugosi and Lillian each relinquished the rights to the inheritance of the other's estate, with Lillian waiving claims to any alimony as well.

Lugosi himself failed to appear on June 24 at the court as ordered in a summons served him on June 9 at the 4601 Rodeo Lane address. He finally appeared on June 30.

The Honorable Samuel R. Blake presided over the testimonies presented on July 17. In addition to Lillian being sworn in, Valeria Springer testified on her behalf. The property agreement was admitted, and Blake quickly awarded Lillian her divorce. She received custody of Bela Jr., with Lugosi given the right of reasonable visitation. An investigation of Lugosi's earning capacity made Blake decide not to order child support at that time. Lillian's $100-a-week salary as a bookkeeper then exceeded Bela's income. The *Los Angeles Daily News* added that Lillian did her best, however, to prevent the court from holding Lugosi responsible for child support. "I know if conditions change Bela Lugosi will support his son without any order to do so," she told Blake. An order for future support was handed down, however, in the event Lugosi's financial situation changed. The clerk entered the case as D-152510.

Again the newspapers grabbed the story, turning it into LUGOSI TERROR, WIFE CLAIMS—GETS DIVORCE and DIVORCES JEALOUS DRACULA. The articles claimed Lugosi had stalked his wife, continually checking on her activities. "He was extremely jealous," Lillian testified. "He kept me under his thumb 24 hours a day. He'd listen in on an extension phone when I talked to my mother; he checked up on me when I went to the dentist's office; he charged me with infidelity."

The marriage finally ended, though the papers incorrectly noted Lillian as Lugosi's third wife. In reality, she had been his fourth. The *Los Angeles Herald-Express* erroneously claimed his first had been a countess. In the end, Bela and Lillian's years together, beginning with a 1933 elopement, constituted Lugosi's most lengthy and important marriage.

11. Voluntary Appearance Before Superior Judge Wallace L. Ware. Psychopathic Ward of the Los Angeles County General Hospital. April 22, 1955.

Judge Ware set up this hearing to consider Lugosi's plea for commitment to a state hospital for a cure from drug abuse. Lugosi had entered the hospital asking for rehabilitation on April 21, but at first the staff thought he was a crank or mental patient pretending to be the famed actor. He told physicians that a private sanitorium where he had been a patient advised him to turn to the county hospital. The hearing was held in the psychopathic ward because Lugosi was "too ill to go into court." He signed the necessary papers for the rehabilitation in advance of the hearing, in hopes that Ware would be agreeable. The hospital allowed him to remain overnight to offer his testimony on April 22.

Lugosi "clearly and resonantly" explained to Ware how he had become addicted to morphine due to pains in his legs. He related that the injections had begun in 1935. He also related that the morphine was used as medication. While Lugosi did not go to the black market to obtain it, he did claim to have smuggled methadone into the country after a tour of Great Britain in 1950. Physicians initially did not reveal the actual drugs to the press, announcing "they are not strong narcotics, but barbiturates." Another newspaper account oddly claimed that he was "not a narcotic addict, however, and that he has been using a narcotic for perhaps twenty years." A hospital counselor described Lugosi's condition as "fairly good, and is able to get around."

The actor also mentioned, "I was afraid to enter the hospital and I was afraid to go home. I knew I would start on the drugs again at home, and I didn't know what kind of treatment I would get at the hospital." Expressing his gratitude to Dr. James E. McGinnis, head of the hospital's psychopathic division, Lugosi added, "Everybody is trying to do everything they can to bring me back to life."

Ware ordered Lugosi's commitment to the Metropolitan State Hospital at Norwalk for a minimum of three months and a maximum of two years. Following this, Ware verbally applauded the actor. "The Court wants to commend you for this very courageous act of yours. It is commendable that you have come forward voluntarily wanting to cure your addiction to the use of drugs. After all, you are only 72 years of age. And it will be wonderful to get well and live the rest of your life as you should."

12. Last Will and Testament of Bela Lugosi. Signed January 12, 1954. Filed September 26, 1956. Admitted to Probate October 18, 1956.

Lugosi appointed Steven S. Weisman of Los Angeles to be executor of his last will and testament. In the event of more than $2,000 or more cash in his estate, Bela bequeathed that exact amount to his nephew, Béla Loosz of Los Angeles. If less than that amount existed in his estate, Lugosi desired Loosz to receive two of the lots at Lake Elsinore that he and former wife Lillian jointly owned. In that event, Weisman was to negotiate with Lillian to secure sole ownership of certain lots, with her being sole owner of the remainder. All the rest of his property went to his "beloved" son, Bela Lugosi, Jr.

Newspapers varied in their accounts of Lugosi's worth at the time of his death. A clipping from The *Hollywood Citizen News* printed a quote from attorney John F. Sheffield, who mentioned the estate was worth "about $4,000 or $5,000, including $1,900 cash, some real estate and paintings." By late September, newspapers mentioned the estate's worth as something closer to $2,900, again citing the cash but estimating the real estate at only $1,000.

Furthermore, under probate law Bela Lugosi, Jr., had to share the property with Hope, who, because she had married Lugosi after the will was written, was not mentioned in the document. She became administratrix of the estate, with her appointment being approved by Judge Clyde C. Triplett. In order to fill the position, Hope posted a bond of $2,000. This was Probate Case No. 382,569, with the Decree of Distribution entered on May 21, 1959. The court discharged Hope Lugosi of her duties on June 8, 1959.

13. *Lugosi vs. Universal Pictures Co.* Case 877975. Superior Court of the State of California for the County of Los Angeles. Los Angeles, California.

Rather than acting, Bela George Lugosi, the actor's only son, became an attorney in Los Angeles. He once described to the press his plans to focus on business law, even joking, "Having Bela Lugosi as a criminal lawyer would be a little too much, wouldn't it?"

In the early sixties, the fledgling attorney spotted an Aurora model kit of his father as Dracula for sale in a department store. Later, he noticed other examples of Lugosi on various products — all commercially licensed by Universal Studios. His legal background helped him quickly grasp a possible infringement on Lugosi's image.

After examining the contracts Lugosi signed with Universal, Lugosi Jr. strongly believed that the studio did not retain the right to his likeness for such products. He and Hope Lugosi engaged the Los Angeles firm of Irwin O. Spiegel to represent their case. They soon discovered that Universal began licensing Lugosi's image for such products during 1960.

On March 6, 1964, Hope filed a petition to reopen the probate of Lugosi's estate because the original order of distribution spoke only of the personal property specifically referenced without consideration of any unmentioned property. Joseph S. Dubin, attorney for the studio, filed objections to the petition on the grounds that there was no property right vested in Lugosi upon his death, that if such a property right existed it could not belong to the estate or be a part of probate proceedings, that there was no Lugosi estate "then in existence subject to further administration," and that no property was found belonging to such an estate.

The court ordered the estate of Lugosi to be reopened on April 29, however. By September 16, 1965, the court decreed distribution of "all property of the estate and all causes of action belonging to the estate, whether described therein or not." One half went to Bela Jr. and the remaining half to Hope. On October 20, 1965, an order for final discharge was made, with the case itself filed on February 3, 1966.

The exact wording of Lugosi's 1930 *Dracula* contract with Universal became important in the events to follow. The right granted to the studio the "right to photograph and/or otherwise produce, reproduce, transmit, exhibit, distribute, and exploit in connection with the said photoplay any and all of the artist's acts, poses, plays and appearances of any and all kinds hereunder, and shall further have the right to record, reproduce, transmit, exhibit, distribute, and exploit in connection with the said photoplay the artist's voice, and all instrumental, musical and other sound effects produced by the artist in connection with such acts, poses, plays and appearances. The producer shall likewise have the right to use and give publicity to the artist's name and likeness, photographic and otherwise, and to recordations and reproductions of the artist's voice and all instrumental, musical, and other sound effects produced by the artist hereunder, in connection with the advertising and exploitation of said photoplay."

This convoluted legalese became the basis for the Lugosis' claim. The contract for *Dracula* gave Universal the right to use the actor's image only in connection with the promotion and exploitation of the film. No merchandising rights were granted, and the Lugosis believed that children's jewelry, pencil sharpeners, and "monster old-maid card games" could not be characterized as the promotion of a film not even in general release. The plaintiffs claimed that Lugosi's right to his likeness was demonstrated by Universal's 1936 attempt to obtain a letter of permission from Lugosi to use his image for the film *Dracula's Daughter*. Minimum damages of $25,000 were sought.

Universal Studios, the defendant in this landmark case, contended that through Lugosi's contracts it had secured all rights to his portrayal of Dracula. The defense also attempted to prove that such rights, even if they had belonged to Lugosi, could not be passed on to heirs in the same manner as tangible property. Moreover, Universal claimed that *Dracula* might be exhibited on television, and thus the kites, shirts, and other products featuring Lugosi's image should be seen as being in connection with the photoplay's exhibition.

The idea of likeness itself became important, with the plaintiffs pointing out Lugosi's creation of an original image. They claimed Universal persisted not in marketing a generic Dracula, who had been portrayed by others like John Carradine, Lon Chaney, Jr., and Christopher Lee, but a very distinctive Lugosi. The Hungarian had, of course, worn little makeup and had portrayed the role as early as 1927 on the stage. Witness Alex Gordon pointed out that this "image" of Lugosi, in full Dracula regalia, became a part of other, non–Universal horror films like *Return of the Vampire*, *Spooks Run Wild*, and *Vampire Over London*.

The plaintiffs suggested that the right Lugosi retained in the 1930 contract was not a right of privacy. Rather, it was a right of property that, upon his death, descended to his heirs. This property had been approved for use in the film *Dracula's Daughter* through a written agreement in 1936. Lugosi's only other contract with Universal concerning the character of Dracula was for *Abbott and Costello Meet Frankenstein* in 1948. This agreement was never provided by Universal, probably due to its loss in an earlier flood of studio files. Since statuettes of Lugosi as Dracula were commissioned by the actor himself, the plaintiffs inferred that the missing 1948 contract must not have altered the rights given by earlier agreements.

The Memorandum Opinion of Superior Court Judge Bernard S. Jefferson stated the following: "It is this court's holding that Bela Lugosi's interest or right in his likeness and appearance as Count Dracula was a property right of such character and substance that it did not terminate with his death but descended to his heirs. Plaintiffs have established that they are the beneficiaries of such property right by distribution under Bela Lugosi's will."

The idea that the merchandise could promote television broadcasts of *Dracula* didn't affect Jefferson's decision. This was due partially to the testimony that the photoplay "might" air commercially. Also, the plaintiffs were able to show that most of the products in question were mere likenesses of Lugosi in costume and did not include references to the film itself.

Several earlier court cases were cited throughout the trial, such as *Zahler vs. Columbia Pictures*, *Fleischer Studios vs. Ralph Freundlich*, *Capitol Records, Inc., vs. Erickson*, and numerous others. *Lugosi vs. Universal Pictures Co.*, however, had no real predecessors. Attorney Irwin Spiegel pointed out that "Judge Jefferson's decision is a first instance ruling (after trial) in California that a performing artist has a protectable 'property' right in the incidents of his personality, such as his likeness, name, etc.; and it is a landmark decision in American jurisprudence (and possibly Anglo-American jurisprudence) that such incidents are descendable to a deceased performer's heirs under the laws of interstate succession and transmissable to them by Will."

The plaintiffs were entitled to recover damages from licensing agreements made by Universal for a period of two years prior to February 3, 1966. Though an interlocutory judgment was filed on April 21, 1972, the final judgment didn't come until July 9, 1974. The plaintiffs were awarded a total of $72,993.86.

Universal Studios appealed the trial court decision to the District Court of Appeals, which overturned the earlier decision. Suddenly, Lugosi was seen unable to transmit any such rights to his heirs. His name and likeness were also seen as part of the public domain. This new ruling found the Lugosis petitioning the California Supreme Court. They claimed the case needed to be considered not only because of Lugosi's rights, but also due to the broader issues the case involved. The Court accepted the case in August 1977.

On December 3, 1979, the Court, in a 4–3 decision, upheld the District Court of Appeals' decision. Lugosi did not have exclusive commercial rights to Dracula, nor could he pass them on to his heirs. Universal Studios won. A 58-page dissenting opinion by Chief Justice Rose Elizabeth Bird argued that the studio had actually infringed upon the rights of the deceased actor. Justices Mathew O. Tobriner and Wiley W. Manuel agreed with Bird.

Yet Justice Stanley Mosk asked in his concurring opinion, "May the descendants of James and Dolly Madison recover for the commercialization of Dolly Madison confections?" An opinion by Justice Lester William Roth proclaimed, "After Lugosi's death, his name was in the public domain. Anyone, including (his heirs), or Universal, could use it for a legitimate commercial purpose." Along with Mosk and Roth, justices William P. Clark, Frank C. Newman, and Frank K. Richardson agreed that Lugosi's image was not a transmissable property.

In 1972, *Time* magazine pronounced "Dracula Lives!" after the Lugosis' success. By December 4, 1979, newspapers read "Lugosi heirs lose 'Dracula' Suit." Justice Mosk himself wrote "Lugosi rises from the grave twenty years after his death to haunt his former employer."

Additional information on the court cases can be found in the USC Law Library's 1973 bound volume of *Lugosi vs. Universal Pictures Company: Memorandum Opinion and Post Trial Brief.* Further records can be obtained in Volume 25 of the *Reports of Cases Determined in the Supreme Court of the State of California*, bound in 1979 by Bancroft-Whitney of San Francisco.

By the nineties, Bela Lugosi, Jr., would himself be licensing Lugosi's image as the "Lugosi estate." He also became a representative for Ron Chaney and Sara Jane Karloff, the respective heirs of Lon Chaney and Boris Karloff. Furthermore, Lugosi Jr. involved himself in other entertainment cases, including a Three Stooges case in which heirs of "Curly Joe" DeRita and Larry Fine sued the heirs of Moe Howard over revenue from merchandising.

4. Lugosi in Politics
by Frank J. Dello Stritto

At different times, Bela Lugosi's political life saw intense activity, though rarely has it been discussed in any lengthy way. One of the few sources to tackle the subject was Robert Cremer's *Lugosi: The Man Behind the Cape* (Henry Regnery, 1976). However, a thorough examination of the issue yields various questions and conclusions on his two major eras of political activity.

The first, when he was in his midthirties, was immediately after World War I. Hungary, like all of Eastern Europe, was in chaos. The collapse of the Hohenzollern, Habsburg and Romanov dynasties left much of Europe's population without their age-old leaders and governments. A rich brew of extremists moved to fill the power void. Lugosi summed up the period in a 1943 interview with *The Boston Globe*, recalling, "You stand a good chance of being hanged." For decades his reminiscences were the only record of that period of his life, and he generally shaded the truth to suit the prevailing political winds.

Lugosi's second political period came during World War II. His native Hungary, which he had not seen for more than 20 years, was no longer in the grip of chaos but of Nazi fascism. No more was Lugosi a struggling actor but a world-famous movie star, whose name and presence could attract thousands to his cause. He used that fame generously — and, in retrospect, perhaps imprudently — in aiding the cause to free Hungary from Hitler. In 1943 Lugosi told the *Boston Herald*, "I am an avowed Roosevelt disciple and I think without a doubt the President is the greatest outstanding personality of the day. I am a firm believer in his ideas and ideals, and you can put that down in spades." A few months later he described himself to the *San Francisco Chronicle* as an "extremely liberal democrat." That characterization intrigued right-wing, conservative watchdogs in the United States who labeled Lugosi a Communist and dogged him through the last years of his life. Those years began with the Hollywood witch-hunt for leftists and ended with Russia's brutal suppression of the Hungarian Revolution, less than three months after Lugosi's death in 1956. Whether the red-baiting of Lugosi prevented him from capitalizing on his brilliant success in *Abbott and Costello Meet Frankenstein* (1948) or otherwise robbed him of acting jobs when he needed them most can only be speculated upon.

A study of Lugosi's early life clearly suggests what attracted him to the political left. He was by nature a soft touch for anyone in need, anyone he could help, and thus he instinctively sided with the downtrodden. He would often offend or alienate those in power — from studio bosses and theater managers who controlled

Along with multiple other guests, Lugosi offered a speech to crowds at this "mass meeting" in 1943. Unlike some events at which he spoke, this "Action to Liberate Hungary" rally seems to have had no links to Communism. (Courtesy of Frank J. Dello Stritto.)

his career, to governments on both sides of the Atlantic which could imprison, exile, or execute him, to his own father.

István Blasko, like his youngest son, Béla, was an ambitious man who often overextended his resources. And, like his youngest son, he controlled his home and family with the firm grasp of a dictator. Young Béla rebelled against the discipline and inflexible regimen of his father. At a tender age Lugosi announced his desire to become an actor; István promptly dismissed such absurdity. In 1894 Lugosi left his father's house and never returned. For years Béla eked out a survival existence as a miner's apprentice, riveter, and engineer's apprentice. Though later in life Lugosi seemed a born patron and patrician, he retained vivid memories of his years of hardship and knew well the lives that most of his audiences led. In the United States, he would often wax poetic on Hungary's system for training and promoting actors, but he bristled under the entrenched seniority system for his whole tenure with the Royal and National theatres.

Thus were the forces that shaped Lugosi's politics: an opposition to autocratic control, going back to his rebellion against his father, as well as a keen appreciation for the underside of life, arising from the desperate, pre-teen years on his own. Rounding out these experiences were a compassion and empathy for anyone who needed his help, a genuine sense of duty that belied his self-indulgent lifestyle, and feelings of inadequacy over his lack of formal education. These traits led him to many selfless acts, but also made him a pawn for those with more savvy.

Arguing politics was a popular pastime for actors who crowded the Budapest cafes before and after performances. Lugosi partook in these "debates," but his first overt political action was joining the Austro-Hungarian army in 1914 at the outbreak of war. As a member of the National Theatre he was exempt from military service, but apparently he never considered any course but defending his homeland. Two years and three wounds later, a presumably disillusioned Captain Lugosi was discharged. He unhappily returned to the autocracy of the National Theatre. The war ended, empires collapsed, and revolts erupted. Lugosi was now poised for a very brief and very costly adventure in politics.

A brewing discord within the Hungarian film industry sparked Lugosi's entree. Artists and technicians made the films; distributors controlled them and reaped most of the profits. A similar labor-management standoff surfaced in the theaters. Lugosi became a leading voice of the actors. Compared with the fledgling Marxist-Leninists whom every labor dispute attracted, Lugosi was practical and free of dogma, rising quickly in the movement. In late 1918 he formed the Free Organization of Theatre Employees. A few months later, he expanded it into the National Trade Union of Actors, which embraced film and theater artists. In March 1919 he galvanized his fellow artists at a conference of industry activists with a stirring speech that called for a mass demonstration. That same month he led the demonstration and shortly after published a very "red" manifesto in the May 15 edition of the *Szinészek Lapja* (*The Actor's Page*).

Hungary was in upheaval in the aftermath of war and the collapse of the Habsburgs. These heady months gave Lugosi the "lead role" in labor movements that the Budapest Theatre autocracy had for years denied him on stage. He was thoroughly sincere in his actions but was as much playing a role as advancing political goals. As in any role, the actor was performing to another's purpose. How much Lugosi then knew or cared about Communist influence in the organizations he founded and promoted is unknown. The Communists, headed by Béla Kun (1886–1937), took power in April 1919, only days after the actors' demonstration. Ousted was Milhály Károlyi, head of the short-lived Hungarian People's Republic. Lugosi initially welcomed one of Kun's first acts, the nationalization of the film industry. Kun would hold power for less than four months, during which time he unsuccessfully tried to stamp his extremist brand of Communism on a country not yet reconciled to postwar realities. As a force in the actors' union, Lugosi had a rather privileged position under Communist rule, but when Kun's "Red Terror" affected his own comrades, he protested.

Kun was soon gone, replaced by Miklós Horthy (1868–1957), an admiral (of which land-locked Hungary produced very few) and as far to the right as Kun had been to the left. "Red Terror" became "White Terror"— Kun supporters and fellow-travelers were in danger. One story claims that on a late night in August 1919 Lugosi and his wife, Ilona, buried themselves beneath a load of straw in a cart and escaped across the border into Austria. Thus ended Lugosi's plunge into politics.

How did Lugosi choose to remember and portray those exciting, terrifying, and disastrous months of 1918–19? A year later, en route to the United States on an Italian freighter, he boasted of his past to his shipmates and was shocked to find hostility among them. His soon tempered his memories. After he gained fame in the United States, he often commented on his part in Hungarian politics to many

Discussing world events with editor Louis Rittenberg. (Courtesy Frank J. Dello Stritto.)

interviewers and publicists. In 1928 he told the *San Francisco Call*, "I am an exile from Hungary, you may know, as I was a follower of Károlyi in the revolution." The *San Francisco Examiner* reported that "Lugosi was one of Count Károlyi's lieutenants in the Hungarian revolution of 1918, and during Károlyi's brief control Lugosi was the government's minister of the theatre." None of this is true. Though Lugosi corresponded with his fellow exile at least through the forties, he was never associated with Károlyi in Hungary. The mass demonstration that Lugosi led in 1919 was in fact against Károlyi's government. By shifting his exile one year back to 1918, Lugosi avoided the implication of Communist ties.

Through the thirties and forties, Lugosi maintained that he fled the "royalist" terror. The pressbook for *White Zombie* (1932) quotes him as saying, "The Royalists regained control of the government, and whenever they could find a member of the Károlyi party, they proceeded to hang him. And so I decided to go away from that place, I had no desire to attend such a necking party." Again, not quite true — Horthy was no more a "royalist" than was Hitler. The quote is perhaps a publicist's creation, but the wording is very much the way Lugosi spoke in English. This version continued in information distributed by Lugosi's publicists. The pressbook for *Black Dragons* (1942) contains an article "Actor Escapes Execution at Hands of Royalist Enemies," which again describes Lugosi's ministry under Károlyi, the return of the royalists, who "in subsequent reprisals hanged 12,000 of the Károlyi followers." By invoking "Károlyi" and "royalists" rather than "Kun" and "reactionaries," Lugosi could hope to win his audiences' sympathy and avoid any implication that he was further left than any lover of democracy.

Though in the United States Lugosi was never shy about recounting his version of his political past, the harrowing experience that cost him everything left its scars. In the midthirties, Lugosi supported the union movement that led to the Screen Actor's Guild, but only clandestinely. The consequences of his 1919 foray into politics weighed heavily upon him when the same muses called 20 years later.

In 1926 a general pardon by the Horthy regime made Lugosi's return to Hungary possible. However, perhaps Lugosi was ambivalent about visiting a homeland that had changed drastically under the man who drove him into exile, Miklós Horthy. Horthy's brutal elimination of his opposition gave Hungary political stability, but the twenties and thirties were decades of grinding poverty for the country. As Hitler would do in Germany, Horthy blamed the hardships on war reparations, using the conditions to promote aggressive but costly foreign policies to regain territories lost after the war. Inflaming nationalism further enabled him to suppress political radicals and ethnic minorities.

Horthy of course gravitated toward his kindred dictators, Hitler and Mussolini, with whom he was allied in all but name. At the outbreak of World War II, Hungary was officially neutral, but definitely pro–Axis. Cooperation with Hitler restored some of the coveted territories to Hungary, but at a terrible cost. Thousands of Hungarians perished on the Russian front fighting with the Nazis. Thousands more faced the horror of deportation and death camps when the Nazis finally occupied Hungary in 1944.

Through the thirties, Lugosi was a reigning patron and leader of the Los Angeles Hungarian community, which at the outbreak of World War II was about 10,000 strong. Hungary declared war against the United States on December 13, 1941, two days after Germany's declaration and only six days after Pearl Harbor. Lugosi, like hundreds of celebrities, immediately joined the war effort and the resistance to fascism. He did the usual rounds at war bond rallies and found a particular niche — given his screen image — at blood drives.

To a degree, Lugosi attempted to use the war effort to change his public image in his never-ending struggle to shed the "Dracula curse." His studio publicity dutifully reported all his civic activities, building a benevolent, fatherly image around them. In the press releases, he often praised the democratic ideals of Franklin Roosevelt, who had been born the same year as Lugosi. "He is constantly extending a helping hand to someone," wrote one of his sheet biographies circulated to newspapers in cities where he appeared. "There is a Hungarian proverb which says you can't receive with a closed fist, and that has been part of his philosophy for life ... Lugosi is a true believer in the democratic principles of our country. Abraham Lincoln is his political ideal. There is a definite Lincolnian air about the strongly civic-minded Lugosi and his activities."

Lugosi's controversial activities during the war were his support and leadership of antifascist organizations. In 1942 Lugosi's publicity claimed that he had formed in Los Angeles the American-Hungarian Defense Federation "for the battle against the so-called 'new order.'" Nothing was heard of this organization again, which may only have been a name coined at a particular rally. He was also a member of American-Hungarian Relief, Inc. His chief affiliation was as "national president" of the Hungarian-American Council for Democracy. The HACD was formed in the summer of 1943 with allegedly strong backing from the Communist Party of the United States (CPUSA).

Lugosi's own publicity described the HACD as "the central organization of Americans of Hungarian descent behind the war effort of our country. At the same time, helping the people of Hungary in their fight against the Nazi-fascist oppressors. This council advocates that Nazism be wiped out everywhere, and by the people and for the people a truly democratic government must be established all over the world for the everlasting peace and prosperity of the United States and rest of the world. There is a genuine cross-section of the Hungarian American population, which under the leadership of Lugosi is standing behind this patriotic movement: college professors, workers, doctors, lawyers, businessmen, farmers, and manufacturers trying to turn Hungary against the Nazi enemies and thus shorten the war, to aid the people of Hungary in writing their own bill of rights, and to help in creating peace and happiness for all mankind."

The years 1943 and 1944 became two of the busiest of Lugosi's career, and thus his later claims to have been a mere figurehead of the HACD are probably correct. As an honorary president, he would have appeared at events and signed various solicitation letters. In the 1990s, with the breakup of the Soviet Union and the release of new information from Moscow itself, the CPUSA's role in such organizations as the HACD becomes clear. Undoubtedly, the CPUSA immersed itself during World War II in a variety of patriotic and special interest groups opposing the Axis powers. Undoubtedly, these movements received support and guidance directly from the Soviet Union. Available information shows that few supporters or organizations such as the HACD knew that the CPUSA was involved in conspiracies and espionage for the Soviet Union.

Could Lugosi have been so utterly unaware or uncaring about the type of people he was associating with? In his interviews and publicity—while praising Roosevelt and drawing parallels to Lincoln—he occasionally refers to himself as an "extremely liberal democrat" working for "100% ideal democracy." What did he mean? Also, there is the conscious avoidance in his publicity of what really happened in Hungary in 1919. There is also the heavy involvement of Eugene and Alfred Neuwald in the HACD, both of whom were—factually or not—widely acknowledged as Communists. Many Hungarians accepted Lugosi's later denials of Communist affiliations; many others did not. As the defeat of the Nazis became more certain and as the Soviet Union dropped the pretense of liberating Eastern Europe to emerge as its oppressor, those in league with the Communists came to be viewed as America's enemy within.

On July 17, 1944, the *New York Daily News* published a column by political writer Frank C. Waldrop entitled, "Why Are They Shy?" an exposé of Communist-affiliated committees headquartered at 23 West 26th Street in Manhattan. That address later became the national headquarters of the U.S. Communist Party. The same month radio commentator Henry J. Taylor blasted the HACD as a

Communist front; many other political writers probably did the same. "Some of them aren't pinks," Waldrop wrote, "they are blushing Reds. But all of them are very, very shy of identification of their true colors. Wherever possible, they speak of themselves as 'democrats,' using the small 'd.'" The article mentions Orson Welles, Charlie Chaplin, Paul Robeson, and Bela Lugosi. "Right next door to Robeson at No. 23 is the celebrated movie murderer and child-frightener Bela Lugosi, performing as president of the Hungarian-American Council for Democracy."

In actuality, Lugosi was rarely in New York during the war years, and certainly was not there in the summer of 1944. But the HACD had offices at 23 West 26th, and Lugosi's name was on their letterhead. He may have visited their offices in April 1944, when he toured the Eastern seaboard in *Arsenic and Old Lace* and spoke at a "liberate Hungary" rally. The rally itself was hardly a pure Communist front, for the other speakers included a U.S. congressman, a rabbi, and a Protestant minister — all of whom outbilled Lugosi in the announcement poster.

A month before the Waldrop column, Lugosi wrote a letter to Milhály Károlyi, then in exile in London, whom Lugosi probably met for the first time when Károlyi visited Hollywood in 1930. The letter mentions Lugosi's HACD work, but there is no hint of leftist conspiracies or hidden agendas within the council. Lugosi's association with Károlyi would be cited as proof of his leftist leanings. Károlyi himself was definitely a socialist, but as the title of his autobiography — *Faith Without Illusion* — suggests, he had no misapprehensions about Soviet-backed Communists. After all, Kun's Communists had toppled Károlyi from power in 1919 (Kun himself later perished in Moscow during Stalin's purges of the 1930s).

A fair assumption is that Lugosi resigned the HACD presidency shortly after the Waldrop article, for mention of the organization in his publicity stops in mid-1944. In 1945 his only political act was signing a petition to President Roosevelt to block the deportation of labor leader Harry Bridges, who had been prominent in the longshoremen's union movement. Bridges's deportation was ordered due to his alleged Communist ties. He vehemently denied the charge, battling against the order throughout 1945. Whether Lugosi thought he was supporting a fellow leftist or a fellow victim of red-baiting is debatable. Publicity supporting Bridges was foolish if Lugosi had anything to hide, and courageous if not.

The year 1947 saw the hearings of the House Committee on Un-American Activities. Lugosi's wartime activities escaped any direct citation made by the committee, but undoubtedly inquiries were made regarding him. Despite his own request that the HACD be investigated, Lugosi's involvement was not forgiven. The January 28, 1949, *Magyarole Vasarpja* (a church weekly) ran this notice, based on a rumor that Lugosi was returning to Hungary: "Adieu, Mr. Dracula! We read in December issue of the *Budapest Kisujsag*: 'Bela Lugosi, the Hungarian actor, who lived in Hollywood for the last twenty years, has written to his sister here at Budapest and advised her that he is coming home for a visit. At the time Lugosi left Hungary he went away because he was expelled from the National Theatre on account of his radical leftist attitude. For twenty years he has not come back!' Thus, the chairman of the so-called Hungarian-American Council for Democracy,

Dracula Lugosi, is proven by a Budapest paper that he is not democratic but extreme leftist, that is, Communist — as we always knew it. We hope he will have such a good time with the Matyas Pakosis that he will never wish to come back to America, which is denounced there as imperialist and inferior."

The Reverend George Borshi, secretary of an organization called the Hungarian Reformed Federation of America, submitted the article to the Senate Judiciary Sub-Committee on Immigration and Naturalization. The sub-committee was then holding hearings on foreign-born political subversives and was considering their denaturalization and deportation. In addition to the Reverend Borshi's testimony, Lugosi is mentioned four times in the massive hearing's transcript. Alfred Neuwald confirmed Lugosi's role as national president of the HACD, and three other Hungarian-Americans described in broad terms Lugosi's Communist links.

Whether legal action against Lugosi — which could have stripped him of his citizenship and led to his deportation and to his imprisonment if he ever lied to the government — was considered beyond the hearings is unknown. The hunt for subversives in Hollywood would run its course through the early fifties. These years were dismal ones for Lugosi's career. Did his documented ties to Communists ever affect his ability to get work? Is an unofficial blacklisting at all responsible for his inability to follow up on his surprise success in *Abbott and Costello Meet Frankenstein* (1948)? The answers are unknowable, since the blacklisting was often a gentleman's understanding among producers and watchdogs.

Of course Lugosi had a myriad of health and personal problems that readily explain his lack of employment, but the suggestive evidence that a blacklisting was in place is great. Ironically, Boris Karloff, who would make two films with the comedians, was the one to profit from *Abbott and Costello Meet Frankenstein*. With the exception of *The Black Sleep* (1955), Lugosi never again worked for a recognized studio. Lugosi had influential Hungarian friends in Hollywood, such as Michael Curtiz and Joe Pasternak, who might have thrown work his way, but they never did. Friends would always give him handouts, but only those outside the Hollywood system like Ed Wood or Alex Gordon associated with him professionally.

Was Lugosi in league with the Communists or an altruist used by them? Could Lugosi have been any more prudent or cunning in managing his political life than he was in managing his acting career? Could political subversives have exploited him as easily as the Hollywood studios? In his life, Lugosi ignored a military exemption to plunge into the bloodbath of World War I, ignored or offended the power brokers of his industry to pursue the life he enjoyed, and ignored the politics of anyone who claimed to be fighting for Hungarian freedom. He always paid a terrible price for such ignorance.

II. Lugosi, the Performer

5. Feature-Length Films

The following entries constitute an exhaustive list of Lugosi's film career. For ease, the movies have been separated into three sections — Hungary, Germany, and the United States and United Kingdom — denoting the country of origin.

For each film, cast and credit listings appear, as well as a short plot summary and notes on the production's history. For his best-remembered and most important films, more depth is given in terms of production information, and cast/credit listings.

Within the credit information of Lugosi's U.S. films, the registration date for the copyright is given alongside the assigned copyright number. Though the production notes offer information concerning the time of each film's release, the copyright date is in many ways more important and exact. Particularly in the earlier days of Hollywood, a film might be previewed one month premiered later, and then over a series of subsequent months it would appear in theaters across the country.

Films appear chronologically. When more than one film was produced within a year, the order is determined chronologically by copyright date (which appears at the end of the credits). When a film was not copyrighted (as in foreign releases or low-budget movies), the order is chronological based on the best information sources available to the author.

Lugosi's appearance in two specific films, *Casanova* (1918) and *Lock Up Your Daughters* (1959), remains questionable. Both are included in this filmography, and surface in the chapter "Unmasking the Mysteries." Careful attention should also be given to *The Last Performance* (1929) and *The King of Jazz* (1930); Lugosi participated only in the Hungarian versions of these two projects.

Hungary

1. *A Leopárd (The Leopard)*

Cast: Arisztid Olt [Béla Lugosi], Annie Góth, Klára Peterdy, Gusztav Turán, Ila Lóth, Peter Konrády.

Credits: Star Company, 1917. Directed by Alfréd Deésy. Screenplay taken from Alphonse Daudet's book.

Plot Summary: Lugosi portrays the title character, an aristocrat who woos the daughter of an immigrant, upper-middle-class financier.

Production Notes: Lugosi's first film expanded into a several-film relationship with the Star Company, which also advertised itself as the Star Film Company. Interestingly, its logo was that of a bat surrounding the company name.

Star followed the same path as most Hungarian film companies by drawing on literature for story material. Director Deésy, under the employ of Star, set a record in Hungary by directing 34 films in approximately three years beginning by late 1915; Star produced the bulk of these in 1917–18. Deésy as a director devoted much of his attention to the business interests. He enjoyed acting as well and had initially met Lugosi on the Debrecen stage.

2. *Álarcosbál (The Masked Ball)*
Cast: Annie Góth, Arisztid Olt [Béla Lugosi (as Rene, the secretary-governor)], Norbert Dán, Robert Fiáth, Richárd Kornai, Viktor Kurd.
Credits: Star Company, 1917. Directed by Alfréd Deésy. Screenplay adapted from Verdi's opera *Ballo in maschera*.
Production Notes: No information is available. Existing photographs show a group of masked men with swords. One in particular has Norbert Dán pointing his blade at Lugosi's heart.

3. *Leoni Leo*
Cast: Arisztid Olt [Béla Lugosi], Norbert Dán, Richárd Kornai, Ila Lóth, Klára Peterdy.
Credits: Star Company, 1917. Directed by Alfréd Deésy. Screenplay by József Pakots. From the play by George Sand.
Production Notes: *Leoni Leo* has almost always found itself left out of Lugosi filmographies, with its discovery by researcher/playwright László Tábori a major contribution to knowledge on this period of the actor's career. Screenwriter Pakots wrote numerous plays, among them *Egy Karrier Története*. Lugosi appeared in the first performance of that play on April 3, 1914. No other information or photographs from *Leoni Leo* are available.

4. *Tavaszi Vihar (Spring Tempest)*
Cast: Arisztid Olt [Béla Lugosi], Myra Corthy, Norbert Dán, Viktor Kurd, Alice Ronay, Aladár Fenyö.
Credits: Star Company, 1917. Directed by Alfréd Deésy. Screenplay by László Bekeffy.
Production Notes: No information available. An existing photograph shows Lugosi, with a straw hat in his hands, talking with other characters in the cast. Trees are visible in the landscape.

5. *Az Ezredes (The Colonel)*
Cast: Béla Lugosi (as the Colonel), Sándor Góth, László Z. Molnár, Károly Huszár, Géza Borosa, Arpad Latabar, Claire Lotto, Zoltán Szeremy, Bero Maly, Janka Csatai.
Credits: Phoenix Company, 1917. Directed by Milhály Kertész. Screenplay by Richárd Falk. Based on a tale by Ferenc Herczeg.
Plot Summary: The Colonel finds himself caught as he breaks into the house of a wealthy man. Rather than have him arrested, the millionaire desires the Colonel to steal a fortune back from his brother. The wealthy man's daughter, Kathe, falls in love with the Colonel and does not want him to return the fortune the uncle had taken. In the end, only the love between Kathe and the Colonel is real.
Production Notes: Lugosi's first film for the Phoenix Company also led to his first film directed by Milhály Kertész, who would achieve much fame as an American director under the name Michael Curtiz. Under that name, Kertész became responsible for *Casablanca* (1943), and many other classic Hollywood films. In 1918 Phoenix considered Kertész its managing director, and his input brought more tales of high adventure and criminal activity to the screen. Kertész helmed 38 films while in his home country, and he was known for his cinematic montage technique. *The Colonel* holds a high place in a list of Kertész's seven most successful films as compiled by historian Istvan Nemeskürty.

Kertész based *Az Ezredes* on a comedy by Ferenc Herczeg, a popular Hungarian author. Lugosi himself had earlier performed in such Herczeg plays as *Ocskay Brigadéros* and *A Dolovai Nábob Leánya*. Scriptwriter Richárd Falk wrote other Phoenix films, including *Alraune* (1918).

Az Ezredes enjoyed great reviews from critics, and in addition to a surviving still from the film, a few minutes of footage exist in the private collection of a Hungarian film collector. For posterity, enlargements have been made of a few frames showing Lugosi.

6. *A Nászdal (The Wedding Song)*
Cast: Arisztid Olt [Béla Lugosi (as Bertram)], Klára Peterdy, Irén Barta, Richárd Kornai, Károly Lajthay.
Credits: Star Company, 1917. Directed by Alfréd Deésy. Screenplay by Ignác Balla and Nándor Ujhelyi. Based on the story *The Wedding Song*.
Plot Summary: Bertram, a famous violinist, honeymoons with his wife in the mountains. One evening, the two are attacked by Izau, a pianist who loves Bertram's wife. The two musicians duel, with Bertram killing Izau and escaping to the forest. For a time, he earns money giving violin lessons. His young wife mourns his death, but when by chance she sees the still-living, bearded Bertram, she has him arrested. She believes he is Izau, but the imprisoned Bertram convinces her otherwise when he plays a melody on his violin that he played to her once before on their wedding night. The two are happily reunited.
Production Notes: Made in 1917 but not released until April of 1918, *A Nászdal* received good notices. Critics paid special attention to the exciting plot, lush cinematography, and the performances of Lugosi and Peterdy. Costars like Ila Lóth went on to perform in Hungarian films after Lugosi left the country; Károly Lathjay became a professional director, making films under the Rex Studio name. The only surviving photograph (from the April 7, 1918, edition of *Színhazielet* magazine) of *A Nászdal* shows the bearded Lugosi, sitting by a wall with his violin, and Peterdy.

7. *Küzdelem a Létért (The Struggle for Life)*
Cast: Arisztid Olt [Béla Lugosi (as Orlay)], Annie Góth, Klára Peterdy, Ila Lóth, Ferenc Virágh.
Credits: Star Company, 1918. Directed by Alfréd Deésy. Screenplay based on Alphonse Daudet's play, *La Lutte pour la vie*.
Plot Summary: An architect named Orlay ruins everyone to further his career. Even his lovers, a countess and a poor girl, don't stand in his way. Eventually, when Orlay believes his career has reached the pinnacle of success, the father of the poor girl shoots him.
Production Notes: *Küzdelem a Létért* became Lugosi's greatest economic success for the Star Company. Some 15 stills from the film survived in Lugosi's personal collection; a three-page advertisement published in the film magazine *Mozihét* also exists. Additionally, the Hungarian Film Institute owns 35mm material from this particular movie.

8. *Casanova*
Cast: Alfréd Deésy (as Casanova), Kamilla Hollay, Marcel Rolla, Norbert Dán, Arisztid Olt? [Béla Lugosi?], Sandy Igalits, Richárd Kornai, Gusztav Turán.
Credits: Star Company, 1918. Directed by Alfréd Deésy. Screenplay by József Pakots and László Bekeffy. Cinematography by Károly Vass.
Plot Summary: The popular story of Casanova unfolds in a twentieth century setting.
Production Notes: Notable for featuring the same person (Deésy) in dual positions as actor and director, *Casanova*—from the standpoint of Lugosi historiography—becomes an area of great contention. More information on the film can be found in the chapter "Unmasking the Mysteries."

9. *Kilencvekilenc (Ninety-Nine)*
Cast: Lajos Rethey, Jenö Balassa, Zoltan Szeremi, Béla Lugosi, Claire Lotto, Gyula Gal, László Z. Molnár.
Credits: Phoenix Company, 1918. Directed by Milhály Kertész. Screenplay by Ivan Siklosi.
Plot Summary: Lugosi, an inspector, uses a variety of disguises to catch a thief. The tale based itself on a story about Monte Cristo, and the artwork for the movie poster shows the number "99" on the sides of a carriage.
Production Notes: István Nemeskürty, a

film historian, named *Ninety-Nine* as one of Kertész's seven most successful Hungarian films in his text *Word and Image: History of the Hungarian Cinema* (Corvina, 1968). Costar Gyula Gal also starred in Kertész's 1918 fantasy film *Alraune*.

10. Lili

Cast: Irén Barta (Lili), Klára Peterdy (Nagymama/Lulu), Béla Lugosi (Tábornok), Ila Lóth (Antoinin), Gusztav Turán (René), Richárd Kornai (Saint Hypothese).

Credits: Phoenix Company, 1918. Directed by Milhály Kertész. Screenplay by Jenö Faragó. Based on an operetta by Hervé. Designer, István Szirontai-Lhotka.

Production Notes: *Lili* became Lugosi's last film for Phoenix and Kertész. Oddly, the film included six of the Star Company's players in its cast. In at least one period advertisement, *Lili* carried the subtitle *Egy Nagymama Naplójából*; more contemporary sources often inaccurately refer to the film as *Lulu*. Lugosi's role in this film was a romantic one, and the Hungarian film historian István Nemeskürty mentioned *Lili* as being one of Kertész's seven most successful films.

11. Az Élet Királya (The Royal Life)

Cast: Norbert Dán (Dorian Gray), Arisztid Olt [Béla Lugosi] (Lord Harry Vatton), Annie Góth, Ila Lóth, Kamilla Hollay, Gusztav Turán, Richárd Kornai, Viktor Kurd.

Credits: Star Company, 1918. Screenplay by József Pakots. Based on Oscar Wilde's *The Picture of Dorian Gray*.

Production Notes: Star released *Az Élet Királya*, Lugosi's final Hungarian film, in September 1918. The film became known as *Dorian Gray Arckepe* for its release outside of Hungary.

Germany

12. Slaven Fremdes Willens (Slave of a Foreign Will)

Cast: Lee Parry, Béla Lugosi (as a hypnotist), Karl Halden, Violette Napierska, Margo Koehler, Gustav Birkholz.

Credits: Eichberg Film, 1919. Directed by Richard Eichberg.

Plot Summary: *Slave of a Foreign Will* apparently bore similarities to Du Maurier's *Trilby*, with a Svengali-like hypnotist. The tale included a violent rape scene.

Production Notes: During the early twenties, critics noted the huge influence of Max Reinhart on the work of Richard Eichberg, whose best known film of the period remains *Monna Vanna* (1922) with Lee Parry and Paul Wegener. Following many dramas, Eichberg moved to comedies, for which reviewers found few kind words. For *Slaven Fremdes Willens*, critics noted the realistic rape scene, though no known record exists of it spawning any moral outrage.

13. Nat Pinkerton

Cast: Olaf Storm, Nestor Pridum, Marian Alma, Sybill de Bree, Béla Lugosi (as a gang leader), E.V. Meghen.

Credits: Dua Film, 1920. Directed by Wolfgang Neff.

Production Notes: Lugosi's first of two films for the Dua Film company found him cast as a seedy gang leader. Star Olaf Storm later portrayed roles in such classics as *The Last Laugh* (1924) and *Metropolis* (1926). Female lead Marian Alma is best remembered for appearing in the 1926 version of *The Student of Prague*.

14. Der Fluch der Menschheit (The Curse of Man)

Cast: Lee Parry, Willi Kaiser-Heyl, Robert Scholz, Gustav Birkholz, Reinhold Pasch, Margo Koehler, Béla Lugosi (as Maelzer, a saboteur), Felix Hecht, Violette Napierska, Paul Ludwig.

Lugosi (second from right) in a scene from *Kilencvekilenc (Ninety-Nine)*, a 1918 Hungarian film.

Credits: Eichberg Film, 1920. Directed by Richard Eichberg.

Plot Summary: After being rejected by his lover, Maelzer commits treason and even attempts sabotage. Electricity kills the traitor before the authorities can reach him.

Production Notes: Eichberg released *The Curse of Man* in two parts, *Die Tochter der Arbeit (The Daughter of Work)* and *Im Rausche der Milliarden (In the Ecstacy of Billions)*. Shooting took place in July 1920, during which Lugosi found himself in an affair with actress Violette Napierska. One love letter he penned to the brunette star still exists.

15. *Der Januskopf (The Head of Janus)*

Cast: Conrad Veidt (Dr. Warren/Mr. O'Connor), Margarete Schlegel, Magnus Stifter, Willi Kaiser-Heyl, Béla Lugosi (as Warren's loyal butler), Margarete Kupfer.

Credits: Lipow Film, 1920. Directed by F. W. Murnau. Cinematography by Karl Freund.

Plot Summary: In an antique store, Dr. Warren purchases a statuette of the Roman god Janus. The two-faced deity appears kindly in one expression, but evil and satanic in the other. The good doctor then begins changing against his will into the vile Mr. O'Connor. The brutish creature then kills a young girl and prostitutes his own fiancée. At the dramatic conclusion, O'Connor takes poison to avoid impending arrest and dies with his hands clutching the bust of Janus.

Production Notes: *Der Januskopf*, which originally bore the subtitle *Eine Tragödie am Rande der Wirklichkeit (A Tragedy on the Border of Reality)*, holds a greater fascination than probably any other of Lugosi's German films. A blatant ripoff of Robert Louis Stevenson's *Dr. Jekyll and Mr. Hyde*, all prints were reportedly confiscated and destroyed by courts due to copyright infringement. Among other titles, exhibitors screened *Der Januskopf* as *Schrecken*

Lugosi as a hypnotist in *Slaven Fremdes Willens (Slave of a Foreign Will)*, a German film of 1919.

(The Terror) and *Love's Mockery*. Austrian spectators saw the film as *Dr. Warren and Mr. O'Connor*.

F.W. Murnau remains a permanent artist of the cinema due to his tremendous film *The Last Laugh* (1924) and the spectacular *Sunrise* (1929). Yet horror fans best remember him perhaps for *Nosferatu* (1922), his unauthorized version of Bram Stoker's *Dracula*, with Max Shreck as a vampire equally representative of pestilence as of sexuality. The eerie film continues to fascinate and even chill some viewers, though the fact it did not share the fate of *Der Januskopf* is amazing. Courts ordered every print of *Nosferatu* destroyed due to copyright infringement; however, the vampire film lived on.

The cast of *Der Januskopf* united several excellent players of German cinema with the famed Conrad Veidt as the tormented Dr. Warren. Veidt rose to stardom following his performance as the sleepwalker in *The Cabinet of Dr. Caligari* (1919), continuing his career until his death in 1943 with such films as *Casablanca* (1943). Actress Margarete Schlegel also appeared in E.A. Dupont's *The Ancient Law* (1923) and in 1931's noted *Berlin-Alexanderplatz*, and Kaiser-Heyl later starred in Wysbar's *Anna and Elizabeth* (1933). Supporting player Margarete Kupfer had already acted in Lubitsch's *Sumurun* (1920) and later appeared in *Nju* (1924), *The Harbor Drift* (1929), and again with Veidt in *Congress Dances* (1931).

Murnau expert Lotte Eisner did not include Lugosi in the credits of her noted book on the director, though his role as the butler can be seen in surviving photos. The notion of a film pairing Murnau, director of *Nosferatu*, and Lugosi, future star of *Dracula*, has great appeal. Certainly postwar Weimar cinema has not loosened its grip on the imagination of film buffs, particularly with its many classic horror films and strong elements of Expressionism. Unfortunately, Lugosi participated little in the classic German cinema, with this lost film possibly his one brush with greatness in that country.

16. Die Frau im Delphin (The Woman in the Dolphin)

Cast: Emille Sannom, Magnus Stifter, Béla Lugosi, Ernest Pittschau, Max Zilzer, and Jacques Wandryck.

Credits: Gaci Film, 1920. Directed by Artur Kiekebusch-Brenken.

Production Notes: Alternately titled *Thirty Days on the Bottom of the Sea*, *Die Frau im Delphin* apparently remains a lost film. Costar Magnus Stifter earlier performed with Lugosi in *Der Januskopf* (1920).

17. Die Todeskarawane (The Caravan of Death)

Cast: Carl de Vogt, Meinhart Maur, and Béla Lugosi (as an Arab sheik).

Credits: Ustad Film, 1920. Directed by Marie Luise Droop.

Plot Summary: A Saharan adventure story featuring an Arab sheik who clashes with a band of European travelers.

Production Notes: Star Carl de Vogt became popular with cinemagoers in Fritz Lang's adventurous *Spiders* (1919), and acted with Conrad Veidt in *The Road of Death* (1917). Costar Maur also appeared in *Spiders*.

18. Lederstrumpf (Leatherstocking)

Cast: Emil Mamelok (Hawkeye), Béla Lugosi (Chingachgook), Herta Heden, Gottfried Krause, Edward Eyseneck, and Margot Sokolowska.

Credits: Luna Film, 1920. Directed by Arthur Wellin.

Plot Summary: A cinematic version of James Fenimore Cooper's *Leatherstocking Tales*, the story covers the exploits of Hawkeye the Deerslayer during the 1740s. Orphaned and later raised by the Delaware Indian tribe in upstate New York, the Deerslayer befriends Chingachgook, the chief's son. The story details a time when "a man's only protection was his rifle."

Production Notes: Though originally 12 reels in length, *Leatherstocking* reached American audiences in 1923 in five reels and titled *The Deerslayer*. A print of the American version exists in the Eastman House, and is marketed on videocassette. Lugosi portrayed the Native American Chingachgook, trusted companion of Hawkeye.

19. Die Teufelsanbeter (The Devil Worshippers)

Cast: Carl de Vogt, Béla Lugosi, Meinhart Maur, Ilja Dubrowski.

Credits: Ustad Film, 1920. Directed by Marie Luise Droop.

Plot Summary: A Karl May tale set in the desert and full of high adventure, the screenplay very possibly contained elements that literary critics found disgusting in the author's novelettes. Though his books were often described as "trashy," May wrote numerous adventure stories in the 1890s, between his periods of poetry and Native American tales in the fashion of James Fenimore Cooper. His popularity in Germany extended well into the twentieth century.

Production Notes: Ustad released *The Devil Worshippers* in December 1920, though little is actually known of the film. Droop's second film based on Karl May's stories almost did not reach completion, as she and star Carl de Vogt fell in love. The two left Berlin together before editors even finished with *The Devil Worshippers*.

20. Johann Hopkins III (John Hopkins the Third)

Cast: Béla Lugosi, others unknown.
Credits: Dua Film, 1920.
Production Notes: Almost nothing is known of this German silent, save that it was Lugosi's second for the Dua company. Principal shooting took place in Berlin.

21. Der Tanz auf dem Vulkan (The Dance on the Volcano)

Cast: Béla Lugosi (as a Parisian aristocrat), Lee Parry, Violette Napierska, Robert Sholz, Gustav Birkholz, Felix Hecht, and Kurt Fuss.

Credits: Eichberg Films, 1921. Directed by Richard Eichberg.

Plot Summary: An aristocrat falls in love with a young lady, but both later perish due to the red flags of the Russian Revolution. Opening credits feature a volcano erupting, with the film itself claiming postrevolution Russia would have to change. The young lady dies when peasants mistake her for the enemy, while the aristocrat is killed on the steps of an enormous staircase as he runs to her corpse.

Production Notes: Eichberg released *The Dance on the Volcano* in two parts, *Sybil Young* and *Der Tod des Grossfuerstens (The Death of the Grand Duke)*. Many of Eichberg's frequent players appeared in the film, including three from *Slave of a Foreign Will* (1920) and *The Curse of Man* (1920), Lee Parry, Violette Napierska, and Gustav Birkholz. *Dance on the Volcano* lasted ten reels, being filmed on a relatively large budget. A print exists in the Eastman House, showing a dashing young Lugosi but exemplifying an outmoded, simple style of filmmaking. It became Lugosi's final German film.

United States and United Kingdom

22. The Silent Command

Cast: Edmund Lowe (Captain Richard Decatur), Belo [*sic*] Lugosi (Benedict Hisston), Carl Harbaugh (Menchen), Martin Faust (Cordoba), Gordon McEdward (Gridley), Byron Douglas (Admiral Nevins), Theodore Babcock (Admiral Meade), George Lessey (Mr. Collins), Warren Cook (Ambassador Mendizabal), Henry Armetta (Pedro), Rogers Keene (Jack Decatur), J.W. Jenkins (the Decaturs' butler), Alma Tell (Mrs. Richard Decatur), Martha Mansfield (Peg Williams, a vamp), Florence Martin (Her Maid), Betty Jewel (Dolores), Kate Blancke (Mrs. Nevins), Elizabeth Mary Foley (Jill Decatur).

Credits: A Fox Picture, 1923. Presented by William Fox. Directed by J. Gordon Edwards. Screenplay by Anthony Paul Kelly. Based on a story by Rufus King. Cinematography by George W. Lane. Running time, 91 minutes (eight reels, 7,809 feet), later cut to 73 minutes (6,820 feet). Copyright number LP19411, August 20, 1923.

Plot Summary: Hisston and a band of enemy agents plan to destroy the Panama Canal and the U.S. Navy's Atlantic Fleet, but fail to obtain needed information concerning mine positions in the canal zone from Captain Richard Decatur. Hisston then hires the adventuress Peg Williams to "vamp" Decatur, putting him at their mercy. Decatur plays along with the spies to gain their trust, even leaving his wife and being dismissed from the navy. Later, he triumphs over the saboteurs at Panama, gaining honorable reinstatement and the thanks of his country.

Production Notes: Basically a propaganda picture to help convince the American public to advocate a larger navy, *The Silent Command* received the full support of the U.S. Navy during production. One possible reason for this collaboration could have been Fox publicity promoter Wells Hawks, who formerly served in a similar capacity for that branch of the military. Fox released the film in September 1923, with period sources mentioning color-tinted sequences. A French release saw the title change to *His Country*.

Lugosi, whose first name is misspelled "Belo" in the credits, portrays Hisston, a "sinister figure in international intrigue, a vulture who feeds on war." Period interviews found him laughing that a Hungarian would help in the trek toward a larger navy, "since Hungary has no navy or needs any!" Tight closeups of his eyes, later used to much effect in horror films, enhance his characterization. Lugosi cuts an elegant figure, leaning back in his chair exhaling great puffs of smoke and mixing with Washington society. Critics also drew attention to a climactic fight scene between him and Lowe. The Hungarian's scenes were shot on the East Coast.

Ads included statements from General Pershing ("An effective, intensely interesting, inspiring picture") and Assistant Secretary of the Navy Theodore Roosevelt ("I wish to congratulate you. I hope that the film may be widely shown throughout the country"). Publicity also claimed, "Thousands of cheering spectators have said 'Great,'" with movie posters announcing "Love, Intrigue and Adventure on the High Seas."

J. Gordon Edwards, the grandfather of Blake Edwards, achieved renown as the director of many Theda Bara and William Farnum vehicles. Star Edmund Lowe, suave male lead with waxed moustache, later appeared opposite Lugosi in *Chandu the Magician* (1932), *Gift of Gab* (1934), and *Best Man Wins* (1935), as well as in such notable films as *What Price Glory* (1926), *The Wizard* (1927), and *Dinner at Eight* (1933).

23. The Rejected Woman

Cast: Alma Rubens (Diane Du Prez), Conrad Nagel (John Leslie), Wyndam Standing (James Dunbar), George MacQuarrie (Samuel Du Prez), Bela Lugosi (Jean Gagnon), Antonio D'Algy (Craig Burnett), Leonora Hughes (Lucille Van Tuyle), Mme. Juliette La Violette (Aunt Rose), Aubrey Smith (Peter Leslie), Frederick Burton (Leyton Carter).

Credits: Distinctive Pictures, 1924. Distributed by the Goldwyn-Cosmopolitan Company. Directed by Albert Parker. Screenplay by John Lynch. Cinematography by Roy Hunt. Art direction by Clark Robinson. Running time, 85 minutes (eight reels). Copyright number LP20175, May 3, 1924.

Plot Summary: Aviator John Leslie makes the acquaintance of Diane Du Prez while seeking shelter in Canada during a storm, though he soon returns home at the news of his father's death. Du Prez soon travels to New York herself, where she meets with John socially. However, both her manners and dress become unacceptable to John's friends. Dunbar, Leslie's business manager, offers her financial aid, which enables her to marry John. After learning of the arrangement, he rejects her. A reconciliaton eventually occurs, with the business manager receiving a well-deserved thrashing.

Production Notes: Shot in the New York area, *The Rejected Woman* found little success at the box office or from critics. The blizzard scenes early in the film apparently struck spectators as impressive, but the film on the whole, despite the title of its production company, was of little distinction. The Goldwyn-Cosmopolitan Company released *The Rejected Woman* in May 1924.

Director Albert Parker achieved greater attention through films like *Sherlock Holmes*

(1922) and *The Black Pirate* (1926). The two leads both were popular with movie audiences, with Rubens being a particularly tragic case. A heroin addict, she died of pneumonia prior to her thirty-fourth birthday. Conversely, the spotlight on Nagel lasted until the fifties, as he moved from popular leads to supporting roles and eventually television. Nagel appeared opposite Lugosi again in *The Thirteenth Chair* (1929).

24. *Daughters Who Pay*

Cast: Marguerite De La Motte (Mary Smith/Sonia), John Bowers (Dick Foster), J. Barney Sherry (His Father), Bela Lugosi (Serge Oumanski).

Credits: Banner Productions, 1925. Directed by George Terwilleger. Screenplay by William B. Laub. Cinematography by Edward Paul, Charles Davis, and Murphy Darling. Running time, 61 minutes (six reels, 5,700 feet). Copyright number LP21211, March 6, 1925.

Plot Summary: Since her profession is a secret agent, Mary Smith must lead a double life. On Sundays she lives in the suburb as "Miss Smith" but works as Russian cafe dancer "Sonia" during the week. Dick Foster, the son of a millionaire, becomes infatuated with Sonia; at the same time, Smith's brother gets caught embezzling $10,000 from Dick's wealthy father. Mary attempts to get the millionaire to show leniency, but when he refuses, she returns as Sonia. The deal now is to let the brother go in exchange for Sonia rejecting Dick's advances. Later, after the arrest of a gang of Russian agents, Smith reveals her true self to the Fosters. Dick and the successful spy decide to wed.

Production Notes: Released in May of 1925, *Daughters Who Pay* found critics and audiences both at a loss for how the title connected to the screenplay itself. Star De La Motte, a brunette dancer supposedly trained under Pavlova, found greatest fame as the female lead in a number of Douglas Fairbanks silent films.

25. *The Midnight Girl*

Cast: Lila Lee (Anna), Bela Lugosi (Nicholas Harmon), Gareth Hughes (Don Harmon), Dolores Cassinelli (Nina), Charlotte Walker (Mrs. Schuyler), Ruby Blaine (Natalie Shuyler), John D. Walsh (Victor), William Harvey (Nifty Louis), Sidney Paxton (Joe), Signor N. Salerno (Manager).

Credits: Chadwick Pictures, 1925. Directed by Wilfred Noy. Based on an original story by Garrett Fort. Screenplay by Wilfred Noy and Jean Conover. Cinematography by G.W. "Billy" Bitzer and Frank Zukor. Running time, 67 minutes (seven reels, 6,300 feet). Copyright number LP2125, March 17, 1925.

Plot Summary: Anna, a beautiful singer, comes to the United States from Russia and finds great difficulty in establishing her career. She meets and falls in love with Don Harmon, an orchestra leader and son of opera impressario Nicholas Harmon. At the same time, Nicholas dismisses the temperamental diva Nina as she loses her voice. Eventually, Nicholas makes a pass a Anna — known as "the midnight girl" — who attempts to shoot him. Instead, she accidentally wounds Nina, who had been hiding behind a curtain in Harmon's study. The situation brings Nicholas to his senses, and he reconciles with Nina. Don and Anna both wed, with the latter becoming a sensation in the Harmon opera.

Production Notes: Melodramatic and at times overacted, *The Midnight Girl* suffered from a lack of promotion and was ignored by many of the major critics. Chadwick released the film in August 1925. The cinematography remains striking, mainly due to Bitzer, who formerly worked hand in hand with D.W. Griffith on classics like *Birth of a Nation* (1915), *Intolerance* (1916), *Way Down East* (1920), and dozens of others. Garrett Fort, who penned the original story, went on to work on scripts for *Dracula* (1931), *Frankenstein* (1931), and *Dracula's Daughter* (1936).

Newspapers announced Lugosi as appearing in the film during March 1925. Lugosi himself appears as "Nicholas Harmon, the immensely wealthy patron [who] loved his weakness — and his favorite weakness was

Nina." Debonair and bearded, the Hungarian delivers a very theatrical performance. Despite that, his presence clearly dominates the film.

Audiences knew actress Lila Lee best perhaps for her starring role in *Blood and Sand* (1922), with Rudolph Valentino, though she had a long career that remained almost unaffected by sound, appearing also in such films as *One Glorious Day* (1922), *The Ghost Breakers* (1922), and *The Unholy Three* (1930).

26. *How to Handle Women*

Cast: Glenn Tryon (Leonard Higgins), Marion Dixon (Beatrice Fairbanks), Raymond Keane (Prince Hendryx), Robert T. Hains (Editor), Bull Montana (The Turk), Cesare Gravina (Tony), E. H. Herriman (as himself), Leo White (Secretary), Mario Carillo (Count Olaff), Violet La Plante (Stenographer), Bela Lugosi (A bodyguard).

Credits: Universal Studios, 1928. Directed by William J. Craft. Based on a story by William J. Craft and Jack Foley. Adapted for the screen by Jack Foley. Story supervision by Joseph F. Poland. Cinematography by Albert Demond. Titles by Arthur Todd. Edited by Charles Craft. Running time, 60 minutes (six reels, 5,591 feet). Silent. Copyright number LP25372, June 12, 1928.

Plot Summary: A commercial artist, Leonard Higgins, helps Prince Hendryx of Volgaria in obtaining a loan in the United States. For security, the prince can offer only his country's enormous peanut crop. By switching places with the prince, Higgins — a peanut lover — cleverly acts the part of royalty and obtains the loan. As a result, he gains recognition for his ingenuity and wins the love of Beatrice Dixon.

Production Notes: Alternately titled *Prince of Peanuts*, this "Universal Jewel" was copyrighted in May 1928 as *Fresh Every Hour*; it had gone under the working titles *Meet the Prince* and *Three Days*. The film apparently hit a few screens in April 1928 under the *Prince of Peanuts* title, though its general release as *How to Handle Women* came in June. The film took very poor reviews due to the actors' "flat pantomime," a story interesting only to the "feeble-minded," and a "poverty of comedy resource."

How to Handle Women was Lugosi's first film in a three-year period. Among other firsts, it became his earliest movie for Universal Studios. The actor found himself among the "large cast of minor players [who] seem to stand about looking on in pained boredom." Given Béla's ongoing success in the Broadway version of *Dracula*, he must have been filmed on the East Coast during either weekends or weekday mornings and afternoons.

The male lead, Glenn Tryon, moved from actor to screenwriter and producer later in his career. Among his better known films was *The King of Jazz* (1930).

27. *The Last Performance*

Cast: Conrad Veidt (Erik the Great), Mary Philbin (Julie), Leslie Fenton (Buffo), Fred MacKay (Mark Royce), Gustav Partos (Theater Manager), William H. Turner (Booking Agent), Anders Randolph (Judge), Sam De Grasse (District Attorney), George Irving (Defense Attorney).

Credits: Universal Studios, 1929. Directed by Paul Fejos. Screenplay by James Ashmore Creelman, Walter Anthony, and Tom Reed. Based on a story by James Ashmore Creelman. Cinematography by Hal Mohr. Edited by Edward Cahn, Robert Carlisle, and Robert Jahns. Running time, 69 minutes. (No copyright records exist for the Hungarian version, which used Lugosi's voice.)

Plot Summary: Erik the Great, a magician, falls in love with his young assistant, Julie; however, her affections go only to Buffo, a thief turned magician's pupil. Mark, another assistant, becomes jealous and exposes the young romance to Erik. Buffo murders Mark and later commits suicide at the trial.

Production Notes: Strong direction and cinematography marked this melodrama, which paired Veidt, the somnambulist of *The Cabinet of Dr. Caligari* (1919), with

Mary Philbin, the heroine of *The Phantom of the Opera* (1925). For overseas distribution, Universal prepared a German version that had Veidt speaking in his native language.

Carl Laemmle, Jr., also decided to release a Hungarian version of the film, which period trades identified as the first "talkie" of the Hungarian tongue. John Auer handled the translation, which was supervised by Paul Kohner. Director Fejos appeared in a brief, filmed prologue. Though Universal prepared the dubbed film for release in Hungary, there is speculation about whether the version could also have played in a few Hungarian communities within the United States.

For this Hungarian version, Lugosi dubbed the part of Erik the Great, probably at the request of fellow expatriate Fejos. At least one article, in the *Los Angeles Times*, spoke of the foreign language production as a "new" film that starred Lugosi. Despite such announcements, it seems quite clear that he merely dubbed Veidt's role. If he appeared at all, it possibly was in the "new" prologue with Fejos.

28. *The Veiled Woman*

Cast: Lia Tora (Nanon), Paul Vincenti (Pierre), Kenneth Thomson (Dr. Donald Ross), Walter McGrail (English Diplomatic Attaché), Josef Swickard (Colonel De Selincourt), Andre Cheron (Count De Bracchi), Ivan Lebedeff (Captain Paul Fevier), Maude George (Countess De Bracchi), Bela Lugosi (A suitor to Nanon), Lupita Tovar (Young girl).

Credits: A Fox Picture, 1929. Directed by Emmett Flynn. Screenplay by Douglas Doty. Based on a story by Julio De Moraes and Lia Tora. Cinematography by Charles Clarke. Assistant Director, Ray Flynn. Running time, 60 minutes (six reels, 5, 192 feet). Silent. Copyright number LP298, April 15, 1929.

Plot Summary: After rescuing a young girl from the clutches of a notorious rake, Nanon tells of the men in her own life. Included among these were a seducer, a gambler, an Englishman on the make, and one man she married who left her after learning of the other men. Following her story, Nanon hails a cab driven by the gambler, who explains that he sacrificed everything to cover up the murder of one suitor. Nanon and the gambler then find happiness together.

Production Notes: Director Emmett Flynn shot this film on the West Coast, despite some period reviews that claimed the film was made in France. In terms of plot structure, *The Veiled Woman* utilized extensive flashback sequences. Audiences first saw the film in April of 1929.

Lugosi portrays a suitor killed by heroine Lia Tora, with most of his notices making the link to his stage success as *Dracula*. One review claimed Fox discovered a new possibility for the talkies in Lugosi, mentioning that *The Veiled Woman* would mark his debut into sound films. Though the released film was apparently a silent, Fox possibly considered adding talking sequences to further the movie's appeal. A notice in *Variety* claimed "Lugozi [*sic*] attracted the attention of film producers when he appeared in a local legit presentation of *Dracula*."

29. *Prisoners*

Cast: Corinne Griffith (Riza Riga), James Ford (Kessler), Bela Lugosi (Brottos), Ian Keith (Nicholas Cathy), Julanne Johnston (Lenke), Ann Schaeffer (Aunt Maria), Baron Hesse (Kore), Otto Matiesen (Sebfi), Harry Northrup (Prosecuting Attorney).

Credits: First National, 1929. Produced by Walter Morosco. Directed by William A. Seiter. Screenplay by Forrest Halsey. Based on the novel by Ferenc Molnár. Cinematography by Lee Garmes. Edited by LeRoy Stone. Titles by Paul Perez. Running time, 87 minutes. Silent, with 10 percent "dialogue." Copyright number LP399, May 21, 1929.

Plot Summary: Riza Riga earns a meager salary as a nightclub showgirl but adds to her wages by stealing. Though she attempts to leave such shameful deeds behind her, Riza steals 300 florins to buy a beautiful dress with which to entice lawyer Nicholas Cathy. Cathy ends up defending her at trial, where she is sentenced to several months in jail. Yet the bond between the two becomes strong, and Cathy promises to wait for her.

Production Notes: *Prisoners,* like several other films of this period, becomes a curious hybrid of silence and sound to cash in on audiences' demand for "talkies." The dialogue makes up only 10 percent of the film, occurring mainly at the film's courtroom climax. First National issued the film in May 1929.

Lugosi portrayed the cabaret owner Brottos, referred to in the film as "the man." The role bordered on being a heavy, and Lugosi himself told the press how delighted he was to appear in a work by the Hungarian novelist and playwright Ferenc Molnár. The actor also explained to another reporter how funny it was that he had purchased a pair of pants in Budapest, then years later ended up wearing them in the film.

To promote the film, First National produced a coming attractions trailer, copyrighted under number MP153. The trailer featured sound and first hit theaters on April 30, 1929.

Although some critics found fault with the dialogue itself, Corinne Griffith's voice struck everyone as quite acceptable. "The world's most beautiful woman," as she had been called, made only a few films following *Prisoners,* however. She later wrote numerous novels, and in 1933 made Walter Morosco, producer of *Prisoners,* one of her many husbands. Costar Ian Keith would later be considered a possibility for the lead in *Dracula* (1931).

30. *The Thirteenth Chair*

Cast: Conrad Nagel (Richard Crosby), Leila Hyams (Helen O'Neill), Margaret Wycherly (Madame Rosalie La Grange), Helen Millard (Mary Eastwood), Holmes Herbert (Sir Roscoe Crosby), Mary Forbes (Lady Crosby), Bela Lugosi (Inspector Delzante), John Davidson (Edward Wales), Charles Quartermaine (Dr. Philip Mason), Moon Carroll (Helen Trent), Cyril Chadwick (Brandon Trent), Bertram Johns (Howard Standish), Gretchen Holland (Grace Standish), Frank Leigh (Professor Feringeea), Clarence Geldert (Commissioner Grimshaw), Lal Chand Mehra (Chotee), Henry Daniell.

Credits: Metro-Goldwyn-Mayer, 1929. Produced and directed by Tod Browning. Assistant Director, William Ryan. Screenplay and dialogue by Elliot Clawson. Based on the 1916 play *The Thirteenth Chair,* by Bayard Veiller. Cinematography by Merritt B. Gerstad. Edited by Harry Reynolds. Settings by Cedric Gibbons and Captain Richard Day. Titles by Joseph W. Farnham. Gowns by Adrian. Recording Engineers, Paul Neal and Douglas Shearer. Running time, 71 minutes (eight reels, 6,571 feet). "All-dialog." Copyright number LP794, October 28, 1929.

Plot Summary: An unsolved murder brings Madame La Grange to the home of Sir Roscoe Crosby. Edward Wales hopes to find the murderer's identity through one of La Grange's séances, yet the spiritualist is a faker, and Wales hopes the séance will merely weed out the killer. Yet when the lights are out so the medium can contact the dead, Wales himself is murdered. Inspector Delzante arrives to take charge, and eventually the killer becomes frightened into a confession.

Production Notes: Based on a popular 1916 Broadway play, *The Thirteenth Chair* proved the first collaboration between Lugosi and director Tod Browning. The latter successfully helmed a series of bizarre films starring Lon Chaney, Sr., as well as later directing such horrors as *Dracula* (1931), *Freaks* (1932), and *Mark of the Vampire* (1935). MGM released its mystery picture in late October 1929. Publicity reports that linked actress Hyams to the number 13 in various ways claimed she attempted to arrange the release date itself for the thirteenth of the month. Browning allegedly claimed the number to be no friend of his and scrapped the idea.

Lugosi and presumably Lia Tora from *The Veiled Woman* (1928). Interestingly, though reviewed as a "silent," still photographs claim this Fox film was an "All Dialog" production.

Browning announced that he was elated over Lugosi, believing him to be a major discovery for the screen. On July 10, 1929, *Variety* noted that MGM had cast Lugosi as the inspector. Though a bit theatrical, the Hungarian is quite memorable in the role, which is made more serious than the detective of Bayard Veiller's play. Additionally, the part allows Lugosi more screen time and dialogue than any of his other pre–*Dracula* talkies. Much of the press that Lugosi received as a result of *The Thirteenth Chair* made the link between the actor and his stage success as the vampire. At least two writers even noted that Lugosi was to play Dracula in a rumored film production.

Advertisements promoted the film as "the weirdest spine chiller of them all," and the press noted the timely release, given the Halloween season. Though the popular horror cinema cycle would begin in 1931 with *Dracula*, publicity for this film proclaimed it to be a definitely terrifying thriller. "All Thrills! All Shudders! All Shakes! All Gasps! O-O-o-o-h!" advertisements exclaimed. The "eerie, scary thriller" helmed by "thrill-wizard Tod Browning" gave Lugosi seventh billing on screen, but newspaper ads featured the Hungarian prominently in their artwork and listed his name fourth in the cast.

Reviews were mixed, but most noted the stagey quality and how odd the English dialects were, especially given the setting of India. While in many ways the film is certainly dated, several moving camera shots make it seem more advanced than other talkies of this period. Among these are a slow, effective track in toward a lone Wycherly, praying in a room, as well as a high angle shot of the cast which not only progresses closer to them but moves down to eye level.

Male lead Conrad Nagel, though essentially

wasted in *The Thirteenth Chair*, went from popularity as a star player to a lengthy career as character actor and even television host. Actress Leila Hyams later appeared opposite Lugosi in *Island of Lost Souls* (1933), as well as in such films as Tod Browning's *Freaks* (1932). Margaret Wycherly, the comical and sometimes eerie medium, achieved renown in such plays as *Tobacco Road* (1933) and through supporting roles in films like *White Heat* (1949). Interestingly, Wycherly reprised the part of Madame La Grange that she had originated in the 1916 play.

31. Such Men Are Dangerous

Cast: Warner Baxter (Ludwig Kranz), Catherine Dale Owen (Elinor Kranz), Albert Conti (Paul Strohm), Hedda Hopper (Muriel Wyndham), Claude Allister (Fred Wyndham), Bela Lugosi (Dr. Goodman).

Credits: Fox, 1930. Directed by Kenneth Hawks. Screenplay by Ernest Vajda. Based on a story by Elinor Glyn. Cinematography by L.W. O'Connell and George Eastman. Music by Dave Stamper. Edited by Harold Schuster. Art Direction by Stephen Goosson. Costumes by Sophie Wachner. Running time, 83 minutes (7,400 feet). Copyright number LP1074, January 25, 1930.

Plot Summary: Ludwig Kranz becomes distraught at his wedding to Elinor when he overhears comments about his unattractive appearance. He eventually fakes his own death and has Dr. Goodman, a plastic surgeon, give him a new and more handsome face. Though Goodman at first refuses, Kranz convinces him by offering the doctor a sizable sum of money. He returns to his former world as a new man, Pierre Kranz.

Production Notes: Originally titled *The Mask of Love*, this became Lugosi's first talkie at Fox. Elinor Glyn's inspiration for the story came from the real-life suicide of a German financier, with Hungarian playwright and novelist Ernest Vajda adapting the story for the screen. Fox released *Such Men Are Dangerous* in March 1930, garnering mixed reviews.

The most notable aspect of the production was a terrible accident in which two planes collided during filming, killing ten men. Three aircraft were some two miles from Redondo Beach, attempting to shoot a sequence in which character Ludwig Kranz parachutes from an airplane. One of the vehicles held a stand-in for Warner Baxter (Jacob Triebwasser), while the remaining planes both contained cameramen to capture the jump on celluloid. The crash supposedly occurred when the wings of the two touched, causing them to turn, hitting nose to nose. Both aircraft immediately fell to waters below, sinking into the depths within moments.

Eyewitnesses remarked at the tremendous explosion, with one comparing it to a "bolt of lightning." Boats quickly sped to the rescue, yet all they found were some twisted and charred pieces of wings and canvas, as well as blazing gasoline marking the spot where the mass of destruction submerged. Three bodies floated on the surface, though later a diver managed to recover two more from the wreckage. Among the dead were two pilots, four cameramen, two property men, an assistant director, and the director himself, Kenneth Hawks. His brother, the famed Howard Hawks, had originally planned to be on the plane as well but backed out at the last minute.

Fox studios related its extreme condolences to the press and to the bereaved, who included Hawks' wife, actress Mary Astor. The coroner held an inquiry into the accident but did not place blame on any specific problem. The pilot of the third, unharmed plane suffered what newspapers termed a nervous breakdown, with the overall situation even receiving comments from aviator Charles Lindbergh. Despite the event, however, the film's production basically continued on schedule.

Lugosi was not present at the disaster, as his character, Dr. Goodman, does not appear in the parachute sequence. As the plastic surgeon, the Hungarian does offer an extremely believable performance, making this film a highlight of his pre-*Dracula* films. Interestingly, Lugosi speaks in German to his cinematic secretary, switching back to English to converse with star Baxter. Also curious is his slight mangling of a few lines ... possible evidence of a need to fine-tune aspects of his own English.

Catherine Dale Owen, who explained to the press how difficult acting in talkies was, received poor notices. Critics did remark favorably on the popular Warner Baxter, who would later be seen with Lugosi again in *Renegades* (1930). Oddly, the actor subsequently appeared in the unrelated *Such Women Are Dangerous* (1934). Hedda Hopper, later to realize fame through her newspaper column on Hollywood, appears in a minor role.

32. *The King of Jazz*

Cast: Paul Whiteman, John Boles, Laura La Plante, Jeanette Loff, Glenn Tryon, Merna Kennedy, Kathryn Crawford, Stanley Smith, William Kent, Grace Hayes, Sisters G, the Brox Sisters, George Ciles, Jacques Cartier, Frank Leslie, Charles Irwin, the Russell Makert Dancers, the Paul Whiteman Orchestra (including Mike Pingatore, Frank Trumbauer, Roy Bargy, Chester Hazlett, Roy Mayer, Wilbur Hall, Harry Goldfield, Joe Venuti, Eddie Lang), the Rhythm Boys (Harry Barris, Al Rinker, and Bing Crosby).

Credits: Universal Studios, 1930. Produced by Carl Laemmle, Jr. Directed by John Murray Anderson. Screenplay by Harry Ruskin and Charles MacArthur. Art direction by Herman Rose. Cinematography by Hal Mohr, Ray Rennahan, and Jerome Ash. Running time of the U.S. release, 95 minutes. (A copyright for the Hungarian version with Lugosi was not registered with the U.S. Library of Congress.)

Plot Summary: *The King of Jazz* is typical of several early musicals, in which music numbers complement short comedic skits. The title refers to bandleader Paul Whiteman, whose orchestra included a number of the twenties' top jazzmen.

Production Notes: Universal Studios approached Paul Whiteman about *The King of Jazz* as early as November 1928, though they did not start rehearsals until November of the following year. Filming ended on March 20, 1930. The studio screened a preview of the film on April 5, though the official release began in May 1930. The Whiteman Orchestra and George Gershwin appeared live at New York's Roxy to promote the film's premiere.

An early use of technicolor and beautiful sets add much to the lush feel of Universal's musical. The songs include Mable Wayne and Harry De Costa's "Ragamuffin Romeo" and "It Happened in Monterey," as well as George Gershwin's "Rhapsody in Blue."

Lugosi's participation came only in the Hungarian version, which added scenes with him speaking in his native language and "translating" the action for a culture relatively unfamiliar with jazz and Whiteman. When Universal shot Lugosi's footage is unclear, though it possibly happened after principal filming for the American version ended on March 20, 1930. Lugosi was probably considered after he had dubbed one voice of *The Last Performance* (1929) into Hungarian for the same studio. Paul Fejos, who acquired his services for that project, had been the original director of *The King of Jazz*.

Some historians doubt whether Universal really filmed Lugosi or whether the actor instead appeared in person with the film in Hungary. The latter case is definitely not true. While a print of the Lugosi-Hungarian version has not surfaced, a 1930 still photograph pictures the actor alongside the rotund Paul Whiteman.

Additionally, surviving reviews indicate that Universal prepared other foreign language versions with filmed hosts speaking the language itself. On December 20, 1930, for example, a French version hit Paris with a "French m.c., who appears several times during the film to tell the public what it is all about." For the German release of November 1930, the studio filmed German actor Arnold Korff as master of ceremonies.

Charles Irwin filled much the same kind of role in the American version. A Hungarian version most likely played theaters of that country in late 1930, with an on-screen Lugosi appearing a handful of times to discuss the action, sandwiched between the skits and musical numbers.

33. *Wild Company*

Cast: Frank Albertson (Larry Grayson), H.B. Warner (Henry Grayson), Sharon Lynn (Sally), Joyce Compton (Anita), Claire McDowell (Mrs. Grayson), Mildred Van Dorn (Natalie), Richard Keene (Dick), Frances McCoy (Cora), Kenneth Thomson (Joe Hardy), Bela Lugosi (Felix Brown, operator of a nightclub), George Fawcett (Judge), Bobby Callahan (Eddie).

Credits: Fox, 1930. Presented by William Fox. Directed by Leo McCarey. Associate Producer, Al Rockett. Screenplay by Bradley King. Based on a story by Bradley King and John Stone. Cinematography by L.W. O'Connell. Art Direction by Stephen Goosson. Edited by Clyde Carruth. Music and lyrics, Jimmy Monaco, Jack Meskill, Cliff Friend, Con Conrad. Recording Engineer, Alfred Bruzlin. Assistant Director, Virgil Hart. Costumes by Sophie Wachner. Running time, 71 minutes (eight reels, 6,666 feet). Copyright number LP1382, June 16, 1930.

Plot Summary: Larry constantly drains his wealthy father for money to lead the life of a Roaring Twenties "flaming youth," spending much of the cash in a nightclub where Sally entertains. Unfortunately, she is the moll of gangster Joe Hardy, who eventually attempts to pin the murder of a nightclub owner on the young man. Larry's own father turns his son over to the police, with the courtroom climax offering words of wisdom and a suspended sentence to the youth.

Production Notes: Originally titled *Road House*, *Wild Company*'s story had its earliest roots in Philip Hurn's short story "Soft Shoulders." The talkie utilized the Movietone sound-on-film process, and used advertising pitches like "Thrills, parties, jazz — where does this mad speedway lead?" Among the tunes Sharon Lynn sang were "Joe" and "That's What I Like About You." Fox issued the film in July 1930, with critics mainly complaining that its moral message was far too overt.

Lugosi appeared as the tuxedoed nightclub owner, with the press again making references to his stage success in *Dracula*. *Variety* first announced his role in the film on May 10. Lugosi's major scene features him walking in on a robbery, with Kenneth Thomson gunning him down.

Director Leo McCarey later achieved fame with his classic comedies like *Duck Soup* (1933) and such sentimental films as *Going My Way* (1944) and *An Affair to Remember* (1957). Star Frank Albertson moved from leading roles to character parts in such films as *Man-Made Monster* (1941) and *Psycho* (1960). Father H.B. Warner had formerly played leads in numerous silent films and later garnered an Oscar nomination for his role in *Lost Horizon* (1937). Sharon Lynn, the gangster's moll, was better known at the time as a singer and comedienne than as a dramatic actress.

34. *Renegades*

Cast: Warner Baxter (Deucalion), Myrna Loy (Eleanore), Noah Beery, Sr. (Machwurth), Gregory Gaye (Vologuine), George Cooper (Biloxi), C. Henry Gordon (Captain Mordiconi), Colin Chase (Sergeant-Major Olson), Bela Lugosi (Sheik Muhammed, the Marabout), Victor Jory (Young Officer), Noah Beery Jr. (Young Legionnaire), Fred Kohler Jr. (Young Legionnaire).

Credits: Fox, 1930. Producer, William Fox. Directed by Victor Fleming. Screenplay by Jules Furthman. Based on Andre Armandy's novel *Le Renegat*. Cinematography by L. William O'Connell. Edited by Harold Schuster. Set Design by William Darling. Costumes by Sophie Wachner. Music and lyrics to "I Got What I Wanted" by Cliff Friend and Jimmy Monaco. Technical Adviser, Louis Van Den Ecker. Running time, 90 minutes (11 reels). Copyright number LP1648, October 3, 1930.

Plot Summary: Deucalion and three companions desert the French Foreign Legion and join a band of thieves after Eleanore, Deucalion's love, breaks his heart. Later, she becomes the mistress of the Marabout, an "uncrowned king of the Riffs." Later, the Riffs side with an Arab guerrilla force attacking the French. Deucalion convinces the Riffs to support the French, however, and the Foreign Legion's fort is saved. Almost everyone dies in the battle, with Deucalion using his last strength to kill the treacherous Eleanore.

Production Notes: Though it was released in November 1930, most audiences did not actually see *Renegades* until early 1931. Victor Fleming, later credited as director of *Gone with the Wind* (1939) and *The Wizard of Oz* (1939), helmed the Foreign Legion epic. Sophie Wachner, who had provided costumes for Lugosi's two previous Fox films, worked in the same capacity for *Renegades*; likewise, cinematographer L. William O'Connell made this his third Lugosi film to shoot. The film was shot in the Mojave desert, and electric refrigerators and water sprayed on the cast's tents helped keep everyone cool. Fox used the Movietone sound-on-film system to provide the "talking."

The film itself pleased most audiences, but critics cried for further editing to quicken the pace of the film. Almost every spectator, however, praised the battle sequences and the desert setting.

Lugosi, despite poor billing, appears in a quite interesting role as the Marabout, uttering colorful phrases ("Muhammed cannot go to mountain; mountain must come to Muhammed"), as well as attempting to keep Loy under control, threatening to flog her if she disobeys his wishes.

Warner Baxter, star of *Such Men Are Dangerous* (1930), returns to star alongside the exotic Myrna Loy. At this point in her illustrious career, Loy found herself frequently portraying vamps, often Asian ones. Later, after appearing in the *Thin Man* series, she became one of the top box office draws in Hollywood. C. Henry Gordon and Victor Jory would later lend their talents to the Lugosi film *The Devil's in Love* (1933), with the former also appearing in *The Black Camel* (1931).

35. *Viennese Nights*

Cast: Alexander Gray (Otto), Vivienne Segal (Elsa), Jean Hersholt (Hochter), Walter Pidgeon (Franz), Louise Fazenda (Gretl), Alice Day (Barbara), Bert Roach (Gus), June Pursell (Mary), Milton Douglas (Bill Jones), Lothar Mayring (Baron), Bela Lugosi (An ambassador).

Credits: Warner Brothers, 1930. Directed by Alan Crosland. Screenplay by Oscar Hammerstein II and Sigmund Romberg. Cinematography by James Van Trees and Frank Good. Filmed in two-color Technicolor. Edited by Harold McLernon. Music Director, Louis Silvers. Choreography by Jack Haskell. Music and lyrics by Sigmund Romberg and Oscar Hammerstein II. Songs include "I Bring a Love Song," "I'm Lonely," "Will You Remember Me Vienna?," "Here We Are," "Regimental March," "Viennese Nights," "Goodbye My Love," and "Yes, Yes, Yes." Running time, 107 minutes (11 reels). Copyright number LP1463, August 4, 1930.

Plot Summary: Three young friends leave their small town to join the Austrian army. One of the group, Franz, becomes a lieutenant and thus ends his association with Otto and Gus. Otto soon falls in love with a cobbler's daughter named Elsa. But, Franz meets and eventually marries the young lady. A heartbroken Otto goes to America, becoming a musician in a theater orchestra, and struggles to support his child. Elsa visits the theater one evening and discovers her former lover. Both express unhappiness in their relationships and make plans to be together, though Elsa declines when she learns of Otto's child. Years later, Elsa's granddaughter avoids marrying a wealthy suitor and elopes with a musician ... Otto's grandson.

Production Notes: Though it was released in November 1930, most exhibitors did not actually screen the film until early the following year. Director Alan Crosland had found success a few years earlier with the first talkie, *The Jazz Singer* (1927). The music team of Romberg and Hammerstein later split up, with the former being immortalized in the screen biography *Deep in My Heart* (1954) and the latter joining with composer Richard Rodgers to write such musicals as *South Pacific* and *Oklahoma!* They wrote the music and lyrics for *Viennese Nights* expressly for the screen, with cinema trades questioning how well the public would go for a "talkie" musical. The storyline itself resembles such novels as Edith Wharton's *Age of Innocence*.

Box office returns on the film were generally poor, but this could be attributed as much to a story Depression-era audiences could relate to as to the music itself. Ads proclaimed the film would be remembered "long after others are forgotten," calling its tale "gay" and "sparkling with the wine of life." Shot in a two-strip Technicolor process, the colors retain a certain pictorial beauty.

Lugosi turned in one of his briefest screen appearances in this musical, taking an unbilled role as an ambassador. *Viennese Nights* remains an interesting relic mainly because it is one of the Hungarian's few color films.

Diva Vivienne Segal starred in few films, finding much greater fame on the stage in operettas and musicals like *Pal Joey*. Male star Walter Pidgeon turned into a popular leading man of Hollywood, acting in such favorites as *How Green Was My Valley* (1941) and *Mrs. Miniver* (1942). Fazenda, who appeared in such films as *The Terror* (1928), retains a place in cinema history due to her comedic roles at Mack Sennett's Keysone studio. Jean Hersholt, best known as "Dr. Christian" on radio and in films, later played opposite Lugosi in *Mark of the Vampire* (1935).

36. *Oh, for a Man*

Cast: Jeannette MacDonald (Carlotta Manson), Reginald Denny (Barney McGann), Marjorie White (Totsy Franklin), Warren Hymer (Pug Morin, the "Walloping Wop"), Alison Skipworth (Laura), Albert Conti (Peck), Bela Lugosi (Frescatti), Andre Cheron (Costello), William B. Davidson (Kerry Stokes), Bodil Rosing (Masseuse), Donald Hall, Evelyn, Althea Henly.

Credits: Fox, 1930. Produced by William Fox and Harold McFadden. Directed by Harold McFadden. Screenplay and dialogue by Philip Klein and Lynn Starling. Based on the *Saturday Evening Post* short story "Stolen Thunder," by Mary F. Watkins. Cinematography by Charles Clarke. Music direction by Arthur Kay. Art Director, Stephen Goosson. Costumes by Sophie Wachner. Edited by Al De Gaetano. Running time (nine reels). Copyright number LP1720, November 5, 1930.

Plot Summary: The great diva Carlotta Manson rejects several suitors and concentrates solely on her career. She returns home after a successful performance to meet Barney McGann, a criminal who plans to rob her home. But the crook actually admires the singer, and the two become friends. Manson even demands that the crook, an amateur singer, be given a job with her opera company. Later Carlotta gives up her career for him, and the wedded couple leave for an Italian villa. They soon become unhappy, however, with Carlotta returning to the United States to sing at the opera again. Barney shows up after a performance and the loving couple reunite.

Production Notes: Initially Fox planned to keep *Stolen Thunder* as the title for this Jeannette MacDonald feature, but changed it before the release in November 1930. *Oh, for a Man* retains much of the short story's plot, though the lead character's name changed from "Madame Cleo Hanni" to "Carlotta Manson." Director Hamilton McFadden directed Lugosi again in *The Black Camel* (1931), with cinematographer Charles Clarke previously filming the actor in *The Veiled Woman* (1929). Clarke later received multiple honors for the technical advances he brought to his profession, including an Academy Award.

Lugosi plays the small part of Frescatti with a goatee, looking dapper, but he was given only a few minutes of screen time and little to do but praise the temperamental MacDonald.

Star Jeannette MacDonald reached greater fame a few years after *Oh, for a Man* by starring in numerous musicals with Nelson Eddy. Her increased appeal made Fox consider reissuing the film, but the Hays Code prohibiting unpunished crime thwarted their plans. In the film, Reginald Denny portrayed a thief who is never penalized for his deeds.

37. *Dracula*

Cast: Bela Lugosi (Count Dracula), Helen Chandler (Mina), David Manners (Jonathan Harker), Dwight Frye (Renfield), Edward Van Sloan (Dr. Van Helsing), Herbert Bunston (Dr. Seward), Frances Dade (Lucy), Joan Standing (Briggs), Charles Gerrard (Martin), Moon Carroll (Maid), Josephine Velez (Nurse), Michael Visaroff (Innkeeper), Wyndham Standing (Surgeon), Jeraldine Dvorak, Dorothy Tree, and Cornelia Thaw (Dracula's vampire brides), Daisy Belmore (English Coach Passenger), Nicholas Bela (Transylvanian Coach Passenger), Carla Laemmle (Sara, a Coach Passenger), John George (Van Helsing's assistant), Donald Murphy (Passenger), Tod Browning (Voice of the Harbor Master).

Credits: Universal Studios, 1931. Produced by Carl Laemmle, Jr. Directed by Tod Browning. Associate Producer, E.M. Asher. Based on the 1897 novel *Dracula*, by Bram Stoker. Adapted from the play by Hamilton Deane and John L. Balderston. Play Script, Garrett Fort. Continuity, Louis Bromfield. Added Dialogue by Dudley Murphy. Adaptation by Louis Stevens. Treatment by Fritz Stephani. Scenario Supervision by Charles A. Logue. Art Direction by Charles D. Hall. Cinematography by Karl Freund. Film Editor, Milton Carruth. Supervising Film Editor, Maurice Pivar. Set Design by Herman Rosse and John Ivan Hoffman. Assistant Director, Scotty R. Beal. Second Assistant Director, Herman Schlom. Assistant Photography by King Gray and Frank J. Booth. Second Unit Photography, Joseph Bretherton. Recording Supervision by C. Roy Hunter. Musical Conductor, Heinz Roemheld. Makeup by Jack P. Pierce. Set Decorations by Russell A. Gausman. Costumes by Ed Ware and Vera West. Casting by Phil M. Friedman. Research by Nan Grant. Script Girl, Aileen Webster. Art titles by Max Cohen. Still Photographer, Roman Freulich. Running time, 78 minutes (nine reels). Copyright number LP1947, February 2, 1931.

Plot Summary: Count Dracula, vampire of Transylvania, purchases a home in London from real estate agent Renfield. The mysterious aristocrat turns poor Renfield into his slave, and the two travel to England. Dracula quickly takes his needed blood supply from local females, including young Lucy. Lovely Mina also attracts his attention, and the bloodthirsty demon attempts to turn her into a vampire. Her lover, Jonathan Harker, and Professor Van Helsing manage to destroy Dracula, however, restoring Mina to her normal self.

Production Notes: Universal Studios first considered *Dracula* for the screen in 1927, though at the time executives believed the material too gruesome to find box office appeal. As Béla Lugosi achieved success on stage, however, various publications in 1928–29 printed the actor's idea that a "talkie" of the Bram Stoker novel could prove highly successful.

By August 22, 1930, the studio obtained full rights to *Dracula*, including two different versions of the stage adaptation. The studio certainly considered Lon Chaney for the lead, with the actor himself having an interest in the tale. But, Chaney's death on August 26 caused Universal to find other talent. They announced a whopping $400,000 budget for the film, and as early as August 7 famed author Louis Bromfield submitted a treatment for the project. Dudley Murphy soon collaborated with Bromfield, resulting in a new script by September 8. Shortly thereafter, Garrett Fort and director Tod Browning continued work on the screenplay, with it transforming more and more into a cinematic version of the stage *Dracula*.

The studio considered Conrad Veidt, William Courtenay, Paul Muni, Ian Keith, John Wray, and others for the title role, initially believing Lugosi carried no name value. At one point, trades even claimed Keith had the part, but by September 20 Lugosi signed a contract. The *Hollywood Filmograph* acted as a major supporter of the Hungarian actor, lobbying extensively in his behalf. Universal also signed Edward Van Sloan and Herbert Bunston, both fresh from the Broadway version of *Dracula*. Helen Chandler, who had appeared in the 1930 film *Outward Bound* and was herself a popular stage actress, took the lead female role. Though the studio first announces Lew Ayres as Jonathan Harker, David Manners became the young male hero shortly before cameras began rolling.

John Hoffman's designs for Castle Dracula's interior became particularly ominous with Karl Freund's cinematography. The latter was Germany's great cinematographer of the twenties, having worked on such films as *The Last Laugh* (1924) and *Metropolis* (1926). Freund had filmed Lugosi in Murnau's *Der Januskopf* (1920) and in 1932 photographed the actor again in *Murders in the Rue Morgue* (1932). Glass shots combined artwork of Transylvanian mountains with horsedrawn carriages. The outside of Dracula's decrepit castle was a miniature. Leftover sets from *The Hunchback of Notre Dame* (1923) and *All Quiet on the Western Front* (1930) further helped give exteriors a much-needed exotic quality.

The studio decided to use a minimal amount of music in *Dracula*, believing that too much could confuse the audiences of talkies. As a result, the film bears not an actual score but passages of Tchaikovsky's "Swan Lake" during the opening credits. While Count Dracula attends a musical concert in London, portions of Schubert's "Unfinished Symphony" and Wagner's "Die Meistersinger" can be heard. The overall lack of music remains a major complaint of cinema historians and film buffs.

Producer Paul Kohner and director George Melford shot a Spanish-language version of *Dracula* on the same sets as the Browning crew. The Mexican cast worked at night after Browning had finished for the day. Carlos Villarias took Lugosi's spot as the vampire, with Lupita Tovar as the lovely female lead. Though this film was long thought to be lost, a restored version from MCA proves it to be even more atmospheric than the Browning version. It falters, however, in its lack of a major presence like Lugosi.

Studio pressbooks suggested theater owners run art contests, with participants sketching in the face of Dracula on a still photograph of Lugosi. Envelopes containing "wolf bane" could be distributed, a theater worker could be cloaked as Dracula with a cape that announced the film title, and quizzes as to what the "Dracula kiss" was could be conducted. Universal made numerous other suggestions to exhibitors, though the latter found no trouble bringing in crowds to theaters.

Dracula's tremendous box office success paved the way for sound horror films, sparking the entire horror film cycle of the thirties. Favorable reviews met *Dracula*, though several critics noted that the film could have even been better than it was. Modern reviewers remark on the same thing, claiming that the film includes unnecessary comic relief and leaves out much of the novel's greatest moments. Browning's version also allows several exciting sequences, such as the Count's death, to take place in off-screen space. Yet the power of *Dracula* remains in Lugosi's performance, which transformed the actor into a 1931 household name. Moreover, the success resulted in typecasting of the actor forever as a horror film star and made his name synonymous with the bloodthirsty Count of Bram Stoker's imagination.

Universal reissued *Dracula* to much success in 1938, helping spur a comeback for the then-unemployed Lugosi. Other reissues came in 1947 and 1951. Releases after 1931 saw the film frame composition cropped to allow space for the dialogue track to be added. An MCA restoration on laser disc finally returned Freund's composition to its original form. Reissue prints also excised a curtain speech by Edward Van Sloan warning audiences that vampires really existed. Though frame blow-ups exist, the speech itself had too much deterioration for MCA to replace it in its restored version of the film.

38. *Fifty Million Frenchmen*

Cast: William Gaxton (Jack Forbes), Olsen and Johnson (Simon and Peter), John Halliday (Michael Cummings), Helen Broderick (Violet), Claudia Dell (Looloo Carroll), Lester Crawford (Billy Baxter), Charles Judels (Permasse), Carmelita Geraghty (Marcelle Dubrey), Nat Carr (Jewish Tourist), Vera Gordon (His Wife), Norman Phillips, Jr. (Their Son), Bela Lugosi (magician who loses his clothes), Evalyn Knapp, Natt Carr, Daisy Belmore, Rolfe Sedan.

Credits: Warner Brothers, 1931. Directed by Lloyd Bacon. Screen adaptation by Joseph Jackson and Eddie Welch. Dialogue by Al Boasberg. Based on the stage musical by Cole Porter, Herbert Fields, and E. Ray Goetz. Cinematography by Dev Jennings. Color by Technicolor. Music by Cole Porter. Edited by Robert Crandall. Wardrobe by Earl Luick. Running time, 68 minutes (nine reels). Copyright number LP2046, March 4, 1931.

Plot Summary: While in Paris, Jack bets $50,000 that he can win the heart of Looloo without spending a single franc. He cannot beg, borrow, or steal, but only work to make money. After a string of embarrassing situations, Jack manages to capture Looloo's affections.

Production Notes: Warner Brothers decided the Cole Porter musical that *Fifty Million Frenchmen* was based on would be box office poison, so the tunes were cut. Porter's music instead is heard only in the background, and the deleted musical sequences later appeared in a 1934 Bob Hope two-reeler entitled *Paree, Paree*. The studio itself had financed the stage version and initially planned to shoot the film in Paris; instead, Hollywood served for the production. Though it was shot in two-strip Technicolor, prints today are often shown in black and white. Warner's first released the comedy in March 1931, with advertisements claiming, "Here's your chance to learn the secrets of la vie Parisien without crossing the ocean and getting your feet wet."

Lugosi appears in an unbilled part as a bearded magician, with his footage having been shot prior to the release of *Dracula*. As a result of his stardom following Universal's vampire film, the Hungarian's name did appear in numerous reviews of this comedy. Reportedly, the studio guaranteed Lugosi one week's salary for his role, which totaled $1,000. Newspaper accounts claimed he spent only some ten minutes rehearsing for the small role.

Cast members Helen Broderick and Lester Crawford were the parents of famed actor Broderick Crawford. Both stars, along with Gaxton, had appeared in the stage version of the comedy. Comedy team Olsen and Johnson achieved greater success with audiences later through the stage and screen version of *Hellzapoppin* (1941).

39. *Women of All Nations*

Cast: Victor McLaglen (Sergeant Flagg), Edmund Lowe (Sergeant Quirt), Greta Nissen (Elsa), El Brendel (Olsen), Fifi D'Orsay (Fifi), Marjorie White (Pee Wee), T. Roy Barnes (Captain of Marines), Bela Lugosi (Prince Hassan), Joyce Compton (Kiki), Jesse De Vorska (Izzie), Charles Judels (Leon), Marion Lesssing (Gretchen), Ruth Warren (Ruth), Humphrey Bogart (Stone).

Credits: Fox, 1931. Directed by Raoul Walsh. Screenplay by Barry Conners. Based on the Flagg and Quirt characters created by Laurence Stallings and Maxwell Anderson. Cinematography by Lucien Andriot. Music by Reginald H. Bassett. Music Direction by Carli D. Elinor. Art Direction

Lugosi and Greta Nissen in a posed publicity still for Fox's *Women of All Nations* (1931).

by David Hall. Production Manager, Archie Buchanan. Sound Recording by George Leverett. Edited by Jack Dennis. Running time, 72 minutes (6,441 feet). Copyright number LP2246, May 15, 1931.

Plot Summary: Formerly having fought side by side in World War I, Flagg and Quirt are reunited after the latter's Turkish bath is raided and he re-enlists in the marines. The two end up in Sweden, both vying for the attentions of the lovely Elsa. From there, Flagg and Quirt move on to an earthquake in Nicaragua, and even later to Egypt. Again they cross paths with Elsa, a member of Prince Hassan's harem. The duo continue to express their affections but find trouble when the prince returns.

Production Notes: Released in May 1931, *Women of All Nations* was the third film featuring the characters Flagg and Quirt. Fox began shooting in February after McLaglen recovered from an illness, and *Variety* announced the film's completion the following month. The studio cut several minutes of footage before issuing *Women of All Nations*, leaving Humphrey Bogart on the cutting room floor. For the French release, the title became *Rivals*.

Lugosi, with moustache and goatee, appears in a turban at the head of a harem. Billed eighth in the cast, he does have a few worthwhile scenes. One even features him "meowing" like a cat to find Flagg and Quirt.

McLaglen and Lowe went on to play the same characters in future films, with silent film director Raoul Walsh continuing his own career in later years through such classics as *White Heat* (1949). Comedian El Brendel, who also appeared in such films as *Just Imagine* (1930), reprised his role of Olsen from a previous Flagg-Quirt outing.

40. The Black Camel

Cast: Warner Oland (Charlie Chan), Sally Eilers (Julie O'Neill), Bela Lugosi (Tarneverro), Dorothy Revier (Shelah Fane), Victor Varconi (Robert Fyfe), Robert Young (Jimmy Bradshaw), Marjorie White (Rita Ballou), Richard Tucker (Wilkie Ballou), J.M. Kerrigan (Thomas MacMaster), Mary Gordon (Mrs. MacMaster), C. Henry Gordon (Van Horn), Violet Dunn (Anna), William Post, Jr. (Alan Jaynes), Dwight Frye (Jessop), Murray Kinnell (Smith), Otto Yamaoka (Kashimo), Rita Rozelle (Lana), Robert Homans (Chief of Police), Louise Mackintosh (Housekeeper).

Credits: Fox Film Corporation, 1931. Produced and directed by Harold McFadden. Adapted by Hugh Stange. Based on Earl Derr Biggers's 1929 Charlie Chan novel, *The Black Camel*. Screenplay and dialogue by Barry Conners and Philip Klein. Cinematography by Joseph August and Daniel B. Clark. Art Director, Ben Carré. Associated Producer, William Sistrom. Recording Engineer, W.W. Lindsay, Jr. Edited by Al De Gaetano. Running time, 67 minutes (6,560 feet). Copyright number LP2301, May 27, 1931.

Plot Summary: A movie being shot in Hawaii stars actress Shelah Fane, though she is soon murdered. Suspects include her fortuneteller, Tarneverro, her ex-husband, her butler, and her maid. Previously, Fane herself killed a director, thus complicating Chan's work all the more. The butler and maid are both guilty, as Chan discovers through his astute investigation.

Production Notes: In addition to being a popular novel of 1929, *The Black Camel* had also been serialized weekly the same year in the *Saturday Evening Post*. The tale later found itself translated into numerous languages, remaining a popular seller for years alongside five other Chan novels by Earl Derr Biggers.

Fox shot *The Black Camel* on location in Hawaii, with the cast staying at the popular Royal Hawaiian Hotel in Honolulu. Oland, originally from Sweden, had previously appeared as the famed detective in *Charlie Chan Carries On* (1931), as well as being the dastardly villain of *The Mysterious Dr. Fu Manchu* (1929); the actor starred in numerous other Charlie Chan vehicles before his death in 1938. The studio announced the picture completed in March, though not releasing it until June 1931.

As Tarneverro, Lugosi supplied proper menace as a murder suspect, though he is not actually the guilty party. The film portrays the fortune-telling character as more mysterious than Biggers's novel did, complementing the actor's screen persona. Press materials made much of the Hungarian's appearing alongside fellow countryman Victor Varconi. The two first met in their native country.

Dwight Frye, another supporting player, etched his way into cinema history by appearing as the maniacal Renfield in *Dracula*

(1931). Leading lady Sally Eilers became an obscure figure in cinema history, never finding tremendous box office appeal.

41. Broadminded
Cast: Joe E. Brown (Ossie Simpson), Ona Munson (Constance), William Collier, Jr. (Jack Hackett), Marjorie White (Penelope), Holmes Herbert (John Hackett, Sr.), Margaret Livingston (Mabel Robinson), Thelma Todd (Gertie Gardner), Bela Lugosi (Pancho), Grayce Hampton (Aunt Polly).
Credits: First National, 1931. Directed by Mervyn LeRoy. Screenplay by Bert Kalmar and Harry Ruby. Based on an original story by Edgar Allen Wolf, Humphrey Pearson, and Henry McCarthy. Cinematography by Sid Hickox. Art Direction by Anton Grot. Wardrobe by Earl Luick. Edited by Al Hall. Running time, 65 minutes (seven reels). Copyright number LP2316, June 26, 1931.
Plot Summary: John Hackett entrusts his playboy son, Jack, to cousin Ossie Simpson, with the latter to act as a chaperone for the flaming youth. As a result, Jack meets with additional chaos, but finds a happy ending with a beautiful girl.
Production Notes: Originally, *Broadminded* was to star James Rennie and Fred Kohler, but eventually First National decided the story was better suited to Joe E. Brown. When the studio announced the comedian to star, they paired his name with director Clarence Badger. Instead, Mervyn LeRoy, director of such films as *Little Caesar* (1931) and *30 Seconds Over Tokyo* (1944), helmed the production. Locations for the film included First National's Burbank studio and Pasadena's Huntington Hotel. *Variety* noted the completion of the shooting in March, with the film itself issued in July.

Lugosi took the role of a Mexican who becomes incensed with the antics of Joe E. Brown. Despite the nonhorror role, several reviews claimed he exuded the mannerisms of Dracula.

Sid Hickox, who later lensed *The Big Sleep* (1946), *White Heat* (1949), and episodes of the television program *I Love Lucy*, acted as cinematographer. Comedian Brown, known to audiences for his particularly large mouth, found himself busy at First National, beginning production on *Broadminded* just after finishing *The Tenderfoot* (1931). Costar Thelma Todd, blonde comedienne of numerous films and short subjects, later died mysteriously of carbon monoxide poisoning in her own garage.

42. Murders in the Rue Morgue
Cast: Sidney Fox (Mlle. Camille L'Espanaye), Bela Lugosi (Doctor Mirakle), Leon Waycoff (Pierre Dupin), Bert Roach (Paul), Brandon Hurst (Prefect of Police), Noble Johnson (Janos, the Black One), D'Arcy Corrigan (Morgue Keeper), Betty Ross Clarke (Mme. L'Espanaye), Arlene Francis (Woman of the Streets), Edna Marion (Mignette), Charlotte Henry (Girl), Polly Ann Young (Girl), Herman Bing (Franz Odenheimer), Agostino Borgato (Alberto Montani), Harry Holman (Landlord), Torben Meyer (The Dane), John T. Murray (Gendarme), D. Vernon (Tenant), Christian Frank (Gendarme), Michael Visaroff (Man), Ted Billings (Man), Charles T. Millsfield (Bearded Man at the Sideshow), Monte Montague (Workman/Gendarme), Charles Gemora (Erik the Ape), Joe Bonomo (Double for Gemora), Hamilton Green (Barker), Tempe Pigott (Crone).
Credits: Universal Studios, 1932. Produced by Carl Laemmle, Jr. Directed by Robert Florey. Associate Producer, E.M. Asher. Screenplay by Tom Reed and Dale van Every. Additional Dialogue by John Huston. Scenario Editor, Richard Shayer. Art Direction by Charles D. Hall. Set Designer, Herman Rosse. Recording Supervisor, C. Roy Hunter. Cinematography by Karl Freund. Edited by Milton Carruth. Supervising Film Editor, Maurice Pivar. Special Effects by John P. Fulton. Special Process by Frank Williams. Music Direction by Heinz Roemheld. Makeup by Jack P. Pierce. Assistant Directors, Scott Beal, Joseph McDonough, and Charles Gould. Technical Adviser, Howard Salemson.

Running time, 62 minutes (six reels). Copyright number LP2804, January 27, 1932.

Plot Summary: The mad Dr. Mirakle attempts to create a bride for his ape, kidnapping young women and injecting them with a serum that generally results in death. The doctor dumps their corpses into a river, leaving the authorities quite confused. At a circus sideshow, Lugosi's ape sees the beautiful Camille, with the doctor later sending the animal to kidnap her. The beast understands Mirakle's intention to inject her with the deadly serum and kills him. The ape then takes Camille and flees across the rooftops of Paris. The young Dupin follows close behind, shooting the ape and saving the girl.

Production Notes: Director Robert Florey initially mentioned the idea of the Poe story for a film to Universal Studios in March 1930, but became director of the project only after being replaced by James Whale on the set of *Frankenstein* (1931). To make room for the Frenchman, the studio dropped George Melford, previously named as *Rue Morgue*'s director. Lugosi himself moved from the *Frankenstein* story to the Poe film, adding the need for Florey to create a character for him. The Poe story featured detective Dupin, with the murderer being an ape. With no villainous role, Florey conceived "Dr. Mirakle" for Lugosi, the name itself coming from an Offenbach opera. The French director wrote a five-page adaptation, with several others (including famed director John Huston) contributing dialogue to the shooting script.

The tale itself resembles elements of *Frankenstein*, but most strongly derives from a German silent film, *The Cabinet of Dr. Caligari* (1919). Along with the plot motifs, *Rue Morgue* adopted much of the Expressionist look of its predecessor, with great attention given to the lighting and shadows, many of which were actually painted to obtain the proper effect. In addition, moving camera work and beautiful composition mark the film. Universal utilized little music for *Rue Morgue*, using Tchaikovsky's "Swan Lake" for the opening credits.

Florey desired an 1845 setting, though Universal wished to spend as little money as possible and thus opted for a modernized version of the tale. The French director protested, and the period costumes and sets were eventually approved. The 23-day shooting schedule began on October 19. The success of *Frankenstein* convinced the studio to spend an additional $23,178.14 on the film, for a grand total of $190,099.45.

The studio re-edited portions of Florey's vision prior to the February 1932 opening, leaving the film somewhat disjointed. Censors also protested certain scenes, particularly those of Arlene Francis, the prostitute tied to crossbeams and writhing in agony at the tortures of Dr. Mirakle. The film did less business than either *Dracula* or *Frankenstein*, though ads promised it would be "grimmer than that grim picture *Dracula*, more gruesome and awe-inspiring than *Frankenstein*," further claiming that *Rue Morgue* would "thrill you to your fingertips." French audiences first saw the film as *The Crime in the Rue Morgue*, with its Italian title being simply *Dr. Mirakle*.

Some spectators wrote angrily to fan magazines that Poe's story had been mangled by the inclusion of "Dr. Mirakle," yet in retrospect it provided Lugosi a tremendous role. Cast and crew both found the Hungarian reclusive, but trade reviews generally approved of the actor. One movie magazine even sponsored a contest in which a lucky winner could meet Béla "Dracula" Lugosi.

Among the crew members was Karl Freund, famed cinematographer of the German Expressionist period and also of *Dracula* (1931). Makeup man Jack Pierce, of *Dracula* and *White Zombie*, returned as well. Ads paired the names of Lugosi and Sidney Fox, with the latter receiving top billing on screen. Formerly the star of *Strictly Dishonorable* (1931), Fox found help with her career and billing through an affair with Carl Laemmle, Sr. Leon Waycoff later changed his name to Leon Ames for such films as *The Postman Always Rings Twice* (1946) and television programs like *Mr. Ed.* Another future television star was a young Arlene Francis, *Rue Morgue*'s "Woman of the Streets." Noble Johnson, as Janos, later appeared in other horror films like *The Mummy* (1932) and *King Kong* (1933). Charles Gemora played the ape, though live shots of a real ape were intercut with his footage.

43. *White Zombie*

Cast: Bela Lugosi (Murder Legendre), Madge Bellamy (Madeline), Joseph Cawthorn (Dr. Bruner), Robert Frazer (Beaumont), John Harron (Neil), Clarence Muse (Coach Driver), Brandon Hurst (Silver), Dan Crimmins (Pierre), Frederick Peters (Chauvin), George Burr MacAnnan (Von Gelder), John Printz (Latour), Claude Morgan (Zombie), John Fergusson (Zombie), Annette Stone (Maid), Velma Gresham (Maid).

Credits: Presented by Amusement Securities Corporation and distributed by United Artists, 1932. Produced by Edward Halperin. Directed by Victor Halperin. Story and Dialogue by Garnett Weston. Cinematography by Arthur Martinelli. Assistant Director, William Cody. Edited by Harold MacLernon. Sound Engineer, L.E. Clark. Art Effects, Conrad Tritschler. Settings by Ralph Berger. Makeup by Jack P. Pierce and Carl Axcelle. Technical Director, Herbert Glazer. Camera Operator, J. Arthur Feindel. Assistant Camera Operators, Charles Bohny and Enzo Martinelli. Production Assistant, Sidney Marcus. Dialogue Director, Herbert Farjeon. Musical Arrangements, Abe Meyer. Original Music by Guy Bevier Williams and Xavier Cugat. Additional Music by Nathaniel Dett, H. Herkan, Gaston Borch, H. Maurice Jacquet, Leo Kempenski, and Hugo Riesenfeld. Running time, 68 minutes (eight reels). Copyright number LP3357, August 1, 1932.

Plot Summary: Neil and his fiancée, Madeline, sail to Haiti for their wedding at the home of Beaumont, who himself loves the soon-to-be-married beauty. After failed attempts to sway her affections, Beaumont seeks the help of zombie master Murder. By use of a zombie powder, Beaumont turns Madeline into the living dead. Murder, however, takes a fancy to the "White Zombie," forming his own plans for her. The villain then turns Beaumont into a zombie, but later finds his plans thwarted by Neil and an old missionary named Dr. Bruner. They arrive to save Madeline and attempt to kill the variety of zombies clustered at Murder's castle. A weak but redeemed Beaumont throws Murder off the castle wall and follows by plunging into the waters below himself. The young couple are then happily reunited.

Production Notes: Independent filmmakers Edward and Victor Halperin realized the potential profits in horror and decided to shoot Garnett Weston's eerie script based on the living dead of Haiti — "zombies." Though the monsters later became a staple of the horror film, Weston's tale was the first to bring them to the screen. The Halperins actually experienced legal trouble before cameras rolled, with playwright Kenneth Webb — author of a short-lived 1932 Broadway tale called *Zombie* — claiming the filmmakers stole their idea from him. The Halperins managed to move forward, however, as Webb did not legally own the rights to the word *zombie*. Shooting lasted only 11 days during March on leftover sets from *Frankenstein* and *Dracula* at Universal Studios, with some exteriors being shot on the RKO-Pathé lot. The final negative cost came to approximately $62,500, with the American Securities Corporation and Phil Goldstone financing the production.

Lugosi headlined the tale as "Murder," the zombie master, with particularly sinister makeup provided by Jack Pierce. His costume, as well as images of the zombies and some plot material, came from a 1929 travelogue by William Seabrook, *The Magic Island*. Seabrook based the book on his firsthand research of Haiti, with a special chapter on "dead men working in the cane fields" which introduced most American readers to the zombie phenomenon.

Silent screen star Madge Bellamy portrayed the title character, hoping the role would lead to a comeback. Robert Frazer, formerly a star in such silents as *Robin Hood* (1912), played Beaumont and later met Lugosi again for *Black Dragons* (1942). Clarence Muse, famed black actor and composer, added much to the film's mood as the coach driver. He also played opposite Lugosi again, in Monogram's *The Invisible Ghost* (1941).

The Halperins believed dialogue should be kept to a minimum of 15 percent of a film, leaving much of *White Zombie* an amalgam of images and music. Arthur Martinelli's atmospheric cinematography, which includes some impressive moving camera shots, complements the interesting optical effects that feature Lugosi's eyes hovering above the countryside. The music ranges from a spiritual called "Listen to the Lambs" to a Spanish *jota* written by Xavier Cugat. Most of the score, however, remains bravura, pseudoclassical music that greatly heightens the action.

Universal Studios attached the negative at the end of May 1932 for some $8,607 in notes owed to it by the Halperins, with Phil Goldstone providing $11,000 in July to solve the problem. Though Educational Pictures originally planned to handle *White Zombie*'s distribution, Goldstone arranged a deal with United Artists. The film premiered in late July, with a majority of critics in the country joining in a chorus of disapproval. Yet *White Zombie* generated crowds at most theaters, becoming the Halperins' most successful film venture.

The Rivoli in New York City hired actors to dress as zombies and enact dramatic sequences outside the theater to draw in audiences. Wonderful and provocative ads featured tag lines like "The Weirdest Love Story in 2000 Years," "She was not dead ... nor alive, yet she walked, breathed, and performed his every wish," and "He Made Her His Slave." Some even featured artwork of Lugosi's eyes beaming down at a nude woman.

French audiences first saw *White Zombie* under the title *The Living Dead*, though a later release rechristened the film *White Zombie: The Day When the Living Dead....* For Italian spectators, it became *The Island of the Zombies*, whereas in Spain *White Zombie* turned up as *The Legion of the Men with No Soul*.

Lugosi's performance remains quite melodramatic, yet for this film his style fits perfectly, turning "Murder" into one of the most dark, evil villains in cinema history. The actor complained later of his paltry fee, given the film's enormous success. Reports vary on his salary, ranging from figures like $500 and $900 to $2,500 and even $5,000. The Halperins attempted to obtain Lugosi again for their sequel *Revolt of the Zombies* (1936), though instead Dean Jagger appeared and the film itself bore few similarities to its predecessor. In the fifties, Lugosi claimed he would appear in another sequel, *Return of the White Zombie*, though the project never got off the ground.

Distributors reissued *White Zombie* in 1936, 1938, 1952, and as part of a double bill with *Freaks* (1932) in the sixties. The film also became one of Lugosi's first to air on television. Though it features a number of poor acting performances, *White Zombie* continues to be one of Lugosi's finest films, and, thanks to a critical re-evaluation, it has found its place as a minor film classic.

44. ***Chandu the Magician***

Cast: Edmund Lowe (Chandu), Irene Ware (Princess Nadji), Bela Lugosi (Roxor), Herbert Mundin (Albert Miggles), Henry B. Walthall (Robert Regent), Weldon Heyburn (Abdullah), Virginia Hammond (Dorothy), June Vlasek (Betty Lou), Nestor Aber (Bobby).

Credits: Fox, 1932. Directed by Marcel Varnel and William Cameron Menzies. Screenplay by Phillip Klein and Barry Conners. Based on a radio program created by Harry A. Earnshaw, Vera M. Oldham, and R.R. Morgan. Cinematography by James Wong Howe. Art Direction by Max Parker. Recording Engineer, Joseph E. Aiken. Edited by Harold Schuster. Running time,

72 minutes (6,350 feet). Copyright number LP3238, September 3, 1932.

Plot Summary: The evil Roxor holds an inventor captive while attempting to understand his death ray machine, which can wipe out civilization. Chandu the Magician steps in to thwart Roxor and win the affections of Princess Nadji.

Production Notes: The magician Chandu came from a popular radio program first heard in Los Angeles in 1932. The show became popular nationally and ran until 1936. Gayne Whitman played the lead in this first incarnation, with the radio program itself revived in 1948–50. The villainous Roxor proved popular enough to be a recurrent character in multiple episodes. The word *chandu* can be traced to the twenties, when it was slang for opium, even becoming the topic and title of a 1927 novel.

The studio first announced a film of the radio program in May 1932. *Chandu*'s cameras began rolling in the second week of July, with Fox releasing the finished product in October. Fox cast Ed Lowe as Chandu as a result of his success as the magician in 1931's *The Spider*. The studio originally cast Ralph Morgan as the inventor, though former D.W. Griffith star Henry B. Walthall replaced him. Codirector Menzies achieved fame later as one of the great art designers of Hollywood through his work on *Gone with the Wind* (1939) and others, and he continued to direct features like *Things to Come* (1936).

Lugosi's Roxor does not clearly die at the film's conclusion, leaving the character available for sequels. Yet, rather than resume the villain again, the Hungarian moved into the hero's spot for the title character of a 1934 serial, the *Return of Chandu*.

As a wax replica of Lugosi's Roxor was placed in Hollywood's Motion Picture Museum and Hall of Fame, Fox awaited strong box office receipts. Radio Pictures even released a comedy short entitled *Sham Poo the Magician*, and trades initially claimed that a sequel to the Fox feature would soon appear. But several factors kept huge returns at bay. For one, Lugosi played Roxor very melodramatically, a far cry from the quite understated Lowe. For another, the film drifts from being a lighthearted romp to taking itself very seriously. Adults were thus alienated from the film that many critics likened to the early-day serials.

45. *Island of Lost Souls*

Cast: Charles Laughton (Dr. Moreau), Bela Lugosi (Sayer of the Law), Richard Arlen (Edward Parker), Leila Hyams (Ruth Walker), Kathleen Burke (Lota, the Panther Woman), Arthur Hohl (Montgomery), Stanley Fields (Captain Davies), Robert Kortman (Hogan), Tetsu Komai (M'Ling), Hans Steinke (Ouran), Harry Ekezian (Gola), Rosemary Grimes (Samoan Girl), Paul Hurst (Donahue), George Irving (The Consul), Alan Ladd (Manimal), Joe Bonomo (Manimal), Randolph Scott (Manimal), John George (Manimal), Larry "Buster" Crabbe (Manimal), Duke York (Manimal), Constantine Romanoff, Jack Burdette, Robert Milasch, Bob Kerr, Evangelus Berbas, Jack Walters.

Credits: Paramount Pictures, 1933. Directed by Erle C. Kenton. Screenplay by Philip Wylie and Waldemar Young. Based on H.G. Wells's novel *The Island of Dr. Moreau*. Cinematography by Karl Struss. Special effects by Gordon Jennings. Makeup by Wally Westmore. Running time, 67 minutes (eight reels). Copyright number LP3518, December 29, 1932.

Plot Summary: Edward Parker finds himself stranded on the island of Dr. Moreau, forced to wait for the next freighter before returning home. He soon learns that the natives of the jungle are really animals transformed into humans by the mad doctor in his "House of Pain." Moreau soon plans to mate his prize experiment, Lota the Panther Woman, with Parker. Eventually, Ruth arrives in search of Parker, her fiancé. A manimal kills the captain of the ship that brought her, with the others rising up against the doctor after having seen blood spilled. Ruth and Edward escape as the manimals drag Moreau to his own House of Pain and perform "surgery" on him.

Production Notes: Originally Paramount slated Norman Taurog to direct *Island of Lost Souls*, but the studio replaced him due to his running behind on *Phantom President*. After he finished the work on the script, the studio recalled writer Philip Wylie in September to do further dialogue work. Cameras then rolled on the horror story during October and November 1932. Paramount shot on location at Catalina Island for some outdoor sequences, with indoor jungle sets being built on a soundstage. Rather than synthetic fog, director Kenton used the natural fog of Catalina mornings, forcing the cast and crew to wake each day at dawn to use the effect. Makeup for many of the "manimals" took over an hour each to apply.

Lugosi appears as a manimal with limited screen time, though the fact that he speaks causes him to stand out. Original makeup left areas of his face bare, but it was discarded in favor of a design that covered his face with hair. Initially, the studio planned George Barbier for Lugosi's role.

Before its release, *Variety* claimed the studio looked for another angle to publicize the film, worried that the "cycle of blood and thunder" and the horror tag could mean poor box office. *Island of Lost Souls* hit theaters in January 1933, having actually turned into one of the most frightening movies of the thirties. Some critics gave nice nods to the film, with one mentioning that it would only please children. Yet the horrific nature and sexual undercurrents caused the film to be banned in England until 1959. Various parts of the United States found the film equally distasteful, and H.G. Wells himself believed the point of his novel — man playing god — was lost among the various monsters. French theaters, however, did screen the film under the title of Wells's book, *The Island of Dr. Moreau*.

Ads questioned, "Woman or Panther — with the body of Venus and the mark of a beast?" Kathleen Burke, the 19-year-old Panther Woman, won a national contest involving 60,000 girls to appear in the film and received a $200-a-week contract. All Paramount-Publix theaters held the contest during July, with Ernst Lubitsch, C.B. DeMille, Rouben Mamoulian, and Norman Taurog judging the finalists. Much publicity came from the chosen young starlet, including such headlines as "Panther Woman laps up blood; No, Malted Milks."

Famed actor Charles Laughton took the lead role of Dr. Moreau, having formerly appeared in *The Old Dark House* (1932). Paramount originally planned Randolph Scott and Nancy Carroll as the young couple of the film, but instead Leila Hyams and Richard Arlen appeared. Future stars Buster Crabbe, Randolph Scott, and Alan Ladd appear as "Manimals."

46. *The Death Kiss*

Cast: David Manners (Franklyn Drew), Adrienne Ames (Marcia Lane), Bela Lugosi (Joseph Steiner), John Wray (Detective Sheehan), Vince Barnett (Officer Gulliver), Alexander Carr (Leon Grossmith), Edward Van Sloan (Tom Avery), Harold Minjir (Howell), Wade Boteler (Hilliker), Al Hill (Assistant Director), Barbara Bedford (Script Clerk), Alan Roscoe (Chalmers), Mona Maris (Mrs. Avery), Edmund Burns (Brent), Jimmy Donlin (Hill), Harold Waldridge (Clerk), Lee Moran (Todd), Wilson Benge (Doorman), Eddy Chandler (Mechanic), Harry Strang (Gaffer), Eddie Boland (Bill), Frank O'Connor (Policeman), Forrest Taylor, Paul Porcasi, King Baggott.

Credits: World Wide Pictures, 1933. Presented by E.W. Hammons. Directed by Edwin L. Marin. Screenplay by Barry Barringer and Gordon Kahn. Based on Madelon St. Dennis's 1932 novel, *The Death Kiss*. Cinematography by Norbert Brodine. Musical direction by Val Burton. Art direction by Ralph M. Delacey. Sound Engineer, Hans Weeren. Supervising Editor, Martin G. Cohn. Film Editor, Rose Loewinger. Running time, 75 minutes. Copyright number LP3967, January 8, 1933.

Plot Summary: An actor is killed during the filming of a movie scene, with screenwriter Franklyn Drew spending much time

An ominous but very beautiful trade advertisement for World Wide's *The Death Kiss* (1933).

attempting to solve the mystery. Drew's own experience writing mystery scripts allows him to investigate more intelligently than the police.

Production Notes: Tiffany shot this film at its own studio, and, given the setting, this offers a unique glimpse into low-budget moviemaking of the thirties. Rushed into production, *The Death Kiss* was finished during November 1932 and released in January of the following year. Though a black-and-white production, the studio added color tints to some prints for occasional effects like fire and smoke from a handgun. Critics generally believed the film had possibilities, but many complained that the comic relief took higher priority than the solution of the crime itself.

Despite top billing, Lugosi's role as a studio exec gave him little to do, other than be one more suspect in the murder investigation. Tiffany cast the actor in October 1932, even before choosing a director. Promotional materials drew strongly on Lugosi's association with *Dracula*, with some ads showing a menacing Lugosi clutching a very scantily clad young woman. Theater managers were told Lugosi "made the two greatest box-office pictures for the exhibitor in *Dracula* and *White Zombie*, and here is the third!"

Director Marin went from *The Death Kiss* (his first film) to directing some 50 movies, including numerous other mysteries. Actor David Manners performed opposite Lugosi in *Dracula* (1931), *The Devil's in Love* (1933), and *The Black Cat* (1934). Edward Van Sloan had formerly appeared in *Dracula* and later acted with Lugosi in a 1939 serial, *The Phantom Creeps* (1939).

47. Night of Terror

Cast: Bela Lugosi (Degar), Sally Blane (Mary Rinehart), Wallace Ford (Tom Hartley), Bryant Washburn (Richard Rinehart), Tully Marshall (John Rinehart), Gertrude Michaels (Sara Rinehart), George Meeker (Arthur Hornsby), Mary Frey (Sika), Matt McHugh, Edwin Maxwell, Pat Harmon, Oscar Smith.

Credits: Columbia Pictures, 1933. Directed by Benjamin Stoloff. Screenplay by Beatrice Van, William Jacobs, and Lester Nielson. Based on an original story by Willard Mack. Cinematography by Joseph Valentine. Edited by Arthur Hilton. Running time, 61 minutes (seven reels). Copyright number LP3811, April 17, 1933.

Plot Summary: This old dark house thriller involves a scientist's formula that supposedly can place people in suspended animation. Various cast members are murdered by unknown hands, though suspects like the Hindu Degar abound. At the conclusion, the killer himself warns spectators not to reveal the ending to potential audience members.

Production Notes: Originally titled *He Lived to Kill*, producers announced this thriller in February 1933. With Lugosi busy shooting *International House* during the day, the cast and crew of *Night of Terror* were forced to work from 2:00 A.M. to 6:00 A.M. The studio pressbook claimed that shooting in the middle of the night and the presence of Lugosi himself caused actress Sally Blane to suffer extreme nervousness throughout the production. The film was released through Columbia in June 1933, receiving generally poor reviews. Publicity materials questioned, "What was this unseen menace that struck in the dark?"

Trades linked the Hungarian to the production from the first mention of the film. Top billed and turbaned, Lugosi portrayed the mysterious Degar to little effect. The role offered him almost nothing to do, other than add to the supposedly chilling atmosphere.

Cast member George Meeker later met Lugosi in *Murder by Television* (1935), and wisecracking Wallace Ford played opposite the Hungarian in *The Mysterious Mr. Wong* (1935) and *The Ape Man* (1943).

48. International House

Cast: Peggy Hopkins Joyce (as herself), W.C. Fields (Professor Quail), Stuart Erwin (Tommy Nash), Sari Maritza (Carol Fortescue), George Burns (Dr. Burns), Gracie Allen (Nurse Allen), Bela Lugosi (General Petronovich), Edmund Breese (Dr. Wong), Lumsden Hare (Sir Mortimer Fortescue), Franklin Pangborn (Hotel Manager), Harrison Greene (Herr von Baden), Henry Sedley (Serge Borsky), James Wong (Inspector Sun), Sterling Holloway (Entertainer in Sailor Uniform), Rudy Vallee (as himself), Colonel Stoopnagle and Budd (as themselves), Cab Calloway and His Orchestra (as themselves), Baby Rose Marie (as herself), Ernest Wood (Newsreel Reporter), Edwin Stanley (Mr. Rollins), Clem Beauchamp/Jerry Drew (Cameraman), Norman Ainslee (Ticket Manager), Louis Vincenot (Hotel Clerk), Bo-Ling (Chinese Girl), Etta Lee (Peggy's Maid), Bo-Ling (Bell-hop), Lona Andre (Chorus Queen), Andre Cheron (Guest).

The very stylish title card from Columbia's *Night of Terror* (1933).

Credits: Paramount Pictures, 1933. Directed by Eddie Sutherland. Screenplay by Francis Martin and Walter DeLeon. Based on an original story by Louis E. Heifetz and Neil Brant. Cinematography by Ernest Haller. Costumes by Travis Banton. Music and lyrics by Ralph Rainger and Leo Robin. Running time, 70 minutes (6,119 feet). Copyright number LP3918, June 3, 1933.

Plot Summary: A Chinese inventor's "radioscope" brings numerous buyers to the International House hotel of Wu Hu, China. Tommy Nash, an American, eventually manages to purchase the device and win the love of Carol Fortescue, only after being treated for illness by Dr. Burns and Nurse Allen and slightly "vamped" by Peggy Hopkins Joyce. Adding to the utter chaos is Professor Quail, who arrives in his "autogyro" (a combination plane and helicopter) not to bid on the radioscope, but simply because he is lost.

Production Notes: *International House* began shooting in the last week of February 1933, with the nine-week production ending in April. Fields, who had made numerous silent films under director Sutherland, became a sensation during the thirties. During the production, an earthquake shook the set, and Fields calmly told everyone to leave carefully. A running camera recorded the event, which later was said to have been faked. Paramount released the comedy in May 1933, with most reviews praising Fields. Other articles drew attention to the use of a televisionlike invention in the plot.

Lugosi portrayed a Russian who sets out to buy the new invention, though he spends most of his time being jealous over former wife Peggy Hopkins Joyce. Studio press materials generally billed the actor seventh in the cast, though some promotional ads listed him fourth.

The impressive cast of *International House* included actress Peggy Hopkins Joyce playing herself. Joyce's role echoed her real-life habit of marrying millionaires. Cab Calloway, popular jazz artist and bandleader, sang "Reefer Man," a tune about marijuana often cut in early television broadcasts.

49. *The Devil's in Love*

Cast: Victor Jory (Lt. Andre Morand), Loretta Young (Margot), Vivienne Osborne (Rena), David Manners (Jean), C. Henry Gordon (Captain Radak), Herbert Mundin (Bimpy), Emil Chautard (Father Carmion), J. Carrol Naish (Salazar), Bela Lugosi (prosecutor for the military), Robert Barrat (Major Bertram), Akim Tamiroff, Dewey Robinson, John Davidson.

Credits: Fox, 1933. Directed by Wilhelm Dieterle. Screenplay by Howard Estabrook. Based on an original story by Harry Hervey. Cinematography by Hal Mohr. Art Direction by Max Parker. Musical Direction by Louis De Francesco. Frocks by Rita Kaufman. Sound Recording by Donald Flick. Edited by Ralph Dietrich. Running time, 70 minutes (6,300 feet). Copyright number LP4025, July 10, 1933.

Plot Summary: After being falsely accused of murder, Doctor Morand joins the Foreign Legion, only to fall in love with Margot, the fiancée of his best friend. Eventually, authorities find Morand and charge him with murder. His innocence soon becomes apparent, however, and he even finds happiness with Margot. Her betrothed had conveniently been killed in battle.

Production Notes: *The Devil's in Love* began shooting in May 1933 and ended in late June. Fox spent a great deal of money on this French Foreign Legion tale, which critics often noted as having a very dated storyline. *The Devil's in Love* premiered shortly after its completion, hitting some theaters by late July.

Lugosi took on a small role as a prosecutor, being added to the cast during mid to late June. *Variety* announced the role during the third week of June, with his scenes coming near the end of the production. His association with the film simply appears to be a minor job, as there is no indication he consciously sought such an insignificant role to escape typecasting. Moreover, while some reviewers noticed him, Fox did not even include the actor's name in the screen credits or movie posters. *The Devil's in Love* then becomes more a reminder of his pre–*Dracula* films at Fox — minor parts with little or no billing.

Along with a host of actors who worked with Lugosi in other films, the cast included Loretta Young, who would find much success through her appearances in Fox productions. Akim Tamiroff, later nominated for two Oscars and a costar of Lugosi's in *The Black Sleep* (1955), also found his way into *The Devil's in Love* cast.

50. *The Black Cat*

Cast: Boris Karloff (Hjalmar Poelig), Bela Lugosi (Dr. Vitus Werdegast), David Manners (Peter Allison), Jacqueline Wells (Joan Allison), Lucille Lund (Karen), Egon Brecher (Majordomo), Harry Cording (Thamal), Henry Armetta (Sergeant), Albert Conti (Lieutenant), Anna Duncan (Maid), Herman Bing (Car Steward), Andre Cheron (Train Conductor), Luis Alberni (Train Steward), George Davis (Bus Driver), Alphonse Martell (Porter), Tony Marlow (Patrolman), Paul Weigel (Stationmaster), Albert Polet (Waiter), Rodney Hildebrand (Brakeman), Virginia Ainsworth, King Baggot, Symona Boniface, Lois January, Michael Mark, Paul Panzer, John Peter Richmond [John Carradine], Peggy Terry (all in small roles as Devil worshippers).

Credits: Universal Studios, 1934. Produced by Carl Laemmle, Jr. Directed by Edgar G. Ulmer. Screenplay by Peter Ruric. Based on a story by Edgar Ulmer and Peter Ruric. Suggested by "The Black Cat," a short story by Edgar Allan Poe. Cinematography by John J. Mescall. Art Direction by Charles D. Hall. Musical direction by Heinz Roemheld. Makeup by Jack P. Pierce. Special Effects by John P. Fulton. Edited by Ray Curtiss. Assistant Directors, W.J. Reiter and Sam Weisenthal. Second Cameraman, King Gray. Assistant Cameraman, John Martin. Script Clerk, Moree Herring. Supervisor's Secretary, Peggy Vaughn. Running time, 65 minutes (seven reels). Copyright number LP4664, May 4, 1934.

Plot Summary: Dr. Werdegast meets the young Allison couple on a train while on his way to visit satanist Hjalmar Poelzig. After a bus crash, all three find themselves guests at Poelzig's house. The occultist had previously stolen Werdegast's wife and then married his daughter while the doctor rotted away as a prisoner of war. Poelzig quickly believes Joan Allison necessary to a devil-worshipping ceremony, though Werdegast attempts to stop him. The two play chess for her life, with the evil Hjalmar winning. Werdegast later binds Poelzig to a rack and skins him alive. The young couple escape the house, which then explodes, destroying Werdegast, Poelzig, and the satanic cult.

Production Notes: Universal began considering the cinematic possibilities of Edgar Allan Poe's "The Black Cat" in 1932, with a variety of treatments landing in studio offices. Director Edgar Ulmer finally convinced Carl Laemmle, Jr., to move ahead on the story, suggesting it serve as an inexpensive teaming of Boris Karloff and Lugosi. Ulmer, formerly an art director for many of F.W. Murnau's German films, turned *The Black Cat* into a story more reminiscent of satanist Aleister Crowley's life than anything resembling Poe. Together with author Peter Ruric, the tale transformed into a cache of necrophilia, sadism, murder, pedophilia, and devil-worshipping. *Variety* announced Ulmer would direct the tale on January 23, 1934.

Shooting began on February 28, the very day after binding the script's final draft. The incredible set designs resemble not the German Expressionism of the twenties, but an ultramodern, overtly Bauhaus style. The production, including several retakes, ended on March 28, at a cost of $95,745. Its highly effective music score included Bach's "Toccata and Fugue in D Minor," as well as a number of Liszt's compositions.

The film's "black cat" took an award at a Universal Studios contest of more than 500 ebony felines. Karloff and Lugosi acted as judges, giving first place to one named Jiggs. First place carried with it a contract for the cat to appear with the duo in the Poe film.

Lugosi received a weekly fee of $1,000 for his role as Werdegast, which gave him semiheroic character. Though he attempts to save the young couple and destroy Karloff, Lugosi's role does allow a dark side to surface, particularly in skinning his adversary alive. Studio publicity claimed, "Great care was extended not to have any of the scenes between Karloff and Bela Lugosi open to any other eyes but those actually employed on the set," adding that for five years Lugosi proudly used the same chair on every movie set.

Lugosi uses effective subtleties of language and gesture often lacking in his later work. Director Ulmer repeatedly told the actor to understate his role rather than overact. The two both spoke German and apparently formed a decent working relationship. Rumors claim, however, that Lugosi as well as the studio demanded changes in the final cut. Lugosi clamored for a more benevolent appearance overall, while Universal worried about the more suggestive, erotic elements of the film.

Universal released the end result in May 1934 to generally disappointing reviews. Advertisements promised audiences "things you never saw or dreamed of before," as played out by Karloff "The Uncanny" and Bela "Dracula" Lugosi. *Billboard* advised exhibitors to sell audiences on the teaming of Karloff and Lugosi in a Poe story, but warned that, due to its poor nature, "on a a longer run this supposed thriller will fail miserably." The film proved such pundits wrong, as it became Universal's top-grossing picture of 1934. Theaters in Spain originally screened the film as *Satan,* and U.S. reissues of *The Black Cat* bore the title *The Vanishing Body.*

51. *Gift of Gab*

Cast: Edmund Lowe (Phillip Gabney), Gloria Stuart (Barbara Kelton), Ruth Etting

(Ruth), Phil Baker (Doctor), Ethel Waters (Ethel), Alice White (Margot), Victor Moore (Colonel Trivers), Hugh O'Connell (Patsy), Helen Vinson (Nurse), Gene Austin (Crooner), Thomas Hanlon (Announcer), Henry Armetta (Janitor), Andy Devin (McDougal), Wini Shaw (Singer), Marion Byron (Telephone Girl), Sterling Holloway (Sound Effect Man), Edwin Maxwell (Norton), Leighton Noble (Orchestra Leader), Maurice Block (Auction Room Owner), Tammany Young (Mug), James Flavin (President of Alumni), Billy Barty (Baby), Richard Elliot (Father), Florence Enright (Mother), Warner Richmond (Cop), Sid Walker, Skins Miller, Jack Harling (trio billed as "The Three Stooges"), Sidney Skolsky, Dennis O'Keefe (Dance Floor Extra), Dave O'Brien (Dance Floor Extra), Boris Karloff (The Phantom), Bela Lugosi (An Apache), Alexander Woolcott (as himself), Paul Lukas, Chester Morris, Richard Pryor, the Downey Sisters, Douglass Montgomery, Candy and Coco, Douglas Fowley, Binnie Barnes, June Knight, the Beale Street Boys, Rian James, Graham McNamee, Gus Arnheim and His Orchestra (as themselves).

Credits: Universal Studios, 1934. Produced by Carl Laemmle, Jr. Directed by Karl Freund. Screenplay by Rian James and Lou Breslow. Based on an original story by Jerry Wald and Philip G. Epstein. Cinematography by George Robinson and Harold Wenstrom. Musical Direction by Edward Ward. Music by Albert von Tilzer, Con Conrad, and Charles Tobias. Edited by Raymond Curtiss. Running time, 68 minutes (seven reels). Copyright number LP4950, September 17, 1934.

Plot Summary: Philip Gabney, after being fired as a radio announcer, devotes his attention to alcohol until girlfriend Barbara helps him back on track by turning him on to a great news scoop. Gabney manages to locate a missing airplane that authorities had been seeking. For the sake of publicity, he even broadcasts while parachuting to the wreckage.

Production Notes: Universal added a tremendous array of stars culled from movies, radio, and music to the cast of this otherwise bland Ed Lowe film, originally titled *Let 'Em Rave* and *Smooth Gab*. Much of the talent appears in bits during radio broadcasts of *Colonel Withers' Chicken Livers* program. Among the names are the Three Stooges, though the team is not the famed trio but a competing group. Universal shot some scenes, such as those featuring singer Ethel Waters and writer Alexander Woolcott, in New York. Released in September, *Gift of Gab* attracted generally good reviews.

Among the many songs were "Talking to Myself," "I Ain't Gonna Sin No More," "Gift of Gab," "Somebody Looks Good," "Don't Let This Waltz Mean Goodbye," "Walkin' on Air," "What a Wonderful Day," "Tomorrow Who Cares?," and "Blue Sky Avenue."

Lugosi appears only briefly as an Apache wearing a checkered hat, with Karloff portaying the "Phantom." Both are in the same sequence, a murder mystery skit for a radio broadcast. The short nature of their parts, as well as their being lost among a huge number of other stars (many of them now-forgotten radio personalities), resulted in poor billing. The original pressbook, however, makes more of their cameos than most of the others, as did several reviews. Universal shot the film during July, with Lugosi concurrently shooting a serial called *Return of Chandu*.

Hungarian Paul Lukas, a friend of Lugosi's, also appeared in the cast, playing a corpse in a skit with Lugosi. The pressbook also notes another costarring acquaintance of the Hungarian's, a black cat who allegedly was the title player in 1934's *The Black Cat*.

52. *Best Man Wins*

Cast: Edmund Lowe (Tobu), Jack Holt (Nick), Bela Lugosi (Dr. Boehm), Florence Rice (Ann), Forrester Harvey (Harry), J. Farrell MacDonald (Captain), Bradley Page, Mitchell Lewis, Esther Howard, Selmer Jackson, Frank Sheridan, and Oscar Apfel.

Credits: Columbia Pictures, 1935. Directed by Erle C. Kenton. Screenplay by Ethel Hill and Bruce Manning. From the story "Mud Turtle" by Ben G. Kohn. Cinematography by John Stumar. Edited by Otto Meyer. Running time, 65 minutes (seven reels). Copyright number LP5240, January 7, 1935.

Plot Summary: Both Tobu and Nick are deep-sea divers, with the former saving the latter's life, only to lose an arm in the process. As a result, Tobu cannot get work and refuses to accept charity. To get back on his feet financially and impress Ann, he becomes involved in a diamond-smuggling operation with Dr. Boehm. Nick, a harbor cop, warns him to leave the crime gang, and when the armless diver does not, Tobu eventually drowns himself 40 fathoms deep to avoid prison. Nick and Ann thus are united.

Production Notes: Titled *The Depths Below* during production, *Best Man Wins* began shooting in late October. Erle C. Kenton, who formerly helmed *Island of Lost Souls* (1933), directed, though critics generally thought more of the underwater photography than anything else. The film hit theaters in January 1935. For its Belgian release, *Best Man Wins* became *Gangsters of the Ocean*.

By early November, trades announced Lugosi as a member of the cast, with the actor already working on *The Mysterious Mr. Wong*. Though a notice in The *Los Angeles Times* promised Lugosi would "cause a whole array of shivers," critics claimed it was the drowning sequence of Lowe that most resembled anything out of the Grand Guignol.

53. *The Mysterious Mr. Wong*

Cast: Bela Lugosi (Mr. Wong, Mandarin), Wallace Ford (Jason Barton), Arline Judge (Peg), Fred Warren (Tsung), Lotus Long (Moonflower), Robert Emmett O'Connor (McGillicuddy), Edward Piel, Sr. (Jen Yu), Luke Chan (Chan Lu), Lee Shumway (Brandon), Etta Lee, Ernest F. Young, Theodore Lotch, James B. Leong, Chester Gan.

Credits: Monogram, 1935. Directed by William Nigh. Supervised by George Yohalem. Based on *The Twelve Coins of Confucius*, an original story by Harry Stephen Keeler. Adapted by Nina Howatt. Continuity by Lew Levinson. Additional Dialogue by James Herbuveux. Cinematography by Harry Neumann. Musical Direction by Abe Meyer. Set Designer, E.R. Hickson. Edited by Jack Ogilvie. Running time, 63 minutes (seven reels). Copyright number LP5244, January 12, 1935.

Plot Summary: The evil Mr. Wong, reminiscent of other Asian villains like Dr. Fu Manchu, understands the power that comes to the one who possesses all 12 coins of Confucius. He stops at nothing to obtain them, and runs a laundry in San Francisco's Chinatown to cover his tracks. Eventually though, journalist Jason Baron and the police thwart his plans.

Production Notes: Mystery and detective writer Harry Stephen Keeler penned "The Twelve Coins of Confucius," published in the October and November 1933 issues of *Great Detective* magazine. Monogram purchased the tale and began shooting on an RKO-Pathé lot in Culver City during mid-October 1934. The production finished the following month, with Monogram releasing the film itself in late January 1935. "Dead Men Tell No Tales," warned the film's advertisements. "Out of the night creeps a shadow striking terror into the heart of Chinatown."

Though most reviewers found the film to be poor, Lugosi received some favorable notices based on his versatility as an Asian character. Trades first announced Lugosi as the lead on October 9, 1934. Dorothy Lee was originally slated as "Peg."

Director William Nigh earlier made such films as *Mr. Wu* (1927) with Lon Chaney Sr., but by the midthirties found himself locked into poverty-row filmmaking. He later directed a series of *Mr. Wong* films at Monogram featuring Boris Karloff, yet the title character was actually a Charlie Chan–style detective and unrelated to the Lugosi film. As well as confusing a few movie buffs, one of films in the Karloff series was even announced in January 1939 as *The Mysterious Mr. Wong.*

54. Mark of the Vampire

Cast: Lionel Barrymore (Professor Zelen), Elizabeth Allan (Irena Borotyn), Bela Lugosi (Count Mora), Lionel Atwill (Inspector Neumann), Holmes Herbert (Sir Karell Borotyn), Jean Hersholt (Baron Otto von Zinden), Carroll Borland (Luna Mora), Donald Meek (Dr. Doskil), Ivan Simpson (Jan), Egon Brecher (Coroner), Henry Wadsworth (Count Fedor Vincenty), Lily Malyon (Sick Woman), Leila Bennett (Maria), June Gittelson (Annie), Michael Visaroff (Innkeeper), Franklin Ardell (Chauffer), Mrs. Lesovosky (Old Woman in Inn), Rosemary Glosz (Innkeeper's Wife), Claire Vedara (English Woman), Guy Belis (English Man), James Bradbury Jr. (bit part), Baron Hesse (Bus Driver), Zeffie Tilbury (Grandmother), Christian Rub (Deaf Man), Torbin Meyer (Card Player), Robert Greig (Fat Man). (Note: Hesse, Tilbury, Rub, Greig, and Meyer appeared in footage cut from the released print.)

Credits: Metro-Goldwyn-Mayer, 1935. Produced by Edward J. Mannix. Directed by Tod Browning. Screenplay by Guy Endore and Bernard Schubert. Contributors to Dialogue, J.S. Kraft, Samuel Ornitz, and John L. Balderston. Based on Tod Browning's original story "The Hypnotist." Cinematography by James Wong Howe. Photographic Effects, Matte Paintings by Warren Newcombe. Photographic Effects, camera by Thomas Tutwiller. Makeup by Jack Dawn, assisted by William Tuttle. Art Direction by Cedric Gibbons. Art Direction Associates, Harry Oliver and Edwin B. Willis. Gowns by Adrian. Recording Engineer, Douglas Shearer. Sound Mixer, Gavin Burns. Effects mixers, T.B. Hoffman, James Graham, and Mike Steinore. Assistant Director and Stand-in for Carroll Borland, Harry Sharrock. Still Photographers, Jimmy Rowe and Clarence Sinclair Bull. Edited by Ben Lewis. Running time, 59 minutes (six reels). Copyright number LP5490, April 15, 1935.

Plot Summary: An old castle owned by Sir Karell Borotyn becomes the site where local townspeople witness mysterious vampires roaming at night to ward off any new residents. Borotyn is found dead and thus Inspector Neumann vows to solve the crime. Baron von Zinden allows young Irena Borotyn to stay at his home rather than in the dreaded castle, with the latter making plans to marry Fedor. Vampire hunter Professor Zelen arrives and, with von Zinden, visits the old castle to see the vampires at work. Confronted by the vampires, the baron believes he is the next to die. Zelen hypnotizes him, only to receive the baron's murder confession. The "vampires" were merely hired to help scare the killer into disclosing his deeds.

Production Notes: Initially titled *The Vampires of Prague,* the film began its casting as the 1935 New Year holiday occurred. Browning started shooting on January 12 with a 24-day production schedule; by January 22, some trades mentioned only Lugosi as the star. *Mark of the Vampire* essentially became a remake of the silent *London After Midnight* (1927), a collaboration of director Browning and silent screen favorite Lon Chaney. With the film's overbudget price tag coming to $305,177.90, MGM unveiled it in May 1935. Before its release, the studio cut *Mark of the Vampire* from 75 to 61 minutes. The film received better than average grosses in New York, with a June issue of *Variety* mentioning that box office receipts nationwide were "fair."

Though modern audiences are often disappointed by the film's conclusion — in which the supernatural elements are shown to be fake and merely an effort to catch a murderer — spectators of the time certainly believed the film to be chilling. One audience member, a physician, even wrote the *New York Times* claiming that such films were far too harmful to the health of theater audiences. The disgruntled moviegoer claimed that *Mark of the Vampire* caused extreme nervousness.

Lugosi received top billed credit in some ads for *Mark of the Vampire,* though generally he was listed third under Barrymore and Elizabeth Allan in movie posters. The role of Count Mora gave Lugosi the chance to look much like the vampire Dracula, though with little to do. He speaks only a few lines, which come at the end of the film after he and Carroll Borland are exposed as "actors" rather than real vampires. Lugosi disliked the film's ending.

A bullet-hole wound on Lugosi's head, applied by makeup man William Tuttle, initially signified Mora's suicide after murdering Luna, his daughter *and* lover. MGM later removed all elements of incest, though the bullet hole itself remained. The studio pressbook claims the music score included French horn notes to indicate Lugosi and a flute to represent Borland, though the released version film no elaborate musical score at all.

Certainly more fearful than the cheat ending was a Universal Studios injunction to block release of *Mark*, claiming it infringed on the *Dracula* (1931). Though Browning's final film with Lugosi bears many similarities to the Universal classic, the now-despised "cheat" ending helped draw a distinction between the two vampire films. As a result, a trouble-free MGM moved ahead with its release.

Tod Browning formerly directed Lugosi in *The Thirteenth Chair* and *Dracula*, and was associated with Lon Chaney, Sr., in a series of bizarre silent films. The famed director had a reputation for being a strong taskmaster. Cowriter Guy Endore achieved renown in the horror genre himself with his novel *The Werewolf of Paris*.

Along with the legendary Lionel Barrymore and Jean Hersholt, of *Dr. Christian* fame, the cast included lovely Carroll Borland as Luna, the vampire daughter of Count Mora. Though she made only a few other film appearances, Borland remains well remembered due to this film. Egon Brecher had appeared in *The Black Cat* (1934), and Michael Visaroff earlier played a small part in *Dracula* (1931).

55. The Raven

Cast: Boris Karloff (Edmond Bateman), Bela Lugosi (Dr. Richard Vollin), Irene Ware (Jean Thatcher), Lester Mathews (Dr. Jerry Holden), Samuel S. Hinds (Judge Thatcher), Inez Courtney (Mary Burns), Ian Wolfe ("Pinky" Geoffrey), Spencer Charters (Colonel Bertram Grant), Maidel Turner (Harriet Grant), Arthur Hoyt (Chapman), Walter Miller.

Credits: Universal Studios, 1935. Produced by David Diamond. Directed by Louis Friedlander. Screenplay by David Boehm. Based on the poem "The Raven" and the short story "The Pit and the Pendulum," both written by Edgar Allan Poe. Cinematography by Charles Stumar. Music by Clifford Vaughn. Choreography (for "The Spirit of Poe" dance) by Theodore Kosloff. Makeup by Jack P. Pierce and Otto Lederer. Art Direction by Albert S. D'Agostino. Edited by Alfred Akst. Assistant Directors, Scott Beal and Vic Noerdlinger. Script Clerk, Moree Herring. Hairdresser, Hazel Rogers. Secretary to Mr. Diamond, E.M. Haskett. Running time, 62 minutes (seven reels). Copyright number LP5606, June 11, 1935.

Plot Summary: After saving her life, Dr. Vollin becomes obsessed with Jean Thatcher. He attempts to woo her away from Jerry Holden but in the end lets his fascination with Poe take control of the situation. Vollin alters the face of a criminal named Bateman into a contorted nightmare, promising to make him handsome in return for helping torture and murder those close to Jean. A pit and pendulum serve almost to kill Jean's father, Judge Thatcher. Vollin also throws Jean and Jerry together into a room with walls that come together, smashing all that is in their path. But Bateman turns against the doctor and sets the victims free. Vollin shoots his unfaithful helper, whose dying strength allows him to shove the evil doctor into the room with crushing walls.

Production Notes: By mid–February, Universal had cast Karloff and Lugosi in their second film together. Universal told the press that copies of the script had been sent to Poe Memorial Societies for feedback.

Lugosi takes a cigar break on the set of MGM's *Mark of the Vampire* (1935).

Writers working on the screenplay included Jim Tully, Clarence Marks, Dore Schary and Guy Endore, though credits bear only the name of David Boehm. Initially, the studio claimed elements of Poe's "The Gold Bug," "The Pit and the Pendulum," and "The Raven" would be combined, though the end result had little to do with any of the tales. Production began on March 20, and finished as scheduled on April 5. Universal allotted $109,750 for the budget, which grew closer to $114,209.91.

Boris Karloff, whose Bateman character had only a fraction of Lugosi's screen time, walked away from the film with twice what Universal paid the Hungarian. Irene Ware of *Chandu the Magician* (1932) again found herself menaced by one of Lugosi's villainous performances, and Samuel S. Hinds—best remembered for his "Andy Hardy" films with Mickey Rooney—played the Judge. Lester Mathews portrayed Jerry, a role originally intended for Chester Morris.

For Lugosi, *The Raven* became his one opportunity completely to dominate a film that costarred Boris Karloff. Dr. Vollin not only provided him with more screen time than his British rival, but also one of the screen's most sadistic and obsessive villains. The actor's contract gave him $1,000 a week for five weeks.

Publicity stories claimed Karloff faced real bullets in the final scene to add realism. No double could be used, and thus Karloff wore a 50-pound bulletproof vest. Universal's ace marksman fired the shot, which allegedly grazed the bulletproof vest and knocked Karloff to the ground. The actor was left with a large bruise.

Other tales claimed that a window broke during one scene, showering glass on the set. While unharmed, actress Irene Ware forgot her lines in the scene.

Clifford Vaughan's music score for the film included such pieces as the "Raven Theme" and the "Bateman Theme." The former composition is associated with the mad Dr. Vollin and is first heard as Lugosi recites Poe's poem for his visiting museum curator.

Critics generally found *The Raven* distasteful and poor, though crowds much enjoyed the new Karloff–Bela Lugosi thriller. One reviewer noted that only once did New York audiences laugh, snickering at Lester Mathews opening a door and nearly falling into a pit. Other viewers took it a bit more seriously, identifying *The Raven* as one of the more sadistic horror films of the day.

56. *Murder by Television*

Cast: Bela Lugosi (Arthur Perry/Professor Houghland's Assistant), June Collyer (June Houghland), Huntley Gordon (Dr. Scofield), George Meeker (Richard Grayson), Henry Mowbray (Chief of Police Nelson), Charles Hill Mailes, Charles K. French, Claire McDowell, Larry Francis, Hattie McDaniel, Henry Hall, Allan Jung, William Sullivan, William Tooker.

Credits: Imperial-Cameo Pictures, 1935. Produced by William M. Pizor. Directed by Clifford Sanforth. Screenplay by Joseph O'Donnell. Based on an original story by Clarence Hennecke and Carl Coolidge. Cinematography by James Brown and Arthur Reed. Music by Oliver Wallace. Art Direction by Lewis Rachmil. Technical Supervisor, Henry Spitz. Associate Producer, Edward M. Spitz. Production Manager, Melville Delay. Edited by Lester Wilder. Running time, 60 minutes. (No copyright records exist for this film.)

Plot Summary: Several experts visit Professor Houghland's home to witness the test of his television invention, but during a second broadcast the inventor dies. Houghland's plans are stolen, along with a device key to the invention. One of the central suspects is the good professor's assistant, who soon dies himself, thanks to a knife through his heart. The assistant seemingly shows back up, however, and solves the murder. The vile Dr. Scofield murdered Professor Houghland, with the amateur investigator actually being the dead assistant's twin brother.

Production Notes: Originally titled *The Houghland Murder Case*, the release title made reference to a much-discussed but then underdeveloped invention: television. The studio shot the tale at the Talisman studio in February 1935. Trades noted $75,000 of TV equipment was used in the film, which itself cost less than $35,000. Imperial-Cameo released *Murder by Television* in October, then reissued it briefly some two years later. Critics pointed out the very stagey look of the film and its lack of music. For a Spanish release, the title became past tense: *Murdered by Television*.

"You'll Gasp! You'll Shudder! You'll Thrill! When Bela Lugosi Throws a Switch Destined to Destroy the World," advertisements promised. Imperial-Cameo proclaimed the film "four-star entertainment," which would produce "one continuous succession of gasps and shudders from thoroughly absorbed audiences."

Lugosi portrayed both Perry brothers, though to little real effect. Pressbooks claimed the actor was a master of makeup and also an expert at photography. As a result, Lugosi could allegedly achieve tremendous effects on screen with even cinematographers unsure how the makeup would appear. For various films, the actor supposedly used 20–30 different colors on his face, employing 43 shades of greasepaint for *Murder by Television*. Though all the information about makeup was sheer publicity, a similar such tale turned up in press materials for *The Dark Eyes of London* (1939).

Costar Hattie McDaniel was still four years away from her Oscar-winning performance in *Gone with the Wind* (1939) when she appeared in *Murder by Television*. Claire McDowell, actress in many D.W. Griffith silents, previously appeared with Lugosi in *Wild Company* (1930).

57. *The Mystery of the Mary Celeste*

Cast: Bela Lugosi (Anton Lorenzen), Shirley Gray (Sarah Briggs), Arthur Margetson (Captain Benjamin Briggs), Edmund Willard (Toby Bilson), Dennis Hoey (Tom Goodschard), George Mozart (Tommy Duggan), Johnnie Schofield (Peter Tooley), Gunner Moir (Ponta Katz), Ben Welden ("Sailor" Hoffman), Clifford McLaglen (Captain Morehead), Bruce Gordon (Olly Deveau), Gibson Gowland (Andy Gilling), Terence DeMarney (Charlie Kaye), J. Edward Pierce (Arian Harbens), Herbert Cameron (Volkerk Grot), Wilfred Essex (Horatio Sprague), James Carew (James Winchester), Monty DeLyle (Portunato), Alec Fraser (Commodore Mahon), Ben Souten (Jack Samson), J.B. Williams (Judge), Charles Mortimer (Attorney-General).

Credits: Hammer Studios, 1935. Produced by H. Fraser Passmore. Directed by Denison Clift. Story by Dennis Clift. Continuity by Till Day. Art Direction by J. Elder Wills. Musical Direction by Eric Ansell. Cinematography by Geoffrey Faithfull and Eric Cross. Running time, 80 minutes (seven reels). Copyright number LP6783, October 19, 1936. (Screened in England in 1935.)

Plot Summary: Captain Morehead and Captain Briggs had once been friends, but that ended when Briggs married the woman they both loved. Morehead plots revenge, using a weather-worn Anton Lorenzen to assist. Lorenzen, who sailed the *Mary Celeste* six years earlier and had been brutally beaten by the first mate, seizes the opportunity to be in charge of his old adversary. The crazed Lorenzen becomes a murderous but tragic old seaman.

Production Notes: Originally titled *Secrets of the Mary Celeste*, the film was based on the real-life mystery of a vessel that set sail from New York on November 7, 1872. Not a soul was on board when it was found adrift four weeks later. Hammer, which became famous beginning in 1957 for its horror films, shot the *The Mystery of the Mary Celeste* at Nettlefold Studios and on a rented ship, the *Mary B. Mitchell*. The film premiered in London on November 14, 1935. American audiences saw the film via a Guaranteed Pictures distribution and with a new title — *The Phantom Ship* — in late 1936 and early 1937. Critics noted some technical problems with the film, such as its audio track, as well as the fact that — in spite of tremendous storms rocking the boat — cabin scenes remained perfectly steady.

On June 28, Lugosi was to sail the S.S. *Aquatania* to England and Hammer Productions to appear in the film, after having signed a contract in early June. However, he and his wife, Lillian, were delayed until after July 4 in order for the actor to appear live at a New York screening of *The Raven*. The actor much enjoyed working in England, returning full of ideas for his own production company. As Lorenzen, Lugosi achieves great pathos in a role much unlike his standard screen fare.

58. *The Invisible Ray*

Cast: Boris Karloff (Dr. Janos Rukh), Bela Lugosi (Dr. Benet), Frances Drake (Diane Rukh), Frank Lawton (Ronald Drake), Walter Kingsford (Sir Francis

Lugosi as Anton Lorenzen in the British film production of *Mystery of the Mary Celeste* (1935).

Stevens), Beulah Bondi (Lady Arabella Stevens), Violet Kemble Cooper (Mother Rukh), Nydia Westman (Briggs), Danell Haines (Headman), George Renavent (Chief of Surete), Paul Weigel (Noyer), Adele St. Maur (Mme. Noyer), Frank Reicher (Professor Mendelssohn), Lawrence Stewart (Number One Boy), Etta McDaniels (Zulu Woman), Inez Seabury (Celeste), Winter Hall (Minister), Snowflake (Frightened Native), Hans Schumm (Clinic Attendant), Lloyd Whitlock, Edwards Davis, Alphonse Martell, Daisy Bufford, Clarence Gordon.

Credits: Universal Studios, 1936. Produced by Edmund Grainger. Directed by Lambert Hillyer. Screenplay by John Colton. Based on an original story by Howard Higgin and Douglas Hodges. Cinematography by George Robinson. Special Effects by John P. Fulton and Ray Lindsay. Art Direction by Albert D'Agostino. Music by Franz Waxman. Makeup by Jack P. Pierce and Otto Lederer. Gowns by Brymer. Assistant Directors, Sergei Petschnikoff and Fred Frank. Sound Supervisor, Gilbert Kurland. Script Clerk, Myrtle Gibsone. Secretary to Producer, Camille Collins. Secretary to Director, June Blumenthal. Technical Adviser, Ted Behr. Running time, 80 minutes (nine reels). Copyright number LP6060, January 14, 1936.

Plot Summary: Dr. Rukh pinpoints the location of a meteor in Africa containing the mysterious "Radium X." In addition to developing a "death ray" from the substance, Rukh begins glowing as a result of exposure. Anyone he touches dies, though Dr. Benet offsets the effect on Rukh with a temporary antidote. Since the radiation also causes him to go insane, the "luminous man" kills many friends and nearly murders his wife. Rukh's mother destroys the antidote, leaving the scientist to jump from a window to his death after bursting into flames.

Production Notes: By mid–September 1935, Universal Studios began production of *The Invisible Ray*, with Lugosi back only a month from shooting *The Mystery of the Mary Celeste* in England. Originally, Universal planned Stuart Walker to direct, though after resigning he was replaced by Lambert Hillyer. At an early stage, the studio called its project *The Death Ray*, but even prior to production trades named it by its release title. Shooting began September 17, 1935, with a budget of $166,875. Hillyer finished a few days late on October 25, overbudget by some $68,000. Among the reasons were "cast overtime," "general set expense," and "process shots" for the special effects. Universal issued the film in January 1936, receiving adequate reviews for its third "KARLOFF and Bela Lugosi" chiller. Many critics quickly noted the story's similarity to *The Invisible Man*.

Publicity claimed that Karloff's radiation "glow" took some six weeks for special effects men to perfect. Studio records show the trick cost only $250 to achieve. John P. Fulton, Universal's top special effects man, had earlier accomplished wonders in *The Invisible Man* (1933).

Franz Waxman, who so beautifully scored *The Bride of Frankenstein* (1935), composed the film's soundtrack. One of the more memorable pieces remains the opening selection, "Castle in Hungary." Waxman's entire score lasts some 25 minutes.

Studio pressbooks for *The Invisible Ray* dubbed Lugosi "the Strangest Man in Hollywood," though the film itself gave him a sincere, nonvillainous role. Yet *The Invisible Ray* also shows a remarkable change in the billing of Lugosi and Karloff. While the latter's name appeared first on publicity materials for *The Black Cat* and *The Raven*, for *The Invisible Ray* his name towers majestically above Lugosi's in much larger letters. Rather than making them a "team," the film headlined Karloff, offering Lugosi in a mere supporting role. The Hungarian received a flat fee of $4,000 for his three weeks' work.

Advertisements exclaimed, "In his brain—the world's most powerful secret," with many calling Karloff the "Luminous Man." Some even concocted an on-screen rivalry between the two horror stars, encouraging audiences to "see how maniac scientists rule the world with their death machine! See love-maddened scientists in a death struggle to possess the invisible ray!" *Billboard* magazine told exhibitors to "play up Karloff and Lugosi, but also stress the fact that it is not strictly a horror yarn, being rather a meller. Also play up the pseudo-scientific end, which offers plenty of chances." Though releases in other countries generally bore the same title, in Spain exhibitors screened it as *The Invisible Power*.

59. *Postal Inspector*

Cast: Ricardo Cortez (Bill Davis), Patricia Ellis (Connie Larrimore), Michael Loring (Charlie Davis), Bela Lugosi (Benez), Wallis Clark (Pottie), David Oliver (Butch), Arthur Loft (Richards), Guy Usher (Evans), William Hall (Roach), Spencer Charters (Grumpy), Hattie McDaniel (Deborah), Marla Shelton (Stewardess), Robert Davis (Pilot), Henry Hunter (Copilot), Billy Burrud (Boy), Harry Beresford (Ritter), Paul Harvey (Lieutenant Ordway), Anne Gillis (Little Girl), Russell Wade (Man), Anne O'Neal (Woman with Nose Machine), Gertrude Astor (Woman with Drum sticks), Flora Finch (Mrs. Armbrister), Margaret McWade (Old Maid), Jerry Mandy (Henchman).

Credits: Universal Studios, 1936. Directed by Otto Brower. Associate Producer, Robert Presnell. Screenplay by Horace McCoy. Based on an original story by Robert Presnell and Horace McCoy. Cinematography by George Robinson. Art Direction by Jack Otterson. Special Effects by John P. Fulton. Musical direction by Charles Previn. Edited by Phil Cahn. Running time, 58 minutes (six reels). Copyright number LP6527, August 14, 1936.

Plot Summary: Benez steals a bag of mail in order to raise money and pay off a loan shark. Postal Inspector Bill Davis eventually manages to pin the robbery on the nightclub owner, while his younger brother Charlie falls for singer Connie Larrimore

Production Notes: This attempt to glamorize U.S. postal inspectors results more in a romance between Michael Loring and Patricia Ellis's characters, as well as a chance to see a tremendous parade of useless mail-order products. Initially, the studio assigned Louis Friedlander of *The Raven* (1935) to direct, but before shooting Otto Brower replaced him. Universal used newsreel footage of New England floods for a chase sequence at the film's climax. The melodrama opened to theaters in September, while a "film consensus" column in *Billboard* magazine found critics' opinions of *Postal Inspector* to be "unfavorable."

Used essentially to get another of his contracted films out of the way, this Universal outing offers a basically uninteresting Lugosi performance. Audiences generally remember hero Ricardo Cortez more for playing opposite Greta Garbo in *Torrent* (1926) or as Sam Spade in the 1931 *Maltese Falcon* than for such films as *Postal Inspector*. Actress Patricia Ellis found more success elsewhere as well, appearing as a leading lady in multiple films at Warner Brothers.

60. *Son of Frankenstein*

Cast: Basil Rathbone (Baron Wolf von Frankenstein), Boris Karloff (The Monster), Bela Lugosi (Ygor), Lionel Atwill (Inspector Krogh), Josephine Hutchinson (Elsa von Frankenstein), Donnie Dunagan (Peter von Frankenstein), Emma Dunn (Amelia), Edgar Norton (Thomas Benson), Perry Ivins (Fritz), Lawrence Grant (The Burgomaster), Lionel Belmore (Lang), Michael Mark (Ewald Neumüller), Caroline Cooke (Frau Neumüller), Gustav von Seyffertitz, Lorimer Johnson, Tom Rickets (Burghers), Edward Cassidy (Dr. Berger), Ward Bond (Guard at Gates), Bud Wolfe (Double for Karloff), Dwight Frye (Villager). (Note: Frye appears in footage deleted from the released film.)

Credits: Universal Studios, 1939. Produced and directed by Rowland V. Lee. Screenplay by Willis Cooper. Cinematography by George Robinson. Art Direction by Jack Otterson. Otterson's Associate, Richard H. Reidel. Musical direction by Charles Previn. Musical Score by Frank Skinner. Assistant Director, Fred Frank. Sound Supervisor, Bernard B. Brown. Techician, William Hedgcock. Set Decorations, R.A. Gausman. Gowns, Vera West. Edited by Ted Kent. Makeup, Jack P. Pierce. Special Effects, John P. Fulton. Musical Arranger, Hans J. Salter. Running time, 94 minutes (11 reels). Copyright number LP8574, January 24, 1939.

Plot Summary: Wolf von Frankenstein arrives in his European homeland from America with his wife and child. Soon, he meets the vile, broken-necked Ygor, as well as the original Frankenstein Monster. Wolf becomes obsessed with the idea of reviving the monster in an attempt to vindicate his father. Thanks to Ygor, however, the monster soon roams free, even paying a visit to the doctor's son. The young doctor confronts and shoots the demented Ygor, leaving a friendly monster to wreak havoc. After kidnapping the doctor's son, the creature threatens to hurl the child into a sulphur pit. Wolf manages to swing a chain at the monster, knocking him into the bubbling sulphur. With the nightmare at an end, Wolf and his family return to America.

Production Notes: Universal made quick plans for a new horror film based on the tremendous success reissues of *Dracula* and *Frankenstein* enjoyed during August and September of 1938, hiring Willis Cooper to draft another sequel to *Frankenstein*. The original script incorporated many elements of the previous sequel, *Bride of Frankenstein* (1935), though much, including dialogue for the monster, was soon discarded.

In early November, the studio told trades that *Son's* budget had doubled, totaling over $500,000. By the end of the month, Universal also doubled its staff in cutting and scoring to attempt a December 30 release, though soon the studio realized the date to be unrealistic. Cast members were subjected to numerous script rewrites on the set. The production, which began on

November 9, finished January 5, 1939, at a final cost of approximately $420,000.

Originally the studio planned for Peter Lorre to play Wolf von Frankenstein, but the actor backed out, and by October 27 Universal signed Basil Rathbone. Along with Karloff, Lugosi, and lovely Josephine Hutchinson, Universal obtained Lionel Atwill through a loan by 20th Century Fox. RKO offered the precocious Donnie Dunagan, who first pleased audiences in *Mother Carey's Chickens* (1938). Dwight Frye, formerly Renfield in *Dracula* and Fritz in *Frankenstein*, found himself in a brief performance as a villager which did not even make the film's final cut.

At first, Lugosi's role as Ygor was small, with the studio hoping to keep the actor on the lot for only one week. Universal also cut his salary from $1,000 to $500 a week. Much to the actor's delight, Rowland V. Lee built up the part until it became more important than either the monster or even the son of Frankenstein. The director left Lugosi on his own to develop the character, which turned out to be a prime example of Lugosi's versatility. The Hungarian remained on the set for the entire production. In addition to third billing, however, Lugosi found himself at the mercy of Karloff's tea break at 4:00 P.M. each day, as well as having to attend his costar's birthday party on the set.

The actor reflected on the popular Ygor, "God, he was cute." Lugosi sat for four hours a day through Jack Pierce's makeup production, which included a rubber broken neck piece, some yak's hair, and a set of jagged teeth. Among those terrified by the makeup was young Donnie Dunagan, who particularly disliked Lugosi's whiskers.

Universal rushed prints to exhibitors to capitalize on the Friday the 13th date. "Frankenstein Hits Boxoffice Jackpot," the *Hollywood Reporter* claimed, announcing that *Son* had reaped bigger returns than any prior horror film in key city openings. The first weekend receipts in Los Angeles, Boston, and Richmond surpassed all previous Universal film openings in those three cities. Heavy grosses came in from across the country, with numerous theaters keeping prints for holdovers. Among the patrons for opening weekend was James Whale, director of the original *Frankenstein* (1931), whom trades delighted in mentioning as a paying customer at one screening. On the whole, critics gave stronger reviews than generally met other horror films.

"To make the stoutest heart quake with nameless dread," ads proclaimed. Publicity also crowned *Son* "four times as fearful as *Frankenstein*," due to "the menace of Rathbone, the frightfulness of Karloff, the terror of Lugosi, and the hate of Atwill."

As a result of *Son of Frankenstein*, a second Hollywood horror film cycle blazed forward. While Karloff vowed never to portray the monster again, Lugosi appeared as Ygor in the next sequel, *Ghost of Frankenstein* (1942). Many countries watched *Son* in 1939, though in Spain the film became *The Shadow of Frankenstein*. Mel Brooks's classic comedy *Young Frankenstein* (1974) later took much of its plot from *Son*.

61. *The Gorilla*

Cast: Jimmy Ritz (Garrity), Harry Ritz (Harrigan), Al Ritz (Mulligan), Anita Louise (Norma Denby), Patsy Kelly (Kitty), Lionel Atwill (Walter Stevens), Bela Lugosi (Peters), Joseph Callela (Stanger), Edward Norris (Jack Marsden), Wally Vernon (Seaman), Paul Harvey (Conway), Art Miles (The Gorilla).

Credits: Twentieth Century Fox Films, 1939. Produced by Darryl F. Zanuck and Harry Joe Brown. Directed by Allan Dwan. Screenplay by Rian James and Sid Silvers. Based on the play by Ralph Spence. Cinematography by Edward Cronjager. Musical Direction by David Buttolph. Art Direction by Richard Day and Lewis Creber. Makeup by Perc Westmore. Edited by Allen McNeil. Running time, 65 minutes. (No copyright records exist.)

Plot Summary: Garrity, Harrigan, and Mulligan are detectives hired by Walter Stevens to guard his life. Stevens receives death threats from a mysterious killer on the loose, known only as "the Gorilla." The three arrive at Stevens's mansion, which not only has its share of secret passages and trap doors but also includes the ominous butler Peters. Meanwhile, a real gorilla escapes and further causes mayhem.

Production Notes: By late October 1938, 20th Century Fox purchased the rights to Ralph Spence's 1925 stage play specifically as a vehicle for the Ritz Brothers. Twice previously, in 1927 and 1931, the tale had been transformed into films. Fox planned to begin production in January, following a personal appearance tour by the Ritzes. By the end of the month, Lionel Atwill, Patsy Kelly, and Wally Vernon signed contracts. The studio initially planned for Kane Richmond to play the romantic male lead, though he was quickly replaced by Edward Norris, who had just signed with Fox for *Charlie Chan in Reno*. To head the crew, Fox chose Allan Dwan, director of some 400 films throughout his career.

The death of the Ritz brothers' father in early January caused a delay, with the trio supposedly dashing for Hollywood on January 14. Problems heightened as the studio leveled a $150,000 lawsuit against the comedy team, charging violation of contract. The picture would have started production January 30, but was postponed when the Ritzes did not show up. The studio argued its losses would be tremendous if it had to abandon the project, as the script was written expressly for the brothers. Fox also placed the trio on suspension, as the team's lawyer claimed that their dissatisfaction with the low-budget vehicle brought about the trouble. By March, the film began shooting as the Ritzes returned to the lot. Though the trio gave kind words about Fox to the press, *The Gorilla* became their last film for the studio.

Fox signed Lugosi in late January, taking Peter Lorre's place as the butler. The latter feigned sickness from pneumonia and needed a month to recuperate. Lugosi did not begin work on the lot until the second week in March, playing a minor role.

62. *Ninotchka*

Cast: Greta Garbo (Lena Yakushova, "Ninotchka"), Melvyn Douglas (Count Leon Dolga), Ina Claire (Grand Duchess Swana), Sig Rumann (Michael Ironoff), Felix Bressart (Buljanoff), Alexander Granach (Kopalski), Bela Lugosi (Commissar Razinin), Gregory Gaye (Count Alexis Rakonin), Richard Carle (Vaston), Edwin Maxwell (Mercier), Rolfe Sedan (Hotel Manager), George Tobias (Russian Visa Official), Dorothy Adams (Jacqueline, Swana's Maid), Lawrence Grant (General Savitsky), Charles Judels (Pere Mathieu, Café Owner), Frank Reicher (Lawyer), Edwin Stanley (Lawyer), Peggy Moran (French Maid), Marek Windheim (Manager), Mary Forbes (Lady Lavenham), Alexander Schonberg (Bearded Man), George Davis (Porter), Armand Kaliz (Louis, the Headwaiter), Wolfgang Zilzer (Taxi Driver), Tamara Shayne (Anna), William Irving (Bartender), Bess Flowers (Gossip), Elizabeth Williams (Indignant Woman), Paul Weigel (Vladimir), Harry Semels (Neighbor Spy), Jody Gilbert (Streetcar Conductress), Florence Shirley (Marianne), Elinor Vandivere, Sandra Morgan, Emily Cabanne, Symona Boniface, Monya Andre (Gossips), Kay Stewart, Jennifer Gray (Cigarette Girls), Lucille Pinson (German Woman at Railroad Station).

Credits: Metro-Goldwyn-Mayer, 1939. Produced and directed by Ernst Lubitsch. Screenplay by Charles Brackett, Billy Wilder, and Walter Reisch. Based on a story by Melchior Lengyel. Cinematography by William Daniels. Music by Werner R. Heymann. Edited by Gene Ruggiero. Art Direction by Cedric Gibbons and Randall Duell. Set Decorations, Edwin B. Willis. Costumes by Adrian. Makeup by Jack Dawn. Running time, 110 minutes (12 reels). Copyright number LP9158, October 2, 1939.

Plot Summary: Three Russian agents travel to Paris in order to sell jewels and purchase farm equipment. The Grand Duchess Swana, who originally owned the jewels, attempts to block their sale. She enlists the aid of Count Leon, who treats the agents to the finer aspects of Parisian life. The Russian government then sends Ninotchka to assist the trio, with her soon meeting Count Leon. The more they see of one another, the more Ninotchka's cold Russian exterior melts into the warmth of love. But the jealous Grand Duchess finally offers to relinquish her hold on the jewels if Ninotchka returns to Russia. Eventually, Leon and Ninotchka are married in Constantinople.

Production Notes: Studios feared that Garbo — in Europe at the time of *Ninotchka*'s announcement — was near retirement, with everyone much relieved when she was signed for the comedy. Garbo received $125,000 for the film, which paired her for the first and only time with Ernst Lubitsch. The director known for the "Lubitsch touch" supposedly told MGM to let them work together. "You tell them, Ernst," Garbo allegedly advised the director. "I'm far too tired to talk with studio executives." Reportedly, studio boss Louis B. Mayer believed the idea to be a mistake, resenting any script that dealt with Communism and thinking Garbo's foray into comedy could be a tremendous mistake.

Consultants at the studio suggested numerous titles for the film, including *We Want to Be Alone*, *A Kiss from Moscow*, *This Time for Keeps*, *The Love Axis*, *A Foreign Affair*, *A Kiss for the Commissar*, *Salute for Love*, *Intrigue in Paris*, *A Kiss in the Dark*, and *Time Out for Love*. The film finally began shooting on May 19, 1939, in Culver City, ending 58 days later.

Advertisements for the film's November 1939 release proclaimed, "Garbo Laughs," much as they had in 1930 with "Garbo Talks." The screen legend made only one film after *Ninotchka*, with the Melchior Lengyel story becoming a musical in *Silk Stockings*. The tale garnered much critical acclaim, with Garbo receiving an Academy Award nomination. Particularly electric were the actress's scenes with Ina Claire, widow of John Gilbert — an actor who had had an affair with Garbo.

Lugosi turned in a sincere portrayal as Commissar Razinin, though reviews made little mention of him. The studio pressbook included the Hungarian's very grateful remarks about being allowed a nonhorror role, with Lubitsch adding that the actor's sympathetic moments on screen would be a surprise to everyone. Interestingly, costar Alexander Granach had performed 17 years earlier in F.W. Murnau's *Nosferatu*, the German silent film version of *Dracula*.

63. *The Dark Eyes of London*

Cast: Bela Lugosi (Dr. Orloff/Dr. Dearborn), Hugh Williams (Inspector Holt), Greta Gynt (Diana Stuart), Edmond Ryan (Lieutenant O'Reilly), Wilfrid Walter (Jake), Alexander Field (Grogan), Arthur E. Owen (Lew), Julie Suedo (Secretary), Gerald Pring (Henry Stuart), Bryan Herbert (Walsh), May Hallatt (Policewoman), Charles Penrose (The Drunk).

Credits: An Argyle British Production, 1939. Produced by John Argyle. Directed by Walter Summers. Screenplay by Patrick Kirwan, Walter Summers, and John Argyle. Based on Edgar Wallace's novel *The Dark Eyes of London*. Cinematography by Bryan Langley. Music by Guy Jones. Edited by E.G. Richards. Running time, 76 minutes (eight reels). Copyright number LP9579, March 1, 1940. (Screened in England in 1939.)

Plot Summary: Dr. Orloff runs an insurance agency in London, becoming the beneficiary on many customers' policies. Scotland Yard finds several bodies drowned in the Thames, realizing that the water in one's lungs was fresh. In the meantime, the dead man's daughter, Diane, gets a job at a home for the blind operated by Dr. Dearborn. Mounting suspicion builds against Orloff and Dearborn, with the former sending a Jake — a blind brute — to kill Diane, who has learned too much for her own good. Orloff disappears, but Diane discovers one of his cufflinks at the home for the blind. Dearborn removes his disguise, revealing his actual identity as the evil insurance salesman. He straps her into a straitjacket and sends for Jake. However, the hulking creature turns on Orloff, learning that the doctor has killed a blind friend of his. Jake throws Orloff out the window, with the doctor sinking slowly into the mud.

Production Notes: Based on the Edgar Wallace novel of the same name, this Argyle Production hit British theaters in November 1939. To help bring to life Wallace's horrifying character "Jake," Wilfred Walter helped create his own highly effective makeup. For Belgian bookings, the thriller became *The Blind Killer*, while American audiences saw the film through a Monogram Studios release in March 1940 as *The Human Monster*.

The tale remains one of the thirties' most gruesome thrillers, making it all the more surprising that it was produced in England — the same country that in 1936 leveled a ban against horror films. During its American run, the National Motion Picture League issued warnings that appeared in the *New York Times* and elsewhere. The group refused to endorse the movie, citing multiple, content-based reasons such as, "many views of drowned body lying in slimy water, throwing vials of gas at people, maniacal sounds, horrible screams as girl is chased, coarse language, drowning man in big tank," and many others.

Lugosi sailed for London on March 29 on the *Queen Mary*, traveling on the same ship as Noel Coward. He portrayed the evil Dr. Orloff in a very understated fashion, with the role becoming one of his best in the horror genre. Wallace's book actually had two Orloff brothers, though the script combined them into Lugosi's character. While he was impersonating the kindly Dr. Dearborn, the Hungarian's voice was dubbed by O.B. Clarence. The actor returned from shooting the film aboard the same ocean liner, sailing from London on April 15. Also on the ship were actor George Sanders and studio executive Adolph Zukor.

64. *The Saint's Double Trouble*

Cast: George Sanders (Simon Templar, "The Saint"/Duke Piato), Helene Whitney (Anne Bitts), Jonathan Hale (Inspector Henry Fernack), Bela Lugosi (Partner), Donald MacBride (Inspector John H. Behlen), John F. Hamilton (Limpy), Thomas W. Ross (Professor Bitts), Elliot Sullivan (Monk), Pat O'Malley (Express Man), Donald Kerr (Card Player), Byron Foulger (Jewel Cutter), William Haade, Walter Miller, Ralph Dunn.

Credits: RKO Radio Pictures, 1940. Produced by Cliff Reid. Directed by Jack Hively. Screenplay by Ben Holmes. Based on a story by Leslie Charteris. Cinematography by J. Roy Hunt. Music by Roy Webb. Special Effects by Vernon Walker. Edited by Theron Warth. Running time, 68 minutes. Copyright number LP9392, January 26, 1940.

Plot Summary: The Saint finds himself in trouble when a jewel thief named Duke Piato turns up looking like an exact double of the detective. Piato attempts to smuggle gems to a college professor by using an Egyptian mummy. The Saint later triumphs and clears up the discrepancies.

Production Notes: This film was the fourth in RKO's series of "Saint" detective stories, with the studio shooting it in only 19 days. The debonair British detective had been played once by Louis Hayward, with Hugh Sinclair taking on the role after Sanders bowed out. Vincent Price later portrayed the detective on the radio, with Roger Moore assuming the character on a sixties' television program. George Sanders, the Saint of this outing, committed suicide in 1972.

By November 6, 1939, RKO announced Lugosi was under contract, with the film itself completed by late December. Lugosi's fourth-billed role in this B movie turns out to be of little interest, with the Hungarian giving one of the more lackluster performances of his Hollywood career.

Reviewers generally believed the film adequate, with the film premiering in February 1940. New York's "Schools Motion Picture Committee" took great offense that the melodrama was double-billed with the animated *Pinocchio* (1940). Even though the Legion of Decency approved the Saint film with an "A-1" rating, the Schools Committee forwarded its complaints directly to Will Hays.

65. Black Friday

Cast: Boris Karloff (Dr. Ernest Sovac), Bela Lugosi (Eric Marnay), Stanley Ridges (Professor George Kingsley/Red Cannon), Anne Nagel (Sunny Rogers), Anne Gwynne (Jean Sovac), Virginia Brissac (Margaret Kingsley), Edmund McDonald (Frank Miller), Paul Fix (Kane), Murray Alper (Bellhop), Jack Mulhall (Bartender), Joe King (Police Chief), John Kelly (Taxi Driver), James Craig (Reporter), Jerry Marlowe (Clerk), Edward McWade (Newspaper File Attendant), Eddie Dunn (Detective Farnow), Emmett Vogan (Detective Carpenter), Edward Earle (Detective), Kerman Cripps (Detective), Edwin Stanley (Dr. Warner), Frank Sheridan (Chaplain), Harry Hayden (Prison Doctor), Dave Oliver, Harry Tenbrook (Cab Drivers), Raymond Bailey (Louis Devore), Ellen Lowe (Maid), Franco Corsaro (Headwaiter), Frank Jaquet (Fat Man at Bar), Dave Willock, Tommy Conolon, Wallace Reid, Jr. (Students), William Ruhl (Man), Victor Zimmerman (G-Man), Jessie Arnold (Nurse), Doris Borodin (Nurse).

Credits: Universal Studios, 1940. Associate Producer, Bert Kelly. Directed by Arthur Lubin. Screenplay by Curt Siodmak and Eric Taylor. Cinematography by Elwood Bredell. Art Direction by Jack Otterson. Associate Art Direction by Harold MacArthur. Musical Direction by Hans J. Salter. Makeup by Jack P. Pierce. Gowns by Vera West. Set Decorations by Russell A. Gausman. Sound Supervisor, Bernard B. Brown. Technician, Charles Carroll. Special Effects by John P. Fulton. Edited by Philip Cahn. Running time, 69 minutes (seven reels). Copyright number LP9479, April 18, 1940.

Plot Summary: Dr. Sovac attempts to save the life of his good friend and college professor Dr. Kingsley, injured in a car crash caused by several gangsters. Sovac takes part of a dead hoodlum's brain and uses it to help save Kingsley. Unfortunately, the result becomes a Jekyll and Hyde character who becomes a gangster part of the time and at others retains his own kindly identity.

Production Notes: Originally titled *Friday the Thirteenth, Black Friday* began a rigorous, 18-day schedule in late December 1939, ending January 18. *Variety* noted the entire film was completed and ready to go to theaters by mid-February. For the teaming of their two top horror stars, Universal had approved a budget of only $130,750. Siodmak's tale of scientists and brains grew into his popular *Donovan's Brain*, first an episode of *Suspense* with Orson Welles, then later filmed as *The Lady and the Monster* (1944) and *Donovan's Brain* (1953).

Unfortunately, the role each actor was to play apparently became switched, moving Lugosi from the part of Dr. Sovac to the gangster Eric Marnay. Karloff went from the Jekyll and Hyde role of Dr. Kingsley to Dr. Sovac. Stanley Ridges stepped in to become Kingsley. Though director Lubin could later not recall why the changes occurred, one possible reason could have been Karloff's unwillingness to play a dual role.

Problems during shooting included Karloff's refusal to work more than eight hours a day, as well as the entire crew racing from one set to another to maintain the short shooting schedule. Weather conditions further impeded progress on the film. The completed film ran $7,000 under budget and opened in March 1940, just in time for Easter. Interestingly, the French title was the moniker first suggested for the American release, *Friday the Thirteenth*.

Along with advertisements that announced "a deadly monster is born to ravage an unsuspecting world," much publicity pointed to Lugosi. Though after the changes he was left in a minor role as a gangster who shared no scenes with Karloff, the actor found his name plastered on headlines after supposedly being hypnotized for a death scene. Lugosi later claimed the hypnosis was faked, but others swore it to be authentic.

The Hungarian's friend Manly P. Hall performed the duty of putting the actor under, with newsreel cameras capturing each moment. Supposedly Lugosi's pulse jumped from 72 to 160. The *New York Times* carried the tale, mentioning that the cameraman accidentally ran out of film in the middle of Lugosi's suffocation scene.

66. *You'll Find Out*

Cast: Kay Kyser (as himself), Peter Lorre (Professor Fenninger), Helen Parrish (Janis Bellacrest), Dennis O'Keefe (Chuck Deems), Bela Lugosi (Prince Saliano), Alma Kruger (Aunt Margo), Kay Kyser's orchestra (as themselves, featuring Ginny Simms, Harry Babbitt, Ish Kabibble, Sully Mason), Boris Karloff (Judge Mainwaring), Joseph Eggenton (Jurgen), Leonard Mudie (The Real Professor Fenninger), Louise Currie, Mimi Forsaythe, Mary Martha Wood, Joan Warner, Mary Bovard, Dorothy Moore, Jane Patten (Debutantes) Joe North, Frank Miller, Bess Flowers, Larry McGrath, Jeff Corey, Eleanor Lawson.

Credits: RKO Radio Pictures, 1940. Produced and directed by David Butler. Screenplay by James V. Kern. Based on an original story by David Butler and James V. Kern. Special Material, Monte Brice, Andrew Bennison, and R.T.M. Scott. Musical Direction by Roy Webb. Musical Arrangements by George Duning. Music and Lyrics by Jimmy McHugh and Johnny Mercer. Cinematography by Frank Redman. Special Effects by Vernon L. Walker. Art Direction by Van Nest Polglase. Associate Art Director, Carroll Clark. Gowns, Edward Stevenson. Set Decorations by Darrell Silvera. Recorder, Earl A. Wolcott. Assistant Director, Fred A. Fleck. Special Sound/Musical Effects, Sonovox. Edited by Irene Morra. Running time, 97 minutes. Copyright number LP10334, November 22, 1940.

Plot Summary: After finishing their radio broadcast, Kay Kyser and Orchestra head to Bellacrest Manor for Janis Bellacrest's twenty-first birthday celebration. The eerie mansion offers an odd collection of artifacts, as well as a drawbridge in the front. A storm rages outside while Aunt Margo plans for Prince Saliano, a medium, to contact her late brother. Retired Judge Mainwaring, the Bellacrest lawyer, hires Professor Fenninger to expose Saliano as a fake. However, Judge Mainwaring, Fenninger, and Saliano actually plan together to murder Janis to keep her from inheriting the Bellacrest estate. Kyser's orchestra discovers the plot, with the evil trio accidentally blowing themselves up with dynamite meant for the others.

Production Notes: Kay Kyser's first film, *That's Right—You're Wrong* (1939), netted unexpectedly high profits, with *You'll Find Out* acting as a follow-up to its success. Originally titled *The Old Professor*, RKO publicists crowned the film "the mystery with music," offering not just Karloff and Lugosi, but also Peter Lorre to help provide the chills. Bandleader Kyser kept his music before the public not only with his records, but also with his very popular radio program. His orchestra, "The Kollege of Musical Knowledge," offered pleasant, danceable music, but lacked the jazz overtones of many other big bands.

You'll Find Out began filming on August 8, 1941, with a higher budget than any other single film that paired Karloff and Lugosi. Trades even claimed that the trio of horror stars would croon the song "The Bad Humor Man," though in the film Kyser's band performed the tune. Shooting ended by October, with RKO premiering the comedy the following month. For its big New York City opening during the week of November 14, Kyser and his orchestra performed live on stage at the Roxy.

The music by Jimmy McHugh and Johnny Mercer includes such tunes as "The Bad Humor Man," "I'd Know You Anywhere," "You've Got Me This Way," "Like the Fella Once Said," "I've Got a One Track Mind," "Don't Think It Ain't Been Charming."

For its Spanish release, *You'll Find Out* became *The Castle of the Mysteries*, while Belgian audiences viewed it under the title *The Villa of the Loonies*.

Many ads and publicity materials gave Lorre, Karloff, and Lugosi — "those three bad humor men" — billing just underneath Kyser's name, though on screen Lugosi received fifth billing under O'Keefe and Parrish. Karloff, though paid less than Lorre, received a special credit by himself on the film. Lugosi signed his contract in July 1941, taking a smaller salary than either of his two companions. *You'll Find Out* became his only film with fellow Hungarian Peter Lorre.

67. *The Devil Bat*

Cast: Bela Lugosi (Dr. Paul Carruthers), Suzanne Kaaren (Mary Heath), Dave O'Brien (Johnny Layton), Guy Usher (Henry Morton), Yolande Mallott (Maxine), Donald Kerr ("One-Shot" Maguire), Edward Mortimer (Martin Heath), Gene O'Donnell (Don Morton), Alec Baldwin (Tommy Heath), John Ellis (Roy Heath), Arthur Q. Bryan (Joe McGinty), Hal Prince (Police Chief Wilkins), John Davidson (Professor Percival Garland Raines), Wally Rairdon (Walter King).

Credits: Producers Releasing Corporation, 1941. Produced by Jack Gallagher. Directed by Jean Yarborough. Screenplay by John Thomas Neville. Based on an original story by George Bricker. Cinematography by Arthur Martinelli. Production Manager, Melville De Lay. Art Direction by Paul Palmentola. Musical Direction by David Chudnow. Sound Engineer, Farrell Redd. Edited by Holbrook Todd. Running time, 68 minutes (seven reels). Copyright number LP10133, December 17, 1940.

Plot Summary: Dr. Paul Carruthers, inventor of numerous cosmetics that made the Heath family wealthy, decides to extract revenge on those who have profited from him. He gives them a new aftershave and, after telling them goodbye, Carruthers releases a giant bat trained to follow and kill whoever emanates the scent. Eventually, the trail of guilt leads to Carruthers, who dies at the hands of his own bat.

Production Notes: PRC, the Producer's Releasing Corporation, entered the horror genre with *The Devil Bat*. The studio reeked of poverty row, shooting its films on meager budgets and often depending on the name value of a star. The special effects in *The Devil Bat*, for instance, are not only less than horrifying but markedly amateurish. David Chudnow's music score also seems less than menacing, opting either for overt, brassy sounds or jazz-style saxophone.

The film opened in January 1941 and was later issued again under the title *Killer Bats*. PRC told exhibitors, "You've made money with him [Lugosi] consistently, and unless your town suffers an earthquake or an attack from Mars, he'll help you make money in *Devil Bat*." Reviewers told a less enthusiastic story, generally pointing to the poor production qualities.

PRC reused the *The Devil Bat*'s plot in 1946 as *The Flying Serpent* with George Zucco. Another 1946 horror film, *The Devil Bat's Daughter*, acted as a semi-sequel Lugosi film, making the deceased Dr. Carruthers out as kindhearted and innocent of any wrongdoing.

Lugosi signed with PRC on October 19, 1940, and he turned the role of Dr. Carruthers into one of his most enjoyable horror film appearances, a performance decidedly better than that of any of his nine B movies at Monogram Studios. Melodramatic and campy, *The Devil Bat* remains popular fare for admirers of the actor. David Linn of the Chicago Horror Club presented both Lugosi and PRC awards in 1941 for *The Devil Bat*. The group studied "fear psychology and suggestive effects upon the human mind" and apparently believed the poverty row chiller to be one of the year's best.

68. *Invisible Ghost*

Cast: Bela Lugosi (Dr. Charles Kessler), Polly Ann Young (Virginia), John McGuire (Ralph), Clarence Muse (Evans), Terry Walker (Cecile), Betty Compson (Mrs. Kessler), Ernie Adams (Jules the gardener), George Pembroke (Detective Lt. Williams), Fred Kelsey (Detective Ryan), Jack Mulhall (Tim), Robert Strange (Coroner Kirby), Lloyd Ingraham (Psychiatrist).

Credits: Monogram Studios, 1941. Produced by Sam Katzman. Associate Producer, Pete Payer. Directed by Joseph H. Lewis. Screenplay by Helen Martin and Al Martin. Cinematography by Marcel Le Picard and Harvey Gould. Production Manager, Ed W. Rote. Assistant Directors, Edward M. Saeta and Harry Slott. Settings, Fred Preble. Musical Direction by Johnny Lange and Lew Porter. Edited by Robert Golden. A Banner Production. Running time, 64 minutes (seven reels). Copyright number LP10440, April 25, 1941.

Plot Summary: In a Jekyll and Hyde-style tale, the kindly Dr. Kessler sees his wife, whom he believes dead, and goes about killing cast members as a result. In reality, his wife is simply a victim of amnesia. Kessler's actions occur while in a trance-like state, without his knowledge and he even assists the police in their attempt to find the killer. When the authorities bring in Kessler's wife for him to see, he falls into the hypnotic state and the case is solved.

Production Notes: *Invisible Ghost*, originally announced under the titles *The Maniac*, *Murder by the Stars*, and *Phantom Monster*, and then produced as *The Phantom Killer*, began filming on March 20, 1941. By April, director Lewis called a wrap. Monogram claimed the tale took its inspiration from the strange but real-life suicide/murder of Walter Krivitsky, whose associations with the Soviet O.G.P.U. resulted in his death.

Reviews varied when Monogram issued *Invisible Ghost* to theaters in May, though most found the plot "feeble." Unlike most Lugosi films, which premiered in New York City or the Los Angeles area, *Invisible Ghost* opened in Chicago, with the actor in a live stage show. Though in some ways its camera work and editing surpass Lugosi's next eight Monogram films, the plot remains particularly outlandish. Pressbooks suggested exhibitors use an "electric nerve tester"—running off a reduced current or batteries—as a promotional item to see whether potential audience members could take the "shock." Also, the studio suggested that theaters use skeletons, swinging them on piano wires between features, though they did not mention whether the desired effect should be gasps or laughs.

Unlike most of the cast members who were signed right before production began, Lugosi contracted to appear in the film well over a month before the cameras rolled. Effective closeups of Lugosi's eyes are among the most memorable shots in the film.

Sam Katzman, earlier associated with the 1936 Lugosi serial *Shadow of Chinatown*, made *Invisible Ghost* the first of nine features he produced with the Hungarian at Monogram. Although the studio was absorbed into Republic during 1935, by the summer of 1937 friction at the new operation resulted in a revived Monogram. Along with Lugosi, other stars like Harry Langdon and Kay Francis found a place at the poverty row studio.

Invisible Ghost's supporting players Polly Ann Young and Clarence Muse had both acted previously in Lugosi thrillers, the former in *Murders in the Rue Morgue* (1932) and the latter in *White Zombie* (1932).

69. The Black Cat

Cast: Basil Rathbone (Hartley), Hugh Herbert (Mr. Penny), Broderick Crawford (Hubert Smith), Bela Lugosi (Eduardo), Gale Sondergaard (Abigail Doone), Anne Gwynne (Elaine Winslow), Gladys Cooper (Myrna Hartley), Cecilia Loftus (Henrietta Winslow), Claire Dodd (Margaret Gordon), John Eldredge (Stanley Grable), Alan Ladd (Richard Hartley).

Credits: Universal Studios, 1941. Associate Producer, Burt Kelly. Directed by Albert S. Rogell. Screenplay by Robert Lees, Fred Rinaldo, Eric Taylor, and Robert Neville. Based on the short story by Edgar Allan Poe. Assistant Director, Howard Christie. Cinematography by Stanley Cortez. Special Photographic Effects by John P. Fulton. Art Direction by Jack Otterson. Set Decorations by Russell A. Gausman. Gowns by Vera West. Technician, Hal Bumbaugh. Edited by Ted Kent. Running time (eight reels). Copyright number LP10437, April 30, 1941.

Plot Summary: Several relatives gather at the old dark house of a wealthy aunt, waiting for her to die and thus receive their inheritance. An unknown killer decides to end the wait and murders the aunt, with the result being a stipulation in the will that claims that no money will be doled out until all of the aunt's cats have died as well. The rest of the film finds all concerned watching their backs until they discover the murderer's identity. Mr. Penny, an antique dealer, helps bring comedy to the doom and gloom.

Production Notes: With a budget of $176,000, Universal began shooting on February 17, 1941, finishing up the following month. Eric Taylor, who cowrote *Black Friday* (1940), and three other writers offered a tale that little resembled the Edgar Allan Poe short story. Before shooting began, Broderick Crawford replaced Richard Carlson, and Basil Rathbone took the lead spot initially intended for Paul Cavanaugh. One report claims that Marlene Dietrich, who dropped by the set occasionally to see Broderick Crawford, stood in for Claire Dodd on one shot in which the latter actress had no dialogue, her back to camera. Though *The Black Cat* itself features above-average camera work and lighting, it remains disappointing. The opening clip of a black cat crawling down the side of a tree turned up in a later horror film, *The Creeper* (1948).

Universal again wasted Lugosi in a minor role that left the whiskered Hungarian merely gazing through windows and attempting to be a source of chills. When the film opened in late April, Lugosi received little mention among reviews that generally believed the film itself to be mediocre.

Director Rogell dabbled in many genres during his lengthy career, including numerous westerns. Along with Rathbone and Crawford, the cast featured Oscar winner Gale Sondergaard, well remembered from the dark, mysterious *Spider Woman* (1944). Anne Gwynne from *Black Friday* (1940) returned to within inches of Lugosi's grasp, and Alan Ladd — still a struggling actor — appeared one year before his breakthrough performance in *This Gun for Hire*.

70. *Spooks Run Wild*

Cast: Bela Lugosi (Nardo), Leo Gorcey (Muggsy), Huntz Hall (Glimpy), Bobby Jordan (Danny), David Gorcey (Pee Wee), Sammy Morrison (Scruno), Donald Haines (Skinny), David O'Brien (Jeff Dixon), Dorothy Short (Linda Mason), Rosemary Portia (Margie), Dennis Moore (Dr. von Grosch), Guy Wilkerson (Constable), Angelo Rossitto (Luigi, the Dwarf), P.J. Kelley (Lem Harvey), Joe Kirk (Man at the Camp Office), Pat Costello (Bus Driver), Jack Carr.

Credits: Monogram Studios, 1941. Produced by Sam Katzman. Directed by Phil Rosen. Screenplay by Carl Foreman and Charles R. Marion. Additional Dialogue by Jack Henley. Cinematography by Marcel Le Picard. Production Manager, Ed W. Rote. Assistant Director, Art Hammond. Musical Direction by Johnny Lange and Lew Porter. Settings by Fred Preble. Edited by Robert Golden. A Banner Production. Running time, 65 minutes (seven reels). Copyright number LP11219, October 24, 1941.

Plot Summary: The East Side Kids briefly escape from the Bowery after being placed in an underprivileged boys' camp. On an evening jaunt through a graveyard, someone shoots Pee Wee. The others quickly carrying their wounded friend to an old house. The mysterious Nardo, who lives in the home with his dwarf assistant, offers his help. After he gives Pee Wee something to ease the pain, the others see their friend walking zombielike through the house and assume Nardo is to blame. Linda Mason shows up looking for the boys with Dr. von Grosch, who claims to be searching for a criminal. But von Grosch is the real killer, with Nardo simply an old magician staying at the old home.

Production Notes: Initially, Monogram cast George Pembroke as von Grosch, but prior to shooting Dennis Moore replaced him. The role seems to include tendencies toward sexual crimes and rape, though this is never outwardly addressed in the film. Oddly, Monogram press materials and period reviews generally listed Pembroke's name rather Moore's. Some reviewers also referred to the film as one of the better East Side Kids flicks, though — given the B status of the series — that slight endorsement could not save *Spooks Run Wild* from more harsh critics. Monogram publicity announced the "screen's Merchant of Menace versus the Tenement Terrors in a spine-tingling battle of shrieks and shudders."

Both Lugosi's attire and elements of the script recall *Dracula*, with the actor providing a strong foil for the East Side Kids' antics. Due to the film's relative success, the Bowery Boys later met Lugosi again in *Ghosts on the Loose* (1943). The Monogram pressbook quoted Lugosi as supposedly saying: "I wouldn't have believed it possible! Here we had all the trappings which made the original *Dracula* such a strange, eerie drama — the cobwebs, the bats, the dank cellars, the coffins, the menacing shadows — and yet the whole thing has become one long roar of laughter. Though I must remain just as serious as before, I found that I could hardly keep my face straight."

The film also marked Lugosi's first appearance with Angelo Rossitto, who later appeared in *The Corpse Vanishes* (1942) and *Scared to Death* (1946). Screenwriter Carl Foreman later moved to such important projects as *High Noon* (1952), *The Bridge on the River Kwai* (1957), and *The Guns of Navarone* (1961).

71. *The Wolf Man*

Cast: Claude Rains (Sir John Talbot), Lon Chaney, Jr. (Larry Talbot), Evelyn Ankers (Gwen Conliffe), Ralph Bellamy (Captain Paul Montford), Warren William (Dr. Lloyd), Patric Knowles (Frank Andrews), Maria Ouspenskaya (Maleva), Bela Lugosi (Bela), Fay Helm (Jenny Williams), Leyland Hodgson (Kendall), Forrester Harvey (Victor Twiddle), J.M. Kerrigan (Charles Conliffe), Doris Lloyd (Mrs. Williams), Olaf Hytten (Villager), Harry Stubbs (Reverend Norman), Tom Stevenson (Richardson, the Grave Digger), Eric Wilton (Chauffer), Harry Cording (Wykes), Ernie Stanton (Phillips), Ottola Nesmith (Mrs. Bally), Connie Leon (Mrs. Wykes), La Riana (Gypsy Dancer), Caroline Cooke (First Woman), Margaret Fealy (Second Woman), Jessie Arnold (Gypsy Woman), Eddie Polo (Churchgoer), Gibson Gowland (Villager), Martha Vickers, Kurt Katch (Gypsy with Bear). (Note: Kurt Katch appeared in footage deleted from the released print.)

Credits: Universal Studios, 1941. Associate Producer and Director, George Waggner. Screenplay by Curt Siodmak. Cinematography by Joseph Valentine. Art Direction by Jack Otterson. Associate Art Director, Robert Boyle. Musical Direction by Charles Previn. Musical Score by Charles Previn, Frank Skinner, and Hans J. Salter. Assistant Director, Vernon Keays. Makeup by Jack P. Pierce. Sound Director, Bernard B. Brown. Technician, Joe Lapis. Gowns, Vera West. Set Decorations, Russell A. Grausman. Special Effects by John P. Fulton. Edited by Ted Kent. Running time, 71 minutes (eight reels). Copyright number LP10910, December 15, 1941.

Plot Summary: Larry Talbot rushes to save Jenny Williams from a vicious wolf, beating the creature to death with a silver-headed cane. Before its death, however, the beast kills Jenny and bites Larry. Police arriving on the scene do not find a dead wolf, but rather the corpse of Bela the gypsy. The gypsy's mother, Maleva, informs Talbot that her son was a werewolf and that Larry himself would transform into such a creature during the next full moon. Though at first he disbelieves her, Talbot does bear the curse of a werewolf. A full moon causes the transformation, and Larry eventually attempts to murder the lovely Gwen. Sir John, his father, kills him with a silver-headed cane. After the life leaves his body, Larry returns to human form.

Production Notes: Though the idea for a film titled *The Wolf Man* drifts back as far as a proposed 1932 vehicle for Boris Karloff, the 1941 project came from a Curt Siodmak screenplay. The film changed titles from *The Wolf Man* to *Destiny* and then back to its first title. Universal assigned the project to George Waggner, who had just directed Lon Chaney, Jr., in *Man-Made Monster* (1940). Ace Universal makeup man Jack Pierce created the design for the lycanthrope; he originally planned very similar makeup for Henry Hull in 1935's *The Werewolf of London*, though the studio rejected it in favor of a design with less facial hair. Jack Otterson, who created a German Expressionist motif for *Son of Frankenstein* (1939), designed *The Wolf Man*'s sets.

Lon Chaney, Jr., son of the famed silent screen star, portrayed Larry Talbot, the poor soul bitten by the werewolf. Chaney achieved success as Lennie in *Of Mice and Men* (1940), and as a result of *The Wolf Man* he became Universal's top horror film star of World War II. Character actor Claude Rains, earlier of *The Invisible Man* (1933), played Larry's father. Russian actress Maria Ouspenskaya became the memorable gypsy woman Maleva, with other key roles filled by future horror film performers like Ralph Bellamy, Evelyn Ankers, and Fay Helm.

Variety announced the filming of *Destiny* on November 5, 1941, listing Lugosi's name first in the lineup of stars. The trade also included Dick Foran, who was replaced by Patric Knowles. Among the other changes was Universal's scrapping of a scene of Chaney wrestling a 600-pound bear.

Lugosi originally hoped to essay the title role, but instead took fifth billing as Bela the gypsy. A werewolf himself, the character Bela proves pivotal to the plot by passing the curse to Lon Chaney, Jr. Lugosi signed a one-picture contract for the film on October 25, 1941.

Ads for the film announced, "The legend of the damned," also naming the creature a "Night Monster! Prowling ... Killing ... Terrifying a countryside!" The film previewed in Hollywood on December 9, 1941, just two days after the bombing of Pearl Harbor. Despite mixed reviews across the country, *The Wolf Man* surprised the studio and trade papers by becoming a tremendous success. Rather than being hurt by the onslaught of World War II, the film drew large audiences and became Universal's biggest hit of the season.

Pressbooks suggested that theaters play records of wolf howls and screams in the lobby, accompanied perhaps by a cheaply made "gypsy wagon." Also suggested was a nurse stationed in the lobby to "test the nerves" of audience members, as well as an ambulance parked in front of the theater and reserved "for those the Wolf Man gets." Along with wolf paw prints on the ground, the pressbook told exhibitors to dress someone as Lugosi's gypsy character to give out "fortunes" that told of the upcoming horror film.

72. Black Dragons

Cast: Bela Lugosi (Dr. Melcher/Colomb), Joan Barclay (Alice Saunders), George Pembroke (Dr. Saunders), Clayton Moore (Don Martin), Robert Frazer (Hanlin), I. Stanford Jolley (The Dragon), Max Hoffman, Jr. (Kerney), Irving Mitchell (Van Dyke), Edward Peil (Wallace), Bob Fiske (Ryder), Kenneth Harlan (Colton), Frank Melton (FBI agent), Joseph Eggenton (Stevens), Bernard Gorcey (Cabby).

Credits: Monogram Studios, 1942. Produced by Sam Katzman and Jack Dietz. Directed by William Nigh. Screenplay by Harvey Gates. Cinematography by Art Reed. Production Manager, Ed W. Rote. Assistant Directors, Arthur Hammond and Gerald Schnitzer. Art Direction by David Milton. Musical Direction by Johnny Lange and Lew Porter. Edited by Carl Pierson. A Banner Production. Running time, 61 minutes (seven reels). Copyright number LP11343, March 6, 1942.

Plot Summary: Dr. Melcher, a Nazi plastic surgeon, treks to Japan to give Asian spies the faces of Americans. The result allows the agents to commit all means of espionage work in the United States while moving unnoticed due to their appearances. The Japanese throw Melcher into a prison to ensure that the experiment remains a secret, but he later escapes and follows the spies to take revenge.

Production Notes: Originally titled *The Yellow Menace, Black Dragons* refers to a historical organization in Japan founded in 1901 which later caused the Russo-Japanese War. Word of an impending attack on the United States and England by the Black Dragon Society came shortly before the attack on Pearl Harbor on December 7, 1941. After the bombing, the topical nature of *Black Dragons* made Monogram rush into production on January 22, 1942, after postponing the cameras from the original January 17 start date. *Variety* announced a 21-day shooting schedule, but the studio made every effort to hasten the production, with many rewrites occurring daily on the set.

Monogram released the film in March 1942 to generally poor reviews, with one mentioning that any child in a "papier-mâché Halloween mask" could cause more chills. Some five decades later, in the early nineties, *Black Dragons* also became one of the few Lugosi films to undergo the colorization process.

Lugosi portrays not only the Nazi scientist Dr. Melcher, but also Colomb, whose identity he assumes in the United States. The Hungarian had earlier played a dual role in *Murder by Television* (1935), but *Black Dragons* offers Lugosi as the same character with merely an altered appearance and a new name better to victimize the "Black Dragons." His new face essentially meant shaving the beard worn while in the service of the Japanese.

Director William Nigh earlier helmed *The Mysterious Mr. Wong* (1935), and actress Joan Barclay found herself terrified by Lugosi a second time, the first being in *Shadow of Chinatown* (1936). Lugosi had victimized Robert Frazer on screen once before as well, in *White Zombie* (1932). Heroic Clayton Moore portrayed the hero of *Black Dragons* some years before he became the Lone Ranger on television.

73. The Ghost of Frankenstein
Cast: Lon Chaney, Jr. (The Monster), Sir Cedric Hardwicke (Dr. Ludwig Frankenstein), Ralph Bellamy (Erik Ernst), Lionel Atwill (Dr. Theodor Bohmer), Bela Lugosi (Ygor), Evelyn Ankers (Elsa), Janet Ann Gallow (Cloestine Hussman), Barton Yarborough (Dr. Kettering), Doris Lloyd (Martha), Leyland Hodgson (Chief Constable), Olaf Hytten (Hussman), Holmes Herbert (Magistrate of Vasaria), Lawrence Grant (Burgomaster of Frankenstein), Brandon Hurst (Hans), Julius Tannen (Sektal), Harry Cording (Frone), Lionel Belmore (First Counsellor), Michael Mark (Second Counsellor), Otto Hoffman (Villager Number One), Dwight Frye (Villager Number Two), Ernie Stanton, George Eldridge (Constables), Eddie Parker (Double for Chaney).

Credits: Universal Studios, 1942. Produced by George Waggner. Directed by Erle C. Kenton. Screenplay by W. Scott Darling. From an original story by Eric Taylor. Cinematography by Milton Krasner and Elwood Bredell. Art Direction by Jack Otterson and Harold H. McArthur. Sound Director, Bernard B. Brown. Technician, Charles Carroll. Musical Score, Hans J. Salter. Gowns by Vera West. Set Decoration by Russell A. Gausman. Assistant Director, Charles B. Gould. Makeup by Jack P. Pierce. Edited by Ted Kent. Running time, 67 minutes. Copyright number LP11129, March 10, 1942.

Plot Summary: Ygor takes the Frankenstein Monster to the peaceful home of Dr. Ludwig Frankenstein, the second son of the creature's creator. The doctor decides to place a good brain in the monster's skull, but Dr. Bohmer — hoping to surpass Frankenstein in glory — secretly provides Ygor's gray matter. Blind but able to speak, the monster wreaks havoc in the laboratory, believing he was tricked by Bohmer. A tremendous fire seemingly deprives the monster of life.

Production Notes: With horror films turning in great profits, Universal decided once again to make a sequel to *Frankenstein* (1931), though the original monster, Boris Karloff, refused to reprise the role following

Son of Frankenstein (1939). Thanks to *The Wolf Man* (1941), Lon Chaney, Jr., became the studio's new reigning horror star, and thus Universal cast him as Mary Shelley's chilling creation. Producers also signed horror star Lionel Atwill as the vile Dr. Bohmer, and lovely Evelyn Ankers, heroine of *The Wolf Man* (1941), as the female lead. Other familiar faces, like Sir Cedric Hardwicke and Ralph Bellamy, took on the remaining roles of importance. Several minor players, including Holmes Herbert, Harry Cording, Dwight Frye, Lionel Belmore, and Michael Mark, had worked with Lugosi on previous projects.

Director Erle C. Kenton headed the production, having formerly directed the particularly gruesome *Island of Lost Souls* (1933). Eric Taylor, who worked on *Black Friday* (1940) and *The Black Cat* (1941), supplied the original story, which was then scripted by W. Scott Darling. George Waggner, director of *The Wolf Man* (1941), produced *Ghost of Frankenstein*, with maestro Hans J. Salter composing a wonderful music score.

The studio affixed various titles to the project, including *The Secret of Frankenstein*, *The Daughter of Frankenstein*, *Destiny*, and *There's Always Tomorrow*, before deciding on the release title. Shooting began on December 15, 1941, and ended just past the original 24-day schedule on January 15, 1942. Universal released *Ghost* in April 1942, to less than enthusiastic reviews, but the film scored well at the box office. For its Italian release, *Ghost* changed titles to *The Terror of Frankenstein*.

"You can't keep a good monster down," Universal told theater owners. The monster was "Universal's 'Midas' ... Out for more gold!" Studio pressbooks advised exhibitors to place an empty chair in the lobby and attach a parchment scroll bearing the question, "Will you loan me your brain?" Circulars announcing the film could be placed in bubble gum wrappers, and a "ghost" hunt would allow townspeople to collect cash prizes by finding the theater's ghost and touching him with the local newspaper.

Potential audiences also read movie posters warning, "He stalks again! The King of all monsters in new terrifying adventures! No chains can hold him! No tomb can seal him!"

The opportunity to portray Ygor a second time pleased Lugosi, whose first appearance as the wretched hunchback came in *Son of Frankenstein* (1939). The actor was rightfully proud of the character, who looked slightly differently in the new sequel. The costume appeared less tattered than before, and Pierce's makeup did not include the rotted teeth used in *Son*.

74. *The Corpse Vanishes*

Cast: Bela Lugosi (Dr. Lorenz), Luana Walters (Pat Hunter), Tristram Coffin (Dr. Foster), Elizabeth Russell (The Countess), Minerva Urecal (Fagah), Kenneth Harlan (Keenan), Vince Barnett (Sandy), Joan Barclay (Alice), Frank Moran (Angel), Angelo Rossitto (Toby), Gwen Kenyon (Peggy), George Eldridge (Mike), Gladys Faye, Pat Costello.

Credits: Monogram, 1942. Produced by Sam Katzman and Jack Dietz. Directed by Wallace Fox. Screenplay by Harvey Gates. Based on an original story by Sam Robins and Gerald Schnitzer. Cinematography by Art Reed. Production Manager, Ed W. Rote. Art Direction by Dave Milton. Musical Direction by Johnny Lange and Lew Porter. Edited by Robert Golden. A Banner Production. Running time, 63 minutes (seven reels). Copyright number LP11282, May 8, 1942.

Plot Summary: Dr. Lorenz, an insane botanist, kidnaps brides from their weddings to obtain glandular material that keeps his old wife, the Countess, beautiful and young. Midget Toby, an old lady named Fagah, and her retarded son, Angel, all assist the doctor. Journalist Pat Hunter investigates the story of the "missing brides," later cracking the mystery. Unfortunately, Lorenz plans to use her for new glandular material, but the police rescue the reporter as the doctor dies from a stab wound inflicted by an underling.

Production Notes: Camera rolled on March 13, 1942, with the ever cost-efficient Monogram designing a 20-day shooting schedule. The studio originally planned to begin on March 10, but delays caused the short postponement, making it all the more amazing that on April 1, *Variety* announced the film as completed ahead of schedule. Despite the bad reviews that met *The Corpse Vanishes* at its May release, Monogram proclaimed the film "horror to make your hair stand on end." The Legion of Decency rated the film a "B," meaning adults only; however, many critics believed the ridiculous tale was better suited for children. For a later, British release, distributor New Realm retitled the film *The Case of the Missing Brides*.

Another dreadful but fun Lugosi film, *The Corpse Vanishes* takes several opportunities to draw on his Dracula image, including a coffin in which Dr. Lorenz sleeps. After actress Elizabeth Russell became too petrified to get into her own casket, Monogram used a double.

Joan Barclay of *Black Dragons* returned to meet Lugosi again, as did Luana Walters of the serial *Shadow of Chinatown* (1936). Frank Moran, the half-witted "Angel," later appeared opposite Lugosi in Monogram's *Return of the Ape Man* (1944). Elizabeth Russell, "the Countess," also appeared in such horror films as *The Cat People* (1942), generally portraying cruel and mysterious characters.

75. Night Monster

Cast: Bela Lugosi (Rolf the Butler), Lionel Atwill (Dr. King), Leif Erikson (Laurie the Chauffeur), Irene Hervey (Dr. Lynne Harper), Ralph Morgan (Kurt Ingston), Don Porter (Dick Baldwin), Nils Asher (Agor Singh), Fay Helm (Margaret Ingston), Frank Reicher (Dr. Timmons), Doris Lloyd (Miss Judd, the housekeeper), Francis Pierlot (Dr. Phipps), Robert E. Homans (Cap Beggs), Janet Shaw (Millie Carson), Eddy Walker (Jeb Harmon), Cyril Delevanti (Torque, Gateman at the Estate).

Credits: Universal Studios, 1942. Produced and directed by Ford Beebe. Screenplay by Clarence Upson Young. Cinematography by Charles Van Enger. Musical Direction by Hans J. Salter. Art Direction by Jack Otterson and Richard Reidel. Set Decorations by Russell A. Gausman and Andrew J. Gilmore. Makeup by Jack P. Pierce. Sound Director, Bernard B. Brown. Technician, Robert Pritchard. Edited by Milton Carruth. Running time, 73 minutes (seven reels). Copyright number LP11597, September 20, 1942.

Plot Summary: Agor Singh, a yogi, materializes objects from faraway places but cannot manage to restore the limbs of paraplegic Kurt Ingston. In the Ingston mansion are more bizarre characters, such as butler Rolf, chauffeur Laurie, and housekeeper Miss Judd. Murders occur frequently, with Dr. King quickly entering the ranks of corpses. In the end, Kurt Ingston, who hoped for revenge against his incapable physicians, turns out to be the murderer.

Production Notes: Originally titled *House of Mystery*, *Night Monster*'s 18-day production started on July 6, 1942. Universal released *Night Monster* in October, with critics noting that the film contained few frights. The British Board of Censors believed otherwise, threatening Universal with censorship. Trades noted that the film scored well at the box office, appearing at many theaters in December on a double bill with *The Mummy's Tomb* (1942).

Lugosi appears in a less than engaging role as butler Rolf, though for the last time he scored top billing in a Universal Studios release. Despite the credits, however, the butler Rolf offers Lugosi little screen time and no real effect on the plot.

Ford Beebe, who earlier directed the 1939 Lugosi serial *The Phantom Creeps*, went on to oversee Universal's *Son of Dracula* (1943). Character actor Frank Reicher earlier appeared with Lugosi in *The Invisible Ray* (1936) and *Ghost of Frankenstein* (1942), as well as acting in other horror films like *King Kong* (1933), *The Mummy's Tomb* (1942), and *House of Frankenstein* (1944).

76. *Bowery at Midnight*

Cast: Bela Lugosi (Professor Brenner/Karl Wagner), John Archer (Richard Dennison), Wanda McKay (Judy), Tom Neal (Frankie Mills), Vince Barnett (Charlie), John Berkes (Fingers Dolan), Ray Miller (Big Man), J. Farrell McDonald (Captain Mitchell), Lew Kelly (Doc Broks), Lucille Vance (Mrs. Malvern), Anna Hope (Mrs. Brenner), George Eldridge (Detective Thompson), Wheeler Oakman (Stratton), Ray Miller (Big Man), Bernard Gorcey (Tailor), Pat Costello (Tramp), Eddie Kane (Police Chief), Ralph Littlefield (Tramp), Snub Pollard.

Credits: Monogram Studios, 1942. Produced by Sam Katzman and Jack Dietz. Directed by Wallace Fox. Original story and screenplay by Gerald Schnitzer. Cinematography by Mack Stengler. Art Direction by Dave Milton. Assistant Director, Arthur Hammond. Edited by Carl Pierson. A Banner Production. Running time, 61 minutes (seven reels). Copyright number LP11590, September 25, 1942.

Plot Summary: Professor Brenner, a psychology professor, leads a double life, running a mission in the Bowery to cover up his criminal activity. When he no longer needs his seedy helpers, the professor has them killed and then buried in the mission's basement. Later, the corpses are revived by a drug addict, and they pull the professor into the basement to his well-deserved death.

Production Notes: Monogram, after discarding a few other ideas for Lugosi vehicles, began shooting *Bowery at Midnight* on August 5, 1942. The studio planned a 14-day production, continually attempting to keep costs low. Gerald Schnitzer, assistant director of *Black Dragons*, penned the often confusing story, which is at least more compelling than most others Lugosi made for the studio. Monogram issued the film in November 1942, with some critics offering kinder words for the film than for many other Monogram efforts. Though often questioning the production values and the plot structure, reviewers gave director Fox and the cast good notices.

While most U.S. reviewers believed *Bowery at Midnight* contained few chills, the British Board of Censors made severe cuts, leaving Monogram wondering whether even to release future horror films in England. Studio advertisements included lines like "Out of the shadows of the underworld comes this diabolical fiend!" Oddly, one little-seen ad depicted artwork of Lugosi that more closely resembled his appearance in *White Zombie*, as well as featuring art of a topless female looking more relaxed than frightened.

Its French release also became interesting, though not due to censors bearing scissors. Fan magazines initially announced the title as *Bowery a Minuit*, though exhibitors realized quickly that this would not work. Few spectators in France would have known what the "Bowery" really was, so the title became *The Monster of Midnight*.

Lugosi again plays a dual part in what is one of his most satisfying performances at the poverty row studio, offering him the chance of a more dignified characterization than most other Monogram melodramas. The studio, in mentioning its upcoming "melodramas" in a *Variety* notice, even placed Lugosi's name beside the genre, as if to suggest that the two words meant one and the same thing. Interestingly, one shot in the released film features a *Corpse Vanishes* movie poster in the background.

Director Wallace Fox, formerly of *Spooks Run Wild* (1941) and *The Corpse Vanishes* (1942), returned to take charge of *Bowery at Midnight*. Actor Vince Barnett also returned from *The Corpse Vanishes*, and lovely Wanda McKay would later appear opposite Lugosi again in *Voodoo Man* (1944).

77. *Frankenstein Meets the Wolf Man*

Cast: Lon Chaney (Lawrence Talbot, the Wolf Man), Ilona Massey (Baroness Elsa Frankenstein), Patric Knowles (Dr. Mannering), Lionel Atwill (The Mayor), Bela Lugosi (The Frankenstein Monster), Maria Ouspenskaya (Maleva), Dennis Hoey (Inspector Owen), Don Barclay (Franzec), Rex Evans (Vazec), Dwight Frye (Rudi), Harry Stubbs (Guno), Adia Kuznetzoff

(Festival Singer), Torben Meyer (Erno), Charles Irwin (Constable), Doris Lloyd (Nurse), Tom Stevenson (Graverobber), Cyril Delevanti (Graverobber), David Clyde (Sergeant), Jeff Corey (Gravedigger), Beatrice Roberts (Rudi's Wife), Martha MacVicar (Margretta, a Village Girl), Moose (Bruno, a Dog in the Gypsy Camp), Eddie Parker (Double for Lugosi).

Credits: Universal Studios, 1943. Produced by George Waggner. Directed by Roy William Neill. Screenplay by Curt Siodmak. Cinematography by George Robinson. Art Direction by John B. Goodman. Associate Art Director, Martin Obzina. Sound by Bernard B. Brown. Technician, William Fox. Set Decorations by Russell A. Gausman. Gowns by Vera West. Musical Direction by Hans J. Salter. Assistant Director, Melville Shyer. Special Photographic Effects by John P. Fulton. Makeup by Jack P. Pierce. Edited by Edward Curtiss. Running time, 74 minutes (eight reels). Copyright number LP11965, December 31, 1942.

Plot Summary: Larry Talbot, the Wolf Man, travels in search of Dr. Frankenstein, whom he believes can offer a cure for lycanthropy. Unfortunately, Talbot discovers the doctor is dead and instead meets the monster he left behind. The two battle, with the townspeople eventually blowing up the dam to wash the monsters away.

Production Notes: The idea for two monsters in one film came from screenwriter Curt Siodmak, who jokingly told producer George Waggner they should make a film called *Frankenstein Wolfs the Meat Man*, or, more accurately, *Frankenstein Meets the Wolf Man*. The producer realized the potential and work on the script soon began. Initially, Universal planned for Lon Chaney, Jr., to portray both creatures, but at the last minute he backed out on that idea, wanting to portray only the Wolf Man. As Boris Karloff refused to play the Frankenstein Monster following *Son of Frankenstein* (1939), the role went to Lugosi.

Siodmak's script, entitled *Wolf Man Meets Frankenstein*, went before Universal's cameras on October 12, 1942. In addition to Chaney and Lugosi, horror star Lionel Atwill appeared as the mayor, after having portrayed Inspector Krogh in *Son of Frankenstein* (1939) and Dr. Bohmer in *Ghost of Frankenstein* (1942). Atwill received a one-year suspended sentence for perjury on October 15, 1942, but — despite pressure from the Hays Office — Universal kept him on the payroll. Character actress Maria Ouspenskaya, best remembered for playing Maleva the gypsy in *The Wolf Man* (1941), reprised her role. Dwight Frye, once an important supporting player in *Dracula* (1931) and *Frankenstein* (1931), enacted a minor role as his career continued to crumble. The actor famous for portraying Renfield died in November 1943.

Studio pressbooks mentioned that Lugosi woke up each day at 2:30 A.M. to arrive at the studio. After a hot bath, rub down, and short break, Lugosi surrendered to the grueling four- to five-hour makeup application by Jack Pierce. Along with the facial changes, Pierce weighted Lugosi's legs to help achieve a "mechanical walking effect."

Despite the fact that stuntman Eddie Parker doubled for Lugosi's more strenuous scenes, the actor collapsed under the monster makeup on November 5, 1942, with director Neill shooting around his scenes until he returned to the set. Certainly Lugosi found it demeaning to take on the role that he had turned down in 1931, but financially he needed the Frankenstein Monster. Possibly Lugosi appreciated the dialogue given to the creature, continuing with the idea from *Ghost of Frankenstein* that the monster's head held the brain of Ygor. Keeping Ygor's brain also meant that the monster could not see, as the beast had been left blind in the previous film.

Thus, director Neill shot much footage of the monster talking and making movements befitting a creature unable to see, though at the studio the result seemed laughable. The idea for a speaking monster was discarded, but much of the same footage, complete with Lugosi's moving mouth, remained in the film. The result made for a particularly embarrassing portrayal for Lugosi, compounded by the fact that the Frankenstein Monster caused the problems. At the studio, he received billing beneath Ilona Massey and Patric Knowles on movie posters, but photographs of theaters prove that exhibitors played up the Chaney/Lugosi team.

Universal faced other problems on the set as well, including Maria Ouspenskaya's being rushed to the hospital the same day as Lugosi. The cast finished on November 11, 1942, with Hans J. Salter then scoring the monster epic with his well-remembered compositions. Universal issued the film in March 1943, advertising it as a "shiver-shudder death duel you'll never forget," adding elsewhere that it contained "all new thrills ... as the screen rocks to the shock of its greatest sensation." Coming attractions warned audiences to "prepare for the shock," guaranteed to be "twice as grim" as anything previously on the screen.

Foreign distribution of the film saw slight title changes, with the less-friendly *Frankenstein Versus the Wolf Man* tacked on for Belgian and French releases. Some audiences in France also witnessed the creature fest as *Frankenstein and the Monster*.

Universal pressbooks gave exhibitors tips on how best to publicize the film, suggesting the title be mixed with metal lettering (for *Frankenstein*) and fur (for the *Wolf Man*) for banner displays. Theaters could also offer a scrim shadowbox for the lobby, with life-size, photographic blowups of each monster lit mysteriously by lightbulbs. Another ploy was to hold a monster "hideout contest," with participants giving ideas for the best places in their town where the horrible duo could conceal themselves. Regardless of the publicity methods chosen, *Frankenstein Meets the Wolf Man* grossed healthy earnings that contributed to a strong year for Universal.

78. *The Ape Man*

Cast: Bela Lugosi (Dr. Brewster), Wallace Ford (Jeff Carter), Louise Currie (Billie Mason), Minerva Urecal (Agatha Brewster), Henry Hall (Dr. Randall), Ralph Littlefield (Zippo), J. Farrell MacDonald (Captain), George Kirby (Butler), Wheeler Oakman (Brady), Emil Van Horn (the Ape), Charles Hall (Barney), Ray Miller (Detective), Jack Mulhall (Reporter), Charles Jordan (O'Toole), "Sunshine" Sammy Morrison (Office Boy).

Credits: Monogram Studios, 1943. Produced by Sam Katzman and Jack Dietz. Associate Producer, Barney Sarecky. Directed by William Beaudine. Screenplay by Barney Sarecky. Based on Karl Brown's story "They Creep in the Dark." Cinematography by Mack Stengler. Art Direction by Dave Milton. Edited by Carl Pierson. A Banner Production. Running time, 64 minutes (seven reels). Copyright number LP11854, February 5, 1943.

Plot Summary: Dr. Brewster, after a failed experiment, becomes an apelike creature needing human spinal fluid to restore himself to normal. He hopes his friend Dr. Randall can help, but the kindly doctor will have nothing to do with murder. With the help of an actual gorilla, Brewster manages to obtain some fresh fluid through murderous means, with reporters Jeff Carter and Billie Mason hot on his trail. Police arrive in the nick of time to help save the journalists, then in Brewster's clutches. Before the film ends, character Zippo reveals himself to be the author of the script and admits, "Screwy idea, wasn't it?" as he rolls up a window that reads "The End."

Production Notes: Initially titled *The Gorilla Strikes*, *The Ape Man* began its 15-day schedule on December 18, 1942. Associate Producer Barney Sarecky wrote the script, with dialogue rewrites on the set occurring daily. Monogram released the film in March 1943, and — even at the time — critics pointed out *The Ape Man*'s unintentional humor. A British issue of the 1950s saw the film retitled as *Lock Your Doors*.

Characters overall show no depth, with Lugosi in a particularly demeaning role. Hunched over with a face half covered by hair, the actor finds himself playing a humiliating role in one of Monogram's most wretched horror films.

Director William Beaudine began his career working on such prestigious films as *Sparrows* (1926), but with the talkies he found himself employed at poverty row studios. Beautiful Louise Currie, who had a small role in *You'll Find Out* (1941) and later appeared in *Voodoo Man* (1944), took the place of actress Amelita Ward as reporter Billie Mason and remains the high point of this dull thriller. Actor Emil Van Horn played apes in other films and in nightclub acts until someone stole his costume. The theft threw Van Horn out of work, leading to his eviction and a new residence in the streets of New Orleans.

79. *Ghosts on the Loose*

Cast: Leo Gorcey (Muggs McGinnis), Huntz Hall (Glimpy Williams), Bobby Jordan (Danny), Bela Lugosi (Emil), Ava Gardner (Betty Williams Gibson), Rick Vallin (John "Jack" Gibson), "Sunshine" Sammy Morrison (Scruno), Billy Benedict (Benny), Stanley Clements (Stash), Bobby Stone (Dave), Minerva Urecal (Hilda), Wheeler Oakman (Tony), Peter Seal (Bruno), Bill Bates ("Sleepy" Dave), Frank Moran (Monk), Jack Mulhall (Lieutenant Brady), Kay Marvis Gorcey (Bridesmaid), Robert F. Hill (Minister), Blanche Payson, Tom Herbert.

Credits: Monogram Studios, 1943. Produced by Sam Katzman and Jack Dietz. Directed by William Beaudine. Original screenplay by Kenneth Higgins. Cinematography by Mack Stengler. Assistant Director, Arthur Hammond. Set Designer, David Milton. Musical Direction by Edward Kay. Edited by Carl Pierson. A Banner Production. Running time, 63 minutes (seven reels). Copyright number LP12102, June 8, 1943.

Plot Summary: The East Side Kids accidentally find their way into a seemingly empty old dark house, which is actually the residence of Nazi Emil. The German attempts to scare them away with the standard haunted house tricks, though the Bowery Boys later help unravel the Fascist conspiracy.

Production Notes: Monogram initially announced this horror-comedy as *Ghosts in the Night*, again pairing Lugosi with the East Side Kids. Just prior to the start of the film, a court sentenced coproducer Jack Dietz to seven months in jail for income tax evasion. Despite the producer's trouble, by April 7, 1943, *Variety* noted the end of this quick production, with the studio releasing it in July. Reissues of the film bore the title *The East Side Kids Meet Bela Lugosi*, with a British release of the film bearing the original moniker *Ghosts in the Night*. Belgian audiences saw the film as *The Enchanted House*.

Lugosi appears as a Nazi, whose most memorable scene comes when he sneezes after breathing dust stirred up by "Sunshine" Sammy Morrison. Audibly, it seems Lugosi says "Oh shit!" rather than "Ahchoo!" The actor receives little screen time, with most footage going to the East Side Kids. For that reason, *Ghosts on the Loose* could very easily be his least interesting film for Monogram Studios.

Ava Gardner, under contract to MGM, found herself loaned to Monogram for this comedy. Gardner herself reached stardom later, though for *Ghosts on the Loose* some theaters advertised her as "Mrs. Mickey Rooney"— even though the real-life couple had already divorced. Minerva Urecal, the creepy old lady from *The Corpse Vanishes* (1942) and *The Ape Man* (1943) returns to portray a Lugosi accomplice.

80. *Return of the Vampire*

Cast: Bela Lugosi (Armand Tesla), Frieda Inescort (Lady Jane Ainsley), Nina Foch (Nicki Saunders), Roland Varno (John Ainsley), Miles Mander (Sir Frederick Fleet), Matt Willis (Andreas Obry), Ottola Nesmith (Elsa), Gilbert Emery (Professor Saunders), Leslie Denison (Lynch), William C.P. Austin (Gannett), Jeanne Bates, Sherlee Collier, Donald Dewar, Billy Bevan, George McKay.

Credits: Columbia Pictures, 1944.

Produced by Sam White. Directed by Lew Landers. Screenplay by Griffin Hay. Based on an idea by Kurt Newmann. Additional dialogue, Randall Faye. Cinematography by John Stumar and L.W. O'Connell. Edited by Paul Borofsky. Art Direction by Lionel Bankes. Set Decorations by Louis Diage. Musical Direction by M.W. Stoloff. Assistant Director, Earl Bellamy. Sound Engineer, H. Fogetti. Makeup by Clay Campbell. Running time, 69 minutes (seven reels). Copyright number LP12353. November 11, 1943.

Plot Summary: Bombing in London during World War II causes the grave of vampire Armand Tesla to gape open. A stake driven through him years before is believed to be the result of the explosion and thus gets removed. Back on the prowl, Tesla takes command of poor Andreas, a werewolf whom the vampire earlier used as a servant. Lady Jane stays hot on Tesla's trail, but his demise comes at the hands of Andreas, whose will becomes strong enough to destroy his master.

Production Notes: Columbia Pictures announced this film in mid-1943, but trades did not mention its completion until December. Lugosi's role in a stage version of *Arsenic and Old Lace* meant that shooting in September caused him to work at the studio in the daytime and then appear on stage at night. Reportedly, *Return of the Vampire* cost $75,000 and took a total of four weeks to shoot. Production began in late August. Universal Studios still owned the rights to *Dracula*, and not only refused permission for the Count's name to be used, but also threatened legal action for *Return of the Vampire*'s similarity to the Bram Stoker tale. Even before its January 1944 release, however, Columbia planned a sequel called *Bride of the Vampire*.

Lugosi appeared for the first time since *Dracula* (1931) as a legitimate vampire in a full-length film, with *Return of the Vampire* (1943) being one of his most enjoyable vehicles of the forties. Columbia announced that the actor would star in August 1943, with Lugosi eventually making $3,500 for his role. The vampire's demise at the end of the film featured an effective melting of Lugosi's head — a wax effigy — which reveals the skull beneath. British censors snipped the scene for the release in England.

Lew Landers, under the name Louis Friedlander, earlier directed Lugosi in *The Raven* (1935), and cameraman L.W. O'Connell lensed a number of Lugosi's pre–*Dracula* films at Fox.

81. *Voodoo Man*

Cast: Bela Lugosi (Dr. Richard Marlowe), John Carradine (Job), George Zucco (Nicolas), Michael Ames (Ralph Dawson), Wanda McKay (Betty Benton), Louise Currie (Stella Saunders), Ellen Hall (Mrs. Evelyn Marlowe), Henry Hall (Sheriff), Dan White (Deputy), Pat McKee (Grego), Terry Walker (Alice), Mici Gota (Housekeeper), Mary Currier (Mrs. Benton), Ralph Littlefield (Sam), Ethelreda Leopold, Claire James, Dorothy Bailer (Zombies).

Credits: Monogram Studios, 1944. Produced by Sam Katzman and Jack Dietz. Directed by William Beaudine. Original story and screenplay by Robert Charles. Cinematography by Marcel Le Picard. Musical Direction by Edward J. Kay. Assistant Director, Art Hammond. Art Direction by Dave Milton. Edited by Carl Pierson. A Banner Production. Running time, 62 minutes (seven reels). Copyright number LP12466, January 15, 1944.

Plot Summary: Dead for two decades, Evelyn Marlowe survives as a zombie, with her husband attempting to revive her through the combined use of black arts and the life force of young girls abducted thanks to a false detour near the Marlowe home. Police discover one girl, Stella, who drifted away from Marlowe's clutches while still in a trance. Voodoo master Nicholas calls her back to the doctor's home, and eventually the villains manage to kidnap another young woman, Betty. The experiment reaches success, but authorities arrive and shoot down Marlowe. Evelyn returns to the world of the dead and the young women recover from their trancelike state. Betty's sweetheart, screenwriter Ralph, then writes a script called *The Voodoo Man* after Marlowe is dead, leaving it on his boss's desk with the advice that actor Bela Lugosi should play the lead villain.

Production Notes: Monogram rolled cameras on *Voodoo Man* starting on October 16, 1943, but only after numerous delays. The studio originally planned to shoot the Andrew Colvin short story under its original title *The Tiger Man* in April 1943, but the project morphed into *Voodoo Man*, announced as an upcoming Lugosi production in June. Monogram hoped to produce it in August 1943, but the film was delayed — possibly due to Lugosi's work on the stage and in Columbia's *Return of the Vampire*. William "One Shot" Beaudine took Phil Rosen's place as director for the film, with the latter being given Lugosi's *Return of the Ape Man* instead. The studio issued *Voodoo Man* to U.S. theaters in February 1944. For its Belgian release, the poverty row thriller became *The Diabolical Spirit*.

Modern viewers often note that Michael Ames's boss in the film, "S.K.," is apparently a takeoff on real-life Monogram producer Sam Katzman. Though the film remains popular fun with movie buffs, *Voodoo Man* saw little kindness from critics all too happy in leveling charges of absurdity against it. Along with the cheap production values, reviewers pointed to the ridiculous plot and childish attempts to frighten. One even thought the film looked as if it had been produced by zombies, rather than just simply being a story about them.

Lugosi makes the most of his bearded Dr. Marlowe, turning in a strong performance, actually one of the best in his series of nine films for Monogram Studios. The script gives Dr. Marlowe more opportuntity for depth than villains in most other poverty row chillers, and Lugosi takes advantage of the potential.

One critic, when pointing out Lugosi's live appearance in a roadshow version of *Arsenic and Old Lace*, suggested that viewers see the actor in the flesh, then flee to the movie theater and reach further heights of fright by viewing *Voodoo Man*. "Gosh, maybe Bela on the screen would scare Bela in the flesh?" the columnist hypothesized. Despite the fact that *Voodoo Man* rates better than other poverty row horrors, the answer to the question, given the film itself, remains a resounding "no."

Costars Wanda McKay, Louise Currie, and Henry Hall appeared with the actor in other Monogram films, with horror stars George Zucco and John Carradine thrown in to make a trio of terror. The latter once called *Voodoo Man* his worst film, probably due to the very demeaning role he portrayed. Barney Sarecky, coproducer of *Black Dragons* and screenwriter of *The Ape Man*, appears in a small role.

82. *Return of the Ape Man*

Cast: Bela Lugosi (Professor Dexter), John Carradine (Professor Gilmore), Frank Moran (the Ape Man), Judith Gibson (Anne), Michael Ames (Steve Rogers), Mary Currier (Hilda Gilmore), Ed Chandler (Sergeant), Mike Donovan (Policeman), George Eldridge (Policeman), Horace Carpenter (Watchman), Ernie Adams ("Willie the Weasel"), Frank Leigh (Husband).

Credits: Monogram Studios, 1944. Produced by Jack Dietz and Sam Katzman. Directed by Phil Rosen. Associate Producer, Barney Sarecky. Screenplay by Robert Charles. Cinematography by Marcel Le Picard. Associate Director, Arthur Hammond. Musical Direction by Edward Kay. Art Direction by Dave Milton. Special Effects by Ray Mercer. Edited by Carl Pierson. A Banner Production. Running time, 60 minutes (six reels). Copyright number 12655, May 13, 1944.

Plot Summary: Professors Dexter and Gilmore find a prehistoric man encased in ice, bringing him back to their laboratory in the United States. The Neanderthal manages to thaw out nicely, with Dexter believing a new brain could help the beast. When Gilmore protests, Dexter murders his fellow professor and implants his brain in the ape man. Though he manages to play the piano as well as Gilmore, the beast soon runs amok until he is finally killed.

Production Notes: Though not released until July 1944, *Return of the Ape Man* was shot in early October 1943 prior to the production of *Voodoo Man*. George Zucco, whose name remained on publicity materials for the film, quit the film due to illness, though one still photo exists with him in the "ape man" makeup. Frank Moran, earlier a costar of *The Corpse Vanishes* (1942) and *Ghosts on the Loose* (1943) took Zucco's place as the prehistoric man. Even though both Zucco and Moran professed that the latter actor alone appears under the makeup in the film itself, various historians continue to claim that the former actually performed in certain scenes.

Studio pressbooks claimed Monogram artists invested much time in researching the "ape man" makeup, as well as claiming that when Los Angeles residents saw the beast being filmed at a vacant theater police were called to the rescue. Additionally, Monogram alleged that actors in the Arctic sequence were actually Eskimos. Standard pressbook fare — it is easy to doubt the more outlandish claims. Certain audience members even received sugar pills called "shock-serum" as an antidote to the horrifying thrills the film did not actually possess.

Some critics found *Return of the Ape Man* acceptable for its genre, though others labeled it ridiculous. Multiple film histories refer to this as a sequel to *The Ape Man* (1943); though possibly an attempt to cash in on the minimal success of the earlier film, *Return of the Ape Man* bears no kinship to the script of its predecessor.

Lugosi turns in a fine performance, with the film remaining one of the more charming of his low-budget efforts. Shortly after a September announcement for the production of the film, Monogram claimed that Lugosi headed its new stable of horror stars, also to include Zucco, Carradine, and Frieda Inescort of *Return of the Vampire* (1943). In actuality, the film became Lugosi's last released performance for the studio.

Phil Rosen, earlier in charge of *Spooks Run Wild* (1941), directed *Return of the Ape Man* after being moved from *Voodoo Man* (1944). Michael Ames (later Tod Andrews) and Mary Currier both performed in *Voodoo Man* (1944), with musical director Edward Kay associated with numerous other Lugosi Monogram films.

83. *One Body Too Many*

Cast: Jack Haley (Albert Tuttle), Jean Parker (Carol Dunlap), Bela Lugosi (Merkel), Bernard Nedell (Attorney Gellman), Blanche Yurka (Matthews), Douglas Fowley (Henry Rutherford), Dorothy Granger (Mona), Lyle Talbot (Jim Davis), Lucien Littlefield (Kenneth), Fay Helm (Estelle), Maxine Fife (Margaret), William Edmunds (The Professor).

Credits: Paramount Pictures, 1944. Produced by William Pine and William Thomas. Directed by Frank McDonald. Screenplay by Winston Miller and Maxwell Shane. Cinematography by Fred Jackson, Jr. Art Direction by F. Paul Sylos. Sound Recording, Paul Schmutz. Set Decorations by Ben Berk. Musical Score by Alexander Laszlo. Edited by Henry Adams. Running time, 74 minutes (eight reels). Copyright number LP13054, October 17, 1944.

Plot Summary: In this old dark house story, insurance salesman Tuttle arrives to sell a recently deceased millionaire a policy, though he is mistaken for a detective hired to guard the corpse until the reading of the will. After becoming acquainted with the lovely Carol Dunlap, Tuttle decides to stay and guard the body, though it soon disappears. Two additional murders occur, with everyone, including the servants, vying for the dead man's money.

Production Notes: Filming began January 12, 1944 on *One Body Too Many*, which Winston Miller wrote while he was still in the marines. He penned the tale on scraps of paper and then mailed them to the producers. No scenes were actually shot at Paramount; the Fine Arts Studio was instead used for the shoot. Though the studio financed *One Body Too Many*, producers

William Thomas and William Pine actually made the film. Paramount issued the film in October 1944 to generally kind reviews.

Lugosi appears as butler Larchmont, though his role becomes more satisfying than those of similar characters in his other old dark house films like *The Gorilla* (1939) and *Night Monster* (1942). Studio pressbooks claimed, "His studied calm endows the most ticklish scenes with an aura of substantial venom. He enters upon every crucial moment with a benign smile of complete misgiving." An ongoing gag finds Lugosi coaxing the principals to quaff poisoned coffee to no avail, only later to drink it himself.

Costar Jack Haley endeared himself forever to film fans as the Tin Woodman in *The Wizard of Oz* (1939), while costar Lucien Littlefield found earlier experience with old dark houses through *The Cat and the Canary* (1927) and *Seven Keys to Baldpate* (1929). Fay Helm earlier appeared with Lugosi in *Night Monster* (1942), and Lyle Talbot later played opposite the Hungarian in *Glen or Glenda* (1953).

84. The Body Snatcher

Cast: Boris Karloff (Gray), Bela Lugosi (Joseph), Henry Daniell (Dr. McFarlane), Edith Atwater (Meg), Russell Wade (Fettes), Rita Corday (Mrs. Marsh), Sharyn Moffett (Georgiana), Donna Lee (Street Singer), Mary Gordon (Mrs. MacBride), Robert Clarke (Richardson), Carl Kent (Gilchrist), Bill Williams (Bit), Jack Welch (Bit Boy), Larry Wheat (Salesman on Street), Jim Moran (Horse Trader), Aina Constant (Maid Servant)

Credits: RKO Radio Pictures, 1945. Produced by Val Lewton. Directed by Robert Wise. Executive Producer, Jack J. Gross. Screenplay by Phillip MacDonald and Carlos Keith. Based on the 1885 short story by Robert Louis Stevenson. Cinematography by Robert de Grasse. Art Direction by Albert S. D'Agostino and Walter E. Keller. Set Decorations by Darrell Silvera and John Sturtevant. Sound Recording by Bailey Fesler. Music by Roy Webb. Musical Direction by C. Bakaleinikoff. Costumes by Renie. Assistant Directors, Harry Scott and Nate Levinson. Rerecording, Terry Kellum. Camera Operator, Charles Burke. Assistant Cameraman, Tex Wheaton. Men's Wardrobe, Hans Bohnstedt. Ladies' Wardrobe, Mary Tate. Makeup by Frank LaRue. Edited by J.R. Whittredge. Running time, 78 minutes. Copyright number LP13340, February 15, 1945.

Plot Summary: Graverobber Gray supplies Dr. McFarlane with fresh bodies to use as cadavers at his medical school, though strong friction exists between the two. Medical student Fettes becomes McFarlane's assistant, with the duo soon needing a fresh body to help a young girl regain the ability to walk. Gray provides one, having turned to murder after police begin carefully guarding the cemeteries. McFarlane later kills the vile graverobber, but traveling in a carriage with what he believes to be Gray's corpse results in the doctor's drifting from the road and killing himself.

Production Notes: Among horror films of the forties, the series produced by Val Lewton at RKO remains subtle, chilling, and classic. After finishing a horror film at Universal Studios, actor Boris Karloff signed a two-picture deal with RKO. The studio initially planned to film *Isle of the Dead* (1945) with Karloff first, though it was postponed after shooting began as several principals were working in other films. Thus, *The Body Snatcher* (mistakenly referred to in many period notices as *Body Snatchers*) went into production on October 25, 1944. Robert Louis Stevenson based his short story on the real-life exploits of nineteenth century graverobbers Burke and Hare, with writer Phillip McDonald taking screen credit alongside Lewton's pseudonym, Carlos Keith.

Lewton considered Albert Dekker, John Emery, George Colouris, Alan Napier, and Philip Merivale for the key role of Dr. McFarlane before casting Henry Daniell. The budget for the film ran close to

$200,000, with a shooting schedule of some 20 days. *The Body Snatcher* used existing sets from numerous other films, such as exteriors from the 1939 *Hunchback of Notre Dame* lot. McFarlane's anatomy instruction room came from 1944's *Experiment Perilous*.

RKO released *The Body Snatcher* in February 1945, getting slapped in May with an "adults only" rating in Illinois by the Chicago Police Motion Picture Censor Board not only due to its "ghoulish theme" but also to its depiction of "blackmailing." Initally, the police board refused to allow exhibitors to screen it in any form. The state of Ohio also found objection to the film, and the Legion of Decency stamped it with a Class B, adults only rating. Yet critics overwhelmingly found it intelligent, atmospheric, and well worth the price of admission.

Coming attractions noted, "The Hero of Horror, Boris Karloff, joins forces with the Master of Menace, Bela Lugosi, in the unholiest partnership this side of the grave!" RKO publicity also promised, "Graves Robbed! Corpses Carved! The Dead Despoiled!"

Despite a few brushes with censors, the film enjoyed tremendous business, premiering at the Hollywood Hawaiian Theatre and coming complete with a body-snatching display in the lobby and an on-stage act featuring an audience member popping out of a ghoul's coffin. A two-page ad in *Variety* announced that test runs in St. Louis hit "within inches of all-time records for first-run Missouri theatre." Reviewers also noted strong audience reaction to various scenes, including multiple screams at the film's finale. Ultimately, *The Body Snatcher* remains a classic horror film and a favorite of cinema buffs. Ted Turner's cable network, TNT, even colorized the chiller in the early nineties.

Lugosi appeared in the small role of a janitor, which had been created specifically for him. Executive producer Jack Gross realized the publicity potential from having both Karloff and Lugosi in one film, with the latter signing on the first day of shooting for half the weekly salary Karloff received and a guarantee of one week only. Cast and crew remembered the Hungarian as being quite ill during production, though the slightly hunched walk he used on screen came as a suggestion by executive producer Gross after remembering the actor's earlier role as Ygor. Despite his near-cameo appearance, Lugosi took second billing after Karloff, and his death scene remains quite chilling. The film became the duo's last together.

Interestingly, *The Body Snatcher* made its way to non–U.S. theaters under a variety of titles, including *The Recuperator of Cadavers* in France, *The Thief of Cadavers* in Belgium, and *The Hyena* in Italy.

Producer Lewton, already known for his horror films like *The Cat People* (1942), went on to finish *Isle of the Dead* (1945) and to produce *Bedlam* (1946) with Karloff. After changing studios, the talented filmmaker died of a heart attack in 1951. Director Robert Wise blazed a tremendous career, later directing such gems as *The Day the Earth Stood Still* (1951), *West Side Story* (1961), *The Haunting* (1963), and *The Sound of Music* (1965).

85. Zombies on Broadway

Cast: Wally Brown (Jerry Miles), Alan Carney (Mike Strager), Bela Lugosi (Professor Richard Renault), Anne Jeffreys (Jean La Dance), Sheldon Leonard (Ace Miller), Frank Jenks (Gus, His Henchman), Russell Hopton (Benny), Joseph Vitale (Joseph), Ian Wolfe (Professor Hopkins), Louis Heydt (Douglas Walker), Darby Jones (Kaloga), Sir Lancelot.

Credits: RKO Radio Pictures, 1945. Produced by Ben Stoloff. Directed by Gordon Douglass. Screenplay by Lawrence Kimble. Based on an original story by Robert Farber and Charles Newman. Cinematography by Jack Mackenzie. Music by Roy Wegg. Musical Direction by C. Bakaleinikoff. Art Direction by Albert S. D'Agostino and Walter E. Keller. Set Decorations by Darrell Silvera and Al Greenwood. Makeup by Maurice Seiderman. Gowns by Edward

Stevenson. Assistant Director, Sam Ruman. Edited by Philip Martin, Jr. Running time, 68 minutes. LP13272, April 20, 1945.

Plot Summary: A nightclub owner sends press agents Jerry and Mike to the Caribbean in a search for zombies promised as an attraction on the club's bill. The duo meet the mysterious Professor Renault, who turns Mike into a zombie. The effect wears off before opening night of the show, but the clubowner himself gets injected with the zombie potion and thus provides the audience with the genuine article.

Production Notes: As a comic follow-up to Val Lewton's *I Walked with a Zombie* (1943) and a chance to get the comedy duo of Brown and Carney on the screen, *Zombies on Broadway* became a mildly amusing horror comedy. Shot in approximately two weeks, the film used sets from an old Sol Lesser *Tarzan* project. The cast featured lovely Anne Jeffreys of *Dillinger* (1945) and "tough guy" actor and future television producer Sheldon Leonard. Darby Jones and Sir Lancelot reprised their roles as zombies from the 1943 Lewton zombie film.

"You'll get the creepin' weebles and the laughing shakes as well from this screamingly hilarious shudder show," RKO promised audiences. Ads also asked, "Ever hunt the walking dead? Boy, some fun!" The Chicago Police Motion Picture Board failed to see the humor, assigning an "adults only" rating to the horror comedy, claiming it was "too scary for the kids."

Lugosi portrays a mad scientist who remains eminently more believable than those of most of his Monogram films, surrounded for once by a laboratory set that looks real. But the film becomes less interesting due to the generally unfunny antics of Brown and Carney, a generally forgotten comedy team. The Hungarian took third billing under the comedy duo.

Director Gordon Douglas, praised by several critics for creating a well-paced film, later directed such films as *Them!* (1954) and *Robin and the 7 Hoods* (1964). No stranger to comedy, Douglas directed numerous "Our Gang" comedy shorts in the thirties. Art director Albert D'Agostino received several Academy Award nominations during his career, and worked on multiple horror films. Among his creations were sets for three Lugosi films, *The Raven* (1935), *The Invisible Ray* (1936), and *The Body Snatcher* (1945).

86. *Genius at Work*

Cast: Wally Brown (Jerry), Alan Carney (Mike), Anne Jeffreys (Ellen), Lionel Atwill (Marsh/The Cobra), Bela Lugosi (Stone), Marc Cramer (Rick), Ralph Dunn (Gilley), Robert Clarke, Philip Warren, Harry Harvey.

Credits: RKO Radio Pictures, 1946. Executive Producer, Sid Rogell. Produced by Herman Schlom. Directed by Leslie Goodwins. Screenplay by Robert E. Kent and Monte Brice. Cinematography by Robert de Grasse. Special Effects by Vernon L. Walker. Music by Constantin Bakaleinikoff. Art Direction by Albert S. D'Agostino and Ralph Berger. Set Decorations by Darrell Silvers. Gowns by Renie. Assistant Director, Harry D'Arcy. Sound Recording, Richard Van Hessen and Roy Granville. Running time, 61 minutes. Edited by Marvin Coil. Copyright number LP706, July 31, 1946.

Plot Summary: Radio detectives Jerry and Mike appear weekly on Ellen's "Crime-of-the-Week" broadcast show. Famous criminologist Marsh assists the radio program in giving the true stories of various crimes. The mysterious villain, known as the Cobra, turns out to be Marsh.

Production Notes: *Genius at Work* rolled before cameras in early 1946, with its script a remake of *Super Sleuth* (1937) tailored to the antics of comedy team Brown and Carney. Critics remained unimpressed when the film hit theaters in August 1946, and it became Brown and Carney's eighth and final film.

Genius at Work wastes Lugosi in the role of Stone, an assistant to the Cobra. The Hungarian received fifth billing in most publicity, under the comedy duo, Lionel Atwill, and Anne Jeffreys. Some reviews even listed him apart from the aforementioned four, offering him in the "supporting players" category. *Genius at Work* fulfilled a three-picture contract Lugosi signed with RKO, the first two being *The Body Snatcher* (1945) and *Zombies on Broadway* (1945).

Lionel Atwill, costar of Lugosi films like *Son of Frankenstein* (1939), *Ghost of Frankenstein* (1942), and *Frankenstein Meets the Wolf Man* (1943), died suddenly in 1946 while filming a serial called *Lost City of the Jungle*. *Genius at Work* was his last completed film. In addition to Brown and Carney, actress Anne Jeffreys of *Zombies on Broadway* returned as the female lead.

87. *Scared to Death*

Cast: Bela Lugosi (Leonide), George Zucco (Dr. Van Ee), Douglas Fowley (Terry Lee), Joyce Compton (Jane), Nat Pendleton (Raymond), Roland Varno (Ward Van Ee), Molly Lamont (Laura Van Ee), Angelo Rossitto (Indigo), Gladys Blake (Lilybeth), Lee Bennett (Rene), Stanley Andrews (Autopsy Surgeon), Stanley Price (Autopsy Surgeon).

Credits: Screen Guild Productions, 1947. Produced by William B. David. Directed by Christy Cabanne. Screenplay by W.J. Abbott. Cinematography by Marcel Le Picard. Filmed in Cinecolor. Cinecolor Director, William Crespinel. Musical Direction by Carl Hoefle. Art Direction by Harry Reif. Edited by George McGuire. Running time, 65 minutes. Copyright number LP963, August 15, 1946.

Plot Summary: A beautiful corpse tells in flashback the story of how she died of fright, giving all the details of the mysterious events. Among the odd array of characters are the bungling Raymond, the sinister Dr. Van Ee, and Leonide, a hypnotist who travels with a dwarf.

Production Notes: Shooting titles of *Scared to Death* included *Accent on Horror* and *The Autopsy*, with an ill Lionel Atwill being replaced by George Zucco as Dr. Van Ee. Christy Cabanne, formerly an assistant to D.W. Griffith, directed the film, which he completed at the Gordon Street Studio in April 1946. *Scared to Death* featured an inexpensive color process, Cinecolor, though its natural hues often look somewhat murky. Exhibitors first screened the film in July 1947, over a year after its completion. In a bizarre twist, *Scared to Death* was one of three Lugosi films offered on videotape during the early nineties in colorized versions, even though the original film was already in color.

Lugosi's only "new" film of 1947 offered not just a muddled plot but also a lackluster role for the actor. On the surface, the idea of color seems appealing, as it was the actor's only horror film shot with that added quality, yet nothing manages to stave off the inevitable boredom. Critics both then and now find the film confusing, dull, and not worth the price of admission. Very possibly this remains Lugosi's worst horror film.

Scared to Death was Lugosi's last outing with horror film star George Zucco, as well as his final pairing with Angelo Rossitto. Douglas Fowley, who portrays Terry, played opposite the Hungarian in *One Body Too Many* (1944) and later appeared as the "director" in *Singin' in the Rain* (1952). Cinematographer Le Picard previously crossed paths with Lugosi as well, lensing a few of his Monogram films.

88. *Abbott and Costello Meet Frankenstein*

Cast: Bud Abbott (Chick), Lou Costello (Wilbur), Lon Chaney (the Wolf Man/Lawrence Talbot), Bela Lugosi (Count Dracula/"Dr. Lejos"), Glenn Strange (The Frankenstein Monster), Lenore Aubert (Sandra Mornay), Jane Randolph (Joan Raymond), Frank Ferguson (Mr. McDougal), Charles Bradstreet (Dr. Stevens), Howard Negley (Mel Harris), Joe Kirk (Man), Clarence Straight (Man in Armor), Harry Brown (Photographer), Helen Spring (Woman at Baggage Counter), Paul Stader (Sergeant), Joe Walls (Man), Bobby Barber (waiter), Vincent Price (The Invisible Man).

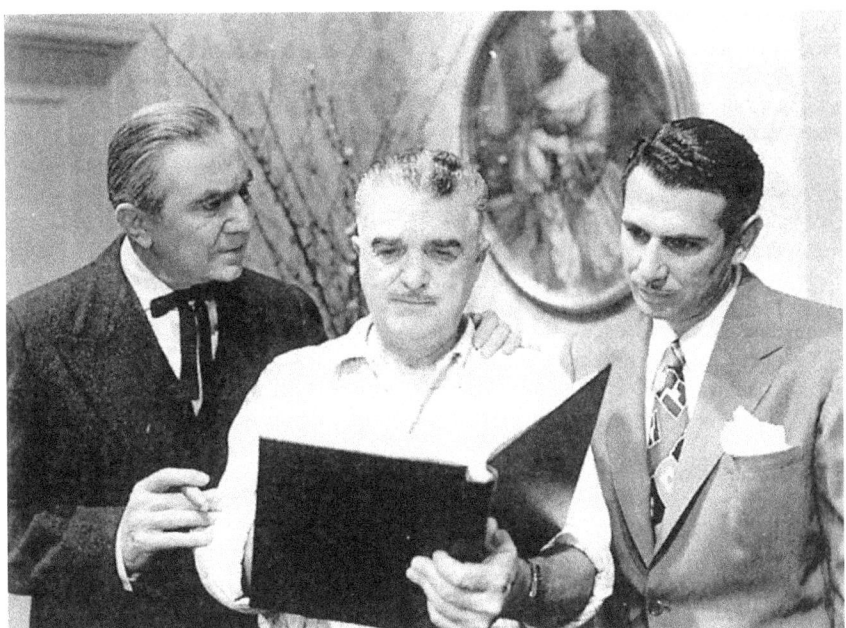

Lugosi with director Christy Cabanne (center) in 1946 on the set of *Scared to Death* (1947).

Credits: Universal-International, 1948. Produced by Robert Arthur. Directed by Charles T. Barton. Screenplay by Robert Lees, Frederic I. Rinaldo, and John Grant. Cinematography by Charles Van Enger. Art Direction by Bernard Herzbrun and Hilyard Brown. Sound by Leslie I. Carey and Robert Pritchard. Set Decorations by Russell A. Gausman and Oliver Emert. Music by Frank Skinner. Orchestrations by David Tamkin. Gowns by Grace Houston. Hair Stylist, Carmen Dirigo. Makeup by Bud Westmore and Jack Kevan. Special Photography, David S. Horsley and Jerome H. Ash. Assistant Director, Joseph E. Kenny. Edited by Frank Gross. Running time, 83 minutes.

Plot Summary: Shipped in wooden crates, Dracula and the Frankenstein monster arrive in the United States at a "House of Horrors." The vampire plans to place a new brain in the monster's skull, hoping in the end to make him more docile. Dracula's female accomplice, Sandra, chooses Wilbur as the brain donor, yet he and Chick are both being watched by an insurance investigator looking for the monsters' bodies. Larry Talbot travels to America to warn Chick and Wilbur, but merely adds to the mayhem when he transforms into the Wolf Man. The ending finds the Wolf Man plunging into the castle's moat with Dracula in his hands, as the Frankenstein monster burns to death and falls through a dock. As Chick and Wilbur find a moment to take a breath, the Invisible Man pops in to give them a final scare.

Production Notes: Universal-International put several writers to work throughout 1947 on a script titled *The Brain of Frankenstein*, which initially brought Abbott and Costello together with Dracula, Dracula's son Alucard, the Frankenstein Monster, the Wolf Man, the Mummy, and the Invisible Man. Eventually, the script dropped the Mummy and Alucard, with the Invisible Man taking a cameo role at the film's gag ending. Director Charles

Barton showed Lou Costello the script, with the comedian refusing to appear. After the offer of a $50,000 advance, Costello's grievances disappeared, and the comedy team headlined the final *Frankenstein* film of Universal's series.

For the Wolf Man, Universal signed Lon Chaney, Jr., who had already played the character in four horror films at the studio. With Boris Karloff uninterested in portraying the Frankenstein monster, the studio brought Glenn Strange back to the role he played twice previously in *House of Frankenstein* (1944) and *House of Dracula* (1945). The voice of Vincent Price became the Invisible Man, as it had in 1940's *The Invisible Man Returns*. Bud Westmore took the reins as head of makeup rather than famed Jack P. Pierce, whom Universal cruelly dropped due to his advancing age. Frank Skinner, who provided the music for *Son of Frankenstein* (1939), composed a sinister but delightful score, with David Horsley and Jerome Ash designed a memorable animated sequence for opening credit caricatures of the monsters and the comedy duo.

Shooting began on February 5, 1948, and stories abound of numerous practical jokes during production, including the gags of Bobby Barber, a comedian hired to help keep the cast happy. Perhaps the wildest day of shooting turned into a tremendous pie fight, wreaking havoc on the set. Few problems occurred, with the worst being an accident that fractured Glenn Strange's ankle. Without complaint, Lon Chaney briefly donned the monster's makeup and stood in for his costar. On the whole, the cast experienced a friendly atmosphere until production ended on March 20.

Memories from one source claim that Lugosi manager Don Marlowe convinced Universal to sign the aging Hungarian for the vampire role just days before shooting began, with the studio itself supposedly more interested in actor Ian Keith. The manager allegedly used guilt as his weapon, informing execs that the actor's success in the 1931 *Dracula* saved Universal from bankruptcy. However, this tale no longer seems plausible, given studio documents that make no mention of Keith and show Lugosi cast in late January 1948, several days before the Marlowe incident supposedly took place.

Animation techniques allowed Lugosi to transform on screen from man to bat and vice-versa. The film also gave Lugosi his second and final chance to appear in a full-length film portraying the character that made him famous. Though he appears somewhat aged, the actor remains highly effective. On the set, he took time to offer actress Lenore Aubert suggestions on how to act hypnotized, and despite occasional stories that claim he disapproved of off-screen gags, photographs and bloopers from the film reveal him as congenial and even joining in the fun.

Universal released *Abbott and Costello Meet Frankenstein* to strong reviews and big box office receipts in July 1948. The comedy became one of Hollywood's top moneymakers of the year and helped reinvigorate the careers of Abbott and Costello. Coming attractions and movie posters announced, "Jeepers! The creepers are after Bud and Lou." To help further promote the film, the studio paid Boris Karloff's hotel bill while he was staying in New York City in order to snap photographs of him buying a ticket for *Meet Frankenstein* and standing beside a movie poster of it.

Non-U.S. exhibitors screened the comedy under a variety of titles, including *Two Simpletons Versus Frankenstein* in Belgium and France, *Abbott and Costello Meet the Ghosts* in Spain, and *The Brain of Frankenstein* in Italy. In another Belgian release the film surfaced as *Abbott and Costello Meet the Monsters*, and though many German issues kept the American title, one took the very odd *My God, Frankenstein!* as a moniker.

89. *Mother Riley Meets the Vampire*

Cast: Bela Lugosi (Von Housen), Arthur Lucan (Mother Riley), Dora Bryan (Tillie), Richard Watts (Police Constable Freddie), Judith Furse (Freda), Philip Leaver (Anton), Maria Mercedes (Julia Loretti), Roderick

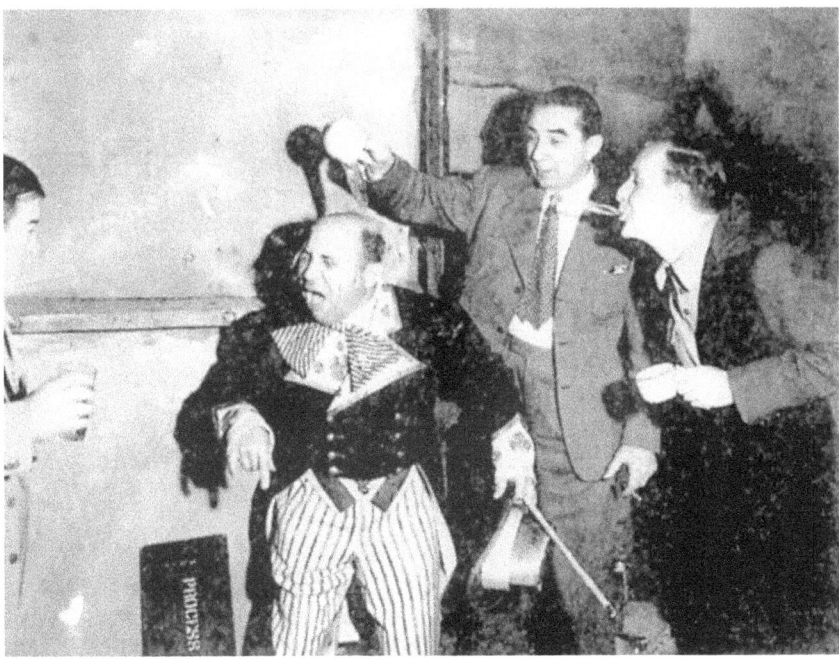

Lugosi is caught clowning around on the set of *Abbott and Costello Meet Frankenstein* (1948). From left to right are Lou Costello, Bobby Barber, Lugosi, and Bud Abbott.

Lovell (Douglas), David Hurst (Mugsy), Hattie Jacques (Mrs. Jenks), Graham Moffatt (Yokel), Dandy Nichols, Arthur Brander, Ian Wilson, Cyril Smith, Charles Lloyd Pack, Peter Bathurst, George Benson, David Hannaford, Bill Shine, John Le Musurier.

Credits: Renown Pictures, 1952. Produced and Directed by John Gilling. Production Manager, Stanley Couzins. Screenplay by Val Valentine. Cinematography by Stan Pavey and Dudley Lovell. First Assistant, Denis O'Dell. Second Assistant, Tony Harris. Continuity, Shirley Barnes. Sound Mixer, W.H. Lindop. Sound Camera Operator, C. Earl. Sound Maintenance, A. Rossiter. Wardrobe Mistress, O. Swinney. Chief Makeup, Eric Carter. Art Direction by Bernard Robinson Assistant Editor, Charles Squires. Edited by Norman Len Trumm. Running time, 72 minutes (6,660 feet). (No copyright records exist at the Library of Congress for this film.)

Plot Summary: The villainous Von Housen plans to take over the world with his army of robots, though to date he has created only one of the thousands needed. Necessary to his plans of domination is a map of a uranium deposit, which causes him to cross paths with Mother Riley. Amazingly, she manages to foil the mad scientist's plans.

Production Notes: Cameras rolled at Nettlefold Studios on October 29, 1951, with *Meets the Vampire* becoming the last of the "Old Mother Riley" series. The studio also filmed location shots around Hampstead and Highgate, with the entire production wrapping up in early December. Female impersonator Arthur Lucan had created "Mother Riley" years before in English music halls, which launched him into a film career. Though the character had previously dabbled in the horror comedy field with *Old Mother Riley's Ghosts* (1947), never before had Lucan played opposite a

Cast and crew members of *Mother Riley Meets the Vampire* (1952) during its 1951 production. Holding hands with Lugosi is Arthur Lucan in his "Old Mother Riley" makeup.

well-known Hollywood star of Lugosi's caliber.

Renown pictures had made three of the many "Riley" films prior to *Meets the Vampire*, issuing the Lugosi entry to British theaters in July 1952. The title of the film had been mentioned as *Old Mother Riley Meets the Vampire* in trades during production, though reviews from the month of release seemingly drop the adjective *Old*.

Unfortunately, plans to distribute the film in the United States found little success, even with title changes to *Vampire Over London* and *Carry on Vampire*. Producers of the popular Gerald Thomas–directed "Carry On" series legally stopped distributor Jack Harris from using the latter title. Prints do exist carrying the *Vampire Over London* name, though whether it saw any real distribution is unclear. By 1963 *Meets the Vampire* was issued briefly in the United States under as *My Son, the Vampire*, including a song of the same name by comedian Allan Sherman for the opening credits. A few theaters also screened the film as *The Vampire and the Robot*. Distributors linked their problems to the very British comedy in the film, with it becoming only one of two "Mother Riley" films ever commercially exhibited in the United States. The film did find its way onto the screens of other countries as well, including a Belgian release as simply *Riley Meets the Vampire*.

Lugosi took the role to help defray his costs in coming back to the United States after a failed British stage tour of *Dracula* left him basically stranded. His role as Von Housen became more a mad scientist bent on world domination than the vampire in the title. As with some of his previous low-budget efforts, *Meets the Vampire* attempts to find ways to cash in on Lugosi's Dracula image, letting him sleep in a coffin and wear a cloak. Though the humor overall presents some decidedly unfunny situations, Von Housen gives a nice glimpse of the Hungarian's comedic skill. Unlike his straight role in *Abbott and Costello Meet Frankenstein*

(1948), for instance, *Meets the Vampire* gave him the chance to crack several punchlines himself. Upon his return to America, Lugosi proudly spoke of the film as *Vampire Over London*, claiming he knew U.S. audiences would enjoy its "very funny" situations.

90. *Bela Lugosi Meets a Brooklyn Gorilla*

Cast: Bela Lugosi (Dr. Zabor), Duke Mitchell (Duke Mitchell), Sammy Petrillo (Sammy Petrillo), Charlita (Nona), Muriel Landers (Salome), Al Kikume (Chief Rakos), Mickey Simpson (Chula), Milton Newberger (Bongo), Martin Garralaga (Pepe Borde), Ramona, the Chimp (as herself).

Credits: Realart Pictures, 1952. Produced by Maurice Duke. Directed by William Beaudine. Screenplay by Tim Ryan. Cinematography by Charles Van Enger. Sound, Dean Thomas. Music by Richard Hazard. Associate Producer, Herman Cohen. Additional Dialogue, "Ukie" Sherin and Edmond G. Seward. Assistant Director, Glenn Cook. Art Direction by James Sullivan. Set Director, Edward Boyle. Dialogue Director, "Ukie" Sherin. Men's Wardrobe, Wesley V. Jeffries. Women's Wardrobe, Esther Krebs. Makeup by Glen Alden. Editor, Phil Cahn. Running time, 74 minutes. (No copyright records exist in the Library of Congress for this film.)

Plot Summary: After falling out of a transport plane, entertainers Duke Mitchell and Sammy Petrillo find themselves stranded on the island of Kola Kola. Dr. Zabor, the resident mad doctor, injects Mitchell with a formula that transforms him into gorilla. Meanwhile, Sammy combs the island looking for his partner, only to discover Mitchell's hairy fate. Zabor attempts to shoot Mitchell, with Petrillo jumping in to catch the bullet. Soon, however, Sammy wakes up and realizes the entire adventure was just a bad dream.

Production Notes: Producer Jack Broder, who from 1947 to 1955 reissued Lugosi's Universal films through his Realart company, decided to pair the aging horror star with a gorilla after the success of another of his movies, *Bride of the Gorilla* (1951). With direction by William Beaudine — who previously shot two of Lugosi's Monogram films — filming began at General Service Studios. The songs included Walter Hirsch and Fred Rose's "Deed I Do" and Nick Therry's "Too Soon." Along with its very long title that cashed in on the horror star's name, the film played some theaters as *The Boys from Brooklyn*. Broder first issued the film in September 1952.

"Brooklyn chumps become island monkeys in a jungle full of laffs!" press materials claimed. The comedy team Duke Mitchell and Sammy Petrillo patterned themselves after Dean Martin and Jerry Lewis, with Petrillo being particularly adept at copying the latter's style. When the film first played New York, Hal Wallis — who then had Martin and Lewis under contract — threatened a lawsuit against *Meets a Brooklyn Gorilla* due to the lookalike impersonations.

Lugosi played Dr. Zabor much as he did most mad doctors, playing a straight role opposite the farcical activities. Behind the scenes, he was actually somewhat ill and kept much to himself. When an opportunity arose, however, he managed to spin stories for the cast and even intentionally blew several takes in order to keep eating a prop ... papayas.

91. *Glen or Glenda*

Cast: Bela Lugosi (The Spirit), Dolores Fuller (Barbara), Tim Farrell (Dr. Alton/Narrator), Lyle Talbot (Inspector Warren), Daniel Davis (Glen/Glenda), Charles Crafts (Johnny), "Tommy" Haynes (Alan/Anne), Captain DeZita (The Devil/Glen's Father), Evelyn Wood (Sheila, Glen's Sister), Shirley Speril (Miss Stevens), Conrad Brooks (Reporter/Pickup Artist/Bearded Drag), Henry Bederski (Man with hat), William C. Thompson (Judge), Mr. Walter (Patrick/Patricia), Harry Thomas (Man in nightmare), George Weiss (Man at transvestite's suicide).

Credits: A Screen Classics Release, 1953.

Produced by George Weiss. Written and Directed by Edward D. Wood, Jr. Cinematography by William C. Thompson. Camera Operator, Bert Shipham. Makeup by Harry Thomas. Sound Technician, Ben Winkler. Music Consultant, Sanford Dickinson. Medical Adviser, Dr. Nathan Bailey. Settings, Jack Miles. Unit Director, Scott McCloud. Running time, 67 minutes. (No original copyright records exist in the Library of Congress for this film.)

Plot Summary: Glen enjoys wearing women's clothes, though he finally must confess to his fiancée, Barbara, whereas Alan, an ex-marine, actually undergoes a sex-change operation to become "Ann." An omniscient spirit offers commentary on the subject. "Beware of the green dragon that sits at your doorstep ... he eats little boys," the spirit warns.

Production Notes: Christine Jorgenson, who made headlines in real life as a successful sex-change patient, turned down offers from exploitation filmmaker George Weiss to appear in *Glen or Glenda*. Director/writer Edward D. Wood, Jr., himself a transvestite, portrayed Glen under the pseudonym Daniel Davis. Working titles during production included *Behind Locked Doors* and *Transvestite*. Various title changes also came with the film's sporadic, limited releases, such as *I Led Two Lives*, *He or She?*, and — for a 1963 run in New York — *I Changed My Sex*. For French and Belgian releases, it became *Louis ou Louise*; for Argentina, *Yo Cambie Mi Sexo*. Theaters in China even screened the film on a limited release.

Allegedly, Lugosi appeared in *Glen or Glenda* without grasping the subject of the entire film, though Robert Cremer's *Lugosi: The Man Behind the Cape* (Henry Regnery, 1976) claims otherwise. Bela's scenes were shot at the Jack Miles Studio in Los Angeles; he reportedly made $5,000 for the role, but some stories claim he earned only $1,000. As the unnamed spirit, Lugosi gives odd advice in a darkly lit but decidedly cheap atmosphere of skulls and other ghoulish decorations.

92. *Bride of the Atom*

Cast: Bela Lugosi (Dr. Eric Vornoff), Tor Johnson (Lobo), Tony McCoy (Lieutenant Dick Craig), Loretta King (Janet Lawson), Harvey Dunne (Captain Robbins), George Becwar (Professor Strowski), Paul Marco (Kelton), Don Nagel (Martin), Bud Osborne (Mac), Jake Warren (Jake), Anne Wilner (Tillie), Dolores Fuller (Margie), William Benedict (Newsboy), Ben Frommer (Police Station Suspect), Conrad Brooks (Policeman/Suspect).

Credits: A Banner Productions Release, 1955. Executive Producer, Donald E. McCoy. Written and Directed by Edward D. Wood, Jr. Associate Producer, Tony McCoy. Cinematography by William C. Thompson and Ted Allan. Special Effects, Pat Dinga. Music, Frank Worth. Technical Adviser, Igo Kantor. Sound, Dale Knight and Lyle Willey. Sound Effects, Ray Erleborn and Mike Pollock. Edited by Warren Adams. Running time, 68 minutes. (No original copyright records exist in the Library of Congress for this film.)

Plot Summary: Dr. Eric Vornoff plans to create a legion of supermen by exposing ordinary people to atomic energy. With the help of his lumbering assistant, Lobo, Vornoff captures Janet Lawson, planning her to be the "Bride of the Atom." The authorities soon begin tracing various events back to the scientist, and eventually chase him into the jungle marsh. Vornoff dies in the grip of an enormous octopus. A bolt of lightning and an atomic blast bring the evil to a close, causing Captain Robbins to remark, "He tampered in God's domain."

Production Notes: *Bride of the Atom*'s first incarnation came as a 1953 script planned as a Lugosi vehicle, *The Atomic Monster*, by Alex Gordon. Lack of financing kept the film from getting off the ground, though later Ed Wood managed to revive the project as *The Monster of the Marshes*. Shooting began in October 1954 at the Ted Allan Studios, but again the film faced money problems. A rancher named Donald McCoy supplied additional funds for production to resume in 1955 at the Centaur Studios and after becoming producer, he also provided his son, Tony, as the film's young hero. Wood picked other cast members from among his own friends, with some returning from *Glen or Glenda*. Vornoff's octopus was a leftover prop found at Republic Studios from *Wake of the Red Witch* (1948), with location shooting at Griffith Park featuring Dr. Vornoff's struggle with an aquatic monster that appears limp and unable to move.

The film premiered as *Bride of the Atom* at Hollywood's Paramount theater in May 1955. It remains best known under a later title, *Bride of the Monster*. Press materials and movie posters carried tag lines such as "The screen's master of the weird in his newest and most daring shocker!" Though it did not cover the "further adventures of Dr. Vornoff," *Night of the Ghouls*, a follow-up film made by Wood in 1958, made reference to the mad doctor's hellish activities, with Tor Johnson again appearing as Lobo.

Lugosi turned in an effective performance as Vornoff, despite the poor production values and the limited acting skills of his fellow cast members. Eddie Parker, who earlier stunted for Lugosi on *Frankenstein Meets the Wolf Man* (1943), doubled in the actor's more strenuous scenes. Lugosi's own most memorable moment was a lengthy speech in which he proclaims, "Now, in this forsaken jungle hell, I have proven that I am all right!" A common remark about Lugosi's performance is that he misread a line, describing Tor Johnson as a gentle "kitchen" rather than "kitten." The error is not Lugosi's, who spouted his dialogue correctly, but that of historians who presumably wrote without carefully viewing the film. Vornoff, a part for which Lugosi received only $1,000, was apparently the actor's last speaking role in a film.

93. The Black Sleep

Cast: Basil Rathbone (Sir Joel Cadman), Akim Tamiroff (Odo), Lon Chaney (Mungo), John Carradine (Borg), Bela Lugosi (Casimir), Herbert Rudley (Dr. Gordon Ramsay), Patricia Blake (Laurie), Phyllis Stanley (Daphne), Tor Johnson (Curry), Sally Yarnell (Nancy), George Sawaya (K-6), Claire Carleton (Miss Daly), Peter Gordon (Investigative Sergeant Steel), Louanna Gardner (Angelina), Clive Morgan (First Bobby), John Sheffield (Scotland Yard Detective).

Credits: United Artists, 1956. Produced by Howard W. Koch. Directed by Reginald Le Borg. Screenplay by John C. Higgins. Based on a story by Gerald Drayson Adams. Cinematography by Gordon Avil. Music by Les Baxter. Costumes by Wesley V. Jeffries and Angela Alexander. Makeup by Volpe and Gordon Bau. Edited by John F. Schreyer. Running time, 82 minutes. Copyright number LP6926, June 8, 1956.

Plot Summary: In order to revive his wife from a coma, Dr. Cadman uses a drug to induce a state resembling death in others. This "Black Sleep" enables him to practice brain surgery on unwitting victims, in hopes that he can learn enough to save his spouse. Several experiments go awry, resulting in numerous scarred creatures that are loosed at the conclusion. As they chant, "Kill, kill," the monsters murder Cadman.

Production Notes: Budgeted at $229,000, *The Black Sleep* united several top-name horror film actors together. Reportedly, producers sought Peter Lorre as well, though for whatever reasons he did not appear. Director Le Borg shot the film at American National Studios, with production beginning on February 9, 1956. By the end of filming on February 23, *The Black Sleep* had run some $6,000 over budget. United Artists released the horror show to decent box office response in June 1956, with television crews covering opening night. The studio reissued the film in 1963 under the new title *Dr. Cadman's Secret*. Non-U.S. releases altered the name as well, with *The Black Sleep* screened as *The Monsters Attack* in Belgium and *The Black Sleep of Dr. Satan* in Italy.

Despite several discussions with the director to allow him dialogue, Lugosi's Casimir remained a mute role. Le Borg later claimed to have shot footage of the actor speaking, but it was not used. Lugosi hoped *The Black Sleep* would act as a springboard for a planned comeback, but the minor part instead became his final film. The studio planned a cast tour to promote the film, but due to his health Lugosi appeared only in San Francisco and Portland. As a further promotion, UA commissioned wax figures of each horror star, with one capturing the Hungarian's likeness as Casimir.

94. *Plan 9 from Outer Space*

Cast: Bela Lugosi (Ghoul Man), Tor Johnson (Inspector Clay), Vampira (Vampire Girl), Tom Keene (Colonel Edwards), Gregory Walcott (Jeff Trent), Dudley Manlove (Eros), Mona McKinnon (Paula Trent), Duke Moore (Lieutenant Harper), Joanna Lee (Tanna), John "Bunny" Breckinridge (The Ruler), Lyle Talbot (General Roberts), Criswell (as himself), Carl Anthony (Patrolman Larry), Paul Marco (Kelton), Norma McCarty (Edith), David DeMering (Danny), Bill Ash (Captain), Conrad Brooks (Patrolman Jamie), Gloria Dea (Mourner), Ben Frommer (Mourner), J. Edward Reynolds (Gravedigger), Hugh Thomas (Gravedigger), Reverend Lyn Lemon (Minister, Clay's Funeral), Don Davis (Drunk), Karl Johnson (Farmer Calder), Dick Chaney (Man Carrying Stretcher), Edward D. Wood, Jr. (Man with Newspaper), Tom Mason (Lugosi's double).

Credits: A D.C.A. Release, 1959. Produced, directed, and written by Edward D. Wood, Jr. Executive Producer, J. Edward Reynolds. Running time, 79 minutes. Associate Producers, Hugh Thomas and Charles Burg. Music Supervisor, Gordon Zahler. Cinematography by William C. Thompson. Edited by Edward D. Wood, Jr. Sound, Dale Knight. Special Effects by Charles Duncan. Makeup by Harry Thomas and Tom Bartholomew. Set Construction, Tom Kemp. Set Designer, Harry Reif. Wardrobe, Dick Chaney. Running time, 79 minutes. (No original copyright records exist in the Library of Congress.)

Plot Summary: Based on a supposedly "true" incident ("sworn testimony of the miserable souls who survived the ordeal"), the story of alien invaders who enact "Plan 9"—an operation that brings the dead back to life—is introduced by prophet Criswell. After getting nowhere in attempts to contact the military and the U.S. government, the aliens believe they have no alternative. Authorities eventually thwart the invaders, but only after they battle a few fresh corpses brought back from the grave.

Production Notes: Shortly before Lugosi's death, Ed Wood filmed a small amount of footage that had the actor stalking a cemetery in his Dracula cape, as well as walking out of a house owned by Tor Johnson. The footage became the selling point of the script, *Grave Robbers from Outer Space*. Wild stories abound of the funding that came from a Baptist church, leading to cast and crew being baptized. Cardboard cemetery gravestones fell over during filming, scenes alternate from night to day with no logic behind them, and characters speak inane dialogue throughout. Cast members included numerous actors from *Bride of the Atom*, as well as the then unemployed television horror hostess Vampira. The film previewed at the Carlton Theater of Hollywood in 1957 as *Graverobbers from Outer Space*, and then went into a DCA release as *Plan 9 from Outer Space* in July 1959. During the eighties it became known as the "worst film ever made," and was presented with a "Golden Turkey Award." Modern critics also dubbed Wood the worst director in cinema history.

While this is usually noted as Lugosi's last film, the actor probably knew nothing of the project itself. Though he had been given other Wood scripts, none of them dealt with the outer space grave-robbing theme of *Plan 9*. Director Wood allegedly had another film idea in mind when he actually shot Lugosi's scenes, *The Vampire's Tomb*. A surviving script of that unmade horror film resembles nothing of *Plan 9*. However, the script also bears no relation to the filmed sequences of Lugosi.

Wood's footage of Lugosi was so short

that he reused it throughout *Plan 9*, with the director also employing a double, Dr. Tom Mason. The chiropractor stands taller than Lugosi, keeps a cape above his face throughout his scenes, and looks so little like the Hungarian that the word *double* seems the wrong term. While most believe that Wood shot the Lugosi footage in 1956, others contend that he filmed the sequences in the spring of 1955. According to Wood, the actor received $1,000 for his trouble.

95. Lock Up Your Daughters

Cast: Bela Lugosi, the Bowery Boys, Polly Ann Young, others unknown.

Credits: New Realm, 1959. Produced by Sam Katzman. Directed by Phil Rosen. Running time, 50 minutes (4,590 feet). Released only in Great Britain.

Plot Summary: Surviving press sheets offer a plot line very similar to that of *Voodoo Man* (1944), though certainly clips of other Monogram Lugosi films appear.

Production Notes: Unfortunately, this film cannot be included in a Lugosi filmography with absolute certainty that footage of him shot specifically for this project appears. No doubt exists that the film was made up of clips from several low-budget Lugosi films of the forties, while Katzman and Rosen almost certainly receive credit due to their affiliation with the original Monogram films used a source material. New Realm issued *Lock Up Your Daughters* only in the United Kingdom, during late 1959 and early 1960. The studio ran a contest during its run, offering money to any audience member who could name the original films from which the clips came.

Much compelling evidence suggests that Lugosi appeared in "new" footage and acted as a master of ceremonies to the old film clips. Such footage would have been shot during the fifties. However, at the time of writing this cannot be verified with complete certainty. Much more information on this film appears in the chapter "Unmasking the Mysteries."

6. Serials

Lugosi appeared in five serials during the thirties, each an inferior product in comparison to his better feature films. Often serials become mixed with movies in historic listings, though the media were very different from one another. As their name suggests, serials appeared over a length of time; generally, studios issued them in 12 or 15 chapters with one being released every week to theaters. The idea of course was to attract repeat customers, who waited on the edge of their seats all week until the theater screened the next chapter. Chapters often left heroes in precarious situations with no possible escape, thus creating a "cliffhanger" ending to build suspense and loyalty in theater patrons. Yet the inexpensive nature of serials caused them often to be very poor in story, acting, and set design. Thus, critics of the thirties usually scoffed at them, and their prime interest came from younger audiences. While enjoyable in their own way, Lugosi's serials highlight low budgets, improbable plots, and essentially juvenile entertainment.

1. *The Whispering Shadow*

Cast: Bela Lugosi (Professor Adam Strang), Viva Tattersall (Vera Strang), Jack Foster (Malcolm McGregor), Henry B. Walthall (President Bradley), Robert Warwick (Detective Raymond), Ethel Clayton (Countess), Roy D'Arcy (Clayton), Karl Dane (Sparks), Lloyd Whitlock (Young), Bob Kortman (Slade), Lafe McKee (Jerome), George J. Lewis (Bud Foster), Jack Perrin (Williams), Max Wagner (Kruger), Kernan Cripps (Foreman), Eddie Parker (Driver), Gordon DeMain (Detective), George Magrill (Mitchell), Tom London (Dupont), Lionel Backus (Jarvis), Norman Feusier (Deane).

Credits: Mascot, 1933. Produced by Nat Levine. Directed by Al Herman and Colbert Clark. Screenplay by George Morgan, Colbert Clark, Wyndham Gittens, Howard Bimberg, Barney Sarecky, and Norman Hall. Associate Producer, Victor Zobel. Cinematography by Ernest Miller and Edgar Lyons. Assistant Directors, George Webster and Theo Joos. Production Manager, Larry Wickland. Musical Direction by Abe Meyer. Edited by Ray Snyder and Gilmore Walker. Running time, 12 chapters (25 reels).

Chapter Titles: "The Master Magician," "The Collapsing Room," "The All-Seeing Eye," "The Shadow Strikes," "Wanted for Murder," "The Man Who Was Czar," "The Double Room," "The Red Circle," "The Fatal Secret," "The Death Warrant," "The Trap, King of the World."

Plot Summary: A gang leader known only as the Whispering Shadow can project his voice and silhouette anywhere, as well as electrocute men from afar. Detective Raymond investigates the arch criminal, as does Jack Foster, whose brother died at the hands of the fiend. Jack manages to capture one of the Shadow's henchmen; he also takes a liking to lovely Vera Strang. Among the many suspects is Professor Strang of a wax museum, Vera's mysterious father. Later, Strang turns out to be a government official on the trail of stolen jewels. Raymond and Jack together find the Shadow actually to be Sparks, who is promptly arrested.

Production Notes: *The Whispering Shadow* became producer Nat Levine's fourth

With cast and crew of the serial *The Whispering Shadow* (1933) in a group portrait, Lugosi remains in costume as the mysterious "Professor Strang."

for the fledgling Mascot Studios. The serial lacked a musical score, and footage of Lugosi was minimal. The 18-day shoot started at the beginning of December 1932, with cameras rolling 12 to 15 hours a day. Even with an animated "Shadow" and an effective use of miniatures, the result remains particularly dull. The first chapters of *The Whispering Shadow* hit theaters in January 1933. Mascot also prepared a six-reel feature version of the footage, though it received few screenings.

Advertisements played up the mystery of the Shadow character, claiming, "No man has ever seen the 'shadow' in the flesh. His fiendish genius for radio and television enables him to project his voice and shadow where he will — to see through doors and hear through walls — to electrocute a squealing henchman by radio death ray! Who is he — Who is the Shadow?"

Lugosi, whom trades announced as the lead player in October 1932, received $10,000 for his services. Professor Strang remains his least interesting role in a serial, as well as a prime example of his tendency to overact in the cinema.

Other cast members included silent screen star Karl Dane, who committed suicide in 1934 by placing a revolver to his head. Henry B. Walthall, another popular actor of silent films, had earlier been associated with D.W. Griffith.

In France *The Whispering Shadow* appeared as a two-part feature, *The Shadow That Kills*. Part one was titled *The Master of Mystery*, with the second installment being *The Lair of the Shadow*.

2. *Return of Chandu*

Cast: Bela Lugosi (Chandu), Maria Alba (Princess Nadji), Clara Kimball Young (Dorothy Regent), Lucien Prival (Vindhyan), Phyllis Ludwig (Betty Regent), Dean Benton (Bob Regent), Bryant Washburn (Prince Andra), Peggy Montgomery (Judy), Wilfred Lucas (Captain Wilson), Cyril Armbrister (Sutra), Elias Lazaroff (Bara), Dick Botiller (Morta), Murdoch McQuarrie (The Voice), Jack Clark (Vitras), and Josef Swickard (Tyba), Frazer Acosta (Nito), Harry Walker (Tagora), Charles Meacham (Mr. James), Isobel LeMall (Mrs. James), Don Brodie (Reporter), Edward Piel (Airline

Agent), Henry Hall (Curator), Beatrice Roberts (Lady), Iron Eyes Cody (Cat Man), Elias Schaffer (Old Man), Merrill McCormick (Sacrificial Aide).

Credits: Principal, 1934. Produced by Sol Lesser. Directed by Ray Taylor. Screenplay by Barry Barringer. Based on the radio serial by Harry M. Earnshaw, Vera M. Oldham, and R.R. Morgan. Cinematography by John Hickson. Dialogue Director, Cyril Armbrister. Assistant Director, Harry Knight. Art Direction by Robert Ellis. Production Manager, Theodore Joos. Edited by Lou Sackin and Carl Himm. Running time, 12 chapters (24 reels).

Chapter Titles: "The Chosen Victim," "The House on the Hill," "On the High Seas," "The Evil Eye," "The Invisible Circle," "Chandu's False Step," "The Mysterious Island," "The Edge of the Pit," "The Invisible Terror," "The Crushing Rock," "The Uplifted Knife," "The Knife Descends."

Plot Summary: Chandu the Magician treks to the mysterious island of Lemuria to save his beloved Nadji, an Egyptian princess, from the murderous Ubasti. The cult plans to sacrifice her to restore life to their ancient goddess Ossanna. However, Chandu joins forces with Tyba the White Magician and eventually triumphs over the evil sorcerers.

Production Notes: Sol Lesser shot *Return of Chandu* at Pathé Studios, as well as location in North Hollywood. *Chandu* utilized leftover sets from *King of Kings* (1927), *King Kong* (1933), and *Son of Kong* (1933). Lesser announced Lugosi as the star in June, though production did not start until mid–July. Cameras finished in late August, with the shoot lasting over five weeks. Lugosi actually performed his small role in *Gift of Gab* (1934) during the filming of this serial. The first chapters of *Return of Chandu* opened at theaters in October 1934. Reviewers generally found the serial (and the subsequent features culled from it) infantile and dull, though some hesitantly gave Lugosi a nice nod.

Lugosi portrays not the evil Roxor, as he had in Fox's 1932 feature film, but the good and kindly Yogi magician himself. As Chandu, the Hungarian brings more mystery to the role than Edmund Lowe had in the earlier film, with the actor relishing his chance to portray a hero. In his later years, Lugosi often offered this project among his most important credits.

Cyril Armbrister, dialogue director and also director for a time of the radio program *Chandu the Magician*, portrayed cult figure Sutra. Silent screen beauty Clara Kimball Young appears, as does the famed Native American actor Iron Eyes Cody. Oddly, one trade announced that "Lionel Atwill, Jr.," had been placed in the film, though Atwill's son had not yet even been born. Perhaps Lesser considered Atwill himself, though no other mention was made of the announcement.

Lesser also edited the serial into a feature, titled *Return of Chandu* and released first in October 1934 with a 76 minute running time. Other theaters exhibited the feature in April 1935 at 65 minutes. The producer also edited half of *Return of Chandu* into a 67 minute feature, *Chandu on the Magic Island*, which he released in January 1935. A few theaters screened *Magic Island* again in 1940. The producer apparently planned the feature versions in advance, filming various takes of each chapter's "cliffhanger" so that the features could be edited more smoothly.

3. *Shadow of Chinatown*

Cast: Bela Lugosi (Victor Poten), Herman Brix (Martin Andrews), Luana Walters (Sonya Rokoff), Joan Barclay (Joan Whiting), Maurice Liu (Willy Fu), William Buchanan (Healy), Forrest Taylor (Captain Walters), Charles King (Grogan), James B. Leong (Wong), Henry F. Tung (Dr. Wu), Paul Fung (Tom Chu), George Chan (Old Luce), John Elliot (Captain), May Ming (Wong's Brother), Jack Cowell (White Chink), Lester Dorr, Henry Hall, Roger Williams, Denver Dixon.

Credits: Victory, 1936. Produced by Sam Katzman. Directed by Robert S. Hill. Story by Rock Hawkey. Screenplay by Isadore Bernstein and Basil Dickey. Special Dialogue by William Buchanan. Cinematography by William Hyer. Production Manager, Ed W. Rote. Set Design by Fred Preble. Edited by Charles Henkel. Running time, 15 chapters (31 reels).

Chapter Titles: "The Arms of the God," "The Crushing Walls," "13 Ferguson Alley," "Death on the Wire," "The Sinister Ray," "The Sword Thrower," "The Noose, Midnight," "The Last Warning," "The Bomb," "Thundering Doom," "Invisible Gas," "The Brink of Disaster," "The Fatal Trap," "The Avenging Powers."

Plot Summary: Sonja, a West Coast representative for a shipping corporation, hires a Eurasian scientist named Victor Poten to conduct a reign of terror against the company's Chinese competition. After his brutal tactics begin, novelist Martin Andrews, reporter Joan Whiting, and Willy Fu investigate. Though Poten attempts to kill the trio, they eventually persuade Sonya to repent. The insane Poten murders his employer, though he is soon captured and given to the authorities.

Production Notes: Sam Katzman shot *Shadow of Chinatown*, his first serial, over some 15 days, keeping the crew working day and night to finish on schedule. Cameramen filmed some location shots in Culver City. The muddled and generally dull serial opened in October 1936. Among its cast was Olympic decathlon star Herman Brix, in his second serial. Brix formerly portrayed Edgar Rice Burroughs's man of the apes in *The New Adventures of Tarzan* (1935). Lovely Luana Walters later played opposite Lugosi in *The Corpse Vanishes* (1942).

Pressbooks for *Shadow of Chinatown* called Lugosi a "human sphynx of mystery," though the serial itself offered him a confusing and vague role. The actor later worked under Sam Katzman's production unit at Monogram Studios for a series of nine features. Production manager Ed Rote worked on several of Lugosi's Monogram features as well, including *Invisible Ghost* (1941), *Spooks Run Wild* (1941), *Bowery at Midnight* (1942), and *The Corpse Vanishes* (1942).

Posters for the serial promised "Thrills and Chills and Shivering Shocks as a Crazed Scientist Terrorizes the Underworld!" In Belgium and Denmark, exhibitors screened the serial under the title *The Mysteries of Chinatown*. Katzman also released a feature version of the film, in which Lugosi's character presumably dies, whereas in the serial the authorities capture him.

4. SOS Coastguard

Cast: Ralph Byrd (Terry), Bela Lugosi (Boroff), Maxine Doyle (Jean Norman), Herbert Rawlinson (Commander Boyle), Richard Alexander (Thorg), Lee Ford (Snapper McGee), John Piccori (Rackerby), Lawrence Grant (Rabinisi), Thomas Carr (Jim Kent), Carleton Young (Dodds), Allen Connor (Dick Norman), George Chesebro (Degado), Ronny Weeks (Wies).

Credits: Republic Pictures, 1937. Directed by William Witney and Alan James. Associate Producer, Sol C. Siegel. Supervised by Robert Beche. Screenplay by Barry Shipman and Franklyn Adreon. Based on an original story by Morgan Cox and Ronald Davidson. Cinematography by William Nobles. Sound Engineer, Terry Kellum. Musical Direction by Raoul Kraushaar. Supervising Editor, Murray Seldeen. Edited by Helene Turner and Edward Todd. Running time, 12 chapters.

Chapter Titles: "Disaster at Sea," "Barrage of Death," "The Gas Chamber," "The Fatal Shift," "The Mystery Ship," "Deadly Cargo," "Undersea Terror," "The Crash," "Wolves at Bay," "The Acid Trail," "The Sea Battle," "The Deadly Circle."

Plot Summary: Mad scientist Boroff attempts to smuggle his secret invention, a poisonous gas, out of the United States and sell it to foreign powers. The first shipment is lost at sea, and the villain soon finds himself facing the U.S. Coast Guard. Boroff escapes after shooting Jim Kent, though his brother, Terry, quickly investigates. Terry keeps Thorg, Boroff's henchman, from retrieving the lost shipment, and eventually

Lugosi as Dr. Alex Zorka in Universal Studios' serial *The Phantom Creeps* (1939).

he even finds the scientist's hideout. Boroff shoots Thorg and escapes on a motorboat. The dying henchman takes his revenge by destroying the scientist's ship.

Production Notes: After cameras rolled in June and July, the studio released *SOS Coastguard* in August 1937 to generally good reviews. Movie posters for the serial promised, "Little known facts about Uncle's Sam's shore guardians revealed for the first time. Smugglers, subs, seething thrills!" Press releases instructed audiences to "see America's valiant protectors of our nation's shores go to battle against sinister forces who want to control the world." A 69 minute feature version later hit theaters in April 1942.

Republic signed Lugosi to the serial in June 1937, with the Hungarian playing the villainous Boroff, the "powerful munitions king," in what coming attraction trailers called a "thunderous explosion of action." Though *SOS Coastguard* remains overall one of his best serials, Lugosi's screen time is relatively limited.

Among the cast members was Ralph Byrd, best known as the Dick Tracy of features and serials. Richard Alexander, the henchman Thorg, portrayed Prince Barin in two serials, *Flash Gordon* (1936) and *Flash Gordon's Trip to Mars* (1938), as well as acting in such features as *All Quiet on the Western Front* (1930). Future director Thomas Carr also appears, portraying the ill-fated Jim Kent.

5. *The Phantom Creeps*

Cast: Bela Lugosi (Dr. Alex Zorka), Robert Kent (Captain Bob West), Regis Toomey (Jim Daly), Dorothy Arnold (Jean Drew), Edward Van Sloan (Chief Jarvis), Eddie Acuff ("Mac"), Anthony Averill (Rankin), Edwin Stanley (Dr. Mallory), Jack C. Smith (Monk), Roy Barcroft (Paker), Forrest Taylor (Black), Karl Hackett (Brown), Robert Blair (Smith), Jerry

Frank (Jones), Dora Clement (Ann Zorka), Hugh Huntley (Perkins), Charles King (Buck), Bud Wolfe (the robot).

Credits: Universal Studios, 1939. Directed by Ford Beebe and Saul A. Goodkind. Associate Producer, Henry MacRae. Screenplay by George Plympton, Basil Dickey, and Mildred Barish. Dialogue Director, Lyonel Margolis. Based on a story by Willis Cooper. Cinematography by Jerry Ash and William Sickner. Art Direction by Ralph DeLacey. Edited by Alvin Todd, Irving Birnbaun, and Joseph Glick. Running time, 12 chapters.

Chapter Titles: "The Menacing Power," "Death Stalks the Highways," "Crashing Towers," "Invisible Terror," "Thundering Rails," "The Iron Monster," "The Menacing Mist," "Trapped in the Flames," "Speeding Doom," "Phantom Footprints," "The Blast," "To Destroy the World."

Plot Summary: Dr. Zorka, a brilliant scientist, invents numerous weapons for warfare, including a mechanical robot and a devisualizer belt that turns the bearer invisible. Additionally, he discovers an element in a meteorite that can freeze an entire army of men into suspended animation. As foreign countries express an interest, Zorka refuses to turn his secrets over to the United States. He moves his laboratory, but after his wife is accidentally killed Zorka declares war on the world. Even though he manages to drop a powerful bomb, the world survives and U.S. authorities prevail.

Production Notes: Director Ford Beebe, who later helmed *Night Monster* (1942) with Lugosi, found himself working with a meager budget on *The Phantom Creeps*. The studio first announced it as *The Shadow Creeps*, a title that stuck with it during production. Though trades mentioned in January that it would be a "mystery-detective thriller," no cast members were signed until some two months later. Universal used much stock footage, including scenes from *The Invisible Man* (1933) and *The Invisible Ray* (1936), an avalanche and explosion from Chapter 11 of a 1934 serial called *The Vanishing Shadow*, as well as footage of the real-life Hindenburg disaster.

Lugosi returned from England and *The Dark Eyes of London* (1939) to portray the mad Dr. Zorka. Beebe planned for cameras to begin rolling on April 24, 1939, just as another Universal serial, *The Oregon Trail*, finished production. Lugosi ran a bit behind, hurrying from New York to the studio "pronto," with the May 10 *Variety* claiming he had joined the production. His melodramatic characterization actually adds much to the serial. At first Zorka wears a heavy beard, though the evil doctor later appears clean-shaven to travel incognito.

Edward Van Sloan, the venerable Professor van Helsing of *Dracula* (1931), appeared alongside Lugosi for the first time since *The Death Kiss* (1933). Another of the Hungarian's former costars signed for the serial, Forrest Taylor of *SOS Coastguard* (1937).

The cast worked through May, with the June 21 *Variety* announcing the serial completed. Universal released *The Phantom Creeps* in August 1939, with trades giving Lugosi good notices while pointing out the more impossible aspects of the plot. The serial found success at small-town theaters in particular, where newspaper ads announcing its chapters and Lugosi's name sometimes took attention away from the top-billed feature. To this day, many film buffs have an affection for the bizarre robot that Dr. Zorka commands.

7. Stage Appearances

The following catalogue of Lugosi's work on the legitimate stage covers performances in four countries: Hungary, the United States, the United Kingdom, and Canada. As the actor performed in the latter two countries in a very limited way, both are cited and identified with United States material. The defining factor of this chapter becomes what trades once referred to as "legit" live work, rather than vaudeville, burlesque, or mere personal appearances. While Lugosi performed numerous condensed adaptations of *Dracula* on the vaudeville circuit, for example, only the full-length versions are covered within these listings.

Lugosi's Hungarian stage career remains a confusing situation, as exact records and playbills do not exist for every performance. Moreover, the actor's own recollections of the period are as little help. In his later days, for example, Lugosi often mentioned that he performed in Molnár's *Liliom*, which cannot be verified. Furthermore, while original printed sources confirm his popularity and success in the provinces of Hungary, it seems he lingered as a minor player at Budapest's National Theater. Again, existing evidence contradicts Lugosi's own accounts of the situation.

As for the performance dates and plays themselves, much effort on the part of Országos Színháztörténeti Múzeum és Intézet, Országos Széchényi Könyvtár, and Somogyi Könyvtár result in the compiled listing that follows. A few dates contradict prior sources on the subject, but they offer the most current data and research available in Lugosi's homeland. Unfortunately, a gap still exists between 1904 and 1910. This period probably saw Lugosi performing in provincial areas of Hungary, but no evidence has yet arisen to confirm that hypothesis.

Another difficult period to trace historically is that of the late forties, when Lugosi appeared in numerous "legit" but minor summer stock performances. Generally, such plays lasted one week and for Lugosi meant either *Dracula* or *Arsenic and Old Lace*. Numerous of these are covered, yet many more are likely missing. The fact that trades gave no publicity, reviews, or even mention to these performances highlights their obscurity as well as their insignificance.

With regard to his best-remembered plays — those that headlined at Broadway theaters in New York — opening nights listed refer to the date of the first actual Broadway performance. Numerous of these plays — such as *The Red Poppy*, *Dracula*, and others — previewed in other cities prior to their New York openings. Such previews are discussed within the individual entries.

Hungary

1. Ocskay Brigadéros (Brigadier General Ocskay)
Opening Night: August 24, 1902, at the Arany-Bárány Restaurant in Hatseg.
Producer: Nándor Benedek.
Author: Ferenc Herczeg.
Lugosi (under the name Béla Blaskó) portrayed Count Königsegg.

2. Házasodjunk (We're Married)
Opening Night: August 25, 1902, at the Arany-Bárány Restaurant in Hatseg.
Producer: Nándor Benedek.
Author: Soma Guthi.
Lugosi portrayed Pokykai. (In this and subsequent listings, unless noted otherwise, he appeared with the stage name of Béla Lugosi.)

3. Felhö Klari (Claire Felho)
Opening Night: September 18, 1902, at the Korona Theater in Szamousújvart.
Producer: Nándor Benedek.
Author: Ratkay.
Lugosi portrayed Vendel Csik, a tailor.

4. Kurucz Féja Dávid (Stubborn King David)
Opening Night: February 10, 1903, in Deva.
Director: György Micsey.
Author: Samu Fényes.
Lugosi portrayed Antonio Caraffa, as part of the Nemzeti Színeszet (National Actor's Company).

5. Maria Stuart
Opening Night: February 26, 1903, in Deva.
Director: György Micsey.
Author: Friedrich Schiller.
Lugosi portrayed Aubespine, as part of the Nemzeti Színeszet.

6. Ezeregy Éjszaka (Arabian Nights)
Opening Night: March 1, 1903, in Deva.
Director: György Micsey.
Author: Feld.
Lugosi portrayed Orias as part of the Nemzeti Színeszet.

7. A Denevér (The Bat)
Opening Night: March 3, 1903, in Deva.
Director: György Micsey.
Author: Meilhac and Helévy.
Lugosi portrayed Frosch, as part of the Nemzeti Színeszet.

8. Monna Vanna
Opening Night: March 4, 1903, in Deva.
Director: György Micsey.
Author: Maurice Maeterlinck.
Lugosi portrayed Marco, as part of the Nemzeti Színeszet.

9. Fedora
Opening Night: March 5, 1903, in Deva.
Director: György Micsey.
Author: Victorien Sardou.
Lugosi portrayed Dr. Lorrck, as part of the Nemzeti Színeszet.

10. Trilby
Opening Night: December 29, 1903, in Temesvar.
Producer: Ignácz Krecsányi.
Author: Du Maurier.
Lugosi portrayed Gecko, Svengali's servant, as part of the Ferencz József Városi Szinház (Franz Josef Repertory Theater).

11. Tartalékos Férj (Husband in Reserve)
Opening Night: January 8, 1904, in Temesvar.
Producer: Ignácz Krecsányi.
Author: Rákosi and Guthi.
Lugosi portrayed Oszkár, as part of the Ferencz József Városi Szinház.

154   II. Lugosi, the Performer

12. *Himfy Dalai (Himfy's Song)*
Opening Night: January 11, 1904, in Temesvar.
Producer: Ignácz Krecsányi.
Author: Berczik.
Lugosi portrayed Fr. Gyorgy Feher, as part of the Ferencz József Városi Szinház.

13. *Az Aranykakas (The Golden Rooster)*
Opening Night: January 14, 1904, in Temesvar.
Producer: Ignácz Krecsányi.
Author: Blumenthal and Kadelburg.
Lugosi portrayed an assessor, Boros, as part of the Ferencz József Városi Szinház.

14. *A Kereszt Jelében (In the Sign of the Cross)*
Opening Night: January 15, 1904, in Temesvar.
Producer: Ignácz Krecsányi.
Author: Wilson (Translated by Gyula Komor).
Lugosi portrayed a messenger, Melos, as part of the Ferencz József Városi Szinház.

15. *Rang és Mod (Rank and Style)*
Opening Night: February 17, 1904, in Temesvar.
Producer: Ignácz Krecsányi.
Author: Jozsef Szigeti.
Lugosi portrayed Baron Oszkar Eltey, as part of the Ferencz József Városi Szinház.

16. *Egyenlöség (The Admirable Crichton)*
Opening Night: February 19, 1904, in Temesvar.
Producer: Ignácz Krecsányi.
Author: Barrie.
Lugosi portrayed Lord Brockelhurst, as part of the Ferencz József Városi Szinház.

17. *A Vasgyáros (The Iron Manufacturer)*
Opening Night: April 6, 1904, in Temesvar.
Producer: Ignácz Krecsányi.
Author: Ohnet.
Lugosi portrayed Dr. Servan, as part of the Ferencz József Városi Szinház.

18. *A Bajusz (The Mustache)*
Opening Night: April 10, 1904, in Temesvar.
Producer: Ignácz Krecsányi.
Author: Verö.
Lugosi portrayed a financier, as part of the Ferencz József Városi Szinház.

19. *Rómeó és Julia (Romeo and Juliet)*
Opening Night: September 1, 1910, in Szeged at the Szegedi Városi Színház (Szeged Repertory Theater).
Author: Shakespeare.
Lugosi portrayed Romeo.

20. *Aranyember (Golden Man)*
Opening Night: September 3, 1910, in Szeged at the Szegedi Városi Színház.
Author: Mór Jókai.
Lugosi portrayed Major Kadisa.

21. *Az Ingyenélök (The Parasites)*
Opening Night: September 4, 1910, in Szeged at the Szegedi Városi Színház.
Author: Vidor.
Lugosi portrayed Pista Balogh.

22. *Az Obsitos*
Opening Night: September 5, 1910, in Szeged at the Szegedi Városi Színház.
Author: Kálmán and Bakonyi.
Lugosi portrayed Joska.

23. *A Kaméliás Hölgy (Lady of the Camellias)*
Opening Night: September 7, 1910, in Szeged at the Szegedi Városi Színház.
Author: Alexander Dumas.
Lugosi portrayed Armand Duval.

24. *A Dolovai Nabob Leana (The Daughter of the Nabob of Dolova)*
Opening Night: September 8, 1910, in Szeged at the Szegedi Városi Színház.
Author: Ferenc Herczeg.
Lugosi portrayed Lieutenant Lorand.

25. *Az Ördög (The Devil)*
Opening Night: September 9, 1910, in Szeged at the Szegedi Városi Színház.

Author: Ferenc Molnár.
Lugosi portrayed János.

26. Taifun (Typhoon)
Opening Night: September 10, 1910, in Szeged at the Szegedi Városi Színház.
Author: Menyhért Lengyel.
Lugosi portrayed an author, Otto Lindner.

27. Bilincsek (Fetters)
Opening Night: September 16, 1910, in Szeged at the Szegedi Városi Színház.
Author: Reichenbach.
Lugosi portrayed Simon.

28. A Postás Fiu és Huga (The Mail Boy and His Sister)
Opening Night: September 18, 1910, in Szeged at the Szegedi Városi Színház.
Author: Buchbinder.
Lugosi portrayed Dr. Emil Csipkés.

29. Amihez Minden Asszony Ert (What Every Woman Knows)
Opening Night: September 20, 1910, in Szeged at the Szegedi Városi Színház.
Author: Barrie.
Lugosi portrayed John Shand.

30. A Vasgyáros (The Iron Manufacturer)
Opening Night: October 10, 1910, in Szeged at the Szegedi Városi Színház.
Author: Ohnet.
Lugosi portrayed Prince Bligny.

31. A Kard Becsulets (Honor of the Sword)
Opening Night: October 19, 1910, in Szeged at the Szegedi Városi Színház.
Author: Kazaliczky.
Lugosi portrayed Landowner Ernö Rozgonyi.

32. A Csikós (The Cowboy)
Opening Night: October 23, 1910, in Szeged at the Szegedi Városi Színház.
Author: Ede Szigligeti.
Lugosi portrayed Asztolf Ormódi.

33. Szigetvári Vértanuk (Martyrs of Szigetvar)
Opening Night: November 1, 1910, in Szeged at the Szegedi Városi Színház.
Author: Mór Jókai.
Lugosi portrayed Confidant Szelim.

34. A Kormánybiztos (The Government Commissioner)
Opening Night: November 11, 1910, in Szeged at the Szegedi Városi Színház.
Author: Guthi.
Lugosi portrayed an assemblyman, Viznemissza.

35. Bánk Bán (The Ban Bank)
Opening Night: November 12, 1910, in Szeged at the Szegedi Városi Színház.
Author: Katona.
Lugosi portrayed a lieutenant.

36. A Sasfiók (The Eaglet)
Opening Night: November 23, 1910, in Szeged at the Szegedi Városi Színház.
Author: Rostand.
Lugosi portrayed Frigyes Gentz.

37. A Balkáni Hercegnö (The Balkan Princess)
Opening Night: November 25, 1910, in Szeged at the Szegedi Városi Színház.
Author: Lonsdale and Curson.
Lugosi portrayed Max Helm.

38. A Balga Szüz (The Foolish Virgin)
Opening Night: November 30, 1910, in Szeged at the Szegedi Városi Színház.
Author: Bataille.
Lugosi portrayed Gaston.

39. A Gyerekasszony (The Child-Woman)
Opening Night: December 6, 1910, in Szeged at the Szegedi Városi Színház.
Author: Bokor.
Lugosi portrayed Ferkó Selyem.

40. Egy Szegény Ifju Története (The Story of a Poor Lad)
Opening Night: December 13, 1910, in Szeged at the Szegedi Városi Színház.

Author: Octave Feuillet.
Lugosi portrayed Bevallan.

41. *Anna Karenina*
Opening Night: December 17, 1910, in Szeged at the Szegedi Városi Színház.
Author: Guiraud and Tolstoy.
Lugosi portrayed Count Vronsky.

42. *Richard III*
Opening Night: December 20, 1910, in Szeged at the Szegedi Városi Színház.
Author: Shakespeare.
Lugosi portrayed George, Prince of Clarence.

43. *Baccarat*
Opening Night: January 8, 1911, in Szeged at the Szegedi Városi Színház.
Author: Bernstein.
Lugosi portrayed Lebourg Amédée.

44. *Narancxvirág (Orange Blossom)*
Opening Night: January 8, 1911, in Szeged at the Szegedi Városi Színház.
Author: Farkas.
Lugosi portrayed a composer, Sidney Clark.

45. *Meguntam Margitot (Tired of Margaret)*
Opening Night: January 14, 1911, in Szeged at the Szegedi Városi Színház.
Author: Wolf and Corteline.
Lugosi portrayed an unknown role.

46. *A Szent Liget (The Sacred Grove)*
Opening Night: January 20, 1911, in Szeged at the Szegedi Városi Színház.
Author: Flers and Caillavet.
Lugosi portrayed Count Zakonskine.

47. *Sárga Liliom (The Yellow Lily)*
Opening Night: February 14, 1911, in Szeged at the Szegedi Városi Színház.
Author: Lajos Biró.
Lugosi portrayed the archduke.

48. *A Medikos (The Medico)*
Opening Night: February 25, 1911, in Szeged at the Szegedi Városi Színház.
Author: Sándor Bródy.
Lugosi portrayed Janos, the medico.

49. *Lotti Ezredesei (Lotti's Colonels)*
Opening Night: March 7, 1911, in Szeged at the Szegedi Városi Színház.
Author: Stonne.
Lugosi portrayed Ramajanah.

50. *Othello*
Opening Night: March 9, 1911, in Szeged at the Szegedi Városi Színház.
Author: Shakespeare.
Lugosi portrayed Cassio.

51. *A Jómadarak (The Scoundrels)*
Opening Night: March 11, 1911, in Szeged at the Szegedi Városi Színház.
Author: Raeder.
Lugosi portrayed Sam Bandheim.

52. *Az Aranylakodalom (The Golden Wedding)*
Opening Night: March 15, 1911, in Szeged at the Szegedi Városi Színház.
Author: Beöthy and Rákosi.
Lugosi portrayed Stanislav Lubomirzki and a law student.

53. *Robin Orvos (Dr. Robin)*
Opening Night: March 16, 1911, in Szeged at the Szegedi Városi Színház.
Author: Premary.
Lugosi portrayed Arthur Malam.

54. *A Tolvaj (The Thief)*
Opening Night: March 23, 1911, in Szeged at the Szegedi Városi Színház.
Author: Bernstein.
Lugosi portrayed Fernande Legardes.

55. *A Vig Özvegy (The Merry Widow)*
Opening Night: March 30, 1911, in Szeged at the Szegedi Városi Színház.
Author: Léhar.
Lugosi portrayed Count Danilo Danilovics.

56. *Hamlet*
Opening Night: March 31, 1911, in Szeged at the Szegedi Városi Színház.

Author: Shakespeare.
Lugosi portrayed Laertes.

57. *A Makrancos Hölgy (The Taming of the Shrew)*
Opening Night: April 2, 1911, in Szeged at the Szegedi Városi Színház.
Author: Shakespeare.
Lugosi portrayed Lucentio.

58. *A Boszorkány (The Witch)*
Opening Night: April 5, 1911, in Szeged at the Szegedi Városi Színház.
Author: Victorien Sardou.
Lugosi portrayed Don Enrique de Palacios.

59. *Viola-Az Alföldi Haramia (Viola, Outlaw of the Lowlands)*
Opening Night: April 10, 1911, in Szeged at the Szegedi Városi Színház.
Author: Szigligeti and Eotvos.
Lugosi portrayed Ákos.

60. *A Becstelen (The Ignominious)*
Opening Night: April 11, 1911, in Szeged at the Szegedi Városi Színház.
Author: Garvay.
Lugosi portrayed Lázló Kápolnay.

61. *Délibáb (Fate Morgana)*
Opening Night: April 21, 1911, in Szeged at the Szegedi Városi Színház.
Author: Sümegi and Kun.
Lugosi portrayed a journalist, Béla Pomándy.

62. *A Kivándorló (The Immigrant)*
Opening Night: April 27, 1911, in Szeged at the Szegedi Városi Színház.
Author: Ferenc Herczeg.
Lugosi portrayed Baron Szentgróthy.

63. *Elnémult Harangok (Silent Bells)*
Opening Night: April 30, 1911, in Szeged at the Szegedi Városi Színház.
Author: Rákosi and Malonyai.
Lugosi portrayed a Presbyterian minister, Pal Simandy.

64. *Botrány (Scandal)*
Opening Night: May 2, 1911, in Szeged at the Szegedi Városi Színház.
Author: Bataille.
Lugosi portrayed Artanezzo.

65. *Bábjáték (Puppet Show)*
Opening Night: May 3, 1911, in Szeged at the Szegedi Városi Színház.
Author: Wolf.
Lugosi portrayed Marquis Roger de Monclars.

66. *A Sárga Csikó (The Yellow Colt)*
Opening Night: May 7, 1911, in Szeged at the Szegedi Városi Színház.
Author: Erkel and Csepreghy.
Lugosi portrayed Peti.

67. *Trilby*
Opening Night: May 8, 1911, in Szeged at the Szegedi Városi Színház.
Author: Potter and Du Maurier.
Lugosi portrayed Prince Rochermartel.

68. *A Tanitónö (The Teacher)*
Opening Night: May 9, 1911, in Szeged at the Szegedi Városi Színház.
Author: Sándor Bródy.
Lugosi portrayed the Judge.

69. *Az Allamtitkam Ur (The Secretary of State)*
Opening Night: May 11, 1911, in Szeged at the Szegedi Városi Színház.
Author: Bisson.
Lugosi portrayed Lambertin.

70. *A Zseni (The Genius)*
Opening Night: May 14, 1911, in Szeged at the Szegedi Városi Színház.
Author: Nagy.
Lugosi portrayed Rudolf.

71. *A Sabin Nök Elrablása (The Rape of the Sabine Women)*
Opening Night: May 17, 1911, in Szeged at the Szegedi Városi Színház.
Author: Schönthan.
Lugosi portrayed Dr. Béla Szilvássy.

158　II. Lugosi, the Performer

72. *Anatol*
Opening Night: May 20, 1911, in Szeged at the Szegedi Városi Színház.
Author: Schnitzler.
Lugosi portrayed Max.

73. *Anna Karenina*
Opening Night: September 3, 1911, at the Magyar Színház (Hungarian Theater) of Budapest.
Producer: László Beöthy.
Author: Guiraud and Tolstoy.
Lugosi portrayed Count Vronsky.

74. *Sárga Liliom (Yellow Lily)*
Opening Night: September 18, 1911, at the Magyar Színház of Budapest.
Producer: László Beöthy.
Author: Lajos Biró.
Lugosi portrayed a lawyer, Asztalos Kálmán.

75. *Az Élet Szava (The Call of Life)*
Opening Night: October 7, 1911, at the Magyar Színház of Budapest.
Producer: László Beöthy.
Author: Schnitzler.
Lugosi portrayed a young officer, Max.

76. *Sárga Liliom (The Yellow Lily)*
Opening Night: November 9, 1911, at the Magyar Színház of Budapest.
Producer: László Beöthy.
Author: Lajos Biró.
Lugosi portrayed the archduke.

77. *A Gésák (The Geisha)*
Opening Night: April 12, 1912, at Budapest's Royal Theater.
Author: Hall.
Lugosi portrayed a navy lieutenant, Reginald Fairfax.

78. *Anna Karenina*
Opening Night: August 22, 1912, at the Magyar Színház (Hungarian Theater) of Budapest.
Producer: László Beöthy.
Author: Guiraud and Tolstoy.
Lugosi portrayed Count Vronsky.

79. *Sárga Liliom (The Yellow Lily)*
Opening Night: September 5, 1912, at the Magyar Színház of Budapest.
Producer: László Beöthy.
Author: Lajos Biró.
Lugosi portrayed the archduke.

80. *A Vasgyáros (The Iron Manufacturer)*
Opening Night: January 5, 1913, at the Nemzeti Színház (National Theater) of Budapest.
Author: Ohnet.
Lugosi portrayed Pontac.

81. *Az Ember Tragédiája (The Tragedy of Man)*
Opening Night: January 20, 1913, at the Nemzeti Színház.
Author: Imre Madách.
Lugosi portrayed Catulus and the Marquis.

82. *Cyrano de Bergerac*
Opening Night: February 3, 1913, at the Nemzeti Színház.
Author: Edmond Rostand.
Lugosi portrayed the second marquis.

83. *Mary Ann*
Opening Night: February 4, 1913, at Pest's Várszinház (Palace Theatre).
Author: Izrael Zangwill.
Lugosi portrayed O'Gorman, a journalist.

84. *Maria Stuart*
Opening Night: February 7, 1913, at Pest's Várszinház (Palace Theatre).
Author: Friedrich Schiller.
Lugosi portrayed Count Belliévre.

85. *Richard III*
Opening Night: February 10, 1913, at the Nemzeti Színház (National Theater) of Budapest.
Author: Shakespeare.
Lugosi portrayed Sir Walter Herbert.

86. *Caesar and Cleopatra*
Opening Night: February 21, 1913, at the Nemzeti Színház.

Author: George Bernard Shaw.
Lugosi portrayed Achilles, an Egyptian commander.

87. *Az Aranyember (Golden Man)*
Opening Night: March 3, 1913, at the Nemzeti Színház.
Author: Mór Jókai.
Lugosi portrayed Major Kadisa.

88. *A Szentivánáji Álom (A Midsummer Night's Dream)*
Opening Night: March 4, 1913, at the Nemzeti Színház.
Author: Shakespeare.
Lugosi portrayed Cardinal Pandolf.

89. *Az Ember Tragédiája (The Tragedy of Man)*
Opening Night: March 5, 1913, at the Nemzeti Színház.
Author: Imre Madách.
Lugosi portrayed Plato.

90. *Tartuffe*
Opening Night: March 10, 1913, at the Nemzeti Színház.
Author: Molière.
Lugosi portrayed Mariann's lover, Valere.

91. *II. Rákoczi Ferenc Fogsága (Francis Rakoczi II in Captivity)*
Opening Night: March 15, 1913, at the Nemzeti Színház.
Author: Ede Szigligeti.
Lugosi portrayed Solári, Commander of Castle Sarospatak.

92. *A Boszorkány (The Witch)*
Opening Night: March 16, 1913, at the Nemzeti Színház.
Author: Victorien Sardou.
Lugosi portrayed Eugenio Fray.

93. *Hamlet*
Opening Night: March 17, 1913, at the Nemzeti Színház.
Author: Shakespeare.
Lugosi portrayed Rosenkranz.

94. *A Fáklyák (The Torches)*
Opening Night: March 28, 1913, at the Nemzeti Színház.
Author: Henry Bataille.
Lugosi portrayed Hervé, a taxidermist.

95. *Bizánc (Byzantium)*
Opening Night: April 8, 1913, at the Nemzeti Színház.
Author: Ferenc Herczeg.
Lugosi's portrayed Folko, mercenary from Genoa.

96. *Drághy Éva Eskuje (The Oath of Eva Draghy)*
Opening Night: April 14, 1913, at the Nemzeti Színház.
Author: Gyula Pekár.
Lugosi portrayed Farkas Weer.

97. *A Fogadott Apa (The Adopted Father)*
Opening Night: May 2, 1913, at the Nemzeti Színház.
Author: Félix Duquesnel and André Barde.
Lugosi portrayed Gilbert Rivers.

98. *Hernani*
Opening Night: May 8, 1913, at the Nemzeti Színház.
Author: Victor Hugo.
Lugosi portrayed Courtier Don Sanebo.

99. *A Kegyenc (The Favorite)*
Opening Night: May 16, 1913, at the Nemzeti Színház.
Author: László Teleki.
Lugosi portrayed Senator Marcus.

100. *La Sorcière*
Opening Night: May 19, 1913, at the Nemzeti Színház.
Author: Victorien Sardou.
Lugosi portrayed Fray Eugenio Calabazas.

101. *Faust*
Opening Night: May 23, 1913, at the Nemzeti Színház.
Author: Goethe.

II. Lugosi, the Performer

Lugosi portrayed Michael and the First Student.

102. Endre és Johanna (Andrew and Joanna)
Opening Night: May 28, 1913, at the Nemzeti Színház.
Author: Jenö Rákosi.
Lugosi portrayed Melazzo.

103. A Kaméliás Hölgy (Lady of the Camellias)
Opening Night: June 3, 1913, at the Nemzeti Színház.
Author: Alexander Dumas.
Lugosi portrayed Varville.

104. Viola
Opening Night: September 13, 1913, at the Nemzeti Színház.
Author: József Szigeti.
Lugosi portrayed the liveried attendant of county dignitaries.

105. Bolondok Tánca (Dance of the Fools)
Opening Night: September 19, 1913, at the Nemzeti Színház.
Author: Leo Birinski.
Lugosi portrayed Malakov, a revolutionary.

106. King Lear
Opening Night: September 29, 1913, at the Nemzeti Színház.
Author: Shakespeare.
Lugosi portrayed a knight.

107. Az Utolsó Nap (The Last Day)
Opening Night: October 3, 1913, at the Nemzeti Színház.
Author: Béla Balázs.
Lugosi portrayed La Spagna, a painter.

108. A Konventbiztos (The Convention Commissar)
Opening Night: October 24, 1913, at the Nemzeti Színház.
Author: Pál Farkas.
Lugosi portrayed a lieutenant of the home guard.

109. Az Attaché (The Ambassador's Attaché)
Opening Night: October 28, 1913, at the Palace Theatre of Pest.
Author: Henri Meilhac.
Lugosi portrayed Lucien de Meré.

110. Essex Graf (Count Essex)
Opening Night: November 17, 1913, at the Nemzeti Színház.
Author: Heinrich Laube.
Lugosi portrayed Count Southampton.

111. Mária Antónina (Marie Antoinette)
Opening Night: November 21, 1913, at the Nemzeti Színház.
Author: Dezsö Szomory.
Lugosi portrayed Breteuille and the Saint Priest.

112. Monna Vanna
Opening Night: December 22, 1913, at the Nemzeti Színház.
Author: Maurice Maeterlinck.
Lugosi portrayed Vedio, Prinzivalle's secretary.

113. Karácsonyi Álom (Christmas Dream)
Opening Night: December 23, 1913, at the Nemzeti Színház.
Author: Géza Gárdonyi.
Lugosi portrayed a man from the theater.

114. Az Egyszeri Királyfi (The Prince in the Tale)
Opening Night: January 4, 1914, at the Nemzeti Színház.
Author: Ernö Szép.
Lugosi appeared as a cowboy.

115. Éva Boszorkány (Eve, the Witch)
Opening Night: January 7, 1914, at the Nemzeti Színház.
Author: Ferenc Herczeg.
Lugosi portrayed Mr. Enzio.

116. Matyó Lakodalom (The Wedding at the Matyo's)
Opening Night: January 16, 1914, at the Nemzeti Színház.

Author: Sándor Garamszeghy.
Lugosi portrayed Pesta, the best man.

117. *Macbeth*
Opening Night: January 30, 1914, at the Nemzeti Színház.
Author: Shakespeare.
Lugosi portrayed Angus.

118. *A Kölcsonkért Kastély (The Borrowed Residence)*
Opening Night: February 6, 1914, at the Nemzeti Színház.
Author: Gyula Pékar.
Lugosi portrayed Clausewitz.

119. *Aesopus (Aesop)*
Opening Night: February 20, 1914, at the Palace Theatre in Pest.
Author: Jenö Rákosi.
Lugosi portrayed Dorsus.

120. *A Nök Barátja (The Woman's Friend)*
Opening Night: February 24, 1914, at the Nemzeti Színház.
Author: Alexander Dumas, Jr.
Lugosi portrayed De Montegre.

121. *Fenn Az Ernyö Nincsen Kas (Spending Spree)*
Opening Night: March 7, 1914, at the Nemzeti Színház.
Author: Ede Szigligeti.
Lugosi portrayed Baron Varkovy.

122. *Liliomfi*
Opening Night: March 9, 1914, at the Nemzeti Színház.
Author: Ede Szigligeti.
Lugosi portrayed a dandy.

123. *Az Igazgató Ur (The Headmaster)*
Opening Night: March 20, 1914, at the Nemzeti Színház.
Author: Edward Knoblauch and Wilfred T. Coleby.
Lugosi portrayed Jack Strahan, a teacher.

124. *Egy Karrier Története (The Story of a Career)*
Opening Night: April 3, 1914, at the Nemzeti Színház.
Author: József Pakots.
Lugosi portrayed the director of an office.

125. *Egy Karrier Története (The Story of a Career)*
Opening Night: April 5, 1914, at the Nemzeti Színház.
Author: József Pakots.
Lugosi portrayed Count Nyrady.

126. *Richard III*
Opening Night: April 6, 1914, at the Nemzeti Színház.
Author: Shakespeare.
Lugosi portrayed Sir Walter Herbert.

127. *A Vasgyáros (The Iron Manufacturer)*
Opening Night: April 13, 1914, at the Nemzeti Színház.
Author: Ohnet.
Lugosi portrayed Baron Préfont.

128. *Liliomfi*
Opening Night: April 21, 1914, at the Nemzeti Színház.
Author: Ede Szigligeti.
Lugosi portrayed a gentleman.

129. *L'Ami des Femmes*
Opening Night: April 24, 1914, at the Nemzeti Színház.
Author: Alexander Dumas.
Lugosi portrayed Montegre.

130. *King John*
Opening Night: April 27, 1914, at the Nemzeti Színház.
Author: Shakespeare.
Lugosi portrayed Prince Limoges.

131. *Julius Caesar*
Opening Night: May 4, 1914, at the Nemzeti Színház.
Author: Shakespeare.
Lugosi portrayed Cinna.

132. *A Trónkövetelök (The Contenders for the Throne)*

II. Lugosi, the Performer

Opening Night: May 15, 1914, at the Nemzeti Színház.
Author: Ibsen.
Lugosi portrayed a vassal, Pál Flida.

133. *A Peleskei Nótárius (The Notary of Peleske)*
Opening Night: June 7, 1914, at the Nemzeti Színház.
Author: József Gaál.
Lugosi portrayed Othello.

134. *Maria Stuart*
Opening Night: April 10, 1916, at the Nemzeti Színház.
Author: Schiller.
Lugosi portrayed Count Belliévre.

135. *The Passion*
Opening Night: April 15, 1916, in Debrecen.
Author: Unknown.
Lugosi portrayed Jesus Christ.

136. *Hamlet*
Opening Night: April 30, 1916, at the Nemzeti Színház (National Theater) of Budapest.
Author: Shakespeare.
Lugosi portrayed Fortinbras, Prince of Norway.

137. *Macbeth*
Opening Night: May 2, 1916, at the Nemzeti Színház.
Author: Shakespeare.
Lugosi portrayed Lenox.

138. *Othello*
Opening Night: May 6, 1916, at the Nemzeti Színház.
Author: Shakespeare.
Lugosi portrayed Lodovico.

139. *Romeo and Juliet*
Opening Night: May 10, 1916, at the Nemzeti Színház.
Author: Shakespeare.
Lugosi portrayed Escalus.

140. *Hamlet*
Opening Night: May 13, 1916, at the Nemzeti Színház.
Author: Shakespeare.
Lugosi portrayed Fortinbras.

141. *Macbeth*
Opening Night: May 16, 1916, at the Nemzeti Színház.
Author: Shakespeare.
Lugosi portrayed Lenox.

142. *A Szökött Katona (The Deserter)*
Opening Night: September 17, 1916, at the Nemzeti Színház.
Author: Ede Szigligeti.
Lugosi portrayed Tengeri.

143. *Henry IV*
Opening Night: October 11, 1916, at the Nemzeti Színház.
Author: Shakespeare.
Lugosi portrayed Lord Mowbray.

144. *Aesopus (Aesop)*
Opening Night: October 14, 1916, at the Nemzeti Színház.
Author: Jenö Rákosi.
Lugosi portrayed Diodor, Prince of Samos.

145. *Hamlet*
Opening Night: October 23, 1916, at the Nemzeti Színház.
Author: Shakespeare.
Lugosi portrayed Laertes.

146. *Zsuzsi (Susie)*
Opening Night: October 27, 1916, at the Nemzeti Színház.
Author: Lajos Barta.
Lugosi portrayed a young man.

147. *Don Carlos*
Opening Night: November 10, 1916, at the Nemzeti Színház.
Author: Friedrich Schiller.
Lugosi portrayed Feria.

148. *Egy Szegény Ifju Története (The Story of a Poor Lad)*

As Jesus Christ in a Passion play in 1916 in Debrecen, Hungary.

Opening Night: November 22, 1916, at the Nemzeti Színház.
  Author: Octave Feuillet.
  Lugosi portrayed Gaston.

149. *A Harom Testor (The Three Bodyguards)*

Opening Night: December 9, 1916, at the Nemzeti Színház.
  Author: Ferenc Herczeg.
  Lugosi portrayed a journalist named Csernay.

150. *A Makrancos Hölgy (The Taming of the Shrew)*
Opening Night: December 19, 1916, at the Nemzeti Színház.
Author: Shakespeare.
Lugosi portrayed Lucentio.

151. *Ünnepi Játék (Festive Play)*
Opening Night: December 30, 1916, at the Nemzeti Színház.
Author: Ferenc Herczeg.
Lugosi portrayed a poet.

152. *Kömíves Kelemen (Kelemen, the Mason)*
Opening Night: January 12, 1917, at the Nemzeti Színház.
Author: Aurél Kárpáti and László Vajda.
Lugosi portrayed the first mason.

153. *Az Ember Tragédiája (The Tragedy of Man)*
Opening Night: January 19, 1917, at the Nemzeti Színház.
Author: Imre Madách.
Lugosi portrayed the first worker.

154. *A Hadifogoly (The Prisoner of War)*
Opening Night: February 9, 1917, at the Nemzeti Színház.
Author: Sandor Hevesi.
Lugosi portrayed Henri Talmont.

155. *A Pártütok (The Insurgents)*
Opening Night: February 12, 1917, at the Nemzeti Színház.
Author: Károly Kisfaludy.
Lugosi portrayed Lieutenant Élosdy.

156. *King John*
Opening Night: March 15, 1917, at the Nemzeti Színház.
Author: Shakespeare.
Lugosi portrayed Louis, the Dauphin.

157. *A Szentivánáji Álom (A Midsummer Night's Dream)*
Opening Night: March 16, 1917, at the Nemzeti Színhás.
Author: Shakespeare.
Lugosi portrayed Demetrius.

158. *A Kaméliás Hölgy (Lady of the Camellias)*
Opening Night: March 30, 1917, at the Nemzeti Színház.
Author: Alexander Dumas.
Lugosi played Varville.

159. *Maria Magdalena*
Opening Night: May 19, 1917, at the Nemzeti Színház.
Author: Friedrich Hebbel.
Lugosi portrayed Leonard.

160. *A Nagymama (The Grandmother)*
Opening Night: May 26, 1917, at the Nemzeti Színház.
Author: Gergely Csíky.
Lugosi portrayed Örkényi Kálmán.

161. *Árva László Kiraly (Lonely King Lazlo)*
Opening Night: October 26, 1917, at the Nemzeti Színház.
Author: Ferenc Herczeg.
Lugosi portrayed László Hunyadi. (Conflicting evidence surrounds this performance, with Robert Cremer's *Lugosi: The Man Behind the Cape* [Henry Regnery, 1976] placing Lugosi in the same play, role, and theater on March 3, 1918.)

162. *Ahogy Tetsik (As You Like It)*
Opening Night: January 18, 1918, at the Nemzeti Színház.
Author: Shakespeare.
Lugosi portrayed Jacques.

163. *Charlotte Kisasszony (Mademoiselle Charlotte)*
Opening Night: February 22, 1918, at the Nemzeti Színház.
Author: Menyhért Lengyel.
Lugosi portrayed Pál Cséfalvi.

164. *II. József Császár (Emperor Joseph II)*
Opening Night: April 5, 1918, at the Nemzeti Színház.
Author: Dezsö Szomory.
Lugosi portrayed Count Hatzfeld.

165. *A Kaméliás Hölgy (Lady of the Camellias)*
Opening Night: April 7, 1918, at the Nemzeti Színház.
Author: Alexander Dumas.
Lugosi portrayed Armand Duval.

166. *Görgötuz (Bengal Light)*
Opening Night: May 3, 1918, at the Nemzeti Színház.
Author: Sándor Hevesi.
Lugosi portrayed Imre Adorján.

167. *Romeo and Juliet*
Opening Night: June 7, 1918, at the Nemzeti Színház.
Author: Shakespeare.
Lugosi portrayed Tybalt.

168. *Bizánc (Byzantium)*
Opening Night: September 18, 1918, at the Nemzeti Színház.
Author: Ferenc Herczeg.
Lugosi portrayed Achmed Khan, a Turkish ambassador.

169. *Richard III*
Opening Night: November 15, 1918, at the Nemzeti Színház.
Author: Shakespeare.
Lugosi portrayed Henry, the Count of Richmond.

170. *Henry VIII*
Opening Night: November 24, 1918, at the Nemzeti Színház.
Author: Shakespeare.
Lugosi portrayed Suffolk.

171. *Bagatelle*
Opening Night: December 29, 1918, at the Nemzeti Színház.
Author: Paul Hervien.
Lugosi portrayed Marsy.

172. *Sancho Panza Királysága (The Kingdom of Sancho Panza)*
Opening Night: January 10, 1919, at the Nemzeti Színház.
Author: Menyhért Lengyel.
Lugosi portrayed the prince in what became his last recorded live performance in Hungary.

United States, United Kingdom, and Canada

173. *Az Ember Tragédiája (The Tragedy of Man)*
Opening Night: April 8, 1922, in New York City, New York.
Cast: Béla Lugosi (Adam), Bella Pogany (Eve), Károly Darvas (Lucifer), Ilona Montágh (Hippia), Margit Lévay (Archangel Gabriel), R. Tóth (Lucifer), A. Zsadanyi (Emperor Rudolph).
Credits: Produced by Lugosi and Serly. Written by Madach.
Production Notes: Lugosi coproduced and starred in this Hungarian version of *The Tragedy of Man* in New York City, with some reviewers in the Hungarian community remembering the actor from the Budapest stage. Lugosi earlier toured Hungarian communities of a few Eastern cities in a version of Imre Foldes's comedy *Hallo*, acting as director, producer, and star. While in New York, he also produced and performed in Hungarian versions of *Bluebeard*, *I Will Die for You!*, *Queen*, *Fata Morgana*, *The Yellow Lily*, and *Happiness*. Such performances generally played to small, lower-class audiences, though *The Tragedy of Man* helped nab Lugosi a role in an English-language version of *The Red Poppy*.

174. *The Red Poppy*
Opening Night: December 20, 1922, at the Greenwich Village Theater.
Cast: Arthur Metcalfe (Prince Sergius Saratoff), Leon Gordon (De Croy), J.J. Greer (Jean and Sergeant de Ville), Estelle Winwood (Claire), Betty Ross Clarke

(Diane), Grace Griswold (Mme. Vali), Byron Russell (Pierre), Gerald Hamer (Duthil), Joan Twain (Francine), Paul Broderick (Footman and a Tough), Frances Eldridge (Friquette), George A. Lawrence (Dudule), Clara T. Bracy (Boule), William Paul (Babe Rose), Blanche Boizon (Lea), Lorna Elliot (Madame Sorel), John H. Brewer (Sorel), Herbert Ashton (Boule), Arthur Lubin (Mimile), Grace Connell (Pauline), Burette Kappes (Becot), Te Ata (Irma), Norris Hobbs (Dede), Bela Lugosi (Fernando), Robert Knight (Rob), Elena Meade (Babo), Beatrice Bradley (Blanche), Elizabeth North (Toto), Marco Mora (Victor), Grace Gordon (A Lady), Ruby Gordon (Another Lady), Kay McKay (A Gentleman), Hubbard Kirkpatrick (Another Tough), Rosario Bogina (An Accordion Player).

Credits: A play by Andre Picard and Francis Carco. Presented by Miss Estelle Winwood. Produced by Iden Payne. Directed by Henry Baron.

Plot Summary: Claire, princess of Russia, resides in Paris and longs for excitement. She finds the luxurious existence of the upper class dull and bothersome, and longs for more excitement than her husband can offer. Fernando, a Spanish cutthroat, soon enters her life, bringing with him an intense and even brutal passion. At the end, however, a man about town kills Fernando.

Production Notes: *The Red Poppy* first played Atlantic City for two weeks, then hit the New York stage. Though critics generally enjoyed Estelle Winwood, they found the overall play less than satisfactory. The play remained in New York for only 13 performances over ten days, with trades reporting very little profit from the Greenwich Village Theater, a house that could apparently make only $500 a week on *The Red Poppy* by playing to capacity each night. No Broadway house was in sight, and Henry Baron's backers removed support. After the first week, no advertisements appeared in newspapers as the play still owed some $230 for its previous publicity. A reported failure to pay salaries caused an abrupt end to the play.

A friend of Henry Baron's informed the director about Lugosi after seeing him in *The Tragedy of Man*. The actor landed a role as the Spanish Fernando, wearing "a scarlet sash and an air of mystery." He and Winwood swept "through those fine passions that are fed by brutal blows and stranglehold kisses, putting to shame the life of the merely tubbed and tailored." Arthur Lubin, who played a small role in the tale and later directed Lugosi in a 1940 film, *Black Friday*, befriended the Hungarian. Though Lugosi certainly had great trouble with the English language at this point, Lubin managed to help him sufficiently grasp his dialogue. The future film director later recalled spending three weeks in an effort to teach Lugosi his lines.

Newspapers and magazines proclaimed Lugosi "an instantaneous hit," with *Theatre Magazine* prophetically announcing that such success "points to his becoming permanently a favorite of American playgoers." Both the *New York Times* and *New York Tribune* also heaped praise upon the Hungarian. Perhaps the most famous tale surrounding the play involves Lugosi's leaving Estelle Winwood with three broken ribs after performing a particular scene. In one interview, Winwood claimed the oft-reported tale was true; in another, she denied it.

175. *The Werewolf*

Opening Night: June 1, 1924, at Chicago's Adelphi Theater.

Cast: Laura Hope Crewes (The Duchess of Capablanca), Marion Coakley (Camilla, her niece), Lennox Paule (Eliphas Leone, President of the Barcelona Society for Psychical Research), Warburton Gamble (Florencio de Viena, State Attorney of Barcelona), Leslie Howard (Paolo Moreira, Professor at the Girl's College at Barcelona), Bela Lugosi (Vincente, the butler), Gaby Fleury (Nina, a maid), Ruth Mitchell (Caterina, a peasant girl), Sydney Paxton (A Priest).

Credits: A comedy play in three acts by Rudolph Lothar. Adapted by Gladys Unger. Produced by George McClellan. Staged by Clifford Brooke.

Plot Summary: The Duchess becomes very disturbed by the notion that the spirit of the late Don Juan roams her castle grounds, with the knowledge that three pretty girls had been attacked in the area adding to her worries. She calls upon Eliphas Leone to investigate, with the psychic convinced that the astral body of Professor Moreira is responsible. The Professor suddenly becomes quite popular, and the Duchess attempts a rendezvous. The following morning, however, she discovers that the culprit is really her butler, Vincente. He is not discharged.

Production Notes: Lothar's German play found great success in Berlin, but the first mention of it for Broadway in the *New York Times* on July 23, 1922, claimed an American production would be "impossible." While acknowledging *The Werewolf*'s brilliance, the rueful verdict came because of the "six seductions and no end of merry quips about rape and the like."

After a tryout in Stamford, Connecticut, on May 27, 1924, however, the Unger adaptation premiered in Chicago. The overt sexual nature of the play perhaps came as a moral affront to a few audience members, but — contrary to some histories — *The Werewolf* turned into an overnight success in the Windy City. The *Chicago Daily News* correctly realized that there would be "no lack of visitors when talk spreads that the work is a bit wicked." The popularity resulted in the *New York Times*' printing a review on June 8, 1924, even though the production was still in Illinois.

At the end of five prosperous weeks, the "most daring comedy of the season" left the Adelphi, beginning its Broadway run on August 26, 1924, with many of the same cast members. Among them was future movie star Leslie Howard. Critics noticed problems with the script, direction, and cast, but quickly pointed out the potential; the nature of its story titillated crowds just as it had in Chicago.

Lugosi saw few of the crowds laugh, as he left during the first week of production, certainly before June 7. Though he rehearsed the part prior to the opening, newspapers got word opening night that the Vincent Serrano would replace Lugosi shortly. Serrano finished the remainder of the Chicago run and then went to Broadway with the production.

Exactly why the replacement occurred is unknown. At least one major reviewer did not speak kindly of Lugosi, so perhaps his unsatisfactory performances during rehearsals led producer McClellan to move toward replacing him with his understudy. However, other newspapers like the *Chicago Evening Post* deemed his performance "exceedingly good." Perhaps Lugosi's troubles in New York City, with a disintegrating marriage and financial difficulties following a court case, made it necessary for him to leave the production and return to the East Coast.

176. *Arabesque*

Opening Night: October 20, 1925, at the National Theatre in New York City.

Cast: Victor Hammond (Ali), Conrad Cantzen (Baba Youssef), Kay McKay (Maroc), Anna Duncan (Dancing Girl), George Thornton (Abs, the Water Carrier), Jacob Kingsbury (Chief Bedouin), Hortense Alden (Laila, a Bedouine from the Desert), Boyd Davis (A Tall Bedouin, to Whom Belongs Laila), Curtis Cooksey (Ahmed Ben Tahar), Bela Lugosi (Sheik of Hammam, a Minor Official), Sara Sothern (M'na, the Pearl in a Bed of Oysters), Olive West (Mabouba, the Mother of the Pearl), Raphael Kados (Coppersmith), Julia Ralph (The Sheik's Mother, Who Would Live in Tunis), Yetta Malamude (Sheik's Aunt), Naoe Kondo (The Sheik's Sister), Helen Judson (Halima, the Professional Matchmaker), Etienne Girardot (Cald of Nadour).

Credits: A play in two acts and ten scenes by Cloyd Head and Eunice Tietjens. Music by Ruth White Warfield. Directed and designed by Norman Bel-Geddes. Produced by Norman Bel-Geddes and Richard Herndon.

Plot Summary: The sensuous Laila

seduces the Sheik of Hammam, who for the sake of policy is betrothed to the lovely M'na. The Sheik's plans become further troubled as Ahmed Ben Tahar desires M'na for his own wife. In the rivalry that follows, Ahmed wins the beautiful M'na's affections.

Production Notes: By finding suitable backing, Norman Bel-Geddes secured approximately $30,000 to spend on this production. Though he was famed as a designer, *Arabesque* marked his American debut as a dramatic director. Coproducer Herndon, who thought little of the story, persuaded Bel-Geddes to drop *Arabesque* and move on to another project. However, authors Eunice Tietjens and Cloyd Head offered to rewrite the play and convinced Herndon to go forward. Bel-Geddes began rehearsals in September, lasting some five weeks. Numerous rewrites occurred throughout the month.

The play then opened at the Teck Theatre in Buffalo on October 8, but some critics offered poor reviews, mentioning that the comedy-drama had little to distinguish it. Many thought the director spent too much time in rehearsals preparing the visuals—including an imaginative set change within full view of the audience—rather than on dramatic elements.

Bel-Geddes hoped to book the Century Theater in New York, but due to their impending Schubert musical he instead opted for the National Theatre on 43rd Street. For his elaborate set, the stage proved too small and the designer then tore out the first two rows of audience seats to extend it. The cast, including numerous extras, numbered over 50, with Kay McKay of *The Red Poppy* (1922) in a small role. After its first week in New York City, the play made under $10,000 at an admission price of $5.50. Its second week took something like $8,000. Notices generally praised the visuals, but denigrated the direction and plot. The play closed after 23 performances at the National, making for an expensive loss.

Even during rehearsals, trades referred to Lugosi as the "Hungarian Barrymore," with the first Buffalo reviews giving kind words to his performance. New York critics also offered generally favorable reports of Lugosi. Moreover, accounts of the play's rehearsals claim that Lugosi realized the lack of attention given to the dramatic line of the play and attempted to help. He and others gave inexperienced cast members advice, and attempted to convince Bel-Geddes that the plot was incoherent. As a result, the director placed more emphasis on the Sheik and Laila, making Lugosi's part a mere foil for M'na.

177. *Open House*

Opening Night: December 14, 1925, at Daly's Theater, New York.

Cast: Frank Martins (Lloyd Bellamy), Ramsey Wallace (Basil Underwood), Albert Andruss (Eugenia Bellamy), Helen MacKellar (Margaret), Eugenia Woodward (Harold), Janice Elgin (Amy), Guy Hitner (Dr. Roger Holt), Bela Lugosi (Sergius Chernoff), Jane Houston (Violet Raymond), Marie Kenrick (Miss Langdon), Robert W. Lawrence (Marsdom).

Credits: A play in three acts by Samuel R. Golding. Produced by Samuel R. Golding. Staged by Henry Stillman and Robert W. Lawrence.

Plot Summary: Lloyd Bellamy insists that his wife, Eugenia, use her charms to help his business. She protests but later agrees to help. However, Eugenia refuses to drop the affections of Russian Chernoff after he signs a contract and completes his business with Bellamy. The husband then accuses his wife of having an affair with Chernoff, and she confesses. She actually had remained pure and loyal to her husband, but by saying otherwise she brings Bellamy to realize the insult he brought upon her.

Production Notes: Golding produced his own stage play, with rehearsals in Fordham, New York, during November and December 1925, following brief performances in Long Branch, New Jersey, beginning October 22. Despite generally poor reviews, the melodrama ran for 73 performances in New

York City. The first week on Broadway took less than $5,000, and a reported $3,000 its third week. The production moved to the Criterion Theater on January 5, 1926, nabbing some $5,000, mainly due to a reduction in admission price.

On January 20, *Variety* mentioned that no cast members received pay, with the exception of Ramsey Wallace, who left the show. Producer Golding begged the remaining cast members to continue, promising to pay them for their prior two weeks of work. All agreed and the show continued. After nine weeks, the show finally closed on February 10, 1926. Though it took in over $5,000 each of its last three weeks, *Open House* proved unprofitable. During its entire run, only one favorable notice appeared in the major newspapers.

Lugosi again found himself cast as a foreigner with a thick accent and an eye for the opposite sex. Critics remembered the Hungarian from *Arabesque* (1925) and noted that he created an authentic performance for the generally clichéd role.

178. *The Devil in the Cheese*

Opening Night: December 29, 1926, at the Charles Hopkins Theater in New York City.

Cast: Fredric March (Jimmie Chard), Dwight Frye (Dr. Pointell Jones), Robert McWade (Joseph Quigley), Catherine Calhoun Doucet (Theodosia Quigley), Linda Watkins (Goldina Quigley), George Riddell (Chubbock), Bela Lugosi (Father Petros), Earl McDonald (Constantinos), Brandon Peters (Min).

Credits: A play in three acts by Tom Cushing. Settings by Norman Bel-Geddes. Staged and produced by Charles Hopkins.

Plot Summary: Mr. Quigley, an archaeologist, accepts Father Petros's suggestion to undertake a dig near an old monastery. He takes his family on the trip, specifically to get daughter Goldina away from Jimmie Chard, a suitor. The daughter rebels; Quigley is unable to understand her attitude. After eating a piece of cheese found along with an ancient vase at the dig, Quigley sees inside Goldina's mind to realize how much in love she really is. Upon waking, Quigley and the others are saved from bandits by Jimmie. The protective father then welcomes the young man to the family.

Production Notes: Though at first the 299-seat Charles Hopkins Theater played to less than capacity, by February 1927 crowds increased. In late April following its twelfth week, *The Devil in the Cheese* moved to the larger Plymouth Theater. During its last month, the play brought in grosses averaging $8,000 a week. *The Devil in the Cheese* closed after 14 weeks and 157 performances, mainly due to cast defections. Critics approved the cast and delighted at the visuals provided by Norman Bel-Geddes, but found the story overall to be awkard and even inept.

Fredric March, portraying the handsome young suitor to Linda Watkins, later became a popular movie star. The thespian took home Academy Awards for both *Dr. Jekyll and Mr. Hyde* (1932) and *The Best Years of Our Lives* (1946). Costar Dwight Frye also entered the cinema, with his most famed role coming as Renfield in *Dracula* (1931).

Lugosi took quite favorable reviews, with the *New York Times* noting that he was "worthy of better things" than Cushing's material. Alexander Woolcott in the *New York World* called Lugosi "excellent," though oddly the critic went on to mention "Miss Lugosi suggests a miniature Phyllis Povah, and that means to you whatever it means to you." The comment seems strange in view of the fact that—at the time of Woolcott's notice—Lugosi was not married.

179. *Dracula*

Opening Night: October 5, 1927, at the Fulton Theatre in New York City.

Cast: Nedda Harrigan (Miss Wells), Terence Neill (Jonathan Harker), Herbert Bunston (Dr. Seward), Edward Van Sloan (Abraham Van Helsing), Bernard Jukes (R.M. Renfield), Alfred Frith (Butterworth), Dorothy Peterson (Lucy Harker), Bela Lugosi (Dracula).

The Devil in the Cheese, on Broadway in December 1925, featured Lugosi as Father Petros.

Credits: A play in three acts, dramatized by Hamilton Deane and John Balderston. Based on the 1897 novel *Dracula,* by Bram Stoker. Produced by Horace Liveright. Staged by Ira Hards. Scenes by Joseph Physioc.

Plot Summary: Dr. Van Helsing suspects a vampire to be the cause of Lucy Harker's problems. He eventually discovers Count Dracula to be the unearthly creature and, after finding the grave, drives a stake through the corpse's heart.

Production Notes: Prior to opening on Broadway, *Dracula* previewed in Hartford, then at Sam Schubert's in New Haven, Connecticut, for September 19–21. Rather than Herbert Bunston, Clarence Derwert played Dr. Seward at both previews.

Though some patrons scoffed at her presence, a nurse stationed by Horace Liveright at the Fulton assisted fainting females in the audience. William Munster, house manager at the Fulton, refused to believe that the women genuinely passed out, but Liveright's office insisted the females were not plants. At any rate, advertisements proclaimed *Dracula* "New York's Newest Shudder."

Reviews varied, but almost all mentioned the play's ability to send shivers through audiences. The *New York Times* found Lugosi "a little too deliberate and confident," and the *New Yorker*'s lengthy review did not even mention the Hungarian's name. On the whole, however, audiences and critics admitted the strength of Lugosi's performance. Others in the cast took good notices as well. By March, however, Helen Mack took Nedda Harrigan's place as the maid. Various script changes, the temporary addition of a second maid, and a well-publicized "trick coffin"— which gave Dracula's body a chance to disappear into fog — were added later in the run as well.

In the end, *Dracula* lasted 33 weeks and 261 performances on Broadway before closing its curtain on May 19, 1928. An average week brought grosses of $13,000, though a few weeks slipped to figures of less than $10,000. *Dracula*'s final month grossed under $40,000.

Liveright supposedly auditioned Lugosi at the recommendation of director Jean D. Williams, who himself attempted to stage *Dracula* in the United States. Presumably Williams noticed Lugosi in *The Devil in the Cheese* (1926) and believed him the only actor capable of portraying the role. Though Williams himself never managed to produce *Dracula*, he crossed paths with Liveright in the summer of 1927 and suggested that the producer consider Lugosi.

Unlike Bram Stoker's description of Dracula and even prior stage versions, Lugosi became aristocratic, gentlemanly, romantic, and sexually charged through his depiction. Makeup added a slight green cast to his face and stage lighting illuminated his eyes for certain sequences. Lugosi's slicked hair and thick accent completed the character, which he would repeat in the 1931 film. The Hungarian gave birth to a cultural icon as a result of the stage play, forever changing the world's view of Dracula and vampires. For this, he reportedly made $100 a week.

In addition to Lugosi, Edward Van Sloan and Herbert Bunston repeated their roles for the 1931 Universal film. Bernard Jukes, the maniacal Renfield, had earlier appeared in a London stage version of *Dracula* and generally scored strong reviews for his portrayal. Though he again worked opposite Lugosi in a 1928 West Coast stage version, Universal Studios instead signed Dwight Frye for the 1931 film.

180. *Dracula*

Opening Night: June 24, 1928, at the Biltmore Theater in Los Angeles.

Cast: Marion Miller (Maid), Terrence Neill (Jonathan Harker), Richard Lancaster (Dr. Seward), Edward Van Sloan (Abraham Van Helsing), Bernard Jukes (R.M. Renfield), Carl Reed (Butterworth), Hazel Whitmore (Lucy Seward), Bela Lugosi (Count Dracula), Francesca Ratoli (Miss Wells)

Credits: A play in three acts, dramatized by Hamilton Deane and John Balderson. Based on Bram Stoker's 1897 novel *Dracula*. Produced and staged by O.D. Woodward.

Production Notes: For its West Coast tour, *Dracula* ran from June 24 to August 18 at the Biltmore in Los Angeles, August 20 to September 8 at San Francisco's Columbia Theater, and then from September 9 to 15 at Oakland's 12th Street Theater. Much publicity greeted the play in Los Angeles, with Hollywood celebrities in attendance at nearly every performance. The play grossed some $10,000 its first week, taking over $12,000 its second and third weeks. The remaining weeks dwindled somewhat, from approximately $10,000 its fourth week, to $9,500 its fourth, then down to $8,000 its seventh week, and $6,000 its final week.

Publicity claimed that the doorman and the much-needed nurse in attendance compiled the following figures for the first seven weeks of *Dracula*'s run at the Biltmore: 110 faintings, 20 shrieks (per performance), 19 left theater scared after the first act, 150 left after the second act, 100 returned after being revived, 10 audience members attended each performance, 10 wives per performance summoned husbands to escort them home, and taxicab use increased 500 percent. Los Angeles theater ads claimed *Dracula* to be "better than *The Gorilla* and *The Bat*," and pronounced the play "The Season's Best Shudder—One You Can't Shake Off."

San Francisco audiences and critics enjoyed *Dracula* as well, with producer Woodward again placing a nurse with smelling salts in the lobby. The play grossed some $14,000 its first week, $14,500 its second, and $12,000 its third. The play then moved for a single week to Oakland.

Much publicity surrounded Lugosi, who gave interviews that detailed why he thought *Dracula* would make a good film, what he thought of the American theater, and how vampires really existed in his homeland. During the Los Angeles leg of the tour, Lugosi met the "It Girl," Clara Bow, and also spent time with various Hungarian members of the film community. The Los Angeles performances also attracted the attention of producers at Fox Studios, with Lugosi soon appearing in such films as *The Veiled Woman* (1928).

181. *Dracula*

Opening Night: May 19, 1929, at the Music Box Theater in Los Angeles.

Cast: Donald Woods (Jonathan Harker), Henry Hall (Dr. Seward), J. Raymond Brown (Abraham Van Helsing), Harry Walker (Renfield), Frederick Pymm (Butterworth), Harriet George/Hazel Whitmore (Lucy Seward), Bela Lugosi (Count Dracula).

Credits: A play in three acts by Hamilton Deane and John Balderston. Based on the 1897 novel *Dracula* by Bram Stoker. Produced and staged by O.D. Woodward.

Production Notes: For its 1929 West Coast tour, *Dracula* played the Music Box Theater in Los Angeles from May 19 to June 9, then moved to the Columbia Theater in San Francisco from July 22 to August 10. *Dracula* next played the Fulton Theater in Oakland, where it opened August 11 and stayed for one week.

Harriet George's San Francisco replacement, Hazel Whitmore, took strong reviews in San Francisco, as did Henry Walker and Henry Hall. Frederick Pymm, who portrayed the title role in a Northern tour, became Butterworth for this edition of the play. The popularity of the play had not diminished, with one former senatorial candidate buying 30 tickets to a single Saturday performance for his party. For the Oakland engagement, newspapers mentioned that George would again essay Lucy Seward.

Between Los Angeles and San Francisco, *Dracula* played four performances in Santa Barbara June 13–15. Harriet George still appeared as Lucy, but Richard Lancaster replaced Henry Hall as Dr. Seward. Santa Barbara theaters had earlier tried to schedule Lugosi in *Dracula* during the summer of 1928, but to no avail.

One of the more notable incidents on the tour came during *Dracula*'s first week in San Francisco. When Dr. Seward clutched at the count's cloak, the vampire was to disappear, leaving a mere wisp of smoke. But the effect misfired one evening, with Lugosi left standing on stage. The actor covered the scene by staring intently at Dr. Seward until an electrician cut the lights. Dracula managed finally to disappear, thanks to the complete darkness.

Lugosi again gave numerous interviews, detailing the evil "Dracula kiss," explaining how many fan letters he received, giving an in-depth definition of a vampire, and even mentioning his thoughts on talking pictures. During the San Francisco leg of the tour, Lugosi married his third wife, Beatrice Woodruff Weeks.

182. *Murdered Alive*

Opening Night: April 2, 1932, at Los Angeles's Carthay Circle Theater.

Cast: Everette Brown (Fangh), Bela Lugosi (Dr. Orloff), Betty Ross Clarke (Sylvia Knight), Eily Nalyon (Mona), W.E. Watts (Professor Steiffitz), Bruce Craden (Bunny Strickland), Lew Kelly (Inspector Quirk), Rodney McLennon (Nicholas Rumsey), David Callis (Duffy).

Credits: A drama in three acts by Ralph Murphy and Helen Baxter. Presented by Arthur Greenville Collins.

Plot Summary: Dr. Orloff, an evil scientist and sculptor, lures men and women to his home, which featured traps, elevators, sliding panels, and secret doors. The mad doctor also spikes wine with embalming fluid, a mixture that leaves guests looking more marble than human. The equally menacing Professor Steiffitz helps create the diabolical potions. On the verge of being captured, Orloff even decapitates one victim; in the end, however, detectives manage to catch up to the crazed scientist.

Production Notes: Ralph Murphy and

Lugosi poses by a billboard for the Los Angeles production of *Murdered Alive* in 1932.

Helen Baxter partially based *Murdered Alive* on a real-life crime investigated by French police. Before its Los Angeles debut, the tale was produced without Lugosi in New York under the title *The Black Tower*.

For its opening night in Los Angeles, numerous celebrities turned out to witness Lugosi's performance. The well-received horror tale allowed actors to take six curtain calls. Critics gave Lugosi's portrayal favorable notices, with the press making much of the actor's continuing his performance after an error in backstage mechanics made him fall 16 feet and break three ribs. Newspapers further publicized the fact that Lugosi himself sculpted a bust of Dr. Orloff used in the production.

Despite disappointing grosses on its Carthay Circle run, the production moved to San Francisco's Orpheum Theater for the week of April 22–28, then returned to Los Angeles in a condensed form. The latter version opened at Los Angeles's Orpheum on April 30, staying until May 5. The theater advertised not just the stage production but also a screening of *The Cohens and Kellys in Hollywood* (1932). Reviewers again remarked on the gruesome nature of the tale, with one mentioning that "Satan himself couldn't think of anything more horrible."

Costar Betty Ross Clarke had appeared with Lugosi nine years before in the New York production *The Red Poppy* (1922), as well as in the 1932 film *Murders in the Rue Morgue*. A few cast changes apparently occurred between the two Los Angeles performances, with newspapers in late April citing such actors as Pat Flannigan who had not appeared in earlier cast listings.

183. *Dracula*

Opening Night: May 29, 1932, at the El Capitan Theatre in Portland, Oregon.

Cast: Norman Fusier (Van Helsing), Henry Hall (Dr. Seward), Marion Clayton (Lucy), Leon Waycoff (Jonathon Harker), Perry Ivins (Renfield), Ruth Lee (Miss Wells), Morry Foster (Butterworth), Bela Lugosi (Dracula).

Credits: Directed by Perry Ivins. Scenic effects by Matt Lermer.

Production Notes: Portland's El Capitan had just emerged from the remains of the Dufwin Theater, with *Dracula* being its second production. The play lasted from May 29 to June 5, 1932. Along with Lugosi in the title role, this version featured "resident El Capitan players," though Waycoff had just performed alongside the Hungarian in the 1932 Universal film, *Murders in the Rue Morgue*.

A publicity portrait for his role as Siebenkase in Earl Carroll's *Murder at the Vanities* of 1933.

Ads and newspaper publicity played up Lugosi's horror image, with one even wrongly claiming that his father was a count. Favorable reviews followed opening night, with the Hungarian's performance called "little short of perfect."

184. *Murder at the Vanities*
Opening Night: September 8, 1933, at the New Amsterdam Theater in New York.

Cast: Charles Ashley (Charles), Pauline Moore (Liane Ware), Frank Kingdon (Mr. Martin), Lew Eckles (Mr. Kerrick), James Rennie (Inspector Ellery), Noami Ray (Miss Jones), Amby Costello (Cornish), Al Webster (Manager), Walker Thornton (Officer Johnson), Billy House (Walter Buck), Beryl Wallace (Hope), Jean Adair (Madame Tangueray), William Fay (Biggies), Robert Cummings (Jack Purdy),

William Balfour (Noomhouse), Olga Baclanova (Sonya Sonya), Lisa Silbert (Hulda), Bela Lugosi (Siebenkase), Barbara Winchester (Scrubwoman), Ben Lackland (Billy Slade), Martha Pryor (Mrs. Forman), James Coughlin (Fred Bernie), Mickey Braatz (Doris), Villi Milli (Vila), Elsie Rossi (Elsie), Charles G. Johnson (Greeves), Helena Rapport (Scrubwoman), Edwin Vickery (Moore), F.X. Mahoney (Tom), Wiley Adams (Fred), Eileen Burns (Scrubwoman), Paul Sheridan (Winchester), Ben Lewis (Mack), F. Raymond (Williams), The Unseen Voice (Mildred Hunt), Al Lee (A Bostonian), Samuel Shaw (Another Bostonian), Woods Miller (Woods Miller), Una Vilon (Una Vilon), Mackie and Lavelle (The Blottos), Lewis and Van (The Dancers), Paul Garrish (The Skater).

Credits: A mystery-musical play by Rufus King and Earl Carroll. Songs by W. Green, Edward Heyman, and Richard Myers. Staged by Burk Symon, Chester Hale, and Stuart C. Whitman. Presented by Earl Carroll.

Plot Summary: During a *Vanities* performance, a murdered showgirl is discovered. Though the show goes on, Inspector Ellery and the entourage search backstage for clues. After some false leads and finding more bodies, they catch the culprit. A wardrobe lady committed the heinous crime in hopes of furthering her daughter's career.

Production Notes: Producer Earl Carroll achieved fame and fortune through his extravagant annual revues that spotlighted beautiful chorus girls. By 1933 his success had faltered somewhat, and he hoped *Murder at the Vanities* could solve his financial troubles. Trades mentioned such problems as a Mutual Life Insurance Company suit to foreclose on the Casino Theater in April, a house in which Carroll owned an interest. Unpaid taxes remained on the property as well. Throughout the summer, Carroll made many visits to court, including an attempted settlement with the United Scenic Artists. A previous Carroll production still owed members of the painters' union some $6,500, and as a result the artisans refused to begin work on *Murder at the Vanities*. Carroll's side initially likened the workers' actions to the unfortunate coal strike of the early thirties, with the producer eventually relying on less-than-lavish sable hangings and figured curtains.

Carroll's devotion to the play began in early 1933, and by March he requested numerous Hollywood agents to find film stars for the leading roles. Though unable to secure certain actors, the production signed Bela Lugosi, who left for New York on July 24 to begin rehearsals. Trades in August added actress Olga Baclanova's name to cast lists as well. Hollywood took an additional interest in Carroll's new play, with Paramount buying the screen treatment in mid–June.

Carroll previewed *Murder at the Vanities* on Philadelphia stages, with the September 5 *Variety* mentioning that critics panned the production. The tryout had opened at the Garrick Theater on August 28 and quickly closed for a rewrite. The revue opened in New York City shortly thereafter, with reviewers continuing to give bad notices. *Variety* prophesied a short run, which it claimed Paramount would probably appreciate. After all, the studio wanted to include Lugosi in its cast, but worried how it could if the stage *Vanities* became a hit and detained the Hungarian on the East Coast.

Despite the critics, however, the show took in generally good business, lasting in New York for 207 performances. The advertisements promised "the most beautiful girls in the world," which led the *New York Herald Tribune* to remark on the "shameless ladies" who "bared their secret charms." The reviewer claimed, "When Mr. Carroll gets a-going [with his scantily clad chorus girls], Minsky is a monk." By contrast, *Stage* magazine spoke of a 16-year-old audience member who thought Carroll's efforts were "child's play next to Minsky's [burlesque shows]" and that the *Vanities* were closer to a "Sunday School charade."

Lugosi received generally kind notices for his role, though apparently he did little more than skulk around looking mysterious. Ads usually billed him fourth, under James Rennie, Olga Baclanova, and Billy House. The Hungarian left the play in November, perhaps planning a return to the coast for the film version. As Paramount had instead cast another actor, Lugosi remained in New York for a vaudeville appearance. William Balfour stepped in to take his place in the stage version of *Vanities*, which by the end of 1933 switched theaters to New York's Majestic.

185. *Tovarich*

Opening Night: March 22, 1937, at the Curran Theatre of San Francisco.

Cast: Osgood Perkins (Prince Mikail Alexandrovitch Ouratief), Eugenie Leontovich (Archduchess Tatiana Petrovna), Fay Helm (Olga), Robert Long (Count Feodor Brekenski), Wedgewood Nowell (Chauffourier-Dubieff), Hans Herbert (Martelleau), Mary Forbes (Fernande Dupont), Melville Cooper (Charles Dupont), Marion Ballou (Louise the Cook), Bruce Campbell (Georges Dupont), Frances Reid (Helene Dupont), Peter Bronte (Concierge), Zoia de Groot (Madame Van Hemert), Meg Sheridan (Madame Chauffourier-Dubieff), Bela Lugosi (Commissar Gorotchenko).

Credits: A comedy-drama in two-acts by Jacques Deval. English adaptation by Robert E. Sherwood. Staged by Pete Mather. Produced by Homer Curran.

Production Notes: The American production of *Tovarich* began on October 15, 1936, though Lugosi only appeared in two Off Broadway runs, the first being in San Francisco from March 22 to April 17, 1937. The second came at Los Angeles's Biltmore Theater from April 19 to May 15, 1937. Eugenie Leontovich headlined the cast, coming from the crest of the British engagement of *Tovarich*, which lasted some 550 performances at London's Lyric Theater. Osgood Perkins, fresh from the New York Theater Guild, took a leading role as well, with Fay Helm, Lugosi's future costar in *The Wolf Man* (1941) and *Night Monster* (1942), appearing in a minor part as Olga.

Before the cast hit San Francisco, they performed a one-nighter in Pasadena to iron out the rough edges. Critics gave favorable notices, though a few mentioned rough spots in the final act. *Tovarich* maintained strong box office appeal throughout its stay in San Francisco, taking about $14,000 a week during the first half of its run. Heavy rains probably kept the first week's take from being even higher. The play closed its fourth and final week with receipts in the $12,000 range. March 25 became a particularly interesting show, with the Hungarian colony of San Francisco turning out to honor Lugosi. The Hungarian consul and his staff also attended, with Lugosi entertaining all his compatriots backstage following the performance. Though newspapers claimed the play could have easily continued its success in San Francisco, the Los Angeles engagement had already been booked.

Opening night in Los Angeles meant a parade of celebrities in the audience seats, including Cary Grant, Norma Shearer, Douglas Fairbanks, Marlene Dietrich, Claudette Colbert, Ginger Rogers, Madge Evans, and others. At $5 a ticket, the Biltmore brought in $4,200, making it the biggest opening night in the history of the house. After selling out, manager Peter Ermatinger removed the Russian band from the orchestra pit and placed them in a box, making room for an additional 40 seats. At $5.50 each, the improvised theater chairs sold out within 20 minutes. Advertisements claimed "all roads lead to one place tonight," meaning the Biltmore for its "gay comedy of Paris."

The first week in Los Angeles took in receipts totalling $18,000, the second week reached $15,000, the third week made $12,000, and the final week grossed $10,000. Film stars continued to pack the audience, and once again critics loved the production. May 12 became "Hungarian Night," with representatives of the Federation of

American-Hungarian Societies attending en masse to support Lugosi. Over 250 members crowded the theater in tribute to their fellow countryman, who hosted them backstage after the show ended.

Just as *Tovarich* delighted critics and crowds, Lugosi appeared to often thunderous applause in his nonhorror role. The play's program noted the "radical departure" the actor had made from the Hollywood chillers in his characterization of Gorotchenko. For interviews, Lugosi bid a fond farewell to Dracula, admitting how glad he was to appear in the play. The journalists also made clear that his Van Dyke was real, with Lugosi calling it much more "authentic" than an artificial beard.

Though the play continued into early 1938 at various U.S. theaters, Lugosi left after the Los Angeles performance. As movie work for the actor had become scarce, perhaps Lugosi jumped at the chance of *SOS Coastguard*, a Republic serial he signed for in June 1937.

186. Dracula

Opening Night: April 30, 1943, at the Klein Auditorium in Bridgeport, Connecticut.

Cast: Mary Stevenson (Miss Wells, Maid), Guy Spaull (Jonathan Harker), Wallace Widdecombe (Dr. Seward), Frank Jacquet (Abraham Van Helsing), Eduard Franz (R.M. Renfield), Len Mence (Butterworth), Janet Tyler (Lucy Seward), Bela Lugosi (Count Dracula).

Credits: Presented by Harry H. Oshrin. Directed by O.D. Woodward. Samuel H. Schwartz, Company Manager. Stage Manager, James Hagan. Scenery designed by H. Gordon Bennett. Electrical equipment by Broadway Stage Lighting Company. Properties by Theatrical Studios.

Production Notes: The 1943 tour of Dracula went from its opening in Bridgeport to the following dates:

The Bushnell Auditorium in Hartford, Connecticut, on May 1

The Plymouth Theatre in Boston, Massachusetts, on May 3–15

Camp Framingham, Massachusetts, on May 9

The Locust Theatre in Philadelphia, Pennsylvania, on May 19–29

Fort Meade, Maryland, on May 23

The Erlanger Theatre in Buffalo, New York, on May 31–June 5

The Hanna Theatre in Cleveland, Ohio, on June 7–13

The Nixon Theatre in Pittsburgh, Pennsylvania, on June 14–19

The National Theatre in Washington, D.C., on June 21–26

Critics generally pointed out that the play lacked its earlier ability to cause chills in the audience, though many still admitted the play had enough novelty to be fun. Others mentioned that supporting players seemed unable to remember their lines very well. Lugosi himself took favorable notices, with one reviewer crowning him the "monarch of all vampires." In Washington, D.C., newspapers actually did claim the play could still frighten theater patrons, adding that the Hungarian was "just tops."

In addition to the various theaters it played, the Lugosi cast performed for two military installations, Camp Framingham in Massachusetts and Fort Meade in Maryland. Surviving reviews show the play made a hit with troops, who generally had only one chance to see the play. The company took off a day from their paid engagements to stage *Dracula* at the bases.

By the appearance in Buffalo, actor Len Mence doubled as stage manager, while even further changes occurred by late June. For *Dracula*'s appearances in Cleveland, Pittsburgh, and Washington, D.C., Joy Nicholson took over as Miss Wells, Charles Francis essayed Dr. Seward, and Mary Heath became Lucy.

As far as its monetary success, *Dracula* took $9,000 its first week in Boston and still nabbed $8,400 its second week. The play made some $15,500 during its entire Philadelphia run, but the box office in

178   II. Lugosi, the Performer

A commonly used advertisement for Lugosi's 1943 stage tour of *Dracula*.

Buffalo took a disappointing $6,000 for its first week. Pittsburgh showed even a greater decline at $5,300, though trades blamed the poor results on the intense outdoor heat. *Dracula*'s final week brought in approximately $8,000 to Washington, D.C.'s National Theatre.

187. *Arsenic and Old Lace*

Opening Night: August 5, 1943, at the Tivoli Theatre in San Francisco.

Cast: Minna Phillips (Abby Brewster), P.J. Kelly (Reverend Harper), Herbert Corthell (Teddy Brewster), James Metcalfe (Officer Brophy), Howard H. Berman (Officer Klein), Ida Moore (Martha Brewster), Louise Arthur (Elaine Harper), Michael Whalen (Mortimer Brewster), Edward Colebrook (Mr. Gibbs), Bela Lugosi (Jonathan Brewster), Harry Sharpe (Dr. Einstein), Charles Jordan (Officer O'Hara), Frank Shannon (Lt. Rooney), Housley Stevens (Mr. Witherspoon).

Credits: A comedy by Joseph Kesselring. Produced by Joe Blumenfield, Robert Goodhoe, and Kline-Howard, Inc.

Plot Summary: Mortimer Brewster, while attempting to commit the insane Uncle Teddy to an asylum, plans to marry lovely Elaine. However, he discovers that Aunt Abby and Aunt Martha have been poisoning various boarders to put them out of their misery. In the midst of the confusion, the evil brother Jonathan arrives with sidekick Dr. Einstein. Jonathan, a murderer himself, finds he is one homicide short of his aunts' record. Eventually, Mortimer manages to work everything out and moves ahead with his new bride.

Production Notes: Lugosi's first appearance as Jonathan Brewster remained at San Francisco's Tivoli August 5–18, 1943, then moved to the Music Box Theater in Los Angeles for August 20–October 24. Lugosi, however, left the latter production during the week of September 22.

Newspapers in San Francisco mentioned the box office rush that met *Arsenic*, with columnists attributing partial success to Lugosi himself appearing on the city's stage. The Los Angeles run also brought in large crowds, taking $8,500 its first week and $8,300 its second.

Allegedly, producers tried to obtain Lugosi for the Jonathan Brewster role in 1941, but the actor turned them down. Boris Karloff had become a huge success on Broadway in the same role, and initially Lugosi did not want to step into a role that his fellow horror film actor had portrayed.

When he did take the part in 1943, however, Lugosi was glad he had never even viewed Karloff's performance, claiming that that helped him create an original side of Jonathan Brewster. Rehearsals lasted for two weeks prior to opening night in San Francisco. Later, during September, the actor found himself working at Columbia Studios in the daytime on *Return of the Vampire* (1943), then rushing to the Music Box in the evening for *Arsenic*.

Critics also seemed happy with the production, though the early days of the Tivoli run were marred by a few supporting actors who fumbled lines and electricians who had not yet learned their lighting cues. Most reviews offered favorable comments for Lugosi, suggesting that he was every bit the equal of Boris Karloff. In fact, producer Blumenfield hoped to put Lugosi on tour across the Pacific Coast in November of that year, but the actor bowed out.

188. *Arsenic and Old Lace*
Opening Night: January 29, 1944, at the Shrine Auditorium in Oklahoma City, Oklahoma.

Cast: Jean Adair (Abby Brewster), Malcolm Beggs (Teddy Brewster), Rutt McDevitt (Martha Brewster), Ann Lincoln (Elaine Harper), Jack Whiting (Mortimer Brewster), Bela Lugosi (Jonathan Brewster), Henry Sherwood (Dr. Einstein), Donald MacDonald (O'Hara).

Credits: A comedy play by Joseph Kesselring. Produced by Howard Lindsey and Russell Crouse.

Production Notes: On January 19, 1944, *Variety* announced Lugosi would assume Boris Karloff's role in the roadshow tour of *Arsenic and Old Lace*, with many believing grosses would drop as a result. However, the show maintained its box office, taking some $23,000 its first week. More than $5,000 came from an appearance in Tulsa. In a visit to Baltimore, the Lugosi version took $13,300, later grossing $12,500 in Boston and $13,000 for a week in Philadelphia. Producers actually noticed an upsurge of ticket sales in many cities when Lugosi headlined the cast. Several articles even noted a larger number of children attending the show than before, with journalists explaining that Lugosi was "one of their particular heroes." Some theaters postponed midweek matinees until 3:30, giving youngsters time to get from school to the theater.

Adults also flocked to the show en masse, with the fascination of Lugosi carrying over to those who had the chance to meet him in the flesh. Photographers in Oklahoma City snapped stills of him "terrorizing" a coffee shop cashier. A young actor in Allentown, Pennsylvania, approached Lugosi, with the elder thespian inviting his admirer to sit beside him at dinner. Diners at the Ritz Carlton received noticeable thrills when Lugosi lunched near them during his appearance in Boston, offering an occasional sinister look in their direction.

Local reviewers made the inevitable comparisons between Karloff and Lugosi, with some claiming the Hungarian lacked his predecessor's subtlety. Yet on the whole the critics praised his performance, and a number believed he outdid Karloff as Jonathan Brewster. Furthermore, crowds greatly appreciated the Hungarian, who lost 11 pounds after the grueling two months on the road.

The roadshow version of *Arsenic and Old Lace* maintained a rapid pace, traveling thoughout the Midwest and East Coast. The schedule left Oklahoma City and toured as follows:

 Convention Hall in Tulsa, Oklahoma, on January 30, 1944
 Robinson Auditorium in Little Rock, Arkansas, on February 1
 The Auditorium in Memphis, Tennessee, on February 2
 Ryman Auditorium in Nashville, Tennessee, on February 3
 The Temple in Birmingham, Alabama, on February 5
 The Municipal Auditorium in New Orleans, on February 7–8
 Lanier Auditorium in Montgomery, Alabama, on February 10
 The Erlanger in Atlanta, Georgia, on February 11–12
 The City Auditorium in Savannah, Georgia, on February 14–15
 The Auditorium in Augusta, Georgia, on February 16
 The Auditorium in Columbia, South Carolina, on February 17
 The Carolina Theater in Charlotte, North Carolina, on February 18
 The Auditorium in Asheville, North Carolina, on February 19
 The Carolina Theater in Greenville, South Carolina, on February 21
 The National Theater in Greensboro, North Carolina, on February 22
 The Carolina Theater in Durham, North Carolina, on February 24
 The State in Winston-Salem, North Carolina, on February 25
 Academy of Music in Roanoke, Virginia, on February 26
 Ford's Theater in Baltimore, Maryland, on February 27–March 3
 The Karlton Theater in Williamsport, Pennsylvania, on March 6
 The Lyric Theater in Allentown, Pennsylvania, on March 7
 The War Memorial Auditorium in Trenton, New Jersey, on March 8
 The Playhouse in Willington, Connecticut, on March 9–11
 The High School Auditorium in Pittsfield, Massachussetts, on March 16
 Memorial Auditorium in Worcester, Massachussetts, on March 17
 Bushnell Auditorium in Hartford, Connecticut, on March 18
 The Colonial Theater in Boston, on March 19–April 1
 The Locust Theater in Philadelphia, on April 9–22
 The Masque Theater in Newark, on April 23–30
 The Civic Theater in Syracuse, New York, on May 24–27
 The Kalaruh Temple in Binghampton, New York, on May 30–31
 The Erie Theater in Schenectady, New York, on June 2–3

189. *No Traveler Returns*

Opening Night: February 26, 1945, at San Francisco's Curran Theater.

Cast: Ann Ainslee (Bhemia, a Hindu Girl), Bela Lugosi (Bharat Singh, a Hindu Servant), George Pembroke (Abdul, a Mohammedan Servant), John Dawson (Gagoram, a Hindu), Harold Johnson (Balkrishna, a Hindu), Ian Keith (Colonel Durant O'Keefe of the Indian Medical Service), P.J. Kelly (Major Cecil Chatteris), Thayer Roberts (William Dane, Officiating Superintendent of the Police), Karen Venge (Audrey Chatteris), Hernrietta Burnside (Laura Parkinson).

Credits: A play in three acts by Richard Goddard. Staged by Rafael Noel. Settings by Edward Fornier. Produced by Ralph Kutsch and Leslie Thomas.

Plot Summary: Set in India, the tale of intrigue features Colonel O'Keefe, who by the third act turns out to less than noble. The essential heavy, Bharat Singh, outdoes O'Keefe through petty larceny, knifing, poisoning, and other crimes. Near the end of the play, the evil Singh dies from bullet wounds.

For both *Dracula* (1931) and *Abbott and Costello Meet Frankenstein* (1948), Lugosi wrested the role of Dracula from Ian Keith. With the ill-fated play *No Traveler Returns* in 1945, the two met on stage.

Production Notes: After a preview in Santa Barbara, *No Traveler Returns* played the Curran Theater of San Francisco from February 26 to March 9. From there, the cast moved to the Metropolitan Theater in Seattle for March 13–19. Publicity contended that writer Richard Gordon spent months in India, gathering mystic and occult information for the play. Ads and programs carried the tag line "The story of a strange obsession."

Reviewers heavily panned *No Traveler*

Returns, with one pronouncing the opening performance as "a saddening and disheartening experience." They considered the tale dull and predictable, and audiences must certainly have agreed. The week in San Francisco nabbed only $5,800, while the first week at Seattle's Metro took a meager $6,000. Management at the latter canceled the play only 6 days into its 12-day run. The cast disbanded after a tour to Chicago via Montana was canceled.

Critics claimed Lugosi merely gave a Dracula-style performance as the turbaned Bharat Singh. He did receive top billing alongside Ian Keith, one of several actors Universal Studios considered in 1930 for the title role in *Dracula* (1931). Costar George Pembroke had earlier appeared with Lugosi in the film *Black Dragons* (1942).

190. *Three Indelicate Ladies*
Opening Night: April 10, 1947, at the Schubert Theater in New Haven.
Cast: Jayn Fortner (Kelly), Elaine Stritch (Roberts), Joey Faye (Mr. Max), Ann Thomas (Morgan), Alexander Clark (Alfred Brook), Ray Walston (Sam Phelps), Jack Arnold (Joe the Heart), Bela Lugosi (Francis O'Rourke), Frances Brandt (Mrs. Henrietta Brook), Katherine Squire (Bernice Desos), Charles Mendick (Gus), Robert Schuler (Police Sergeant), Stratton Walling (Paul Astin).
Credits: A mystery farce in three acts by Hugh Evans. Produced by Hunt Stromberg, Jr., and Thomas Spengler (in association with Irving Cooper). Directed by Jessie Royce Landis. Setting and lighting by Stewart Chaney. Production associate, Thomas Elwell.
Plot Summary: Three women, the office staff of a deceased private detective, find themselves nearly bankrupt and thus run a blind ad soliciting clients. A murder takes place, and the trio become involved with Francis O'Rourke, a crook who falls in love with one of the girls and then "goes honest." Bodies fall out of closets and the murder count soars.
Production Notes: *Three Indelicate Ladies* stayed at the Schubert Theater from April 10 to 12, then moved to the Wilbur Theater in Boston for April 14–19. Hunt Stromberg told the press he had eyed the script for nine months and finally acquired the rights. Though critics mentioned numerous points that needed to be improved upon, *Three Indelicate Ladies* faced nothing of the wrath *No Traveler Returns* received. Publicity claimed the production was headed for Broadway, but it actually went no farther than Boston.

Reviewers offered kind words to Lugosi, though given that his character was Irish, they found him to be unusually cast. The actor received top billing and expressed relief to reporters at the chance to portray a comedic role.

191. *Arsenic and Old Lace*
Opening Night: June 30, 1947, at the Bucks County Playhouse in New Hope, Pennsylvania.
Cast: Bela Lugosi (Jonathan Brewster), Viola Roache and Dorothy Sands (the Brewster sisters), Walter Coy, Wallace Acton, Will Hare, Pam Gillespie, David Leland, Leslie Austin, Paul Lilly, Michael Barrett, Philip Tonge, and Harry Gribbon.
Credits: A comedy play by Joseph Kesselring. Staged by Don Hershey. Set design by S. Syrjala.
Production Notes: The New Hope run of *Arsenic and Old Lace* lasted one week, ending July 5. By June 25, Lugosi arrived in the city for rehearsals. The actor stayed at the Logan Inn and even put in a guest appearance at New Hope's state fair. Lugosi perhaps made a string of appearances in the New England area throughout the summer in this play, *Dracula*, or various other personal appearances.

192. *Dracula*
Opening Night: Early July 1947 at the Norwich Playhouse in Norwich, Connecticut.
Cast: Bela Lugosi (Dracula), Simon Oakland (Abraham Van Helsing), Dick Kiley (Jonathan Harker), others unknown.

Credits: Produced by Alden Wilkes and Herb Neeter.

Production Notes: Lugosi portrayed the title role in a full-length version of the play in Norwich, Connecticut, probably starting shortly after the conclusion of New Hope's *Arsenic and Old Lace*. That would place the show during the second week in July, just before he appeared in another version of *Dracula* at a Long Island theater. The appearance received no coverage in major publications that listed summer stock performances, and the city of Norwich has little archival material or newspapers to make clear the vague nature of the date.

The short run apparently broke local records and probably lasted six days. One of the more memorable anecdotes of this engagement claims Lugosi slept in the coffin prop at his hotel room, with the actor explaining it helped his back pains.

193. *Dracula*

Opening Night: July 14, 1947, at the John Drew Theater in East Hampton, Long Island.

Cast: Elizabeth Ross (Miss Wells), Frank Baxter (Jonathan Harker), Wallis Roberts (Dr. Seward), Bram Nossen (Abraham Van Helsing), Ray Walston (Renfield), Patrick McVey (Butterworth), Elaine Stritch (Lucy Seward), Bela Lugosi (Dracula).

Credits: Stage Manager, Fred Ross. Staged by Jerome Coray. Settings by Frederick Stover. Produced by Francis I. Curtis.

Production Notes: Unlike Lugosi's vaudeville versions of *Dracula*, the John Drew Theater hosted the full-length play, as it took place the same month in Norwich, Connecticut. *Dracula* remained at "America's most beautiful summer theater" until July 19, 1947.

194. *Dracula*

Opening Night: July 21, 1947, at the Boston Summer Theater in Boston, Massachusetts.

Cast: Gertrude Flynn (Miss Wells), Casey Walters (Bill Harker), Allan Tower (Dr. Seward), William Mendrek (Abraham Van Helsing), Robert Foster (R. M. Renfield), William Becker (Butterworth), Connie Morehead (Lucy Seward), Bela Lugosi (Dracula).

Credits: Presented by Lee Falk and John Huntington. Staged by Lee Falk. Setting by Matt Horner.

Production Notes: The Boston Summer Theater held this performance of Dracula at the New England Mutual Hall in Boston between July 21 and 26, 1947. Along with evening performances, the Wednesday and Saturday dates featured matinees.

Critics and audiences received the performances well enough, lauding Lugosi and Robert Foster. The *Boston Globe* did find more amusement from the story than fright, and mentioned that the updated script featured Dracula traveling to England by plane rather than ship.

195. *Dracula*

Opening Night: July 28, 1947, at the Cambridge Summer Theater in Cambridge, Massachusetts.

Cast: Gertrude Flynn (Miss Wells), Casey Walters (Bill Harker), Allan Tower (Dr. Seward), William Mendrek (Abraham Van Helsing), Robert Foster (R.M. Renfield), Bernard Kates (Butterworth), Connie Morehead (Lucy Seward), Bela Lugosi (Dracula).

Credits: Unknown.

Production Notes: Period sources give little information on this stock performance, though the Cambridge Summer Theater announced it shortly before Lugosi's appearance in Boston during the week of July 21, 1947. The cast, with the exception of Bernard Kates taking William Becker's role as Butterworth, remained the same from the previous week in Boston. The performance lasted from July 28 to August 2, 1947. Archival data unfortunately does not reveal the credits for the Cambridge appearance.

196. *Arsenic and Old Lace*

Opening Night: August 5, 1947, at the Spa Summer Theater in Saratoga Springs, New York.

Cast: Bela Lugosi (Jonathan Brewster), Lucia Seger (Abby Brewster), Clyde Waddell (Rev. Dr. Harper and Lieutenant Rooney), Ted Allegretti (Teddy Brewster), John Lupton (Officer Brophy), William Becker (Officer Klein), Judith Elder (Martha Brewster), Ruth Homond (Elaine Harper), Ford Rainey (Mortimer Brewster), John W. Brothers (Mr. Gibbs and Mr. Witherspoon), Bruce Adams (Dr. Einstein), Richard Boone (Officer O'Hara).
Credits: A comedy by Joseph Kesselring. Presented by John Huntington. Staged by Ford Rainey.
Production Notes: Initially, the Spa Summer Theater announced Lugosi would star in yet another version of *Dracula*, though for reasons unknown a switch was made to the popular Kesselring play. Critics noted generally strong perfomances, but at the same time chided the cast for not knowing their lines very well.

One review in the *Saratogian* gave the blame to Ford Rainey, saying, "Perhaps it is too much both to direct and play a major part in such a play." In a smaller part, Richard Boone — years before the *Have Gun Will Travel* television program — himself received an acceptable nod from critics.

Though the first review in Saratoga Springs' newspaper accused Lugosi of being the most guilty at fumbling lines, all notices pointed out his overall presence and skill as Jonathan Brewster. While in the area, Lugosi made an appearance on television in *Arsenic and Old Lace* and met with Robert Ripley of *Believe It or Not* fame.

197. *Dracula*
Opening Night: Summer stock, 1948.
Cast: Bela Lugosi (Dracula).
Credits: Unknown.
Production Notes: Lugosi reportedly turned up in numerous cities during the summer of 1948, appearing in full-length versions of *Dracula*. Lugosi's agent Don Marlowe recalled booking such cities as Green Bay, Wisconsin, and the Coronado Theatre in Rockford, Illinois. Though little information has come to light, it is not difficult to imagine that Lugosi made various one-week summer stock appearances at minor theaters. Certainly these performances would have been prior to his vaudeville tour in August of that year.

John Wulp designed the sets, with his memories helping to corroborate the reality of such appearances. In 1977 he mentioned that Lugosi knew his part so well that he did not usually rehearse with the other players. Wulp commented that the actor was one of the "strangest and most mysterious" he had ever met and remembered Lugosi saying, "You must not make fun of this play, because *Dracula* is my *Hamlet*."

198. *Arsenic and Old Lace*
Opening Night: August 9, 1948, at the Sea Cliff Summer Theater in Sea Cliff, New Jersey.
Cast: Bela Lugosi (Jonathan Brewster).
Production Notes: In another of his many summer stock appearances, Lugosi apparently met Richard and Alex Gordon during this production. They both became friends with the actor, later helping him in numerous professional situations. This particular version of *Arsenic and Old Lace* lasted until August 14.

199. *Arsenic and Old Lace*
Opening Night: July 11, 1949, at the Famous Artists Country Playhouse in Fayetteville, New York.
Cast: Bela Lugosi (Jonathan Brewster), John Larson (Mortimer Brewster), Catherine Cosgriff (Abby Brewster), Florence Beresford (Martha Brewster), Florenz Ames (Dr. Einstein), Helen Marcy (Elaine Harper), Tom Reynolds (Teddy Brewster), Carl Schmid (The Reverend Dr. Harper), Jack Kenny (Mr. Gibbs), Keith Burnett (Officer Brophy), David Yellin (Officer Klein), Rick Ricker (Officer O'Hara), Kenneth Bowles (Lieutenant Rooney), Gordon Alderman (Mr. Witherspoon).
Credits: A comedy by Joseph Kesselring. Directed by David Yellin. Playhouse Directors, Murray Bernthal and E.R. Vadebon-

conur. Managing Director, John Larson. Scenic Designer, John Blankenchip. Consultant, Paul Crabtree. Stage Manager, Burry Fredrik.

Production Notes: Lugosi's summer stock appearance at Fayetteville came during the first season of the Country Playhouse, which held the performances at the Fayetteville high school. The local Firemen's Association sponsored not just Lugosi's appearance but an entire "Famous Artists Series" that summer. *Arsenic and Old Lace* itself ran from July 11 to 16, with local newspapers printing large ads headlining "Dracula in the Flesh." Lugosi reportedly played another summer stock version of the same play in St. Louis, Missouri, during 1950, but no corroborating evidence can be found to support it.

200. *The Devil Also Dreams*

Opening Night: July 24, 1950, at the Somerset Summer Theater in Somerset, Massachusetts.

Cast: Claire Luce (Effie), Francis L. Sullivan (Quill), Bela Lugosi (Alexander Martin Petofy), Richard Waring (Bernard), Oswald Marshall (Dr. Woodruff).

Credits: A comedy melodrama by Fritz Rotter and Elissa Rohn. Staged by Reginald Denham. Presented by H. Clay Blaney and C. Peter Jaeger. General Manager, Lester Al Smith. Stage Manager, Ray Parker.

Plot Summary: Quill, a famous playwright, finds himself on a losing streak, and actress Effie returns his affections only when his plays become hits. The playwright plans to steal the work of the unknown Bernard and pass it as his own. Quill later even decides to poison the obscure author after Effie falls in love with him. However, the inept butler Petofy uncovers the murderous plot.

Production Notes: *The Devil Also Dreams* made its world premiere in Somerset, staying July 24–29, 1950. From there the play followed the following schedule:

Famous Artists Country Playhouse in Rochester on July 31–August 5

The Country Playhouse in Fayetteville, New York, on August 7–12

The Royal Alexandria Theatre in Toronto on August 14–19

The Capitol Theatre in Montreal on August 21–26

Producers signed Lugosi in June 1950 after having first considered the actor during May. They also hoped to secure either Angela Lansbury or Alexis Smith for the female lead, which eventually went to Clare Luce. Sullivan, Luce, Lugosi, and Waring took equal star billing in the final production. Rehearsals began July 1, 1950.

Lugosi himself enjoyed the nonhorror role, mentioning it in nearly every interview he gave. Reviewers found him animated, humorous, and delightful as the nutty butler who believes himself an actor. His character quoted Shakespeare and remarked at how much more rich the Bard's words became in Hungarian. Critics mentioned the excitement of hearing the actor speak lines from *Hamlet* in his native language.

Box office receipts of $6,200 in Toronto proved disappointing, as did $4,500 in Montreal. Critics generally enjoyed the performances and the story idea, but often suggested that the script needed severe rewrites. Authors Rotter and Rohn trekked to Toronto to do just that, but problems arose. By September 1, trades mentioned that Francis L. Sullivan and Clare Luce were in New York looking for new vehicles. Producer Blaney hoped to recast the roles and move *The Devil Also Dreams* through Boston and Philadelphia on the way to Broadway opening in September. The play never made it; the entire production folded.

201. *Dracula*

Opening Night: April 30, 1951, at the Royal Theatre in Brighton, England.

Cast: Joan Winmill (Mary Wells), Richard Butler (Jonathan Harker), David Dawson (Dr. Seward), Arthur Hosking (Van Helsing), Eric Lindsay (Renfield), John Saunders (Butterworth), Sheila Wynn

(Lucy Seward), Bela Lugosi (Count Dracula).

Credits: Presented by John C. Mather and W.H. Williams on behalf of Chartres Productions Ltd. Production and lighting by Richard Eastham. Stage director, Thomas Muschamp. Stage Manager, Janet Gray. Decor by Bertram Tyrer.

Production Notes: *Dracula* moved from Brighton to Lewisham's Hippodrome by the second week in May, then to the Golders Green Hippodrome for a week beginning May 14, then to the Dudley Hippodrome by the end of the month. The company then toured Scotland for part of the following month, premiering at the King's Theatre in Glasgow on June 18. By mid–July, the company performed at the Manchester Hippodrome, Leicester for the week of July 30, the Alma in Luton for the week of August 20, and the Lyceum in Sheffield the second week of September. As the company toured provincial areas in Britain and Scotland, it is very safe to assume the production played additional theaters.

Lugosi and his wife, Lillian, traveled to England on the *Mauritania*, reaching London the morning of April 11. For the early part of his visit, the actor found himself surrounded by the press, giving multiple interviews. Among numerous stories and jokes, newspapers also heard that the play had been updated to the present day for the British tour. Count Dracula now flew to Heathrow airport with his six boxes of earth, rather than traveling by ship as he had in earlier productions.

Critical reactions were mixed, though the play received encouraging notices in Brighton. However, both reviewers and audiences observed amateurish acting among some supporting players, as well breaking into giggles at moments that years before inspired chills. Despite such responses, Eastham maintained the publicity ploy of keeping a nurse in attendance.

Over three months of touring found multiple cast changes. For much of the tour, Joan Harding rather than Joan Winmill played Mary Wells, and by mid–August Ralph Wilson took over Hosking's role as Van Helsing. During at least part of July, John Martin portrayed Harker, though by August 20 Richard Butler resumed his place in the role.

202. *Arsenic and Old Lace*

Opening Night: January 19, 1954, at the Empress Playhouse in St. Louis.

Cast: Ruth Hermansen (Abby Brewster), Velma Royton (Martha Brewster), Gordon Peters (Teddy Brewster), Ken McEwen (Mortimer Brewster), Gena Bantle (Elaine Harper), Vincent Vernon (Officer O'Hara), Don Lochner (Dr. Einstein), Bela Lugosi (Jonathan Brewster).

Credits: Unknown.

Production Notes: The Empress Playhouse presented the full-length play with Lugosi, as always, in the Jonathan Brewster role. Ads touted the fact that *Arsenic and Old Lace* had lasted for three years on Broadway, with local newspapers interviewing "this Dracula ... who looks more like a banker ... or a statesman." Box office receipts totaled $11,000 for the week's performance, with the production ending on January 25.

203. *The Devil's Paradise*

Opening Night: June 8, 1956, at Hollywood's Troupers Green Room.

Cast: Bela Lugosi (as an international drug smuggler), Anthony Thomas, Pat Rogan, Howard Amacker, Sally Jones, Eleanor Ames, Margo Strange, Leo Como, Linda Phillips, Kid Mitchell, Marilyn Marshall, Jackie Mandell, Jacky Superata, Carlos Gomez, Paphy Manning, Jeff Hodges, Nancy Mathews, Richard Engriquez, Marilyn Zack, Duane Puett, Judy Lake, Bill Lamm, Helen Scott, Don Wilson, Dorothy Lloyd, John Wardy, Evelyn Bunn. Additional singing and dancing staged by Miss G. Boucher's groups.

Credits: Produced and directed by James B. Leong. Players furnished by C.A.S.T. Assistant Director, Mary Daugherty.

Plot Summary: An advance program/handbill for the play offered the following information: "A dramatic play written for teenagers and adult audiences. Two girls saved and one girl sold her soul to the devil. The story deals with the methods of how the vast international underworld recruit [*sic*] the wholesale distributors for distribution of narcotics in the United States. It then takes you behind the scene — gives you the background — their methods of recruting the teenagers as prospective victims. Touching every home and family. What are you doing to prevent it?"

Production Notes: *The Devil's Paradise* was staged only three times, beginning on Friday evening, June 8. The next day featured a matinee and then one final evening performance. Trades ignored the production, with no reviews surfacing in the major newspapers. Publicity encouraged audiences to meet the actor following the curtain call.

8. Vaudeville and Live Appearances

In addition to his "legit" stage work, Lugosi made numerous vaudeville appearances across the United States, ranging from big-budget acts at New York theaters to very minor appearances with various "spook shows." Trade publications often did not list his routes, with the overall history of vaudeville being one that lacks proper documentation. By the late forties and into the fifties, the Hungarian definitely traveled more routes than are currently known, though the nature of the act itself changed little over the years. His wife, Lillian, remembered that most acts through the forties contained an excerpt of the *Dracula* stage play; by the following decade, the act was transformed into a variation of the "spook show" that Bill Neff and others popularized in the nation's movie theaters. Almost every situation capitalized on Lugosi's association with Bram Stoker's vampire.

While this listing contains his most important appearances, others remain unverified or simply unknown. For example, one of Lugosi's friends recalled his making a promotional tour of Europe in 1928. Memories of those who knew him usually include vague data, such as supposed "spring and summer" vaudeville tours in 1944, with no indication as to cities and dates. Other oral histories and even a few notices in Hollywood publications place him in vaudeville acts that simply do not hold up under the examination of primary sources like the newspapers of individual cities.

For example, trades claimed Lugosi appeared in a San Diego comedy act in the early fifties; archival materials in that city cannot confirm the performance. Conversely, there is little doubt that especially in the late forties — particularly near the dates of known appearances — the actor played many other theaters than what are catalogued in this listing.

In addition to such vaudeville acts, Lugosi's major public appearances at movie premieres, important social gatherings, civic events, and wartime rallies are chronicled as well. In the case of movie premieres, for example, he supposedly appeared with director Tod Browning at Grauman's Egyptian on December 4, 1929, but no known source verifies his actual attendance.

Certainly many more personal appearances occurred, though a large number are at this point lost to history. As an avid supporter of efforts during World War II to help free Hungary from Fascist elements, Lugosi also definitely made more speeches than listed.

1. The Apollo Theater of Budapest
On March 28, 1919, Lugosi gave a speech at this against the problems Hungary's artistic community faced. Three days later he appeared at the same theater for a protest march.

2. Screening of the Spanish-language *Dracula*
On January 10, 1931, Lugosi appeared at a Universal Studios screening of the Spanish-language *Dracula* (1931), reportedly claiming the film was "beautiful, great, splendid."

3. *Dracula*
In late November 1933 New York City newspapers announced Lugosi's availability as a vaudeville act, and as a result Loew's State soon booked the actor. Lugosi appeared as the featured vaudevillian starting December 5 in an 18-minute capsule version of *Dracula*. The excerpts included Dracula's first meeting with Mina and the tale's climax. Afterward, Lugosi slipped out of character into a comedic curtain speech. Reviews claimed the act superior to that of many Hollywood stars, but bestowed few kind words on his costars.

The Lugosi act appeared alongside the Paul Muni film *The World Changes* (1933), Alex Hyde's orchestra, Ruth Brent and the Four Rhythm Queens, singers Al Wohlman and Harry Carroll, a gymnastic group called the Five Gay Boys, and several comics. Lew Parker, one of the latter group, followed Lugosi and built a few jokes around the vampire act.

Following the Loew's State appearance, Lugosi played the Loew's Stanley in Baltimore December 16–19, then Loew's Fox Theater in Washington, D.C., December 22–28, 1933. For the Fox Theater, the Lugosi act even performed on Christmas day.

It is possible that a similar act took place earlier the same year on the West Coast. In her later years, actress Carroll Borland spoke fondly of having worked with Lugosi in *Dracula* on stage. She initially mentioned that such appearances took place prior to the release of the 1931 vampire film. However, a letter that surfaced in her scrapbooks from Lugosi asking her to join his troupe is dated November 1932. The two cities she remembered on the "tour" were San Francisco and Santa Barbara. However, newspapers and archives in those areas offer no collaborative information. Her memories and one tangible letter remain in support of some kind of appearance; many scholars, however, have since begun to doubt the validity of her tales. Thus, if she indeed was on stage with the actor, it is possible that it was a less-promoted vaudeville performance of the type he performed on the East Coast.

4. Hungarian Artists' Ball
On February 10, 1934, Lugosi appeared as guest of honor at this New York City function held at the prestigious Pennsylvania Hotel.

5. *Black Cat* contest
More than 500 cats paraded during this 1934 contest held at Universal Studios, with the winning feline receiving an award and a contract to appear in *The Black Cat* (1934).

6. *The Black Cat* premiere
On May 3, 1934, Lugosi, along with Boris Karloff and Jacqueline Wells, made a live appearance at the Hollywood Pantages for this premiere of the Universal film.

7. Los Angeles Police Department presentation
At an official meeting in late 1934, Mayor Shaw presented Lugosi with a badge as reserve captain in the police force. "Civic-mindedness is one of the finer attributes of every American, and civic leadership a Democratic quality which has been a bulwark of this great nation's present strength," Shaw said at the presentation. The mayor continued to cite the award as a result of Lugosi's "splendid leadership of the Los Angeles colony of Hungarians, honorable citizens, who have come from your native land."

8. San Diego Exposition

On May 29, 1935, newsreel cameramen captured Lugosi's live act at this California exposition, which featured him "filming a scene" at the Hollywood Pavillion in a mock-up movie set. Other stars at the expo included Warren William, James Gleason, Francis Lederer, Thelma Todd, Lee Tracy, Ralph Morgan, and Robert Young.

9. Premiere of *The Raven*

Lugosi arrived in New York City at the beginning of July 1935, taking an on-stage bow at the Roxy Theater's Fourth of July premiere of *The Raven* (1935).

10. Max Factor Building

Lugosi and numerous other celebrities turned out for the grand opening of this site in November 1935, located at 1666 Highland Avenue in Hollywood. The exact building remained a Max Factor museum until 1996, and included a Lugosi autograph from his appearance that day.

11. American Syrian Society fundraiser

In the midthirties, Lugosi appeared at the Mayan Theater to help raise money for this society.

12. *Tovarich* Day at the Tanforan Racetrack

On April 1, 1937, the Tanforan Racetrack in San Francisco honored Lugosi and the stars of the *Tovarich* touring company. As well as declaring the event "*Tovarich* Day," the Tanforan titled each race after a cast member's name.

13. Regina Theater live appearances

Since the Beverly Hills' Regina scored tremendous success in 1938 with a triple-bill reissue of *Dracula* (1931), *Frankenstein* (1931), and *Son of Kong* (1933), the management contacted a down-and-out Lugosi to make live appearances with the films. The actor took the stage at 10:00 P.M. daily, though the exact dates are unclear, as the Regina's huge crowds gave them little reason to do extensive advertising. The *Hollywood Reporter* first mentioned Lugosi's appearance in its August 11 edition, and one Regina ad on August 19 claimed the actor would continue with the films for another week.

Trades also reported that Lugosi would make a West Coast tour with the horror films, then hit theaters across the rest of the country. While very probably he appeared at theaters after the Regina date, it is unclear when and where such personal appearances took place. As studios soon wished again to place Lugosi in films, his "tour" would most likely have been relatively short.

14. On Stage with Hamilton Deane

As Hamilton Deane appeared as *Dracula* on a West End stage in London, British producers filmed *The Dark Eyes of London* with Lugosi. Sometime during the first two weeks of April 1939, Lugosi attended Deane's performance, appearing on stage with the actor following the play. As Deane reached to shake the Hungarian's hand, he instead found himself in an embrace with the silver screen's Dracula.

15. *Stardust Cavalcade*

Opening Night: Dayton Ohio's Colonial Theater on March 30, 1940.

Cast: Ed Sullivan, Arthur Treacher, Bela Lugosi, Marjorie Weaver, Helen Parrish, Douglas McPhail, Betty Jaynes, Vivian Fay, Peg Leg Bates.

Credits: Presented by Ed Sullivan.

Production Notes: After Sullivan's *Stardust Cavalcade* opened in Dayton to run March 30–April 3, 1940, the company traveled the following dates:

The Stanley Theater in Pittsburgh, Pennsylvania, on April 4–11
The Stanley Theater in Hartford, Connecticut, on April 12–15
The State Theater in New York on April 18–24
The Capitol Theater in Washington, D.C., on April 26–May 2

Sullivan, at the time known primarily as a columnist, wanted to include actress Jean Parker and actor Lon Chaney, Jr., in the unit, but neither signed a contract. Furthermore, famed African American dancer Peg Leg Bates merely appeared alongside the *Cavalcade* in Dayton, though the following week found him incorporated into Sullivan's show. In each of its appearances, *Stardust Cavalcade* played movie theaters, billed with popular new films.

After an opening act by Bates (performing such numbers as *Rhythm on the Peg*), Betty Jaynes and Douglas McPhail sang duets of such tunes as *Where or When* and *Indian Love Call*. Arthur Treacher entered from the audience seats to exchange banter with Sullivan, as well as to point out his disbelief in "bogeymen." Lugosi then entered to "convince" his costar and meekly request an autograph, while all three later crooned *Ragtime Cowboy Joe*. Vivian Fay performed a toe dance, with Helen Parrish, Betty Jaynes, and Marjorie Evans teaming up to warble *Wives of the Horror Men*. The tune, set to the music of *Oh Johnny*, again brought Lugosi to the stage.

Along with acting as master of ceremonies, Ed Sullivan narrated a film compilation of silent stars before bringing everyone back to the stage for a finale. The last act began with each star wearing the disguise of his or her favorite celebrity (with Lugosi donning a Frankenstein monster mask), though later in its run the artists instead spoke of what they would like to do professionally outside of their present activities. The overall order of events varied from date to date, with a planned opening at Indianapolis's Lyric on March 22 apparently canceled.

Along with generally kind words from critics, *Stardust Cavalcade* played to large audiences. For example, the show grossed $17,000 in Pittsburgh and $18,000 in Washington, D.C. The unit itself cost Sullivan approximately $7,500 a week. The troupe found great attention everywhere it went, including a cocktail party at New York's Carlton on April 25.

Toward the end of its Pittsburgh run, *Stardust Cavalcade* went on without Lugosi for two days, due to the actor's illness. He took favorable reviews overall, with at least one critic suggesting the actor be given a monologue/solo act of his own. The May 22, 1940, *Variety* reported Lugosi's return to Hollywood.

16. Speech at the Hungaria House

Lugosi gave a speech at the inauguration of the Los Angeles Hungaria House on Washington Boulevard, which the *Californiai Magyarsag* reprinted on September 28, 1940. The actor spoke of his dedication to Hungary and his duty to attend Hungarian-sponsored events in the United States.

17. *You'll Find Out* preview

By November 20, 1940, trades reported that Lugosi, along with Boris Karloff and Helen Parrish, attended a premiere of their RKO film. Rather than the New York premiere on November 14, this seems to have been a preview in the Los Angeles area.

18. *One Night of Horror*

For the world premiere of *Invisible Ghost* (1941), Lugosi appeared in a live act at Chicago's Oriental Theater for the week of May 2–8, 1941. *One Night of Horror* became a "shock and shudder show," with a "cast of thirty-three" that headlined the bill. The Oriental featured six other acts as well, including Stuart and Taylor, Marie Bartell and Company, the Youngman Sisters, Zoe Kennedy, and Diane Moore. Ads featured artwork of Lugosi from *Dracula* and *White Zombie*, with each adding the name of Bram Stoker's vampire for the Hungarian's middle name.

19. Wartime appearances at Defense Plants

Special Services officer Buddy Hyde organized World War II tours in which stars appeared at West Coast plants to bolster workers' spirits and enthusiasm. Lugosi appeared on numerous occasions, one time reportedly stealing the show from comedian Eddie Cantor and others on the bill.

For the week of May 2–8, 1941, Lugosi appeared in a live stage show called *One Night of Horror*. The act coincided with the "world premiere" of Monogram's new Lugosi chiller, *Invisible Ghost* (1941).

20. Anti-Nazi Rally at the Riverside Breakfast Club

Lugosi gave the keynote address at this World War II rally in Los Angeles, delivering his speech in Hungarian. Despite the fact that many in the audience could not even understand the language, crowds cheered his appearance and passionate rhetoric. The exact date of the speech is unknown.

21. *Ghost of Frankenstein* cast tour

Universal concocted a short cast tour to promote its fourth Frankenstein film, with

Lugosi and Evelyn Ankers taking to the road in March 1942.

22. American Hungarian Defense Federation rally
Lugosi headlined this 1943 bond rally, with 10,000 Hungarians in attendance. The crowds purchased some $65,000 in war bonds, donated $1,600 to the Red Cross, and equipped an ambulance for wartime action.

23. Action to Liberate Hungary mass meeting
Lugosi spoke at this afternoon "mass meeting" in New York on April 23, 1944, along with Congressman Emanuel Celler, Rabbi Steven Wise, Reverend Géza Takaró, Antal Balásy, Professor Oscar Jaszi, and Professor Vámbéry Rustem. The famed opera star Margaret Bokor appeared as "guest singer."

24. Loew's Melba Theatre
Maria Rigo told historian Forrest J Ackerman of Lugosi's appearance at this Brooklyn theater in 1946. The actor performed a capsule version of *Dracula*, then even claimed he would come into the audience to "get some blood." After the audience screamed, Lugosi laughed and went off stage.

25. Spook Show
The January 22, 1947, edition of *Variety* claimed agent Irving Yates was agenting an entire Lugosi show, asking $7,500 a week of potential theaters. San Diego would first witness the act, with the unit breaking in a two-day stand at the Orpheum starting February 7. The show must have been short-lived, as by February 19, *Variety* mentioned Lugosi on his way from Los Angeles to New York, with the actor starting in rehearsals for *Three Indelicate Ladies* on March 19.

26. *A Nightmare of Horror*
For February 7–8, 1947, Lugosi appeared at San Diego's Orpheum Theater in a skit called *A Nightmare of Horror*. An article in the San Diego Union carried Lugosi's promise that "Dracula will turn into a bat and that he will hold a fiesta with Frankenstein up and down the aisles of the theater." The show started each evening at the "stroke of 12," with Lugosi advertised as "Dracula the Batman." The "spine twisting" performance offered a live "Frankenstein the Mad Monster" as a second-billed attraction.

27. Boston University lecture
In 1947, while headlining *Three Indelicate Ladies*, Lugosi gave a lecture on abnormal psychology to students of Boston University's College of Practical Arts and Letters. Newspaper coverage mentioned that the actor's April 17 talk would offer his observations on criminology.

28. New Hope, Pennsylvania, State Fair
While portraying Jonathan Brewster in a New Hope, Pennsylvania, revival of *Arsenic and Old Lace*, Lugosi made a guest appearance at the state fair on July 3, 1947.

29. Cocktails aboard the *Mon Lei* with Robert Ripley
During an August 1947 summer stock run of *Arsenic and Old Lace* in Saratoga Springs, New York, Lugosi attended a well-publicized cocktail party with columnist Robert L. Ripley. The "Believe It or Not" creator docked a Chinese junk—the *Mon Lei*—some 15 miles from Albany, where three Civil Air Patrol planes welcomed him on the morning of August 8. Local newspapers invited members of the Albany Yacht Club to welcome the famed adventurer. After lunch that same day, Ripley broadcast his daily radio show from the junk, with the cocktail party itself beginning at 4:30. Lugosi promised newspaper reporters that he had some "Believe It or Not oddities" of his own to share with Ripley, communicated to him from "another world."

30. *Bill Neff's Madhouse of Mystery*
Lugosi definitely toured with Neff's

194   II. Lugosi, the Performer

Shaking hands with an unknown acquaintance against advertisements of a World War II rally in which Lugosi may well have participated.

popular spook show, appearing during the 1947 season at various movie theaters. Yet, given the actor's activities during the earlier part of the year, most likely his association with Neff came during the autumn months.

31. *The Tell-Tale Heart*

Opening Night: November 19, 1947.
Cast: Bela Lugosi.
Credits: Written and produced by Don Marlowe. Based on the short story by Edgar Allan Poe.
Production Notes: Don Marlowe, Lugosi's manager in the late forties, printed posters and sent out press releases for this production. Advertisements read, "The Screen's Master of Horror — In Person!" while also promising crowds a full-length Lugosi film. A notice in a November 1, 1947, *Motion Picture Herald* announced *The Tell-Tale Heart* as a personal appearance tour, mentioning that the shows would begin at midnight. While a lack of substantial information, such as exact playdates, has led some historians to question whether the tour ever took place, at least one audience member recalled Lugosi performing *The Tell-Tale Heart* in New Jersey as a monologue.

Marlowe wrote the script, adapting the story to a modern setting. The agent also claimed to have played a drum backstage each night to reproduce the sound of a heartbeat. Lugosi and Marlowe definitely signed a contract, which guaranteed the Hungarian $1,000 a week against 10 percent of the top gross, as well as transportation from New York to the engagements. The contract further stipulated that the agent would provide Lugosi return transportation to his choice of New York or

8. Vaudeville and Live Appearances   195

Offering a spooky look for the cameras while making a guest appearance on July 3, 1947, at the New Hope State Fair in Pennsylvania.

California, and would pick up the tab for all hotel rooms along the way. The two signed the contract on November 1, with the engagements to begin on November 19, 1947.

If *The Tell-Tale Heart* played many theaters, most likely they were very minor, as the trades printed no further information on the tale. Marlowe's book *The Hollywood That Was* (Branch Smith, 1974) claims the adaptation ran 40 minutes and played alongside a reissue of the film *Dracula*

(1931). Furthermore, his writings do indicate that the performances took place in second-rate, insignificant locations.

The agent's memoirs also recount an evening in which the drum-beating Marlowe accidentally fell from backstage into full view of the audience. Lugosi supposedly slipped out of character long enough to introduce theatergoers to his agent, then proceeded with the drama as if nothing had happened.

32. *Abbott and Costello Meet Frankenstein* promotional tour

Lugosi definitely appeared on a promotional tour for this 1948 Universal film, though no exact playdates are known. Very probably the "tour" could have meant taking a quick bow at a handful of theaters screening the film.

33. Bela Lugosi Company vaudeville tour

For this short tour, Lugosi first appeared during the week of August 20–26, 1948, at the Broadway-Capitol Theater in Detroit on a bill with Rose Murphy, Harry Babbit, Barney Grant, and the Four Evans Whirlwind Dancers. Lugosi's act found him engaging in a bit of small talk and then re-enacting a scene from *Dracula*. Reviewers claimed his effort to be more humorous than horrifying.

The Olympia Theater in Miami next hosted the act, publicizing it as the "Bela Lugosi Company." Beginning September 1, the Lugosi group remained on the bill for one week, headlining with comedienne Ada Lynn, Tato and Julio, Johnny Woods, and the Levernes. Again, critics pointed out that the Lugosi *Dracula* routine inspired more giggles than shrieks.

On September 22, *Variety* reported the act booked at Atlantic City's Steel Pier, with Marilyn Frechette, Sonny Sparks, the Four Elgins, and Pansy the Horse. The next and last mention of the group came on October 20, with the company slated for the Valley Arena in Holyoke. Also on the bill would be Helene and Howard, the Dewey Sisters, Barney Grant, and the Gene Krupa Orchestra.

Advertisements for the act generally gave Lugosi top billing, with the name "Dracula" often above the Hungarian's. Biographer Arthur Lennig recalled seeing Lugosi on October 29, 1948, at the Manhasset Theatre in New York with comedian Sonny Sparks, so perhaps the act continued at lesser theaters in some form with trades no longer even printing the route.

34. Bela Lugosi Company

The November 16, 1949, *Variety* announced that the Fox Theater in St. Louis booked the Lugosi Company on a bill with the Four Stamps, Bredice and Olson, Minda Lang, Hal Menkin and Madalyn, the Three Edwards Brothers, Steve Evans, the Three Appletons, and Aunt Jemima.

On November 23, the trade listed the Lugosi Company at Wichita's Orpheum Theater, headlining with Menkin and Madalyn, the Three Edwards Brothers, Aunt Jemima, Steve Evans, and the Three Appletons.

In both 1948 and 1949, Lillian Lugosi generally played the hypnotized female in a *Dracula* act. The company itself probably played many other dates, but if so the trades completely ignored them.

35. State Theatre vaudeville act

The March 8, 1950, edition of *Variety* announced Lugosi on a vaudeville bill at the Torrington State Theatre in Torrington, Connecticut. The theater also scheduled Bert Gilbert and the Quinlans for the same date.

36. Gamut Club dinner

On May 24, 1950, the Gamut Club of New York City hosted guest of honor Bela Lugosi at its last dinner of the season. Among those present that evening at the Old Garden restaurant were President Essex Dane and Vice President Grant Mitchell.

37. *Bela Lugosi's Horror and Magic Stage Show*

8. Vaudeville and Live Appearances 197

Theatergoers in Miami buy tickets to see the Bela Lugosi Company's live appearance during the first week of September 1948.

Variety first announced the formation of Lugosi's traveling act on December 6, 1950. The trade mentioned the influence of Bill Neff's *Asylum of Horrors* on the Lugosi attraction, as well as claiming renowned producer Mike Todd backed the show. The initial playdate became Capitol in Trenton, New Jersey, with a number of other theaters along the Atlantic seaboard booking the act to bolster pre–Christmas business. Among these were a number of Westchester and Brooklyn RKO houses. Though the Trenton show was postponed, Lugosi did appear in Yonkers on December 28, 1951, and in New Rochelle on December 29.

Much of the planned schedule — which would have taken the actor to 17 theaters between New Year's and January 30, 1951— was canceled. On January 3, the *New York Post* announced that an ill Lugosi had bowed out for at least most of the month.

The *Horror and Magic Show* did play the Regent Theater in Paterson, New Jersey, on February 9, 1951, then moved to the RKO Proctor's Theater in Newark, New Jersey, for February 20. The act also appeared in Camden, New Jersey, at the Stanley Theater on March 15, 1951.

According to publicity and newspaper articles, this touring show must have been slightly more elaborate than the Lugosi vaudeville routines of 1948–49. Lugosi rose from a coffin, the stage filled with "the beauty and the monster, ghosts, and goblins." Imps flew through the air and demons burned the beautiful girl alive. "Vampire maidens and voodoo magic" added to the performance, with posters and ads promising "Lugosi and the bloody guillotine." Ads claimed that the show featured "thirteen breath-taking scenes to hold you spellbound." One particularly elaborate advertisement featured a "vampire's eye" that could permit free entry to the show, providing that it turned red after being breathed upon. Another photo montage for the show depicted numerous poses of Lugosi as Dracula, as well as one of a cloaked actor who definitely was not Lugosi.

On most occasions, theaters offered only a single performance of the show, which generally started at 8:30 P.M. The Camden performance, however, began at midnight. Along with the live act and a supposed "carload of scenery," the show included a screening of "Bela Lugosi in *They Creep in the Dark*," a retitled Monogram film — probably *The Ape Man* (1943). The act played for a percentage of the theater's take, which by some accounts must have been very little. Actor Charles Stanley usually portrayed the show's ape.

Film historian William K. Everson commented that the show consisted of nothing more than Lugosi, a laboratory, and a manacled ape. The film apparently played before the live act, giving no real buildup at all. Crowds seemed unappreciative and sometimes quite disrespectful. Lugosi generally felt embarrassed when he left the theater, with the show coming to an end due to the actor's leaving for England and a stage version of *Dracula*.

38. Tour with Kim Yen Soo

Though Lugosi made a short "spook show" tour in 1952 with this "Oriental wizard," the duo must have played minor theaters, but no trades covered their appearances.

39. *The House of Wax* premiere

On April 16, 1953, Lugosi went with Alex Gordon and a man costumed as a gorilla to the Paramount Theatre premiere of *House of Wax* in downtown Los Angeles. The premiere began at midnight, with Gracie Allen, Eddie Cantor, Broderick Crawford, Irene Dunne, Judy Garland, Merv Griffin, Rock Hudson, Ginger Rogers, Shelley Winters, and numerous others slated to attend. Another screening, minus the stars, took place at the Hollywood Paramount the same evening.

Lugosi wore dark glasses, and later drank milk at a Red Cross booth. At first, Lugosi wrongly believed he was supposed to bite a nurse on the neck, which resulted in the milk itself being spilled. In the lobby, a female interviewer cornered the actor, though not asking her questions in the order in which the hard-of-hearing Lugosi had previously memorized the answers. The result proved unfortunate, with the actor leaving after the film started.

40. San Bernardino, California, appearance

Writer/director Ed Wood booked Lugosi to appear at the West Coast Theatre's New Year's Eve show for 1954. Rather than a "spook show" act or *Dracula* excerpts, the actor gave a well-received speech. He remained to shake hands and sign autographs. Manager Albert Stetson sandwiched Lugosi between several films, including *When the Daltons Rode* (1940), *Pagan Love Song* (1950), and *Arabian Nights* (1942).

41. *Bela Lugosi Revue*

Opening Night: February 19, 1954, at the Silver Slipper Saloon in Las Vegas, Nevada.

Cast: Bela Lugosi, Hank Henry, Sparky Kaye, Bill Willard, Jimmy Cavanaugh, Virginia Dew, Joan White, Terre Sheehan, and the George Redman Orchestra.

Credits: Produced by Eddie Fox. Directed by Edward D. Wood, Jr. Writers included Eddie Fox, Hank Henry, Bill Willard, and allegedly Edward D. Wood, Jr.

Production Notes: Costumed as Dracula, Lugosi appeared alongside comedian Hank Henry for a series of comedic skits to make up a 60-minute revue. According to Ed Wood, Eddie Fox initially signed Lugosi for one week at $1,000, though the enormous response found him extending the show. In the seventies, Wood told an interviewer that several shows sold out, with the actor getting $2,000 for each subsequent week. He also mentioned that the show received a seven-week extension, though in a 1954 letter to Lugosi Wood spoke only of an additional three weeks. Critics and patrons alike found the *Bela Lugosi Revue* a tremendous joy. Ads indicate the actor appeared twice an evening, and the entire run lasted until April 1, 1954.

The revue included a *Dragnet* skit, with Jimmy Cavanaugh as Sergeant Friday, Sparky Kaye as a maid, Bill Willard as a corpse, and Hank Henry, Virginia Drew, and Joan Mann; Lugosi portrayed a gloating butler. Critics referred to another skit as "Be-Bop." Several histories incorrectly list stripper Lili St. Cyr as appearing on the bill, when in actuality it was Terre Sheehan. Sheehan, a blonde whom period critics did in fact compare to St. Cyr, emerged on stage from an enormous, bubbling champagne glass. After parading through the audience and giving away a pair of champagne bottles, Sheehan stripped and reclined back into the glass.

The Last Frontier Hotel operated the Silver Slipper, with Kaye, Cavanaugh, and Henry regulars in their live acts. Ads generally billed the latter as "the funniest man in the world." Producer Fox generally charged no cover, with the club reaching capacity at 200.

42. Bela Lugosi benefit

On May 12, 1955, the Paramount Hollywood Theater screened *Bride of the Atom* (1955) as a benefit for Lugosi, with proceeds building a trust fund for the actor. Though Lugosi did not appear, Bela Lugosi, Jr., Maila Nurmi, Ed Wood, Paul Marco, and Richard Sheffield attended the benefit. Prior to the film, Dolores Fuller hosted a cocktail party at the Gardens restaurant.

A plan formed by actor/producer Tony McCoy and theater operator Marco Wolff ensured that a certain amount of money would be paid to Lugosi each week after his release from the Metropolitan hospital. Price Waterhouse handled all receipts, which supposedly were quite meager.

In addition to the benefit, Lugosi himself allegedly appeared at a few Los Angeles–area movie theaters with Maila Nurmi and Tor Johnson, attempting to promote *Bride of the Atom*. In the 1990s Nurmi recently remembered the Pic Theater and another in Inglewood as stops. Such appearances could have taken place during the film's limited release in 1956. Nurmi further recalled that audiences proved tremendously disrespectful to the film and its lead actor.

43. Carmel Museum Theatre opening

On November 3, 1955, the Carmel Museum Theatre opened, with *Tillie's Punctured Romance* (1914) and a tribute to Mack Sennett. The silent "king of comedy" reminisced about the Keystone Kops, who — via Andy Clyde, Heinie Conklin, and Al Thomson — appeared in a live skit. Criswell acted as host, introducing the numerous special guests. Mary MacLaren, Raymond Griffith, Rose Tapley, Bert Wheeler, the Duncan Sisters, Francis McDonald, Jack Oakie, Minta Durfee, Jack Mulhall, and Mrs. Tom Mix attended as special guests, as did Lugosi — accompanied by his close friend Richard Sheffield. Even Groucho Marx allegedly made a brief appearance.

44. *The Black Sleep* luncheon

To help publicize the film, Lugosi, John Carradine, and other cast members traveled by hearse on February 23, 1956, to the Tail o' the Clock restaurant in Hollywood. Each came in his or her makeup used for the film, with the gruesome luncheon acting as an opportunity for press attention.

45. *The Black Sleep* premiere

Director Reginald LeBorg, producer Howard Koch, historian Forrest J Ackerman, and others cited Lugosi and other cast members at the premiere of United Artists' *The Black Sleep* (1956). Ackerman himself remembered pointing Lugosi in the direction of a television crew when the actor had difficulty seeing where the interviewer stood. "We didn't really have a premiere," Koch recalled. "It was just a regular opening." Yet the date of the opening they cite is difficult to pinpoint. The film opened at 18 Los Angeles–area theaters on June 27,

1956, usually coupled on a double bill with *The Creeping Unknown* (1956).

Newspaper ads noted the "opening" of the "All-New Double-Horror Super Shock Show," with the publications themselves running articles about television horror host Vampira (Maila Nurmi) and Tor Johnson appearing live in the lobbies of the Orpheum, New Fox, Uptown, and Fox Inglewood. No mention is made of Lugosi, and such "openings" actually came after screenings in San Francisco, Portland, and elsewhere. Though the *Los Angeles Times* and other papers seemingly do not corroborate the possibility, the cast perhaps appeared at a Los Angeles–area preview in early June.

46. *The Black Sleep* cast tour

Lugosi left Hollywood for only a few days on this June 1956 tour, appearing first in San Francisco. Press agent Chuck Moses accompanied the actor and his three colleagues, Lon Chaney, Tor Johnson, and John Carradine. While in his hotel, an intoxicated Lugosi supposedly screamed that he could "fly" while standing on a window ledge. Moses managed to pull him back into the hotel room safely.

Shortly thereafter, on the afternoon of June 7, the four actors appeared at a Portland, Oregon, press conference in the Aloha Room of the Heathman Hotel. The group then went on stage that night at the Paramount Theater, which screened *The Black Sleep* on a double bill with *The Creeping Unknown* (1956). Lugosi collapsed after walking off stage.

Allegedly, inebriation caused the actor to fall, rather than any serious health problem. If true, this helps explain how he was able to perform in the stage version of *The Devil's Paradise* on the evening of June 8. Moreover, the fact that the play was scheduled for that day means Lugosi must have intended a quick return to Hollywood even before his collapse.

9. Radio Performances

Unfortunately, with such scant records for the history of radio, it is almost impossible to assume that a truly "complete" list of Lugosi's programs could ever be assembled. Furthermore, despite his individual and commanding voice, many sources indicate that Lugosi did not perform on numerous programs. Those that do survive have often been saved through mere luck and have been transferred from the 16-inch transcription discs that were used at the time. A few have even been commercially marketed to the modern public.

Lugosi and horror film actors Lon Chaney, Jr., George Zucco, and Lionel Atwill all seem to have had limited work in the "theater of the mind." This is direct contrast to actors Peter Lorre and Boris Karloff. Lorre appeared on a large number of programs like *Suspense* and had his own programs like *Mystery in the Air*. His comedy appearances included a guest shot on *The Fred Allen Show*, where he claimed that he and Lugosi gave donations to the blood bank every day ... but it wasn't their own blood that was contributed! Similarly, Sydney Greenstreet once told Fred Allen about a baseball team he played on that used Lugosi as "bat boy." Boris Karloff fared quite well in radio by appearing as a guest dozens of times and hosting his own programs like *Starring Boris Karloff* and *Boris Karloff's Treasure Chest*. Besides surpassing Lugosi in this medium, Karloff once remarked on the comedy program *Duffy's Tavern* that he knew Bela before he had a "coffin to cough in," adding that he had had to loan a down-and-out Lugosi a nickel so he could "buy some plasma."

Furthermore, unlike many stars of that era, Lugosi never appeared on the programs like *Lux Radio Theater* which adapted films for radio listeners. Most programs of that kind, like *Screen Director's Playhouse* and others, adapted "A" films. Almost never were horror films used as source material, and one nonhorror Lugosi film, *Ninotchka* (1939), aired on the *Screen Guild Players* in 1940 without his assistance. Lugosi did help secure radio time in Hungary during the war era for the Hungarian-American Council to broadcast.

Commercials for his films certainly aired on radio stations, with press materials occasionally sending written copy to movie theaters that might wish to run ads on the radio. For example, a March 15, 1932, *Film Daily* mentioned the script that Universal Studios was sending to exhibitors in conjunction with *Murders in the Rue Morgue*. Some pressbooks, however, such as that for *Mark of the Vampire*, included no such copy, but instead mentioned that horror film commercials on the air were not popular with some parents and radio listeners.

Radio has thus been a sketchy and overlooked side note to Lugosi's career, and discussion here is at times more brief than might be desired. Several photos exist showing him at radio mikes, including several with unidentified interviewers. Lugosi himself once even expressed a dislike for doing radio shows on a 1935 personal information form for Imperial-Cameo Pictures. Yet his few existing "appearances" show him generally adept in the medium.

1. *Dracula,* late 1927–early 1928

In a July 24, 1929, article printed while he was performing in San Francisco, Lugosi commented that one broadcast had been made of the tale when he was still in New York City, placing it presumably during the run of the Broadway version. Lugosi told the *San Francisco Call* that *Dracula* was aired only once because of listeners' indignation. One woman supposedly telephoned the station in an attempt to stop the broadcast, claiming she had six terrified children at home.

2. KFI radio speech, March 27, 1931

A transcript of this speech, written in quite eloquent English, exists in Lugosi's own hand-typed copy. The speech was broadcast from the Los Angeles station KFI, but in an era of uncluttered airwaves it could easily have been heard throughout much of the country. Obviously this speech was given to promote the film *Dracula.*

3. *Shell Chateau,* spring 1934

A little-known radio credit of Lugosi's that seems not to exist. At times, Al Jolson hosted this variety program.

4. *Tovarich* interview, 1937

While he was appearing at the Curran in San Francisco, local radio transmitters carried interviewers with Lugosi and "practically every member of the [*Tovarich*] cast," according to *Variety* on April 7, 1937. The broadcasts apparently took place between opening night on March 27 and the date *Variety* hit newsstands.

5. *Seein' Stars in Hollywood,* March 18, 1938

Along with part of the broadcast, a still exists showing Lugosi, Boris Karloff, Ozzie Nelson, and Harriet Hilliard singing in front of a radio mike. Portions of the episode—which unfortunately survives without credits—find the two horror stars joking with the Nelsons and singing (somewhat off-key) "We're Horrible, Horrible Men." Lugosi also acted out a short skit with the bandleader and his wife; during another part of the show Karloff recited a poem.

6. *The Tuesday Program with Walter O'Keefe,* October 17, 1939

Lugosi guest-starred on this program while staying at the Essex House in New York City. Along with comedian O'Keefe and Lugosi, the program featured singer Mary Martin and strongman Charles Atlas. Béla played a werewolf with a "terrible case of rabies" on this program, which was mentioned as airing on CBS in a *New York World-Telegram* article. O'Keefe's program has also been referred to as *The Packard Show,* after his sponsor of the time. Another interview with Lugosi from the October 19 *New York Post* claimed that the actor came to the coast to do a "couple" of broadcasts, so he very possibly appeared on another program during the same period.

7. *Texaco Star Theater,* November 15, 1939

Hosted by Ken Murray, this hour-long CBS variety show featured Lugosi and Burgess Meredith as guests for one episode. Lugosi appeared in a short skit called *Dracula on Sunnybrook Farm,* with "Mr. Dracula" causing innumerable screams as a boarder at a farmhouse. One by one he murders the family's children, with the calm parents reacting nonchalantly to inspire laughs. Meredith starred in a separate drama called *The Criminal Code,* with singer Kenny Baker included as an added attraction.

8. *Kay Kyser's Kollege of Musical Knowledge,* September 25, 1940

Lighting one of his favorite cigars while being interviewed on station WHUM of Reading, Pennyslvania.

Lugosi guest-starred on the bandleader's popular program along with Boris Karloff and Peter Lorre to plug the film *You'll Find Out*, which starred all four. Lugosi probably did not enjoy the zany humor and music of the Kyser band, but this is the only known radio show he did with fellow Hungarian Peter Lorre.

9. *Play Broadcast*, May 2, 1941

While Lugosi was appearing live at Chicago's Oriental Theater, WGN asked him to appear on its popular quiz program. Bill Anson "and his impersonations" acted as quizmaster, with announcer Guy Savage, home economist June Baker, character actors Marvin Mueller and Dorothy Roberts, and the WGN Dance Orchestra also taking part. In addition to being heard in Chicago, *Play Broadcast* aired over the Mutual Broadcasting System.

10. *Suspense*, February 2, 1943

Béla had the leading role in J. Donald Wilson's tale "The Doctor Prescribed Death," which was the twenty-seventh installment of CBS's long-running program. Lugosi played Antonio Bassille, a psychologist who contends "that a person who has decided to kill himself can very easily be turned from that desire to the desire of taking the life of another." Bassille finds a willing subject and convinces her to murder Lugosi's publisher (who is supposedly his wife's lover). To keep listeners in "suspense," Bassille's scheme is not discovered by the authorities until the last moment. *Suspense* was directed by Ted Bliss and produced by William Spier. As always, the "Man in Black" hosted what became one of radio's best-loved mystery programs. Lugosi was only one in a series of big-name guest stars *Suspense* had in its 20-year run.

11. *Texaco Star Theater (The Fred Allen Show)*, April 25, 1943 (Armed Forces Radio Service #22)

Lugosi guest-starred on the legendary, Fred Allen comedy show in a skit that had Béla trying to sell Allen a house. The usual horror/comedy gags are employed. For one, Lugosi says he is going to make a new Frankenstein monster, using the brain of Red Skelton, the body of Skinnay Ennis, the singing voice of George Jessel, and the nerves of Fred Allen, because, Béla mentions, Allen has so much nerve each week to tell his jokes. The show was broadcast live from New York while Lugosi was starring in the revived theatrical version of *Dracula*. Lugosi seems to enjoy himself, and Allen mentions having seen him in the 1927 version of the play *Dracula*. The show was aired later as the twenty-second in the Armed Forces rebroadcasts of Allen's program.

12. Lugosi speech for Columbia Studios transcribed October 21, 1943

This speech lasts only a few minutes and on the surface does not seem to act as a promo for another show or as an advertisement of any kind. However, Columbia Studios recorded it presumably to help promote *Return of the Vampire*. As Columbia did not release the film until January 1944, transcriptions may not have been sent to radio stations until December 1943 or later. Lugosi explains tongue in cheek that there are such things as the supernatural. A complete transcript of the speech follows:

> [Laughing] Good evening ... I hope you're not frightened. I'm your old friend Bela Lugosi, better known as the fiendish vampire, Count Dracula. If I have frightened you in this character, it is because I portrayed it just as I learned about it in my birthplace in Transylvania. And, as the legend goes, if you believe in it, don't think that you are safe from vampires. Oh no!
>
> Supernatural beings are not chained to their graves. They are free to roam the entire world and even to seek their victims right here. [The] vampire feeds by night on the blood of the living and at daybreak goes back to its coffin, which is filled with the earth of its native soil, and there awaits the nightfall when it can go forth to prowl the land. Once it has chosen you as its victim, you will be pursued relentlessly until it has fastened its teeth in your throat and have drained your veins of all your blood.
>
> [Laughs] But there is a way to destroy a vampire. All you have to do is to track it by day to its lair and catch it as it lies sleeping in the coffin. Then, drive a stake through its heart. Very simple, isn't it!
>
> So, when you lie in bed in your darkened room tonight and these thoughts give you nightmares, and you dread to look behind the curtains for fear of seeing my horrible face appear at the window, just pull yourself together and remember ... after all, there are such things! [Laughs]

13. *Inner Sanctum*, early 1940s (?)

This favorite horror radio show, well-known for its "creaking door" and host Raymond, featured many famous guests like Boris Karloff and Agnes Moorehead. Lugosi, when on Fred Allen's radio show in 1943, mentioned having recently been on *Inner Sanctum*. No details were given, and it is probable that it was merely part of the Allen script. Other sources have also indicated that he guest-starred on the popular horror show. Yet the show's mastermind, Himan Brown, clearly refuted in an interview the claim that Lugosi ever entered the *Inner Sanctum* for any broadcast.

14. *Mail Call*, March 11, 1944

This popular wartime show was a variety program for the U.S. troops. Lugosi was a guest on an episode along with Orson Welles and the Mills Brothers. He was featured in a skit with Gregory Ratoff and Edward Everett Horton. Ratoff is shooting a new film, and he casts Horton as a werewolf and Lugosi as the victim. The exact date of this episode is unknown, but it was an honor to be on this show, as guests had to be requested by mail from the listeners.

Performing in an unidentified radio show in the forties.

15. *Creeps by Night*, summer 1944

The Blue Network created this program in early 1944, which headlined Boris Karloff for the first 12 episodes. The tales were "dramatic explorations into the vast and unknown darkness of the human mind." From the existing handful of programs, it seems that the scripts were quite good. After Karloff left, an anonymous host ("Dr. X") took over. On the "Walking Dead" episode of May 16, 1944, it was mentioned that Lugosi would be the upcoming guest. Others such as Rathbone and Lorre were to be guests as well. Unfortunately, the Lugosi episode itself does not seem to exist.

16. *Mystery House*, transcribed during autumn 1944

Perhaps the most interesting aspect of Lugosi's radio career is this — an attempt at his own program. It hoped to feature Lugosi in the leading role of various "Grand Guignol" tales. Ken Carpenter, a well-known radio personality at the time, gave introductory and closing remarks. Among the planned episodes was a story about a woman who had been buried alive, with producers hoping for Simone Simon as a guest. "The Thirsty Death," a "pilot" episode, survives and features John Carradine and Lureen Tuttle as guests. Lugosi played a jealous husband who injects his wife or Carradine — her presumed lover — with a poison, only to find out too late that the two were innocent of infidelity. This particular recording is seemingly the only one actually produced and recorded. The Mystery House press would have sponsored it, so why the show never reached the air remains a question.

The stories on *Mystery House* were to be from "the greatest mystery theater the world has ever known, the Grand Guignol of Paris." The only recorded show claims

Lugosi was to star in a series of *Mystery House* films for Universal Studios. If produced, they would have echoed the *Inner Sanctum* series of films Universal made with Lon Chaney, Jr. Some 14 episodes of *Mystery House* exist without Lugosi, surviving artifacts from another of the program's incarnations.

17. *Command Performance*, July 16, 1946

This edition of *Command Performance* featured a "Superman" sketch with Bob Hope as Clark Kent and Paulette Goddard as Lois Lane. Lugosi portrayed the villainous Dr. Bikini, aided by his "insane assistant professor," Sterling Holloway, Lugosi spent most of his time menacing the musical King Sisters, whom he forced into his evil soap machine. Unfortunately, they make only a few bars, with Lugosi explaining that "no matter how you slice them, you can only get eight-to-the-bar." His biggest laughs on this program aimed at the "fighting men overseas" came from simply asking in regard to the King Sisters, "You know what we can do with those girls?"

18. *The Rudy Vallee Show*, October 22, 1946

Lugosi guest-starred in a short skit with Billie Burke on Vallee's program, sponsored by Phillip Morris. Playing a vampire called, appropriately enough, "The Bat," Lugosi attempts to get Burke's brain for use in his mindless monster. Burke has a difficult time grasping Lugosi's vampire status, and when he asks her what eats "red raw meat three times a day," she replies, "A capitalist." A surviving transcription of this program's rehearsal audibly shows Lugosi almost breaking up with laughter when, in response to mentioning that he and Burke have "dallied" long enough, she flitters out that they hadn't even "dillied" yet.

19. *Candid Microphone*, July–August, 1950

Allen Funt's popular television show *Candid Camera* started out by this name on radio, once featuring Lugosi in a gag setup. Funt produced the 30-minute show, with Joe Graham acting as director and Don Witty as editor. ABC carried the series, which Funt recorded in New York.

Lugosi portrayed the "King of the Zombies," running a quite curious curio shop of skulls, shrunken heads, and other "ghoulish knickknacks." When the unsuspecting victim of the gag remarks on Lugosi's collection as being "peculiarly sadistic," Bela gleefully replies, "Isn't it!" He proceeds to tell of a skull shortage before complimenting his guest on how nice her own skull is. When the joke is revealed and the "victim" says she doesn't believe he is really Bela Lugosi, he offered to bite her on the neck as proof.

20. *The Tell-Tale Heart*, 1947 (?)

Although now apparently lost, a 16-inch transcription disc did exist, complete with radio call numbers, of Bela doing a dramatized monologue of the Poe story. The actual program and its purpose remain unclear; presumably the disc was recorded in conjunction with the short-lived 1947 roadshow version that starred Lugosi. From the reports of a listener and previous owner of the disc, the actor performed the tale as a monologue, with the main sound effect being the beating of a heart. The description greatly resembles the style of the 1947 live act. During this same period, agent Virginia Doak attempted to get Lugosi for some "radio recording platters" (his words), apparently for syndication. *The Tell-Tale Heart* could easily have been one of them.

21. *The Abbott and Costello Show*, May 5, 1948

For this program, aired on ABC and sponsored by Camel Cigarettes, Lugosi's presence was probably done due to his role in the film *Abbott and Costello Meet Frankenstein* (1948). Actor Sidney Fields played the part of a ghost, and Lou Costello played a sheriff who inspects the haunted house Lugosi lives in. The show was broadcast from Hollywood, with Lugosi coming off as genuinely funny. Lon Chaney, Jr., who also starred in *Meet Frankenstein*, made a guest appearance on the duo's radio show later the same summer.

22. *House Party*, October 6, 1949

For this October episode, Art Linkletter interviewed Lugosi on his popular program *House Party*. In addition to talking about the role of Dracula, Lugosi mentioned his hopes that no younger fans would be scared of him in real life. He also signed Linkletter's guest book with Franklin D. Roosevelt's famous remark that there is "nothing to fear but fear itself." Lugosi further spoke of a *Dracula* stage revival, which probably refers to manager Don Marlowe's attempt to promote a new version of the play.

23. *Crime Does Not Pay*, February 17, 1951

Crime Does Not Pay ran from 1949 to 1952, and was produced by MGM. The tales were based on a series of short films released under the same name. On the episode "Gasoline Cocktail," Lugosi plays an arsonist named Nick Segadin, who delights in watching tall fires and chasing fire engines. Ever since his childhood in Budapest, Hungary, Nick has been obsessed by fires. He begins cheating on his wife, but eventually burns his mistress's house to the ground after a quarrel. Nick leaves his wife and flees to a boardinghouse, though the police eventually capture him. At the end of the story, an out-of-character Lugosi explained to audiences, "If we see to it that the roots of crime — the social conditions that breed warped gangsters and people like Nick — are removed, we will have taken a long step on the way to a better world." John Gart wrote the tale, which was directed by Ira Marion. John Gart directed the music.

24. Joe Franklin Interview, 1950s (?)

Bela's presence on Franklin's radio show has been rumored for some time but never verified. When asked, Franklin said he believed that the Hungarian once guested on his show, but he thought the date was 1959; however, Lugosi certainly did not give interviews three years after his death. Doubt hovers over any alleged radio encounter between the two.

10. Television Appearances

Lugosi's television work was limited, due probably to the overall state of his career by the late forties and fifties. Whether he enjoyed working in the medium is not really clear, but certainly at that time he would have welcomed almost any widespread publicity.

Curiously, a fifties *TV Guide* magazine mentioned that Lugosi could have become the king of "terrorvision" if only he had retained the rights to his old films as Hopalong Cassidy did. Apparently he felt the same way because, when some of his films certainly aired on television before his death, Lugosi was embittered that he received no royalties for the broadcasts. *The Black Camel* (1931), *White Zombie* (1932), *The Body Snatcher* (1945), and many of his Monogram horror films hit the airwaves prior to 1956.

In any event, Lugosi certainly did not dominate or even take much part in this medium. Don Marlowe tried to interest CBS in *The Bela Lugosi Show* during late 1948, but the network did not move ahead. A television scout named George Clark attended a Providence performance of *The Devil Also Dreams* in July 1950 to investigate the television possibilities of both Lugosi and Francis L. Sullivan, but nothing came of it. Additionally, Lugosi himself mentioned that he was to star in a television series called *Dr. Acula* in 1953, but it never hit the airwaves.

Biographers long believed that Bela had guest-starred on *The Colgate Comedy Hour* with Abbott and Costello. However, Bob Furmanek and the Lou Costello estate have proved this rumor false. Another rumor insists that the actor appeared on *What's My Line*, though existing archival data emphatically refutes the tale. Other tales claim Lugosi performed on a television program with Vin Scully in 1955; even further hearsay speaks of a toothpaste commercial. Proof of either still evades researchers.

In fact, Lugosi made few television appearances and even fewer exist. Perhaps the actor's advancing years and fading popularity, in combination with his poor reviews from *Suspense* and unsure performances on programs like *The Red Skelton Show*, eliminated any real chance of prolonged success in the medium.

These credits are presented chronologically. Relevant dates are included in the annotations.

1. *Backstage at the Spa Theater*

While appearing in *Arsenic and Old Lace* at the Saratoga Springs, New York, Spa Summer Theater, Lugosi made a personal appearance on television station WRGB on August 7, 1947, at 7:20 P.M. Duff-Brown directed and Ted Beebe arranged this program, in which John Huntington appeared with Lugosi. The ten-minute program apparently featured Lugosi plugging the Spa

Lugosi out to get actor Romney Brent in the "Cask of the Amontillado" episode of *Suspense* on October 11, 1949. Primary materials, including critical reviews, suggest that Lugosi portrayed a Fascist; given Brent's costume in this still, both actors must have essayed characters with such a background. (Photo courtesy of Buddy Barnett.)

Theater performances, as well as perhaps an interview or a scene from the Joseph Kesselring play. *Backstage at the Spa Theater* was inaugurated the night Lugosi appeared, going before the cameras at General Electric's television studio.

2. Guy Lebow interview

Lebow, a pioneer of early television, claimed in his autobiography to have interviewed Lugosi on the air, with the Hungarian's latest film being *Abbott and Costello Meet Frankenstein*. If the story is accurate, the broadcast probably occurred in 1948. Among the details Lebow gave was Lugosi's announcement of his favorite role: Santa Claus, at which he was so convincing he fooled even his own son. Also, an off-camera Lugosi kissed a model's hand and supposedly blamed Boris Karloff for having ruined him at the studios. Lebow's account oddly (and incorrectly) claims that Lugosi was Jewish.

3. *Suspense*

Suspense, whose radio counterpart lasted some 20 years, customarily received good reviews for its transition to television. The October 11, 1949, episode paired Bela Lugosi and the British actor Romney Brent for a modernized adaptation of Poe's "Cask of Amontillado." In occupied Italy, the victim of the tale (Brent) finds himself walled up alive by a Fascist general (Lugosi). Robert Stevens directed and produced the 30-minute program, which was sponsored by Electric Auto-Lite and broadcast from New York over CBS. Announcer Rex Marshall handled the commercials, and Hank Sylvem directed the music.

A period review remarked on an unscheduled head shot of Brent that appeared on the screen, as well as the overuse of a circular stairway into the wine cellar. Brent received favorable comments, but the reviewer expounded at length on Lugosi's poor performance. Critic Jerry Franken claimed the Hungarian walked through his part, destroying any existing tension and failing to instill any sense of reality into his own role.

4. *Texaco Star Theater*

Lugosi appeared as a guest on Milton Berle's popular show on Tuesday, October 27, 1949, wearing a cape and trying to hypnotize the comedian. The 60-minute program does exist, replete with many trite horror jokes and Berle's ad-lib about Lugosi's ability to ruin jokes. A surprise ending found Olsen and Johnson, as well as a midget, popping out of a mummy case. The skit took good reviews in the trades.

The same episode featured a reprise of the *Ziegfeld Follies*, with Billie Burke narrating. Additionally, Bill "Bojangles" Robinson tap danced and engaged in small talk with Berle and Jackie Robinson. Critics bestowed favorable comments on the entire program.

5. *Starlit Time*

On May 21, 1950, Lugosi guest-starred on this musical/variety program, which was part of the Dumont Network offerings. Bill Williams and Phil Hanna acted as emcees, with Cy Coleman and Reggie Bean providing the music. The program began on May 9, 1950, with a running time of two hours. By the last episode, on November 26 of that year, the length had dwindled to 60-minutes. Pat Fay directed and Bob Loewi produced Starlit Time, which was also known as *The S.S. Holiday*.

6. *Ship's Reporter*

The *Ship's Reporter* appeared on New York station WJZ as early as the summer of 1949, produced by Chick Vincent. Jack Mangan interviewed a variety of celebrities during the show's run, ranging from Joe E. Lewis and Arthur Treacher to Dinah Shore and Otto Preminger. Each program, which usually aired on Thursdays at 7:00 P.M., lasted 15 minutes and featured more than one interview. The crew filmed each in advance of the program, apparently on 16mm.

When *Ship's Reporter* featured Lugosi in December 1951, the actor had just returned to the United States from his British tour of *Dracula*. He spoke about a film he had made in England (*Mother Riley Meets the Vampire*, which he refers to as *Vampire Over London*), about his career in general, and about being typecast as a horror star. The Lugosi episode aired probably a week or two after the interview was conducted. Film prints of the interview have been passed around on 16mm under such titles as *Tribute to a Star!* and *Meet Bela Lugosi and Oliver Hardy*. The latter simply edited the Lugosi interview together with one Mangan conducted separately with Hardy.

7. *The House of Wax* premiere

Leading an "ape" around on a leash, Lugosi appeared at the Los Angeles premiere of this 3-D horror film on April 16, 1953. Television cameras broadcast a portion of the opening, including an interview with Lugosi. Unfortunately, he had prepared answers in advance, and Shirley Thomas, who had lost her list of questions, did not follow the original order. The result was disastrous.

8. *You Asked for It*

Viewers wrote to this 30-minute ABC program with requests for the guest stars or entertainment acts they wanted to see. In 1953 Harriet Frazier penned a letter from Springfield, Massachusetts, mentioning Lugosi as her choice. Shortly thereafter *You Asked for It* featured the actor in full Dracula regalia. The program was aired for the West Coast on July 27, 1953, and rebroadcast for the East Coast on August 9, 1953. For his short sketch, Lugosi made actress Shirley Patterson disappear from a magic cabinet, leaving a bat in her place. After the skit, Lugosi told audiences and host Art Baker that he was to star in his own television series and in a 3-D film called *The Phantom Ghoul*. Neither project came to light.

9. *The Red Skelton Show*

For Halloween in 1953, Lugosi appeared as a guest on Skelton's program, with Peter Lorre and Lon Chaney, Jr. Apparently the Hungarian disliked Skelton's habit of ad-libbing and did not fare well in dealing with it on the air. Accounts vary in detailing this program, with period sources not listing the trio as Skelton's guests for the Halloween 1953 episode, broadcast on October 27. One story claims the broadcast occurred closer to June 1954. That tale involves television horror hostess Vampira (Maila Nurmi) as a guest alongside Chaney and Lugosi, with Ed Wood acting as the latter's dialogue coach. Again, no period sources verify the date.

10. *The Spade Cooley Show*

Though Lugosi made a guest shot on this very popular but now largely forgotten KTLA variety program, the date is unknown. Very possibly the appearance came during 1954. Cooley himself had a Western swing band similar to Bob Wills's Texas Playboys; his television program often featured such personalities as John Carradine, Rudy Vallee, and Frank Sinatra.

11. Metropolitan Hospital interview

Interviewed on August 1, 1955, just prior to his release from the hospital, Lugosi spoke about his drug use and his future plans. Information surrounding the interview (such as its actual air date) is scant, but an unedited print survives. The interviewer himself questioned Lugosi for information about obtaining drugs through the black market, even though the actor claimed he did not ever do so. Lugosi's alcohol abuse and marital problems were topics as well.

12. *The Tom Duggan Show*

Friends of Lugosi's and his fourth wife both recalled that Tom Duggan invited Lugosi as a guest on his KTLA program to discuss the evils of drug abuse following Lugosi's release from the hospital. Supposedly, Duggan treated Lugosi with very little respect. Los Angeles–area television listings do not offer a date for his appearance; however, Duggan's 10:45 P.M. program on KCOP, Channel 13 began on May 14, 1956. An additional 6:15 P.M. Duggan's show first aired on July 16, 1956, but no period information corroborates the claim of a KTLA program during Lugosi's life. It would then seem that Lugosi appeared not immediately after his release from the Metropolitan Hospital, but instead during the summer of 1956 on KCOP. At that time, the interview would perhaps have coincided with the release of *The Black Sleep* or the play *The Devil's Paradise*.

13. *The Black Sleep* Premiere

Forrest J Ackerman recalled television interviewers speaking to Lugosi at the premiere of this film in June 1956. The actor's sight was poor at this time, but Ackerman helped direct him to the camera, where he came off quite gallantly.

11. Other Celluloid Appearances

1. *The Last Performance* dubbing session, 1928

Paul Kohner filmed some of the dubbing session that Lugosi did for the Hungarian release of this film. Supposedly, the studio planned to release the footage along with the dubbed film.

2. Screen test with Gloria Swanson, 1928

Lugosi tested with the popular Swanson, but nothing came of it, as his height made him tower over the silent screen favorite. Swanson and actor/filmmaker Erich von Stroheim costumed Lugosi in various bizarre uniforms for the filming.

3. *Dracula* trailer, 1931

The original coming attraction trailer for the Lugosi version includes a few film clips not seen in the released film, notably a scene with Edward Van Sloan that did not appear in any form in the released film. The sequence is now believed to be Van Sloan's screen test. Also, the trailer features an alternate take of a scene with David Manners and Helen Chandler.

4. *Frankenstein* test footage, 1931

Before director Robert Florey and Lugosi were taken off the project and moved to *Murders in the Rue Morgue*, various footage, including the creation scene, was shot. Edward Van Sloan and Dwight Frye also appeared in the test. This raw footage was then edited into a reel lasting some 20 minutes. It is possible that a second test could have been shot with Lugosi under James Whale's direction.

5. Spanish language *Dracula*, 1931

The Spanish version of *Dracula* with Carlos Villarias includes approximately five shots of Lugosi that were not in the Tod Browning version. These include a hand and a partial face seen as a coffin opens in Transylvania, two shots outside of a concert hall, Dracula walking on a street past a policeman, and — possibly — the establishing shot at Trafalgar Square with Dracula walking toward the camera.

6. *Island of Lost Souls* trailer, 1933

The trailer for this film includes a few wide shots showing Lugosi and others which did not make it into the final film. Numerous other trailers for Lugosi films also feature brief clips not seen in the films, since often coming attractions were built around alternate takes. Examples of this include trailers for *The Invisible Ray* (1936) and *Son of Frankenstein* (1939).

7. *Mark of the Vampire* trailer, 1935

The original coming attraction trailer of this film had on-screen narration by Lugosi in a vampire costume, "summoning" patrons back to the theater to see the MGM chiller. From a scroll, Lugosi also read the names of the film's cast, including his own.

8. *Charge of the Light Brigade* test, 1936

Warner Brothers gave Lugosi a screen test for this Errol Flynn adventure, though he did not appear in the film.

9. *House of 1000 Candles*, 1936

Before Irving Pichel replaced an ill Lugosi, a week's worth of footage with the Hungarian was shot in mid–January.

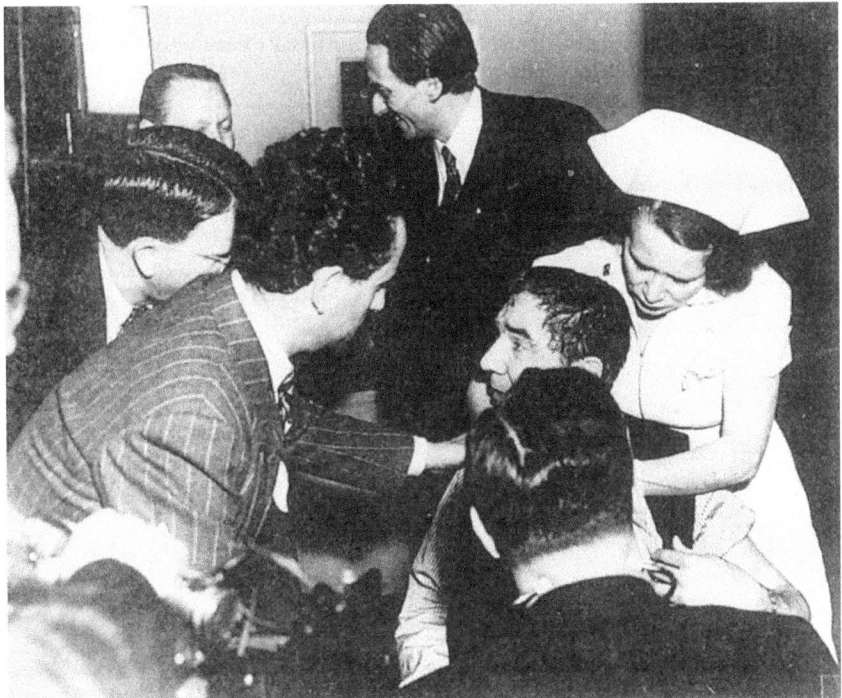

Supposedly coming out of a hypnotic state for Universal Studios' *Black Friday* **(1940). At the least, it brought press attention and footage that turned up in the coming attraction trailer for the film.**

10. *Black Friday* **trailer, 1940**

Original and rerelease trailers for the film showed on-the-set clips of Lugosi being hypnotized for his role as gangster Eric Marnay.

11. *Fantasia*, **1940**

Walt Disney hired Lugosi to model for the demon in *Fantasia*'s "A Night on Bald Mountain" sequence. Wilfred Jackson shot live footage of Lugosi, which animator Bill Tytla planned to use as the basis for the character and its movement. In an interview printed in Frank Thomas and Ollie Johnston's *Disney Animation: The Illusion of Life* (Abbeville, 1981), Jackson recalled, "We got him [Lugosi] and he looked upon it as an actor's job, but this is not what Bill [Tytla] wanted. He was interested in the movement. Lugosi started showing him how he would unwrap his wings like that, and we were getting along great, but Bill was having an awful time — he was telling Lugosi how he should do it. Finally, Bill gave up and went over in the corner and sulked, so I got the best stuff I could out of it and after it was all over Bill said, 'Jack, I don't like what he's done. I like the way you do it. Won't you take your shirt off and get in front of the camera?' So I took off my shirt, he ran the music and we used that stuff. Yeah, the photostats of skinny me. We never told Walt. Bill and I made it up in the music room before Lugosi ever came, then I just went through what I'd been doing with Bill and he'd say fine."

12. *You'll Find Out* **home movies, 1941**

Approximately ten minutes of color home movies showing Lugosi, Boris Karloff,

Peter Lorre, and Kay Kyser were filmed during the production of this RKO farce. The camera caught Lugosi arriving at the studio, laughing with Peter Lorre, and standing beside Boris Karloff.

13. Lugosi home movies, forties through fifties

Color home movies of Lugosi were taken in the late thirties and early forties, which are now owned by the actor's son. Another occasion caught Lugosi and his cape on silent black-and-white 16mm footage, shot in the fifties by some young friends of the actor.

14. Bloopers, out-takes, and alternate takes, various periods of career

Bloopers, alternate takes, and out-takes of at least some of Bela's American films no doubt exist. Bloopers from *Abbott and Costello Meet Frankenstein* (1948), for example, survive and have surfaced among collectors.

12. Newsreels and Short Subjects

1. *Punchinello*, 1926

Lugosi appeared in a cast featuring Duncan Renaldo and Ronda Rainsford. The silent short subject found Lugosi portraying Pierrot, with Renaldo as the unfortunate Punchinello, who grieves for the love of a pretty girl while listening to the sounds of his rival's serenade. The Famous Lovers Production, directed by Renaldo, built itself around highly effective pantomime. Great Arts Pictures later released the 20-minute short subject with recorded music and spoken information as *The Mask*.

2. *Intimate Interviews*, 1932

Interviewed by Dorothy West in his backyard, Lugosi spoke of Hungary and of the types of roles he hoped to play in future films. While talking, Béla showed West some stills of himself before "scaring" her in an obviously staged ending.

3. *Hollywood on Parade*, #A-8, 1933

Lugosi is Dracula, a wax figure at Charles Pressley's Motion Picture Museum and Hall of Fame, which comes to life and bites Betty Boop (Mae Questel) on the neck. "You have booped your last boop," he tells her as she screams. Eddie Borden, Rex Bell, Dorothy Burgess, George Sidney, Charlie Murray, Gayne Whitman, and forgotten silent screen actress Marie Prevost also appear. This was the eighth in a series of 24 short subjects at Paramount.

4. *Screen Snapshots*, #11, 1934

Béla Lugosi and Boris Karloff appear together playing a friendly game of chess, with the winner to lead the "parade of the film stars' frolics." This short also included segments with James Cagney, Pat O'Brien, and Eddie Cantor.

5. *The Hollywood Movie Parade*, 1934

Released in December by Educational Pictures, *The Hollywood Movie Parade* included Lugosi, Jackie Cooper, George O'Brien, and others. Neither an interview nor "real-life" clips of the stars, this short (according to a period review) had a thin plot line.

6. *Black Cat Parade*, March 16, 1934

Filmed at Universal City, a short clip of Béla and Boris Karloff judging a contest of children's black cats surfaced in newsreel form. The clip was seen again in a 1959 newsreel called *Twenty-Five Years Ago Today*. In this publicity ploy for *The Black Cat* (1934), the duo appeared in costume from the Universal film.

7. *San Diego Exposition Opened*, June 1, 1935

Following general clips of the exposition, the camera moves to the Hollywood Pavilion exhibit. Scenes of Lugosi and an unidentified thespian on a movie lot being "filmed" are included in this newsreel. Lugosi's voice is not heard, but he is seen kissing the hand of an actress while pushing away a jealous suitor. Another actor views the events.

8. *Bela Lugosi Hypnotized*, January 18, 1940

Lugosi's hypnotism for the 1940 Universal film *Black Friday* is shown in complete

216   II. Lugosi, the Performer

Serenading Ronda Rainsford in the Famous Lovers' short subject of *Punchinello* (1926).

form, along with added narration. From a variety of camera angles, Lugosi is seen being prepared, going under hypnosis, then coming back to consciousness. At present, this newsreel seems to be lost, as the National Archives' copy burned some years ago in a fire. Similar or possibly some of the same footage turned up in the *Black Friday* coming attraction trailer.

9. *Screen Snapshots*, 1943

In this Columbia newsreel hosted by Alan Mowbray, Lugosi is seen briefly giving blood for the war effort and afterward having a doughnut. Lugosi is not heard, but he does give a nice smile for the camera. Jerry Colonna appeared in another segment of this short.

10. Pathé Newsreel, 1953

Along with apparent television coverage, the *House of Wax* premiere of 1953 drew the newsreel cameramen. This Pathé newsreel, released on April 27, 1953, featured a brief shot of the theater's exterior, as well as a shot of Lugosi and Steve Calvert (inside a gorilla suit) entering the Paramount theater.

13. Unfinished Projects and Canceled Roles

1. Karl May/Saharan Adventure Film Series

In 1920 Lugosi performed in two German films based on Karl May's Saharan adventure stories. Directed by Marie Luise Droop and costarring Carl de Vogt and Mainhart Maur, *The Caravan of Death* and *The Devil Worshippers* were the first in a projected series of five films. Lugosi seemingly would have performed in the remaining three, but director Droop fell in love with de Vogt and the series ended.

2. *The Right to Dream*

Lugosi won the position of director on this 1924 New York play, only to lose the job because of his limited English skills. After he was dismissed, Lugosi unsuccessfully sued producer Hubert Henry Davis for breach of contract.

3. *Luxury*

Trades claimed in mid-1930 that Lugosi was to portray a principal role in this Fox drama with Clare Luce, but the film was not made.

4. *Dracula*

Lugosi was preparing for a vaudeville version of *Dracula* in the fall of 1930, but canceled it when he was signed for the Universal film of the same story.

5. *Frankenstein*

By April 8, 1931, *Frankenstein* and *Murders in the Rue Morgue* were listed in *Variety* as upcoming films. Two weeks later, the same trade mentioned Universal's purchase of the John Balderston and Peggy Webling play *Frankenstein* from Horace Liveright. Despite earlier plans and even a preliminary movie poster headlining his name, Boris Karloff succeeded Lugosi in the role of the monster shortly after director James Whale replaced Robert Florey. At one point, the studio also considered Lugosi for the part of Dr. Frankenstein. *Variety* made reference to this when informing readers of Colin Clive's contract for the same part.

Before being switched exclusively to *Murders in the Rue Morgue*, Florey worked on the *Frankenstein* script and even shot test footage. Lugosi was on the *Frankenstein* project for a short time longer, and certainly Carl Laemmle, Jr., desired to see the new "Chaney" in the monster role. Stories vary as to why Lugosi did not appear. For one, the Hungarian actor, with his newfound stardom, did not wish to portray a mute and heavily made-up monster. And while Whale may not have been against Lugosi from the start, his attentions definitely diverted to the unknown William Henry Pratt, better known as Boris Karloff. In later years, Lugosi claimed that it was he who had suggested Whale test the British actor, but this has not generally been accepted as truth.

6. *The Hunchback of Notre Dame*

Universal announced a talkie remake of the 1923 silent film in July 1931, with Lugosi playing the hunchback. By the end of that year, the studio claimed that it would have to spend at least $1 million to produce adequately the film, and Universal officials were undecided as to whether to spend such an amount. The studio mentioned Boris

Karloff's name along with Lugosi's in December 1931 as possibilities for the title character. RKO would later consider Lugosi as the lead for their 1939 version before deciding on Charles Laughton.

7. *The Invisible Man*

A 1931 idea for a Lugosi film with Robert Florey as director. By 1932 the studio considered Boris Karloff and director E.A. Dupont. The filmed version of the H.G. Wells novel featured Claude Rains and was helmed by James Whale, resulting in a Universal film of 1933.

8. Garrett Fort screenplays

On January 12, 1932, trades announced that Lugosi was to sign a long-term contract with Universal and would appear in two films scripted by Garrett Fort.

9. Edgar Wallace "thrillers"

The January 1932 issue of *The Cast* highly suggested that RKO "tie" Lugosi to a contract based on his appearance in *Murders in the Rue Morgue* in order to combine his acting with the "thrillers" of Edgar Wallace, who had already signed with the studio.

10. *The Suicide Club*

Universal planned this as a Lugosi film, to be based on the Robert Louis Stevenson story. Another abandoned project, this was mentioned as early as January 1932 and again in a 1933 press release. Shortly after its initial announcement to the press, Boris Karloff's name was added to the lineup. After the completion of *The Black Cat*, trades again spoke of this as an upcoming film for the duo, even speaking of Laemmle Jr.'s attempting to get Lionel Atwill as a "third topper" for the film.

11. *The Empty Chair*

Variety mentioned *The Empty Chair* with *The Suicide Club* in 1932 as a Universal horror film, pending production. Lugosi would certainly have been considered for this little-known project. Some have suggested that this could have been an early version of *The Electric Man,* but that seems incorrect, since the tale had not even been written by 1932.

12. Series of shorts based on the poems of Poe

In 1932 one trade announcement held that Lugosi would soon appear in a series of short subjects based on the poems of Edgar Allan Poe and others.

13. *Conception*

Béla would have starred with Lady Marjorie Burton in this play at the Los Angeles Biltmore in April 1933, but plans were dropped due to financial trouble. Oliver Morosco would have produced, and the rest of the cast was to include Helen Mitchell, Arthur Rankin, and Judith Vosselli.

14. *Murder at the Vanities*

Lugosi had performed in the 1933 version of Earl Carroll's *Vanities* on the New York stage. Even before the play opened, the *Los Angeles Times* mentioned that it was "practically assured that Lugosi will do the same role on the screen." *Variety*, after realizing in late September that *Vanities* would not find long life on Broadway, commented that "this will probably suit Paramount just as well, incidentally, for among the preliminary summer dog-day worries were how to release Lugosi for the film version." The 1933 film, however, did not use the Hungarian's talents. On December 5, 1933, *Variety* told readers, "Victor McLaglen plays the lead ... [he] has Bela Lugosi's role in the stage version."

15. *Pagan Fury*

Lugosi obtained the rights to this play by S.J. Warshawsky and intended to star in it on the stage at the conclusion of his vaudeville tour. Plans were announced in the *New York Times*, with Lugosi to produce as well as star. Scheduled for spring 1934, the plans were canceled after Lugosi signed a three-picture contract with Universal for *The Black Cat, Dracula's Daughter*, and *The Suicide Club*.

16. *Chandu* projects

Producer Sol Lesser planned other Chandu the Magician vehicles for Lugosi after the 1934 *Return of Chandu* serial, but none were filmed.

17. *Vampire of the Skies*

Embassy Films discussed this project as a production for George King, to star Lugosi and Jean Batten. The studio considered it in July 1935, but *Vampire of the Skies* never went before the cameras.

18. *Cagliostro*

Announced in September 1935, this would have been the first film of Lugosi's own production company, but it was never made due to financial constraints. Lugosi's idea of producing his own films was quite modern, with the venture to have been managed by Al Kingston. *Cagliostro* was written by Andre de Soos and based on Lugosi's "extensive historical research" on Guiseppe Balsamo, the Italian charlatan. Following its release, the actor planned to produce and star in a series of 10 or 12 historical romances.

"Every time I get my thoughts centered on a role that I believe fits me, some other actor — and always great actors — gets there first," Lugosi told the press. "So what am I to do? I figured out that one, so now I'll finance my own company and star in pictures that I want to play in." Curiously, a version of *Cagliostro* had been mentioned by Universal Studios in early 1932 as a Karloff horror film, displaying a "1,000 year-old accumulation of evil." The proposed Karloff film would have been a drastically different project from what Lugosi planned.

19. *Dracula's Daughter*

Initially, Lugosi and Jane Wyatt were to star in the sequel to the 1931 *Dracula*. Universal also considered Boris Karloff and Colin Clive for parts, with both James Whale and Edward Sutherland mentioned as possible directors. None would participate in the film. Among other difficulties was the problem of the story. David Selznick had made a provisional sale of a script to Universal, made on the basis that *Dracula's Daughter* would begin shooting before October 1, 1935. A two-month extension was given, but even that deadline was not met. *Variety* reported that Selznick would thus nab a percentage of the gross.

By January 29, 1936, trades announced that Lugosi was "off the Universal lot, with Cesar Romero slated to take his role." Eventually, Lambert Hillyer became director, with Gloria Holden and Irving Pichel assuming lead roles. The released film of 1936 shows only a brief shot of Dracula in his coffin, played not by Lugosi, but by a wax bust fashioned after his likeness. Some reference works claim Lugosi was paid as much as $4,000 for his trouble even though he didn't appear in the film. This, however, seems unusual, given a one-page letter agreement between the actor and Universal Studios dated February 20, 1936. In it, Lugosi allowed Universal to use his likeness for the wax bust "without compensation." Photographs do exist of him visiting the cast, however, as well as lunching with Gloria Holden in the Universal Studios commissary.

20. *The Mysterious Abbe*

Another Manly Hall idea, a treatment of which was presented to Warner Brothers in late 1935 as a potential Lugosi starrer. Hall once claimed that this detective tale would have been reminiscent of Don Camille. The studio even made wardrobe tests for the project, in which Lugosi was to play a French clergyman who solved crimes through offbeat scientific knowledge.

21. *The Cabinet of Dr. Caligari*

In 1935 Concordia Films considered Lugosi for the title role in a remake of the 1919 German classic, but they never produced the project.

22. *The Emperor of Atlantis*

Researched and prepared by Manly Hall, this film idea supposedly interested Lugosi

Premature Universal artwork for *Dracula's Daughter* (1936), a film without Lugosi's participation. (Courtesy of the Lynn Naron collection.)

a great deal. Nothing ever came of the tale, however, which was considered in 1935.

23. *The Return of Frankenstein*

A 1933 press notice claimed that Lugosi would costar with Karloff in the *Frankenstein* sequel. Supposedly, Lugosi was to play a role similar to that of Dr. Praetorious, but the studio instead signed Ernest Thesiger for what became a 1935 Universal release, *The Bride of Frankenstein*. Some reports claim Lugosi simply changed his mind about playing the role, but this seems unlikely due to the important nature of the film.

24. *Werewolf of London*

The studio considered Lugosi for the role of Dr. Yogami, but instead Warner Oland assumed the part for this 1935 Universal Studios release.

25. *Bluebeard*

A would-be film with Boris Karloff and Lugosi, to have been shot in 1936 at Universal. The studio envisioned Karloff as the title character.

26. *The Electric Man*

Another possible Karloff-Lugosi film planned by Universal for 1936. Harry J. Essex sold this story for little more than $3,000 in August 1935, retitled *The Man in the Cab* for its planned celluloid incarnation. Sid Schwartz and Len Golos coauthored the story. Universal scrapped the idea, though it later resurfaced as the Lon Chaney, Jr., film *Man-Made Monster* (1941).

27. *The House of a Thousand Candles*

Republic Pictures signed Lugosi to play Sebastian, an espionage agent in this spy film of 1936, yet a bad cold made him bow out after the first week of filming. Irving Pichel replaced him in late January of that year. Arthur Lubin, director of *House of a Thousand Candles*, knew Lugosi during the early twenties in New York and subsequently directed him in *Black Friday* (1940).

28. *Faust*

Max Reinhardt chose Lugosi to portray Mephistopheles in what might have been a 1936 Warner Brothers film. Reinhardt later directed a lavish stage version of Goethe's tale in Hollywood in 1938. The stage version featured Conrad Nagel, with Angelo Rossito in a supporting role. Manly Hall, Lugosi's friend, also prepared a story for Lugosi based on the damnation of Faust around the same time period. As with Reinhardt's cinematic plans, Hall's never came to pass.

29. *Cyrano de Bergerac*

Lugosi very much wanted to portray Cyrano in a film version, but a London film company instead announced Charles Laughton for the lead role.

30. *Revolt of the Zombies*

Negotiations between Lugosi and the Halperin Brothers fell through for this sequel to *White Zombie* (1932). The released film of 1936, which bore no similarity to the earlier movie, used Dean Jagger in the Lugosi part. Clips of Béla's eyes from *White Zombie* were incorporated in the film, however.

31. *Ferrari*

Trades announced in September 1937 that Lugosi had nabbed the lead part for the stage version, written by Earl Cortis and to be produced by Jack Linder. He did not appear.

32. *Tovarich*

Lugosi, who had appeared in a West Coast stage version of this play, hoped to repeat his role in the 1937 film. Instead, Basil Rathbone signed the contract.

33. *Jack the Ripper*

A November 1938 *Hollywood Reporter* mentioned that A.P. Waxman was "dickering" with Universal and Paramount for a deal on a proposed production of *Jack the Ripper*. "Slated to star in the picture are John Barrymore, Bela Lugosi, and Boris Karloff," the trade announced. This project never came to fruition, but apparently Lugosi had some interest in the subject. The Hungarian and his wife Lillian, later expressed regret in the forties that he did not get to play in *The Lodger*, a 1944 version of the Ripper tale.

34. *The Vampire*

In England, Argyle Films' *The Dark Eyes of London* headlined Lugosi, the same company wished to bring him back to England to appear in an adaptation of Alexander Dumas's *The Vampire*. This announcement hit *Variety* on April 26, 1939.

35. *The Return of Dr. X*

Warner Brothers tried to cast Boris Karloff in the lead for this horror film, only to have him back out at the last minute due to a scheduling conflict. Claude Rains was mentioned as Karloff's potential costar. Lugosi and James Stephenson were also considered for the title role. The released film of 1939 instead starred Humphrey Bogart.

36. Horror film series for John Argyle, British producer

In February 1940, John Argyle announced plans to film a series of Edgar Wallace novels for which he had acquired the movie rights. He wished to use Lugosi in each, as the two had already collaborated on 1939's *The Dark Eyes of London*. Argyle intended to move his activities from Britain to the West Coast for the series after completing two films in London.

37. Follow-up to *You'll Find Out*

In early November 1940 trades claimed that Lugosi, Boris Karloff, and Peter Lorre would team with Kay Kyser for a second film. Their first together, *You'll Find Out*, had not even premiered in New York City, but RKO noticed tremendous response at sneak previews in San Francisco and Oakland. The studio announced that David Butler would direct and that the "trio of cold-shiver artists" would begin shooting in February 1941. The studio did not proceed on the project.

38. *King of the Zombies*

Lugosi was to be "head zomby" in this Monogram film, according to a January 22, 1941, issue of *Variety*, but instead Henry Victor eventually starred as the heavy.

39. *Arsenic and Old Lace*

Lugosi was apparently considered for the part of Jonathan Brewster in the film version when Boris Karloff could not be obtained, but instead the studio cast Raymond Massey. The Frank Capra–directed comedy underwent production in 1941, but did not become a Warner Brothers' release until 1944.

40. *The Monster of Zombor*
Universal planned this as a 1941 film with Karloff and Lugosi. The studio shelved the project, but a preliminary movie poster still exists.

41. *Eyes of the Underworld*
Variety claimed in August 1942 that Lon Chaney, Jr., Claude Rains, and Lugosi were starring in this Universal production. Curiously, this title can also be found in Lugosi's listing in the 1942 *Academy Players Directory*. By September, the trades no longer listed Lugosi or Rains in the cast. The released film starred Chaney.

42. *The Phantom Killer*
Lugosi offered this as one of his screen credits in multiple interviews. When he underwent a cure for drugs in 1955, the flurry of press attention gave numerous lists of his film work; *The Phantom Killer* found its way into many of them. More than one obituary mentioned this film, and Lugosi filmographies printed shortly after his death also catalogued it. Yet Lugosi did not appear in the Monogram film when its shooting finished in August 1942. The released product became a B mystery, with Dick Purcell and John Hamilton playing duel roles.

Since Lugosi was never announced for this Karl Brown screenplay, why the confusion? Most likely *The Phantom Killer*, as it was with Purcell and Hamilton, is not really an "unfinished or canceled role." Rather, the mistake has probably occurred due to *The Phantom Killer*'s being a shooting title for *Invisible Ghost* (1941), a completely different project that did star the Hungarian.

43. *Night of Horror*
Monogram planned *Night of Horror* for the 1942-43 season as a Lugosi film; the poverty row studio shelved the project.

44. *Torment*
Monogram Studios announced this never-made horror film for their 1942-43 season, with Lugosi slated to star.

45. *Chamber of Horrors*
Variety claimed in June 1943 that Karloff, Lugosi, Chaney, Lorre, and George Zucco would team up in this multi-monster extravaganza at Universal Studios. In addition to Dracula and Frankenstein, the Wolf Man, the Mad Ghoul, and the Mummy were to have wreaked havoc as well. The *Hollywood Reporter* even went further, claiming Lionel Atwill, Henry Hull, and Claude Rains would also appear. *Chamber of Horrors* was transformed into *The Devil's Brood*, a tale with fewer monsters and name actors than were announced for *Chamber*. John Carradine, rather than Lugosi, portrayed the vampire count in the produced film, released as *House of Frankenstein* (1944).

46. *Star-Strangled Rhythm*
The Hollywood Reporter told readers in June 1943 that Lugosi, Karloff, and Lorre would be teamed in this RKO comedy. Lugosi and Karloff would supposedly play actors whose bodies are unfortunately possessed by the horrific characters they portrayed in their horror movies.

47. *Bride of the Vampire*
In December 1943 *Variety* announced the filming of this sequel to Columbia's *Return of the Vampire*. Griffin Jay's script was to be produced by Wallace McDonald and to star Lugosi.

48. *Dracula Meets the Wolf Man*
The year 1943 saw consideration of this project, based on the *Frankenstein Meets the Wolf Man* mix of monsters. Producer Paul Malvern recalled that Lugosi was considered for the vampire lead, and that the story idea later saw life in *House of Dracula* (1945).

49. *Revenge of the Zombies*
Monogram originally hoped Lugosi would star in this zombie film. The produced

film of 1943 instead featured John Carradine as Dr. von Alterman.

50. *The Monster's Warning*

Announced by Monogram to be part of its 1943-44 season, this never-made film was mentioned in press releases along with *Voodoo Man* (1944).

51. *Dark Continent*

Albert de Courville, producer and coauthor (with P.H. Powell) of *Dark Continent*, desired a film lead for his Broadway production. The story itself unfolded as a psychological drama about prewar England. Lugosi wired de Courville on July 10, 1944, saying he would accept the role if a slight alteration in the character's accent could be made. The delighted producer approved of the change and was to send Lugosi a revised script the following week. Despite mutual enthusiasm, Lugosi did not appear.

52. *The Gold Bug*

Lugosi was to essay Legrand in Poe's tale for what would have been his tenth Monogram film produced by Sam Katzman. It appeared on the 1944 schedule; the studio canceled it for reasons unknown.

53. *Mystery House* films

In 1944 an announcement came that Universal planned a series of movies based on Lugosi's radio show *Mystery House*. This never-realized project would have been similar to the *Inner Sanctum* series at Universal with Lon Chaney, Jr.

54. *House of Dracula*

While Lugosi had been considered for this film's earlier incarnation (the never-made *Dracula Meets the Wolf Man*) in 1943, some press releases also mentioned his name in connection with the 1945 project. One particular article in the *Oakland Tribune* claimed that Lugosi had to rush to Universal to make the film after finishing his association with the play *No Traveler Returns*. Instead, John Carradine donned the cape as he had in *House of Frankenstein* (1944).

55. *Dracula*

Another project Don Marlowe mentioned to Lugosi in late 1947 was a revival of the stage *Dracula* in England. Although the Hungarian toured that country in 1951, it was through the efforts of Richard Gordon rather than Marlowe. What remains curious about Marlowe's plans are the notices in *Variety* that indicate that such a tour almost occurred. On February 4, 1948, the trade claimed, "Bela Lugosi leaves April 15 for London to open a revival of *Dracula*." Plans apparently fell through between those dates.

56. Don Marlowe projects

When Lugosi signed a contract with manager/agent Don Marlowe, the latter mentioned such projects as (in Lugosi's words) "an MGM picture—the Columbia '*Chandu*' serial and different other things." After *Abbott and Costello Meet Frankenstein* found success at the box office, Marlowe tried to interest Universal Studios in a script called *The Return of Dracula* as a sequel to the 1931 film *Dracula*. Marlowe's listing in the October 1948 *Player's Directory Bulletin* included "an Invisible Man" film at Universal-International and *The Bela Lugosi Show* on CBS as the current Lugosi projects.

One trade announcement during this period held that Lugosi would star in a 3-D motion picture, presumably another of Marlowe's plans. The January 1949 listing again claimed *The Bela Lugosi Show* as being in the works, as well as *The Inner Sanctum* at MGM. None of these projects ever got off the ground, with the exception of *The Inner Sanctum* ... a film that bore no trace of Lugosi or Marlowe.

57. Spook show with Kim Key

Lugosi and Alexander Great (aka Kim Key) thought about forming a spook show in 1948 when they ran across one another in Detroit. "My idea is to build a midnight show, a spook show, with your mystery and my magic," Great told Lugosi. The two discussed it and even made some photos of the Hungarian in a magic store. Lugosi, however, had to leave town for his next personal appearance, and Great never saw him again.

58. Dracula

Variety claimed on October 3, 1951, that Lugosi had been made an offer to tour Australia for a year in the stage version of *Dracula*. The play would have opened in January 1952 in Sydney, but nothing became of the idea.

59. Return of the White Zombie

During the early fifties, Lugosi told reporters he was soon to star in a sequel to his 1932 classic *White Zombie*, to be titled, appropriately enough, *Return of the White Zombie*. He jokingly mentioned that it was a film, *not* a drink.

60. The Six Arms of Siva

Lugosi himself wrote to author Walter C. Brown, who had penned a novel called *The Six Arms of Siva*. In December 1953 Brown declined Lugosi's offer to enter an agreement that would supposedly bring the tale before movie cameras. "I would much rather make an outright sale of movie rights to a film studio then enter into any speculative arrangement," he responded to Lugosi. "I too have to make a living, and as my business is writing, I am not in a position to handle complicated financial arrangements that are centered thousands of miles away."

61. Dr. Acula

Ed Wood planned to write scripts, with Ted Allan producing, for this television program. The Hungarian planned to star. Lugosi mentioned this while guest-starring on the *You Asked for It* television program in 1953.

62. Dracula

In his last years, Lugosi strongly hoped to remake *Dracula* (1931) in color and in 3-D. Efforts by Richard Sheffield, who then had a Lugosi fan club, were made in 1953; he circulated a petition and gathered signatures from theatergoers who wanted to see the film produced. Sheffield mailed the petition to Universal Studios, but nothing came of it.

63. King Robot

In 1953 producer Alex Gordon, a friend of Lugosi's, planned this as a combination of scenes from *Mother Riley Meets the Vampire* (1951) and new footage of Lugosi. Gordon soon scrapped the idea, as Lugosi appeared too ill to match the earlier footage.

64. Sequel to *Mother Riley Meets the Vampire*

In late 1953 newspapers mentioned that Lugosi was to head to England to make a "sequel" picture for J. Arthur Rank, presumably a follow-up to *Mother Riley Meets the Vampire*. The film was never shot.

65. Dracula

In January 1954 Ed Wood attempted to obtain the rights to the play from Samuel French, desiring to produce a new stage version with Lugosi.

66. The Bowery Boys Meet the Monster

While appearing in Las Vegas in late February and early March 1954, Lugosi was asked to costar with Leo Gorcey once again. The trades said that the only question was one of "moola." Rather than Lugosi, however, the finished film would spotlight John Dehner as the heavy.

67. Frank Winkler film project

While promoting "fights, wrestling, and ice-skating" in Seattle, Ed Wood befriended an agent named Frank Winkler. In March 1954, after having known him for some seven years, Wood tried to interest Winkler in a picture deal with Lugosi. The idea remained just that ... an idea.

68. Ron Ormond film project

Ron Ormond was a friend of Ed Wood's and eventually the coauthor of two books with Ormond McGill, *Into the Strange*

Unknown and Religious Mysteries of the Orient. In March 1954 the transvestite filmmaker wrote to Lugosi claiming that he could "swing one of his pictures your way." Wood was also trying to interest Ormond in an "island" script called *Enchanted Isle.*

69. The Vampire's Tomb

Many have erroneously referred to this unmade Lugosi/Ed Wood film as *Tomb of the Vampire.* In March 1954 Wood told Lugosi that Ford Beebe would direct the project for Allied Artists and that the title had been shortened to "The Vampire." When this didn't pan out, Wood officially announced its shooting (which would have been done over six days and with the original title) in August 1954. *Variety* claimed that Bela Lugosi, Loretta King, Lyle Talbot, Dolores Fuller, and Hazel Franklin had been signed for the project. On September 9, the *Hollywood Reporter* claimed that production was to begin in October. Wood apparently would have directed this incarnation.

Bela's character in the tale, "Dr. Acula," is hired to help prove that a character's death was due to murder. The rest of the cast was planned to include Tom Keene, Bobby Jordan, Lyle Talbot, Loretta King, Dolores Fuller, Duke Moore, and "Devila." Instead of filming this script, however, Wood began *Bride of the Atom.* A few silent scenes of Lugosi in a cape were actually shot in 1956, when Wood possibly revived plans for the film. The footage taken later appeared in *Plan 9 from Outer Space* (1959), a very different film from the script for *The Vampire's Tomb.*

70. Bela Lugosi comic book

In late March 1954 Ed Wood contacted a number of comic book companies on Lugosi's behalf (referring to himself as "Lugosi's manager"), and attempted to interest them in a Bela Lugosi comic, but nothing came of the matter. Among the companies to which Wood sent letters: St. John Publishing Company, Quality Comics, Toby Press, Inc., National Comics Publications, Ziff-Davis Publications, Fiction House, Dell Publications, Lev Gleason Comics, Ace Publications, and Crestwood Publications.

71. The Terror

Ed Wood had plans for a 15-minute radio show in April 1954 and even mailed Lugosi one script. The subsequent stories, as he mentioned 12 more to Lugosi, were to be written or bought by Wood. The show itself fell through.

72. Jailbait

Ed Wood planned the role of Dr. Boris Gregor for Lugosi, who was unable to appear. Herbert Rawlinson, a former silent screen actor, assumed the part of Gregor, a physician who alters the face of criminal Steve Reeves. The film opened in May 1954.

73. Doctor Voodoo

Another potential Ed Wood–Bela Lugosi film project, though for this one Boris Karloff was also to star. In 1954 the president of Allied Artists turned down the script, which was reminiscent of 1934's *The Black Cat.* Friends of Wood's have also alluded to this project as *Voodoo Doctor.* Wood told Lugosi that Harold Merish and Ford Beebe at Allied decided the fate of this project.

74. Ed Wood film project

In 1954 Wood mentioned to Lugosi that he had access to $1,000 to promote a film, under the agreement that he, Lugosi, and the "friend" with the money be equal partners. The director told Lugosi it would be a great situation because "you should own a good piece of one of your own films since they always make good money." The film never came to fruition.

75. Revenge of the Dead

Ed Wood first proposed this idea during the midfifties as a Lugosi film. After the actor's death, the idea germinated into the Wood film *Night of the Ghouls* (1960), which acted as a semisequel to *Bride of the Atom* (1955).

76. *The Ghoul Goes West/The Phantom Ghoul*

Planned as a horror–Western with Lugosi and Gene Autry, this was to be shot following the Hungarian's 1955 release from the Metropolitan Hospital. It was to incorporate both color and widescreen. When Autry backed out, Ed Wood considered Bob Steele and Ken Maynard. Harold Daniels would have directed, with Wood producing.

The project had earlier been known as *The Phantom Ghoul*, which Ed Wood considered in 1953 as a possible 3-D film project for Lugosi. Wood regarded Lon Chaney, Jr., Tor Johnson, and John Carradine as potential costars. The script, which Wood wrote, had Lugosi playing a mad "professor," bearing a few similarities to Wood's film *Bride of the Atom* (1955). The professor spoke lines like, "I profected [*sic*] the way to make a giant of a man — a man any country would give a fortune in money and glory to possess. With such a giant man whichever country gave enough, could rule over the world...."

77. *The Final Curtain*

Written by Ed Wood, this script was in Lugosi's possession at the time of his death in August 1956. The plot features a vaudevillian who dies on stage and then meditates over his entire career. His coffin summons him at the conclusion. One intriguing but false Lugosi story claims that a copy of *The Final Curtain* was in his hands at the moment he died.

78. Michael Jon Spencer film idea

Michael Jon Spencer and Richard Sheffield befriended Lugosi in 1953. When they met Ed Wood once at Lugosi's home, the director became excited by Spencer's one-paragraph idea for a Lugosi film. Wood gave the two a token $1 payment to make the sale legal. The story featured an aging horror film actor married to an ailing wife. The actor requests work from his former directors, each of whom refuses. When his wife dies, the actor plans the deaths of the directors along the same lines as the plots of the films they made together. Wood supposedly sold the tale to another filmmaker, with elements of the story later becoming *How to Make a Monster* (1958).

79. *Undead Masses/Ghouls on the Moon*

Ed Wood's idea for this film began to circulate immediately following Lugosi's death. One of the two above titles would have been attached to a selection of previously unused Lugosi footage. The problem with this story is that Wood was later forced to use very limited Lugosi footage repetitiously throughout *Plan 9 from Outer Space* (1959). If Wood truly had enough film of the Hungarian to make anything close to a feature, the question remains why it did not surface in *Plan 9 from Outer Space* (1959), when he resorted to using the same short sequences of Lugosi over and over again.

III. Works By or About Lugosi

14. Reviews, Articles, and Pamphlets

The following is a selective bibliography of articles and pamphlets pertaining to Bela Lugosi which have been printed over a span of almost a century. Due to the large number of magazine articles written on Lugosi since his death, those that are repetitive in their information and photographs have been left out. Moreover, articles that contain numerous errors have been excluded. Unfortunately, most literary works in the horror film genre have been very derivative; thus, they have been intentionally overlooked. The articles listed offer unique historical information, interesting critical insight, or rare photographs. Annotations following the bibliographic entries explain the value of each.

Critical reviews of Lugosi's films and plays are also included. Rather than being a descriptive entry, quotes pertaining to Lugosi from the original review are given, following the bibliographic information. For a broader view, one should obtain and examine the entire review. In cases where the review did not specifically address Lugosi, comments on the production as an entity are quoted.

His better-known work is represented here by multiple reviews, selected for a variety of reasons. For one, more widely read publications hold a certain priority because of their importance and circulation, as well as the ease with which the original reviews can be obtained at libraries and archives. At times, diverse reviews (as in the case of *The Mystery of the Mary Celeste*) have been included specifically to show the opposing opinions given of Lugosi's work. One should keep in mind that those reviews often did not coincide with the film's popularity.

Biographical and interview-style articles written during Lugosi's lifetime (such as the fascinating series of articles by Gladys Hall) should be taken with a grain of salt in terms of their accuracy. A 1933 article in *Vanity Fair* noted that some 5 million people bought movie magazines every month, despite their "furious exaggeration." These kinds of articles were intended as fan material and should be regarded as such. They are included, however, to illustrate how audiences perceived Lugosi while he was a major star. This aspect is historically important to consider, given that Lugosi was often viewed publicly as a mystery man, very close to his on-screen image.

Being Hungarian, Lugosi received much press in his homeland and in Hungarian journals printed in the United States. Some of the more interesting ones are catalogued, but many are overlooked because of their limited accessibility, as well as their need for translation. Moreover, a few of the dates for articles from 1920 and before vary from what has been printed in earlier sources; the dates used represent the most accurate information currently available in Hungarian archives.

Taken as a whole, these articles complement greatly the books that have dealt with Lugosi. Furthermore, the selective nature of this compilation should serve to divert attention from inaccurate and uninteresting pieces that do not add to the world of Lugosi knowledge.

1. *Temesvári Színpad* (*The Temesvar Stage* of Temesvar, Hungary), 29 Dec. 1903.

Review of the play *Trilby*: "Béla Lugosi as Svengali's evil henchman was absolutely spellbinding."

2. *Temesvári Színpad*, 17 Feb. 1904.

Review of the play *Rang és Mod* (*Rank and Style*): Lugosi was acknowledged as "titillating women with a strong undercurrent of passion seldom experienced on the Temesvar stage."

3. *Mai Színlap* (*Today's Playbill* of Szeged, Hungary), 2 Sept. 1910.

"Last night, Béla Lugossy, a new member of the troupe, demonstrated his artistic talent in the role of Romeo, which will undoubtedly destine him as the permanent replacement for Milhály Kertész. The pleasant, handsome actor will certainly become one of the greats, judging by audience reaction to his performance."

4. *Szeged Napló* (*Szeged Journal* of Szeged, Hungary), 3 Sept. 1910.

Review of the play *Rómeó és Juliet*: "It was evident that he [Lugosi] prepared his part diligently, knew his lines well. Yet sometimes he spoke so quickly I couldn't understand a word. His exuberance was excessive, and I have never seen such a youthful portrayal of the role. Nevertheless, his youthfully naughty lovelorness was accented by burning, thirsty lust, and the audience clapped enthusiastically for the young Lugosi who, I feel, might better use his qualities in a modern role."

5. *Színházi Újság* (*The Theatre News* of Szeged, Hungary), 14 May 1911.

The Theatre News printed a speech by Béla Kalmany, drama critic of Szeged, who paid tribute to "Lugosy's" talents and bade him farewell as he left for Budapest.

6. Lugosi, Béla. "The Structure of the Formation of Our Union." *Színészek Lapja* (*The Actor's Page* of Budapest, Hungary), 1 May 1919.

Lugosi offered his own defense of an actor's worth and importance for this Budapest journal.

7. "*Der Fluch Der Menschheit*" (*The Curse of Man*). *Film Magazin* (*Film Magazine* of Germany), 11 Jan. 1920.

"Richard Eichberg directs with satisfactory results, although the action is a bit awkward at times. Violetta Napierska, Béla Lugosi, Robert Scholz, and Willi Kaiser-Heyl are to be praised in the main roles."

8. "*Slaven Fremdes Willens*" ("*Slave of a Foreign Will*") *Erste International Filmzeitung* (*First International Film Newspaper* of Germany), 11 Jan. 1920.

This review of the German film mentions that Lugosi gives an "uncanny portrayal of demoniacal passion."

9. Corbin, John. "The Red Poppy." *New York Times*, 21 Dec. 1922.

"Bela Lugosi is a newcomer of quite splendid mien, romantically handsome and young. Hungarian though he is said to be, he looks every inch the Spanish pirate of romance. He is a stranger to the crew at *The Red Poppy*, awaiting the blond moll, who has at first sight enchanted him, and the habitues try every means to pick a quarrel. With a forward thrust of the shoulder, with a mere glance, he quells them. Equally convincing is his passion of kicks and clenches. In the final scene he is not without a touch of the truly noble spirit. Here is an actor of fine achievement and possibly greater promise."

10. Hammond, Percy. "Miss Estelle Winwood Is Satisfactory Even If *The Red Poppy* Is a Trifle Otherwise." *New York Herald-Tribune*, 21 Dec. 1922.

"Played as he is by Bela Lugosi, of the National Theater, Budapest, Fernando submits, we suspect, few reasons for the Princess' feverish deportment. A tall, sallow, lugubrious and earnest person, with luscious eyes and an accent, he strove last night to please. But we thought him the least likely of all the other criminals present to inspire desperate behavior in the breast of this or any other naughty princess."

11. "Bela Lugosi." *Theatre Magazine*, May 1923.

"A virile young Hungarian actor whose personal success in *The Red Poppy* with Estelle Winwood points to his becoming permanently a favorite of American playgoers." A beautiful portrait of Lugosi accompanies the short piece.

12. "*The Silent Command.*" *New York Times*, 5 Sept. 1923.

"There is a great deal of acting by turning the pupils of the eyes back and forth. The villain, of course, turns his eyes at times into mere slits. The splashing waters, the uniforms, and the sea pictures are very good."

13. "*The Silent Command.*" *Variety*, 9 Sept. 1923.

"It's a red-fire, flag-waving picture that relies on the real old sure fire hoke to get over. In the cast are a lot of names that sound imposing but they really amount to little."

14. "*The Rejected Woman.*" *New York Times*, 5 Mar. 1924.

"It is a rambling story with weird subtitles. There are some effective blizzard scenes in the first portion of this photodrama, but they are not particularly interesting, owing to the lack of real suspense in the narrative."

15. "*The Rejected Woman.*" *Variety*, 7 May 1924.

"As a hokum production in the cheaper grade of house it will serve well enough, but as a pre-release in a Main Stem house it runs for Sweeney."

16. Donaghey, Frederick. "Here's a Bold, Gay Piece of German Make—And It's Nothing for the Facile Blushers." *Chicago Tribune*, 2 June 1924.

Review of the stage play *The Werewolf*: "Mr. Lugosi, evidently a good actor, was a bit heavy; and his dialect was not a beneficence in a cast which varied uncommonly in its attitude toward English diction."

17. Collins, Charles. "Oh How European the Clark Street Drama Is Getting!" *Chicago Evening Post*, 24 June 1924.

Review of the stage play *The Werewolf*: "Warburton Gamble, as a Spanish man of the world, Lennox Pawle, as the droll expert in occultism, and Bela Lugosi, as the sleek Don Juanish butler, are exceedingly good. This is a brilliant company, giving an adept interpretation of a play that requires the utmost finesse in light cynicism."

18. *The New York Telegraph*, 15 Mar. 1925.

The *Telegraph* printed an interesting profile photograph of Lugosi, along with an announcement of his upcoming part in *The Midnight Girl.*

19. "*Daughters Who Pay.*" *Variety*, 13 May 1925.

"The result is a picture full of action and should please in the daily houses."

20. "*Arabesque* Reveals Pictorial Beauty." *New York Times*, 21 Oct. 1925.

"The performance is quite sufficient."

21. "A Sheik, a Lovely Lady, and a Grand Duchess on Parade." *New York Herald-Tribune*, 25 Oct. 1925.

This article includes a section on the reviewer's desire to meet Lugosi, who immediately informed him that he hadn't eaten or slept for 48 hours. A group including Lugosi and the *Herald-Tribune* columnist then scurried to a Hungarian restaurant on Eighty-second Street and Second Avenue. The meal, accompanied by live music, consisted of noodles, chicken, and paprika. Lugosi spoke to them of the language barrier he faced with English, as well as of his views on acting.

22. Atkinson, J. Brooks. "*Open House* a Naive Play." *New York Times*, 15 Dec. 1925.

"The plot is developed with little ingenuity and much artificiality."

23. "*Open House* Mechanical and Consistently Tedious." *New York Herald-Tribune*, 15 Dec. 1925.

"The two principal actors in the cast are not unknown to Broadway. They are Ramsey Wallace and Bela Lugosi. Mr. Lugosi made the most recent appearance locally, being seen as the Arabian Sheik in *Arabesque*."

24. Atkinson, J. Brooks. "*The Devil in the Cheese.*" *New York Times*, 30 Dec. 1926.

"As the chief bandit, Mr. Lugosi acts with an authority and a cadence worthy of better things."

25. Hammond, Percy. "*The Devil in the Cheese*, a Sweet and Novel Frolic by Tom Cushing, at the Charles Hopkins Theater." *New York Herald-Tribune*, 30 Dec. 1926.

"An earnest, unaffected actor named Fredric March plays the hero handsomely, and a foreigner, Bela Lugosi, impersonates a Greek brigand, masked under the habit of a monk, better than I have ever seen a character of the kind portrayed."

26. "*Punchinello.*" *Motion Picture Today*, 1926.

"As a class short, this one rates with the best."

27. Anderson, John. "*Dracula.*" *New York Post*, 6 Oct. 1927.

"Mr. Lugosi performs Dracula with funeral decorations suggesting a little more an operatically included but cheerless mortician than a bloodsucking fiend."

28. Atkinson, J. Brooks. "*Dracula.*" *New York Times*, 6 Oct. 1927.

"Played more swiftly, fiercely and mysteriously, *Dracula* could doubtless scare the skeptics out of several years' growth into complete submission. Sometimes Mr. Lugosi, as Dracula, is, like the performance, a little too deliberate and confident."

29. Hammond, Percy. "The Theaters." *New York Herald-Tribune*, 6 Oct. 1927.

"The torments of the first American performance [of *Dracula*] might have been more alarming had the demon been illustrated less stiffly than he was by Mr. Lugosi. It was a rigid hobgoblin presented by Mr. Lugosi, resembling a wax man in a shop window more than a suave ogre bent on nocturnal mischief-making. Nothing more blithely bloodcurdling has happened in the Drama since *The Bat*."

30. "The Theatre." *The New Yorker*, 15 Oct. 1927.

"The play [*Dracula*] could be even more terrifying without some of the arrant hokum which has been introduced, but it is quite terrifying enough, and supplies that long felt need of the New York stage, a shudder that you can't shake off."

31. Whitaker, Alma. "Lugosi, Creator of Dracula Role, Is Courtly Hungarian." *Los Angeles Times*, 17 June 1928.

Printed in anticipation of *Dracula*'s opening at the Los Angeles Biltmore on June 25, this article mentions Lugosi's stay at the Ambassador Hotel and also his screen test with Gloria Swanson. Whitaker also mentions that Lugosi spent his free time in Los Angeles swimming, playing tennis and golf, and associating with fellow Hungarians in the entertainment business. Vilma

Banky, Lya de Putti, Victor Varconi, and Michael Curtiz are among the notables listed.

32. "*Dracula* Is at Biltmore." *Los Angeles Times*, 24 June 1928.

This article, accompanied by elaborate artwork of the play, mentions the plot of the West Coast version starring Lugosi.

33. "*How to Handle Women*." *Variety*, 28 June 1928.

"An utterly tiresome comedy that couldn't amuse any audience of intelligence."

34. "Hollywood Likes Vampire Actor." *Los Angeles Record*, 29 June 1928.

Brief article examines Lugosi's immediate acceptance in Hollywood, mentioning that he was "much sought after in the best homes of the movie colony."

35. "*Dracula* Is Discussed as Picture." *Los Angeles Times*, 22 July 1928.

Unique story in which Lugosi contends that *Dracula* would make for a great sound film. Universal Studios is not mentioned, nor is any other. The "discussion" is completely from Lugosi and the Biltmore Theater cast.

36. "Return to Native Accent Retards Actor's English." *Los Angeles Times*, 29 July 1928.

Lugosi prophesied the doom of many silent screen stars, while seeing talkies as holding great potential for stage actors. Furthermore, he claimed that the part of Dracula, since he used a "south–Hungary accent," had actually set back his progress in English diction "two years."

37. "They Shriek, Faint Daily at *Dracula*." *Los Angeles Times*, 11 Aug. 1928.

Statistics compiled by a nurse and a Biltmore Theater doorman concerning the first seven weeks of *Dracula*'s run in Los Angeles list the following information: "Faintings 110; shrieks 20 (per performance); left theater (first act 19); left theater (second act) 150, left theater (third act) 1; returned (after revival) 100; returned visit 10 (per performance); husbands summoned to escort home wives 10 (per performance); taxicab increase 500%."

38. Johnson, Fred. "*Dracula* Escapes Coffin, Reveals in S.F." *San Francisco Call*, 25 Aug. 1928.

An interviewer found Lugosi in his Mark Hopkins Hotel bedroom and inquired about his thoughts on the theater. Lugosi commented how unfortunate it was that the American stage sought "types" rather than training actors to portray multiple kinds of roles. He also happily mentioned finding a California wine that was similar to one he enjoyed in Hungary. Turning the tables on the reporter, Béla asked his own questions, inquiring about the best bridle paths and golf courses.

39. "Nurse with Smelling Salts Regular Adjunct to Staff." *San Francisco Chronicle*, 25 Aug. 1928.

According to this article, the ammonia-carrying nurse at the Columbia Theater run of *Dracula* handled about 14 faints per evening. The story stated, "Largely responsible for that sinking feeling as experienced by Columbia patrons is Bela Lugosi as suave Count Dracula."

40. Waite, Edgar. "*Dracula* Practices Mysteries Off Stage." *San Francisco Examiner*, 26 Aug. 1928.

A nervous reporter—who was "too scared" to interview Lugosi in his hotel or dressing room, wishing to be in a more public place—tracks the actor's career, including such erroneous stories as one about Lugosi's having been "government supervisor of all theatrical activity in Hungary." The reporter also nabbed Lugosi's tales about those in his homeland who actually believed in vampires, supposedly plunging an occasional stake into hearts of the undead.

41. "*The Veiled Woman*." *The Free Press* (Detroit, Michigan), 18 Nov. 1928.

"If this actor [Lugosi] gives talking pictures a fair trial I predict he will be a strong sensation as he is one of the strongest personalities of the stage."

42. "*Dracula* Comes to Music Box: Lugosi in Lead Again." *Los Angeles Record*, 18 May 1929.

During the 1929 Los Angeles run of *Dracula*, Lugosi gave his definition of what a vampire really is, in response to "hundreds of letters" asking for an explanation.

43. "'Dracula Kiss' to Be Popular Among Villains." *Los Angeles Record*, 18 May 1929.

Lugosi noted that the evil "Dracula Kiss" would become the kiss for villains and was itself responsible for the play's success at L.A.'s Music Box Theater.

44. "Vampires and Bats in Foray." *Los Angeles Times*, 20 May 1929.

"To a rising crescendo of shrieks and half-suppressed ejaculations, Bram Stoker's thriller, *Dracula*, noised its way into the Hollywood Music Box Theater last night. *Dracula* is the vampire play first seen here at the Biltmore last summer. Bela Lugosi portrays his original role of 'Dracula' with sinister suavity. He does easily the outstanding work of the play and seems even more malevolently predatory with his ghostly, phosphorescent make-up and Satanic mannerisms than he did last summer."

45. "Lugosi Flouts Superstition." *Los Angeles Times*, 24 May 1929.

This short article brought attention to the fact that since he smashed a looking glass every evening in the stage version of *Dracula*, Lugosi dispelled the belief in bad luck that comes from breaking a mirror. "He has been doing it for two years, which have been replete with good fortune."

46. "*Dracula*." *San Francisco Examiner*, 23 July 1929.

"Bela Lugosi moves through the drama with sinister suavity. He endows his portrait of the immortal man who rises from the earth at night to live on the blood of the living, with imagination and an authority born of traditional lore. His make-up is an achievement."

47. "Shudders Fill Tale of Old, Wicked Count." *San Francisco Chronicle*, 23 July 1929.

"Essentially this presentation of O. D. Woodward [of *Dracula*] is not good drama, but it provides entertainment of the variety that should prove lucrative."

48. Johnson, Fred. "*Dracula* Sees No 'Talkie' Future." *San Francisco Call*, 27 July 1929.

Lugosi announced to this reporter that "speakies" were a novelty, claiming that silent pictures would continue to be produced and that the "flesh-and-blood" stage would further its popularity. He also spoke of his love for sculpture, painting, dancing, and singing, each being a help to his stage presence. The article claimed that his home — "one of the most artistic in Hollywood" — was designed in no particular period or design.

49. Hanifin, Ada. "Dracula Found Out; Secret of Lugosi Revealed." *San Francisco Examiner*, 28 July 1929.

An interview with Lugosi, conducted at the Columbia Theater, covers his views on the theater in Hungary and his marriage to Beatrice Woodruff Weeks. When asked whether his wife was blonde or brunette, Lugosi answered that he did not know. "You see, it is like this. The eyes got in the way. You understand." Prefacing the interview material is an introduction that paints him as very much the mystery man.

50. Shaffer, Rosalind. "Talkie Language Difficulties Met." *San Francisco Chronicle*, 28 July 1929.

Quotes from Lugosi are included in this article, which examines Lugosi's efforts to learn English, ranging from his work in

1922's *The Red Poppy* to the film *The Thirteenth Chair* and his touring version of *Dracula*, then headlining at San Francisco's Fulton Theater.

51. "Hungarian Stage Star Weds Widow of S.F. Architect." *San Francisco Examiner*, 28 July 1929.

Short article from Redwood City, California, mentions the wedding of Lugosi to Beatrice Woodruff Weeks on the prior day. The ceremony was presided over by Justice of the Peace Edward I. McAuliffe, and many local citizens waited outside for the wedded couple to appear.

52. Jimerson, Royal. "*Dracula* Advised for Pleasantly Horrific Night." *San Francisco Examiner*, 4 Aug. 1929.

"Thousands of spectators have viewed *Dracula* with widely variant emotions during its two runs at the Columbia Theater, with the formidable Bela Lugosi in the title role of the Transylvanian vampire. And, while many were disappointed, a far larger number succumbed without a struggle to the weird titillations it induces on the spine and flesh of the beholder."

53. "*Prisoners*." *Variety*, 21 Aug. 1929.

"The grizzled book wormers know well how Ferenc Molnar stands in the batting files of the literary league, yet in the filming of his novel, *Prisoners*, the celluloid fans will be disappointed. Some nice photographic shots and some of the scenes set a Hungarian background on a Hollywood lot."

54. Hall, Gladys. "True Hollywood Ghost Stories: The Case of the Man Who Dares Not Fall Asleep." *Motion Picture*, Aug. 1929.

Wonderful photos of Lugosi from the stage version of *Dracula* complement this article. The first of Gladys Hall's articles on Lugosi makes strong mention of "real" vampires. One brown-eyed, female vamp in particular supposedly haunts Lugosi, and thus he dares not sleep and cannot love. Unbelievable, yet a sign of the building public image of Lugosi as a real-life vampire mystery man.

55. "*Prisoners*." *Motion Picture*, Aug. 1929.

"This is one of those hybrids in which characters suddenly burst into disconcerting speech after several reels of subtitles. Bela Lugosi makes a very European villain."

56. "The Kiss That Kills." *Motion Picture Classic*, Oct. 1929.

Beautiful Duncan photograph of Lugosi complements a paragraph that rumors Lugosi will star in a film version of *Dracula*. This is particularly interesting in view of the fact that Lon Chaney, Sr., was still living at the time.

57. Scheuer, Philip K. "Veiller's Thriller a Talkie." *Los Angeles Times*, 1 Nov. 1929.

Review of *The Thirteenth Chair*: "In this cast of unusually promising calibre [is] ... the frowning Bela Lugosi of *Dracula* fame."

58. "Lugosi Wins Heart of Clara Bow, Says Second Wife, Seeking Divorce." *New York Daily Mirror*, 5 Nov. 1929.

This scandal sheet mentions Lugosi's affair with Clara Bow and his impending divorce from Beatrice Weeks. Quotes allegedly from Weeks are included in this very inaccurate article, claiming for instance that Lugosi was a real count and that Weeks was his second wife; in reality, she was his third. The *Daily Mirror* featured a photograph of Weeks and Lugosi on the cover.

59. "Wife of *Dracula* Star Says Role Carried Too Far." *San Francisco Chronicle*, 10 Dec. 1929.

Front-page article describes the divorce court testimony in which Lugosi's third wife, Beatrice Woodruff Weeks, mentions how temperamental, sullen, and morose he was.

60. Hunter, Helen Unity. "Screen's Spotlight." *Los Angeles Record*, 17 Dec. 1929.

Short article on Lugosi, who mentions

he believes it is much easier to become a movie star in the United States than in Europe.

61. "*The Thirteenth Chair.*" *Variety*, 22 Jan. 1930.

"As usual, the one least suspected turns out to be the culprit. Finish itself is weak, after two killings, with the second murder left unexplained. The scenes are laid in India, and the characters speak with that broad, overdone English accent that has become unwelcome to American audiences."

62. Hall, Mordaunt. "*Such Men Are Dangerous.*" *New York Times*, 8 Mar. 1930.

"Bela Lugosi gives a sincere performance as Dr. Goodman."

63. "*Such Men Are Dangerous.*" *Variety*, 12 Mar. 1930.

"With all of its exploitation possibilities and newspaper hookups, it remains mediocre fare for the better first runs."

64. "**Producers Have Their Eyes on Him.**" *Hollywood Filmograph*, 2 Aug. 1930.

An interesting piece that argues Lugosi is the logical choice for the lead in Universal's upcoming filming of *Dracula*. Quotes from various newspapers are used, including one from the *Oakland Post-Enquirer*, which mentioned that Louis Bromfield, E.M. Asher, and Dudley Murphey had all three viewed Lugosi at the Fulton Theater to consider him further for the role. Several articles appeared subsequently in this pro-Lugosi film magazine.

65. "**Bela Lugosi.**" *Hollywood Filmograph*, 9 Aug. 1930.

The *Filmograph*, one of Lugosi's prime supporters, printed his picture on its cover.

66. "**Bela Lugosi.**" *Hollywood Filmograph*, 16 Aug. 1930.

A short paragraph and photograph again establish support for Lugosi and lobby for his gaining the role of *Dracula* at Universal Studios.

67. "**Universal Has Made Test of Bela Lugosi for *Dracula* Talkie.**" *Hollywood Filmograph*, 30 Aug. 1930.

Lugosi's initial screen test for *Dracula* excites the *Filmograph*, which mentions that Carl Laemmle's approval had not yet been heard.

68. "**Pulling for Him.**" *Hollywood Filmograph*, 6 Sept. 1930.

Brief mention that "everybody that is anybody is pulling for Bela Lugosi to play *Dracula.*"

69. "**Ian Keith to Play Dracula: Rumored.**" *Hollywood Filmograph*, 13 Sept. 1930.

This premature announcement was incorrect, but despite the announcement of Ian Keith the article still exhibits a pro-Lugosi sentiment.

70. "**Bela Lugosi Signed by Universal for *Dracula*.**" *Hollywood Filmograph*, 20 Sept. 1930.

The *Filmograph* tells of Universal Studios' final choice for the lead in *Dracula*, and mentioned how the magazine's editor had even said to "everyone that had any power" that the role should be Lugosi's. Several successful camera tests are given as one of the prime reasons Universal signed Lugosi.

71. "**Bela Lugosi Praises Director Tod Browning.**" *Hollywood Filmograph*, 18 Oct. 1930.

Lugosi speaks about his stage personification and Browning's help in molding his performance of Dracula for it to transfer well to the medium of film. His remarks on director Browning are particularly complimentary.

72. "*Renegades.*" *New York Times*, 8 Nov. 1930.

"Although it is endowed with impressive desert scenes and capable acting, *Renegades*, an audible pictorial adaptation of Andre Armandy's novel of the French Foreign Legion, is a muddled and tedious offering."

73. "*Renegades.*" *Variety,* 12 Nov. 1930.
"For general release and showing in the average theatre, it should net a satisfactory return."

74. "*Oh, for a Man.*" *Variety,* 3 Dec. 1930.
"Picture is hardly of deluxe house calibre, but in the neighborhood spots with some judicious cutting of the draggy opening sequence it should get by nicely."

75. "*Viennese Nights.*" *Variety,* 3 Dec. 1930.
"Plenty of good production all in acceptable color, direction beyond reproach, well assembled cast and everything, but it's a musical."

76. Hall, Gladys. "The Feminine Love of Horror." *Motion Picture Classic,* Jan. 1931.
Another of the intriguing and sometimes outrageous Hall articles, again building a mystique of solitude around Lugosi. The author presents Lugosi as a man who "lives alone in his darkened house. The man who never sleeps at night. The man to whom no woman can stay married." An interesting curio, but far from reality.

77. "Is He the Second Chaney?" *Silver Screen,* Jan. 1931.
An interesting comparison of Lugosi to the silent screen star printed shortly before the release of *Dracula.*

78. Thirer, Irene. "*Dracula.*" *New York Daily News,* 13 Feb. 1931.
"It is superbly photographed and presented to audible screen audiences at the capable movie direction of Tod Browning—megaphoner of so many mysteries that he knows every trick of the type. Bela Lugosi's performance as Count Dracula is a repetition of his stage role. He's simply grand."

79. Watts, Richard Jr. "*Dracula.*" *New York Herald-Tribune,* 13 Feb. 1931.
"Bela Lugosi is even more effective than he was on the stage, which is something of a tribute."

80. Hall, Mordaunt. "*Dracula.*" *New York Times,* 14 Feb. 1931.
"Mr. Browning is fortunate in having in the leading role in this eerie work, Bela Lugosi, who played the same part on the stage when it was presented here in October 1927. What with Mr. Browning's imaginative direction and Mr. Lugosi's makeup and weird gestures, this picture succeeds to some extent in its grand guignol intentions. Most of the excitement takes place in Carfax Abbey and other places in England. Helen Chandler gives an excellent performance as one of the girls who is attacked by the 'undead' Count. Dwight Frye does fairly well as Renfield. This picture can at least boast as being the best of the many mystery films."

81. "*Dracula.*" *Film Daily,* 15 Feb. 1931.
"It is not a picture for too squeamish people to see, but there is no denying its dramatic power and tingling thrills. Bela Lugosi creates one of the most unique and powerful roles of the screen in this one."

82. Harris, Sidney. "*Dracula.*" *Billboard,* 21 Feb. 1931.
"Popular *Dracula* is now seen on the screen after a success as a Bram Stoker novel and a play by Hamilton Deane and John Balderston. It has been done splendidly, yet it is doubtful as to how it will react on the variety of audiences attending film houses. Bela Lugosi is Count Dracula and gives a brilliant portrayal, with his original stage work in that role meaning much."

83. Hall, Mordaunt. "*Dracula* as a Film: Tod Browning in His Element in Directing Stoker Fable—Other Productions." *New York Times,* 22 Feb. 1931.
"Mr. Lugosi succeeds in revealing the man-vampire as a hideous creature, one that few would like to encounter within the

moss-covered walls of an old English abbey. Mr. Browning endeavors to add to the pallid fiend's general spine-tingling effect by devoting special lighting to Dracula's eyes."

84. "The New Pictures." *Time*, 23 Feb. 1931.

"*Dracula* is an exciting melodrama, not as good as it ought to be but a cut above the ordinary trapdoor and winding sheet type of mystery film."

85. Tinee, Mae. "Awed Stillness Greets Movie About *Dracula*." *Chicago Tribune*, 21 Mar. 1931.

"Bela Lugosi, as photographed in the title role, is a weird looking creature. Edward Van Sloan does a better job, however, as Dr. Helsing — which role he played on the stage. The direction appeared not all what it should have been, considering Tod Browning megaphoned — and I wonder why? But — *Dracula*, as a whole, is quite a satisfactory thriller."

86. Schallert, Edwin. "*Fifty Million Frenchmen* — Spirited Comedy." *Los Angeles Times*, 29 Mar. 1931.

"Warner Brothers' presentation of a stage success has capital values of entertainment. Others [in the cast] include ... Bela Lugosi [who was not billed on the film itself]."

87. Scheuer, Philip. "Adventures of *Dracula* Now in Film Form." *Los Angeles Times*, 30 Mar. 1931.

"Many of the 'shots' seem 'posed,' especially those of Count Dracula — who, of all the company, should have been the most elusive, steeped as he is in the tradition of the Undead. Then, too, the dialogue is peculiarly artificial, although I admit that 'modernizing' it would have robbed it further of its claim to illusion. Music, perhaps, would have helped; but that is something to concern its creators more than the casual spectator, who can only report his own responses to the finished version."

88. Strauss, H. David. "*Fifty Million Frenchmen*." *Billboard*, 4 Apr. 1931.

"Usual musical comedy story, not as well adapted for the screen as some of those that have gone before."

89. "Spirits of Darkness." *True Mystic Crimes*, Apr. 1931.

The pulp magazine printed several pen-and-ink drawings of scenes from the film *Dracula* in appreciation of Lugosi.

90. Scheuer, Philip K. "Flagg and Quirt Go on Tour." *Los Angeles Times*, 1 June 1931.

Review of *Women of All Nations*: "In energy, if not altogether humor, they have succeeded."

91. "*Women of All Nations*." *Variety*, 2 June 1931.

"Far short of smash rating and winds up as merely program fare which the men will like more than the women, and the males won't be overly impressed."

92. "*The Black Camel*." *New York Times*, 4 July 1931.

"Tarnevarro — the man everyone but Charlie suspects — is played by Bela Lugosi."

93. "*The Black Camel*." *Film Daily*, 5 July 1931.

"There are bits of clever comedy and much good humor. Oland is perfectly cast and the remainder of the players give convincing readings."

94. "*Broadminded*." *Film Daily*, 5 July 1931.

"Bela Lugosi plays a Mexican with whom Brown gets into various trouble."

95. "*The Black Camel*." *Variety*, 7 July 1931.

"Bela Lugosi, the crystal peeker, and Victor Varconi as the first husband, are boys who can always look guilty under the right conditions and in this instance conditions are perfect between dialects and scowls."

14. Reviews, Articles, and Pamphlets 239

96. "*Broadminded.*" *Variety*, 7 July 1931.
"It's an exceptionally good comedy program talker."

97. *Film Daily*, 25 July 1931.
The *Film Daily* mentions Lugosi will star in Universal's *Frankenstein*.

98. "Weird Films: Character Changes in *Rue Morgue*." *New York Times*, 10 Jan. 1932.
This article informs the *Times*' readers that director Robert Florey made numerous changes in filming Poe's *Murders in the Rue Morgue* (1932).

99. Sinclair, John. "Master of Horrors." *Silver Screen*, Jan. 1932.
Though less than accurate, this piece is not as outlandish as the Gladys Hall articles. Sinclair crowned Lugosi with the "Master of Horrors" title just as Boris Karloff became a household name.

100. "*Murders in the Rue Morgue.*" *New York Times*, 11 Feb. 1932.
"The entire production suffers from an overzealous effort at terrorization, and the cast, inspired by the general hysteria, succumbs to the temptation to overact."

101. Watts, Richard Jr. "*Murders in the Rue Morgue.*" *New York Herald-Tribune*, 12 Feb. 1932.
"Bela Lugosi fails to be properly frightening as the mad doctor."

102. "*Murders in the Rue Morgue.*" *Film Daily*, 14 Feb. 1932.
"Bela Lugosi gives an intense characterization of the fanatical scientist who attempts to combine the blood of an ape with that of a white girl."

103. "*Murders in the Rue Morgue.*" *The Times* (London), 30 Mar. 1932.
"There is plenty of blood in this film, but the thunder lacks resonance and conviction ... poor acting and puerile production."

104. Schallert, Edwin. "Shivery Show Enjoyed." *Los Angeles Times*, 5 Apr. 1932.
Review of the Lugosi play *Murdered Alive*: Schallert mentioned, "It's a very fair horror play, and if you like them, you'll undoubtedly like it."

105. "Lugosi Plays with Three Broken Ribs." *Los Angeles Examiner*, 9 Apr. 1932.
The *Examiner* claimed that Lugosi broke three ribs after a 16-foot fall while performing in *Murdered Alive*, due to an "error of backstage mechanics." A physician was able to help with injuries, and Lugosi continued his work in the last act of the play.

106. *Los Angeles Examiner*, 10 Apr. 1932.
Short, untitled mention that Lugosi, then the star of *Murdered Alive*, was displaying his own sculptures at various Los Angeles exhibitions.

107. "Bela Lugosi Stars in Horror Play." *San Francisco News*, 23 Apr. 1932.
"*Murdered Alive* fails to gain distinction even by the presence of Bela Lugosi. The audience laughed at his lines. But that was no singular slight to Mr. Lugosi alone. It laughed at practically everybody else's, including Betty Ross Clarke's screams."

108. Warren, George C. "Thriller Is Hit on Orpheum Stage." *San Francisco Examiner*, 23 Apr. 1932.
Review of the stage play *Murdered Alive*: "What menace, I ask you, could impersonate the demented surgeon half so well as Bela Lugosi. His performance is skilled and smooth."

109. "Bela Lugosi Is Splendid in Dracula." *Oregon Daily Journal*, 30 May 1932.
Review of a Portland revival of the stage *Dracula*: "Of the players, Mr. Lugosi's splendid acting may almost be taken for granted, and passed without comment. He

is not only a veteran actor, but he played the film version of *Dracula* and has perfected his part until his performance is little short of perfect."

110. "Lugosi Gives Weird Drama Tense Touch." *Portland Oregonian*, 30 May 1932.

Review of a Portland version of *Dracula*: "His [Lugosi's] is one of the most finished performances ever given here by any actor in any role. Every tone of his voice, every gesture and every attitude is invested with a depth of meaning, and it is chiefly to his credit that such an impossible character seems for two hours very real."

111. "Cal York's Monthly Broadcast from Hollywood." *Photoplay*, May 1932.

A photo of Lugosi and Boris Karloff in street clothes accompanies an extensive caption.

112. Watts, Richard Jr. "*White Zombie*." *New York Herald-Tribune*, 29 July 1932.

"Bela Lugosi, as the amiable Mr. Murder, proves that good makeup cannot conceal a bad actor and the rest of the playing isn't altogether what it should be."

113. "*White Zombie*." *New York Times*, 29 July 1932.

"The screen, shuddering slightly, can go on; it can forget [*White Zombie*], it can be a Zombie too."

114. "*White Zombie*." *Variety*, 2 Aug. 1932.

"Bela Lugosi, as Murder, the sorceror, is the chief figure, and a dominant one with a not too horrible make-up and a sinister air he never loses. He gives an exceptionally good performance, but the producers wisely did not place their entire dependence on him."

115. Lusk, Robert. "*White Zombie* Panned but Attracts Crowds." *Los Angeles Times*, 7 Aug. 1932.

"Though panned by critics in the ringing unison of an anvil chorus, *White Zombie* is attracting excellent business to the Rivoli Theater [New York City]. Hasty preparation and quick direction are evident throughout, while the acting is more often overwrought than authoritative."

116. *New York Times*, 7 Aug. 1932.

Untitled paragraph on Lugosi gives a career background of his stage credits and mentions *White Zombie*, then playing at the New York City's Rivoli Theater.

117. "The New Pictures: *White Zombie*." *Time*, 8 Aug. 1932.

"Bela Lugosi, who looks like a comic imbecile, can make his jawbones rigid and show the whites of his eyes. The acting of everybody in *White Zombie* suggests that there may be some grounds for believing in zombies."

118. Skinner, Richard Dana. "*White Zombie*." *The Commonweal*, 17 Aug. 1932.

"There is no such artistry in the writing or filming of *White Zombie*—no more than in the clap-trap play of *Dracula* which also dwelt on the theme of the undead. It is obsessed with the idea of the 'twelve year old mentality'—forgetting that with the twelve year old mind go an imagination and an instinctive response to artistry as deeply rooted as the life of humanity. *White Zombie* is interesting only in the measure of its complete failure."

119. "*Chandu the Magician*." *Film Daily*, 16 Sept. 1932.

"There's plenty of conflict and suspense before Lugosi gets his just desserts."

120. "*Chandu the Magician*." *New York Times*, 1 Oct. 1932.

"This is hocus-pocus week at the Roxy, where most of the photographic tricks known to Hollywood have been assembled to startle and confound the enemies of Chandu. Roxor, a baleful character whose behavior may be described with the simple

is not only a veteran actor, but he played the film version of *Dracula* and has perfected his part until his performance is little short of perfect."

110. "Lugosi Gives Weird Drama Tense Touch." *Portland Oregonian*, 30 May 1932.

Review of a Portland version of *Dracula*: "His [Lugosi's] is one of the most finished performances ever given here by any actor in any role. Every tone of his voice, every gesture and every attitude is invested with a depth of meaning, and it is chiefly to his credit that such an impossible character seems for two hours very real."

111. "Cal York's Monthly Broadcast from Hollywood." *Photoplay*, May 1932.

A photo of Lugosi and Boris Karloff in street clothes accompanies an extensive caption.

112. Watts, Richard Jr. "*White Zombie*." *New York Herald-Tribune*, 29 July 1932.

"Bela Lugosi, as the amiable Mr. Murder, proves that good makeup cannot conceal a bad actor and the rest of the playing isn't altogether what it should be."

113. "*White Zombie*." *New York Times*, 29 July 1932.

"The screen, shuddering slightly, can go on; it can forget [*White Zombie*], it can be a Zombie too."

114. "*White Zombie*." *Variety*, 2 Aug. 1932.

"Bela Lugosi, as Murder, the sorcerer, is the chief figure, and a dominant one with a not too horrible make-up and a sinister air he never loses. He gives an exceptionally good performance, but the producers wisely did not place their entire dependence on him."

115. Lusk, Robert. "*White Zombie* Panned but Attracts Crowds." *Los Angeles Times*, 7 Aug. 1932.

"Though panned by critics in the ringing unison of an anvil chorus, *White Zombie* is attracting excellent business to the Rivoli Theater [New York City]. Hasty preparation and quick direction are evident throughout, while the acting is more often overwrought than authoritative."

116. *New York Times*, 7 Aug. 1932.

Untitled paragraph on Lugosi gives a career background of his stage credits and mentions *White Zombie*, then playing at the New York City's Rivoli Theater.

117. "The New Pictures: *White Zombie*." *Time*, 8 Aug. 1932.

"Bela Lugosi, who looks like a comic imbecile, can make his jawbones rigid and show the whites of his eyes. The acting of everybody in *White Zombie* suggests that there may be some grounds for believing in zombies."

118. Skinner, Richard Dana. "*White Zombie*." *The Commonweal*, 17 Aug. 1932.

"There is no such artistry in the writing or filming of *White Zombie*— no more than in the clap-trap play of *Dracula* which also dwelt on the theme of the undead. It is obsessed with the idea of the 'twelve year old mentality'— forgetting that with the twelve year old mind go an imagination and an instinctive response to artistry as deeply rooted as the life of humanity. *White Zombie* is interesting only in the measure of its complete failure."

119. "*Chandu the Magician*." *Film Daily*, 16 Sept. 1932.

"There's plenty of conflict and suspense before Lugosi gets his just desserts."

120. "*Chandu the Magician*." *New York Times*, 1 Oct. 1932.

"This is hocus-pocus week at the Roxy, where most of the photographic tricks known to Hollywood have been assembled to startle and confound the enemies of Chandu. Roxor, a baleful character whose behavior may be described with the simple

14. Reviews, Articles, and Pamphlets   239

96. "Broadminded." *Variety*, 7 July 1931.
"It's an exceptionally good comedy program talker."

97. *Film Daily*, 25 July 1931.
The *Film Daily* mentions Lugosi will star in Universal's *Frankenstein*.

98. "Weird Films: Character Changes in *Rue Morgue*." *New York Times*, 10 Jan. 1932.
This article informs the *Times*' readers that director Robert Florey made numerous changes in filming Poe's *Murders in the Rue Morgue* (1932).

99. Sinclair, John. "Master of Horrors." *Silver Screen*, Jan. 1932.
Though less than accurate, this piece is not as outlandish as the Gladys Hall articles. Sinclair crowned Lugosi with the "Master of Horrors" title just as Boris Karloff became a household name.

100. "*Murders in the Rue Morgue*." *New York Times*, 11 Feb. 1932.
"The entire production suffers from an overzealous effort at terrorization, and the cast, inspired by the general hysteria, succumbs to the temptation to overact."

101. Watts, Richard Jr. "*Murders in the Rue Morgue*." *New York Herald-Tribune*, 12 Feb. 1932.
"Bela Lugosi fails to be properly frightening as the mad doctor."

102. "*Murders in the Rue Morgue*." *Film Daily*, 14 Feb. 1932.
"Bela Lugosi gives an intense characterization of the fanatical scientist who attempts to combine the blood of an ape with that of a white girl."

103. "*Murders in the Rue Morgue*." *The Times* (London), 30 Mar. 1932.
"There is plenty of blood in this film, but the thunder lacks resonance and conviction ... poor acting and puerile production."

104. Schallert, Edwin. "Shivery Show Enjoyed." *Los Angeles Times*, 5 Apr. 1932.
Review of the Lugosi play *Murdered Alive*: Schallert mentioned, "It's a very fair horror play, and if you like them, you'll undoubtedly like it."

105. "Lugosi Plays with Three Broken Ribs." *Los Angeles Examiner*, 9 Apr. 1932.
The *Examiner* claimed that Lugosi broke three ribs after a 16-foot fall while performing in *Murdered Alive*, due to an "error of backstage mechanics." A physician was able to help with injuries, and Lugosi continued his work in the last act of the play.

106. *Los Angeles Examiner*, 10 Apr. 1932.
Short, untitled mention that Lugosi, then the star of *Murdered Alive*, was displaying his own sculptures at various Los Angeles exhibitions.

107. "Bela Lugosi Stars in Horror Play." *San Francisco News*, 23 Apr. 1932.
"*Murdered Alive* fails to gain distinction even by the presence of Bela Lugosi. The audience laughed at his lines. But that was no singular slight to Mr. Lugosi alone. It laughed at practically everybody else's, including Betty Ross Clarke's screams."

108. Warren, George C. "Thriller Is Hit on Orpheum Stage." *San Francisco Examiner*, 23 Apr. 1932.
Review of the stage play *Murdered Alive*: "What menace, I ask you, could impersonate the demented surgeon half so well as Bela Lugosi. His performance is skilled and smooth."

109. "Bela Lugosi Is Splendid in *Dracula*." *Oregon Daily Journal*, 30 May 1932.
Review of a Portland revival of the stage *Dracula*: "Of the players, Mr. Lugosi's splendid acting may almost be taken for granted, and passed without comment. He

information that Bela Lugosi plays the part, is a madman who wants to possess himself of a death ray and destroy the world."

121. Watts, Richard Jr. "*Chandu the Magician.*" *New York Herald-Tribune*, 1 Oct. 1932.

"His [Lugosi's] efforts to be frightening are somewhat less terrifying than Mr. Lowe's attempts to be mysterious and romantic."

122. "*Chandu the Magician.*" *Variety*, 4 Oct. 1932.

"*Chandu* carries the fantastic, the inconsistent, and the ludicrous to the greatest lengths yet achieved by the screen. Were it to be taken seriously, there'd be no enjoyment for anyone. If it's accepted strictly as hoke growing out of the development of the horror cycle, it's not so bad, but it's still hoke. [Lugosi] looks more himself than in any other picture, not going in for too much menace on makeup."

123. "*Chandu the Magician.*" *The New Yorker*, 8 Oct. 1932.

"…none of the atrocities described seem as fearful as the acting."

124. "The New Pictures: *Chandu.*" *Time*, 10 Oct. 1932.

"Thrilling drama for children, splendid farce for adults … Lowe out-eyes Lugosi and the death-ray explodes, leaving civilization untoasted."

125. "Lugosi Broke, with Furniture Main Asset." *Variety*, 25 Oct. 1932.

Short article mentions Lugosi's bankruptcy petition, listing some $2,965 in liabilities and $600 of posssible assets. *Variety* lists Lulu Shubert's wage claim for housekeeping services at $700, an entire year's salary.

126. LeBerthom, Ted. "Demons of the Film Colony." *Weird Tales*, Oct. 1932.

A "fright-duel" between Lugosi and Boris Karloff, staged for this popular magazine of the bizarre. This obviously fabricated tale questions which horror film star can "outscare" the other.

127. Hall, Mordaunt. "*Island of Lost Souls.*" *New York Times*, 13 Jan. 1933.

"Although the attempt to horrify is not accomplished with any marked degree of subtlety, there is no denying that some of the scenes are ingenuously fashioned and therefore interesting."

128. "*Island of Lost Souls.*" *Variety*, 17 Jan. 1933.

"With such actors as Charles Laughton, Richard Arlen, and Bela Lugosi in the cast, *Souls* is provided with a mainstay assuring wider patronage than had their roles been filled at random."

129. "*Island of Lost Souls.*" *Billboard*, 21 Jan. 1933.

"It's a fairly chilling picture, but it's too hokey to have much of an adult appeal. The kids will probably go for it big."

130. *New England Film News*, 26 Jan. 1933.

The cover of this trade featured Lugosi in a shot from *The Death Kiss.*

131. "*The Death Kiss.*" *Variety*, 31 Jan. 1933.

"A weak picture despite a first-rate cast of standard names and a workman-like physical production."

132. Barry, Barbara. "Meet the Vampire." *The New Movie Magazine*, Jan. 1933.

Fascinating piece on Lugosi uses numerous interview quotes, including descriptions of his home and stories about Hungary.

133. "*Dracula* Creator Domestic: Hungarian Actor and Bride at Home." *Los Angeles Times*, 2 Feb. 1933.

A photograph of Lugosi and his third wife, Lillian Arch, accompanies a short article on their marriage.

134. "Kiddie Revue, Thriller, and Stage Show for Fun Club." *The Morning Press* (Santa Barbara), 24 June 1933.

"It [*The Whispering Shadow*] is said to be one of the most exciting [serials] yet seen on the screen."

135. "Wild Fun: *International House.*" *New York Times*, 27 May 1933.

"Bela Lugosi, with the sinister eyes, is on hand to represent Russia at the demonstration."

136. "*International House.*" *Variety*, 30 May 1933.

"Cast includes enough names ... to offset the effects of an otherwise second-rate picture."

137. Troy, William. "*International House.*" *The Nation*, 21 June 1933.

"The effect of the whole is to make one wonder whether Hollywood is not sinking beneath its own worst level in turning out such a picture as this."

138. "*The Night of Terror.*" *Variety*, 27 June 1933.

"Another of those efforts in which Bela Lugosi wears a turban and a mysterious look. Comes too late in the cycle to be an outstander. Not for ambitious booking and a risk among the top B spots."

139. "*The Devil's in Love.*" *Variety*, 1 Aug. 1933.

"Given any kind of a break, returns at the box-office should be fair when the final count is in nationally."

140. "*The Devil's in Love.*" *Billboard*, 5 Aug. 1933.

"If it weren't for the photography and the cast, you'd swear the picture had been made in 1910."

141. "Defaulting Romeo Gave Lugosi His Chance on Stage." *Philadelphia Public Ledger*, 13 Aug. 1933.

This article, printed in anticipation of his appearance in *Murder at the Vanities* on August 28, wrongly claims that Lugosi's first-ever appearance on the stage was in *Romeo and Juliet*. As with so many biographical pieces of the period, little of the truth surfaces.

142. Atkinson, Brooks. "*Murder at the Vanities.*" *New York Times*, 3 Sept. 1933.

"The combination of musical and mystery yields a desultory evening. It retains little of the pomp and gayety of the one or the excitement of the other."

143. "The Theater: Music and Murder." *The New Yorker*, 23 Sept. 1933.

"Admirers of Bela Lugosi's strange, pale-green talent will probably feel that the emotional transition from his hypnotism-and-dagger scene to the spectacle of the Most Beautiful Girls in the World gaily singing 'Who Committed the Moider?' is rather more than they can comfortably make, while serious students of anatomy are surely going to be distracted by the sudden screams of the dying."

144. "Feed Pepper to Your Little Boy." *Stage Magazine*, Nov. 1933.

"The plot [of *Murder at the Vanities*] was awful hooey, of course; Bela Lugosi sneaking around."

145. "Bela Lugosi, Film Villain, Playing at Loew's State." *New York Herald-Tribune*, 9 Dec. 1933.

"The enterprising Loew book department, looking about for worthy headliners, has picked Bela Lugosi, sinister motion picture and stage villain, as the featured player of the vaudeville show this week at Loew's State Theater. With proper regard for his fans, Mr. Lugosi offers the most thrilling parts of *Dracula* for his variety vehicle. His act, somewhat more novel than the ordinary headline piece, should be a treat for variety goers."

146. "New Acts: Bela Lugosi." *Variety*, 12 Dec. 1933.

A review of Lugosi's vaudeville version

of *Dracula* at the State Theater in New York. "Better than the usual 'When I was in Hollywood' style of personal appearance, but the excerpts show how much the screen was able to do for the play."

147. "Bela Lugosi Acquires Play." *New York Times*, 15 Jan. 1934.
Short article mentions that Lugosi obtained the rights to stage the Warshawsky play *Pagan Fury*.

148. "U's Chiller with Lugosi, Karloff, and Atwill in It." *Variety*, 27 Mar. 1934.
Brief announcement claims Lugosi would be teamed with Boris Karloff and Lionel Atwill in the never-made Universal chiller *The Suicide Club*.

149. Hoffman, Jerry. "Frankenstein Meets Dracula in *Black Cat*." *Los Angeles Examiner*, 4 May 1934.
"Bela 'Dracula' Lugosi is an avenging prodigal, come to confront Boris 'Frankenstein' Karloff. Throughout most of the movie, both try to outstare each other, with Karloff having a bit of an edge. Lugosi never concedes victory — for he can stare, too."

150. Barnes, Howard. "*The Black Cat*." *New York Herald-Tribune*, 19 May 1934.
"It is undoubtedly the presence of these masters at curdling one's blood that makes the screen drama less than triumphant as a mystery. Unfortunately, there is little significant action until the very climax of the production, leaving much of their overacting rather pointless."

151. *New York Times*, 20 May 1934.
Short, untitled biography of Lugosi, "the big shiver and shudder man," written at the time of *The Black Cat*'s release. Along with incorrectly printing his birthdate, the story claims that Lugosi's "most bizarre activity is a merry habit of calling up his friends on the telephone at 3 A.M. and serenading them with the ballads of his native Budapest."

152. "*The Black Cat*." *Variety*, 22 May 1934.
"Because of the presence in one film of Boris Karloff, that jovial madman, and Bela Lugosi, that suave fiend, this picture probably has box office attraction. But otherwise and on the counts of story, novelty, thrills and distinction, the picture is subnormal."

153. "*The Black Cat*." *Billboard*, 26 May 1934.
"Occasionally a black cat does wander around a bit in the picture, but it is far from being the thriller your audiences will expect with Boris Karloff and Bela Lugosi in the cast.…on the whole, it's a pretty gruesome mess of celluloid."

154. "*The Black Cat*." *Newsweek*, 26 May 1934.
"Two major monsters perform all the cute antics of deviltry in this Universal film which has little to do with Edgar Allan Poe's Brainchild."

155. "*Gift of Gab*." *Film Daily*, 25 Sept. 1934.
"In addition to having enough name stars to bowl over almost any audience, this production has been given a story to string the sequences together, so that between the dramatic suspense and musical specialties there is never a dull moment."

156. "*The Return of Chandu*." *Film Daily*, 9 Oct. 1934.
"This is the good old hoke, but is done with class and intelligence, and with strong story interest building logically to a tense climax."

157. "*Best Man Wins*." *Variety*, 8 Jan. 1935.
"Bela Lugosi heads the gem thieves, and [is] okay."

158. "*Best Man Wins*." *Billboard*, 12 Jan. 1935.
"This one might go over on a dual bill program but is too weak to stand alone."

159. *"The Mysterious Mr. Wong." Film Daily*, 15 Jan. 1935.

"There is nothing artistic or delicate about the theme or presentation. So it is out for the class trade. Then there is terrifying Mr. Wong as played by Bela Lugosi, who knocks off a murder every few hours."

160. *"The Mysterious Mr. Wong." Variety*, 13 Mar. 1935.

"Lugosi, despite a marked slavic accent, clicks impressively as an Oriental menace. His performance during the big torture scene packs enough scary stuff to get a long way, particularly with the kids."

161. "Horror Story Well-Written and Acted: *Mark of the Vampire*." *Hollywood Reporter*, 23 Mar. 1935.

"It's a well-produced, well-acted, well-directed [film] by that old master of the screaming thrill, Tod Browning. Bela Lugosi is just elegant as Count Mora. It's the first in the new series of horror-mystery-murders and it ought to make the customers more respectful of the powers of darkness for awhile at least."

162. "*Return of Chandu* Dull Hocus-Pocus." *New York Daily News*, 14 Apr. 1935.

Review of a feature film cut from the 1934 serial: "The dialogue is crudely written and the direction is none too deft. Lugosi's Chandu is much less effective than the dreadful vampire he presented on the screen in *Dracula*."

163. "*Sons of Steel*." *New York Times*, 15 Apr. 1935.

"Our ten-year-old great-grandson informed us that *Return of Chandu*, featuring Bela Lugosi, has been playing the neighborhood houses in serial form. It seems all too likely. Mr. Lugosi and his magic ring, which permits him to vanish into thin air, much to his enemies' dismay, saves an Egyptian princess from a sacrificial altar of a sinister Eastern cult. Elementary melodrama, my dear Watson."

164. "*Return of Chandu*." *Variety*, 17 Apr. 1935.

Review of the feature film cut from the 1934 serial: "Bela Lugosi is wasted. Even at that he stands shoulders above rest."

165. "*Mark of the Vampire*." *New York Times*, 3 May 1935.

"Like most good ghost stories, it's a lot of fun, even though you don't believe a word of it."

166. Mitchell, Helen. "The Philosophy of Bela Lugosi: The Horror Man of Hollywood." *To You!* 2:3 (May 1935).

Lugosi's interview gives him the opportunity to talk about how much he reads, how he considers sex the most important thing in life (from the standpoint that it is the "basic principle of life ... all life"), and also about how much he would like to portray Don Quixote and Don Cesar de Bazan on the screen.

167. "Log of the Good Ship Life." *Alhambra Post-Advocate*, 17 June 1935.

Article speaks out against the terrible nature of Bela Lugosi and Boris Karloff horror films.

168. Thirer, Irene. "Bela 'Dracula' Lugosi a Regular Fellow — Pokes Fun at Jinx." *New York Daily News*, 3 July 1935.

Thirer interviewed the actor a few days before he sailed to England and the production of *The Mystery of the Mary Celeste*. She quotes the actor speaking about his wife, Lillian, the horror film business, and his "very good friend" Boris Karloff.

169. "*The Raven*, with Boris Karloff and Bela Lugosi, Is a Horror Film in More Than One Sense." *New York Times*, 5 July 1935.

"Of course, it must be said that Lugosi and Karloff try hard, even though, both being cultured men, they must have suffered at the indignity of being visited upon by the helpless Edgar Allan."

A portrait of Lugosi from *The Black Cat* (1934), which *Billboard* called a "pretty gruesome mess of celluloid."

170. "Dracula Without His Cape." *New York Times*, 7 July 1935.

Short interview conducted in New York City while Lugosi was visiting to take an on-stage bow at a showing of *The Raven*.

171. Lugosi, Bela. "I Like Playing Dracula." *Film Weekly*, July 1935.

Whether Lugosi actually wrote this is very questionable, but in any event it details how much he enjoys portraying supernatural parts and hopes to continue doing so.

172. "*The Raven*." *Motion Picture Reviews*, July 1935.

"It is, technically, well-done, but will appeal only to those who enjoy the type.

Adolescents twelve to sixteen, impossible. Children eight to twelve, absolutely no."

173. "*The Raven.*" *The Times* (London), 5 Aug. 1935.
"Like any chamber of horrors, there is neither life nor horror in this film."

174. Bordages, Asa. "Being Horrible Is a Good Business to Bela Lugosi, but He Enjoyed Being Lovable in New British Role." *New York World-Telegram*, 28 Aug. 1935.
"Scaring Folks Allows Him to Buy Drinks for the Boys" was the subtitle to this newspaper interview with Lugosi. He speaks of *The Mystery of the Mary Celeste*, the British film industry, and England in general.

175. "Lugosi Branches Out." *Variety*, 18 Sept. 1935.
Lugosi's independent "producing organization" announced that *Cagliostro* would be its first release. The story would have been based on an original by Andre de Soos.

176. "*Mark of the Vampire.*" *Los Angeles Examiner*, 20 Sept. 1935.
"A fantastic horror picture, *Mark of the Vampire* is in a class by itself. Marked by splendid acting and a coherence in plot, *Mark of the Vampire* attains its intensity in drama through a series of cleverly contrived situations."

177. "*The Raven.*" *Motion Picture Herald*, 28 Sept. 1935.
"A shocker all right and pleased the Saturday crowds."

178. *New York Times*, 29 Sept. 1935.
Untitled article mentions Lugosi's own production company and the plans to film *Cagliostro*. Hopes for it to be a major release were made clear.

179. Barnes, Eleanor. "Bela Lugosi to Produce Here." *Illustrated Daily News*, Sept. 1935.
Lugosi's concern about losing dramatic roles to others brought about a desire to produce films himself, which he discussed with this reporter.

180. *Photoplay*, Sept. 1935.
A photograph of Lugosi (striped pants, checkered sports jacket, and bow tie) is accompanied by a caption informing readers that he "is one of the quietest and most retiring persons you could ever find."

181. "*Murder by Television.*" *Monthly Film Bulletin* (England), Oct. 1935.
"The actors are stiff and appear to be ill at ease with their parts; their voices are sometimes monotonous."

182. "*Dracula*'s Troubles." *Variety*, 20 Nov. 1935.
With Eddie Sutherland listed as director and Lugosi as star, Universal slated *Dracula's Daughter* to go into production by December 1 due to a clause in the story's purchase.

183. "*Mystery of the Mary Celeste.*" *Variety*, 4 Dec. 1935.
"[An] outstanding role is played by Bela Lugosi as a seaman ... very strong for those who like tragic entertainment."

184. *New York Evening Journal*, 2 Jan. 1936.
An untitled *Journal* article explains that Lugosi backed out on a two-picture deal in Great Britain upon learning that the British would quarantine his four dogs for six months.

185. "*The Invisible Ray.*" *Motion Picture Daily*, 11 Jan. 1936.
"On the whole the film is good entertainment, interest-holding and saleable, and largely without the 'horror' theme which has featured many of the films of Karloff and Lugosi."

186. "*The Invisible Ray.*" *Variety*, 15 Jan. 1936.

Reading a newspaper on the set of *Best Man Wins* (1935). Note the can of Sackett cigars on the table.

"It is different and fairly entertaining. He [Karloff] and Lugosi stand away out in an otherwise average cast."

187. "*The Invisible Ray.*" *Billboard,* 18 Jan. 1936.

"A weird mess of pseudo scientific abracadabra."

188. "*The Invisible Ray.*" *Motion Picture Herald,* 25 Jan. 1936.

"This production is a typical Karloff-Lugosi shudder picture and therein lies its entertainment values."

189. "Karloff's Year at U." *Variety,* 29 Jan. 1936.

Karloff's new one-year contract is announced, with additional mention of Lugosi not only being out of *Dracula's Daughter* (Cesar Romero was mentioned as his replacement) but entirely off the Universal lot.

190. "Vampires, Monsters, Horrors!" *New York Times*, 1 Mar. 1936.

An early and fascinating examination of horror film history, detailing the 1931 *Dracula* and mentioning Lugosi's other Universal chillers.

191. "Horror on the Screen." *The Times* (London), 4 Aug. 1936.

This article does not directly mention Lugosi, but it is key to the mindset that established the British ban on horror films. The ban had a tremendous affect on Lugosi's career.

192. "Postal Inspector." *Film Daily*, 1 Sept. 1936.

"The cast is good, but the story is too obvious in destination to carry much suspense."

193. "Phantom Ship." *Film Daily*, 15 Feb. 1937.

"Bela Lugosi is the main character, and his part does not develop till the film is three-quarters over. All the characters are realistically portrayed."

194. "Tovarich." *San Francisco Bulletin*, 23 Mar. 1937.

"In the role of Soviet commissar appears that old film horror man, Bela Lugosi, sinister by playwright's command, but as often as possible with tongue-in-cheek. His continental bearing and actorial skills make the character surefire in his hands."

195. "Phantom Ship." *Philadelphia Exhibitor*, 1 Apr. 1937.

"This is pretty poor. The actors are positively hammy; the recording, the photography are awful; Lugosi is an unbelievable, silly menace; the editing leaves out whole scenes so that the story is annoyingly choppy."

196. "So Long, Dracula — Nice to Have Met You." *San Francisco Call-Bulletin*, 3 Apr. 1937.

With his straight role in *Tovarich* and the British ban on horror films, Lugosi asks, "Why won't they let me be human?" of film producers. He also relates that if the horror films resume, they'll have to "get another boy" for the parts. Lugosi also pleaded that audiences not consider his role in *Tovarich* that of a villain, even if it was a Russian Communist.

197. LaBelle, Claude A. "Those Gorotchenko Whiskers on Bela Lugosi Are Genuine." *San Francisco News*, 5 Apr. 1937.

Lugosi's resolve to find nonhorror parts is made clear to the reporter, as is the fact that his beard in *Tovarich* was authentic.

198. Schallert, Edwin. "*Tovarich* Well Played at Biltmore." *Los Angeles Times*, 20 Apr. 1937.

"The performances are calculated to highlight its attributes and one surmises that the play will be much enjoyed during the next few weeks, for its engagement is destined to last that long at least."

199. "SOS Coastguard." *Variety*, 25 Aug. 1937.

"*SOS Coastguard* is a natural for the urchins and any adult who wanders in will also be kept on the edge of his seat."

200. "Lugosi for Broadway?" *Film Daily*, 17 Sept. 1937.

Short piece about the Earl Cortis play *Ferrari*, which was never produced.

201. Starr, Jimmy. *Los Angeles Herald Express*, 24 Nov. 1937.

Starr's column asks the question "What's happened to Bela Lugosi, who used to do a lot of swell acting around town?"

14. Reviews, Articles, and Pamphlets

202. Wallace, Inez. "Dracula's Castle in Hollywood." *Cleveland Plain-Dealer*, 16 Dec. 1937.

This female reporter believed she got the true story of Lugosi, which "debunks this Dracula stuff," even though her cameraman allegedly retreated in fear to their car. Before her own nerves were calmed, however, Wallace was chilled by Lugosi's reference to her as "mademoiselle"—all too reminiscent of his lines in *Murders in the Rue Morgue*. The end result of Wallace's interview included her believing Lugosi had a true home, a lovely wife, and four dogs.

203. Parsons, Louella. "Chatter in Hollywood." *San Francisco Examiner*, 8 Jan. 1938.

Parsons, the quintessential Hollywood gossip columnist of the period, questions why Lugosi is out of work. Why isn't he in films anymore? This sympathetic piece was written during Lugosi's dry period, which resulted from the British ban on horror films.

204. Coulter, H. "Cold Chills and Cold Cash." *Cinema Progress*, May–June 1938.

"Why do we enjoy being scared to death?" Coulter asks in this article. To help answer the question, he interviewed Lugosi, who offers his own explanation. Overall, this piece is unique, given the fact it was written at a time when Hollywood was not making horror films and Lugosi was not working.

205. "Bela Lugosi Scaring 'Em Again on Comeback Trail with *Dracula*." *Hollywood Reporter*, 11 Aug. 1938.

The *Hollywood Reporter* announced Lugosi's personal appearances at the Regina Theater in conjunction with the revival of 1931's *Dracula*. "The big chills and fever man" would also appear on a prolonged personal appearance tour with the film.

206. "Universal Planning New Horror Films." *Daily Variety*, 10 Oct. 1938.

This article mentions Universal Studio's plans to produce new horror films and details the enormous success double-bills of *Dracula* (1931) and *Frankenstein* (1931) achieved across the country.

207. "New Universal Horror Picture Ready; Lorre, Karloff, Lugosi Star." *Daily Variety*, 13 Oct. 1938.

Announcement of *Son of Frankenstein*'s shooting includes Lorre's name in the cast, though he would turn down the title role and be replaced by Basil Rathbone.

208. "Revival of the Undead: The Monster and the Vampire Go Barnstorming and Scare Up Business." *New York Times*, 16 Oct. 1938.

This piece points out the huge success and profits *Dracula* (1931) and *Frankenstein* (1931) reaped from their national rerelease. Chronicled are the various theaters where sellouts occurred with the films' reissue. At the time this was written, both were a day from opening on a double bill at the Rialto.

209. "Huge Horror Pic Take Shoves U's Graveyard Production Upward." *Daily Variety*, 17 Nov. 1938.

Daily Variety chronicles the amazing grosses of *Dracula* and *Frankenstein* reissues and speculates that the initial horror film "epidemic" ended before the public "had had its fill." Universal's upping the budget of *Son of Frankenstein* is mentioned, along with the news that Willis Cooper was already working on another Frankenstein script, *After Frankenstein*.

210. *Variety*, 18 Jan. 1939.

An untitled *Variety* article mentions Lugosi's signing of a new, five-year contract with Universal.

211. "Oh, You Beautiful Monster." *New York Times*, 29 Jan. 1939.

The *Times* chronicles makeup man Jack Pierce's career, with both *Son of Frankenstein* and Lugosi's Ygor being mentioned.

250   III. Works By or About Lugosi

212. Barnes, Howard. "*Son of Frankenstein.*" *New York Herald-Tribune*, 30 Jan. 1939.

"The acting, like the photoplay itself, works hard for chilling effects without achieving them. Mr. Karloff's monster is far from loathesome and Bela Lugosi is not much more convincing as Ygor of the broken neck who is his buddy and sends him out on errands of assassination."

213. "*Son of Frankenstein.*" *New York Times*, 30 Jan. 1939.

"With a pit of boiling sulphur in the basement and Bela Lugosi living there as a combination monster-nurse and janitor, what could be cozier? ... Bela Lugosi is only an assistant bogyman."

214. "*Son of Frankenstein.*" *Film Daily*, 31 Jan. 1939.

"It is far better constructed than the first *Frankenstein*, and with Basil Rathbone in the cast in addition to Karloff and Lugosi, it is one of the finest acted thrillers ever produced. All of the five principles give grand performances."

215. "The *Son of Frankenstein* Starts a New Horror Cycle." *Look*, 28 Feb. 1939.

Look previews the third *Frankenstein* film with numerous still photographs.

216. "Father Keeps Son Out of Footsteps." *San Francisco News*, 4 Mar. 1939.

A reporter overheard Lugosi telling director Allan Dwan that he intended his son, Bela Jr., to pursue a career outside the entertainment field.

217. "*Son of Frankenstein.*" *Movie Comics*, 1 (Apr. 1939).

The first issue of *Movie Comics* adapts *Son of Frankenstein* (1939) as well as *Gunga Din* (1939), and *The Great Man Votes* (1939), into comic book form.

218. "*Son of Frankenstein.*" *Photoplay*, Apr. 1939.

"Success of the revival of horror pictures inspired this up-to-date chiller. The interesting thing about it is that the material is excellent, not cheaply done for commercial purposes."

219. "*The Gorilla.*" *Variety*, 24 May 1939.

"Production is standard throughout."

220. "*The Gorilla.*" *New York Times*, 28 May 1939.

"It's all supposed to be either funny or shockingly thrilling depending on how you look at it. We couldn't see it either way."

221. Fiddler, Jimmie. "In Hollywood." *Los Angeles Times*, 29 July 1939.

Fiddler discusses Lugosi's period of unemployment, mentioning the actor's attempts to pay back a benefactor who helped him during the rough period of 1937–38.

222. "*The Phantom Creeps.*" *Variety*, 9 Aug. 1939.

"Lugosi, as the mad scientist, develops his characterization convincingly, even to the more impossible situations."

223. "*The Phantom Creeps.*" *Movie Comics*, 6 (Sept.-Oct. 1939).

An adaptation of *The Phantom Creeps* (1939), this comic book takes various liberties with the serial's plot.

224. Smith, H. Allen. "Bela Lugosi Can Imagine No Horror Quite So Bad as Having a Horror That Runs Out on You." *New York World-Telegram*, 17 Oct. 1939.

Lugosi, wearing a bright red robe and drinking imported mineral water, gave this interview while in New York to guest-star on a radio show with Walter O'Keefe. In addition to speaking about his comeback with the second horror film cycle, he discusses his thoughts on Greta Garbo. "She is mysterious by publicity and I am mysterious by trade. I thought she would be a spoiled badness, but she was not," Lugosi said. "I did not fall in love with her at first, but later, yes. She is so damn human it is wonderful."

225. Mok, Michael. "Horror Man at Home." *New York Post*, 19 Oct. 1939.
Article briefly chronicles Lugosi's career, containing quotes from the actor and also two very curious *Post* photographs of him.

226. "Great Garbo's Giggles: Taciturn Star Laughs in Tale of Converted Commissars." *Newsweek*, 30 Oct. 1939.
Review of the film *Ninotchka*: "The film sparkles with the subtle innuendo and satirical touches that are the trademark of a Lubitsch comedy."

227. "The New Pictures: *Ninotchka*." *Time*, 6 Nov. 1939.
"A literate and knowingly directed satire which lands many a shrewd crack."

228. Nugent, Frank S. "*Ninotchka*." *New York Times*, 10 Nov. 1939.
"Stalin, we repeat, won't like it; but, unless your tastes hew too closely to the party line, we think you will, immensely."

229. "Bela Lugosi Son Fetes Birthday." *Los Angeles Times*, 14 Jan. 1940.
The short *Times* article mentions a party held for Bela Lugosi, Jr.'s second birthday.

230. Hopper, Hedda. "Horror Men of Screen Just Pair of Home-Loving Folks, After All." *Los Angeles Times*, 14 Jan. 1940.
In her column, Hopper speaks to both Karloff and Lugosi. "Lugosi made me feel at home," she writes. He talks about marriage, what kind of cigars he smokes, and more.

231. "Saint Is Back in Rather Good One." *Hollywood Reporter*, 20 Jan. 1940.
Review of *The Saint's Double Trouble*: "Bela Lugosi is his unexcelled best as a menace. He handles any part ... and handles it well."

232. Churchill, Douglas W. "Here We Go Folks!" *New York Times*, 28 Jan. 1940.
A *Times* journalist covers the supposed hypnotism of Lugosi by Dr. Manly Hall for a scene in Universal's *Black Friday*. In this article, director Arthur Lubin proclaims that Lugosi's main scene, shot under hypnosis, which had his character dying of suffocation, was 100 percent better than on a previous take. Churchill further mentions that "the effect on Lugosi was so amazing that the studio's exploitation engineers believe that hypnosis can be practiced on writers to make them finish scripts, but most of all on actors."

233. Kerr, Martha. "Horror Men Talk About Horror." *Modern Screen*, Jan. 1940.
Lugosi describes what "horror" means to him for readers, after Boris Karloff and Basil Rathbone had earlier spoken on the same subject. The definition offered by Lugosi is not one that translates into the supernatural but is rather "fear for those I love."

234. "*Black Friday*." *Variety*, 13 Mar. 1940.
"It's a standard programmer for lower dual spotting in the secondary houses. Lugosi is seen briefly as a gang leader."

235. "*Black Friday*." *New York Times*, 22 Mar. 1940.
"Lugosi's terrifying talents are wasted in the role of a mere gangster, an un-supernatural mug."

236. Crisler, B.R. "*The Human Monster*." *New York Times*, 25 Mar. 1940.
"All Mr. Lugosi has to do is look at people and they either get hypnosis or cramps from laughing."

237. "*The Human Monster*." *Variety*, 27 Mar. 1940.
"Additional asset is the presence of Bela Lugosi in a more villainous characterization than he's been in for some time."

238. "Schools Film Group Opposes Double Bill: Letter Takes Exception to Linking *Pinocchio* with Melodrama." *New York Times*, 27 Mar. 1940.

The Schools Motion Picture Committee, a voluntary organization, protested a New York double-bill of Disney's *Pinocchio* with the Lugosi film *The Saint's Double Trouble*. This article mentioned that because the Lugosi film had been approved by the Legion of Decency, the pairing of the movies would remain.

239. *PIC Broadway Magazine*, 2 Apr. 1940.

PIC features Lugosi's hypnotism for *Black Friday* on its front cover.

240. "*Black Friday*." *Film Daily*, 5 Apr. 1940.

"Action is swift, stirring, and ... impossible, but nevertheless it's all entertaining."

241. "Ed Sullivan Unit: Stanley, Pittsburgh." *Variety*, 10 Apr. 1940.

"Long-planted meeting of Lugosi and Treacher follows, with the former supposedly scaring Treacher only to ask for his autograph, and then the two of them joining Sullivan for a comically corny song and dance to 'Ragtime Cowboy.'"

242. "Ed Sullivan Leads Show of Film Stars at State." *New York Herald-Tribune*, 19 Apr. 1940.

"Fast moving, lively and honestly entertaining, it is a tribute to the showmanship of Sullivan, who again assumes his familiar role of master of ceremonies. Miss Jaynes also appears with Miss Parrish and Miss Weaver and the three girls sing a humorous tune called 'The Wives of the Screen's Horror Men.' It is a perfect buildup for Bela Lugosi, who enters in his 'frightening' role of 'Dracula,' scaring the girls offstage and finally winding up by meekly asking for Treacher's autograph."

243. "Ed Sullivan Unit: Colonial, Dayton." *Variety*, Apr. 1940.

"Bela Lugosi's sepulchral voice is heard off stage with its gruesome haw-haw-haw to the accompaniment of flickering lights, and later he sneaks up behind Treacher, who, turning around and facing him suddenly extends his hand and cracks, 'Dr. Lugosi, I presume.' ...something in the way of a skit for Lugosi would improve the setup."

244. "Film News and Comment." *New York Times*, 5 May 1940.

The *Times* prints a "warning note" for readers with regard to *The Human Monster* with Lugosi, pointing out that the National Motion Picture League, Inc., refused to endorse the film for a variety of reasons, which ranged from "tatooed arm" to "drowned bodies thrown out window into river."

245. "*You'll Find Out*." *New York Times*, 15 Nov. 1940.

"On the whole, the picture is just routine and dull."

246. "*You'll Find Out*." *Variety*, 20 Nov. 1940.

"Boris Karloff, Bela Lugosi, and Peter Lorre form a strong setup of sinister villainy, to provide plenty of trouble and conflict for Kyser to combat."

247. "*The Devil Bat*." Hollywood Reporter, 2 Feb. 1941.

"With Bela Lugosi performing in style, as the mad doctor, the picture moves along at good pace under the direction of Jean Yarbrough. The affair is not without humor, and doesn't take itself too seriously."

248. "*The Black Cat*." *Hollywood Reporter*, 25 Apr. 1941.

"The strangest role of all falls to Bela Lugosi."

249. "*The Black Cat*." *New York Times*, 26 Apr. 1941.

"Basil Rathbone, Gale Sondergaard, and Bela Lugosi are properly menacing."

250. "If You Care for Murders, They're Here." *Chicago Daily Tribune*, 8 May 1941.

Review of the film *Invisible Ghost*: "Mr. Lugosi scares the wits out of you. And he can strangle! Direction, photography, and dialog do very well. And the piece *does* have suspense."

251. "The [sic] Invisible Ghost." *New York Times*, 8 May 1941.

"The motivation is as wild as the wind and the performances are as incredibly amateurish as The [sic] Invisible Ghost is silly."

252. "Invisible Ghost." *Variety*, 14 May 1941.

"Except for Bela Lugosi's name for the marquee, this would-be chiller adds up to approximately zero. It's undoubtedly one of the feeblest pictures of the season."

253. Hall, Gladys. "Memoes of a Madman." *Silver Screen*, July 1941.

Extensive quotes attributed to Lugosi form this biographical piece that Hall compiled. Lugosi speaks of his childhood, his family, and his career in both the United States and Hungary. *Famous Monsters of Filmland*, a fan magazine, later reprinted the article in its issues numbered 115 and 116.

254. "Spooks Run Wild." *Hollywood Reporter*, 6 Oct. 1941.

"Lugosi's performance and the background provide a field day for the capers of the youngsters and the laughs come thick and fast when they go into action."

255. "Spooks Run Wild." *New York Times*, 1 Nov. 1941.

"Mr. Lugosi, by turns, is a necromancer, a murderer, and a magician. Perhaps the whole business is supposed to be as authentic as a papier-mache skeleton. Anyway, in this case, its not the spooks who are wild."

256. "The Wolf Man." Daily *Variety*, 10 Dec. 1941.

"Here is a film that will take the minds of patrons off the Japanese war, thoroughly and effectively — at least for the time they are in the theatre. Wherever a good, old-fashioned killer diller of a murder meller will go, *The Wolf Man* should do a thumping business."

257. "The Wolf Man." *Hollywood Reporter*, 10 Dec. 1941.

"Destined to be brought to sudden ends are the roles in which Bela Lugosi and Fay Helm appear."

258. "The Wolf Man." *New York Times*, 22 Dec. 1941.

"Sharing his [Lon Chaney, Jr.'s] embarrassment are Maria Ouspenskaya, Claude Rains, Bela Lugosi, Warren William, Ralph Bellamy, and Evelyn Ankers."

259. "Death Makes His Payday: 'It's a Living,' Actor Says." *New York Morning Telegraph*, 31 Dec. 1941.

Lugosi's many "deaths" highlight this piece, which claims the actor "has died in more than 100 stage and screen plays." He offers his "favorite" death scene as *Son of Frankenstein* because — even though he was merely shot — he had "the chance to act all over the place for several hundred feet of film." The article mentions that "Lugosi has been murdered in every conceivable way known to men, and a few special methods have been invented for his particular benefit."

260. "Black Dragons." *Hollywood Reporter*, 2 Mar. 1942.

"Bela Lugosi finds himself disadvantageously spotted as the Nazi surgeon. When all else fails, an audience may find some slight measure of amusement in counting the entrances and exits that substitute for action in the film. How the yellow men turned white remains unexplained."

261. "The Ghost of Frankenstein." *Daily Variety*, 2 Mar. 1942.

"Full measure of melodramatic hoke for

254   III. Works By or About Lugosi

those susceptible to this type of film entertainment. Bela Lugosi is the warped Ygor."

262. "*The Ghost of Frankenstein.*" *Hollywood Reporter*, 2 Mar. 1942.
"Nothing will kill Frankenstein's Monster, which is, of course, to the monstrous delight of Universal. Bela Lugosi is again a splendid Ygor."

263. "*Black Dragons.*" *Daily Variety*, 3 Mar. 1942.
"Lugosi is his usual competent, black browed self."

264. "Horror Actor Favors Fun." *New York Morning Telegraph*, 9 Mar. 1942.
While Lugosi admits portraying maniacs and monsters "offers a compelling challenge," he explains that comedy, travel subjects, and cartoons represent his interests in film fare.

265. "*Black Dragons.*" *Motion Picture Exhibitor*, 11 Mar. 1942.
"With a topic uppermost in the minds of the public, and cashing in on the recent expose of the Black Dragon in Japan, this has suspense and plenty of creepy situations to hold the audience."

266. "*Black Dragons.*" *Harrison's Reports*, 21 Mar. 1942.
"This espionage drama is best suited for small towns and neighborhood theatres, where the patrons are not too exacting in their demands for story values.... Intelligent audiences will hardly find it acceptable."

267. Crowther, Bosley. "*The Ghost of Frankenstein.*" *New York Times*, 4 Apr. 1942.
"The thought that he [the monster] may yet return for further adventures with his body and Lugosi's sconce fills us with mortal terror. That is the most fearful prospect which this picture manages to convey."

268. "*SOS Coastguard.*" *Variety*, 15 Apr. 1942.
Review of the serial feature: "Lugosi gives the best performance...."

269. Hale, Wanda. "Two Horror Helpings at New York Theatre." *New York Daily News*, 27 May 1942.
"There's suspense enough to keep the picture [*The Corpse Vanishes*] going, but we couldn't take it seriously."

270. "*The Corpse Vanishes.*" *Variety*, 3 June 1942.
"A dull murder mystery with all the cliches that usually accompany a second grade story of this kind. On the end of double bills, it might be of interest to youngsters, but it insults the average intelligence. Dully told, minus thrills, poorly directed for sustaining of suspense, and not well acted. Lugosi does most of his acting with his eyes."

271. "*The Corpse Vanishes.*" *Harrison's Reports*, 6 June 1942.
"This is another 'dish' of program horror in the Lugosi manner, but only mildly terrifying. There is enough suspense and weird doings to satisfy the horror-seeking fans, but other audiences may find it to be more amusing than spine-chilling."

272. Barnett, Hoyt. "The House That Horror Built." *Hollywood Magazine*, July 1942.
Barnett's article shows two photographs from Lugosi's home on 10841 Whipple Street, with his text describing the house. Several quotes from Lugosi explain why the architecture and interior design fit his personality "perfectly."

273. "*Bowery at Midnight.*" *Daily Variety*, 28 Sept. 1942.
"Lugosi does his usual masterful menace."

274. "*Bowery at Midnight.*" *Hollywood Reporter*, 28 Sept. 1942.
"Horror fans will find an offering that should be to their liking in *Bowery at*

Midnight. As a fantastic chiller-diller, it has its points of popularity and Bela Lugosi in the starring role under capable direction by Wallace Fox."

275. "*Night Monster*." *Hollywood Reporter*, 19 Oct. 1942.

"The name values of Bela Lugosi and Lionel Atwill with the horror addicts will bring good money returns for *Night Monster*. Lugosi, however, is merely ominously planted as a butler to draw conclusions of guilt."

276. "*Night Monster*." *Variety*, 21 Oct. 1942.

"Cast, headed by Bela Lugosi and Lionel Atwill, is adequate, while direction by Ford Beebe drags at times and he seemed to have a tough time in shaking up the static script."

277. "Bela Lugosi Collapses Under 'Monster' Make-up." *Hollywood Reporter*, 6 Nov. 1942.

Brief article mentions Lugosi's being ordered home by his physician following his collapse on the set of *Frankenstein Meets the Wolf Man*.

278. "H'Wood Chillers Get Chill from British Censors; Too Jittery." *Variety*, 25 Nov. 1942.

The British Board of Censors, the group that helped bring an end to the first horror film cycle during the thirties, balked again at Hollywood horrors during World War II. In particular, *Bowery at Midnight* needed "severe trimming," with *Night Monster* and *Frankenstein Meets the Wolf Man* mentioned as potential problems as well.

279. "*Night Monster*." *New York Times*, 30 Nov. 1942.

"And last but not least, Bela Lugosi as the butler with the evil eye. When all these characters get going, is it any wonder strange things begin to happen?"

280. "*Frankenstein Meets the Wolf Man*." *Daily Variety*, 19 Feb. 1943.

"Here is a strong dish for the mass of customers who go for the bizarre, the weird, the creepy ... one of the most plausibly handled in the whole series of *Frankenstein* and *Wolf Man*."

281. "*The Ape Man*." *Daily Variety*, 22 Feb. 1943.

"*The Ape Man*, latest horror entry from Monogram, is expertly figured for its market. Bela Lugosi continues his bloodthirsty ways as a pseudo-scientist."

282. "*The Ape Man*." *Hollywood Reporter*, 22 Feb. 1943.

"Bela Lugosi, in a 'horrible' makeup, gives another of the performances that addicts of the gruesome expect of him and applaud."

283. Crowther, Bosley. "*Frankenstein Meets the Wolf Man*." *New York Times*, 6 Mar. 1943.

"We confess a great disappointment."

284. "Lugosi Occupies Strangest House in Film Capital." *Hartford Daily Courant*, 25 Apr. 1943.

Printed before Lugosi appeared at the Bushnell Memorial on May 1 in *Dracula*, this article describes his home in North Hollywood. "I really feel," Lugosi said, "that I have a home to match and express my personality, the same as I feel when I play parts that call for very hard and arduous work."

285. Lugosi, Bela. "Bela Lugosi, Star of *Dracula*, in Person." *Boston Herald*, 2 May 1943.

Published the day before he opened in *Dracula* at Boston's Plymouth Theatre, Lugosi explains why he believes *Dracula* remains popular, as well as taking time to express his "firm" belief in President Roosevelt's policies.

286. Eager, Helen. "Bela Lugosi in *Dracula* Revived at Plymouth." *Boston Evening Traveller*, 4 May 1943.

"Fifteen years ago when Count Dracula first paid a visit to Boston, sucking his victim's blood nightly at the Hollis Theater, women fainted and strong men blanched. Last evening Count Dracula, this time in the person of Bela Lugosi, returned to the Plymouth with quite the opposite effect. Everyone had a lovely time at the corny old melodrama with its demonical villain, its madmen, its offstage howling dogs, its wolfsbane."

287. "*Dracula* Revival Opens at Locust." *Philadelphia Record*, 18 May 1943.

"There are too many strange and terrifying things going on in the world today for the mock-horrific doings of *Dracula* to seem very important or convincing. The drama serves to bring Bela Lugosi back from Hollywood's filmpots to play the role of the Count which he created in 1927. He plays it, too, to good effect, suave and sinister by turn for a sharp characterization."

288. Finn, Elsie. "Menace with Cold Feet — That's Bela Lugosi." *Philadelphia Record*, 19 May 1943.

Finn speculates that Dracula Lugosi, with the "Red Cross demands and war shortages," has turned from blood to the glue on stamps. Quotes from Lillian Lugosi explain her husband's stamp collection and his need for nightly foot massages.

289. "*Ghosts on the Loose* Slimsy Material." *Hollywood Reporter*, 9 June 1943.

"Bela Lugosi receives a vacation from playing vampires who sink their fangs into the soft throats of heroines and mad scientists who lurk amidst laboratory retorts seeking an elixir of youth in *Ghosts on the Loose*. However, as Lugosi is always Lugosi, and as this time he's teamed up with the East Side Kids, Monogram still has somewhat of a horror feature on its hands."

290. Crowther, Bosley. "Old Black Magic." *New York Times*, 13 June 1943.

Crowther's article informs the *Times*' readership of Universal's plan to put all its movie monsters into a horrifying epic called *Chamber of Horrors*. The article also gives a brief chronology of the horror film, placing *Dracula* in an important historical light.

291. "*Dracula* Still Chills at National, with Lugosi in Original Role." *Washington Post*, 20 June 1943.

Review of the *Dracula* stage revival: "As for Bela Lugosi, there's only one thing to say. Lugosi is to the business of scaring the hell out of the customers as Petty is to the production of pin-up girls, as Count Fleet is to racing. Just tops."

292. "*Ghosts on the Loose*." *Variety*, 7 July 1943.

"Okay for supporting feature ... Bela Lugosi, as the principal menace, is the Nazi chief, but has little to do."

293. Whitney, Dwight. "*Arsenic and Old Lace* Revived." *San Francisco Chronicle*, 7 Aug. 1943.

"I think, undoubtedly, Bela Lugosi has in him the makings of a Jonathan Brewster which is the equal, or perhaps the superior, of Boris Karloff's masterful reading of the demented Brewster brother with a propensity for manslaughter."

294. Whitney, Dwight. "The World of Drama: Bela Lugosi." *San Francisco Chronicle*, 8 Aug. 1943, Sunday supp. ed., *This World*.

Whitney interviewed Lugosi while the actor lunched on a parsley omelette. He described himself to Whitney as an "extreme liberal Democrat," and listed his favorite newspaper on the Coast as Los Angeles's liberal *Daily News*. Lugosi told Whitney that there is definitely a place for a good horror film, as it "supplies a need which is best explained in the Greek theory of tragedy, a catharsis." Lugosi explained the unfortunate tendency of Hollywood to forget that "what you can see, no matter how horrible, is not half as frightening as what you can't see." Whitney also described the Lugosi home and the actor's interest in sculpture.

295. Hanna, David. "*Arsenic and Old Lace.*" *Los Angeles Daily News*, 21 Aug. 1943.

"Lugosi, for instance, an experienced stage actor, endows his role of the murderer looking for a hideout with a vitality that was lacking in Boris Karloff's portrayal. The result is a faster, more acceptable pace."

296. Schallert, Edwin. "*Arsenic* Again Affords Diabolical Enjoyment." *Los Angeles Times*, 21 Aug. 1943.

"...plenty of praise may be bestowed on Lugosi for his sinister, brilliant and satirical portrait."

297. "Tragedy-Comedy Tradition Safe with Bela Lugosi." *Los Angeles Times*, 6 Sept. 1943.

Lugosi admits to having fun starring in a stage version of *Arsenic and Old Lace*, though his schedule was certainly rushed by shooting *Return of the Vampire* in the daytime before heading to the Music Box Theater at night. Between bites of his salad, Lugosi told the *Times* that burlesquing horror stories would not hurt the tradition. He also explained that children like horror stories due to a "subconscious, atavistic feeling born in them through catastrophes which befell their forebearers centuries ago. Children like to see fearsome happenings from a safe position."

298. **Bela Lugosi in** Dracula. Horowitz, 1943.

Published as a souvenir program for Lugosi's 1943 appearance in a stage revival of *Dracula*, the 16-page booklet offers photographs not only of that play but from numerous Lugosi films. Artwork of Lugosi, reprints of various movie magazine articles on the actor, and cast information on the play itself accompany the images.

299. "*Return of the Vampire.*" *Daily Variety*, 28 Jan. 1944.

"Lugosi is his usual bogey self as the vampire, but Matt Willis takes the honors as the wolfman slave of the bloodsucking gent."

300. "*Return of the Vampire.*" *Hollywood Reporter*, 28 Jan. 1944.

"The performances of Frieda Inescort and Matt Willis are outstanding, but secondary to that of Lugosi, the master of horrors ... it is probably one of the best horror pictures Hollywood has made to date."

301. "Any Blood Donors?" *New York Times*, 29 Jan. 1944.

Review of the film *Return of the Vampire*: "All right, we'll tell you that Bela Lugosi rises again from the grave to go about sucking transfusions from the throat of a beautiful girl in the dark of the night, while mists rise again from around the English mansion and dogs howl mournfully on the hill."

302. "*Voodoo Man.*" *Motion Picture Exhibitor*, 9 Feb. 1944.

"With Lugosi, Zucco, and John Carradine — as a half wit, this should satisfy the thrill followers, and fit into the lower half. It has a saleable title, and the fans who like this sort of thing won't complain even though the story is far fetched."

303. "*Voodoo Man.*" *Variety*, 8 Mar. 1944.

"*Voodoo Man* is negligible as a chiller."

304. Christoph, M. Oakley. *Hartford Daily Courant*, 17 Mar. 1944.

"By the way, Bela Lugosi who is starred in the play at Bushnell, Saturday, is also starred in *Voodoo Man* at the State Theater. So if you want to scare yourself to death, first see him in the flesh at Bushnell and then go to the State and see him on the screen. Wonder if he will go to the State and see his own film? Gosh, maybe Bela on the screen would scare Bela in the flesh, could he?"

305. Finn, Elsie. "Beauty Hung a Hex Sign on Bela Lugosi." *Philadelphia Record*, 9 Apr. 1944.

Finn tells a bizarre tale of a beautiful Hungarian actress who cursed Lugosi after he spurned her. Lugosi's reason for coming to the United States, the author claims, was to escape her spell. "Often he has tried to break the spell. Once, he even shackled a wife to a 5th avenue bus bench ... but he couldn't stop her from going to Reno." Lillian broke the curse, "at least so far as marriage is concerned." Reminiscent of Gladys Hall's articles, Finn's tale is fun but unbelievable.

306. "Lugosi Stars in *Arsenic* at Locust." *Philadelphia Inquirer*, 11 Apr. 1944.

Review of the stage version of *Arsenic and Old Lace*: "If anything, Mr. Lugosi, who was last seen here on the stage in the revival of *Dracula* last May, plays the part of the killer escaped from an institution for the criminally insane along even broader lines than Erich von Stroheim and Boris Karloff, his predecessors here, as Jonathan Brewster. Which makes even more amusing a play that extracts heaps of hilarity from murder and madness."

307. Lee, Laura. "Murder with a Great Big Smile." *Philadelphia Bulletin*, 12 Apr. 1944.

A short biography written while Lugosi appeared as Jonathan Brewster in *Arsenic and Old Lace*. His interests in stamp collecting, imported mineral water, and detective stories are all mentioned. Lillian Lugosi mentions how they were both disappointed in Lugosi's not starring in the film *The Lodger* (1944).

308. Quirk, David. "Bela Lugosi Slated for Broadway Role." *New York Daily News*, 11 July 1944.

Quirk claimed Lugosi was to be featured in the play *Dark Continent*, with revisions in the script being made to accommodate Lugosi's accent.

309. "U Finds Ghouls Pay Off in Gold." *Variety*, 26 July 1944.

Horror films netted "around $750,000 annually" for Universal, accruing steady profits despite "foreign regulations which have confined horror pictures largely to the American continent." *Variety* listed *Dracula* and *The Wolf Man* among the films.

310. "Wife Sues the Monster." *New York Daily News*, 19 Aug. 1944.

Short article details the separation of Lugosi and his wife, Lillian, who claimed he was an "inhuman husband." In the divorce proceedings, Lillian was asking for custody of their son, Bela Jr.

311. "Return of the Ape Man." *Daily Variety*, 3 Sept. 1944.

"Designed to meet horror picture standards, what starts out as a fanciful premise is so ineptly developed and a barrier of poor screenplay and hammish acting reared that *Return of the Ape Man* enters the realm of the ridiculous from which it never emerges."

312. "Return of the Ape Man." *Hollywood Reporter*, 3 Sept. 1944.

"...in its feverish reaching for new sensations and effects, it crosses into the utterly absurd and unacceptable, even for this type of picture."

313. "One Body Too Many." *Hollywood Reporter*, 18 Oct. 1944.

"Bela Lugosi, as the butler, has too little to do but ... [he] ably carried out the best sustained gag in the picture."

314. "Beyond the Limit." *New York Times*, 25 Nov. 1944.

Review of the film, *One Body Too Many*: "This film is a wretched exhibition of trashy film construction and clowning."

315. "*One Body Too Many* Found at Rialto Theatre." *New York Post*, 25 Nov. 1944.

"It all depends on how you feel about these things. Do you go for secret panels and passages? When the electric lights go off and the storm outside blows open the French windows, thus putting out the candles, do you shiver with delight? Is the mere presence of Bela Lugosi sufficient?"

316. "*The Body Snatcher.*" *Daily Variety*, 14 Feb. 1945.
"Bela Lugosi is excellent as Daniell's snooping houseman."

317. Johnson, Fred. "But Playwright Was Survivor!" *San Francisco Call-Bulletin*, 27 Feb. 1945.
Review of the play *No Traveler Returns*: "Any printed recital of the intrigues and superstitions involved would be just as boring as they proved in their trans-footlight projection, even though such accomplished players as Bela Lugosi and Ian Keith were concerned with them."

318. "*No Traveler Returns.*" *San Francisco News*, 27 Feb. 1945.
"Mr. Lugosi played his usual role of a heavy, and while sinister, lost much of the effect through our inability to discover what he was saying."

319. Fried, Alexander. "*No Traveler Returns* Proves Dull Fare on Curran Stage." *San Francisco Examiner*, 28 Feb. 1945.
"To play the role of Bharat Singh, a servant, Lugosi hides his identity under a dark skin and native white dress and turban. He is supposed to be an overpowering presence, hovering on and off the scene, filling the air with fright and mystery. He never succeeds in being any such thing."

320. "*Zombies on Broadway.*" *Daily Variety*, 17 Apr. 1945.
"*Zombies on Broadway* is a screwball comedy that kids Hollywood's regular crop of horror epics. As such it should provide an okay dualer. All [cast and crew] work well."

321. "*Zombies on Broadway.*" *New York Times*, 27 Apr. 1945.
"Bela Lugosi, glaring evilly as any of the zombies he creates, is the scientific genius behind all the goings on. *Zombies on Broadway* is no laughing matter."

322. "Chi Censors Nix RKO's *Body Snatchers* [sic] and Give Adult's-Only to *Zombies.*" *Variety*, 9 May 1945.
Short article mentions that the Chicago police movie censor board refused to pass the film *The Body Snatcher*. The same group rated *Zombies on Broadway* as "adults-only."

323. Agee, James. "The New Pictures: *The Body Snatcher.*" Time, 21 May 1945.
"...there is a grisly shot of Lugosi's slaughtered head, distorted beneath brine. *The Body Snatcher* shows a humane sincerity and a devotion to good cinema unfortunately rather rare in U.S. movies."

324. Hubler, Richard G. "Scare 'Em to Death—And Cash In." *Saturday Evening Post*, 23 May 1945.
Written near the end of the horror film cycle, this piece is an early but intelligent overview of the genre. The author includes quotes from Curt Siodmak regarding *Frankenstein Meets the Wolf Man*.

325. "*The Body Snatcher.*" *New York Times*, 26 May 1945.
"Bela Lugosi, surprisingly unsinister for a change, works industriously to achieve fame as a blackmailer."

326. "RKO's *Body Snatchers* [sic] Now OK for Adults-Only." *Variety*, 6 June 1945.
Short piece mentions the Chicago police censor board's decision to lift a ban on *The Body Snatcher* and replace it with an "adults-only" pass. The censor board in that city continued to hold its "adults-only" stance on *Zombies on Broadway*.

327. Hartung, Philp T. "*The Body Snatcher.*" *The Commonweal*, 15 June 1945.
"It has a subtle psychological insight that will interest and satisfy serious adult audiences as well as those looking only for the touch of the macabre. Because the characters are well portrayed and psychologically sound, the gruesome story becomes very real indeed."

328. Madden, Oden and Olivia. "The Screamy-Weamies." *Colliers*, 12 Jan. 1946.

This article described many of Universal's publicity ploys used for its horror films, with quotes from a Mr. Eustace and a Mr. Sharick, who supposedly helped formulate various stunts. Much mention is made of *Dracula* (1931). This piece becomes curious historically in that a major magazine printed an article on horror films during a low ebb of the genre's productivity.

329. "*Genius at Work.*" *Daily Variety*, 1 Aug. 1946.

"...run-of-the-mill programmer, dull moments far outnumbering its laughs. Atwill and Lugosi provide suitable menace, but are made too much on the buffoon side."

330. "Spook in Person." *Variety*, 22 Jan. 1947.

Variety announced Lugosi's 1947 "spook show," with the first appearance listed as San Diego's Orpheum.

331. "*Three Indelicate Ladies.*" *Variety*, 6 Apr. 1947.

"Bela Lugosi attempts to shoulder the incongruous burden of a Hungarian accent tied to an Irish character named Francis X. O'Rourke."

332. Hughes, Elinor. "*Three Indelicate Ladies.*" *Boston Herald*, 15 Apr. 1947.

"Mr. Lugosi, usually cast as Dracula or similarly improbable characters, had a cheerfully cockeyed role which he played with a pleasantly light touch, submitting cheerfully to being pushed around by three ladies and making very much out of not very much."

333. Adams, Marjorie. "Bela Lugosi Glad of Respite from Horror-Inspiring Roles." *Boston Globe*, 17 Apr. 1947.

Lugosi told Adams of his real name, Blaskó, and said that Lugosi is pronounced something like "You-Go-She" in Hungarian. Adams also noted other names — "Pop," which he was called by his wife, "Lil." Additionally, Lugosi responded to the question of why fewer horror films were being made by mentioning that studios were using mainly contract players and that neither he nor Boris Karloff was under contract at the time.

334. "Lugosi in Boston University Talk." *Boston Herald*, 17 Apr. 1947.

This article informed readers about Lugosi's lecture on abnormal psychology given at Boston University's College of Practical Arts and Letters.

335. "*Dracula.*" *Boston Globe*, 22 July 1947.

Review of a summer stock performance of *Dracula*. "*Dracula* today seems a period piece — a thriller that belongs to another decade. We have grown sophisticated and amused at too elaborate eeriness. Mr. Lugosi as the ghostly vampire ... should terrify children under 10 and delight those come to scoff."

336. Eaton, Fred G. "Humor Survives Flaws in *Arsenic*'s First Night." *The Saratogian*, 7 Aug. 1947.

Review of a summer stock version of *Arsenic and Old Lace* in Saratoga Springs, New York: "It survives a rather ragged performance at the Spa Theater with its flag of humor still flying. Mr. Lugosi, after a slow beginning, works up until he is in full stride through act three."

337. "Shiver-Giver to Trade 'Rip' Tales." *Albany Times Union*, 7 Aug. 1947.

Article discusses the forthcoming meeting of Robert L. Ripley and Bela Lugosi aboard a Chinese junk at a cocktail party on August 8, 1947.

338. "Dracula in Person." *Motion Picture Herald*, 1 Nov. 1947.

This short article covers Lugosi's personal appearance tour in a dramatization of Poe's *The Tell-Tale Heart*.

339. Brady, Thomas F. "Old Ghoulish Friends Roam the Sets at Universal/Larry Parks vs. Columbia." *New York Times*, 14 Mar. 1948.

Article discusses the making of *Abbott and Costello Meet Frankenstein*, including quotes from Lugosi transcribed while the actor was "scrambling on the floor of his dressing room for a missing shirt stud."

340. "*Abbott and Costello Meet Frankenstein.*" *Hollywood Reporter*, 28 July 1948.

"Lon Chaney, as the wolf man, and Bela Lugosi, playing his old role of Count Dracula, make excellent foils, as does Glenn Strange in the spot of the monster."

341. "*Abbott and Costello Meet Frankenstein.*" *New York Times*, 29 July 1948.

"The notion of having these two clowns run afoul of the famous screen monster is a good laugh in itself. But take this gentle warning: get the most out of the one laugh while you can, because the picture itself does not contain many more."

342. Hartung, Philip. "*Abbott and Costello Meet Frankenstein.*" *The Commonweal*, 6 Aug. 1948.

"Bud and Lou make the most of this triple threat; and their director doesn't let you miss an expected laugh or thrill."

343. Weitschat, Al. "The Screen in Review." *Detroit News*, 21 Aug. 1948.

Review of a vaudeville bill with Lugosi at Detroit's Broadway Capitol Theatre: "Temporarily done with the business of spreading goose pimples among movie fans, Bela Lugosi comes out to indulge in a bit of uncomfortable chit-chat, and then re-enact a *Dracula* scene, which is more humorous than horrifying."

344. "Olympia, Miami." *Variety*, 8 Sept. 1948.

Review of a live appearance Lugosi made in Miami, Florida: "Bela Lugosi, marquee lure for the package, offers the Hollywood personal, complete to the uninteresting reminiscing and a 'scene' which in this case is supposed to be a scary bit but which doesn't come off, inspiring giggles instead. In fact, the aisle sitters seemed to be looking for laughs rather than 'horror character' stuff done straight."

345. "Tele Follow-up Comment." *Variety*, 5 Oct. 1949.

Review of the September 27, 1949, episode of *The Texaco Star Theatre*, with Milton Berle and guest Bela Lugosi: "Two other skits came off well. A hoke horror bit with Bela Lugosi with a surprise ending in which Olsen and Johnson, plus a midget, came out of a mummy case, provided a good supply of yocks."

346. Franken, Jerry. "*Suspense.*" *Billboard*, 22 Oct. 1949.

Review of the October 11, 1949, televised episode of *Suspense* with guests Bela Lugosi and Romney Brent: "This was the role [an Italian Fascist] played by Bela Lugosi and the show's greatest weakness for he failed to bestow an iota of reality on what appears to have been a fine and meaty part."

347. "Gamut Club to Honor Lugosi." *New York Times*, 23 May 1950.

Short article mentions Lugosi's being the guest of honor at a New York organization's dinner.

348. "Lugosi Wants to Reform." *New York Herald Tribune*, 8 June 1950.

Short piece mentions Lugosi's wanting to escape horror roles through the Fritz Rotter play *The Devil Also Dreams*.

349. "New Play Draws Top Executes." *Providence Journal*, 23 July 1950.

Among other notables, television scout George Clark attended the premiere of *The Devil Also Dreams*, observing the television potential of Francis L. Sullivan and Lugosi.

350. "*The Devil Also Dreams.*" *Variety*, 2 Aug. 1950.

"Present billing has a tendency toward greater expectation on the part of the viewer. When it doesn't materialize, despite the cleverness of the fairly simple plot and the suspense it generates, there is a letdown. This piece is doubtful Broadway material."

351. "Bela Balks at Blood, Lives for Laughs." *Ottawa Journal,* 21 Aug. 1950.

Lugosi, wearing "a most unsinister bow tie," spoke to reporters during his association with *The Devil Also Dreams.* "I'm having the best time of my life making people laugh," he told reporters of his role.

352. *"The Devil Also Dreams."* *Montreal Daily Star,* 23 Aug. 1950.

"Bela Lugosi of *Dracula* fame has never been seen here in a domestic role. His exits, muttering implications, are all notes of comedy for the audience learns to wait. Mr. Lugosi is always the schooled and experienced actor."

353. "Lugosi's Horror Show Set to Hypo Nabe Biz." *Variety,* 6 Dec. 1950.

Variety describes Lugosi's live East Coast horror show tour.

354. "Dracula Gloats So — Over His Stamps." *Daily Mirror* (London, England), 11 Apr. 1951.

Lugosi excitedly spoke of appearing in *Dracula* for the first time on the British stage, while his wife, Lillian, mentioned that he "loves cartoon films" and that stamp collecting was "the only thing he really gets worked up about."

355. "Dracula Is So Charming and Easy to Live With." *London Daily Graphic,* 11 Apr. 1951.

Lillian Lugosi told British reporters that her husband was very romantic, kind, and lazy. She also commented that "he crushed the ribs of leading lady Estelle Winwood, so he turned to horrors."

356. *"Dracula."* *Brighton Standard* (England), 2 May 1951.

"What with the magic of Bela Lugosi's personality, and it is a powerful personality indeed, and the sumptuous production on which things are so brought up to date that Dracula flies from Transylvania to Hampstead, that this is a sort of time of your life show."

357. "Bela 'Dracula' Lugosi at Lewisham." *Lewisham Journal* (England), 11 May 1951.

An interviewer for the *Journal* drew much attention to Lillian Lugosi's reference to her husband as "Bel," pronouncing it the same "as the French pronounce their 'belle' for beautiful." Among other topics, Lugosi mentioned that he found England cold after the warmth of California.

358. *"Dracula."* *Birmingham Mail* (England), 29 May 1951.

"Those who have seen his [Lugosi's] films will find this production an anticlimax. It lacks the effects upon which the screen can call."

359. MacKay, Colin Neil. "This Is Really *Dracula.*" *Scottish Daily Express,* June 1951.

"This is melodrama in the Henry Irving tradition, magnificent, macabre, and glorious bloodcurdling; not staged, but invoked and declaimed rather than acted. Hollywood could never provide realism like this. At a lesser theatre, it would be capacity twice nightly."

360. "New *Dracula* Tones Down Horrors." *The Star* (Sheffield, England), 7 Sept. 1951.

"Bela Lugosi is a most effective Count Dracula. Here is a true master of his craft. His acting is just and not overdone."

361. *"Mother Riley Meets the Vampire."* *Today's Cinema* (England), 26 Jan. 1952.

"The production work is modest but efficient, and the various comedy-thriller gags are effectively managed. The exuberant clowning of Arthur Lucan in the title

362. "*Bela Lugosi Meets a Brooklyn Gorilla.*" *Daily Variety*, 8 Sept. 1952.

"Lugosi provides dark and threatening looks. William Beaudine didn't stand a chance with the Tim Ryan screenplay in his direction."

363. "*Bela Lugosi Meets a Brooklyn Gorilla.*" *Hollywood Reporter*, 8 Sept. 1952.

"William Beaudine's direction merely proves that the best of directors are helpless when given a hopeless story and a weak cast."

364. "*Bela Lugosi Meets a Brooklyn Gorilla.*" *Variety*, 10 Sept. 1952.

"This low-budgeted, long-titled comedy-horror pic is destined for a quick demise. Lugosi is menacing."

365. "Bela Lugosi Accused of Cruelty in Divorce Suit." *Los Angeles Times*, 3 June 1953.

Article covers the divorce suit filed by Lillian Arch Lugosi, mentioning the accusation of her husband's cruelty.

366. "Divorces Jealous Dracula." *Los Angeles Herald-Express*, 17 July 1953.

Newspaper story mentions Lugosi's fourth wife, Lillian, winning an uncontested divorce.

367. "What One Monster Could Do." *TV Guide*, 14–20 Aug. 1953.

Bela Lugosi could have been the "king of terrorvision," this tongue-in-cheek article claims. Along with a short biography of Lugosi, the article offers the idea that the actor could have made a fortune from his movies and merchandising on television if only he had retained the rights to some of them.

368. Thomas, Bob. "For a Halloween Story, He Went to an Expert." *Los Angeles Mirror*, 30 Oct. 1953.

Thomas interviewed Lugosi in his apartment, shortly after his divorce from Lillian Arch. The actor claimed to be friends with Boris Karloff, though admitting to not having seen him for "two or three years." On the subject of Karloff, he also remembered having suggested Boris for the lead in *Frankenstein* (1931). Thomas noticed a "willowy nude" hanging on the wall and commented that Lugosi had auctioned numerous personal belongings only a few days prior to the interview.

369. Geltzer, George. "Tod Browning." *Films in Review*, Oct. 1953.

In covering director Browning's career, Geltzer discusses such Lugosi films as *The Thirteenth Chair*, *Dracula*, and *Mark of the Vampire*. Though somewhat outdated, the comments — given that this was one of the few serious critical discussions of the films while the actor was still alive — remain interesting.

370. Kimbrough, Mary. "Bela Lugosi a Gentle Dracula Off-Stage." *St. Louis Post-Dispatch*, 21 Jan. 1954.

Lugosi gave this short interview while he was performing *Arsenic and Old Lace* in St. Louis. The article, which became the main publicity Lugosi received while in Missouri, quickly chronicles his career.

371. Clemens, Bob. "Inside Las Vegas." *Las Vegas Sun*, 25 Feb. 1954.

Review of the *Bela Lugosi Revue* at the Silver Slipper in Las Vegas: "By the way, Bela Lugosi has assuredly found himself a new career, and mayhap will wind up burlesque-ing on film his old horror roles. We hope so. This old horror man is such a gentle, lovable guy, the entire Slipper cast to a man can't do enough for him. And since those changes, the *Bela Lugosi Revue* is a show you can see again and again for new experience every time."

372. "Bela Lugosi Will Joust with Bowery Boys." *Los Angeles Times*, 2 Mar. 1954.

This article claims that Lugosi was hired for *The Bowery Boys Meet the Monster*, though he did not appear in the movie.

373. "Silver Slipper, Las Vegas." *Variety*, 10 Mar. 1954.

"Dracula is burlesqued in a series of skits for big yocks as Bela Lugosi scores with patrons no matter what he does. Lugosi is no mean ad libber ... there is no doubt he has the affection of the audience, which is aware that the 72-year-old actor still has plenty of that old spark left."

374. "Bela Lugosi Surrenders Self as Narcotic Addict." *Los Angeles Examiner*, 22 Apr. 1955.

Photograph of police officer R.W. Hastings and an amiable Lugosi accompanies the *Examiner*'s article on Lugosi's request for a cure.

375. Heard, Roby. "Bela Lugosi Describes 20 Years of Shame." *Los Angeles Mirror-News*, 22 Apr. 1955.

An article on Lugosi's drug addiction, printed before Judge Ware approved his desire to be committed to the state hospital.

376. "Bela Lugosi Seeks Cure." *New York Times*, 23 Apr. 1955.

Mention is made of Lugosi's entering the state hospital at Norwalk after the hearing with Judge Ware.

377. "Bela Lugosi Tells Long Dope Ordeal." *Los Angeles Times*, 23 Apr. 1955.

Another piece on Lugosi's drug use, printed just after Judge Ware approved his request for help.

378. "Lugosi Benefit Slated Tonight." *Los Angeles Times*, 11 May 1955.

The *Times* gives brief mention to the *Bride of the Atom* premiere in Los Angeles, which served as a benefit for Lugosi to help defray his medical costs.

379. "*Bride of the Atom*." *Daily Variety*, 13 May 1955.

"Even the least discriminating audiences will find it dull. Bela Lugosi's histrionics are reduced to the ridiculous through over-direction."

380. "Bela Lugosi Nearing Freedom as Dope Case." *Los Angeles Times*, 30 July 1955.

Article discusses Lugosi's three months in the hospital, noting that he was soon to appear before the staff physicians for release consideration.

381. "Lugosi Drug Cure Progresses." *New York Times*, 3 Aug. 1955.

This newspaper story mentioned that Lugosi had "passed with flying colors" a staff examination at the Metropolitan State Hospital, thus paving the way for his release from their care.

382. "Bela Lugosi Plans Quick Return to Movie Work." *Los Angeles Times*, 4 Aug. 1955.

In this article printed the day before his release from the hospital, Lugosi happily told of his upcoming films, like the never-made *Ghoul Goes West*. He also related how many letters and phone calls of encouragement he had received while being cured.

383. "Bela Lugosi Leaves Hospital to Begin Movie Comeback." *Los Angeles Herald-Examiner*, 6 Aug. 1955.

This article focused on Lugosi's hopes for new movie roles after his release from the Metropolitan Hospital.

384. "Cured." *Newsweek*, 8 Aug. 1955.

Short paragraph mentions Lugosi's rehabilitation from drug use.

385. "Bela Lugosi, 73, Marrying His Hospital Pen Pal, 40." *New York Post*, 24 Aug. 1955.

Nice article covers Lugosi and Lininger's meeting and subsequent wedding with quotes from both. The same newspaper printed a very nice photo from the matrimonial services the following day, with the header "Hope's Hopes Come True."

386. "Actor Bela Lugosi, 72, Takes His Fifth Bride, 39." *Los Angeles Times*, 25 Aug. 1955.

A photograph shows Lugosi toasting his new bride, Hope Lininger, and is accompanied by an article about their wedding.

387. "Lugosi to Wed His Letter Pal." *New York Daily News*, 25 Aug. 1955.

Another story on the Lugosi-Lininger marriage, with quotes from Lugosi transcribed shortly before the wedding. The *Daily News* printed a photo of the couple on the front page.

388. Skolsky, Sidney. *This Was Hollywood* 1:1 (1955).

This short biography of Lugosi (which erroneously claimed he was born in 1888 and had begun his screen career in 1915) includes Bela's story that playing Dracula so many times was hazardous due to the compounded chemicals used to create the effect of fog. "I am now more resurrected than real," Lugosi allegedly stated as a result of his exposure to such chemicals.

389. "The Black Sleep." *Daily Variety*, 7 June 1956.

"Chaney, Carradine, and Lugosi prove okay bogeyman."

390. "The Black Sleep." The *Hollywood Reporter*, 7 June 1956.

"There are not many good horror pictures these days and *The Black Sleep* is a good one. ...well-made and should be popular with audiences who seemingly have a perennial appetite for good horror productions."

391. "Bela Lugosi Collapses, Dies at Home." *Los Angeles Examiner*, 17 Aug. 1956.

The *Examiner* paid tribute to the actor with this obituary.

392. "Bela Lugosi Dies; Created Dracula." *New York Times*, 17 Aug. 1956.

Lengthy obituary printed with a 1955 photograph of the thespian. Like many of the obituaries, this one inaccurately states his age at the time of death.

393. "Obituaries: Bela Lugosi." *Daily Variety*, 17 Aug. 1956.

Daily Variety published this very brief obituary the day following Lugosi's death.

394. "Bela Lugosi Shroud to Be Dracula Cape." *Los Angeles Times*, 18 Aug. 1956.

Brief article mentions the time and date of Lugosi's funeral, as well as explaining his wish to be buried in the cloak of Dracula.

395. "Mr. Bela Lugosi." *The Times* (London), 18 Aug. 1956.

The British obituary of Lugosi, which erroneously mentions him being age 67 at the time of death.

396. "Last Farewell." *Los Angeles Times*, 19 Aug. 1956.

A photo of Hope Lugosi and A.G. Holloway, mortician, is printed with another mention of the funeral.

397. "Meghalt Lugosi Béla." *Magyar Nemzét* (Hungary), 19 Aug. 1956.

One of the main Hungarian obituaries; brief but quite respectful.

398. "Milestones: Died." *Time*, 27 Aug. 1956.

Short obituary mentions only two of Lugosi's films, one being *The Ghost of Frankenstein*.

399. "Transition: Died." *Newsweek*, 27 Aug. 1956.

A short obituary accompanied by two photographs of the actor.

400. "Lugosi Widow to Handle Estate." *Hollywood Citizen-News*, 19 Oct. 1956.

The *Citizen-News* mentions that the court appointed Hope Lininger administrator of Lugosi's estate. This article places its worth from $4,000 to $5,000, some

$1,900 of which was in cash and the remainder in real estate and paintings.

401. Beaumont, Charles. *The Magazine of Fantasy and Science Fiction*, Dec. 1956.

Beaumont's obituary of Lugosi remains one of the most memorable, possibly because he actually knew the actor.

402. Lichello, Bob. "For Twenty Years Hope Lininger Was a Fan! Then … 'I Married Dracula and He Was Afraid of Me!'" *National Enquirer*, 17 Nov. 1957.

Extensive quotes from Lugosi's final wife and actor Paul Marco describe the actor's last year of life.

403. Ackerman, Forrest J. "Public Vampire Number One." *Famous Monsters of Filmland*, 2 (1958).

Subsequently reprinted numerous times, this article is an early and touching biographical statement written by a friend of Lugosi's. Ackerman's tribute had also appeared in a 1956 British publication, *A Book of Weird Tales*, issue no. 1.

404. "A Wellsian Film: Horror on Dr. Moreau's Island." *The Times* (London), 7 Feb. 1959.

Review for a British release of *The Island of Lost Souls* (1933): "For collectors of horror films, *The Island of Lost Souls* would seem to be a natural. …available for exhibition in England for the first time since it was made more than twenty years ago."

405. Brooks, Conrad. "Bela Lugosi's Life Story." *World Famous Creatures*, 3 (Feb. 1959).

Short text, printed with several photographs, was written by an actor who appeared in the Lugosi–Ed Wood film *Glen or Glenda*. Mentions some of the projects Lugosi was slated to do at the time of his death.

406. *Famous Monsters of Filmland*, 5 (Nov. 1959).

Beautiful Albert Nuetzell cover art of Lugosi in the test makeup for *The Island of Lost Souls* adorns the cover of Forrest Ackerman's horror film magazine. This magazine, the first and best of early such publications, became a prime factor for renewing interest in Lugosi during the sixties.

407. "Lugosi's Secret Terror." *Famous Monsters of Filmland* 9. (Nov. 1960).

This intriguing but unbelievable story told of a woman with yellow eyes who followed Lugosi throughout his life. It is a reprint of a 1929 article by Gladys Hall.

408. Boullet, Jean. "Bela Lugosi: Prince de la terreur et reincarnation du Count Dracula." *Bizarre* (France), 1962.

This article is typical of Boullet's writing, which was far from accurate and led many European fans to believe Lugosi the actor and his screen characters were one and the same.

409. *Famous Monsters of Filmland Yearbook*, 1 (1962).

The Lugosi cover from *Famous Monsters of Filmland* no. 5 appears in a cover montage with three other artworks.

410. *Midi Minuit Fantastique* 4–5 (Jan. 1963).

Lugosi as Dracula graced the cover of this special, double-sized French publication that devoted the entire issue to discussing Dracula in film and literature.

411. "*Dracula*: Fact and Fiction." *Famous Monsters of Filmland*, 22 (Apr. 1963).

Famous Monsters featured Lugosi on the cover in a scene with Dwight Frye from *Dracula*, while the article itself contained numerous quotes out of Lugosi's own scrapbook concerning the 1931 *Dracula*.

412. *Fantastic Monsters of the Films*, 2:1 (1963).

The pull-out cover pictures Lugosi in Ygor makeup and Boris Karloff as the monster, taken from *Son of Frankenstein*.

413. Gordon, Alex. "My Favorite Vampire." *Fantastic Monsters*, 2:5 (1963).

This very interesting article deals with Lugosi's life in the early fifties. Gordon's memories cover *Mother Riley Meets the Vampire*, *The House of Wax* premiere, and Lugosi's guest shot on Red Skelton's television show.

414. *Mad Monsters* 5 (1963).

Artwork of Lugosi as the Frankenstein Monster and Lon Chaney, Jr., as the Wolf Man adorns the cover.

415. *Castle of Frankenstein*, 4 (May 1964).

Wonderful cover art of Lugosi as Dracula was used for this issue of Calvin T. Beck's horror film magazine.

416. *Famous Monsters of Filmland*, 28 (May 1964).

Great cover art of Lugosi from *The Island of Lost Souls* complements a "filmbook" of same, which was concluded in the July 1964 edition, issue no. 29.

417. *Famous Monsters of Filmland*, 30 (Sept. 1964).

Excellent Russ Jones art of Lugosi as Dracula decorates the cover.

418. "Beatles vs. Lugosi." *Variety*, 28 Oct. 1964.

This brief article chronicles the numerous Lugosi fan clubs in the southern Florida region, which attests to the level of his renewed popularity in the sixties.

419. *Fantastic Monsters of the Films*, 7 (1964).

Cover art by Larry Byrd features Lugosi as Ygor.

420. Smith, Gene. "A Sentimental Journey to Dracula's Home Town." *Saturday Evening Post*, 27 Mar. 1965.

A tourist's view of Romania and the real-life Dracula territories, this major article is complemented by numerous Lugosi photographs. Even during Christopher Lee's popularity in the role of Dracula, Lugosi remained to many the definitive visualization of Stoker's creation.

421. "When Dracula Invaded England." *Famous Monsters of Filmland*, 35 (Oct. 1965).

Lugosi in Vic Prezio cover art compliments a story on the 1951 British tour in the play *Dracula*.

422. Jordan, Harold. *The Films of Bela Lugosi*, 1965.

Jordan published his booklet — only a handful of pages — in Great Britain. Though it offers no unique information, the monograph is one of the few "all–Lugosi" publications.

423. Brown, Barry. "The True Facts Behind Lugosi's Tragic Drug Addiction." *Castle of Frankenstein*, 10 (Feb. 1966).

Four-page story on Lugosi's drug use, now interesting mainly due to several good photographs that accompany the text.

424. "Inside Lugosi's Haunted House." *Famous Monsters of Filmland*, 37 (Feb. 1966).

A reprint of an old movie magazine article, this tale featured a woman who had a vampirelike power over Lugosi, causing the actor to leave Hungary and two sons he had supposedly fathered.

425. "*Son of Frankenstein*: His Heritage Was Horror." *Monster World*, 7 (Mar. 1966).

Lugosi, Boris Karloff, and Basil Rathbone are all pictured in cover artwork painted by Gary Morrow, as well as in a large number of photographs that accompany the article on the film *Son of Frankenstein*.

426. Everson, William K. "The Last Days of Bela Lugosi." *Castle of Frankenstein*, 8 (Apr. 1966).

Everson, noted film historian, writes on

Lugosi's life in the early fifties. The author became friends with Lugosi while the actor lived in New York City.

427. Borland, Carroll. "What Makes Luna Tick." *Famous Monsters of Filmland*, 39 (June 1966).

Forrest J Ackerman interviews Carroll Borland, Lugosi's costar from *Mark of the Vampire*. She discusses at length her friendship with Lugosi, as well as working with him on the film and in a touring stage version of *Dracula*.

428. *Modern Monsters*, June 1966.

Modern Monsters, a fan publication, featured a pen-and-ink drawing of Lugosi as Dracula on the cover of this issue.

429. "Great Lugosi Mystery." *Famous Monsters of Filmland*, 40 (Aug. 1966).

Reprint of an old movie magazine article claims that a specter haunted Lugosi.

430. Bojarski, Richard. "The Bela Lugosi Story." *For Monsters Only*, 2 (Sept. 1966).

An intelligent overview of Lugosi's life as told by the man who later authored *The Films of Bela Lugosi* (Citadel Press, 1980).

431. "Bride of the Monster." *Monster World*, 5 (Oct. 1966).

A *Bride of the Monster* plot summary and numerous stills accompany cover artwork of actor/wrestler Tor Johnson. It is curious that such a meager and (at that time) little-known film would command several pages in a nationally read magazine.

432. *Famous Monsters of Filmland*, 42 (Jan. 1967).

Cover artwork by Ron Cobb features Lugosi and Lon Chaney, Jr. from the film *Frankenstein Meets the Wolf Man*.

433. *Castle of Frankenstein Monster Annual*, 1967.

A Russ Jones painting of Lugosi graces the cover in a montage with several other horror film stars.

434. *Famous Monsters of Filmland*, 61 (Jan. 1970).

Lugosi and Carroll Borland, in art by Peter Green, are featured on the cover in a pose from *Mark of the Vampire*. The magazine also includes the first half of an article on the same film, which was concluded in *Famous Monsters* 62 (February 1970).

435. Marlowe, Don. "Lugosi." *Classic Film Collector*, Winter 1970.

Written by Lugosi's manager of the late 1940s, this article covers his association with the actor during that period. The text later appeared in Marlowe's book *The Hollywood That Was* (Branch Smith, 1974).

436. "Essai Bela Lugosi pour *Frankenstein*." *Midi Minuit Fantastique* (France), 23 (1970).

Short but fascinating article on the Lugosi test footage for the 1931 *Frankenstein*. Quotes from Florey accompany an advertisement for the footage itself. Don Marlowe, Lugosi's manager in the late 1940s, attempted to sell the footage for $4,000.

437. *Famous Monsters of Filmland Yearbook*, 1970.

Famous Monsters featured wonderful Lugosi art from *Dracula* on the cover of this issue.

438. Luther, Claudia. "Lugosi House to Be Razed: It's a Bloody Shame." *Beverly Hills Citizen*, 14 July 1971.

Attorney Frank Saletri, then owner of Lugosi's three-story home and of a terrier named after the actor, spoke with sadness about having to move from the house.

439. del Olmo, Frank. "Afraid of Dracula? His Son Never Was." *Los Angeles Times*, 19 July 1971.

Quotes from Bela Lugosi, Jr., recount stories about his father. *Classic Film Collector* later reprinted the article in its Fall 1971 issue.

440. Barbour, Alan G. *Lugosi* (Screen Facts Press, 1971).
Some 50 pages of Lugosi stills, printed on heavy stock. No text or real rarities, but a fine magazine/booklet tribute. *Lugosi* appeared on microfilm in 1987.

441. "Dracula Lives!" *Time*, 14 Feb. 1972.
Short article mentions the decision of the Los Angeles Supreme Court ruling in favor of Bela Lugosi, Jr., and Hope Lininger Lugosi, entitling them to share in money made by Universal Pictures from games, shirts, models, and other merchandise bearing Lugosi's likeness.

442. "Lugosi: The Life of Filmland's Dracula." *Famous Monsters of Filmland*, 92 (Sept. 1972).
The above title refers to the entire magazine, devoted exclusively to Lugosi. The issue included an interesting piece called "Count Dracula's Vampire Ring," featuring a close-up of Lugosi's ring. "Bela Lugosi: 14 Fantastic Pages of Facts You'll Never Forget!" offered Alex Gordon's remembrances along with a unique caricature in pen-and-ink that had belonged to Bela himself. Ackerman also reprinted his own Lugosi biography, "Public Vampire Number One." Cover featured Lugosi in art by Barry Morgan.

443. *Remember When*, 9 (Nov. 1972).
A still of Lugosi and Carroll Borland from *Mark of the Vampire* graced the cover, with an article on the film contained within this nostalgia magazine.

444. Pinsker, Simon. "Some Bloody Lines for Bela Lugosi." *Harper's*, Oct. 1973.
A 21-line poem in honor of Lugosi evokes memories of Dracula, Transylvania, and even the Dead End Kids.

445. Ackerman, Forrest J. "*Such Men Are Dangerous*, Especially If They're Born in Lugos, Hungary!" *Famous Monsters of Filmland*, 112 (Dec. 1974).
Article discussed information from the *Murder by Television* pressbook, as well as reprinting a personal information form Lugosi filled out in his own handwriting for that film's producer, Imperial-Cameo Pictures.

446. Noel, Gerard, ed. "Bela Lugosi: Le Plus grand de tous?" *Horror Pictures* (France), 1974.
Noel featured Lugosi on the cover of this European horror film magazine, which also included an article on the actor.

447. Isaacs, Stuart. "Lugosi Book: Labor of 'Love.'" *Atlantic City Sunday Press*, 2 (Feb. 1975).
Isaacs interviewed Arthur Lennig, author of G.P. Putnam's *The Count*, finding out how and why Lennig wrote the first Lugosi biography.

448. "The Book of Bela." *Famous Monsters of Filmland*, 115 (Apr. 1975).
The first in a two-part article (concluded in the May issue, no. 116) reprints the 1941 Gladys Hall article "Memoes of a Madman."

449. Mitchell, Lisa. "Lugosi at the Midnite Deli." *Famous Monsters of Filmland*, 123 (Mar. 1976).
The remembrance of a fan who encountered Lugosi late in his life, seeing him numerous times at the Midnite Delicatessen, a store on the south side of Hollywood Boulevard.

450. Cremer, Robert. "If It's Midnight, This Must Be Transylvania." *Famous Monsters of Filmland*, 125 (May 1976).
The first in a two-part article by the author of *Lugosi: The Man Behind the Cape* chronicles his search for Lugosi information, as well as his association with Lugosi's fourth wife, Lillian Arch.

451. Mitchell, Lisa. "I Remember Bela." *New West* 1:4 (7 June 1976).
Mitchell quickly examined the marketing

industry that built itself up around Lugosi before mentioning how she met the actor at Price's Shoe Store on Hollywood and Ivar in the fifties.

452. Maronie, Samuel James. "Things You Never Knew about the Unholy Two." *Famous Monsters of Filmland*, 127 (Aug. 1976).

Actors Lyle Talbot, Leon Waycoff, and Huntz Hall each share their memories of costarring with Lugosi.

453. Blankenhorn, Richard. "The Great Lugosi." *Famous Monsters of Filmland*, 132 (Jan. 1977).

Insight and anecdotes come from Alexander Great (aka Kim Key), a magician who claimed to have first met Lugosi in Budapest when he was a small child, then again years later in the United States.

454. Sheffield, Richard R. "Lugosi's Last Years: The Boy Who Befriended Bela." *Famous Monsters of Filmland*, 133 (Apr. 1977).

A wonderful personal history of Sheffield's three-year friendship with Lugosi. An indispensable look at Lugosi's final days, written by his closest companion of the period.

455. Dello Stritto, Frank. "In Search of Bela Lugosi." *Photon*, 27 (1977).

Highly astute reviews of Arthur Lennig's *The Count* and Robert Cremer's *Lugosi: The Man Behind the Cape*. This article is perhaps the best and most informative criticism on the two Lugosi books.

456. Guy, Gordon, ed. *The Castle Dracula Quarterly*, 1:1 (1977).

A marvellous publication devoted to Bela by one of the major contributors to Lugosi lore. Guy includes excellent artwork, unique stills, and reproductions of rare items like Lugosi's Screen Actor's Guild card and the program from his funeral. Memories of meeting Lugosi in person by fan Jack Miller and an article by Carroll Borland (of *Mark of the Vampire*) are among the highlights.

457. Ross, T.J. "The Lugosi Touch." *Quarterly Review of Film Studies*, Spring 1978.

This extensive review of Robert Cremer's *Lugosi: The Man Behind the Cape* focused not only on the book itself but also on Ross's own evaluation of the Hungarian.

458. *Los Angeles Times*, 23 Apr. 1979.

A short, untitled article mentions George Hamilton's salute to Lugosi at his "Hollywood Walk of Fame" star, in honor of the movie *Love at First Bite* (1979).

459. Hager, Philip. "Bela Lugosi's Heirs Lose *Dracula* Suit." *Los Angeles Times*, 4 Dec. 1979.

Newspaper article explained a court decision regarding the Lugosi family's loss in the struggle for rights to the exclusive commercial usage of the Lugosi/Dracula likeness.

460. "Films So Bad, They're Good." *Newsweek*, 28 Apr. 1980.

An early and widely read article on a "worst" film festival and the "so bad they're good" quality of the Ed Wood movies.

461. "Who Can Inherit Fame?" *Time*, 7 Aug. 1980.

A short article in *Time*'s "Law" section mentions the reversal of the California Supreme Court ruling on Lugosi merchandising.

462. *Film Collector's World*, 98 (Nov. 1980).

This publication featured Lugosi on its cover in a still from *Dracula* (1931).

463. "*Glen or Glenda*." *Variety*, May 27, 1981.

Review of one of Lugosi's last movies, which the trade had not previously critiqued: "Most ['mad flights of fancy'] involve a weird scientist, delightfully played by Bela Lugosi in eye-popping fashion."

14. Reviews, Articles, and Pamphlets

464. *Dun's Business Month*, Sept. 1982.
Lugosi as Dracula adorns the cover, symbolizing an evil aristocrat causing financial woes to publicize an article called "The Bankruptcy Scare."

465. *Famous Monsters of Filmland*, 188 (Oct. 1982).
Art of Lugosi, Lon Chaney, Jr., and Boris Karloff takes the cover spot, with the Lugosi painting a reprint from *Famous Monsters of Filmland Yearbook*, no. 8.

466. Telotte, J.P. "A Photogenic Horror: Lewton Does Robert Louis Stevenson." *Literature-Film Quarterly*, 10:1 (1982).
Examines Lewton and Wise's approach and alterations to the Stevenson tale *The Body Snatcher* from a historical and theoretical standpoint. The author does not discuss Lugosi, but the text is an important discussion of the 1945 film.

467. Rosar, William. "Music for the Monsters: Universal Pictures' Horror Film Scores of the Thirties." *Quarterly Journal of the Library of Congress* 40:4 (Fall 1983).
In-depth article delves into the music scores (or lack thereof, in some cases) for the Lugosi films *Dracula*, *The Black Cat* (1934), *The Raven*, and *The Invisible Ray*.

468. Williams, Tony. "*White Zombie*: Haitian Horror." *Jump Cut*, 28 (1983).
An intriguing theoretical analysis of the 1932 Lugosi film, written in such a way as to connect aspects of the film's plot to U.S. relations with Haiti throughout the twentieth century.

469. Mandell, Paul. "Edgar Ulmer and *The Black Cat*." *American Cinematographer*, Oct. 1984.
A massively researched article, this is the definitive work on the 1934 Karloff-Lugosi chiller. Production history, budget and shooting schedules, and memories of Lugosi by Ulmer's widow highlight the essay.

470. Gallagher, John. "Wise Fantastica." *Fangoria*, 44 (1985).
An interview with director/editor Robert Wise reveals interesting information on *The Body Snatcher* (1945) and Lugosi's health during the production.

471. Friedman, Drew and Josh Alan. "Bela Lugosi's Scariest Role." *National Lampoon*, Jan. 1986.
A one-page pen-and-ink comic covers Lugosi's career in brief. Tongue-in-cheek strip later saw print in a Fantagraphics booklet entitled *Warts and All* (1994).

472. *Filmfax* 3 (June 1986).
Wonderful cover art of Lugosi complements a series of articles on the Hungarian, such as a trivia section. Most valuable, though, is an interview with Reginald Le Borg, who discusses Bela's role in *The Black Sleep* (1955).

473. Gardella, Kay. "A Look at Lugosi." *New York Daily News*, 11 July 1986.
An overview of the documentary film *Lugosi: The Forgotten King*.

474. "It's Bad Video." *Video Times*, Aug. 1986.
Poor insight led this article to proclaim Lugosi the king of bad films, mentioning only his lesser efforts. The actor appears on the cover of this magazine.

475. Mank, Gregory William. "Universal's Golden Age: Some Facts and Figures." *Midnight Marquee*, 35 (Fall 1986).
In-depth piece covers shooting schedules and budgetary information for such films as *Murders in the Rue Morgue*, *The Black Cat* (1934), *The Raven*, *The Invisible Ray*, and *Son of Frankenstein*.

476. "The Big Little Man." *Fangoria*, 50 (1986).
Angelo Rossitto, costar of three Lugosi films, recalls his friendship with the Hungarian in this interview.

477. Taves, Brian. "Universal's Horror Tradition." *American Cinematographer*, Apr. 1987.

Fascinating article describes the never-made Robert Florey/Bela Lugosi version of *Frankenstein* and their collaboration on *Murders in the Rue Morgue* (1932). Taves also discusses the mysterious *Frankenstein* test footage of Lugosi at length.

478. Weaver, Tom. "Kelton the Cop Sez: Don't Knock on Wood." *Fangoria*, 64 (June 1987).

This interview with Paul Marco, one of Ed Wood's regular players, sheds light on Lugosi movies like *Bride of the Monster*.

479. Rhodes, Gary Don, ed. *The World of Bela Lugosi*, 1 (Aug. 1987).

This first issue of the Bela Lugosi Society newsletter featured an interview with *Black Friday* director Arthur Lubin, an article on Lugosi's radio shows, book reviews, artwork, and various stills.

480. "Dracula a Nightmare for General Mills." *USA Today*, 16 Oct. 1987.

Short article recounts General Mills' trouble with consumers over the use of Lugosi in Dracula regalia for Count Chocula cereal boxes. The handful of complaints had nothing to do with the actor, but rather the medallion he wore which resembled the Star of David. The company exerted much effort to deny any anti–Semitic motives.

481. Rhodes, Gary Don, ed. *The World of Bela Lugosi*, 2 (Dec. 1987).

An interview with *Mark of the Vampire* costar Carroll Borland, an analysis of Lugosi books, video reviews, and mention of Lugosi's likeness on General Mills' Count Chocula cereal boxes make up the bulk of this newsletter.

482. Noel, Gerard, ed. *Bela Lugosi: 1882–1956*. (France: Horror Pictures, 1987).

This slick, 32-page booklet devoted to the Hungarian includes Lugosi stills, a photograph of a Lugosi lifemask, and a reprint of a 1932 letter written by the actor.

483. Rhodes, Gary Don, ed. *The World of Bela Lugosi*, 3 (Apr. 1988).

Includes articles on the various homes Lugosi owned, the history of Lugosi's "Dracula" ring, the collection of Forrest J Ackerman, and the discovery of the 1936 Lugosi serial *Shadow of Chinatown*. The newsletter reprints Gladys Hall's 1929 article "True Hollywood Ghost Stories," while a previously unpublished shot of Lugosi from *The Thirteenth Chair* decorates the cover.

484. Turner, George. "The Two Faces of Dracula." *American Cinematographer* (May 1988).

This history of the American and Spanish versions of *Dracula* (1931) relates various production information, as well as an observation of how the studio recorded the sound for each. Frame blow-ups from Edward Van Sloan's curtain speech accompany the text.

485. Rhodes, Gary Don, ed. *The World of Bela Lugosi*, 4 (Aug. 1988).

Important articles on the authenticity of Lugosi autographs, the rediscovery of three Lugosi newsreels, and an investigation into Lugosi's financial troubles in the early 1930s highlight this issue. *WBL* also reproduced the 1939 *Look* magazine piece on *Son of Frankenstein*.

486. Broeske, Pat H. "Face Off." *Los Angeles Times*, 2 Oct. 1988.

Carroll Borland discussed Lugosi and her role in *Mark of the Vampire* (1935) with this *Times*' reporter.

487. *The Prowler in White Zombie*, 1 (Forestville, Calif.: Eclipse Comics, Oct. 1988).

Written by Michael H. Price and drawn by Gerald Forton, this one-shot comic book pits a superhero called "The Prowler" against Murder Legendre, Lugosi's character from *White Zombie* (1932).

488. Rhodes, Gary Don, ed. *The World of Bela Lugosi*, 5 (Dec. 1988).

Three *White Zombie* articles (one mentioning the fate of the film's lost footage) set the tone for this issue. Various unpublished stills of Lugosi from his Hungarian days are included, and Gregory Mank discusses his book *Karloff and Lugosi*. Another article on Lugosi's radio shows updates new information, and a short piece on the Dracula medallion Lugosi wore tells its history.

489. Rhodes, Gary Don, ed. *The World of Bela Lugosi*, 6 (Apr. 1989).

An article on *Plan 9 from Outer Space* relates numerous stories from its costars on Lugosi, a theoretical investigation of *The Black Cat* (1934) offers insight into the film, and an interview with Patric Knowles covers *Frankenstein Meets the Wolf Man*. Unpublished photos from Lugosi's early New York stage era, information on Lugosi's billing in *Murders in the Rue Morgue*, and a reproduction of the 1917 *Leopard* film poster complete the issue.

490. Rhodes, Gary Don, ed. *The World of Bela Lugosi*, 7 (Sept. 1989).

An extensive section on Lugosi's Hungarian films, complete with rare photographs, results in the first complete and accurate account of his early film career ever published. The newsletter also includes articles on Lugosi's 1947 play *Three Indelicate Ladies*, the never-made *Ghoul Goes West*, and *The Silent Command*.

491. Brosch, Robert, ed. *Color Collector's Guide* (Allen Park, Mich.: Archival Photography, 1989).

Brosch's color magazine features a multitude of Lugosi movie posters and lobby cards reprinted alongside those of numerous other horror and science fiction films. Includes a foreword by film historian Forrest J Ackerman.

492. Noel, Gerard, ed. *Le Retour de Bela Lugosi* (France: Horror Pictures, 1989).

This follow-up to Noel's 1987 Horror Pictures booklet on Lugosi includes a tribute article by Jean-Claude Michel and color movie poster reproductions of *The Phantom Ship* and *Black Dragons*. Noel also prints a large number of photographs, including a color still of Lugosi (from the film *Scared to Death*).

493. Copner, Mike and Buddy Barnett, eds. *Bela Lugosi: Then and Now!* (Hollywood, Calif.: Videosonic Arts, Jan. 1990).

The first edition of Videosonic Arts, which later became *Cult Movies* magazine, devoted itself entirely to Lugosi. The booklet reprints Lugosi's own article from the *Return of Chandu* pressbook and Lisa Mitchell's "Midnite Deli" piece, as well as entries on Lugosi's old "Hollywood Haunts" and his friend Manly P. Hall. Though unfortunately no captions are given, the collection of photos remains one of the best ever presented on Lugosi.

494. *Forrest J Ackerman's Monsterama*, 1 (Spring 1991).

A photo of Lugosi, as well as photos of Karloff and both the Chaneys, peers out at the reader of the sole issue of this horror film magazine.

495. *Midnight Marquee*, 42 (Summer 1991).

A painting of Lugosi adorns the cover of this well-respected film magazine.

496. *Filmfax*, 30 (Dec. 1991-Jan. 1992).

Lugosi, in a pose from *Black Dragons*, appears on the cover.

497. Mank, Gregory. "*Mark of the Vampire*: When MGM Challenged Universal ... and Lost!" *Midnight Marquee*, 44 (Summer 1992).

Very well researched article covers the shooting and release information on the 1935 Lugosi film. The piece itself is an excerpt from Mank's book *Hollywood Cauldron: Thirteen Horror Films* (McFarland, 1994).

498. *Filmfax*, 35. (Oct.-Nov. 1992).

Lugosi as Dracula appears on the cover alongside Karloff's Frankenstein monster, and the magazine includes an interview with Dwight Frye's son. Information from David Skal on the play *Dracula* in the article "The Monsters and Mr. Liveright" also addresses Lugosi. Skal's article is an excerpt from his book *The Monster Show* (W.W. Norton, 1992).

499. *Classic Images*, Jan. 1993.

Classic Images prints movie poster for *Son of Frankenstein*, which displays Lugosi as Ygor, on the cover.

500. MacGillivray, Scott, and Ted Okuda. "Play It Again, Jack! Remembering 'Realart,' the Re-Releasing Company." *Filmfax*, 39 (June-July 1993).

Important article on Realart, a company that reissued most of Lugosi's Universal horror films. The article also points out the title changes that were occasionally made (1934's *The Black Cat* became *The Vanishing Body*).

501. "The Holy Grail." *Movie Collector's World*, 10 Sept. 1993.

Article mentions the sale of a style–A, *Dracula* (1931) one-sheet movie poster that broke all records at the time for its auctioned price of $77,000. A color photo of the poster decorates the magazine's cover.

502. Lilley, Jesse. "Carroll Borland." *Scarlet Street*, Fall 1993.

Lilley interviews Borland, who speaks at length on her involvement with *Mark of the Vampire* and Lugosi.

503. Smith, Don G. "The Road to Dracula: The Bela Lugosi Scrapbook." *Scarlet Street*, Fall 1993.

Reprints several notices, reviews, and pictures from Lugosi's personal scrapbooks which chronicle his pre–*Dracula* (1931) American films.

504. Brosch, Robert, ed. *Color Collector's Guide: Volume Two* (Allen Park, Mich.: Archival Photography, 1993).

Brosch's follow-up to his *Color Collector's Guide* (Archival Photography, 1989) includes numerous color reproductions of Lugosi movie posters and lobby cards. Includes Don Cullen Smith's short essay "Collecting Bela Lugosi Lobby Cards."

505. Dello Stritto, Frank J. "The Summer of '31." *Cult Movies*, 9 (1993).

Engaging piece covers the months of Lugosi's life when he was being considered for the part of the monster in *Frankenstein*.

506. Vado, Dan. *Dracula*. Dark Horse Comics, 1993.

Adapted by Vado and with art by Jonathon D. Smith, this is a comic book version of Lugosi's *Dracula* (1931). Universal licensed the rights to this full-color, one-shot booklet, which recreates Lugosi's likeness very well.

507. Lockwood, Charles. "Bela Lugosi: A Modest Hollywood Bungalow for the Star of Dracula." *Architectural Digest*, Apr. 1994.

Architectural Digest devoted most of this issue to the homes of yesteryear's movie stars. Photos of Lugosi at home highlight the short article on the actor.

508. Chad, Norman. "Monster Mesh." *Entertainment Weekly*, 19 Aug. 1994.

Article mentions the efforts of Bela Lugosi, Jr., Sara Jane Karloff, and Ron Chaney to see their fathers immortalized on a U.S. postage stamp.

509. McCarthy, Todd. "*Ed Wood*." *Daily Variety*, 7 Sept. 1994.

Review of Tim Burton's film, *Ed Wood*: "Lifting all this enormously is Landau's astounding performance as the old Hungarian. Looking (thanks to a tremendous makeup job) and sounding very much like the real thing, Landau brilliantly conveys the ego, pride, hurt, and gratitude of the man in his twilight and, despite his character's grand theatricality, gives the film its most human moments."

510. Kipen, David. "Bela of the Ball." *Los Angeles Daily News*, 28 Sept. 1994.
Article details Martin Landau's portrayal of Lugosi in the film *Ed Wood*, featuring numerous quotes from Landau himself.

511. Thomas, Karen. "*Ed Wood* Gives Landau a Big Break." *USA Today*, 6 Oct. 1994.
Article chronicles Landau's preparatory techniques for playing Lugosi in Tim Burton's film *Ed Wood*, as well as describing the makeup used for transforming him into the Hungarian actor.

512. Kenny, Glenn. "The Man, Wood: Who? B King!" *Entertainment Weekly*, 7 Oct. 1994.
Review of the Ed Wood documentary film *Ed Wood ... Look Back in Angora*, as well a video release of *Plan 9 from Outer Space*.

513. "Kitsch as Kitsch Can: A Sad, Funny Salute to the Master of Ineptitude." *Newsweek*, 10 Oct. 1994.
Review of Tim Burton's film *Ed Wood*: "Landau's Lugosi is a towering, touching creation — a hilarious, pathetic, imperious old pro, imprisoned by opiates and his 'Dracula' persona, still gamely pursuing the limelight. It's tempting to say that Landau does Lugosi better than Lugosi."

514. "Landau and Lugosi Meet Shakespeare." *Newsweek*, 10 Oct. 1994.
Short article discusses Landau's preparation and portrayal for the role of Lugosi in the film *Ed Wood*.

515. Hoover, Will. "Bela and Ed and the Gang." *Honolulu Advertiser*, 15 Oct. 1994.
Article features Hope Lugosi's view and review of the film *Ed Wood*.

516. Clark, John. "The Wood, the Bad, and the Ugly." *Premiere*, Oct. 1994.
Premiere offers an in-depth look at Tim Burton's film *Ed Wood*, and the real-life persons it depicts. The article gives attention to Bela Lugosi, Jr.'s dislike of the portrayal of Lugosi in *Ed Wood*.

517. *Venice*, Oct. 1994.
Martin Landau, in Rick Baker's Lugosi makeup, appears on the cover of this magazine, a publication of "Los Angeles Arts and Entertainment."

518. *Collecting Hollywood*, 8 (Oct.-Nov. 1994).
Lugosi and Carroll Borland, via a color-tinted pressbook cover of *Mark of the Vampire*, grace the cover of this collectors' magazine.

519. Engel, Joel. "He Vill See You in Court." *New York Times*, News Service. 10 Nov. 1994.
Many newspapers throughout the country printed this article, dispatched from Los Angeles, during the second week of November. The author describes Bela Lugosi, Jr., and his battle for the Three Stooges' heirs' right to their famous fathers' likenesses, along with a history of Lugosi Jr.'s fight to secure the right to his father's image.

520. Weaver, Tom. "Fuller Brushes with Fame." *Fangoria*, 38 (Nov. 1994).
Interview with Dolores Fuller, Ed Wood's first wife. Several unique photographs accompany her quotes on Lugosi and the film *Ed Wood*.

521. Weaver, Tom. "Man with the Plan (9)." *Starlog*, Nov. 1994.
Weaver covers the history of Ed Wood's films and Lugosi's involvement in them, including quotes about the actor from such persons as Alex Gordon. The article addresses discrepancies in the various recollections of Wood's cohorts, as well as inaccuracies in the film *Ed Wood*. Wonderful Drew Friedman artwork of Lugosi and Wood accompanies the article.

522. Smith, Gavin. "Punching Holes in Reality: Tim Burton." *Film Comment*, Nov.-Dec. 1994.

Interview with director Burton reveals his thoughts behind *Ed Wood*, as well as his conception of the film character Bela Lugosi. *Film Comment* featured Martin Landau in Bela Lugosi makeup on the cover.

523. Ackerman, Forrest J. "Lugosi Lives Infernal: Those Who Knew Bela Take Exception to *Ed Wood* Artistic 'Lie-Sense.'" *Famous Monsters of Filmland*, 205 (Dec. 1994).

Editor Ackerman, an acquaintance of Lugosi's, examines the inaccuracies presented by Martin Landau's character in the Tim Burton film *Ed Wood* (1994).

524. Stein, Michael. "Landau's Lugosi." *Outré*, 1 (Dec. 1994).

Filmfax editor Stein cornered actor Martin Landau to discuss his role as Lugosi in *Ed Wood*. *Outré* itself sprang from the publishers of *Filmfax* to cover the world of "ultramedia."

525. Dello Stritto, Frank J. "The Road to Las Vegas: Bela Lugosi in American Theater." *Cult Movies*, 11 (1994).

Engrossing article details Lugosi's American stage career, giving reviews and precise dates for most of his appearances from the twenties through the fifties. The text also covers roadshow productions and some of Lugosi's vaudeville acts as well.

526. Dello Stritto, Frank J. "Whatever Became of Beatrice Woodruff Weeks?" *Cult Movies*, 10 (1994).

Dello Stritto investigates the courtship, brief marriage, and divorce proceedings of Lugosi and his third wife, as well as Lugosi's screen test with Gloria Swanson and his appearances in a stage version of *Dracula* in San Francisco. This absorbing piece was originally titled "What Ever Happened to Beatrice Weeks," in the same grammatical meter as the non–Lugosi horror film classic *Whatever Happened to Baby Jane* (1962).

527. *Famous Monsters of Filmland*, 206 (Jan.-Feb. 1995).

Lugosi, portrayed as Dracula in a cover painting originally seen on early sixties merchandising, invites readers into the magazine.

528. *National Review*, 17 Apr. 1995.

Lugosi as Dracula peers out at readers of this magazine, symbolizing this time the specter of the Internal Revenue Service and asking, "Ready for your audit?"

529. Madison, Bob. "Lugosi at the Academy Awards." *Scarlet Street*, 19 (Summer 1995).

Madison's article describes the renewed interest in Lugosi as he chronicles Martin Landau's triumph at the 1995 Academy Awards, where the actor accepted a Best Supporting Oscar for portraying Lugosi in Tim Burton's film *Ed Wood* (1994).

530. Parnum, John and Gregory William Mank. "House of Carradine: Why Isn't Lugosi in the House?" *Midnight Marquee*, 49 (Summer 1995).

Parnum and Mank briefly speculate as to why Lugosi did not appear in *House of Frankenstein* (1944), a Universal horror film that cast John Carradine as Dracula. The magazine's cover features a beautiful oil painting of Lugosi as Dracula, painted by Lorraine Bush.

531. Dello Stritto, Frank J. "At Long Last Lugosi" *Cult Movies*, 13 (1995).

Subtitled "Film History's Evolving View of Bela Lugosi," this article covers critical assessments of Lugosi since the time of his death. Dello Stritto breaks down the changes in published criticism into phases, turning his article into a fascinating history of evolving judgments on Lugosi.

532. Dello Stritto, Frank J. "H: The 1937 British Ban on Horror Films." *Cult Movies*, 14 (1995).

An amazing article that presents almost all that is missing from most horror film literature: careful, painstaking research, an extended discussion of the topic; and insightful, interpretative comments. The article also stands as the definitive work on the British ban on horror films, which sent Lugosi's career into a quick, downward spiral during 1937 and 1938.

533. Orrison, Katherine. "Bela's Baby Leading Lady." *Cult Movies,* **16 (1995).**

Orrison's interview-style piece presents quotes from Helen Richman, an actress who appeared with Lugosi in a summer stock performance of *Arsenic and Old Lace* in Reading, Pennsylvania. Additionally, this article features quotes from Ted Post, who directed a stage version (presumably summer stock) of *Dracula* with Lugosi.

534. Rhodes, Gary Don. "*Dracula* (1931): Addenda to the Children of the Night." *Cult Movies,* **13 (1995).**

In addition to covering the essential resources on the 1931 *Dracula* (David J. Skal's book *Hollywood Gothic,* for example), Rhodes examines many sidenotes to that film which had not previously been discussed in print. Among other items, Rhodes details promotional gimmicks and comments from 1931 theater managers concerning the Lugosi film.

15. Books

The following annotated bibliography is in some respects quite selective. All full-fledged Lugosi biographies are included, as are numerous fictional works that refer to the actor. Furthermore, various film histories and bound scripts are covered.

Only a handful of books have actually dealt with Lugosi exclusively. Several other Lugosi biographies have been attempted without seeing the light of publication. Two authors borrowed a large number of handwritten notes dictated by Lugosi himself from Richard Sheffield. The "authors" never returned the material. Another writer, after spending a great deal of time at work on a manuscript, came home one afternoon to find it stolen. A second biographer, frustrated by a lack of interest from publishers, cast his text into an incinerator.

Existing biographies tend to age somewhat, as new information comes to light. Moreover, critical reactions change over time, devaluing some theoretical analyses of Lugosi films. On the whole, however, the biographies retain much needed insight, rare photographs, and some wonderful memories of Lugosi.

In addition to describing all works that specifically cover Lugosi, this listing includes multiple works on stage and film history. The chosen volumes either include valuable memories, rare information, or unique photographs that relate to Lugosi. Among these are several books on the horror film. While dozens of authors have tackled the genre, only a few offer particularly original insight or rare information.

Detailed also are various novels that refer to Lugosi, illustrating the actor's role in popular culture. Furthermore, the many published scripts from Lugosi and Lugosi-related films are chronicled, as such volumes offer insight into production history.

Biographies

1. Lennig, Arthur. *The Count: The Life and Films of Bela "Dracula" Lugosi* (New York: Putnam, 1974).

Written by film historian Arthur Lennig, *The Count* became the first full-length biography of Lugosi, and at the time it proved ground breaking in its research. Lennig's work remains invaluable, but some of his data has been superseded by more modern research. The photographs included are a joy, including one of a young Lennig with the "Count" himself. The critiques of Lugosi's films are also of interest, though somewhat outdated, given renewed interest in the actor's B movies. This volume must be investigated for a comprehensive look at Lugosi.

2. Cremer, Robert. *Lugosi: The Man Behind the Cape* (Chicago: Henry Regnery Company, 1976).

Cremer's work is the most integral work yet on Lugosi the man. Written with the assistance of Lugosi's fourth wife, Lillian — and with a foreword by Bela Lugosi, Jr. — this is a very moving and accurate portrayal of his struggles, achievements, and failures. Particularly of note are the time and care put into examining Lugosi's drug addiction. Cremer pays close attention to Lugosi's Hungarian past, but he devotes little time to a discussion of the actor's films. It is instead a biography of a man ... and one that is quite well written.

3. Bojarski, Richard. *The Films of Bela Lugosi* (Secaucus, N.J.: Citadel Press, 1980).

With an introduction by actress Carroll Borland and an inviting cover photograph of Lugosi from *White Zombie*, this is one of the best in Citadel's "Films of..." series. Rather than dwell on Bela's personal life, it centers (as the title suggests) on his cinematic efforts. A massive number of photographs are used, resulting in the best single collection of Lugosi stills in one place. Moreover, Bojarski's lengthy research offers much production information on the films and quotes from those who worked on them. Cast and credits are given for all of his motion pictures, and all films from 1931 to 1959 are listed with a movie review. This important reference book is a nice companion to Cremer's *Lugosi: The Man Behind the Cape*.

4. Mank, Gregory William. *Karloff and Lugosi: The Story of a Haunting Collaboration* (Jefferson, N.C.: McFarland, 1990).

This well-researched book chronicles the films made by the Lugosi/Karloff duo, and to a lesser extent follows their separate careers. Much interesting information on the studio budgets for their films is given, and such Lugosi associates as actress Carroll Borland, director Robert Wise, author Curt Siodmak, director Charles Barton, the late Lillian Lugosi, and others gave their input. Mank treats Lugosi with loving respect, giving attention to the resurgence in the actor's popularity during the eighties. Well-written and very worthwhile.

5. Svehla, Gary, and Sue, eds. *Midnight Marquee Actor's Series #1: Bela Lugosi* (Baltimore: Midnight Marquee Press, 1995).

Though actually a compilation of essays rather than a narrative biography, *Bela Lugosi* covers some 28 of the actor's films, by the following authors: Tom Weaver, Bruce Hallenback, Don Smith, Gregory Mank, Bryan Senn, David H. Smith, John Soister, Dennis Fischer, Don Leifert, Bret Wood, Gary Don Rhodes, John Stell, David Hogan, Mark A. Miller, Bob Madison, and Gary Svehla. Producer Richard Gordon covers his memories of Lugosi in an additional chapter.

Film and Stage Histories

6. Tietjens, Eunice. *The World at My Shoulder* (New York: Macmillan, 1938).

Author Tietjens's autobiography spends an entire chapter on the 1925 stage production of *Arabesque*. Along with lengthy production information, she includes her memories of Lugosi.

7. Ormond, Ron. *Your Career in Hollywood* (Hollywood: Screen Guild Press, 1954).

With uncredited help from Ed Wood, Bela Lugosi wrote a short foreword to this text, as did Marie Windsor, Julia Adams, Jerry Colonna, and Raymond Hatton. Along with offering a quick summary of his Hollywood successes, Lugosi writes of his pride in being an actor. Ormond's book itself is not actually a film history but rather a "how to get into movies" handbook.

Lugosi at home in the thirties, with part of his book collection behind him.

8. Ludlam, Harry. *A Biography of Dracula: The Life Story of Bram Stoker* (London: W. Foulsham and Company, 1962).

This wonderful biography of Stoker includes a section on Lugosi. Features information on the *Bela Lugosi Revue* of Las Vegas in the fifties and a personal remembrance of Ludlam's meeting with the Hungarian.

9. Lennig, Arthur, ed. *Classics of the Film* (Madison, Wis.: Wisconsin Film Society Press, 1965).

This compilation of essays covers a variety

of films and acted as a companion volume to *Film Notes*, published in 1960 by the same press. Lugosi's future biographer Lennig includes his own important treatise on *White Zombie*.

10. Clarens, Carlos. *An Illustrated History of the Horror Film* (New York: Capricorn Books, 1967).

One of the best critical surveys of horror movies, this also remains an indispensable book for students of film history. Among the learned opinions and nice selection of photographs is a very significant discussion of Lugosi and such films as *White Zombie* (1932).

11. Marlowe, Don. *The Hollywood That Was* (Fort Worth, Tex.: Branch Smith, 1969).

Several stories about Lugosi, particularly on the roadshow version of *The Tell-Tale Heart* of the late forties, are included in this book by Bela's one-time manager. Though the complete validity of Marlowe's stories has come under much scrutiny, the book is a crucial oral history of the actor's career in the late forties.

12. Gifford, Denis. *A Pictorial History of Horror Movies* (New York: Hamlyn Publishing Group, 1973).

Important look at horror movies, offering numerous photos and movie posters from Lugosi films. Gifford assembled a revised edition of the text a decade later, published in 1984 by Exeter Books (New York).

13. Bojarski, Richard and Kenneth Beale. *The Films of Boris Karloff* (Secaucus, N.J.: Citadel Press, 1974).

Covers all the Karloff and Lugosi film collaborations in detail and features many stills of each.

14. Everson, William K. *Classics of the Horror Film* (Secaucus, N.J.: Citadel Press, 1974).

In this overview of many favorite horror films, Lugosi titles like *White Zombie*, *Mark of the Vampire*, *The Black Cat* (1934), and *The Body Snatcher* are given intelligent critiques. The book is one of the most respected on the subject, and Everson, a well-known film historian, remains one of the field's best authors.

15. Beck, Calvin T. *Heroes of the Horrors* (New York: Macmillan, 1975).

Authored by the editor of *Castle of Frankenstein* magazine, this book devotes an entire chapter to Lugosi. The analysis of his films continues to be worthwhile (particularly the discussion of *White Zombie*), and Beck complements the text with many photographs.

16. Brosnan, John. *The Horror People* (New York: St. Martin's Press, 1976).

Also published in London the same year by MacDonald and James, Brosnan's work on the horror film includes a chapter on Karloff and Lugosi. His investigation of the Hungarian covers the obsessive qualities of some fans, and discusses Lugosi's own personality at length.

17. Castle, William. *Step Right Up! I'm Gonna Scare the Pants off America* (New York: Putnam, 1976).

Subtitled *Memoirs of a B-Movie Mogul*, Castle's autobiography includes his extensive memories of watching Lugosi perform, meeting the actor for the first time, and receiving his help in getting his earliest job in the theatrical profession. Pharos reprinted *Step Right Up!* in 1992 with a new introduction by filmmaker John Waters.

18. Turner, George E. and Michael H. Price. *Forgotten Horrors* (San Diego: A.S. Barnes, 1979).

Fascinating work that centers on poverty row horror films of the thirties, with chapters on such Lugosi projects as *White Zombie*, *The Death Kiss*, *The Whispering Shadow*, *The Return of Chandu* (serial and feature), *Chandu on the Magic Isle*, and *The Mysterious Mr. Wong*.

282   III. Works By or About Lugosi

19. Oakie, Jack. *Jack Oakie's Double Takes* (Portland, Ore.: Strawberry Hill Press, 1980).

Oakie's autobiography includes his memories of Lugosi, particularly his first meeting with the actor. In 1928 Oakie accompanied actress Clara Bow to a Los Angeles stage version of *Dracula*, which turned into the "It" girl's first meeting with the Hungarian, who became her lover.

20. Mank, Gregory William. *It's Alive: The Classic Cinema Saga of Frankenstein* (San Diego: A.S. Barnes, 1981).

A wonderful chronicle of the Frankenstein films, with coverage of each that included Lugosi, as well as the 1931 version, which did not. Along with in-depth production information and insightful commentary are many fascinating stills, such as those of Lugosi with director James Whale and Lugosi with all of Universal's key stars of late 1938.

21. Warren, Bill. *Keep Watching the Skies!: Volume One* (Jefferson, N.C.: McFarland, 1982).

This well-written reference work covers the science fiction films made during 1950–57. *The Black Sleep* and *Bride of the Monster* are included in extensive entries.

22. Grant, Barry Keith, ed. *Planks of Reason: Essays on the Horror Film* (Metuchen, N.J.: Scarecrow, 1984).

Planks of Reason includes Edward Lowry and Richard deCordova's theoretical treatise "Enunciation and the Production of Horror in *White Zombie*" in its collection of analytical essays.

23. Larson, Randall. *Musique Fantastique: A Survey of Film Music in the Fantastic Cinema* (Metuchen, N.J.: Scarecrow, 1985).

Larson's detailed account of the music and composers for the history of horror films covers the soundtracks of various Lugosi films. Also, Larson includes biographies of many composers who scored films starring Lugosi.

24. Everson, William K. *More Classics of the Horror Film* (Secaucus, N.J.: Citadel Press, 1986).

In this follow-up to his book *Classics of the Horror Film*, Everson analyzes many overlooked and forgotten fright films. Very intelligent critiques become examples of changing views on B horror films. Lugosi titles such as *The Thirteenth Chair* and the Monogram Studios series are covered, along with numerous stills.

25. Warren, Bill. *Keep Watching the Skies!: Volume Two* (Jefferson, N.C.: McFarland, 1986).

Covering science fiction films from 1958 to 1962, this edition includes production information on *Plan 9 from Outer Space*.

26. Taves, Brian. *Robert Florey: The French Expressionist* (Metuchen, N.J.: Scarecrow, 1987).

Taves includes a wonderful chapter on the never-made Lugosi/Florey version of *Frankenstein* and an in-depth look at *The Murders in the Rue Morgue* (1932).

27. Weaver, Tom. *Interviews with B Science Fiction and Horror Movie Makers* (Jefferson, N.C.: McFarland, 1988).

Excellent collection of interviews includes quotes from Lugosi associates Richard Gordon, Howard W. Koch, Reginald Le Borg, Paul Marco, Curt Siodmak, and Harry Thomas.

28. Brunas, Michael, John Brunas, and Tom Weaver. *Universal Horrors: The Studio's Classic Films, 1931–1946.* (Jefferson, N.C.: McFarland, 1990).

Exhaustively researched volume, covering all of the Lugosi horror films done at Universal from 1931 to 1945. Though it is not always flattering to the Hungarian actor, the historical data and insight are important.

29. Skal, David J. *Hollywood Gothic: The Tangled Web of Dracula from Novel to Stage to Screen* (New York: Norton, 1990).

An amazing research effort, *Hollywood Gothic* stands as one of the best-written books in the cinema studies field. It includes much information on the stage version of *Dracula* with Lugosi, and the actor's struggle to nab the lead in the Universal Studios film version. Ultimately fascinating in its information and photos, the book is a necessity.

30. Gaines, Jane M. *Contested Culture: The Image, the Voice, and the Law* (Chapel Hill: University of North Carolina Press, 1991).

Gaines thoroughly covers the California Supreme Court case of *Lugosi v. Universal Pictures, Inc.*, becoming an intriguing investigation into entertainment law commentary. Lugosi as Dracula graces the cover, though his face in the photograph, much like the question of inheritable rights, appears blurred.

31. Borst, Ronald V. *Graven Images* (New York: Grove Press, 1992).

Graven Images constitutes perhaps the best collection of color Lugosi movie posters gathered in a single, deluxe hardcover volume. The book covers horror movie posters in general and features chapters by such authors as Robert Bloch, Harlan Ellison, and Forrest J Ackerman. The posters used have each been carefully restored to their original splendor, and a beautiful poster of Lugosi's *Murders in the Rue Morgue* adorns the cover.

32. Grey, Rudolph. *Nightmare of Ecstasy: The Life and Art of Edward D. Wood, Jr.* (Los Angeles: Feral House, 1992).

Many important memories of Lugosi's final years and his association with director Wood make this a necessary volume to grasp fully the history behind films like *Glen or Glenda* and *Bride of the Monster*.

33. Weaver, Tom. *Poverty Row HORRORS!* (Jefferson, N.C.: McFarland, 1993).

Weaver's volume includes very informative discussions of Lugosi's low-budget films of the forties, including PRC's *The Devil Bat* (1941) and nine of his Monogram efforts. Weaver's unique and often witty critiques are sprinkled with fascinating historical data and a quiz/survey of Lugosi fans describing their favorite Lugosi Monograms.

34. Skal, David J. *The Monster Show: A Cultural History of Horror* (New York: Norton, 1993).

A very engrossing discussion of the horror film, this volume includes much worthwhile Lugosi information. Production data on the film *Dracula*, Lugosi's affair with Clara Bow, and Horace Liveright's production of *Dracula* on Broadway are all discussed at length.

35. Mank, Gregory William. *Hollywood Cauldron: Thirteen Horror Films from the Genre's Golden Age* (Jefferson, N.C.: McFarland, 1994).

Mank's text includes an important chapter on the 1935 Lugosi film *Mark of the Vampire*.

36. Weaver, Tom. *Attack of the Monster Movie Makers: Interviews with 20 Genre Giants* (Jefferson, N.C.: McFarland, 1994).

Weaver's compilation of interviews includes numerous memories concerning Lugosi. Included are Lupita Tovar (Mina from the 1931 Spanish language version of *Dracula*), Samuel Arkoff (who comments on *Bride of the Monster*), Herman Cohen (producer of *Bela Lugosi Meets a Brooklyn Gorilla*), and Herbert Rudley (the "hero" of *The Black Sleep*).

37. Skal, David J. and Elias Savada. *Dark Carnival: The Secret World of Tod Browning, Hollywood's Master of the Macabre* (New York: Anchor Books, 1995).

Skal and Savada's biography covers *The Thirteenth Chair* (1929), *Dracula* (1931), and *Mark of the Vampire* (1935) — the three Tod Browning–directed Lugosi films — in considerable detail. Among the more interesting inclusions are Hays Office documents concerning *The Thirteenth Chair*, the text of a letter from Lugosi to agent Harold Freedman requesting help in landing the title role of *Dracula*, and previously unpublished interviews with actress Carroll Borland and screenwriter Bernard Schubert on *Mark of the Vampire*. Illustrations include a previously unpublished candid shot of Lugosi on the *Dracula* set with Browning and actress Helen Chandler.

38. Svehla, Gary and Sue, eds. *Guilty Pleasures of the Horror Film* (Baltimore: Midnight Marquee, 1996).

This collection of essays includes Gary Don Rhodes's analysis of *Voodoo Man* (1944), which also provides much insight into the television broadcasts of Lugosi's films in the early fifties.

39. Weaver, Tom. *It Came from Weaver Five: Interviews with 20 Zany, Glib, and Earnest Moviemakers in the SF and Horror Traditions of the Forties, Fifties and Sixties* (Jefferson, N.C.: McFarland, 1996).

One of Tom Weaver's entertaining books of interviews with cinema talent, this edition offers conversations with such Lugosi associates as Aubrey Schenck (executive producer of 1956's *The Black Sleep*) and Robert Wise (director of 1945's *The Body Snatcher*).

40. Weaver, Tom. *Monsters, Mutants, and Heavenly Creatures: Confessions of 14 Classic Sci-Fi/Horrormeisters* (Baltimore: Midnight Marquee, 1996).

Yet another of Weaver's interview tomes, this edition includes an interview with William Witney, director of the 1937 serial *SOS Coastguard*.

Novels and Film Novelizations

41. Biggers, Earl Derr. *The Black Camel* (New York: Grosset and Dunlap, 1931).

Printed in 1931 but bearing only the original 1929 copyright date, *The Black Camel* includes numerous photographs of Lugosi from the Fox film. The photoplay edition is a rare but intriguing item used to promote the Charlie Chan film.

42. Stoker, Bram. *Dracula* (New York: Grosset and Dunlap, 1931).

This photoplay edition of Stoker's novel features artwork of Lugosi, printed in connection with the film. The jacket read, "Never before has a play so remarkable in its thrills and so completely overwhelming in every respect been staged in this town ... an ample feast of the uncanny and supernatural ... these were some of the press notices which preceded the play *Dracula* from London where it ran for three years ... New York theatergoers, hardened to sensational mystery plays, were skeptical. Yet at every performance of this weird, uncanny piece, women shrieked and men gripped their chairs at the blood-freezing scenes before them."

Lugosi's image as the vampire Dracula became so strong that, despite his dissimilarity to Stoker's description of the Count, artwork and photographs of him have appeared with numerous subsequent editions of the novel. This trend runs from artwork on Pocketbook's first printing of the book in 1947 to Barnes and Noble's use of a Lugosi still on a 1992 hardback. An image of Lugosi even appeared on the cover of a 1968 paperback edition of *Dracula's Curse and the Jewel of the Seven Stars*, a compilation of works by Bram Stoker.

43. Poe, Edgar Allan. *Murders in the Rue Morgue and Other Tales of Mystery* (New York: Grosset and Dunlap, 1932).

This book featured Lugosi on the cover and multiple illustrations from the 1932 film *Murders in the Rue Morgue*. The text itself, however, is not a novelization of the film's plot, but rather a collection of Poe's stories, including the original short story "Murders in the Rue Morgue."

44. *Chandu the Magician* (Akron, Ohio: Saalfield Publishing Company, 1935).

This children's "Big Little Book" features photographs of Lugosi as well as the plotline of *Return of Chandu*.

45. Mauro, John F. *Rhapsody in Death* (New York: Fortuny's, 1940).

Lugosi wrote a preface to Mauro's horror novel, mentioning his enjoyment of the tale and giving a brief background of the Magyar people.

46. Brower, Brock. *The Late, Great Creature* (New York: Atheneum, 1971).

A novel about Brower's character Simon Moro which includes references to Lugosi.

47. West, Paul. *Bela Lugosi's White Christmas* (New York: Harper and Row, 1972).

A fictional story about a character named Alley, who is placed in an insane asylum for murder. He becomes obsessed with such things as moon rocks, the dying words of famous men, and actor Bela Lugosi.

48. Pynchon, Thomas. *Gravity's Rainbow* (New York: Viking, 1973).

Pynchon's outstanding yet difficult novel includes references to Lugosi and *White Zombie*.

49. Anobile, Richard J., ed. *Ninotchka* (New York: Universe, 1975).

This is one in a series of books that retold the plots of films by reprinting dialogue along with appropriate photographs.

50. Thorne, Ian. *Dracula* (Mankato, Minn.: Crestwood House, 1977).

Thorne takes the of plot of the 1931 classic and complements it with numerous stills and production information, turning the Lugosi film into a popular children's book of the seventies.

51. Thorne, Ian. *The Wolf Man* (Mankato, Minn.: Crestwood House, 1977).

As part of the same series as Crestwood's *Dracula*, this edition aims toward a young audience. Many photographs and a plot summary of the 1941 Universal film are combined with production information.

52. Kaminsky, Stuart. *Never Cross a Vampire* (New York: St. Martin's, 1980).

Never Cross a Vampire concerns the fictitious Toby Peters and the detective's attempt to help character Lugosi, who has received numerous death threats. Entertaining fiction.

53. Thorne, Ian. *Frankenstein Meets the Wolf Man* (Mankato, Minn.: Crestwood House, 1981).

Another of Thorne's books aimed at children, this one summarizes the plot of Universal's 1943 film. Multiple photographs from the movie accompany the text.

54. Green, Carl R. and William R. Sanford. *Ghost of Frankenstein* (Mankato, Minn.: Crestwood House, 1985).

Crestwood House's success with its earlier children's books built around classic horror films prompted this volume. Numerous stills of the film complement a summary of *Ghost*'s plot.

55. Sanford, William R. *Murders in the Rue Morgue* (Mankato, Minn.: Crestwood House, 1987).

Another of the many Lugosi film adaptations by Crestwood. As with the earlier volumes, Sanford targets *Rue Morgue* at grade school children. The plot is from Florey's film and is supplemented with stills from the production.

56. Campbell, Ramsey. *Ancient Images* (New York: Charles Scribner's Sons, 1989).

A novel by the author of *Obsession* and *The Influence*, *Ancient Images* gives a fictional account of a search for a lost, British-made film starring Lugosi and Boris Karloff, *The Tower of Evil*. In addition to the tale being a work of fiction, *The Tower of Evil* is itself a fabrication.

57. Beath, Warren Newton. *Bloodletter* (New York: TOR, 1994).

Beath's vampire novel includes references to Lugosi.

58. Borland, Carroll. *Countess Dracula* (Absecon, N.J.: Magicimage, 1994).

Borland wrote *Countess Dracula*, her sequel to Bram Stoker's vampire novel, in 1929. The book, which Borland once read to Lugosi himself, was finally published some 65 years later through the efforts of Charles Heard. Many items from Borland's scrapbook concerning Lugosi and *Mark of the Vampire* are also printed, as is Gregory William Mank's extensive biography of Borland, which touches on her relationship with the Hungarian.

59. French, Philip and Ken Wlaschin, ed. *The Faber Book of Movie Verse* (London: Faber and Faber, 1994).

French and Wlaschin catalogue much cinema-related poetry in this volume, including David Meltzer's *15th Raga for Bela Lugosi* and R.H.W. Dillard's *Bela Lugosi: Three Lines.*

60. McMurtry, Larry and Diana Ossana. *Pretty Boy Floyd: A Novel* (New York: Simon and Schuster, 1994).

McMurtry and Ossana's novel includes a wonderful two-page passage in which outlaw Floyd and his wife take their son, Dempsey, to see Bela Lugosi in *Dracula* (1931).

Published Scripts

61. Cushing, Charles Cyprian Strong. *The Devil in the Cheese* (New York: Samuel French, 1927).

The complete script to the Broadway play, with Lugosi's name listed among the cast.

62. Deane, Hamilton. *Dracula: The Vampire Play in Three Acts* (New York: Samuel French, 1933).

Copyrighted by French in 1933, this edition has been reprinted numerous times. Notes on the production and diagrams for stage props are included, along with the complete dialogue and stage directions from the 1927 theatrical version of the play.

63. Brackett, Charles, Billy Wilder, and Walter Reisch. *Ninotchka* (New York: Viking, 1972).

The script of the 1939 film with Garbo, Melvyn Douglas, and Lugosi is reprinted in complete form.

64. Riley, Philip J., ed. *Son of Frankenstein.* Universal Filmscripts Series, vol. 3 (Absecon, N.J.: Magicimage, 1989).

With production background by Gregory Mank, this volume reprints the original script, many production photos, and the original film pressbook.

65. Mason, Tom, ed. *Plan 9 from Outer Space: The Original, Uncensored, and Uncut Screenplay by Edward D. Wood, Jr.* (Newbury Park, Calif.: Malibu Graphics, 1990).

The complete script is reprinted, along with an introduction by author John Wooley and cast information by Kregg Sanders.

66. Riley, Philip J., ed. *Abbott and Costello Meet Frankenstein.* Universal Filmscripts Series. Classic Comedy Films, vol. 1 (Absecon, N.J.: Magicimage, 1990).

Magicimage reprints the revised, final script for the film — still under the title *The Brain of Frankenstein* — along with the complete pressbook and production stills. Production background by Gregory W. Mank complements archival materials from Bob Furmanek. Bud Abbott Jr., Vickie Abbott

Wheeler, Chris Costello, and Paddy Costello Humphreys offer forewords, accompanied by filmmaker John Landis's introduction.

67. Riley, Philip J., ed. *Dracula.* **Universal Filmscripts Series, vol. 13 (Absecon, N.J.: Magicimage, 1990).**

This includes a reprint of Lugosi's personal copy of the script, but also never-before-published production stills, the complete pressbook, and contributions from historian Forrest J Ackerman, actor David Manners, and the late Edward Van Sloan. *Dracula's* production history receives coverage from George Turner.

68. Riley, Philip J., ed. *Frankenstein Meets the Wolf Man.* **Universal Filmscripts Series, vol. 5 (Absecon, N.J.: Magicimage, 1990).**

The original pressbook, production photos, and pages of the Hans J. Salter score accompany the script itself. A written introduction by Curt Siodmak and a chapter of production information by Gregory Mank are also part of this volume.

69. Riley, Philip J., ed. *The Ghost of Frankenstein.* **Universal Filmscripts Series, vol. 4 (Absecon, N.J.: Magicimage, 1990).**

Production information by Gregory Mank, a foreword by composer Hans J. Salter, and an introduction by actor Ralph Bellamy complement the reprint of the script. Production stills, photos of cut scenes, and pages of Salter's music score are also included.

70. Riley, Philip J., ed. *The Wolf Man.* **Universal Filmscripts Series, vol. 12 (Absecon, N.J.: Magicimage, 1993).**

Accompanying Curt Siodmak's original shooting script to the classic 1941 film is a 1974 article by actress Evelyn Ankers, the original studio press sheet, a production history by Gregory Mank, a study of makeup artist Jack Pierce by Douglas Norwine, and a reprint of an article Pierce himself wrote on "Character Makeup." Additionally, this volume includes an article on Hans J. Salter's musical score for the film and reprints of the original sheet music. Multiple stills and production photos further illuminate this very complete volume in the Magicimage series.

71. Skal, David J., ed. *Dracula: The Ultimate, Illustrated Edition of the World Famous Play by Hamilton Deane and John L. Balderston* **(New York: St. Martin's, 1993).**

Skal uses many rare photos, some previously unpublished, along with many astute annotations to complement the text from Hamilton Deane and John Balderston's 1927 stage version of *Dracula*. Skal also reprints Deane's previously unpublished script from 1924.

72. Alexander, Scott and Larry Karaszewski. *Ed Wood* **(London: Faber and Faber, 1995).**

The published script for Tim Burton's 1994 film *Ed Wood* includes multiple photographs from the movie and a cast/credit listing. The authors include a lengthy introduction in which they detail why they wrote a screenplay based on Wood's life, and explain their depiction of Lugosi.

16. Quotations from Lugosi

The following is a cache of various writings by and quotations from Bela Lugosi. However, these materials need to be taken with an academic grain of salt. Bela's wife, Lillian, often answered some mail, and some of the articles and speeches included could possibly have been the work of a studio publicist. Lugosi's full grasp of the English language has often been questioned; in later years, actor Boris Karloff would often describe Bela's supposedly unfortunate language problems. Actress Carroll Borland once remarked that some of his costars found him to be quiet for this very reason, though instead they sometimes took it as a kind of arrogance.

While certainly in his early years in the United States he was learning some lines phonetically, by the time of his death he obviously could speak and read English with no real problems. For example, stories abound of his voracious reading habits, with friends of his later years remarking that he never even misspelled words. By 1932 Bela remarked to an interviewer, "I know how to say 'okay,' 'cat's whiskers,' 'baloney,' and 'and how!'" Yet the strongest command of the language and its colloquialisms may have been skills he did not fully attain.

A deeper investigation of his language difficulties reveals numerous articles printed in the late twenties when Lugosi enjoyed success on the stage. Titles varied from "Mastery of English Put Lugosi on Way to Stardom" to "Dracula Villain Still Struggles with His English." In one interview, Lugosi claimed to have avoided Hungarians for a time so that he would translate his thoughts only into English. He later mentioned that as a result a few of these acquaintances apparently believed he was giving them the "high hat." Another interview spotlighted Lugosi's feeling that the role of Dracula—in which a thick accent was expected of him—actually affected his progress with English and set him back "two years." Even an early Hungarian stage review commented on Lugosi's thick accent within the bounds of his own language; oddly, a 1925 article on *Arabesque* claimed he had "no trace" of an accent.

In many ways, the actor's work itself becomes the most revealing. His live appearances on radio programs often highlight little emotion, showing him to be less than adept at reading a script cold. Moreover, a few lines in his films offer minor problems. For example, in *Such Men Are Dangerous* (1930) he reads two lines incorrectly: "I can do too much good with this money," meaning more accurately "I can do *so* much good with this money"; and "Wait a little minute," when he probably intends "Wait a minute" or "Wait a bit," rather than suggesting that a minute can come in different sizes and lengths. A decade later, in *Black Friday* (1940) he misuses a preposition, resulting in "Red's been dead *since* two months." Though very minor, these examples suggest that some details of English grammar — as for so many who take the language as their second — escaped him. Whether the problem was even larger in the thirties — as director Edgar Ulmer's wife once suggested — remains unclear.

As for his "words" themselves, Lugosi wrote a few articles on political subjects for the *Magyar Jovó*, a Hungarian daily newspaper, in addition to the articles printed in this listing. Moreover, Lugosi and Ed Wood co-wrote a preface to a book by Ron Ormond, though Lugosi alone received credit in the published volume.

In any event, this smattering of various writings of Lugosi represents his entire career in brief. Grammar and spelling have been left identical to the originals when taken from source material. Further examples of his letters can be found in Robert Cremer's book *Lugosi: The Man Behind the Cape* (Henry Regnery, 1976). Also, numerous articles, particularly Gladys Hall's 1941 "Memoes of a Madman" in *Silver Screen*, feature extended quotations.

1. Lugosi, Béla. "The History of the Formation of Our Union." *Színészek Lapja* (The Actor's Page, of Budapest, Hungary), 15 May 1919.

Author's Note: The following is one of several politically oriented articles that Lugosi wrote prior to leaving Hungary. He uses very convoluted, politicized language that is very similar to Communist literature of post–World War II Hungary. The document — which is quite "red" (and also naive) by most standards — is much the same as a piece Lugosi wrote for *Népszava*, a leftist political newspaper.

Lugosi speaks at length of the unions with which he has been instrumental in evolving, though he never makes his exact role in each very clear. The article also covers his plans for a state-run theater. Lugosi submitted his ideas to Zsigmond Kunfi just before Béla Kun rose to power. By the time this article saw print, the Kun regime was in place. Kunfi immediately rose to political power and gave Lugosi's plans to Belát Reinitz, a well-known musician who also received a position in the Kun regime. The intention was certainly to make the theater state-run; how many of Lugosi's ideas were seriously considered is unknown.

An earlier and partial translation of this article appeared under the erroneous title "Love the Actor." Dr. Tibor Herczeg made this content-based translation, which appears here in condensed form. Lugosi's full-length article uses much space offering thanks to long lists of individuals who helped in the cause. His final "thank you" went to the "steady hand" of Rudolf Pajor, who was to help with the new union; Pajor had an article in the same journal alongside Lugosi's.

The year before the October revolution of 1918, in the party organization of the first precinct to which I belonged, the mood was very strained and hot, and I saw the time coming to reorganize the actors of the country on the basis of the class struggle to introduce them into a union and further their proletariat conscience. Actors are carved from the socialist ideology; there is only a need for clarification and a little socialist education, only because as artists they did not occupy themselves much with social sciences. They were blinded by the many colorful political lifestyles around them. The actors are in a position of slavery and need to discover how low and oppressed they really are. They do much important work, but go unrewarded and are kept among the poorer layers of society. Thanks go to Jenö Landler and Albert Király, who supported us with their socialist knowledge and prestige, and it would be unjust not to mention those members of the National Theater who immediately joined us early.... It was a courageous and manly act for them to join.

On December 2, the union of theater employees was formed on behalf of the general counsel of the country's unions. Shortly thereafter, Albert Király [who held a major position in the general counsel] gave a lecture telling the actors how important it is to organize into a union and consider the ideological basis of class struggles. Also, the formation of the union went very fast and arose despite heavy problems and fighting before this.

The majority of the National Theater was also convinced of the importance and urgency of the unionization. The aim of the organization was to raise the moral, financial, and cultural level of the society of actors. I worked out a draft for these ideals and gave it to Zsigmond Kunfi. He was the secretary for cultural affairs and later became the people's commissar [under Béla Kun]. To socialize the theater and make it state run is my primary aim. Why and how can we make the theater state run?

The financial aims: to improve the state theaters without unduly burdening the budget of the state. Earlier, most of the provincial theaters were in private hands. You can improve the lot of the actors without burdening the budget by making theaters state run because in the private world there is huge personal waste. A great profit goes into the pockets of the owners. The few already state run theaters had yearly deficits simply because they were poorly run.

This would also help cultural problems. The real aim would occur thru culture and a directed education of the people, helping them to appreciate a very high level of cultural entertainment. It would be important that talented students receive direct support from the state and enter the theater at an appropriate level. The state running of theaters would enable the state as far as means are present to improve the number of theaters in the whole country. With this comes the possibility of improving the layers of the populace by exposing them to culture and also reducing the unemployment among those in the theater.

Already, most of the theater buildings are in the hands of local communities. As with schools, the state should maintain this without asking for payment. Stage scenery at this moment is the private property of directors ... this should go to the state, which could establish a factory for the accessories necessary for putting on a stage production. Such solutions would be profitable for the morals of the people and will bring material profit to the state.

After the second revolution on March 21, 1919, Kunfi, now the people's commissar, gave this proposal to Bélát Reinitz, a high level administrator, as well as giving him the task of organizing the theater to make it state run. On March 27, the association of the actors considered that they join the artists division of the union of state employees. At a meeting on March 26, the union dissolved itself; the next day it fused with the union and association of those already in the state employees artists' division and formed a new union for actors statewide.

2. Lugosi, Béla. Comments to a theater reporter. *New York Herald-Tribune***, 25 Oct. 1925.**

I do not care that my private face should be handsome, as long as I can buy several dollars' worth of grease paint and make a good face for the stage. That is what is important, is it not?

3. Lugosi, Béla. Remarks on perfecting a role. *Los Angeles Record***, 23 June 1928.**

Would you like to know what I have found is the best way for my work toward perfecting a characterization since I have been in this country? I first get a part in my own Hungarian, thinking it out as though I were going to act it in my native tongue ... you see? I study it and seek to perfect it as though I were going to act it in Budapest for Hungarian audiences.

Then, when I begin to feel quite at home in it, I begin to concentrate on the English diction, so that I may speak the part as it should be spoken for the American audiences.

4. Lugosi, Béla. Comments on American theater. *San Francisco Call*, **25 Aug. 1928.**

I like your Calee-fornia, and who knows — I may go into pictures here. I made manee of them in pioneer days of the cinema in Berlin and Budapest. Your American people — I like their sportsmanship. Your theater — I like not so well. You hunt for actor types, instead of training your actors so they may play manee roles. In the Academy of Theatrical Arts in Budapest that I attended we had such training. Before leaving the continent six years ago, I appeared in romantic parts, but in this country, you know, the foreigner is nearly always the heavy.

5. Lugosi, Béla. Definition of a vampire. *Los Angeles Record*, **18 May 1929.**

Dracula ran a whole season in New York. During that time, and also playing recently in Los Angeles, I had hundreds of letters asking me to kindly explain origin of the meaning of "vampire." During the Middle Ages, a person supposed to have been changed, or to have the power to change himself into a wolf at will, was known and feared as a "werwolf" [sic]. Related to the werewolf, but distinct, was the vampire, who was said to be a dead person who rose from the dead to suck the blood of the living during sleep.

6. Lugosi, Béla. Speech. Los Angeles, California, KFI radio, 27 Mar. 1931. (Transcript in the Forrest J Ackerman Archives.)

I read the book, *Dracula*, written by Bram Stoker, eighteen years ago, and I always dreamed to create and play the part of *Dracula*. Finally the opportunity came. Horace Liveright, stage producer of New York, acquired the stage rights of the novel and he chose me for the part. I have played the role of Dracula about a thousand times on the stage, and people often ask me if I still retain my interest in the character. I do — intensely. Because many people regard the story of *Dracula* simply as a glorified superstition, the actor who plays the role is constantly engaged in the battle of wits with the audience, in a sense, since he is constantly striving to make the character so real that the audience will believe it.

Now that I have appeared in the screen version of the story which Universal has just completed, I am of course not under this daily strain in the depiction of the character. My work in this direction was finished with the completion of the picture, but while it was being made I was working more intensely to this end than I ever did on the stage.

Although *Dracula* is a fanciful tale of a fictional character, it is actually a story which has many essential elements of truth. I was born and reared in almost the exact location of the story, and I came to know that what is looked upon merely as a superstition of ignorant people, is really based on facts which are literally hair-raising in their strangeness — but which are true. Many people will leave the theater with a sniff at the fantastic character of the story, but many others who think just as deeply will gain an insight into one of the most remarkable facts of human existence.

Dracula is a story which has always had a powerful effect on the emotions of an audience, and I think that the picture will be no less effective than the stage play. In fact, the motion picture should even prove more remarkable in this direction, since many things which could only be talked about on the stage are shown on the screen in all their uncanny detail.

I am sure you will enjoy *Dracula*. I am sure you will be mightily affected by its strange story, and I hope that it will make you think — about the weirdest, most remarkable condition that ever affected mankind.

I thank you.

7. Lugosi, Béla. Remarks on theatergoers. *San Francisco Examiner*, **24 Apr. 1932.**

Theatergoers always will be interested in the unusual. It is that thrill of witnessing something entirely foreign to normal lives, of being part of some highly imaginative plot that stirs their senses and leaves them with the feeling of having really been entertained.

8. Lugosi, Béla. Comments on why "women love horror." *Murders in the Rue Morgue.* **Universal Studios pressbook, 1932.**

When I was on the stage in *Dracula*, my audiences were composed mostly of women. They came again and again, thrilling to the shocking story. True, many men were in the audience, but most of them had been brought by women, who craved the subtle sex intimacy brought about when both sat watching the terrifying incidents of the play. In the same way, women were most thrilled and intrigued by the screen version of *Dracula*. The blood-sucking monster of the story excited strange thoughts and strange feelings.

Women are the ones who constantly visit cemeteries, ostensibly to grieve for departed ones, but subconsciously to gloat over death. A woman will repeatedly detail the circumstances of a husband's death, deriving a certain savage satisfaction from her recital of the circumstances that might better be forgotten. Women are in the majority as spectators at murder trials, and the more gruesome the killing, the more breathless will be their attention to the horrible details revealed by witnesses.

Women put forth every possible effort in their frantic desire to get to the front line trenches during the World War. Granted that their great wish was to give aid and comfort to the wounded. But subconsciously they sought the savage thrill that came from being in the midst of suffering and horrible mutilation. It was not that they entered the service from any unworthy motives; they were simply being guided by a feeling which has from time immemorial been an attribute of the feminine sex.

9. Lugosi, Béla. Statement to a reporter. *Californiai Magyarsag,* **9 Nov. 1934.**

I don't know how you feel, but I think I emigrated to America too late. I left Hungary thirteen years ago. When I crossed the Hungarian border, I thought I could start a new life in the West. I was determined to change countries and to blow up my bridges behind me. I resolved to forget about everything that was Hungarian — memories, feelings, and culture. But it seems that I deceived myself, for I came to realize that I could not start an entirely new life anywhere — not in Berlin, not in New York, or Hollywood. Everywhere I was compelled to lead a Hungarian life. Everywhere I had Hungarian friends; I devoured news from Hungary; I sought out Hungarian ties, a reawakening of my own Hungarian spirit; I needed a Hungarian heart. I will never suppress my Magyar nostalgia. We read English language newspapers but scour them for news from home. We are soldiers of the movie industry, but our hearts rally to Hungarian-sponsored events. The papers here announce our successes, but our hearts leap at the thought — the hope — that perhaps our brothers and sisters read of them in Hungary. This is nothing but our eternal identity as Hungarians who are thrown out into a foreign world. This is not red, white and green patriotism, but rather the immutability of our ties and emotions as Hungarians. Despite thousands upon thousands of miles that separate us from Hungary, the distance is bridged by our Hungarian thoughts and feelings.

10. Lugosi, Béla. Acting on the stage versus the screen. *The Black Cat.* **Universal Studios pressbook, 1934.**

While the stage is near and will always be dear to me, I cannot truthfully say I would rather be back on the stage. While it is true that a screen actor has no audience before him, other than his fellow workers, he is nevertheless compensated in the knowledge that millions will see his performance at one time where only hundreds could see it on the stage.

11. Lugosi, Béla. "I Welcome the Romantic Role After Being Typed as Heavy." *The Return of Chandu.* **Principle Studios pressbook, 1934.**

In the Greek language the terms "stranger" or "foreigner" and "enemy" are identical. It is assumed that a foreigner must be a barbarian and foe.

A little of that sentiment endures today. At least I found it to be so, coming to America from Hungary.

Though it is egotism, I hope pardonable, when an artist has achieved recognition in his own country to take it for granted that his name is not entirely strange in other centers of culture, and perhaps to resent it when he finds out that he is quite unknown and must begin again, as you say in this eloquent country, "from scratch."

The roles with which my name was most closely identified in Budapest, where for many years I was a leading player, were those of heroic and romantic character. I think my most popular performances in Hungary's capital were as Romeo, Cyrano de Bergerac, and Hamlet, than which, I think you will agree, there could hardly be mentioned roles more romantic in quality. If the reader is surprised at the mention of two Shakespearean characters, I am proud to say that in my country, it is of statistical record, there are more performances of Shakespeare's plays in any other country in the world; for the Theater in Hungary is under the direction of the Ministry of Education, and is an honored institution whose cultural influences are thoroughly appreciated.

In spite, however, of the predominance of romantic roles in my repertoire when I came to America, I found that, because of my language and the pantomime (gestures) with which most Europeans accompany their speech, that I was catalogued as what you call "a heavy." And at once I became identified with that class of performances. Particularly was this true in pictures, where, strangely enough, no accent could then be registered, since pictures in those days were silent. If my accent betrayed my foreign birth it also stamped me, in the imagination of producers, as "an enemy." Therefore, I must be a "heavy."

However, it was during my appearance on Broadway in *The Red Poppy* that I was approached by a picture organization and asked if I would care to undertake a film debut. I naturally said yes and was assigned to the role of the spy in *The Silent Command*, which was a propaganda picture seeking to convince the American people that they needed a large navy. I used to smile at the thought that for this preachment a Hungarian star has become chosen as the chief propagandist, since Hungary has no navy nor needs any!

It is needless to speak of two years on the stage in *Dracula* which role I created in America, nor of *The Black Cat* in which I was able to persuade a producer that I could play a romantic or at least benign role. *The Black Cat* was the picture that secured for me my present stellar part in which I am at last permitted to appear before American audiences in a distinctly romantic characterization, that of Chandu in Mr. Lesser's production of the *Return of Chandu*.

12. Lugosi, Béla. "I Like Playing Dracula." *Film Weekly,* **July 1935.**

I like playing "horror" parts on the screen. This may surprise you, but let me explain my point of view.

There is a popular idea that portraying a monster of the Dracula type requires no acting ability. People are apt to think that anyone who likes to put on a grotesque mask can be a fiend. That is wrong.

A monster, to be convincing, must have a character and a brain.

The screen monster produced by mere tricks of make-up and lighting will never thrill an audience. It will make them laugh! It is just a machine which does not understand what it is doing.

Now, imagine this creature with a character, with reasoning power and certain human mental faculties. It is no longer a machine. It can think.

Reading a speech in April 1943. Rarely did photographers catch Lugosi in his reading glasses.

Such a monster is able to thrill an audience. It can plot against the hero and heroine. It is a menace which must be combated by brains, not by running away.

We are all more afraid of cunning than brute force. Therefore, the monster must have cunning to trap his victims — physical strength is not enough to convince an audience.

Now, perhaps, you begin to see why I find the playing of fiends interesting!

When I am given a new role in a horror film, I have a character to create just as much as if I were playing a straight part.

Whether one thinks of films like *Dracula* as "hokum" or not does not alter fact; the horror actor must believe in his part. The player who portrays a film monster with his tongue in his cheek is doomed to failure.

An example of this occurred not very long ago. An actor, whose name I will not mention, played the part of a sinister foreigner. He had been used to straight parts, and he went into this film laughing at himself. He did the correct villainous actions, but he had his tongue in his cheek all the time.

The villain was completely unconvincing and as a result the film was a flop at the box office. Later, an almost exactly similar character was played by another actor. He took it seriously. Audiences believed in the villain and the film was a success.

I am not saying that I personally take seriously these vampires and monsters as such. I am saying that one must take them seriously when one is portraying them.

In playing Dracula, I have to work myself up into believing that he is real, to ascribe to myself the motives and emotions that such a character would feel. For a time I *become* Dracula — not merely an actor playing at being a vampire.

A good actor will "make" a horror part. He will build up the character until it convinces him and he is carried away by it.

There are, of course, plenty of tricks of the trade to be employed, such as effective make-up, clever photography, a threatening voice and claw-like gestures with the hands. These are important in the "hokum" film and must be used. But even they must be employed with intelligence or they will fail to thrill.

To leave the theoretical discussion of so-called monsters, there is another reason why I do not mind being "typed" in eerie thrillers.

With few exceptions, there are, among actors, only two types who matter at the box office. They are heroes and villains. The men who play these parts are the only ones whose names you will see in electric lights outside the theater.

Obviously, I cannot play a juvenile part — you will not find me competing with Clark Gable or Robert Montgomery! Therefore, I have gone to the other extreme in my search for success and public acclaim.

Every year a number of films with fantastic or supernatural characters are made, and will, it seems, continue to be made, whatever may happen to the horror "cycle" of pictures. I have deliberately specialized in such characters — and I firmly believe there will be suitable roles for me for a long time to come!

13. Lugosi, Béla. Comments on Great Britain. *New York World-Telegram*, 28 Aug. 1935.

I think that England, if they would have the sense to buy the technicians of Hollywood, they would be very, very keen competition to Hollywood on account Hollywood doesn't let authors, writers exploit and deliver their talents and imaginations. It has to go through the mill, not be passed by one individual talent, right or wrong.

There is something in England we do not have in the matter of courtesy. Whether they like you or not, they feel if they would not be kind, courteous, they would offend themselves.

I observed a lot in England in the way of courtesy I would like to spread here. They don't curtail authors so much. They work more at leisure. They are rested people working. That is why they sometimes get the results they do.

14. Lugosi, Béla. Interview in *The Film Star* (London), 30 Aug. 1935.

I am made in the same mold as everyone else. I don't grow horns for ears, nor do I sprout bat wings on my back. Fan letters come to me from all parts of the world, from people who have heard strange tales about my childhood in the Hungarian town of Lugos. The writers ask if my parents were hypnotists, if I commune with ghosts, and whether or not I practice the supernatural in my private life. They say my eyes have an expression unlike the eyes of a human being! As a matter of fact, my childhood in the Black Mountains was the usual husky, healthy life of any country boy and there was nothing weird or extraordinary in my family background.

15. Lugosi, Béla. Comments on being typecast. *San Francisco Call-Bulletin*, 3 Apr. 1937.

It's about time the film producers were shown I can play roles like this in *Tovarich*, or those I did for twenty years before coming to Hollywood. I wouldn't expect them to remember I played a Spanish lover in *The Red Poppy* in New York fifteen years ago, or everything from Hamlet to Liliom in Budapest ... comedy, tragedy, tragi-comedy — everything old Polonius named. But perhaps after *Tovarich*, they'll call me for something half-way civilized — no Draculas, White Zombies, Chandus, or Mysterious Mr. Wongs, I hope.

16. Lugosi, Béla. Reflections on his comeback. *New York World-Telegram*, 17 Oct. 1939.

One day, I drove past and see my name [on a theater marquee], and big lines people all around. I wonder what is giving away to the people — maybe bacon or vegetables. But it is the comeback of horror, and I come back.

17. Lugosi, Béla. Interview by Hedda Hopper. "Horror Men of Screen Just Pair of Home-Loving Folks." *Los Angeles Times*, 14 Jan. 1940.

Even the part of the bloodthirsty "Dracula" didn't haunt me. This may sound like a publicity story. But during the making of *Dracula*, I had an infected finger and when the doctor cut it and it bled a little, I fainted and couldn't go back to being "Dracula" for two days.

18. Lugosi, Béla. Comments on what he believed "horror" to be. "Horror Men Talk About Horror." *Modern Screen*, Jan. (Excerpts from an article written not entirely by Lugosi, but based on quotes from him.)

Horror to me, is losing our home as we did. Our home into which I had put all of my savings. Horror, to me, is learning that you cannot influence your Destiny. Horror, to me, is the reptilian sting of the knowledge of my own stupidity, my own lack of foresight, my belief that because I had always worked, I would always work.

No, I am not afraid of the supernatural. I am afraid only of the horror I have just described. Now horror, to me, concerns my baby. Horror that an automobile may pass over him when he is old enough to run about at play. Horror that a hand may snatch him from where he sleeps. Fear, of course, fear is what I am trying to say. Fear is horror. Not for one's self — fear for those you love better than yourself. Fear lest through your failure, they may go hungry, go cold, go homeless, or be hurt. Fear for those I love — that is what horror means to me.

19. Lugosi, Béla. Preface for a book by John F. Mauro. *Rhapsody in Death* (New York: Fortuny's, 1940).

Mr. Mauro has spun an admirable fantasy in his *Rhapsody in Death*. I could not sleep until I had finished reading it — and then I could not sleep. Such is the hypnotic grasp it exerts on the imagination.

In one sense it is quite understandable that I should find it a fascinating story: I have a natural and inborn affinity for the slightly weird and morbid. As a small boy in Transylvania, I heard many tales of vampires, werewolves, and other strange animals and monsters of the dark. I listened, not frightened, but enthralled and spell bound.

This peculiar allergy to things supernatural has its origin in that strange race of people of whom I am a part — the Magyars. We accept it as neither fortune nor misfortune, but merely as fact, that there are no others in Europe like us. When we are happy, we are always a little sad. As we love the mysterious because we understand it and feel its influence in our lives. To us, it is very real and tangible. It is part of the psychology of all Transylvanians.

Yet, for all of my natural sympathies, it has become second nature with me to view weird drama with the calculating eye of an expert. Starting with the stage and screen versions of *Dracula*, I have frequently played strange and mysterious characters, vested with super-natural and incredible powers. Thus, for some years past such stories have been the mainstay of my livelihood, and, perforce, I have read them by the score.

So, as both an expert and as a lover of these exciting tales, I pay tribute to *Rhapsody in Death* as an outstanding work, constructed with good craftsmanship and adequate suspense. It should succeed admirably as a book, a play or a motion picture.

It is not often that an actor writes prefaces for books. Therefore, I plead indulgence, for I must express in a language that is not my own. I sincerely hope that Mr. Mauro's book will have the success that it merits, and that the fine and horrible characters that he has conceived will come to be known by all who appreciate a good yarn gruesomely told.

B.L.

20. Lugosi, Béla. "Bela Lugosi, Star of *Dracula*, in Person." Article accompanying news of Lugosi opening in *Dracula* at the Plymouth Theater. *Boston Herald*, 2 May 1943.

Having run all the alarming Hollywood fright gamuts from Georgian monsters to baying werewolves, it is certainly rather relieving to find myself back in the role of the relatively innocuous bloodsucking vampire. I have sort of an affection for this role and since to this day people refer to me as "Dracula's" Lugosi, I feel a paternalism to the character very much akin to that which Frankenstein must certainly have felt for the monster he created.

Ordinarily I am a very pleasant, softspoken gentleman, I think, affably observing the world from my six-feet-two-inches. I love gypsy music, dogs, and Hungarian food, which is natural, I think you will agree. However, I am an avowed Roosevelt disciple, and I think without a doubt the President is the greatest outstanding personality of the day. I am a firm believer in his ideas and ideals and you can put that down in spades. I really believe this is a propitious time for a revival of *Dracula*. I think audiences need the emotional release and a certain stimulus which this kind of escapist entertainment provides. Now you take after a session of pure, undiluted stage horror, like this, the public is better equipped to cope with the realities of the day.

It is also interesting to me to see that the treatment of this thriller is now being approached in a very different manner by a new cast of people, some of whom have never even seen the play. Unlike me, they have no preconceived notions of how the dramas should be projected, and they are all eager to contribute something of their own ideas, which is not bad and at times very interesting, I think.

21. Lugosi, Béla. Opinions on his family. *Philadelphia Record*, 9 Apr. 1944.

I'm just a simple, old fashioned man who loves his home and family. And, I mean to protect them.

22. Lugosi, Bela. Memories of choosing his stage name. *Boston Globe*, 17 Apr. 1947.

My hometown was Lugos, so I picked [for my name] Lugosi, which merely means a resident of Lugos. In Hungarian, it sounds something like You-Go-She.

23. Lugosi, Bela. Excerpts from a letter to Virginia Doak at Hollywood 28, California, 8 Oct. 1947.

My darling friend Virginia:—

The reason why I am putting the sugar on so thick in addressing you is to make you accept the bad news that on Sept. 18th I signed an exclusive contract with Don Marlowe, which naturally means that if he can't realize even one of his promises in four months that contract expires.

It is easy for people that have a steady income from some source to be able to wait for the help and achievement of their friend who is in the managerial business. But it is close to two years that have had some many projects in view which unfortunately — naturally not your fault — did not realize. That would have been alright [sic] if I would have had money to cover my overhead expenses — which I didn't — and especially that I was not working for two years and getting very deep in the red. I had to borrow money on my last collateral to escape from Hollywood and try to cash in on my popularity and box office value in the east.

I couldn't help signing with him for a year which means four months if he can't deliver. But I signed for motion pictures only and the radio field is still free for you. So as far as motion pictures are concerned he is entitled for full commission of anything he knows and is able to deliver but if you should know of anything of which he does not — naturally you should receive full commission regardless of my obligations to Marlowe.

So I would suggest, my dear, to cooperate with Marlowe for the time being and believe me I would not disappoint you. I need a job very badly and am just human when I say that I do not mind who helps me to get my bread and butter I have to take it. So when I return to make a picture arranged by whom-ever I can make the radio recording platters and finally try to get out of the red.

Please answer by air mail and believe me, we are your sincere but desperate friends.

Truly,
Bela

24. Lugosi, Bela. Statements to the press concerning *Abbott and Costello Meet Frankenstein*. *New York Times*, 14 Mar. 1948.

There is no burlesque for me. All I have to do is frighten the boys, a perfectly appropriate activity. My trademark will be unblemished.

25. Lugosi, Bela. Letter to Representative John S. Wood, Chairman, House Committee on Un-American Activities, 19 Jan. 1951.

My belief in the principles of democracy and personal freedom is firm and unshakable. My entire life in America has been guided by these principles. I am unalterably opposed to the Communist menace against these ideals. Communist totalitarianism has always been abhorrent to me. I have never knowingly or willfully given it aid or comfort in any way.

During the war I was one of several artists of Hungarian birth asked to sponsor an organization. Shortly thereafter I learned the so-called Hungarian-American Council for Democracy was in reality a Communist front. I promptly resigned. Its high-sounding platform was deliberately phrased to avert suspicion from its true auspices.

My indignation at such deception impelled me to communicate with the FBI. I reported all I knew. My judgment proved correct. Four years later the Attorney-General cited this organization as subversive and disloyal.

Actors are usually too busy to pay much attention to organizations that request their sponsorship. These are times of sharpening conflict between freedom-loving people and Red Fascism. We must act and speak boldly against this brutalitarianism. I urge my fellow — artists to carefully scrutinize groups before giving their endorsement, lest they fall into a Communist booby-trap.

26. Lugosi, Bela. *Los Angeles Herald-Examiner*, 6 Aug. 1955.

I'm no longer addicted to drugs. I've licked a habit of 20 years and I'm a happy man again.

27. Lugosi, Bela. Remark to Richard Sheffield while watching one of his own films on television, c. 1955–56.

Goddamit, what a good-looking bastard I was!

28. Lugosi, Bela. Observations on the set of *The Black Sleep*. *Newark Star-Ledger*, 15 Feb. 1956.

There is Basil [Rathbone] playing my part. I used to be the big cheese. Now I'm playing just a dumb part. I have no dialogue because I was a bit worried whether I could do justice to the expectations. I'm still recuperating.

29. Lugosi, Bela. One of his last notes. Undated.

I wish you all the success in the world and perhaps some day when after all the struggle you will anchor at the harbour of your dreams — we may be together again soon — who knows?
      Sincerely yours,
      Bela

17. Quotations About Lugosi

Lugosi the man is in many ways much more elusive than the often mysterious or fantastic roles he portrayed on the screen. In speaking with those who knew him, a disjointed picture emerges, almost like an oral history when more than one person and one viewpoint are involved. The picture at first seems as skewed and confusing as that of the newspaper magnate in *Citizen Kane* (1941). The only consistent comments regarding Lugosi are those from actors with whom he worked, with an almost constant refrain being that Lugosi was quiet and hard to know. As with any real investigation, the resulting image is a complicated one. Lugosi lived a complex life, and with many levels of association, friendship, and love. The following quotes taken as a whole offer not so much conflicting stories as a collage of insight into Lugosi as a person.

The arrangement in this section departs from chronological as is favored elsewhere. The organization is alphabetical by speaker's last name.

1. **Ames, Leon.** Film actor. Interviewed by Samuel James Maronie, "Things You Never Knew About the Unholy Two." *Famous Monsters of Filmland* 127 (Aug. 1976).

Bela and I costarred in one of the first films I ever made, *Murders in the Rue Morgue*, a perfectly awful film which still pops up on TV to haunt me. Lugosi was a very quiet fellow and kept to himself during most of the shooting. At that time, he had not yet mastered English and was having a bit of difficulty with the language. I was very "green" in the acting profession then and to me as a young man, Bela seemed very much like the eerie Dracula character of his films.

2. **Arch, Lillian.** Lugosi's fourth wife. Quoted by Robert Cremer, "If It's Midnight, This Must Be Transylvania." *Famous Monsters of Filmland* 125 (May 1976).

He loved just about any kind of music, but he loved folk music the best. We often went to the record stores to pick out music together and that was a chore. Bela insisted on listening to every record before he bought it. At that time, they had booths where you could listen to the records. We made three piles ... a "yes" pile, a "no" pile, and a "maybe" pile. He listened to that "maybe" pile until he could make up his mind about them. I thought I would go crazy.

Bela was a health food fanatic long before it became a fad. He liked his vegetables raw and his meat blood rare. And when it came to delicacies from Hungary, he ate only the best. When he was at his peak following *Dracula*, he ordered crates of imported goose liver, Egri Bikaver wine, and sulfur water that he liked to mix with his red wine. It made the wine an inky-black color and smelled horrible, but he always insisted that it was healthy. We just stacked everything in our cellar.

3. **Arkoff, Samuel Z.** Movie producer. Quoted in Tom Weaver, *Interviews with B Science Fiction and Horror Movie Makers* (Jefferson, N.C.: McFarland, 1988).

Lugosi is about to bite his friend Richard Gordon on the neck at Nettleford Studios in this 1951 photograph taken on the set of *Mother Riley Meets the Vampire*.

I had a number of conversations with Lugosi, who was very interesting; by this time, he was "playing the role" of Lugosi—you know what I mean.

4. Bellamy, Madge. Film actress. *A Darling of the Twenties: Madge Bellamy* (New York: Vestal, 1989).

During the making of *White Zombie*, my father took over the role of my chauffeur and helper. He and Bela Lugosi became friends. They were both rather ceremonial in manner. When I am asked so often what Bela Lugosi was like, I am tempted to say that I almost had my neck bitten.

5. Bishop, Joey. Comedian. Quoted in Paul F. Boller, Jr., and Ronald L. Davis, *Hollywood Anecdotes* (New York: Ballantine, 1987).

When a member of a poker game asked the comedian, "Did you hear Bela Lugosi died?" Bishop responded without looking up from his cards. His response was simply, "He'll be back."

6. Bloch, Robert. Novelist, author of *Psycho*; Radio interview with Warren James on the *Hour 25* radio show. KPFK radio, 1993.

Lugosi — as the world's most recognizable vampire, he celebrated the career of the nocturnal prowler. He symbolized the Continental seducer, kissing hands and then biting necks.

7. Borland, Carroll. Film actress. "Bela Lugosi and *Mark of the Vampire*." *Castle Dracula Quarterly* 1 (1977).

We often ate at the Hollywood Roosevelt Hotel ... wined and dined, rather. There was a good orchestra and both Bela and I were good dancers. It was wonderful to dance with him. I recall his strength, his height, the whiff of good cigars, and the rumble in his chest under my ear as he spoke to me. We would often take a late walk down Hollywood Boulevard, window-wishing, spouting theatrical theory, and quoting plays. At that time I never wondered why I was chosen as his companion. I just knew that he knew that I admired him greatly. I found him fascinating, intimidating, charming, exasperating, demanding, and generous all at the same time.

8. Borland, Carroll. Film actress. Interview with Gary Don Rhodes. *The World of Bela Lugosi* 2 (1988).

When I was about fourteen years old, he was playing in *Dracula*. I had already started writing a sequel to it ... *Countess Dracula*. I went to the theater and went backstage and told him about it. He said he would like me to come down and tell him about it at the hotel where he was staying. He invited me and my mother to lunch. He said he wanted to hear it read to him because he didn't read English too well. And so, he would come out to the house in a taxi cab from downtown Oakland and sit and smoke and drink coffee as I read him the novel. He liked it very much. We kept up a correspondence and when I was sixteen or seventeen, he wrote me a letter saying that they were dissatisfied with the "Lucy" [in a roadshow version of *Dracula* Lugosi was starring in], and would I come down and read for it. I did, and it got as far as Santa Barbara before the company broke up.

Well, of course he was sort of a practical joker. In one scene, when the cape came up and you couldn't see what was happening behind the cape, he dropped a piece of ice down my back! You know, Lugosi was such an extreme professional. He was never temperamental or anything. It was very comfortable.

9. Brooks, Conrad. Film actor and friend of Ed Wood. Interview with Steve Randisi, *Filmfax* 47 (Oct.-Nov. 1994).

He was a serious man — quiet, pleasant, well-spoken and very polite. He was nice to everybody and the whole crew liked him. In the beginning, he had forgotten my name when I was working for him as a stand-in. I saw him walk over to someone to ask what my name was. Then he called me over, by name, and asked if I'd hold his cigar for him as he looked over the script. It was enjoyable just being there with the man and watching him perform before the cameras.

10. Carradine, John. Film actor. Quoted by Bob Lichello, "I Married Dracula! And He Was Afraid of Me." *National Enquirer,* 17 Nov. 1957.

As for the part we both played, he was the better vampire. He had a fine pair of eyes.

11. Carradine, John. Film actor. Interviewed by Terry Pace. *Fangoria* 52 (1986).

The English critics said I was the best Dracula, which was very nice considering that I had been preceded by Bela [Lugosi], who did a hell of a job. He was a charming man and a hell of an actor. He used to come to the set with a bottle of claret, which he supped at a little bit all day long. He never got drunk, never lost a line, never lost his tempo or his accent, which was native to him.

12. Castle, William. Movie producer. *Step Right Up! I'm Gonna Scare the Pants Off America* **(New York: Pharos, 1976).**

Bela Lugosi was a very humble, gentle man, quite unlike the roles he portrayed. I knew what I wanted to do with my life. I wanted to scare the pants off audiences. Bela Lugosi was to make it all possible. When I was fifteen, I received a call from a producer who was getting ready to do a road company tour of *Dracula*. Mr. Lugosi had suggested me as the assistant stage manager. Amazed that Lugosi had remembered me, I excitedly accepted and promptly dropped out of high school.

13. Clarke, Robert. Film actor. Interviewed by Tom Weaver. *Interviews with B Science Fiction and Horror Movie Makers.* **(Jefferson, N.C.: McFarland, 1988).**

During the time that I was involved on *The Body Snatcher* he hardly came out of his dressing room unless the assistant director called him. They had a daybed in there, and he was flat on his back on that couch nearly all the time. He talked very little to anyone, and obviously he wasn't well at all. It was very difficult for him to perform.

14. Cohen, Herman. Movie producer. Letter to Gary Don Rhodes. 22 June 1987.

He was not well [during the filming of *Bela Lugosi Meets a Brooklyn Gorilla*] and was with his son on the set all the time. Bela always knew his script and was at work on time and ready to go each day.

15. Currie, Louise. Quoted by Gregory Mank. *Karloff and Lugosi: The Story of a Haunting Collaboration* **(Jefferson, N.C.: McFarland, 1990).**

I remember long chats with Lugosi. He was a very educated, polished, interesting man. It was amazing to me that he got into the horror end of Hollywood; he could easily have been a serious actor and have gone in another direction.

16. Disney, Walt. Movie producer. Quoted in a *Castle of Frankenstein* **magazine, 1960s.**

Sometimes I think he [Lugosi] was touched by the Devil himself when I see him up on the screen.

17. Everson, William K. Film historian. Conversations with Frank J. Dello Stritto, 11 Dec. 1972, and 28 Jan. 1973.

Lugosi was a bad source of information. If he was asked the same question two weeks apart, he would give totally different answers. He talked mostly about his stage career and was not interested in his film past. He was not bitter, but he had a chip on his shoulder, especially concerning the television rights of his films. Lugosi would phone late at night from Los Angeles to New York and answer questions I had written him, rather than bother to write back.

18. Florey, Robert. Quoted in James Curtis, *James Whale* **(Metuchen, N.J.: Scarecrow, 1982).**

After seeing Max Shreck in Murnau's *Nosferatu* [1922], I had not been particularly impressed by Lugosi in *Dracula* [1931].

19. Gardner, Ava. *Ava: My Story.* **(New York: Bantam, 1990).**

Bela was a gentle man who wouldn't frighten a nervous kitten, but as Dracula, honey, he'd filled every movie house in the country.

20. Gordon, Alex. Movie producer. "My Favorite Vampire." *Fantastic Monsters* **5 (1963).**

When he was on tour, he could not stand the hard mattresses in most of the hotels as he had trouble with his back. So he would place his beautiful silk-lined coffin from the theater in the middle of his hotel room and sleep in it. This is absolutely true and no publicity story. It was not done for effect, just plain comfort.

Bela was a delightful companion, gracious and kind and with a good sense of humor. He was also a man of many moods, and sometimes he would sink into deep despair. Bela loved good cigars, and he became interested in religion, hypnosis, and philosophy. He was very particular about many little things. He once asked me to sort out his desk and papers, and I found receipted bills and other statements going back twenty years, which he thought he should keep for tax and book-keeping purposes. He also kept a large collection of stills from his movies in scrapbooks.

21. Gordon, Alex. Movie producer. Quoted by Tom Weaver, "Man with the Plan (9)." *Starlog* **(Nov., 1994).**

Lugosi did *not* like gays — anything to do with gays, he would abhor — and he never *dreamed* for a moment that Eddie was a transvestite. But had he known Eddie had those kind of tastes, it would have been hands off. Lugosi wouldn't have touched him with a mile-long pole, because Lugosi was very much a womanizer and very straightforward and old-fashioned in his beliefs.

22. Gordon, Richard. Movie producer. Letter to Gary Don Rhodes, 20 Aug. 1986.

He was an extraordinarily warm-hearted and generous person, always ready to help anyone in need even when he could not afford it. When he was paid for a TV guest shot or a personal appearance, he would spend a substantial part of the money immediately entertaining his friends and fellow workers. He "lived" his Dracula role with dignity and respect. One of my greatest regrets is that I became a producer myself too late to be able to make a picture with Bela that might have been worthy of his former status and career. He was never unprofessional, and when I knew him, he was not a drug addict. He liked to drink, although he had a chronic stomach ailment, and when the combination of rich food and too much alcohol caused him great pain, Lillian [his fourth wife] would administer injections to relieve his agony. His favorite drink was a mixture of whiskey and beer, which can certainly be lethal even for someone who doesn't have a health problem.

23. Great, Alexander (aka Kim Key). Interviewed by Richard Blankenhorn, *Famous Monsters of Filmland* **132 (Mar. 1977).**

So I told him, "We have some good steak houses [in Detroit]. He said, "I'm not interested in that. What I would like is to go to a Hungarian place where I can have Hungarian food like dried sausage or paprika bacon. That's what I would like." I said, "I have exactly the right place," and we went into this Hungarian neighborhood and walked into this place and sat down. The owner came up to us with a funny look on his face. He said, "Can I talk to you, Alex?" So I excused myself and went with him. He asked who the man was who was with me. He said, "He looks like Bela Lugosi, the man who plays Dracula in pictures." I told him it should be because that was who it was. The man got so excited he almost jumped to the ceiling. He said, "Oh my God, how did he get here?" I said: "With me." So I introduced the owner to Bela Lugosi. Before we knew it the place was filled with people (how it got around I don't know). Soon there were five or six gypsies playing and the place was jammed.

A young lady wanted to meet him. I said: "This young lady would like to meet you." She said: "Mr. Lugosi, I am very happy to meet you. I've seen all your pictures." He said, "Do you like me?" He turned slowly and looked at her and said, "It looks like you are afraid of me." The young lady was shying away from him. He said, "Don't worry, I'm not going to hurt you ... I'm only after your heart." At that the young lady fell off the stool from leaning back away from him. He helped her to stand up but she never sat back on the stool again.

24. Hall, Huntz. Film actor, one of the "Bowery Boys." Interviewed by Samuel James Maronie, "Things You Never Knew About the Unholy Two." *Famous Monsters of Filmland* 129 (Aug. 1976).

"Well, Mr. Lugosi, what do you think of the Bowery Boys?" I asked. Lugosi raised his eyebrows theatrically and said, "Scum!" Bela had a great sense of humor. He loved to laugh, but not to be laughed at. That would make him more angry than anything.

25. Howe, James Wong. Cinematographer. Quoted in Charles Higham, *Hollywood Cameramen: Sources of Light* (New York: Garland, 1970).

Bela Lugosi was funny; he lived the part of the vampire.

Interestingly, Howe once told Dick Cavett that Lugosi was a gracious man who gave no impression of Dracula off camera.

26. Knowles, Patric. Film actor. Interview with Gary Don Rhodes, *The World of Bela Lugosi* 6 (Apr. 1989).

A quiet and lonely man ... seemed unhappy.

27. Landau, Martin. Film actor who portrayed Lugosi in Tim Burton's film *Ed Wood* (1994). Interviewed by Michael Stein, "Landau's Lugosi." *Outré* 1 (1994).

I wanted to bring some new insight into Lugosi — the pain, the difficulty, the lack of glamor in his life. I don't believe it's ever been done before. I really became very fond of Lugosi; I liked him.

28. Lee, Christopher. Actor who portrayed Dracula in a series of films. Interviewed by Garry Parfit. Distributed by the Christopher Lee Fan Club, 1970s.

Bela was in his younger days such a wonderful looking man. He had tremendous presence and personality. Not the right person to play Dracula from the point of view of nationality. Because Transylvania is in Rumania and he was an Hungarian from the town of Lugos, hence his name.

29. Lee, Christopher. Film actor. Quoted in Leonard Wolf, *A Dream of Dracula* (Boston: Little, Brown, 1972).

Anyhow, about the Lugosi Dracula. I was so disappointed. I was absolutely. I had been wanting to see it for a long, long time. There are aspects of it, for instance, that I considered ridiculous. ... Dracula is played too nice at the beginning. Practically no menace in the character ... There is no shock or fright in it ... Lugosi's hands too ... He held them out stiffly ... making him look like a puppet. His smile was not always sinister either.

30. Lubin, Arthur. Director. Interview with Gary Don Rhodes, *The World of Bela Lugosi* 1 (1987).

Well, he was a powerful looking man ... very tall. He had a fantastic smile, but spoke practically no English at all. It was my job, assigned by the director [of the 1922 play *The Red Poppy*], to teach Bela English before the opening ... and I must say he spoke pretty good English with a Hungarian accent. [In 1940] I did one picture with him called *Black Friday*. He was still a very popular actor. He was still drawing big audiences. Out here among the colony, he was very well liked.

31. Lubitsch, Ernst. Director. *Ninotchka*. MGM Studios pressbook, 1939.

People are so accustomed to him as a "Dracula" that I thought a sympathetic moment [in the film *Ninotchka*] would surprise audiences as much as it did him.

32. Lugosi Jr., Bela. Quoted on *Suspense—Bela Lugosi*. LP 611, Mark 56 Records, 1976.

I remember, oh I think it was when I was age twelve, I had the most wonderful summer of my life when my Dad took me on a summer stock tour with him around the East. During that summer is when I learned more about my Dad. I remember him being very conscientious with his work — very demanding of himself as an artist. Taking pride in his work, being impatient with those that flubbed scenes and did not bring themselves up to the quality of acting that he thought ought to be given by performers. My Dad never did compromise his quality. He was a great artist and great actor in my estimation. I think he realized his powers over people — his magnetism. I just remember observing him; I was just fascinated with the reaction of others to my father. Everybody remembered him; they had to. I could just see his influence over people.

33. Lininger Lugosi, Hope. Lugosi's fifth wife. Quoted by Bob Lichello, "I Married Dracula! And He Was Afraid of Me." *National Enquirer,* **17 Nov. 1957.**

He used to scare people. He had long sofas in his living room, and when reporters from fan magazines came around, he would swear them to secrecy and tell them he had his three wives buried in them. I was never afraid of him. For personal reasons, I made him afraid of me. I had to show him who was boss. He was afraid of my sister, Pat. She told him what to do and what to wear, and he did it meekly. She dressed him for the wedding. He was afraid of me. I told him I was a witch and I know he believed me. He was afraid of cats. Now I have a black cat sitting in front of his painting. If he knew that, he'd die all over again.

He dramatized everything. If a lamb stew were cooking, he'd dramatize it. When the meal was done he would invariably kiss my hand and say, "That was a truly marvellous dinner." He was the perfect host when company came. Very gracious. He kissed all the ladies hands. And yet he was annoyed by company, but he never showed it. He liked to go to bed early.

I made a very unfortunate remark one time. I got so sick of his eternal religious arguments that I said, "You know, Bela, I don't think I even believe in God." He was furious. He had a memory like an elephant, you know, and he would always throw it up to me.

He was just terrified of death. Toward the end he was very weary, but he was still afraid of death. Three nights before he died he was sitting on the edge of the bed. I asked him if he were still afraid to die. He told me that he was.

34. Marco, Paul. Film actor and friend of Ed Wood. Quoted by Bob Lichello, "I Married Dracula! And He Was Afraid of Me." *National Enquirer,* **17 Nov. 1957.**

When he came to a party at my house, he saw our black Christmas tree. He waved his hand dramatically and said, "Now I feel at home."

35. Marlowe, Don. Lugosi's agent in the late 1940s. *The Hollywood That Was* **(Fort Worth, Tex.: Branch-Smith, 1974).**

[Lugosi was] ... the only man I ever knew who lived life to the fullest.

36. Oakie, Jack. Film actor and comedian. *Jack Oakie's Double Takes* **(Portland, Oregon: Strawberry Hill, 1980).**

Suddenly she [Clara Bow] came running out. "Come on, everybody! We've got tickets!" she said. "We're going down to the Biltmore to see *Dracula.*" She was so excited she didn't stop to dress. She just threw a long mink coat over her swimsuit and we all got into her chauffeur-driven black Packard limousine. Bela Lugosi was starring in *Dracula* on the stage of the Biltmore Theatre downtown [in 1928]. He couldn't speak English, but no language barrier could hide his thrill at meeting Clara Bow. He was overwhelmed with the Redhead. "How do you know your lines?" Bow asked him immediately. We finally understood the Hungarian's explanation. He told us that he memorized each word from a cue and, if by mistake another actor should ever give him a wrong line, he would be lost for the rest of the night.

Bow invited him to her home and they became very good friends.

37. Pavey, Harold. Silent film actor. Interviewed by Michael J. David, May 1985.

I met him at Universal Studios and he was very kind—just like Mr. [Rudolph] Valentino was to a boy. He used to take my hand and say, "Harold, would you like to come to the commissary and have a sandwich with me?" His eyes were so piercing, I was frightened. I liked him, but I feared him.

38. Quarry, Robert. Film actor and star of *Count Yorga, the Vampire* (1970). Interviewed in *Monsters of the Monsters* (Aug. 1974).

Looking back at the 1931 *Dracula* now, I must say, in all honesty, Bela Lugosi was a very dear man, but I think he was one of the worst actors I ever saw on God's green earth! *Dracula* is really a terrible film; it's just that it was a first. In those days people weren't so selective. If that movie were made today it would be laughed off the screen! Bela was sometimes effective ... but as Dracula? I think if I was ever *that* terrible an actor I'd *kill* myself! You just couldn't work now if you acted like that. It was a poorly made film ... I always thought of Bela's *Dracula* as something to poke fun at. Even as a kid that film didn't scare me.

39. Rossitto, Angelo. Film actor/midget. "The Big Little Man." *Fangoria* 50 (1986).

Lugosi told me, "Angelo, you are my greatest free advertisement. When they see you they've got to say to themselves, 'There's the little guy who works with the monster.'" He even told his son, the lawyer, to come and visit me after he died. Lugosi was a sweetheart of a guy and he loved me.

40. Sheffield, Richard. Close friend of Lugosi. "Lugosi's Last Years: The Boy Who Befriended Bela," *Famous Monsters of Filmland* 133 (April 1977).

He was at times an extremely heavy drinker but according to him he hated drinking. He told me with tears in his eyes that he hated the taste of Scotch but couldn't be without it. Hope [his fifth wife] tried to curb his drinking, but he had the Scotch and beer in every nook and cranny of the apartment. He did go a few times to Alcoholics Anonymous, even inviting Forrest Ackerman, a teetotaler, to accompany him but didn't stay with it.

41. Sheffield, Richard. Close friend of Lugosi. Letter to Gary Don Rhodes, 23 June 1987.

One evening we went to Blums in Beverly Hills for Ice Cream. Bela was recognized by all. On that particular occasion, Danny Thomas saw Bela and came over and introduced himself, remarking how much he had always admired him, and Bela loved every second of it. When he was sober, Bela was an incredibly exciting and fun person to be with. We watched several of Bela's films with him: some on TV, some in theaters, and once we projected *Abbott and Costello Meet Frankenstein*, which he had never seen previously. He'd watch himself intently and on one occasion came out with, "Gauuuud Damn, vat a gud luking bastard I vas." He had a great sense of humor and used to totally crack us up with his jokes.

42. Strange, Glenn. Film actor. Recorded speech for the Count Dracula Society Banquet, 22 Apr. 1972.

Strange summed up Lugosi by saying he was "hard to get to know."

43. Talbot, Lyle. Film actor. Interviewed by Samuel James Maronie, "Things You Never Knew About the Unholy Two," *Famous Monsters of Filmland* 129 (Aug. 1976).

Lugosi was a nice man—a very intelligent man. He did have a slight accent though—but a very fine actor. We got into several conversations while shooting this picture [*One Body Too Many*] because he had just started smoking a pipe. Bela had never smoked one before and was all enthused about getting this pipe. But Lugosi allowed so much "cake" to accumulate in his pipe that he could hardly get any tobacco in it. "Bela," I said, "your pipe will crack if you put too much carbon inside." So he was very grateful to hear this and I cleaned out his pipe. Then, everything was okay between us.

44. Tovar, Lupita. Film actress. Interview in Tom Weaver, *Attack of the Monster Movie Makers* **(Jefferson, N.C.: McFarland, 1994).**

Oh, yes, Lugosi, he was terribly nice. I used to see him, usually on weekends. All the Europeans used to get together for a koffeeklatsch — they'd have coffee and pastries, and talk.

45. Ulmer, Edgar G. Director. Interviewed by Peter Bogdanovich. *Film Culture* **58-60 (1974).**

You had to cut away Lugosi, continuously to cut him down. But there was the huge success of *Dracula* on stage and films.

46. Vampira (Maila Nurmi). Television "horror hostess" and actress in Ed Wood's *Plan 9 from Outer Space* **(1959). Interviewed by Robert Rees. "The Vampira Chronicles."** *Cult Movies* **11 (1994).**

I worked with him a number of times and we were friends, I think. No human I have ever met has made me feel so regal and precious. He was a gentleman of infinite dignity and refinement. His last days were tragic. He was too dignified a person to sink to "milking" sympathy. And he got no sympathy ... only smears and jeers. I'd say Bela was a victim of Ed Wood, society, and himself. Bela was very sick and would crawl out of his deathbed, at the last, to tub thump Ed Wood movies, only to be insulted by a public who had been poisoned by a smear campaign.

47. Weeks, Beatrice Woodruff. Lugosi's third wife. Quoted in "Lugosi Wins Heart of Clara Bow, Says Second Wife, Seeking Divorce." *New York Daily Mirror,* **5 Nov. 1929.**

He slapped me in the face because I ate a lamb chop he had hidden in the icebox for his after-theatre, midnight lunch. "If you want lamb chops — buy your own," my husband said. He told me that he was King, that in Hungary a wife and all she possessed were placed at the husband's disposal; that, in effect, she was nothing but a servant. Of course, I objected to this, and we quarreled. His table manners were terrible. He would break an apple in half and crowd one of the portions in his mouth, unable to speak or to swallow, until he had chewed it up fine. He constantly used his fingers in place of a fork and was addicted to similar habits that simply frayed my nerves.

48. Winchell, Walter. Newspaper columnist. Quote circulated on publicity during the late 1940s by the Don Marlowe Agency.

[Lugosi gave the] most electrifying performance I have ever witnessed.

49. Wise, Robert. Director. "Wise Fantastica." Interview with John Gallagher. *Fangoria* **44 (1985).**

It had to be a part [in *The Body Snatcher*] that was not too demanding, because Bela was not a well man. He had been ill for some time and his English wasn't terribly good and he didn't seem terribly well when I was working with him on the film. I had no major problems with him but it was just hard to get through because of the language problem and his illness.

50. Wood, Edward D., Jr. Director. Quoted in Rudolph Grey, *Nightmare of Ecstasy* **(Los Angeles: Feral House, 1992).**

I was his front pallbearer. I touched his hand and the large ring of Count Dracula as he lay in the coffin ... I said "Goodbye, dear friend Bela."

18. Quotations About Lugosi and Karloff

The following is an assortment of verbal artifacts from the relationship between Bela Lugosi and fellow actor Boris Karloff. Though Lugosi worked with other stars frequently, including Lionel Atwill, Lon Chaney, John Carradine, and George Zucco, the alleged rivalry with Karloff holds an important place in most historiography on the subject. The fact that Lugosi turned down the role of the monster in *Frankenstein* (1931) and thus opened the door of stardom to Karloff remains a popular tale of film histories, which often claim that that single error became the greatest mistake of Bela's life. Some have gone as far as claiming that Lugosi and his representatives should be maligned for creating potential competition in the burgeoning horror genre.

Yet a version of *Frankenstein* with Lugosi, especially if helmed by the original choice of director Robert Florey, would have been far different from the highly successful film with Karloff. The critical and popular appeal of the Karloff film might have eluded a Lugosi version. Moreover, while hindsight shows the thirties to have been the golden age of horror films, in 1931 when *Frankenstein* went into production, a Hollywood "horror genre" did not yet exist. To presume that Lugosi or any agent should have been thoroughly aware of the profitable years ahead in horror and would intentionally thwart competition in advance of its very existence is a less-than-reasonable argument. Even if someone had prophesied such information, halting competition at every studio would have been impossible. Additionally, Lugosi the actor had prerogatives outside those of Universal Studios, and, if anything, newspapers commenting on the success of both *Dracula* and *Frankenstein* highly questioned how long audiences would care to see such topics at the cinema.

At any rate, Karloff found stardom and success at Universal Studios, soon moving to such films as *The Mummy* (1932) and *The Old Dark House* (1932). Trades called him the cinematic heir to Lon Chaney, with Lugosi being rapidly overshadowed in a genre that did in fact find a home at the nation's theaters. Of the films the two made together, advertisements moved from equal billing in early ads for *The Black Cat* (1934) to Karloff's name towering over Lugosi's in *The Invisible Ray* (1936). By their last collaboration in *The Body Snatcher* (1945), Lugosi had become not merely second-billed but a minor player in the cast, scenery for a truly Karloff film.

Furthermore, as horror films fell out of fashion at times during the next three decades, Karloff easily moved into character roles and continued working; Lugosi

At their first meeting in 1932, Lugosi and Boris Karloff have fun picking on a "non-monster" for the cameras.

did not. Horror typecast both men, but for Lugosi alone it became an inescapable trap. When the two first met in 1932 on the set of *Night World* (1932), both were new to Hollywood's spotlight. By 1935 the *London Daily Telegraph* described Lugosi not by any character trait or film title, but as "Boris Karloff's chief rival."

The "rivalry" between the two transformed into standard horror film history, yet the term itself hardly describes the actual relationship. Every indication shows an outwardly friendly, if not warm, association. Though the two did not socialize, their interests and hobbies outside studio sound stages were far different. Even away from a movie set, however, evidence shows a polite duo, either judging children's pets during the production of *The Black Cat* (1934) or being jointly interviewed in 1940 by Hedda Hopper in Karloff's Coldwater Canyon home.

Additionally, a rivalry would suggest actual competition for the same roles, though again this was not the case. Following *Frankenstein*, the two essentially were not striving for the same parts. Rather, Karloff's status as a major star surpassed Lugosi's, making the British actor the sole choice in the eyes of studios hoping for assured box office success. Moreover, comparisons of the duo would become endlessly debated only after Lugosi's death in fan magazines. During Lugosi's lifetime, the primary comparisons were connected to their separate portrayals of Jonathan Brewster in the stage versions of *Arsenic and Old Lace*. As with the Frankenstein Monster, Lugosi found himself portraying the murderous Brewster brother after Karloff had achieved renown with the role.

The question remains as to what rivalry really existed. If not quarrels between the two in public places or strong competition for precisely the same roles, what then caused such a cloud of strife? The answer cannot be found with Karloff. Existing evidence shows that even though the British actor did not socialize with the Hungarian, he certainly admired Lugosi's talent and sympathized with the tragic qualities of his life. No malice seemingly came from Karloff's side of the association.

Despite portrayals of the type in Tim Burton's film *Ed Wood* (1994), however, malice might not best describe Lugosi's view of Karloff. If memories of those from the thirties show the proud Hungarian quickly moved from the spotlight of attention and angered by the mention of *Frankenstein*, no available information reveals Lugosi decrying Karloff's talent or even using obscenities to describe him personally. Instead, 25 years of witnessing Karloff's image towering over his own seems to have quietly embittered Lugosi. Perhaps this is best exemplified by the fact that shortly before he died Lugosi awoke in the middle of the night, telling his wife, Hope, that he had to meet his fellow actor ... that Karloff was "waiting for him."

The "rivalry" in retrospect seems more one-sided, with Lugosi feeling the pain of Karloff's success through the failings of his own career. The British actor — despite the many others like Lon Chaney, Jr., also known for their work in the genre — became an outlet for Lugosi for envisioning the success he desired, complicated further not just by his bitterness over *Frankenstein* but particularly by his own inability to escape the horror genre and find other kinds of roles. Karloff then symbolized the success Lugosi did not eventually find more than any desire on the Hungarian's part to be the most sought-after star of horror films.

The following is a list of examples of the two actors speaking to one another and about one another, and of other parties recalling memories or opinions of their relationship. Additionally, reviews of *Arsenic and Old Lace* which make direct comparisons of Karloff and Lugosi are included. The concluding piece is a complete reprint of a 1932 *Weird Tales* article, "Demons of the Film Colony." Though very much an unbelievable tale, it represents the two meeting head-to-head in a "fright duel," literally vying to see which is the greater monster. The result offers a variety of evidence from which to build a picture of Lugosi and Karloff's "rivalry."

1. Lee, Christopher. Interview by Garry Parfitt. Distributed by the Christopher Lee Fan Club. 1970s.

Boris always referred to him as "Poor Bela."

2. Karloff, Boris. Quoted in an article by Robert C. Roman. *Films in Review*. Aug.-Sept. 1969.

He [Lugosi] was very suspicious on the set, suspicious of tricks, fearful of what he regarded as scene stealing. Later, when he realized I didn't go in for such nonsense, we became friends. He had real problems with his speech and difficulty interpreting lines. I remember he once asked a director what a line of dialogue meant. He spent a great deal of his time with the Hungarian colony in L.A., and this isolated him.

3. Borland, Carroll. Quoted in Gregory Mank, *Karloff and Lugosi*. (Jefferson, N.C.: McFarland, 1990).

We were walking down Hollywood Boulevard [in the early thirties], and in those days the celebration for Christmas meant that every streetlight was decorated with a circle of lights, and tinsel, with a star's picture inside. It was after *Frankenstein* had been released. Lugosi looked up ... and there, in a circle of lights, was a picture of Boris Karloff. And I'll never forget Lugosi, looking up at that picture of Karloff, glaring at it, taking his cigar from his mouth. I'll never forget that look on his face. And I'll never forget the sound he made ... "Grrr ... Arrgh."

4. Borland, Carroll. Interviewed by Forrest J Ackerman. *Famous Monsters of Filmland*, 39 (June 1966).

As Roosevelt said, "You don't talk about rope in the house of a man who was hanged" ... and we didn't say *Frankenstein*. You could say, "Boris Karloff," because they played in some films together and had respect for each other, but *Frankenstein* was the source of ... I think he felt that it would have been he.

5. Bela Lugosi and Boris Karloff. *Screen Snapshots* newsreel 11 (1934).

Lugosi and Karloff found themselves playing chess for the cameramen in this short subject, the result reminiscent of a similar scene in *The Black Cat* (1934). The duo played the game in street clothes, however, and the set itself was different from that in the Poe film. Karloff began the segment, asking, "Ready for the test, Dracula?" Lugosi answered, "I'm ready ... Frankenstein." Karloff: "Then ... let us begin. [*Laughter*.] You understand, Bela, don't you, that the one who wins this little game of chess is to lead the parade at the Film Stars Frolic." Lugosi: "Okay, Boris. Your move." Karloff: "Right."

6. *The Raven*. Universal Studios pressbook, 1935.

Lugosi in spite of his fearsome screen reputation is really a simple soul, much like his *Raven* costar Karloff, who, according to Lugosi, is too gentle to be cast in horrendous roles. His rivalry with Karloff for the place of leading screen fiend is entirely a friendly one devoid of hogging the camera or stealing scenes.

7. Lugosi, Bela. Interviewed by Irene Thirer. "Bela 'Dracula' Lugosi a Regular Fellow — Pokes Fun at Jinx." *New York Daily News*, 3 July 1935.

We're very good friends [Boris and I]. In fact, we're costarred in *The Raven*, and when we were celebrating the completion of *The Raven*, we laughed over my sad mistake and his good fortune as far as *Frankenstein* is concerned. The difference in the way we work is that I believe solely in illusion, and Karloff uses heavy makeup with which I'm not in sympathy at all.

8. Lindsey, Cynthia. *Dear Boris*. (New York: Knopf, 1975).

I personally remember Boris' attitude toward Lugosi. In the late 1930s, the Karloffs, Jimmy and Lucille Gleason, Russell, and I were riding in the Santa Claus sleigh down Hollywood Boulevard, which becomes "Santa Claus Lane" during the holiday season. Every night the sleigh carries so-called celebrities who wave to the populace as Santa "Ho-ho-ho's" through a scratchy microphone. The night we rode, Santa was very, very drunk and commenting loudly on people in the profession, neglecting at times to switch off his microphone. Suddenly, a voice from the crowd cried, "Boris, Boris, down here!" It was Bela Lugosi loyally applauding his "compatriot." Boris waved back and shouted, "Bela, how are you, old boy!" "Boo," hiccuped Santa.

9. Karloff, Boris. Quoted in *Famous Monsters of Filmland*, 47 (Nov. 1967).

When a reporter inquired if he had been close friends with Lugosi, Karloff replied, "No, we really didn't socialize. You see our lives, our tastes, were quite different. Ours was simply a professional relationship. I'll tell you a story on myself and Bela. It was during the making of *Son of Frankenstein*, the third and last time I played the Monster. Bela was a big man, and I was supposed to pick him up and carry him. I put one wrist beneath his knees, the other behind his neck ... and lifted. I hadn't lifted a pound."

10. Hopper, Hedda. "Horror Men of Screen Just Pair of Home-Loving Folks, After All." *Los Angeles Times*, 14 Jan. 1940.

Lugosi told Hopper of his son's birth, saying, "I went through hell when our boy was born. It gave me such a scare and I was so nervous I took to smoking cigars." "But Bela," Karloff said, "I thought cigars made you more nervous?" Lugosi responded, "Not me; I smoke cigars without nicotine. It's the nicotine that makes you nervous."

11. Churchill, Douglas W. "Here We Go, Folks!" *New York Times*, 28 Jan. 1940.

To reassure doubters [of Manly Hall's hypnotism of Lugosi for a scene in *Black Friday*], Boris Karloff, costar of the epic, stated he was positive Lugosi was hypnotized because he had never seen his fellow actor keep his back to the camera for so long.

12. Underwood, Peter. *Karloff: The Life of Boris Karloff, with an Appendix of the Films in Which He Appeared* (New York: Drake, 1972).

Underwood's book includes a tale of director Arthur Lubin from the making of *Black Friday* (1940). When they met for the film, they realized each would be sans makeup in the new production. Karloff was wearing formal morning dress as Lugosi approached him in a plain blue suit. "Get away, I'm seeing a ghost," Karloff yelled. Lugosi responded, "Change your brand. It's only me and you ought to know!" Karloff answered, "Why ought I to know? I've never seen you before in my life." The Hungarian retorted, "I've never seen you without makeup either, if it comes to that," adding as he turned to Lubin, "and you can say for me that Karloff is definitely terrifying."

13. *The Devil Bat*. PRC Studios pressbook, 1941.

In Hollywood, scene of so many artistic and jealous feuds, the conduct of the leading Horror Men is a refreshing change from the usual pattern for these artists — rather than being envious of and embittered at each other — are not only friendly, but thoroughly interested in each other's work. They never fail to see their rivals' pictures and their discussions have helped each of them to improve their work which accounts for the amazing betterment of the quality of their type of production. Thus it was quite natural for Bela Lugosi to drop into a neighborhood theater one evening where one of Hollywood's other Bogey-Men

This beautiful lobby card from *Black Friday* (1940) illustrates the common billing of the two actors' names, with Lugosi's again following Karloff's.

was attempting to scare the audience out of its collective wits. "He was doing a mighty fine job, too," commented Lugosi, "for suddenly in a particular savage and horrifying scene, the young lady on my left, a perfect stranger, gave a terrific gasp and the next thing I knew she had thrown her head around and against my shoulder."

14. *"Arsenic and Old Lace." San Francisco Chronicle*, 7 Aug. 1943.

Bela Lugosi has in him the makings of a Jonathan Brewster which is the equal, or perhaps the superior, of Boris Karloff's masterful reading of the demented Brewster brother with a propensity for manslaughter.

15. *"Arsenic and Old Lace." San Francisco Examiner*, 7 Aug. 1943.

His [Lugosi's] interpretation [of Jonathan Brewster] was different from the already familiar one of Boris Karloff, but — barring occasional uncertainty — about equally effective.

16. Whitney, Dwight. "The World of Drama — Bela Lugosi." *San Francisco Chronicle. This World* Sunday Supplement, 8 Aug. 1943.

He [Lugosi] has never seen Boris Karloff play Jonathan Brewster in *Arsenic and Old Lace*. This he deems fortunate because an actor will automatically pick up certain mannerisms from watching another actor play the part, no matter how hard he may try to keep his interpretation absolutely original. Lugosi will play a role as he sees it; as far as he is concerned he's working in virgin territory.

17. "Bela Lugosi to Be Star of Hit Comedy at Ford's." *Baltimore News-Post*, 24 Feb. 1944.

A rather interesting surprise has been that the grosses since Bela Lugosi took over from Boris Karloff [in *Arsenic and Old Lace*]; they have been larger than before.

18. "The Theater—*Arsenic and Old Lace*." *Baltimore Sun*, 27 Feb. 1944.

This Mr. Lugosi, as any film fan can tell you, is no slouch, no understudy, no second fiddler. There was never a day when he couldn't stand toe to toe with Mr. Karloff on the screen and swap snarl for snarl, tooth gnash for tooth gnash, curse for curse, and murder for murder. He has been more active in pictures, particularly in recent years, than has Mr. Karloff; while the latter was absent on Broadway, Mr. Lugosi kept right on slaying ingenues, elderly extras, G-men and frightened women at a terrific rate; and his sinister phiz is quite as well-known as that of Mr. Karloff.

19. Watts, A.E. "Lugosi Now in *Arsenic*." *Boston Traveler*, 21 Mar. 1944.

Mr. Lugosi lacks the subtlety of Karloff's villainy [in *Arsenic and Old Lace*], but leaves no doubt when he gets sinister.

20. Eustace, Edward J. "A Witches' Sabbath." *New York Times*, 10 Dec. 1944.

In answer to J. Carroll Naish's statement that he started "all this monster business," Boris Karloff said, "No, not quite. Bela Lugosi started it in the talkies with the first, *Dracula*, a few months before I did *Frankenstein*. But it all goes back to Lon's [Chaney Jr.] dad."

21. Adams, Marjorie. "Bela Lugosi Glad of Respite from Horror-Inspiring Roles." *Boston Globe*, 17 Apr. 1947.

When asked "why no pictures of the shocking character are being made right now, Lugosi said it was because neither he nor Boris are under contract, and, due to labor troubles, the film companies have cut down on the number of productions and are using their contract players to save money."

22. Marlowe, Don. *The Hollywood That Was* (Fort Worth, Tex.: Branch-Smith, 1974).

It was about ten o'clock [in the late forties] and practically all of Rockford's inhabitants were indoors on this cold, snowy November night. As Bela and I walked briskly along the street, we noticed a brightly lighted stretch ahead of us. This turned out to be a long bridge, right in downtown Rockford [Illinois]. In the distance, we could make out the lone figure of a young boy about ten, coming toward us from the opposite direction. Lugosi, usually a modest man, but now in an elated mood, turned to me with a twinkle in his eye, and said: "He will spot me any minute, watch." As the boy approached us we could both see his expression of disbelief as he recognized Bela Lugosi. Bela was smiling and as we got near to the boy he said in a gentle voice: "Good evening, my young man." The astonished boy timidly returned the smile and managed to blurt out: "Could I have your autograph, please?" "Certainly," said Lugosi, turning to me with a triumphant grin. The boy took a piece of paper out of his pocket and I offered my pen to Bela. As he was about to sign his name, Bela paused momentarily and said to his young fan: "And, young man, what is my name?" Without hesitation, the boy said: "Boris Karloff."

23. Gordon, Richard. Letter to Gary Don Rhodes, 20 Aug. 1986.

I had also met Boris Karloff [in addition to Lugosi] and we had become friends. In my office, I had several autographed photos on the wall, including Karloff and Lugosi. I soon learned that it was wise, whenever I expected Bela at the office [during the early fifties], to remove the photo of Karloff and substitute someone else. Bela and Boris had been friends in their heyday at Universal but later Bela became bitter about Karloff's greater success and versatility, especially because he had originally turned it [*Frankenstein*] down because the part was a non-speaking one. As a result, James Whale found Boris Karloff for the film.

24. Lugosi, Bela. Quote, circa 1951, reprinted in "When Dracula Invaded England." *Famous Monsters of Filmland*, **35 (Oct. 1965).**

The horror business is certainly not what it used to be. Boris Karloff, a great horror specialist ... look what he is driven to do ... comedy stuff in New York.

25. Johnson, Erskine. "Bogey Man Has Way with Kids." *New York World-Telegram*, **5 June 1952.**

There's only one cross that bears over his merchant of menace character which started twenty years ago when he stepped out of romantic roles and played Dracula. "Every time I get into a cab — and this is without exception — the driver looks at me and says, 'Aren't you Boris Karloff?'"

26. Beaumont, Charles. Lugosi's comments to him in a 1952 conversation.

I called a friend of mine in New York [Karloff]. He was starving. I told him the part [in *Frankenstein*] was nothing, but perhaps he would make a little money. He came to Hollywood. He made the picture. Now Boris Karloff is on top and I am on the bottom. It is very funny.

27. Thomas, Bob. "For a Halloween Story, He Went to an Expert." *Los Angeles Mirror*, **30 Oct. 1953.**

"What about holding a wake with Boris Karloff," the reporter asked Lugosi. "Are you two on speaking terms?" Lugosi responded, "I haven't seen Boris for two or three years. I started him out as a bogeyman. After I did *Dracula* at Universal, they wanted me to do the monster in *Frankenstein*. But when I tested the makeup, it was heavy and painful. Then I read the script. I did not have a word of dialogue. I got out of the role by having my doctor say it would be bad for me. I suggested Karloff for the role. You might say I created my own Frankenstein monster ... competition for horror roles."

28. Sheffield, Richard. "Lugosi's Last Years: The Boy Who Befriended Bela." *Famous Monsters of Filmland*, **133 (Apr. 1977).**

Only twice do I recall him mentioning Karloff [in the years 1953–56]. He complained that Karloff had to stop at 4:00, no matter what, to have his tea. This seemed to annoy Bela. A few days before Bela died, he woke in the middle of the night insisting he had to get dressed and go into the living room as Karloff was there waiting to see him. [Lugosi had been drinking.]

29. Karloff, Boris. Interviewed by Collin Edwards in Carmel, California, (1959).

I worked with Bela Lugosi in, oh, probably, three or four pictures, but outside of the studio we didn't meet. In those days, I used to play a lot of cricket, which I don't think would have appealed to Bela. He had a tragic, tragic life that man. He really did. I've always felt extremely sorry for him. In a way, he was his own worst enemy. He was a fine actor, a brilliant technician in every sense of the word. He just didn't move with the times. When he came to America, he didn't really learn the language as well as he might have. I'm afraid those things were bad for him. An unhappy man ... an unhappy life.

30. Borland, Carroll. Letter to the Editor. *Monsterland*, **15 (Dec. 1986).**

I think that comparing Karloff and Lugosi is like comparing apples to oranges. They had different personalities, techniques and accents.

31. Lugosi Jr, Bela. Quoted in Lisa Mitchell's "*Wood* Tarnishes a Great Man — Lugosi." *Los Angeles Times*, **24 Oct. 1994.**

The so-called animosity between my father and Karloff existed in the publicity mills ... not in real life.

32. LeBerthom, Ted. "Demons of the Film Colony." *Weird Tales*, **(Oct. 1932).**

Was a gigantic hoax perpetrated on the author by "Dracula" Lugosi and "Frankenstein" Karloff, aided and abetted by the photographer?

For ten years I have been writing about the activities of the motion picture colony for what are known as the "fan" magazines, and, in strict justice to the one that befell me recently — for there is nothing weird, preternatural or otherwise affrighting about most motion picture people, from the child Jackie Cooper to the more elderly Marie Dressler. There have been, it is true, curious legends about Greta Garbo, but she stays away from interviewers. Whatever her secret, she keeps it.

Obviously, I could not relate the experience I had in the pages of a "fan" magazine. The readers of these magazines are too accustomed to sunshine to relish shadows. So I decided to submit to the readers of *Weird Tales* the ghastly details of gigantic hoax perpetrated on me by Bela Lugosi, star of the films *Dracula* and *Murders in the Rue Morgue*, and Boris Karloff, who played the monster in the film *Frankenstein*.

Candidly, for reasons which the reader may surmise before he finishes reading, I have hesitated considerably about writing of just what happened, but now I feel I should make what happened public.

I was just leaving Universal City one rainy, dreary morning when John Leroy Johnstone, Universal publicity director, called to me.

Ted, don't go away. I just happened to think that our two demons, "Dracula" Lugosi and "Frankenstein" Karloff, are coming here in a few minutes. A demons' rendezvous ought to interest you. I might add that they're hustling here from opposite directions, to meet for the first time. They actually have never met. You see, *Dracula* and *Murders in the Rue Morgue*, in which Lugosi starred, were made here at different times than *Frankenstein* in which Karloff played the ghastly, man-made monster. And that's why they've never met professionally. Nor have they ever met socially, although both have been in Hollywood, on and off, for several years. But you know the film colony. All split up into little groups and circles.

I didn't mind sticking around. For one thing, a murky drizzle had begun to fall outside. The mammoth Universal stages, seen through a window seemed in the grayness to be enormous squat tombs, unadorned sarcophagi in which giants five hundred feet tall stretched in death could be laid. It might not be a bad idea, I concluded, to wait around a little, if only to give the rain a chance to stop.

"Doggoned if it isn't just the kind of a morning for a couple of monsters to meet," laughed Johnstone. "And do you know something, I've a queer hunch something funny'll happen when they meet. Not that there's any professional rivalry between them in the demon field, as far as I know, but there's been a lot of banter going around the studio about the weird possibilities, you know, the things that could happen when Dracula meets the Frankenstein monster! Candidly, I wouldn't be surprised if they try to frame each other."

"What do you mean?" I chuckled nervously.

"Well," he countered, "it's natural that this meeting should strike them both as funny. And you know what actors are for pulling gags on each other."

The rain, increasing, muttered against the ground outside.

Boris Karloff was the first to arrive — and, fantastically enough in evening clothes, worn under a rain flecked overcoat which he tossed off with a mischievous, almost boyish fling.

We were introduced. And I learned, from his accent, then his admission, that his name is not Karloff, but that he is an Englishman with a most unfortunate name. But we won't go into that.

He is slender, debonair, graceful, with powerful shoulders and large strong hands, smooth iron-gray hair, darkly tanned skin, and lucent, deep-set brown eyes. A witty, casual, well-bred fellow, with one of those strong-boned, hollow-cheeked countenances that seems carved out of hickory, and is characteristic of so many well-traveled, weather-beaten, distinguished-appearing Britishers.

He joked waggishly, this Englishman from God knows where whose name is not Karloff, about his coming meeting with Bela Lugosi.

As he was talking and Johnstone and I were absorbed in his high spirits, the door leading to the studio outside evidently opened. No one saw it open. In fact, we did not see anything until Karloff, who faced the door as he chatted with us, suddenly looked up and asseverated startlingly, "Oh, my God!"

Johnsone and I looked around and I don't know what he thought or felt. I do know I became visibly disconcerted, to put it lightly.

There stood Lugosi, filling the doorway, quiet as death, and smiling in his curiously knowing way. It is the smile of a tall, weary, haunted aristocrat, a person of perhaps fallen greatness, a secretive Lucifer who sees too clearly and knows too much, and perhaps wishes it were not so, and would like to be gracious. He, too, was in evening clothes — on a rainy morning! He advanced with a soft springy tread.

Karloff stood up as if galvanized by some sudden irrevocable plan of action. Then he turned on the advancing Lugosi a cold, unbelieving stare that would have riveted another man in his tracks. But the tall, taper fingered Hungarian, drawing himself erect, continued to smile with unmistakably ghastly knowingness.

It was Lugosi's hand which was thrust forward first. As they shook hands they seemed to lock horns with their eyes. Only for a moment, however, for both broke into ear-to-ear grins.

"I hope I didn't scare you to death," Lugosi smiled, narrowing his eyes, and seeming to look right through the quondam monster.

"I hope I didn't scare you," parried Karloff mirthfully.

I could not be certain, but I thought Lugosi bristled, as if his demonical prowess had been challenged by a tyro in demonism.

Finally he said slowly,

"I think I could scare you to death."

Karloff struck a match, lit a cigarette, puffed a couple of times, and retorted with an air of whimsical scorn,

"I not only think I can scare your ears right off, Mr. Dracula, I'll bet you that I can."

Within the next few minutes a wager of a hundred dollars had been made. They would go into a deserted set within one of the vast, empty, tomb-like stages squatting in the rain outside. No lights would be turned on. They would tell each other stories — such stories of darkness, terror and madness that one or the other would either faint or cry out for the other to stop. The other would then be pronounced victor.

Publicist Johnstone, grinning a bit uncomfortably, as if he were somewhat ill, protested:

"There should be a referee. You go along, LeBerthom, and decide which one out-scares the other. And I'll tell you what. Take Ray Jones, the photographer, along. He can get incontrovertible evidence."

"I don't want to oppose your wishes," put in Lugosi, his eyes widening like wrathful alarm signals, "but I would rather be alone with Mr. Karloff. You won't need any evidence. All you may need is a doctor, a nerve and heart specialist. You see only one of us will walk off that stage. The other will be ... er ... carried off."

He said this with some heat, yet with a growing twinkle in his eyes, which gradually narrowed again. But Johnstone was obdurate.

And so, two tall actors in evening clothes, a photographer and a writer walked with bowed heads and hunched shoulders in the rain to reach the stage building with its unfortunate resemblance, for me, to a colossal sepulcher.

We entered a small door in the side, nearly tripping over cables that coiled like lifeless serpents about the floor in the dank, dusty atmosphere. Photographer Jones lit a match. We found our way to a set where, among other articles of furniture, there was a davenport. It was then agreed that Jones could take photographs if he and I would stand twenty-five feet away in a dark corner, and if he would use only noiseless flash powder.

The tall actors in evening clothes sat on the davenport. In the obscure gloom, we scarcely could discern their figures. But soon we were to hear a mournful voice, Lugosi's.

"Boris," he began in a gloating sonority. "What would say if this set, this stage, this studio, suddenly vanished, and you found that in reality you and I were sitting at the bottom of a pit? Ha! That would be convenient for you, wouldn't it? But of course I might provide some charming company—I might drag down into this pit an exquisite young woman. And I should indulge in a curious experiment that would cause your hair to turn white—and your stomach to turn inside out."

"Boris," he went on in a ghoulish, sickeningly exultant tone. "Women are thrilled by Dracula, the suave one. Women love the horrible, the creepy, more than men. Why does a woman always tell the story of her husband's death so often and with such relish? Why does she go to cemeteries? Tenderness? Grief? Bah! It's because she likes to be hurt, tortured, terrified! Yes, Boris! Ah, Boris, to win a woman, take her with you to see *Dracula*, the movie. As she sees me, the bat-like vampire, swoop through an open casement into some girl's boudoir, there to sink teeth into neck and drink blood, she will thrill through every nerve and fiber. That is your cue to draw close to her, Boris. When she is limp as a rag, take her where you will, do with her what you will. Ah, especially, Boris, bite her on the neck!

"The love bite, it is the beginning. In the end, you too, Boris, will become a vampire. You will live five hundred years. You will sleep in moldy graves by day and make fiendish love to beauties at night. You will see generations live and die. You will see a girl baby born to some woman and wait a mere sixteen to eighteen years for her to grow up, so that you can sink fangs into a soft white neck and drink a scarlet stream. You will be irresistible, for you will have in your powerful body the very heat of hell, the virility of Satan. And someday, of course, you will be discovered—a knife, after centuries, will be plunged into you, you will drop like a plummet into the bottomless sulphur pit. Yes Boris, that's the end—for you! For us! For, look at me, Boris ..."

"Ha! Ha! Ha! You fool, Bela," came Karloff's scornful pealing laugh in the darkness. "Why try that kindergarten stuff on me? You ask me to look at you, Bela. Well, look at me! Look ... look ... look ... and take an occasional glance upward, Bela. These two hands of mine, clenched together above my head, could descend at any moment, in a second, ay, even before I finish this sentence, if I wanted them to, they'd bash your distinguished head in as if it were an egg. Your brains would run out like the yolk of an egg and spatter your pretty tuxedo.

"Bela, a monster created by Frankenstein is not worried by your stories of sucking blood from beauties' necks. But did you see the movie *Frankenstein*, Bela? Did you see me take an innocent like girl, a child playing among flowers, and drown her? Some sentimentalists said I did it unknowingly. Bosh! I have done it a thousand times, and will do it a thousand times again. Bela, it's dark in here, but you know me. You know it was no accident or chance, but significant, that I—the Englishman from God knows where whose name is not Karloff—was called on to play that monstrous role! You know me, Bela, you know me. What's that bosh about five hundred years old! You know that both of us are nearly six thousand years old! And that we've met many times before, the last time not more than two hundred years ago. ... And you shouldn't have made that foolish wager. Admit it, Bela!" Karloff's voice shook with deep agitation.

"I wonder," came Lugosi's reply, dreary as a fog-horn in the semi-darkness. In the meantime, photographer Jones in his scarce-visible corner kept snapping pictures. The noiseless powder recurrently rose in puffs, so that — spookily enough — the scene resembled the laboratory of a medieval alchemist.

"Come, Bela — let's go. Er — Jones, LeBerthom," Karloff shouted hoarsely. "are you ready to go? Bela and I have found we're members of the same — well, we say lodge. We're therefore, quite unable to scare each other to death, for reasons you might not understand, even to oblige you. You'll just have to call it a draw."

"All right, we're ready to go," responded Jones, nervously enough for that matter. "And — say — I've used up my last match. Will one of you fellows strike one?"

I shall never know whether it was Lugosi or Karloff who struck the match. All I do know is that when the match was struck it apparently revealed, not Lugosi and Karloff on that davenport, but two slimy, scary monsters, dragon-like serpents, with blood-red venomous eyes. The apparitional things flashed before me so suddenly that I became sick to my stomach and made a rush, on buckling legs, for the exit — and the cool air.

Just as I reached it and noted fleetingly that the rain had stopped, and that my heart was pounding to the bursting point, and that I was strongly weak and giddy, Jones and the two tall actors in evening clothes came through the door. Jones was rather sober and unconcerned, but Lugosi and Karloff were laughing heartily over something or other.

"Will you have lunch with us?" Lugosi asked me, still grinning but with something of a physician's tender concern.

"No thank you," I replied, scarcely looking either at him or Karloff. "I have to hurry away."

And I did hurry away.

I am, of course, now convinced that what happened was their idea of a practical joke, that the slimy, scaly things I had seen, the things which had so frightened and sickened me in that fleeting moment were either the imaginings of my over-wrought mind — or some mechanically contrived illusions in which Jones had some share.

There are, of course, some who will wonder if I do not merely prefer this simple, comforting explanation to one that might cause Hollywood hostesses to fear to invite Lugosi and Karloff to social functions — and fear not to invite them!

Many people, deep down, still are superstitious. And there are many things in life we do not fully understand, such as why it is the destiny of certain human beings to portray certain roles — whether in real or "reel" life.

19. Sources and References

This chapter, divided into various sections, attempts not only to catalogue the modern coverage Lugosi has received through audio/visual means such as videotape and compact discs, but also to examine the history of documentary sources pertaining to him. Furthermore, likenesses of the actor in animated films, as well as verbal and visual references in motion pictures, are also covered. Arrangement is chronological in this chapter, except for the Visual Sources and Archival Sources sections which are alphabetically arranged.

Audio Sources

1. Bob Crosby Orchestra. *I'd Know You Anywhere* and *I've Got a One Track Mind.* **Decca, 1940.**

Decca placed both tunes — written by Jimmy McHugh and Johnny Mercer — on a single 78 rpm by Bob Crosby's big band; the tunes not only came from *You'll Find Out*'s score, but they mentioned the RKO film on their label. Bregman, Vocco, and Conn, Inc., printed sheet music for the film in 1940 as a 20-page booklet, including both of the above mentioned tunes and "The Bad Humor Man," "Don't Think It Ain't Been Charming," "Like the Fella Once Said," and "You've Got Me This Way."

2. Sherman, Allen. *My Son, the Vampire.* **Warner Brothers 5419, 1952.**

Written by Linda Southworth and sung by Sherman, the song on this 45 rpm record became the theme song for *Mother Riley Meets the Vampire* in its limited American release under the same title as Southworth's composition.

3. Dell, Gabriel. *Famous Monsters Speak.* **A.A. Records, 1963.**

A popular offering of the Captain Company through *Famous Monsters of Filmland* magazine, this LP featured Dell, a former "Bowery Boy," imitating various horror stars, including Lugosi in a skit called "Dracula's Return." Cherney Berg scripted this album, which pictured Lugosi and Boris Karloff on its cover.

4. Karloff, Boris. *An Evening with Boris Karloff and His Friends.* **Decca DL 74833, 1967.**

Boris Karloff narrated soundtrack clips from various Universal horror films, including *Dracula* and *Son of Dracula*. Decca contracted Forrest Ackerman to write the script for this album and released it in March 1967.

5. Bruce, Lenny. *Interviews of Our Time.* **Fantasy 7001, 1970s.**

This comedy LP ("a new orthopedic sound recording") includes brief imitations of Lugosi and Boris Karloff by Bruce.

6. *Boris Karloff/Bela Lugosi*. Command Performance LP-5, 1974.

This is an unimpressively packaged LP, releasing Lugosi's 1942 appearance on the *Suspense* radio program, with the flipside of Karloff starring in a radio version of *Arsenic and Old Lace*.

7. *Suspense/Bela Lugosi.* Mark 56 Records 611, 1975.

Produced by George Garabedian, this was another issue of Lugosi's 1942 *Suspense* episode. However, with beautiful cover art and a short speech by Bela Lugosi, Jr., recorded specifically for this LP, Mark 56 definitely surpassed the Command Performance album.

8. *The East Side Kids Come Out Fighting.* Murray Hill Records 57393, late seventies.

A three-record boxed set, this is nothing more than dialogue soundtracks from a trio of public domain East Side Kids B movies. Lugosi's *Spooks Run Wild* finds itself in the mix. No copyright date.

9. *The Great Radio Horror Shows.* Murray Hill Records 933977, late seventies.

Another Murray Hill three-record set, again released without a printed copyright date. "The Thirsty Death" episode of Lugosi's radio show *Mystery House* sees its only commercial release in this boxed collection.

10. Salter, Hans J., composer. *Music for Frankenstein, Dracula, the Mummy, the Wolf Man, and Other Old Friends.* Citadel Records CT 6026, 1978.

Hans J. Salter's various compositions (including *Black Friday* and *Son of Frankenstein*'s "Lament") are incorporated into a 24-minute suite called "Horror Rhapsody" for one side of this LP. Citadel Records reissued it in 1979 (CT 7012) as Horror Rhapsody, along with a French pressing (Decca 900-411) as *Horror Rhapsody/Malpertuis.*

11. Salter, Hans J., composer. *The Film Music of Hans J. Salter: The Ghost of Frankenstein, Magnificent Doll, Bend of River, Against All Flags.* Tony Thomas Productions TT-HS-1/2, 1979.

A suite from 1942's *Ghost of Frankenstein* is included on this LP, with music from Salter's scores for other, non–Lugosi films.

12. Salter, Hans J., composer. *The Ghost of Frankenstein.* Tony Thomas Productions TT-HS-3, 1980.

Another of the Salter LPs that Tony Thomas released, this one devotes itself entirely to the classic score from *Ghost of Frankenstein.*

13. Bauhaus. *Bela Lugosi's Dead* (picture disc). Teeny 2P, early 1980s.

The British rock band Bauhaus found much success with their song "Bela Lugosi's Dead," with it featured not only in their own music video, but also in the soundtrack of Tony Scott's 1983 film *The Hunger* (neither of which featured visuals of Lugosi). The tune was issued on an analog 45 rpm and stereo 12-inch disc in 1979, as well as on the LP collection *Bauhaus* 1979–1983, released on Bega 64. The picture disc LP, which became a picture compact disc single in the nineties, featured photos of Lugosi and the song title in glow-in-the-dark lettering. Teeny 2P released the picture disc LP, but no copyright date is listed on the actual record.

14. *Abbott and Costello Double Feature.* Metacom, Inc. 1985.

This audiocassette included Lugosi's appearance on Abbott and Costello's radio show, paired with Lucille Ball's guest shot on the same program. Artwork of Lugosi and Costello graced the cover.

15. The Manimals. *Blood Is the Harvest.* Rock River, Ohio, 1985.

A rock group called the Manimals cut this very obscure album, which originated from Rock River, Ohio. The tunes used such horror films as *White Zombie* and *Island of Lost Souls* for inspiration.

16. *Bela Lugosi Meets Alfred Hitchcock (On the Radio).* Radiola Records MR-1162, 1987.

Released as an LP and as an audiocassette, this represented the nineteenth in Radiola's "crime series." The two titans do not actually "meet," except in the cover artwork. Instead, this is merely another issue of Lugosi's 1942 *Suspense* episode, coupled with a non–Lugosi program helmed by Hitchcock.

17. *Plan 9 from Outer Space: Original Motion Picture Soundtrack*. Performance Records 391, 1989.

Producer Wade Williams released the dialogue track to Ed Wood's film on LP and later on compact disc through Performance. Another issue of the dialogue had been made in 1986 by Hippo Records, featuring Monroe Kidd's liner notes and the tag line commemorating the "thirtieth anniversary" of the film.

18. Alwyn, Kenneth, conductor. *The Bride of Frankenstein*. Silva Records, 1993.

This compact disc features the complete music to *The Bride of Frankenstein*, as played by the Westminster Philharmonic Orchestra. In addition a 5-minute, 54-second "Invisible Ray Suite," taken from Franz Waxman's 1936 score, rounds out the disc.

19. Penny, Andrew, conductor. *Hans Salter: Music for Frankenstein*. Marco Polo, 1993.

This CD edition of Marco Polo's "Film Music Classics" features the complete Salter score from *Ghost of Frankenstein* (1942), as well as that of a non–Lugosi film, *House of Frankenstein* (1944). Andrew Penny conducts the RTE concert orchestra of Dublin through each piece.

20. Alan, Josh. *The Worst!* Black Cracker Music, 1994.

This compact disc represents all musical numbers from Alan's stage musical *The Worst!*, based on the life of Edward D. Wood, Jr. Along with Alan are guest stars Cafe Noir, Phoebe Legere, Jennifer Griffin, Sara Hickman, and Kim Pendleton. Two numbers are devoted to Lugosi, one a violin instrumental entitled "Bela's Funeral Dirge," and the other a vocal number called "Bela Lugosi." Alan himself sings the latter, with such lyrics as "Got my top hat, got my cape ... got my vampire fangs on straight." The Lugosi pieces, as well as the entire musical, are both poignant and well performed. Artwork of Lugosi by Drew Friedman appears on the cover and throughout the CD booklet.

21. *Creepy Classics*. Warner Brothers, 1994.

Various horror-related compositions, such as Mussorgsky's "A Night on Bald Mountain," find their way onto this compact disc. Though no compositions from Lugosi films are included, Lugosi and Helen Chandler are featured on the cover photo.

22. Shore, Howard, composer. *Ed Wood: Original Soundtrack Recording*. Hollywood Records, 1994.

Shore, the composer, also produced this soundtrack to Tim Burton's film *Ed Wood*, released by Touchstone Pictures. In addition to the music associated with the Lugosi character in the film ("Mr. Lugosi/Hypno Theme" and "Eddie, Help Me," for example), Martin Landau's renditions of Lugosi's speeches from *Glen or Glenda* ("Pull the String!") and *Bride of the Monster* ("I Have No Home") are included.

23. Stromberg, William T., conductor. *The Music of Hans J. Salter and Frank Skinner*. Marco Polo, 1995.

This Marco Polo CD features the complete scores from *Son of Frankenstein* (1939) and *The Wolf Man* (1941), as well as the non–Lugosi film *The Invisible Man Returns* (1940). Stromberg conducts the Moscow Symphony Orchestra through each piece.

Visual Sources

Early sources of Lugosi films for home use were those companies actually duplicating 16 mm, 8 mm, and Super 8 mm motion pictures. For example, the National Cinema Service was responsible for duping numerous Lugosi titles on 16 mm. The monster craze of the sixties led Castle Films in particular to release Lugosi films onto such formats, usually in an abridged form. Super 8 mm was probably the most widespread, due to its low cost for equipment and purchasing prints. The majority of buyers at the time were younger readers of horror film magazines. *Dracula, The Human Monster, Son of Frankenstein, Frankenstein Meets the Wolf Man, Return of the Vampire,* and *Abbott and Costello Meet Frankenstein* were among the numerous Super 8 mm issues. Due to the brief nature of these versions, sometimes new names were given to segments of Lugosi films. For instance, portions of *Ghost of Frankenstein* became *Frankenstein's New Brain* and *The Trial of Frankenstein*. Super 8 mm remained a popular format into the later seventies, until the videocassette began to replace it.

In some ways, the canon of Lugosi's films has received the best representation on videotape and laser disc. While a few Lugosi horror films are noticeably absent from commercial release — specifically *Night of Terror* and *Chandu the Magician* — most are readily available from reputable companies. Several of his earlier American films have not been officially issued — such as *The Silent Command, Viennese Nights, Such Men Are Dangerous, Wild Company, Oh, for a Man, Renegades,* and *Best Man Wins* — though they often pass into the hands of collectors on tape formats like VHS.

Educational purposes have occasionally brought about the issue of Lugosi footage as well. In 1968, Teacher's Disc distributed 30 minutes of *Return of the Vampire* under the title *Return of Count Dracula*. The footage was dubbed into Spanish and released specifically for use in language courses. The Creative Film Society of Reseda, California, aimed several 16 mm compilation reels at the educational world during the seventies, including one named *Abbott and Costello Meet the Monsters*; it featured clips of Lugosi's 1948 film with the comedy duo. Another was *Monster Mosaic*, a 27-minute montage of clips from *Son of Frankenstein* and other horror films.

A few Lugosi films, *Dracula* in particular, were marketed briefly on RCA videodisc (a format far different from and much more primitive than laser disc). Also, though it has become outmoded in terms of widespread use, the Betamax ½-inch format embraced a large number of Lugosi films, though — with the exception of Sinister Cinema's catalogue — these have fallen out of print.

In addition to the popularity of Lugosi's Universal horror films and his outings with Ed Wood, one reason for the large number of Lugosi VHS videocassettes is the many Lugosi titles in the public domain. A number of his low-budget films, such as *White Zombie, The Devil Bat,* all nine Monogram films of the forties, and others, fall under the category of unrenewed copyrights. At present, anyone can sell duplicates of these films at will. Unfortunately, that means that poor source material, low-quality tape stock, and cheap packaging mark many of the "companies" releasing such films. Furthermore, such outfits have a tendency to drift in and out of business, making the availability of their product difficult to ensure.

Another problem is the various running times offered on certain Lugosi titles by various companies. Between typographical errors and occasional deceptiveness, many of the same companies releasing inferior products also shortchange buyers of footage. This problem is compounded by the variety of some film lengths, due to cuts made for early television, theatrical reissues, and so forth. *White Zombie*, for example, has been sold through numerous companies. Most of 13 such companies investigated provided copies of a visual quality inferior to that provided by more reputable dealers, the greater number being on low-quality tape and often recorded at slower speeds (a process that conserves tape, but at the same time degrades the quality of the duplication). Running times ranged from 59 minutes to 93 minutes, the former copy suffering the loss of numerous scenes and the latter proving a bold overstatement of the 68 minutes actually on the cassette. The packaging of one even declared the film's director to be Edgar O. Ulmer; in reality the director was Victor Halperin (and Ulmer's middle initial was actually G).

Similar problems and inconsistencies surface with many of Lugosi's other public domain titles, which are so often released by low-caliber companies. Other titles that fall into this category are *The Death Kiss, Murder by Television, The Mysterious Mr. Wong, The Dark Eyes of London* (aka *The Human Monster*), *The Gorilla, The Devil Bat* (aka *Killer Bats*), *The Invisible Ghost, Spooks Run Wild, The Ape Man, Black Dragons, The Corpse Vanishes, Bowery at Midnight, Ghosts on the Loose, One Body Too Many, Scared to Death, Mother Riley Meets the Vampire* (aka *Vampire Over London* and *My Son, the Vampire*), and *Glen or Glenda* (aka *I Led Two Lives* and *I Changed My Sex*).

As with the Super 8 mm films, videotapes and laser discs have not been shown to increase in value, but rather act as media to view these films at home. Certainly other media will follow and include in their selections Lugosi titles. In addition to the innumerable versions of his public domain thrillers, copyrighted Lugosi films have often been issued by the owners in different forms with various packaging. *Dracula* (1931) has been issued with a variety of packaging designs, including a laser disc bearing the "restored" label and as part of a VHS double-cassette boxed set with the 1931 *Frankenstein*. A listing of this kind is destined to become obsolete quickly given the rapid changes in the electronic world, but it is hoped that the following can act as a guideline to what films are available and through what reputable dealers they have been released. The listing covers standard, ½-inch VHS videocassettes, unless specifically marked "laser disc."

1. Bosko Video, 3802 East Cudahy Avenue, Cudahy, Wisconsin 53110-1234.

Bosko's issue of *The Phantom Ship*, which is matted so as not to crop any of the image, comes from an excellent print.

2. Discount Video Tape, P.O. Box 7122, Burbank, California 91510.

The Death Kiss as sold by Discount remains the essential commercial release with the color tints intact.

3. Feature Creature Home Video, P.O. Box 197, Montgomery, Illinois 60538.

Feature Creature took great pains to bring *The Deerslayer* to video, making it the only available Lugosi film of his German output.

4. Hollywood Home Theater, 19528 Ventura Boulevard, #320, Tarzana, California 91356.

You'll Find Out has been made available on videotape through this company.

5. Image Entertainment, 9330 Oso Avenue, Chatsworth, California 91311.

Image, which has licensed laser disc rights from various companies, has released *The Gorilla*, *You'll Find Out*, *Return of the Vampire*, *The Body Snatcher*, *Zombies on Broadway*, and *Plan 9 from Outer Space* (issued by itself and in the *Ed Wood Collection*, two-disc set) onto disc. The *Ed Wood Collection, Volume Two*, featured the first laser disc appearances of *Glen or Glenda* and *Bride of the Monster*. In 1995 Image released *The Val Lewton Collection*, which offered *The Body Snatcher* with a special audio track by director Robert Wise.

6. Lumivision, 1490 Lafayette Street, Suite 305, Denver, Colorado 80218.

Lumivision released a double-feature laser disc set of *Scared to Death* and *The Devil Bat*. Both were of outstanding quality and came with well-written liner notes by Buddy Barnett.

7. MCA/Universal, 70 Universal City Plaza, Universal City, California 91608.

Dracula, *Son of Frankenstein*, *The Invisible Ray*, *Murders in the Rue Morgue*, *Island of Lost Souls*, *The Wolf Man*, *Frankenstein Meets the Wolf Man*, *Ghost of Frankenstein*, *Abbott and Costello Meet Frankenstein*, *Night Monster*, *Black Friday*, *The Black Cat* (1934), and *The Raven* have all been issued through MCA. The first seven titles can also be obtained on laser disc, with *Dracula* having a particularly clean soundtrack, the rerelease trailer, and a collection of images (movie stills and posters) that can be accessed after the film ends.

Abbott and Costello Meet Frankenstein was issued on laser disc not only by itself, but also in the *Abbott and Costello Meet the Monsters* boxed set. MCA also paired *Murders in the Rue Morgue* and *Island of Lost Souls* for a laser disc issue that included coming attraction trailers along with the feature-length films. *The Black Cat* and *The Raven* were initially made available on one cassette and laser disc as a double feature, yet the frame rate had to be sped up just slightly to fit both into a two-hour time slot. Subsequent VHS releases found them issued separately.

8. Media Home Entertainment, 510 West 6th Street, Suite 1032, Los Angeles, California 90014.

This company issued *The Saint's Double Trouble* on VHS.

9. MGM/UA Home Video, 10000 West Washington Boulevard, Culver City, California 90232.

The 1935 classic *Mark of the Vampire* found new audiences through this videocassette release, as did *Ninotchka*. The latter has been issued on laser disc as well.

10. RCA/Columbia Home Video, 3500 West Olive Avenue, Burbank, California 91505.

Videocassettes of *Return of the Vampire* have been offered by RCA/Columbia.

11. Republic Pictures Home Video, 1236 Beatrice Street, Los Angeles, California 90066-0930.

Through Republic, colorized versions of *White Zombie*, *Black Dragons*, and *Scared to Death* were sold, though the latter is an odd case, as it was originally shot and released in natural color in 1946. Republic also released four Lugosi serials: *Return of Chandu*, *SOS Coastguard*, *The Phantom Creeps*, and *The Whispering Shadow*. Of the group, only *SOS Coastguard* has made it to laser disc.

12. Rhino Home Video, 10635 Santa Monica Boulevard, Los Angeles, California 90025-4900.

Rhino's home video selection includes a nice print of *Ed Wood's Plan 9 from Outer Space* and *Glen or Glenda*.

13. The Roan Group, P.O. Box 1615, Thomasville, Georgia 31799.

The Roan Group's 1995 laser disc of *White Zombie* far surpassed any previous offering of the film, garnering critical raves for its restoration. In addition to improved audiovisuals, the film was coupled with a sepiatoned 1951 reissue trailer, and came with booklet on the film written by Gary Don Rhodes and a reproduction of the 1932 campaign book.

The same company issued a laser disc of *The Human Monster* in 1996, pairing it with a non–Lugosi horror film called *Chamber of Horrors*. Again, the company succeeded in offering a superior version of a public domain Lugosi film.

14. Sinister Cinema, Box 4369, Medford, Oregon 97501-0168.

The oldest video company that specifically targets horror film fans, Sinister Cinema offers a multitude of Lugosi titles. *The Midnight Girl*, *White Zombie* (sold with a 1955 Lugosi television interview), *The Death Kiss*, *Return of Chandu* (serial and serial feature), *The Mysterious Mr. Wong*, *Murder by Television*, *The Phantom Ship*, *Postal Inspector*, *Shadow of Chinatown* (serial and serial feature), *SOS Coastguard* (serial and serial feature), *The Gorilla*, *The Phantom Creeps* (serial and serial feature), *The Human Monster*, *The Devil Bat*, *Invisible Ghost*, *Spooks Run Wild*, *Black Dragons*, *The Corpse Vanishes*, *Bowery at Midnight*, *The Ape Man*, *Ghosts on the Loose*, *One Body Too Many*, *Return of the Ape Man*, *Scared to Death*, *Vampire Over London*, and *Bela Lugosi Meets a Brooklyn Gorilla* have all been made available on VHS and Beta by Sinister. Furthermore, this company has compiled numerous tapes of coming attraction trailers, many of which include Lugosi titles.

15. Turner Home Entertainment, One CNN Center, Box 105366, Atlanta, Georgia 30348-5366.

Turner's catalogue includes *The Body Snatcher*, *Zombies on Broadway*, and *Genius at Work*.

16. Video Yesteryear, Box C, Sandy Hook, Connecticut 06482.

Video Yesteryear became involved in selling classic films on videocassettes early in the medium's consumer history. Among the Lugosi selection are *The Midnight Girl*, *White Zombie*, *The Death Kiss*, *Return of Chandu* (serial and serial feature), *The Mysterious Mr. Wong*, *Murder by Television*, *The Phantom Ship*, *The Gorilla*, *The Phantom Creeps* (serial and serial feature), *The Human Monster*, *The Devil Bat*, *Invisible Ghost*, *Spooks Run Wild*, *Black Dragons*, *Bowery at Midnight*, *The Corpse Vanishes*, *The Ape Man*, *Ghosts on the Loose*, *One Body Too Many*, *Scared to Death*, *The Boys from Brooklyn*, *Glen or Glenda*, and *Bride of the Monster*.

Documentary Sources

Various television and video documentary films have referenced Lugosi in some form or fashion, though most have used a few film clips and offered little — and sometimes erroneous — information. A large number of television programs have included features on Lugosi as well. Historian and collector Forrest J Ackerman has donned Lugosi's cape from *Plan 9 from Outer Space* for innumerable televised interviews, including appearances on *The Merv Griffin Show*, *The Tomorrow*

Show, and *Entertainment Tonight*. The latter allotted part of its Halloween program in 1984 to Lugosi clips, and a segment on the 1931 *Dracula* in its 1987 "Masters of Terror" series hosted by Vincent Price. Actor Louis Gossett, Jr., appeared in Lugosi's cape once on a program devoted to the hundredth anniversary of Hollywood. The Nostalgia Channel devoted a short *Starclips* program to Lugosi in the late eighties. Many television programs gave coverage to the release of Tim Burton's 1994 film *Ed Wood*, as well as to the struggle for a Lugosi postal stamp. The following represents the most important of these programs.

1. "Monsters We've Known and Loved." *Hollywood and the Stars*, broadcast 6 Jan. 1964.

This episode of David Wolper's 30-minute Hollywood and the Stars program included clips from *Return of the Vampire* and others.

2. *The Horror Hall of Fame*, broadcast 1972.

The Horror Hall of Fame and host Vincent Price offered a tribute to Lugosi, screening clips from *Mark of the Vampire* and *Return of the Vampire*. Price, Frank Gorshin, and makeup artist William Tuttle spoke about the Hungarian as well.

3. *The Mike Douglas Show*, broadcast Oct. 1975.

Arthur Lennig, author of *The Count*, Lillian Lugosi (the actor's fourth wife), and Bela Lugosi, Jr., guest-starred on Douglas's program shortly before G.P. Putnam's Sons printed Lennig's biography.

4. *In Search of Dracula*, broadcast 1975.

Hosted by Christopher Lee, this documentary found limited theatrical release and has since been aired numerous times on television. The entire history of the Dracula character is examined, from Vlad the Impaler to the present. A short segment on Lugosi's influence uses clips from *The Midnight Girl* and *Return of Chandu*. This documentary is not to be confused with the 1970s television program *In Search* of, with Leonard Nimoy which once "searched" for vampires and also screened a Lugosi film clip.

5. *The CBS Horror Show*, broadcast 6 Feb. 1979.

Host Anthony Perkins took CBS television viewers on a two-hour trip through the history of horror films, drawing on footage of such Lugosi films as *Dracula* and *Island of Lost Souls*. Lugosi and Karloff's chess game from a *Screen Snapshots* short subject was among the highlights of this documentary.

6. *Bela Lugosi: Behind the Cape*, W.I.L.L. Champaign-Urbana, Illinois, recorded 26 Aug. 1981, broadcast 2 Sept. 1981.

Lugosi fan Brian Cook and film historian Maurice Terenzio appeared on this episode of "Reeling It," showing clips of Lugosi (drawn from coming attractions and short subjects like *Intimate Interviews*) and sharing Lugosi stories. Cook was the producer of this program and Steve Izzo the director.

7. *Coming Soon*, 1982.

Hosted by Jamie Lee Curtis, this compilation of horror film clips acted as a tribute to coming attraction trailers. *Coming Soon* received a limited theatrical release before making its way to video. Clips from *The Wolf Man* and *Dracula* surface in this sinking documentary.

8. *Temps X* (France), broadcast Jan. 1986.

This program, presented weekly by two brothers named Igor and Grichka Bogdanoff, devoted an entire episode to Lugosi using the help of French film historian Jean-Claude Michel. The idea was to dispel the innumerable inaccuracies about Lugosi promoted to the French by the late

A fascinating portrait of Lugosi as the vampire from the midthirties.

Jean Boullet. Boullet had claimed Lugosi was exactly in private life as he was on the screen, living in a castle with black ceilings, red walls, and so forth. Michel must be lauded for correcting the erroneous "historical" rantings of Boullet.

9. *Hollywood Ghost Stories*, Warner Brothers, 1986.

John Carradine hosts this documentary, which features clips from such films as *You'll Find Out* (1941).

10. *Horrible Horrors*, Goodtimes Home Video, 1986.

Zacherley, famed television horror film host, provides on-screen narration and takes viewers through a series of film clips, including numerous bloopers from *Abbott and Costello Meet Frankenstein*.

11. *Lugosi: The Forgotten King*, MPI Home Video, 1986.

Operator 13 produced this documentary, written and directed by Mark Gilman and Dave Stuckey, in 1983, later broadcasting it on various PBS syndicates and the Discovery Channel. The 45-minute documentary draws on public domain clips of Lugosi, as well as interviews with Ralph Bellamy, Carroll Borland, John Carradine, and Alex Gordon. Forrest J Ackerman acts as the host for this production.

12. *Sinister Cinema*, KMEL cable access, San Jose Bay area, broadcast 1986.

Sonny Joe Fox (in reality Greg Luce) interviewed Bob Cremer, author of *Lugosi: The Man Behind the Cape*, on this program during 1986. That same year William K. Everson appeared and also spoke on Lugosi.

13. *The Lugosi Files*, Sinister Cinema, 1987.

Similar to *Mondo Lugosi*, this is another video compilation of Lugosi short subjects, trailers, and his appearance on the *You Asked for It* television show.

14. *Mondo Lugosi*, Rhino Home Video, 1987.

Not actually a documentary, *Mondo Lugosi* is instead a VHS collection of short subjects (including *Tribute to a Star!* and *Intimate Interviews*), as well as various coming attraction trailers for Lugosi films.

15. *Best of the Monsters*, Video Yesteryear, released to video in the late eighties.

Wayne and Schuster's examination of horror movies, broadcast in the days of black-and-white television included separate tributes to Lugosi and Boris Karloff. Video Yesteryear released this program to VHS and Beta videocassette during the late eighties.

16. *Monsters and Maniacs*, Donna Michelle Productions, 1989.

Written and directed by Ted Newsome of Heidelberg Films in 1988, this documentary is an outstanding series of clips from the history of horror films. Hostess Brinke Stevens exposes viewers to much information about and footage of Lugosi, as well as other horror film stars.

17. *Bela Lugosi: Then and Now*, Videosonic Arts, 1990.

This 50-minute film takes a walking tour of Lugosi's various homes and hangouts in the Hollywood area. Filmmakers Mike Copner and Buddy Barnett also use clips from a 1943 newsreel, with Lugosi donating blood to the war effort.

18. *Hollywood Heaven: Tragic Lives, Tragic Deaths*, Goodtimes Home Video, 1990.

"There's more to the stars than meets the eyes!" this documentary proclaimed. With clips compiled by Sandy Oliveri, this film includes a five-minute segment on Lugosi's career and drug addiction.

19. *Hooray for Horrorwood!* Dynacomm Home Video, 1990.

Forrest J Ackerman stars in this tour of his collection, reminiscing about the various horror film stars he knew. Memories and collectibles relating to Lugosi make up a part of this Ray Ferry documentary.

20. *The Horror Hall of Fame*, syndicated Oct. 1991.

This syndicated television awards program featured a tribute to Lugosi, with his grandson accepting on his behalf.

21. *Dracula: A Cinematic Scrapbook*, Rhino Home Video, 1991.

Writer/director Ted Newsome compiled

this collection of clips and photographs in an attempt to cover the history of Dracula in the cinema. Various footage of Lugosi is used, as is also the case with the companions to this documentary, *The Wolf Man: A Cinematic Scrapbook* and *Frankenstein: A Cinematic Scrapbook*.

22. *The Horror of It All*, **MPI Home Video, 1991.**

Produced by Wombat Productions and shown on PBS in the seventies, this documentary was directed by Gene Feldman and narrated by Jose Ferrer. Clips from *White Zombie* are seen, as well as photographs from *Dracula*, *The Gorilla*, and others.

23. *Monsters We've Known and Loved*, **Burbank Home Video, 1991.**

Not to be confused with the episode of *Hollywood and the Stars* which used the same title, this documentary includes a quick segment about Lugosi.

24. *On the Trail of Ed Wood*, **Videosonic Arts, 1991.**

From the makers of *Bela Lugosi: Then and Now* comes this investigation into the world of Ed Wood. Conrad Brooks speaks extensively about Wood, mentioning also his acquaintance with Lugosi.

25. *Fear in the Dark*, **Pacific Arts Video, 1992.**

This compilation of clips features scenes from *Dracula* (1931), as well as various non-Lugosi horror films.

26. *Flying Saucers Over Hollywood: The Plan 9 Companion*, **Atomic Pictures, 1992.**

Produced by Mark Carducci, this documentary covers not only *Plan 9 from Outer Space* but the world of Ed Wood. Many of the transvestite's cronies speak about their acquaintance with Lugosi. Lee Harris narrates this 111-minute videotape. Subsequent releases of the film appeared under the title *The Ed Wood Story*.

27. *Famous Monsters of Filmland World Convention*, **Dynacomm Entertainment, 1993.**

A visual scrapbook of the *Famous Monsters* convention held in Washington, D.C., in 1993, this Ray Ferry–directed video includes such figures as Bela Lugosi, Jr., Carroll Borland, and screenwriter Curt Siodmak.

28. *Ed Wood: Look Back in Angora*, **Rhino Home Video. 1994.**

A lighthearted romp through the world of Ed Wood, this film interviews his widow, Kathy Wood, and is narrated by Gary Owens. Many photographs and film clips of Lugosi find their way into this 50-minute documentary.

29. "Bela Lugosi: Hollywood's Dark Prince." *Biography*, **Arts and Entertainment, broadcast 27 Oct. 1995.**

Written by David Skal and produced by Kevin Burns, *Biography* covers the entire life and career of Lugosi. Film clips include color home movies, the actor giving blood for the war effort, and various excerpts from his films. On-camera interviews with Bela Lugosi, Jr., Ray Walston, Richard Sheffield, Forrest Ackerman, and Martin Landau add further insight.

30. "Frankenstein vs. Dracula." *Rivals*, **Discovery Channel, broadcast 27 Oct. 1995.**

Produced by Hearst Entertainment, *Rivals* looks at the relationship between Lugosi and Boris Karloff. Among those interviewed are Sara Jane Karloff, Richard Sheffield, Gary Don Rhodes, and Gregory Mank. Rare footage includes clips from a 1934 newsreel of Bela Lugosi and Boris Karloff judging black cats.

Multimedia Sources

1. ***Microsoft Scenes: Hollywood Collection*, Microsoft Corporation, 1994.**

In addition to the multiple audio bites and photographs traded via cyber sources like the Internet and America Online, Lugosi meets the computer age through this IBM-compatible CD-Rom featuring information and actual film clips of Lugosi and a host of other stars.

Theatrical References

1. Viaggio, Vincent. *The Man Who Is Dracula.* **Nat Horne Theater, New York City, 12 Jan.-Feb. 1979.**

Peter Umbras portrayed Lugosi under Robert Fuhrman's direction for this production of Viaggio's play.

2. Tábori, László. *Love the Actor! A Drama in Two Parts.* **Written in Hungary during the eighties.**

Written by playwright Tábori, this play (which by 1996 had not seen production in the Western Hemisphere) features Lugosi during a low ebb of his career, matching wits with the ghost of Bram Stoker.

3. Alan, Josh and Richard Jaccoma. *The Worst! A Low Tech Musical.* **First draft completed on 24 Dec. 1993.**

Alan and Jaccoma's musical, with music and lyrics by Alan, refers to itself as a "musical fantasy based on the career of Ed Wood, Jr." Lugosi appears as a prominent character throughout, crooning a song after purchasing morphine from a "reefer man." Though no production had occurred by the end of 1996, a compact disc of Alan's music has been pressed.

4. Gooch, Peter, with music by Little Jack Melody. *Hubcaps Afire Over Hollywood: The True Fantasy of Ed Wood, Jr.,* **Hip Pocket Theatre, Fort Worth, Texas, 7–30 Oct. 1994.**

Gooch not only wrote this two-act play, but also directed the Fort Worth production and starred as "Older Ed Wood, Jr." Dick Harris took the role of Lugosi. One review called it a "jumbled, but lovable tribute."

Animation References

1. ***Mickey's Gala Premiere*, Walt Disney Studios, 1933.**

This short cartoon features caricatures of almost every major star of the thirties attending the premiere of a new Mickey Mouse cartoon. Lugosi, Karloff, and Fredric March are represented respectively as Dracula, Frankenstein's monster, and Mr. Hyde. Though the likeness of Lugosi is not terribly strong, clearly it is meant to be him ... as these are supposedly actors attending a movie premiere.

2. ***G-Man Jitters*, Terrytoons, 1939.**

Released on March 10, 1939, this Gandy Goose short cartoon presented Dracula and Frankenstein, with the vampire looking much more like Lugosi than in *Mickey's Gala Premiere.* Interestingly, Lugosi rarely became a cartoon caricature in animated films, whereas Peter Lorre was a very prominent villain. Perhaps this is due as much to Lorre's connection with Warner Brothers — producers of "Looney Tunes" — as anything else.

"I was fascinated, enthralled... His hands, his voice, his gestures"—Richard Sheffield.

3. *Fantasia*, **Walt Disney Studios, 1940.**
One segment of this feature-length cartoon built itself around Mussorgsky's composition *A Night on Bald Mountain*. The studio hired Lugosi to perform in live-action footage, which was then supposedly used by Bill Tytla in animating Tchernabog, the Black God in the Mussorgsky sequence. Later, those who worked on the project claimed Tytla did not use the Lugosi footage for reference. Leopold Stokowski conducted the Philadelphia Orchestra for this powerful piece of animation.

Visual References

1. *Revolt of the Zombies*, **1936.**
Though Lugosi was not signed to play in this Halperin Brothers follow-up to *White Zombie*, closeups of his eyes from his 1932 zombie outing are used.

2. *Dr. Terror's House of Horrors*, **1943.**
Clips from some five horror films, *Vampyre*, *The Living Dead*, *The Golem*, and Lugosi's *White Zombie* and *Return of Chandu*, were re-edited into a "new" story for this little-seen roadshow effort. Producer Max

Rosenberg was evidently so pleased with the title that when he worked with Hammer Studios in the sixties it became the moniker for a 1965 Christopher Lee film.

3. *The Blob*, 1958.

Though Lugosi is not seen, his name appears on the marquee of the film theater that the audience flees from as the Blob oozes from the projection room.

4. *The World of Abbott and Costello*, 1965.

Narrated by Jack E. Leonard, this compilation of Abbott and Costello comedy clips included segments from *Abbott and Costello Meet Frankenstein*.

5. *Games*, 1967.

Footage of *Dracula* (1931) appears in this late sixties film with Simone Signoret.

6. *Head*, 1968.

The Monkees romped through this feature film with the aid of *The Black Cat* (1934) footage.

7. *The Love Machine*, 1971.

Dyan Cannon and Jackie Cooper star in this mediocre film, which used clips from *Dracula* (1931).

8. *Fade to Black*, 1980.

Dennis Christopher portrays a film buff gone insane in this thriller, dressing up as his favorite screen villains to go on murder sprees. He patterns himself after Lugosi in one sequence.

9. *It Came from Hollywood*, 1982.

John Candy, Cheech and Chong, Dan Aykroyd, and Gilda Radner introduce clips to bad movies in this somewhat unfunny film. The film targets *Plan 9 from Outer Space*, *Glen or Glenda*, and *Bride of the Monster* for would-be laughs.

10. *Rumble Fish*, 1983.

Francis Coppola's direction of Mickey Rourke, Matt Dillon, and Diane Lane results in a moody, stylish adaptation of S.E. Hinton's novel. *Shadow of Chinatown* surfaces in quick clips.

11. *Fright Night*, 1985.

Portraying an aging horror film star, Roddy McDowell faces vampire Chris Sarandon. While McDowell is shivering at his apartment, his movie memorabilia is seen to include a painting of Lugosi.

12. *Into the Night*, 1985.

Jeff Goldblume and Michelle Pfeiffer star in this John Landis film; footage from *Abbott and Costello Meet Frankenstein* is also featured.

13. *Amazon Women on the Moon*, 1987.

Directors Joe Dante, John Landis, and others helmed various segments of this comedy, which starred everyone from Steve Allen to B.B. King to Michelle Pfeiffer. Footage from *Island of Lost Souls* finds a home in this comedy.

14. *Basket Case 3*, 1992.

Frank Henelotter's third installment in the *Basket Case* series used clips of *The Devil Bat*.

15. *The Hand That Rocks the Cradle*, 1992.

Annabella Sciorra headlined this popular but predictable thriller, which thrilled movie buffs by using footage of *White Zombie*.

16. *Innocent Blood*, 1992.

John Landis, director and horror film buff, fits a few seconds of *Abbott and Costello Meet Frankenstein* into this vampire flick.

17. *The Runestone*, 1992.

Critics heavily panned writer/director Willard Carroll's B horror film, but many audiences enjoyed seeing clips of *White Zombie*.

18. *Ed Wood*, 1994.

For years, biographical films about Bela

Lugosi have been planned. Ed Wood was to direct Peter Coe in a concept from Blue Dolphin Records, which also wanted Wood to write a book about Lugosi. Another project was to use a script by Anthony Shaeffer. In 1985 trades announced that Michael Callan and Phil Marshak had purchased the screen rights to the Lugosi story. At one point, rumors claimed Robert DeNiro would portray Lugosi for a film. Marc Cramer penned yet another American script based on the Hungarian, while rumors of a French biopic surfaced in the eighties.

The first dramatized version of Lugosi's life on film, however, is in this Tim Burton–directed effort, with Martin Landau starring as the aging Lugosi. Johnny Depp played Ed Wood, with George "the Animal" Steele starring as Tor Johnson. The stark, black-and-white film, though it failed at the box office, became a critical success and won numerous awards. Photos of the real Lugosi can be seen in Landau's home, as can clips from *White Zombie*.

Many of Lugosi's friends were disappointed at the erroneous portrayal: having Landau use foul language, being harassed at the premiere of *Bride of the Monster*, being thrown out of the hospital for lack of money, and scowling terribly at the mention of Boris Karloff. In addition, several high points of Lugosi's last years, such as his marriage to Hope Lininger, his friendship with Richard Sheffield, and his role in *The Black Sleep*, are conveniently left out. However, the part comes alive through Landau's acting and Rick Baker's makeup. Despite the dramatic license, the portrayal is transformed into a sympathetic and respectful one.

Landau subsequently won Best Supporting Actor awards from the Los Angeles Critics, New York Critics, the Golden Globes, and the Academy Awards. He accepted his Oscar on March 27, 1995, though producers cut his speech before he could thank Lugosi. The film, however, failed at the box office, grossing only $5.8 million on its initial theatrical run.

19. *Possessed by the Night*, 1994.

Fred Olen Ray's low-budget horror effort costars Lugosi, via the cover of Ronald Borst's book *Graven Images*.

20. *Midnight Son*, 1995.

Director Jerome Cook's surreal, experimental short subject becomes a quite unusual tribute to Lugosi. Within the film's 12 minutes, Cook offers shots of Lugosi from *Dracula* and an array of other images, ranging from a 1991 fire to clips from *Nosferatu* (1922). Vilem Krinz offers bizarre narration in Czech, drifting into English for the line "Actor, Addict; Dracula, Morphine."

21. *Nadj*a, 1995.

An unusual vampire film, *Nadja* integrates images of Lugosi from *White Zombie* (1932) into its plot.

22. Christopher Lee Dracula films.

For many of the Hammer series of Dracula films, including *Dracula Has Risen from the Grave* (1968) and *Scars of Dracula* (1970), actor Chris Lee wore an exact replica of Lugosi's Dracula ring. Forrest J Ackerman, owner of the original, gave Lee the replica.

23. Television programs.

Clips of Lugosi have been incorporated into numerous television programs, including Rod Serling's *Night Gallery*, in which *Island of Lost Souls* appeared briefly. *The Twenty-First Century* used footage from *The Mysterious Mr. Wong*, while HBO's comedy program *Dream On* often used quick clips of Lugosi.

Verbal References

Lugosi, certainly an icon of twentieth century entertainment, has been referred to in a large number of television programs and feature films. References to him in relation to horror or Dracula have been made in passing innumerable times. In feature films, his name has been heard in Rouben Mamoulian's *Golden Boy* (1939), Joseph Mankiewitz's *Somewhere in the Night* (1943), John Huston's *Casino Royale* (1967), Woody Allen's *Sleeper* (1973), Boris Sagal's *Diary of Anne Frank* (1980), and the unfortunate comedy *Weekend Pass* (1984). Also, while Lugosi's name is not directly used in *Love at First Bite* (1979), George Hamilton's portrayal shows the Hungarian's major influence. Hamilton himself paid respects to the Hungarian that year at Lugosi's star on the Hollywood Walk of Fame.

In television, his name has been mentioned on *M*A*S*H**, *The Honeymooners*, *Sledge Hammer*, *Seinfeld* (in an episode about *Plan 9 from Outer Space*), and twice on *Sanford and Son*. Frankie Avalon once even did an impression of Lugosi on *Here's Lucy*, asking "what if" Bela—rather than Jimmy Cagney—had starred in *Yankee Doodle Dandy*. Furthermore, his name was mentioned on a television documentary called *Abbott and Costello Meet Jerry Seinfeld*.

Television Sources

From the early days of television to advertisements for the Sci-Fi Channel in the nineties, Lugosi has long been a staple of television fare. Even though he performed on only a handful of television programs, his movies have been constantly generating new fans since the fifties. A few Lugosi movies surfaced on television before his death, and the actor himself watched several with his friend Dick Sheffield; he also balked at receiving no monetary remuneration for the broadcasts. At any rate, television has helped keep alive the canon of Lugosi's horror films, with innumerable broadcasts through the years. Cable expansion in the nineties meant networks like the Sci-Fi Channel, which have held "festivals" and "tributes" to his work.

Many "horror film hosts" have shown Lugosi's work, from Bob Wilkins to Elvira. One short-lived horror hostess, Jo Rowan, was even known as "Stella Lugosi." But, perhaps the most important broadcasts became the early "Shock" packages, which exposed television audiences to his Universal films for the first time. Ninety major cities broadcast "Shock Theater," though the most popular host was certainly "Zacherley" of WABC–New York, formerly "Roland" of WCAU–Philadelphia. Renewed interest in classic horror films and Lugosi occurred, and the monster craze of the sixties, helped also by *Famous Monsters of Filmland* magazine, took off.

1. The *Shock* television package, 1957.
This package included the following Lugosi films, shown on television for the first time that year: *Dracula, Murders in*

the Rue Morgue, *The Black Cat* (1934), *The Raven*, *The Invisible Ray*, *Son of Frankenstein*, and *The Wolf Man*. Universal's agreement with Screen Gems to allow television broadcasts of the films constituted the studio's first distribution deal of old films to the new medium. New York City's debut of Shock began with *Dracula* on October 3, 1957.

2. The *Son of Shock* television package, 1958.

The second package of Universal horror films sold to television, which was also sprinkled with a number of Boris Karloff/Columbia Pictures efforts, included two Lugosi films, *Black Friday* and *Ghost of Frankenstein*.

Archival Sources

Various archives have been maintained for the preservation of motion picture history. Often these attempt to preserve films and keep files on those who participated in the productions. Now, with the easy availability of most Lugosi titles on videocassette, and the large output of written material that has almost exhausted the information in such files, most of these archives are not of critical interest to the Lugosi enthusiast, though much praise should be given to them. Also, in addition to files buried in museums, various exhibits focusing on the horror film have been shown, including *Screams on Screen: 100 Years of the Horror Film*, at the New York Public Library for the Performing Arts (October 31, 1994 to April 29, 1995). A great many of the rarest items, such as artifacts owned by Lugosi (including pipes, letters, cigarette cases, paintings, ration books, scrapbooks, furniture, the cape from *Abbott and Costello Meet Frankenstein*, pants from *Voodoo Man*, and much more), are in the hands of private collectors. The following should offer the most pertinent sources available to the researcher and collector.

1. The Ackerman Archives, Hollywood, California.

Ackerman's collection, touted for decades as the most extensive archive of horror film memorabilia, was in 1953 visited by Bela Lugosi himself. In addition to thousands of still photographs, movie posters, and books, the collection includes a multitude of "one of a kind" items, such as Lugosi's "Dracula ring," and the cape he wore in *Plan 9 from Outer Space*. Despite an Ackerman auction in 1989, and the multiple thefts from the collection through the years, the Ackerman Archives remain an incredible and vastly important collection.

2. Hungarian Film Institute and Film Archive, Budapest, Budakeszi, Hungary.

This collection holds 35 mm prints of portions of both *Casanova* (1918) and *Küzdelem a létért* (1918), as well as various photographs and clippings on Lugosi's Hungarian period.

3. International Museum of Photography at the George Eastman House, Rochester, New York.

Among this museum's collection of films are two very rare Lugosi titles, *Dance on the Volcano* and *Daughters Who Pay*.

4. Library of the Performing Arts, Lincoln Center, New York City, New York.

This archive features the performing arts holdings of the New York City Public Library. Among its collection are original playbills from all of Lugosi's English-language stage appearances in New York, microfilm copies of pressbooks for almost every U.S. and British Lugosi film, and a large photo collection. The Lugosi clipping file has been thoroughly ravaged by thieves over the years, but it still has historical value.

5. Margaret Herrick Library, Academy of Motion Picture Arts and Sciences, Beverly Hills, California.

The library for the Motion Picture Academy of Arts and Sciences has an extensive Lugosi file on microfilm, as well as most film publications and trade journals that covered the actor and his films. Unfortunately, before its Lugosi file was transferred to its present form, many items were stolen.

IV. Critique and Appreciation

20. Image, Apparition, and Icon

Though on the surface Lugosi's fate echoes the all-too-familiar story of the rise and fall of a "star," in many ways he can be viewed as a unique figure. Certainly after his ascendancy via *Dracula* (1931) Lugosi refused to become what the studio and press desired: a second Lon Chaney. Similarly, he could not attain his own goal as an actor; instead, he became trapped and typecast due to the image he created. Lugosi the professional actor virtually became the professional Dracula. The Hungarian's plight became problematized further not just by studios, critics and censors, but by the public at large. Changing tastes of moviegoers resulted in changing views toward their Dracula.

In other words, earlier attempts to find a single reason for his decline fail in their naïveté toward history; more accurately, there were several key factors in the fall of Lugosi's dimly lit star. The image, steeped as it was in the generally popular Transylvanian vampire, found agreeable multiplicity only after Lugosi's death. While this provides a firm ground for the Bela "Dracula" Lugosi legend and birth of an icon, the actor rarely shared its success during his lifetime.

A major factor in Lugosi's stardom immediately following *Dracula* (1931) was the desire to designate him as the heir to Lon Chaney, Sr., the "man of a thousand faces" who captivated audiences in the twenties with his grotesque but amazing makeup and acting through roles in *The Hunchback of Notre Dame* (1923), *The Phantom of the Opera* (1925), *London After Midnight* (1927), and others. Though most of Chaney's films might not immediately be considered "horror films," his bizarre characterizations on the whole embodied the closest American cinema in the twenties came to the genre. The classic supernatural films of Europe such as *Witchcraft Through the Ages* (1922), *Nosferatu* (1922), *The Student of Prague* (1926), and others were little seen by audiences in the United States. Therefore, some Chaney films acted as proto-horror cinema for the Roaring Twenties.

Moreover, Chaney's star shone brightly enough to command tremendous appeal at theaters, with his death in 1930 prematurely ending studio profits. "Clara and Lon Are 'It' with Theatre Owners," a January 1930 *Exhibitor's Herald-World* announced. Bow and Chaney were the top box office moneymakers for the previous year. In addition to Chaney's being a dominant image of the bizarre, he meant money to studios. His popularity extended even beyond his premature death, with tremendous amounts of fan mail still arriving at the studio in 1931 and 1932. Both years also saw *Photoplay* print more on the late pantomimist than on either Lugosi or Boris Karloff. Clearly, Universal Studios desired a replacement.

This publicity shot highlights the slicked hair, aristocratic profile, tarantula-like fingers, and hypnotic eyes that associated the actor so closely with the Dracula image he created.

Therefore, the determination for Lugosi to become the next Lon Chaney was not slight. Universal Studios' hopes for a replacement for the "man of a thousand faces" were clear not just in the initial desire for Lugosi to be the monster (rather than the doctor) in *Frankenstein*, but in such immediate thoughts about a remake of Chaney's masterpiece, *The Hunchback of Notre Dame* (1923). Universal's plans were of course motivated by purely economic ambitions.

Furthermore, magazines and newspapers strove obsessively to bestow Chaney's crown. An article by John Sinclair in January 1932 asked pointedly, "Has Bela Lugosi inherited the mantle of Lon Chaney?" The actor himself quickly responded, "I have always said I would rather play — say Percy Marmont roles than Lon Chaney types of things." His aversion to portraying the monster of Shelley's *Frankenstein* (1931) exemplifies the action he took consciously to avoid the Chaney syndrome in its rudimentary form: heavy makeup. Later, as in Paramount's *Island of Lost Souls* (1933) and Universal's *Son of Frankenstein* (1939), Lugosi did find himself buried alive under an avalanche of makeup. Jack P. Pierce cited the latter film as an example of an actor's inability to escape his own fate. Yet even though Lugosi on other occasions fell into this category, in *Frankenstein Meets the Wolf Man* (1943) and *The Ape Man* (1943), the use of a "thousand faces" through makeup really was not his cinematic fate.

The same month that Sinclair's article hit newsstands, much of America saw *Frankenstein* (1931) animated into life by Boris Karloff. By late August 1932 columnists moved in their quest from Lugosi to Karloff, asking if the latter were "Filling Chaney's Shoes?" On August 27, for example, the *Los Angeles Times* proclaimed, "He is well on his way to being Lon Chaney's successor." *Photoplay* said of the film *Frankenstein*, "It introduces a successor to the late Lon Chaney, who out-horrors anything Chaney ever gave us." *Vanity Fair* also spoke of Karloff as the true heir to Chaney's throne.

By September 1, 1932, Mollie Merrick's column mentioned that Charles Laughton, star of *Island of Lost Souls* (1933), would soon "occupy something of the place Lon Chaney had in films." Even later, in a December 3, 1932, article, a journalist announced that Lionel "Mystery" Atwill, headlining Warner Brothers' *Mystery of the Wax Museum*, was fast becoming "the best successor to Lon Chaney the colony has ever found and that Boris Karloff—the present king of the weird and wonderful—is no longer alone in his field."

Dracula underscored Lugosi's romantic possibilities, but due to the burgeoning horror genre, the same qualities instead led to horror. Nonetheless, the potential was present. *Vanity Fair* spoke of the 1927 stage *Dracula* in very sexual terms, claiming Lugosi to be the "masterworker of those Ghosts de Gotha who stir up such pleasurable fits and desires, in the current dramatization of Bram Stoker's most shudderful romance of Dracula, that celebrated commuter from the grave to the bedside." Speaking of the film, the same publication called Dracula's life one of "amourous dalliance," that he possessed the erotic "love bite." Lugosi himself once referred to the power of the tale as "a biological thing," speaking also of the sexually charged "Dracula Kiss." Universal publicity called *Dracula* a "love story," with numerous magazines referring to the enormous amount of mail the actor received from women.

Yet even beyond such popular descriptions of Dracula in a romantic and sexual light, the most telling evidence comes in the Lugosi performance itself. Along with the vampire-victim relationship in which the former pursues the latter in an attempt not only to control but to captivate, the obvious similarity between blood and semen exists. The penetration of the teeth and complete domination further suggest a sexual encounter. To these qualities, the image of Lugosi added a romantic quality. Rather than the pestilence of Murnau's vampire in *Nosferatu* (1922) or the old man of Stoker's novel, Lugosi offered not just the sexuality of a vampire but a romantic and charming incarnation of it. Juxtaposed against this is the fact that Dracula remains a sexual criminal, exerting his influence without necessarily obtaining permission.

However, just as Lugosi did not become the "new Chaney," he also did not move from Dracula to romantic roles. His image and its irrevocable connection with Dracula's more horrifying elements left him helpless in the vampire's clutches. He continued as Dracula, with publicists seizing on the opportunity just as they had earlier attempted with the Chaney name. One side of this problem occurred through his screen and stage billing, with many advertisements of the thirties and forties crowning him Bela "Dracula" Lugosi. "The original Dracula," "our friend

Lugosi beams confidence and a smile to the newsreel cameraman in the film *International House* (1933).

Dracula," "the most experienced of bat-men," and so many more phrases also became attached to his name in publicity materials and critical reviews. On the LP record *An Evening with Boris Karloff* (Decca, 1967), the British actor pronounced, "Count Dracula. Bela Lugosi. One and the same."

Lugosi realized very well the effects of the situation, once asking, "Suppose you were introduced as a vampire bat every place you went? Well, that's the way it is with me. It's gotten so almost nobody but my wife calls me by my right name." Yet at times he embraced what he called the "Dracula curse," naming one of his dogs Dracula, referring to one of his homes by that name, and even by the late forties calling the image he created a "trademark." On another occasion, he said, "I feel a paternalism toward the character very much akin to that which Frankenstein certainly must have felt for the monster he created." Perplexed whether to think of it as a "fortune or a curse," the cloak of Dracula even went with its owner to the grave.

"Give 'em a couple of tons of makeup and — ooh!" *Photoplay* said of Karloff and Lugosi in May 1932. Still another aspect of his complete association with Dracula can be shown through his essential lack of makeup as the vampire count. "The difference in the way we work is that I believe solely in illusion," Lugosi once explained, "and Karloff uses heavy makeup with which I'm not in sympathy at all." Obviously, the use of heavy makeup resulted in Lugosi's disdain for the Frankenstein Monster role in 1931; yet his own face, voice, and dress forever became Dracula. Lugosi's own image was a mask from which he could not escape.

Lugosi's appearance and that of Dracula bore no distinction from one another. The slicked-back hair, tarantula-like hand movements, tall and trim physique, and mysterious and penetrating eyes became qualities forever associated with the vampire count; the same characteristics were Lugosi's own personal traits. The image profoundly affected future cinematic portrayals of Dracula, as well as Halloween decorations and costumes, children's toys, and even dust jackets for Bram Stoker's novel — which describes a very different image from Lugosi. László Tábori's stage play *Love the Actor!* points to the power of the latter case, with the Lugosi character proclaiming to Bram Stoker that the author lived after death only through the power of the Hungarian's own image.

Many writers have attached the term "poor Bela" to Lugosi, used in retrospect to comment on the tragic elements of his life and career. Such qualities were most illuminated — though somewhat inaccurately — in Tim Burton's 1994 film *Ed Wood*. Sometimes these depictions overemphasize or skew the tragic qualities of Bela's final years, leaving out key points like his friendship with Richard Sheffield, his fifth marriage, and his appearance in United Artists' *The Black Sleep* (1955). Moreover, some texts, such as McNally and Florescu's *In Search of Dracula* (Warner, 1972), incorrectly paint Lugosi's drug addiction as a black market situation involving heroin.

Yet, it was Boris Karloff who coined the phrase, using it as early as the late thirties. Karloff's use of the term was not simply more sympathetic than later detractors; it pointed to the real problem. The famed British actor recognized that Lugosi's accent had become a real impediment to his career. Yet, Karloff's analysis that Lugosi simply should have been better instructed in the language does miss the mark. The Lugosi voice, the accent, became indelibly linked with America's (and the world's) conception of the vampire character. Innumerable imitations, ranging from comedians and impressionists to "The Count" of PBS's *Sesame Street*, exemplify the qualities of Lugosi's voice that became inseparable from the Dracula image. Lenny Bruce's mimicking of Lugosi's voice on the LP *Interviews of Our Time* shows strongly how even the Lugosi voice alone connotes the cinema vampire.

A critical backlash against horror films and Lugosi occurred following the first few genre efforts of the early thirties, making the actor's position even worse. *The New York Daily News* mentioned in early 1932 that "Carl Laemmle Jr. is trying to end the depression by scaring everyone to death." Numerous critics applauded *Dracula* and *Frankenstein*, but subsequently began taking a more dim view of the genre. When *Photoplay* announced 50 picks for 1931's best pictures, *Dracula* did not even appear. Instead, Pare Lorentz, critic and later famed documentary filmmaker, deemed *White Zombie* and *Murders in the Rue Morgue* runners-up for the worst films of 1932.

As Lugosi became linked with the genre, critical reactions to his work grew less tolerant. Indicative of this are Richard Watts's reviews of both *Dracula* and *White Zombie*. "Bela Lugosi is even more effective than he was on the stage, which is something of a tribute," he wrote in the *New York Herald-Tribune*. Yet less than one year later, the critic proclaimed, "Bela Lugosi proves that a good makeup cannot conceal a bad actor." Condemnation followed tribute at the hands of horror.

Columnist A.L. Woodridge wrote in 1932 that he heard a female theatergoer shout in response to horror films, "If I don't see a picture before long with a laugh in it, I'll scream." Woodridge added that "possibly a dozen heard it and openly voiced approval." Other instances of everyday spectators displaying a dislike for Lugosi's style of horror made their way into the public eye. "Why can't pictures of frenzied horror such as *Dracula* be eliminated entirely from the screen," Ethel Cook of Alabama wrote to *Photoplay* in 1931. "Life is hectic enough without tormenting us with pictures of this kind." Another puzzled movie patron wrote to the same magazine after viewing *Murders in the Rue Morgue*, "Why invent that erratic figure, Dr. Mirakle, and those absurd experiments with gorilla's blood?"

The controversy over horror films of the Lugosi ilk took many forms. Those worried about the morals of children in this country and especially England took strong positions against the cinema genre, resulting in the British ban on horror movies in 1936. For many adults, such films as *Dracula* were off-limits for children, a taboo often broken of course. Others worried over the potential medical harm that horror films could cause. Dr. William J. Robinson of New York City, for example, wrote to the *New York Times* in 1935, incensed over one Lugosi chiller. "There is a good deal of criticism of obscene and vulgar movies," the good doctor wrote. "But a dozen of the worst obscene pictures cannot equal the damage done by such films as *The Mark of the Vampire*. I do not refer to the utter senselessness of the picture. I do not even refer to its effect in spreading and fostering the most obnoxious superstitions. I refer to the terrible effect that it has on the mental and nervous systems of not only unstable but even normal men, women, and children. I am not speaking in the abstract; I am basing myself upon facts. Several people have come to my notice who, after seeing that horrible picture, suffered a nervous shock, were attacked with insomnia, and those who did fall asleep were tortured by the most horrible nightmares. In my opinion, it is a crime to produce and present such films. We must guard not only our people's morals — we must be careful of their physical and mental health."

Protests came in even more bizarre and specialized forms as well. One Gabriel Stanley wrote to the *Cleveland Plain-Dealer* in March 1931, enraged over the cinema depiction of *Dracula*: "I saw in the *Plain-Dealer* the other day where you are giving a recommendation to a Hungarian, namely Bela Lugosi, who is demonstrating his stupidity and ignorance to the far more ignorant American public about Dracula ... Lugosi would have the puerile and credulous Americans believe Dracula was a prince of Transylvania. Of this stupidity could be cured with education."

Simply put, critics and various sectors of the public found problems with horror films and often Lugosi in particular. All the while, the Hungarian's name grew closer to that of Dracula. "Mr. Lugosi ... is still trying to play Dracula," the *New York Herald-Tribune* said of *Chandu the Magician* (1932). Eleven years later, the *New York World-Telegram* said of *Return of the Vampire* (1943), "He is not called

"Lugosi the Mysterious," as Universal Studios once dubbed him, is mysteriously out of camera range, with his hypnotic hand motions scaring — or perhaps entertaining — the three women in the photograph.

Dracula this time — but what's the difference? Dracula or Tesla? It's still Bela Lugosi." The *Boston Globe* pronounced him that year the "monarch of all vampires."

Fan magazines of the thirties also helped solidify Lugosi and Dracula into one person. The well-remembered articles by Gladys Hall in *Motion Picture*, *Modern Screen*, and *Silver Screen* promoted Lugosi as a real vampire, a man who could not sleep at night, a man haunted "with the lore of demonlogy, the dark secrets of the state of trance a part of his daily life." On other occasions, Hall painted an actor pursued by "the Woman with the Yellow Eyes," a bloodsucker from his home country of Hungary. The author became confused enough to ask, "Is Bela Lugosi Dracula?" after stating, "Dracula is Bela Lugosi." The pens of other journalists wrote equally bizarre tales, which for the most part are more fantasy than fact. But these played an important role in molding the public image of Lugosi. Studio publicity added to this, with pressbooks crowning him with titles like the "human sphynx of mystery."

Even in the thirties, the "Dracula curse" did not necessarily help Lugosi's career. Before the association drove him to bankruptcy with the British ban on horror films, it often mired him in a narrow and unimportant position. A *Film Daily* poll of theater manager responses to the "players who drew the greatest number of patrons into your theater" gave managers a chance to push Boris Karloff into the 10 percent range; Hungarian actor Paul Lukas showed 3 percent of the votes, and near-forgotten actors like Ned Sparks and Kent Taylor placed in the 1 percent category. Lugosi's name appeared nowhere.

As for Karloff, the studio admittedly planned to continue building him as a star player. If anyone became another Lon Chaney, it was Karloff, portraying various unfortunates in a variety of makeups. Universal Studios saw the early box office appeal of the British actor and exploited it. Lugosi became overlooked, mentioning as early as 1936 that he had created his own Frankenstein monster with Boris Karloff by turning down the role of Mary Shelley's creature in 1931. Much speculation about Lugosi insists bad management caused problems, and — while possibly true to an extent — the actor himself aggravated this difficulty more than anyone by so frequently changing agencies due to his constant impatience for work.

Furthermore, by the end of 1932, Lugosi found no single studio behind him and supporting him to the fullest degree. He also lacked the ability to promote himself to the greatest possible extent, developing an aversion to radio shows and posing for promotional photographs. Karloff and other actors in the horror field also helped erode Lugosi's status and ability to headline films. Regardless of such facts, Lugosi still could not escape Dracula. Josh Alan's 1994 musical *The Worst!* allows the Lugosi character to sing of this plight, moaning, "The only part they'll hire me for is to play this old vampire whore, ever more."

While thousands of theatergoers loved *Dracula* (1931) for its thrills and mythic qualities — as in the case of some men — or its sexual undercurrents — as in the case of many women — the appeal changed by the forties. Lugosi's aging qualities and features exuded less of the sexual electricity than years before, just as Val Lewton and others brought a higher level of intelligence to the maturing horror film genre of America. Dracula began losing his punch, turning up without Lugosi in the more juvenile *House of Dracula* (1945) and others, with Lugosi stage tours sometimes drawing as many giggles as gasps. A review of the latter in May 1943 simply deemed Lugosi and the play *Dracula* "not effective."

A Seattle review of the roadshow *No Traveler Returns* (1945) claimed, "Those who expected Lugosi to scare hell out of them probably were disappointed." *The*

Detroit News said the Hungarian was "more humorous than horrifying" as *Dracula* in a 1948 stage act. Although determining the reaction of spectators to him is difficult, unintentional laughs sometimes formed in adult audiences for Lugosi on stage as the vampire or in his numerous B films of the period. Such effects on audiences seemingly increased in later public appearances of the 1950-period.

Through his Monogram films and other lesser efforts, Lugosi moved from acceptance with adult audiences to hero status among many children frequenting Saturday double features. Many of these films featured the actor in roles similar to that of Dracula (*Spooks Run Wild*, 1941), elements of the vampire (the coffins in *The Corpse Vanishes*, 1942), the image of a bat (*The Devil Bat*, 1941), and numerous others. If critics dismissed such films even more quickly than Lugosi chillers of the previous decade, young audiences flocked to them. Confirmation of this is clear with reports of Lugosi's 1944 stage tour of *Arsenic and Old Lace*. Theater manager after theater manager noted moving matinees to 3:30 P.M., giving the adoring children a chance to buy tickets to see their "master of horror" in the flesh. To a large degree, the cinema image found new viewers to witness and appreciate it.

The substantive nature of the films' plot became as much a formula as the B Westerns of the forties. Though each was an individual movie, in many ways the Lugosi films of World War II were simply "Lugosi films." Nothing exceptional distinguished them from one another; instead, such chillers seemed almost assembly-line products — the Fordism of the cinema. "It was push a button and get Lugosi," the actor once said. "I was like an automation [*sic*]." Like much other formula entertainment, its audience dwindled after the war ended.

By the forties, artists' caricatures of Lugosi often moved from the suave and handsome to images much more ugly than the actor himself. In addition to the nature of his roles, the actor's advancing age certainly brought this about. One of the more famous such caricatures, a 1954 Hirschfeld montage, ironically shows Karloff towering above the Hungarian. As his looks continued to decline with age, the romantic potency of the image suffered as well. Historian David J. Hogan pointed to this problem in his text *Dark Romance: Sexuality in the Horror Film* (McFarland, 1986). Lugosi, he claims, became "victimized by his own sexuality" as it slowly departed during the actor's later years.

By the late forties, Lugosi's situation worsened in other ways. After World War II ended, American studios stopped producing horror films en masse for the rest of the decade. After wading through numerous summer stock presentations of *Dracula* and *Arsenic and Old Lace*, the actor portrayed Dracula in *Abbott and Costello Meet Frankenstein* (1948). Though he considered his "trademark unblemished," irony exists in the fact that his last major film featured him playing the Stoker vampire in a comedy. His biographical portrait in the 1947-48 *Motion Picture Almanac* highlights the problem: the entry under his name is only half the length it had been the prior decade.

The fifties resulted in even more complete oblivion. The actor portrayed Dracula in a cheap live appearance tour, being heckled by teens who held little respect for his work. Ads promised horrifying sights like "Lugosi and the Bloody Guillotine!" but patrons chided the futile attempts to scare. His other serious attempt at the vampire, in a British stage tour, also failed. To raise funds for his return voyage to the United States, the actor had to lampoon his Dracula image in a film alongside a female impersonator. In general, Lugosi's minor success that decade came from spoofing his vampire alter ego; even then, television offers were few, and only his short-lived Las Vegas act attracted any real attention. Lugosi had spoofed the image previously, including biting Betty Boop in a 1933 short subject. But by this period he was almost forced to do so, as serious attempts with the vampire generally faltered. The image's potency faded to a shadow, a mere apparition of what it had been.

Following the end of World War II, Lugosi's ability to chill the spine proved less constant than ever. The fifties, scarred by the reality of atomic power and frothing with xenophobia as a result of the Red Scare and outer space invaders, offered no real opportunities for the actor. Patrick Lucanio's *Them or Us: Archetypal Interpretations of Fifties' Alien Invasion Films* (Indiana University Press, 1987) makes quite a valid point in claiming Lugosi was conspicuous in the fifties for only one thing: his "near absence" from the public eye. The barren world of Ed Wood embraced him, but it remained a cinematic wasteland far removed from the reality of Hollywood. One of Wood's key Lugosi projects, the ridiculous *Dr. Acula*, intended to plunder the same vampire image; it never came to fruition. Of his earlier performances, one of the few critical comments of note that decade came in George Geltzer's treatise on Tod Browning in an October 1953 *Films Review*. His verdict was simply "Today, *Dracula* (1931) seems weak."

Television in the fifties often broadcast his low-budget efforts of the prior decades, but mainly because of their accessibility to stations' budgets; viewers — outside perhaps of some children — did not cry for them to be aired. Movie theaters revived his films, but again only young children walked away scared. For teens, spook shows were generally for laughs; to adults, Lugosi was essentially a "has-been." When one middle-aged audience member requested his appearance on a television program called *You Asked for It*, she pointed out his disappearance from the limelight. The Lugosi name still registered horror, but precious few in the public really cared.

Obviously Lugosi's numerous personal problems heighten the unfortunate aspects of his career; however, the nature of the classical Hollywood paradigm almost dictates that a star's brightness dim significantly. Lugosi's career remains unique in that as Dracula he faced an extreme form of typecasting. The problems he battled as part of the unstable horror genre were not unique, nor were problems of public interest and studio production unknown to other cinema genres of the thirties and forties.

In 1930 as Lugosi neared signing a contract with Universal for *Dracula*, a *Los Angeles Times* feature story read, "Film Stars Shy at Future." A journalist asked a dozen major stars what they expected to be doing ten years in the future. "Each and all of them gave a queer little shudder ... what a disturbing question." Columnist Alma Whitaker pronounced cinema acting a "cruel and treacherous profession," and also stated what became true in the careers of Lugosi and dozens of others: "There isn't anywhere to go after the top ... except down."

Perhaps in May 1932 Lugosi read of Maurice Costello, the early screen idol who collapsed in a Beverly Hills drugstore. Even by the thirties, America had forgotten the actor. *Photoplay* remarked that his "glory waned," that "his adorers spent all their admiration for him so intensely that it was quickly used up," and that due to competition he "slowly found himself crowded out." Costello was "left completely alone," save for the "memories of his once glorious past."

Though certain aspects of *Photoplay*'s analysis evoke similarities with Lugosi (for example, horror film competition, short-lived attention from female spectators and youthful audiences), a precise comparison is unnecessary. Costello remains an early example of the almost inevitable nature of the Hollywood star system. Generally performers reach an apex of popularity which then begins to erode. That Lugosi remained in front of the public eye in major Hollywood films for 17 years in some ways breaks out of the mold; that he forged a major comeback in 1938 after having been nearly forgotten once definitely surpassed the fate of many other Hollywood stars.

Yet Hollywood's cruelty toward Lugosi seems razor sharp, most likely given its root: the dominant image of Dracula that loomed over its popular creator. No Hollywood stars visited the actor's funeral, but the cloak of Dracula embraced his restful body forever. Ted LeBerthom's 1932 *Weird Tales* article on Lugosi and Karloff spoke of "fallen greatness"; the phrase applies well to the Hungarian's career.

Speculation sometimes insists Lugosi's hoped-for comeback could have occurred in the monster-crazed sixties, with its movie magazines like *Famous Monsters of Filmland*, its "monster" model kits and toys, its late-night television airings of thirties horror films, and its use of aging horror stars in movies at American International Pictures. While audiences of all ages often enjoyed the "new" films with Boris Karloff, Peter Lorre, and Basil Rathbone which AIP produced, the motivating force behind the renewed popularity of such stars was again the youth. America's children became infatuated with the classic movie monsters, starting fan clubs, watching films, buying memorabilia, and especially reading monster movie magazines.

Though a generation of new audiences discovered Lugosi, on the whole they were youths infatuated with old horror films. The sexual and romantic aspects in more mature audiences were diverted to the color, blood, and nudity of British horror films, produced by Hammer Studios. For those viewers, Christopher Lee became Dracula, and while he at least indirectly shared Lugosi's influence, at the time the British actor fulfilled such visual and psychological pleasures more readily for many adult audiences due to improved film technology (widespread use of color stock revealed the red color of blood) and relaxed censorship.

By the late eighties and nineties, however, the history of the horror film, as well as cinema and culture, revealed overt and numerous changes. The video revolution offered easy access to almost the sum total of Lugosi's Hollywood canon. Increased academic work in the horror film genre led to important empirical studies as well as to cultural analysis. The classic horror cinema of the thirties revealed its relationship to the Great Depression, while Lugosi's Dracula became a symbol. The sexual qualities of his Dracula have only strengthened with time, framed forever in the romance of black-and-white film. Lugosi can simultaneously appear on a financial magazine symbolizing economic problems or the Internal Revenue Service, emerge within a sexually charged film like *Innocent Blood* (1992) as the ultimate vampire icon, headline a magazine's list of the "Kings of Bad Video," and surface in academic coursework as worthy of critical and artistic study. He endures as a historical figure through novels like Larry McMurtry's *Pretty Boy Floyd: A Novel* (Simon and Schuster, 1994), while keeping a strong grasp on the modern mind for Thomas Pynchon's *Gravity's Rainbow* (Viking, 1973). The image also teaches children how to count on PBS and sells breakfast cereal on television commercials.

During his Hollywood career and subsequent decades, the pronunciation of Lugosi's name — as well as its spelling — plagued the actor. From "Belo" and "Zela" to "Laguna" and "Lugoosa," the name has suffered. Though not the central problem to an actor better known as Dracula during his own lifetime, the minor problem remains. However, more to Lugosi's favor is the mantra of quotes from his films which stand as classic lines of the cinema. Repeated television viewings and monster magazines in the sixties help give certain quotes from his movies the mantle of familiarity. Easy access to his films via the video revolution of the eighties furthered this circumstance. In this familiarity's most extreme form, a fan recited from memory the entire script of *Bowery at Midnight* on a 1982 episode of NBC's *Late Night with David Letterman*. Yet its common incarnation finds almost everyone recognizing lines like "I never drink ... wine." Such quotes might well be clichéd from overuse, but audience familiarity with them generally results not in nausea but instead a kind of aural pleasure associated with famous words and phrases.

Modern fans themselves range from those of the prior *Famous Monsters* generation who remain obsessed with the classic Universal horror films, to admirers of forties B movies, to viewers interested in the Ed Wood era. For example, interest in the subject spawns collectors who sacrifice much of their lives and money in pursuit of artifacts to place them closer to the Lugosi aura. The fascination results in various but layered levels of attention. Though some writers wrongly claim Lugosi is more popular in this more modern period than in his own lifetime — when marquee lights sporadically chased around his name on major Hollywood film releases — the interest itself is in less flux. Lugosi the icon carries numerous meanings for various groups of fans, collectors, scholars, and the general public.

Interestingly, the icon became so strong as to merit study within the courts of California. *Lugosi vs. Universal Pictures Co.* saw the actor's son and fifth wife join forces to claim the icon as their inheritable right. The two accused Universal Studios of infringing on their family by marketing Lugosi as a model kit, school notebook, and every other imaginable product. Numerous authors build metaphors of Lugosi rising from the grave to protect his birthright, though the icon in question was still very much alive. Jane M. Gaines's *Contested Culture: The Image, the Voice, and the Law* (University of North Carolina, 1991) addressed this issue. With regard to Universal Studios' victory in the trial's final outcome, Gaines mentions, "It is quite possible that the Lugosi family could never establish a clear right to Lugosi as Dracula because Universal's motion picture character had so thoroughly taken over the Lugosi persona." While probably a correct legal analysis, in a cultural sense the Lugosi image had merged with Stoker's character. The two danced together and formed the icon, rather than any character usurping Lugosi's personality.

In retrospect, while Lugosi consciously attempted to become Universal's *Dracula* in 1931 and subsequently endeavored at times to capitalize on the image, a program for the 1945 play *No Traveler Returns* best sums up the history by claiming, "Dracula pursued *him*." The unstable image that often plagued Lugosi's pocketbook became an icon capable of multiple meanings and reactions only after his death. During the thirties, forties, and fifties, the image contained the possibilities of multiple readings, but only decades later has the potential become reality. The result moves Lugosi beyond mere cinema history to a permanent place within Western culture.

21. Authority Survey

A cross-section of the major collectors, writers, and researchers in the field of Lugosi studies and collecting participated in the following survey during 1994. The first section of the survey is rather subjective, querying the "best" and "worst" Lugosi films. The second portion of the survey offers the tallied answers to numerous questions which, while again subjective, might be of value in discerning the most worthwhile sources for information, films, and collectibles relating to the actor. Though obviously this section is less than scientific, it is hoped that the results yield useful opinions concerning Lugosi's work. Moreover, it offers insight into those who have kept the actor's memory alive.

Films and Performances

In terms of Lugosi's "best" and "worst" films and performances, a variety of responses were made, demonstrating the varied manner in which the actor still commands interest. As for his finest performances on film, *Dracula* (1931) received the largest response, followed closely by *White Zombie* (1932), *The Raven* (1935), and to a lesser degree *Son of Frankenstein* (1939).

From the standpoint of tabulated answers, the same four films, as well as *Murders in the Rue Morgue* (1932), *The Black Cat* (1934), *Mark of the Vampire* (1935), and *Abbott and Costello Meet Frankenstein* (1948), numbered the highest for responses to the "best" films. Those surveyed most often mentioned such low-budget films as *The Mysterious Mr. Wong* (1935), *Scared to Death* (1947), and *Bela Lugosi Meets a Brooklyn Gorilla* (1952) as Lugosi's "worst." On the basis of this information alone, collectors and researchers believe Lugosi's bigger budget films — particularly those of the early thirties — to be the most important, while holding disdain for lower-budget efforts.

But the situation reveals itself to be more complex under closer examination. The bulk of writers and collectors of the horror film genre grew up during the sixties reading *Famous Monsters of Filmland* and viewing television revivals of Universal Studios' classic monster movies. For that reason, the numbers almost automatically show favoritism to those films, which certainly do rank as minor classics of the cinema.

A second group of collectors and writers, though in smaller numbers, tend particularly to remember and enjoy the B movies of the forties. In Lugosi's case, this translates into films like *Spooks Run Wild* (1941) and *The Ape Man* (1943). Thus, when responding to such questions, author John Wooley cites *The Corpse Vanishes*

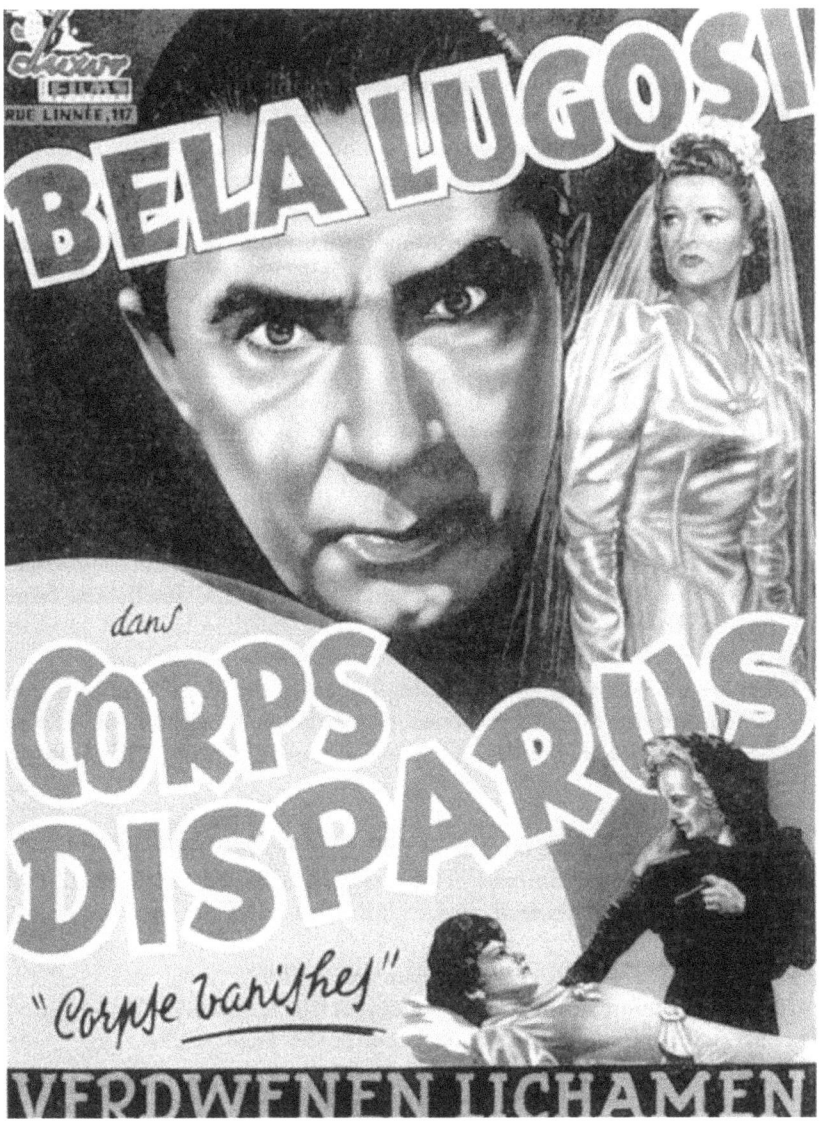

A Belgian poster for *The Corpse Vanishes* (1942), one of several B movies that is generally either well loved or strongly disliked by Lugosi fans.

(1942) as one of his favorite Lugosi films, while writer Gordon Guy lambasts it as one of the actor's worst. At any rate, the low-budget films of Monogram, PRC, and other such studios hold strong interest for certain fans. A third category of Lugosi enthusiasts is interested in the collaborations between the actor and Ed Wood. Some cite *Glen or Glenda* (1953) or *Bride of the Monster* (1955) as among the best Lugosi efforts, though others noted great dislike for the same titles.

Such categories should *not* indicate that enthusiasts cannot bridge the gap between each, automatically defending any of the actor's films. "I don't believe any Lugosi film is bad," biographer Richard Bojarski wrote. "The bad films would be the boring ones, but of course this would be no fault of Lugosi's." Michael Copner of *Cult Movies* magazine echoed that sentiment, claiming, "I don't personally believe there are any worst films if Lugosi appears in them." Lugosi's friend Richard Sheffield also chimed in, mentioning, "His simple presence lifted any flick."

Perhaps the most essential conclusion to draw from the overall responses is that Lugosi's cult of personality is vigorously displaying its strength decades after his death. Mounting fascination has led to a re-examination of the entire Lugosi canon, with enthusiasts generally finding points of interest in all his work.

Tabulated Responses

1. What is the most valuable single book you own for Lugosi research?

Lugosi: The Man Behind the Cape received the most votes, with *The Count* and *The Films of Bela Lugosi* close behind. *Karloff and Lugosi* and *Poverty Row Horrors* also received attention.

2. What are the best magazines covering Lugosi in the nineties or in the past?

Famous Monsters of Filmland proved the most popular, with *The World of Bela Lugosi, Filmfax, Castle of Frankenstein, Cult Movies,* and *Scarlet Street* following close behind.

3. What is the best source for Lugosi stills and movie memorabilia?

Cinema Collectors, located in Hollywood, was far and away selected as the prime business for such material.

4. What is the finest archive of Lugosi memorabilia?

Again, an almost unanimous response proclaimed the collection of Forrest J Ackerman to be the greatest single archive of Lugosi memorabilia.

5. What companies offer the best videocassette releases of Lugosi films?

MCA/Universal and Sinister Cinema won the greatest respect from those surveyed.

Participants

1. Barnett, Buddy. Collector; writer for such publications as *The World of Bela Lugosi*; publisher of *Cult Movies* magazine.

2. Bojarski, Richard. Researcher and author of *The Films of Boris Karloff* and *The Films of Bela Lugosi*.

3. Camacho-Romo, Dr. Juan Jose. Collector; author of numerous articles on Lugosi in both the United States and Mexico.

4. Chacon, Mario. Collector and fan, with a special interest in autographs.

5. Copner, Michael. Videographer of the documentary *Bela Lugosi: Then and Now*.

6. Cremer, Robert. Author of *Lugosi: The Man Behind the Cape*.

7. Dello Stritto, Frank J. Researcher and author of many important Lugosi articles in *Photon* and *Cult Movies*.

8. Evans, Philip R. Collector, fan, and author of *Bix: Man and Legend* and several other books.

9. Michael Ferguson. Collector, researcher, and writer for *The World of Bela Lugosi*.

10. Guy, Gordon. Researcher; writer for *The World of Bela Lugosi*; editor of *The Castle Dracula Quarterly*.

11. Hand, Jon. Research assistant on Arthur Lennig's book *The Count*; collector, with a special interest in still photographs.

12. Heard, Charles. Collector and fan; responsible for getting Carroll Borland's novel *Countess Dracula* published.

13. Kaffenberger, Bill. Collector and fan; "rediscovered" three Lugosi newsreels at the National Archives.

14. Kohl, Leonard. Collector, researcher, and writer for such publications as *Filmfax*.

15. Liquori, Frank. Collector and fan.

16. Luce, Greg. Collector and fan; president of the Sinister Cinema video company.

17. Mank, Gregory William. Author of such books as *Karloff and Lugosi, The Hollywood Hissables, It's Alive*, and others.

18. Michel, Jean-Claude. Researcher; collector; author, responsible for bringing accurate biographies of Lugosi to French-reading audience; star of the *Temps X* episode on Lugosi.

19. Naron, Lynn. Collector, fan, and researcher.

20. Noel, Gerard. Writer, researcher, and publisher of two French booklets about Lugosi (*Bela Lugosi: 1882–1956* and *Retour de Bela Lugosi*).

21. Nye, James. Collector and fan; writer for *The World of Bela Lugosi*.

22. Obbaggy, Bill. Collector and fan; president of the International Bela Lugosi Fan Club during the sixties.

23. Payne, Dennis. Collector and fan; artist whose pen-and-inks of Lugosi have appeared on the covers of such journals as *The World of Bela Lugosi* and *The Big Reel*.

24. Pirola, Bill. Fan and collector, with a special interest in personal items.

25. Rees, Robert. Collector and fan; writer for such journals as *Scream*.

26. Sheffield, Richard. Collector, fan, author, founder of the Official Bela Lugosi Fan Club, and a close friend of the late actor.

27. Terenzio, Maurice. Collector; writer; star of the *Behind the Cape* television program.

28. Toland, Mario. Collector and fan.
29. Weaver, Tom. Writer, researcher and author of such books as *Poverty Row HORRORS!* and *Attack of the Monster Movie Makers*.
30. Wooley, John. Writer and researcher; author of the comic book *Plan 9 from Outer Space: Thirty Years Later*.

22. Advertising Lugosi

During his Hollywood career, Lugosi conjured visions of horror to theater audiences, with his name and image generally a signal for the kind of film one would witness. Historians have often drawn a strong connection, however, between Lugosi's billing on certain films and his apparent popularity with the public at that exact moment. All too often, however, advertisements shifted him to the center of focus of a ticket buyer, even if the on-screen credits billed him beneath other actors.

Lugosi himself knew well the power of advertising, sometimes actually buying ads for himself. Upon the actor's arrival in Berlin, for example, an ad for him appeared in *Film Magazin* to announce his availability. Over a decade later, the actor purchased ads in *The Cast* to promote himself again.

A few in the business world also realized his potential in advertising, though he endorsed fewer products than did most of his Hollywood colleagues. During the forties, Lugosi did pose for KOOL cigarettes, Royal Crown cola, and Remington razors. In the midfifties, while hoping for a comeback, the actor even appeared in a California promotion for Epicurean Reese of California, Inc., Fine Foods. The company's six "Spooky Foods" included alligator soup, rattlesnake meat, Mexican fried agave worms, natural snails, fried grasshoppers, and boiled quail eggs. Lugosi's image guaranteed the delicacies to be wonderful appetizers.

Yet, the advertising of Lugosi and his own films shows much disparity. Immediately after the phenomenal success of *Dracula* (1931), the comedy *Broadminded* (1931) and the horror film *Murders in the Rue Morgue* (1932) denied him star billing. While much has been made of such on-screen credits, movie posters for *Broadminded* often featured larger images of Lugosi than of star Joe E. Brown. And, while Sidney Fox's affair with studio head Carl Laemmle, resulted in her name appearing above the Hungarian's on the Poe film itself, newspaper and trade publication ads diverged. For such promotions, Lugosi — the recent star of *Dracula* — almost invariably took top honors.

By the time of his teaming with Karloff, Lugosi did hold the lesser status at Universal Studios. The earliest exhibitor ads for *The Black Cat* actually appear differently from those finally seen on movie posters, reading either "Boris Karloff the uncanny and Bela Lugosi the mysterious" or "Boris (Frankenstein) Karloff and Bela (Dracula) Lugosi." While the studio often retained the moniker "Uncanny" for his colleague, Lugosi's tag "Mysterious" quickly disappeared. Posters also generally deleted Karloff's first name, listing the Hungarian with full name and "Dracula" label. Rather than a move against Lugosi, however, this should be seen more as Universal Studio's attempt to build Karloff into a major star.

Throughout their many films together, Lugosi not only continued his second-

The Realart rerelease of Universal's *The Black Cat* (1934) became a rare case of inverted billing. In lobby cards for its retitled incarnation, Lugosi's name topped Karloff's.

billed status, but in some ways declined further in name value on posters. Karloff's name dwarfed the Hungarian's for *The Invisible Ray* posters in 1936, doing the same years later for *The Body Snatcher* (1945). Yet, newspaper ads in New York and elsewhere often (in equally sized lettering) mention simply "KARLOFF and LUGOSI" as the stars of the former film, with Lugosi taking a part in the latter simply because RKO Studios knew he retained marquee value. Oddly, the only time Lugosi's name appeared above his rival's came on scene cards for *The Vanishing Body*, a reissue of *The Black Cat* (1934), during a period when Lugosi's career had definitely reached a lower ebb than Karloff's.

For *Mark of the Vampire* (1935), MGM coming attraction trailers found Lugosi himself reading off his name under those of Lionel Barrymore and Elizabeth Allan. Posters also carried his name under Barrymore's. But for many newspapers and some trade magazines, the ads offered "Bela (Dracula) Lugosi" above all other cast members, a fact that Lugosi later recalled with pride.

Other examples of studio billing seem equally bizarre. On the crest of his comeback in 1938, producers quickly signed Lugosi to take Peter Lorre's place in *The Gorilla* (1939). On-screen billing and even a title card from the film list his name beneath the three Ritz Brothers, Anita Louise, Patsy Kelly, and Lionel Atwill. However, a one-sheet poster not only listed Lugosi immediately under the comedy

Despite his even greater love of good cigars, the forties found Lugosi plugging KOOL cigarettes for the cameras.

trio but also offered as its only artwork a towering image of the Hungarian's face. Moreover, his marquee value certainly caused his name to appear in place of Lorre's.

For *You'll Find Out* (1941) the screen credits show the Hungarian listed under Kay Kyser, Peter Lorre, Dennis O'Keefe, and Helen Parrish (with Karloff receiving a special billing card of his own). Yet posters and publicity materials offer Lugosi's name following Kyser, Karloff, and Lorre, with the three horror stars depicted together in striking and equally sized images.

Other unusual discrepancies occurred with Lugosi's Universal films of the early forties. In *Ghost of Frankenstein* (1942), for example, Lugosi took billing beneath Lon Chaney, Sir Cedric Hardwicke, Ralph Bellamy, and Lionel Atwill. For *Frankenstein Meets the Wolf Man* (1943), posters list the actor beneath Lon Chaney, Ilona Massey, and Patrick Knowles. Yet existing photographs highlight theater publicity that often paired Lugosi's name with Chaney's, apparently to capitalize on the Hungarian's marquee value and association with the genre to attract potential audience members. Some ads devised by the newspapers and local theaters occasionally gave Lugosi top billing on such films, such as one for *Frankenstein Meets the Wolf Man* in the *Chicago Tribune*.

Moreover, studio pressbooks and publicity materials generally made much mention of the actor. For the most part, visual materials like movie posters distinctly displayed Lugosi's image, even if his billing was of less than star status. His likeness meant horror (and more specifically Dracula), and even if his roles and salaries did not reflect his unique qualities, the promotional materials certainly did.

One of the few consistent aspects of materials advertising the actor came with the much-used "Bela (Dracula) Lugosi" label. From *White Zombie* (1932) and *Murders in the Rue Morgue* (1932) through *The Invisible Ghost* (1941) and various vaudeville acts of the forties, the title remained with him. In addition to the mere words, some films and live appearances offered images of Lugosi as the vampire rather than an accurate depiction of his then-current role. The use of "Dracula" as a middle name slowed down in the forties, though few other tag lines took its place. Occasionally, Lugosi became "The Master of Horror" (for reissues of *Dracula*), "The Master of Menace" (for 1945's *The Body Snatcher*), the "Master of the Weird" (for 1955's *Bride of the Atom*), "Mr. Horror Himself" (for a 1951 live appearance tour), or even the "Man of 1000 Horrors" (for Monogram Studios' publicity), but his name alone became identified with B horror films more than ever in the forties. By the time of *Bela Lugosi Meets a Brooklyn Gorilla* (1952), his name and the film title became one to announce and advertise the nature of the story.

Ultimately, the manner in which studios promoted Lugosi should not be seen as a concerted attempt to thwart his success. Rather, it represents the mixed ideas of strategists at studios and theaters alike hoping to bring success to individual films. These varied attempts to ensure box office grosses obviously caused inconsistencies between the point of production and consumption, but the object was simply to bring in profits. The image and name of Lugosi became a useful but not always well-used aspect of such promotions.

23. Collecting and Merchandising Lugosi

Interest in Bela Lugosi has spawned a huge collecting and merchandising operation that only seems to grow as time goes by. Earliest and most important in this hobby was probably Forrest J Ackerman, who realized quite prophetically the historic nature of lobby cards, movie posters, and studio props. The collecting bat has since bitten an untold number of unsuspecting victims, most joining the ranks in the sixties, with Ackerman's magazine *Famous Monsters of Filmland* guiding them. Other forces include the video revolution of the eighties, which generated interest in Lugosi as so many of his films became easily accessible.

Studio props, costumes, and personal items are of course at the top of any collector's list, yet such items are limited in number and sometimes command exorbitant prices. The Ackerman collection, for example, includes such material as the Dracula cape Lugosi wore in *Plan 9 from Outer Space* and the Dracula-crest ring that Lugosi used. Other items, ranging from pipes, cigar holders, canes, ink pens, World War II ration books, scrapbooks, and much more, are sprinkled throughout various Lugosi collections. For example, a monocle used in the 1931 *Dracula*, Lugosi's tails from *The Invisible Ray*, his pants from *Voodoo Man*, and the vampire cape from *Abbott and Costello Meet Frankenstein* are all privately owned.

Autographs are within the financial reach of many collectors but prices on these have also continually risen during the last 20 years. Signatures on Dracula photos, or autographs signed "Bela 'Dracula' Lugosi," particularly excite collectors and have price tags that reflect this. Handwritten letters, which sell at high prices, are also of great interest. Lowest on the price scale are usually the signatures on scraps of paper rather than on photos or collectibles. This aspect of the hobby is fascinating, exciting, and also dangerous. Only a few collectors are true experts at proving an autograph to be authentic, and unfortunately many fakes find their way into the marketplace. Along with recent forgeries, Bela's own wife, Lillian, penned a large number of bogus "Bela autographs" during their lengthy marriage.

Signatures from early in Lugosi's Hollywood career tend to have strong underlines beneath his name, with an acute accent mark over the *e* in Bela. The *a* in his first name often appeared as a quick curve, extending occasionally into the line stricken under his autograph. By the late forties and fifties, Bela signed his name somewhat bigger, with a large, bulbous *B* and an open *a*. The European-style accent over the *e* disappeared. These changes, particularly the size of the signature, possibly reflected Lugosi's deteriorating eyesight.

Paper items from the Lugosi films have also been a long-established point of

One of Lugosi statuettes the actor commissioned of himself to give as gifts to friends. (From the Charles Heard Collection; photo taken by Sherry Childress.)

interest. Movie posters in all their many shapes, sizes, and varieties, can also command a variety of prices. One-sheets are, given their 27" × 41" size, most familiar to moviegoers of today, yet varieties like the insert (14" × 36"), the three-sheet (41" × 81"), and the six-sheet (81" × 81") are also popular with collectors. The 22" × 28" half-sheet was also common in Lugosi's heyday, as were 11" × 14" lobby cards. Lobby cards usually came in sets of eight for films, with one being a title card and the rest being scene cards. Original 8" × 10" stills, window cards (often hung in businesses near the theater), and pressbooks (sent to theater owners, complete with clip art, photos, and advertising ideas) remain favorites of collectors as well, but perhaps less so than the lobbies and one-sheets. Also, since only a handful appeared at the time, original movie magazines featuring articles on Lugosi generally intrigue collectors.

As far as Lugosi is concerned, movie paper has steadily increased in price, far surpassing material associated with Boris Karloff, Peter Lorre, and other horror film stars. An original, style "A" *Dracula* one-sheet from 1931 broke all prior records in 1993 when auctioned for $77,000. Rarity, Lugosi's prominence in the poster itself, and popularity of the particular film have much to do with the price tag. Original material from the Universal films, cult movies like *White Zombie*, and the Ed Wood pictures tend to excite collectors the most.

Amazingly, in the nineties paper material from even the poorest Lugosi films can command nice sums, even if the artwork features little of Lugosi himself. Reissue posters of his Monogram films can bring in dollars and cause bidding wars at auctions. Values have steadily increased during the years, with large jumps occurring during the eighties and nineties.

Indeed, to capitalize on the interest in movie posters, several companies have issued reproductions of the originals. Not to be confused with the "real article," these reprints have generally been of either the one-sheets or the lobby cards. For example, Portal Productions marketed reprints of the *Dracula* and *The Black Cat* (1934) posters in the seventies. By the nineties, Robert Brosch's Archival Photography offered innumerable reproductions of Lugosi lobby cards.

Along with the standard material used to promote his films, a variety of products using the Lugosi image appeared during his own life. A pop-up matchbox heralding the release of *Murders in the Rue Morgue*, a color-tinted cigarette card from 1938, a *Phantom Creeps* comic, and an "official" 1947 collector's stamp were among these products. Lugosi himself commissioned 25 statuettes of himself as Dracula, allegedly made by his sister-in-law. A number of these continue to pass through the hands of collectors.

Life-size wax figures are also included among the Lugosi-based products. One, sculpted in approximately 1928, found itself publicizing the touring *Dracula*. Another, at Charles Pressley's Motion Picture Museum and Hall of Fame, went on display in the early thirties. Though it later burned in a fire, the wax likeness made it to celluloid in a 1933 *Hollywood on Parade* short. Subsequently, wax figures of Lugosi as Dracula have turned up in a number of museums. The Hollywood Wax Museum, for example, has long displayed such an effigy. Most only slightly resemble Lugosi, and many are simply "Draculas" with no direct association with the Hungarian. Furthermore, a wax facsimile of Lugosi came in a series of *The Black Sleep* characters used to promote the 1956 film.

The fans whose interests have generated such collecting are not the only ones who cause Lugosi to be continually commercialized. Widespread interest in horror films has been a part of Americana since the thirties, perhaps heightening in the sixties with *Famous Monsters of Filmland* magazine. Although most people won't necessarily be buying expensive movie posters, many will purchase a Lugosi videotape or school notebook adorned with his picture at a local department store. Such merchandising has proved to be an intriguing industry, with both financial and legal ups and downs.

The early sixties saw much of this begin with the success of numerous horror movie magazines. In 1963 Hasbro made a Lugosi three-ring school binder and a Bela "paint by numbers" set. The same year the company manufactured a Lugosi "Dracula Mystery Game," along with a Lugosi wallet in which young fans could keep their *Famous Monsters* funds. Along similar lines, Jaymar put out a Lugosi "Frame Tray Puzzle," with Yankee Products releasing its "*Famous Monsters* Photo Printing Set" later that decade. With the latter, product a filmmonster fan could develop Lugosi stills in a bathroom turned photo lab.

To help reproduce the moving image itself, Multiple put out a "Horror Scope Movie Viewer" in the sixties which featured clips of *Dracula* (1931). Furthermore, during the heyday of *Famous Monsters*, many companies sold silent and sound 8 mm condensations of Lugosi's films. In addition to watching clips of his movies, a fan could become Lugosi via the Don Post Studios' Lugosi mask. Issued in 1967, these have since become collectors' items.

Monster trading cards have long been a staple as well, going back to a Nu-Cards 1961 set called "Movie Monsters." Topps's popular "You'll Die Laughing" series, originally printed in 1963 and rereleased in 1970, featured Lugosi on several cards. Along with these sets, a pair of "Monster Old-Maid Cards" from 1964 included an image of the actor. In the nineties, Lugosi appeared on several of Raygem's "Ackermonster Cardiacards," featuring movie posters from Forrest Ackerman's collection. "Michael H. Price's Hollywood Horrors" set, released by Shel-Tone in 1993, spotlighted an artwork montage of Lugosi on card #19. Furthermore,

Lugosi signing one of the autographs that would later command high prices.

Starline's 1992 "Hollywood Walk of Fame" set included one Lugosi card, as did the same year's "Edward D. Wood, Jr., Players" released by the Kitchen Sink Press. Halloween of 1992 even found him on one of Pizza Hut's four-card, hologram set of Universal Monsters. Artwork from Lugosi's *Dracula* can also be seen as part of Topps's 1994 card set of Universal horror films, with the back of each giving historical information and stills from the 1931 film.

Tracing back almost as far as trading cards are Lugosi model kits, allowing young fans to conjure up their own monster with the aid of paint and ordinary household glue. The Universal-licensed Aurora models remain the best known and best loved of such kits, with their series including Lugosi as *Dracula*. The company manufactured the model from 1962 to 1968, using the same mold for the 1969 "Frightening Lightning" series. It also appeared in their "Glow-in-the-Dark" series from 1969 to 1975. Revell/Monogram reissued the kit again in 1991 as part of its "Luminators" line of glow-in-the-dark models. Indeed, it was the original Aurora model that brought about a court case, pitting Bela Lugosi, Jr., and Hope Lininger Lugosi against Universal Studios in the seventies for capitalizing on Lugosi's image.

In the late eighties and nineties, much more detailed model kits began surfacing, with their market often the same people who had bought Aurora kits 20 years before. For example, Horizon and Biliken both manufactured vinyl Lugosi/

Dracula kits, while Dimensional Designs created a caricature called "Bela the Vampire." A further Dracula model based on the Hungarian is a 1994 Dark Horse kit sculpted by Thomas Kuntz. Moreover, Resin from the Grave created a resin "Lugosi as Ygor" model, sold by itself or in a *Son of Frankenstein* set with a Karloff monster. Also in the nineties, Resin from the Grave released a kit of *The Devil Bat*, and the Janus Company created a *White Zombie* model. Additionally, Cinema Art Models and Dimensional Designs both marketed variations on the *Phantom Creeps* robot. Though sold to limited audiences, the kits generally show extreme detail. As a result, models of this period are referred to as "garage kits," playing off the small size of their manufacturers.

Additionally, action figures and statuettes constitute yet another aspect of such merchandising. Remco's 1979 doll, the 1980 "Mini-Monster," and the "Glow-in-the-Dark Mini-Monster" were Universal-licensed likenesses of Lugosi as Dracula. Imperial released an eight-inch figure in 1986, and Just Toys put out a "Bend-Em" Lugosi figure in 1991. Placo's ten-inch doll of 1991 became part of a Universal "60th Anniversary" series, celebrating the original releases of *Dracula* and *Frankenstein*. The various statuettes of Bela Lugosi include the Rene D. Lyon Company's re-creation sold through the Count Dracula Society. In the nineties Esco Products also created a sculptured Lugosi/Dracula.

Comic books have also been invaded by the Lugosi likeness. Most Dracula comics have avoided use of the Lugosi image, with a notable exception being the 1993 Dark Horse adaptation of the film licensed by Universal Studios. With regard to his other portrayals, Eclipse Comics' *The Prowler* series in the late eighties used the "Murder" character from *White Zombie* as a villain. In addition, Malibu Graphics released a comic adaptation of *Plan 9 from Outer Space* in 1990. The following year, John Wooley's *Plan 9 from Outer Space: Thirty Years Later* also used Lugosi as a character. Various comics have also briefly referenced Lugosi through the years, such as *Power Man and Iron Fist* #118, *Green Lantern* #196, and the newspaper strip *Gasoline Alley* on October 30, 1994.

The seventies overall were less productive of Lugosi merchandising produced than the movie-mag sixties or the video-deluged eighties. The "Universal Movie Monsters Lunch Box" was sold in 1973, complete with Dracula artwork and a Universal-licensed Thermos; however, its Dracula did not at all resemble the Hungarian. The landmark *Lugosi vs. Universal Studios Co.* case was decided by Judge Bernard Jefferson in 1972, making clear that the actor's image was a property right belonging to Lugosi's heirs.

Among the items mentioned in the plaintiffs' suit were: kites, children's phonograph records, plastic toy pencil sharpeners, greeting cards, talking greeting cards, model plastic figures, T-shirts, sweatshirts and patches, jump picture rings, jump picture pins on packages and boxes, soap and detergent products, Halloween costumes and masks, casting and enlargograph sets and kits, target games and sets, mechanical walking toys, ink-on transfers, an LP record album, trading cards, Halloween candy and gum, small comic books, self-erasing magic slates, punch-out novelty mask books, a Monster Mansion vehicle, wax figurines, candy dispensers, transparencies, calendars and prints, plastic sliding square puzzle games, children's and ladies' jewelry, belts and belt buckles, biking buddies, animated flip books, juvenile luggage, wall plaques, wallets, campaign type buttons, stirring rods and spoons, toy horoscope viewer with flip cards, and photo printing kits.

For a time, Universal backed away from using Lugosi's image, though the initial court decision was later overturned by a district court of appeals. Later, in 1979, Universal won the case when it went before the California Supreme Court. In 1974, shortly after the appeals court claimed Lugosi's image was public domain, Walt Disney released plastic "flicker" rings with images of the actor as Dracula.

Over time, the law made it easier to merchandise Lugosi's likeness, and more products appeared. For example, the eighties saw a Lugosi/Dracula color "Bop Bag" that stood about four feet high. Movie poster magnets of films like *Dracula* and even *Black Dragons* could creep onto refrigerators. World Candies of New York sold "Monster Candy," packaged with art of Lugosi and other well-known movie monsters. Hallmark Cards put a Lugosi still on a Halloween card, and Admit One Video pictured *The Phantom Creeps* on postcards. The One-Stop Poster company used Lugosi on a bookmark, and stickers for the Bauhaus rock tune "Bela Lugosi's Dead" made the rounds. The Centric Corporation of Hollywood offered a Lugosi cardboard standup. Bumper stickers of *Lugosi: The Forgotten King* could be stuck on any automobile, and, as always, pinback buttons of Lugosi were available. At school, the student could even use Poster Books' 1980 three-subject Lugosi notebook, and at home play Milton Bradley's 1981 "Universal Monster Mansion" board game.

Another eighties product that prominently featured Lugosi was General Mills' Count Chocula breakfast cereal. Clips from the 1931 film *Dracula* were used in 30-second television spots, and the cereal box featured artwork of Lugosi in full Dracula regalia. Shortly after the promotion began in 1987, however, many of the Jewish faith took issue with the medallion worn by Lugosi. Detractors claimed that this part of his costume appeared too similar to the sacred Star of David. To protect customer relations, General Mills removed the medallion, leaving the rest of the design untouched. However, the company did not recall the 4 million released boxes with the star. "We are not anti–Semitic," William Shaffner, manager of the General Mills' public relations office, proclaimed. The version sans medallion did not last either, though. Another advertising scheme took hold, and Lugosi parted ways with the cereal-maker.

Despite the General Mills incident, new Lugosi/Universal Dracula items continued to flood stores in the early nineties. Rubie's Costume Company made Universal horror star costumes for Halloween, Unique industries did party goods, Fun-Wear manufactured T-shirts, and Impact put out a large line of pencils, stencils, memo pads, binders, whistles, and much more. Pizza Hut even offered Universal Monsters plastic cups during the Halloween of 1992. While the Universal Studios "monster" logo featured faithful artwork of the Hungarian in 1990 and 1991, their "Dracula" soon became a vampire that bore no resemblance to him. Not due to any legal encounter, this change occurred in an attempt supposedly to modernize the look of the classic movie monsters. With Lugosi's growing cult status and ability to sell Universal-licensed merchandise since 1960, the decision to drop his image from the logo was indeed bizarre.

Taken straight from a Lugosi still is the Western Publishing 1991 puzzle, available as a 200-piece set or in a children's version. Also using a Lugosi photograph is the 1991 Harlo wristwatch. In 1993 Ready-Made Rubber of Downieville, California, peddled rubber stamps featuring Lugosi in Rick Geary artwork, while Classic Casting, Inc., sold a life mask of the actor during 1992. During this period, a mail order outfit offered perhaps the most outlandish and disrespectful merchandise, packets of soil supposedly taken from Bela's grave.

During the same decade, nostalgia for the sixties brought a revived "Captain Company" in a reincarnation of Ackerman's *Famous Monsters of Filmland*. The firm manufactured coffee mugs and computer mouse pads in 1994, along with reproductions of Lugosi's Dracula ring on a lapel pin. The same year — apparently to capitalize on Tim Burton's film *Ed Wood* — Stephen Dee released his "Irish Connection" sculpture of Ed Wood, Tor Johnson, and an unflattering representation of Lugosi.

Also during 1994, some products finally credited the "Lugosi Estate," including full-color "pogs" of Lugosi movie posters. Bela Lugosi, Jr., also became involved with Ron Chaney and Sara Jane Karloff in the struggle for a U.S. postal stamp featuring all three of their famous relatives.

Throughout the many decades of "Lugosiana," a more diehard section of the audience generated several fan clubs and organizations devoted to Lugosi. One Julia Skrupsky started an official fan club as early as 1936, and Richard Sheffield began an endorsed fan club in 1953 that sent out a newsletter, membership cards, and an autographed photo of Lugosi. The sixties found William Obbaggy helming the International Bela Lugosi Fan Club, which grew to a membership of more than 1,000 at its peak. Members were residents not only of the United States, but also of Australia, Canada, Germany, England, and France. His group published two *Bela Lugosi Bulletin*s and two *Bela Lugosi Journal*s, as well as sending out membership certificates and cards. The group even met on two occasions for "Bela Bashes," both held in Cleveland, Ohio. The first was in 1965, and the second, the following year, was held in conjunction with Tricon (sponsored by the three major cities of Ohio). The club was "official" and lasted from 1960 to 1969.

The same decade brought several other groups, like Chuck Luxemburg's 1963 group, the Bela Lugosi Fan Club in Sepulveda, California. The Boris, Bela, Lon Jr. Fan Club of Long Island, New York was another, short-lived club. Later, in 1986, Gary Don Rhodes formed the Bela Lugosi Society. In addition to pinback buttons and membership cards, the authorized organization published the *World of Bela Lugosi* newsletter from 1986 to 1989. In addition to members in almost all 50 states, the group included Lugosi fans from such countries as Austria, Germany, Japan, England, Australia, France, Canada, and Mexico.

In retrospect, the entire scope of collecting and merchandising, from well-meaning organizations to movie memorabilia and children's toys, represents a broad range of activity and interest. While Lugosi's popularity wanes occasionally, the world of Lugosi — and indeed the products it spawns — has never yet truly died.

24. Unmasking the Mysteries

To explore, unearth, and analyze data becomes the goal of historical research. However, missing pieces of information — as well as streams of misinformation — often keep precise answers at bay, just out of the researcher's grasp. Poorly documented accounts, "lost" artifacts, and forgotten memories create gaps in the historical record. Unfortunately, such problems are occasionally compounded by *fakirs*, who disseminate false data into the historical community — from the Konrad Kujaus that pen "Hitler's diaries" to the author that invents facts simply to excite readers.

Bela Lugosi's life and career presents numerous mysteries — riddles yet to be thoroughly solved. Thus, unmasking these historical phantoms to understand what is and is not known becomes necessary. Some of the following instances might forever remain lost to history, while others seem virtually unraveled. As a result of these investigations, however, the research trail can be blazed and the body of knowledge will grow.

1. The *Casanova* of Hungary, 1917

In discussing his Hungarian career with journalists and friends, Lugosi conjured images of a virile and dapper romantic lead. During the twenties, a few critics dubbed him the "Hungarian Barrymore"; the actor himself cited his success as Romeo and similar other roles in his homeland. Such tales painted a historical picture of Lugosi resembling a Casanova — a great lover igniting passion in his theatrical and screen audiences. The extent to which the portrait accurately renders his days in Budapest remains debatable. A more direct but equally difficult historical question asks whether he really appeared in the often-mentioned Hungarian film production of *Casanova* (1918).

Various histories of Hungarian cinema — some written years prior to any book-length biographies of the actor — place Lugosi in the cast of *Casanova*, including *Magyar Filmográfia* (Magyar Filmtudományi Intézet és Filmarchivum, 1962) and *Új Filmlexicon* (Akadémiai Kiadó, 1973). However, primary sources offer little help in verifying his role, with such journals as *Film Szemle*, *Mozgófénykép Hiradó*, and *Mozihét* providing no definite answers.

In May 1976, *Famous Monsters of Filmland* magazine published the article "If It's Midnight — This Must Be Transylvania," which carried an account of surviving footage from the original film at the Hungarian Film Institute. "The lights dimmed and *Casanova* flashed on the screen," the article mentioned. "A few minutes later, Lillian [Lugosi, the actor's fourth wife] whispered, 'That's him! That's Bela.' Sure enough, Bela was sitting on the edge of a marble bench romancing a young lady. Tears welled up in Lillian's eyes as she watched Bela wooing the young maiden. Just moments later, the screen flickered to white and the projector stopped, plunging the room into darkness."

Another reference appears in the biography *Lugosi: The Man Behind the Cape* (Henry Regnery, 1976), claiming, "The one third of *Casanova* which still survives, proves clearly that Bela's reputation as a romantic idol was well founded in every respect. In this film, he played the fiancé of a rich industrialist's daughter, and the few extant scenes of Bela wooing a beautiful, young actress on marble benches and chaise lounges scattered around a country estate only serve to whet the appetite for his more volatile stage performances and romances." An appendix in the same reference offers Lugosi, Annie Góth, and Viktor Kurd as cast members, with Cornelius Hintner as director for the Star Film production.

Yet, others that viewed the *Casanova* footage at the institute cannot discern Lugosi in the surviving fragments. Lugosi biographer Arthur Lennig screened the film, believing the Hungarian simply could not be seen. Playwright László Tábori watched the same 35 mm print on two separate occasions, unable to pinpoint Lugosi in any moment of the film. In the midseventies, Dr. István Molnár — the director of the institute itself — commented that Lugosi did not appear in their archive's footage.

Additionally, some period sources refer to *Casanova* as a Star Film directed not by Hintner, but rather Alfréd Deésy. Cast listings show not Góth and Kurd, but instead Kamilla Hollay, Marcel Rolla, Norbert Dán, Sandy Igalits, Richárd Kornai, and Gusztav Turán. Research also reveals Deésy, an actor and director, headlined the cast as Casanova. Though not listed in available reviews from 1918, if Lugosi had appeared most likely it would have been under the pseudonym Arisztid Olt, which he used in all of his other Star Film productions.

Hintner, a German director, definitely worked in Hungary during 1917 and 1918, remaining even after Miklós Horthy seized power. His productions for Budapest film companies include *Az Elrabolt Szerencse* and *Marion de Lorme*. Whether a second version of the Casanova tale was filmed in 1917 remains doubtful; no available records connect Lugosi and the German director in a professional or social situation.

In 1970, László Panczel — an acquaintance of Lugosi's during his Hungarian cinema career — remembered viewing *Casanova* in 1918. He told researcher Jon Hand that Lugosi definitely appeared in the film, but not in a leading role. As further evidence, Lugosi's own collection of stills contained several marked in his handwriting as *Casanova*.

Questions, however, remain unanswered, with Hungarian archives — at least for now — able to offer no more than what has already come to light. In some ways, the confusion adequately mirrors not only the political and artistic chaos Hungary experienced following the end of World War I, but also the problematized history of the nation's early cinema. Stored in German vaults, many Hungarian films were destroyed during the Nazi regime and World War II. Fragments remain of a few films; many titles unfortunately exist as mere names. Print sources and surviving photographs often offer the only insight into the content and merit

372   IV. Critique and Appreciation

Checking not for a vampire bite, but instead his tie. Lugosi appears here in a photo allegedly from *Casanova* (1917).

of a given film. For the most part, the moving images were stilled decades ago, and even their memory slowly fades to black.

2. *He Who* (Possibly) *Gets Slapped*, 1924

In 1924, on the heels of such successes as *The Shock* (1923) and *The Hunchback of Notre Dame* (1923), silent film icon Lon Chaney, Sr., took the title role in *He Who Gets Slapped*. After spending $172,000 on the budget, MGM saw a handsome profit of $349,000. It became one of the actor's great successes — both artistically and financially.

Three decades later, Bela Lugosi had befriended Richard Sheffield. The teenager visited his hero/friend regularly, often examining the actor's old files and clothing used in his films. One afternoon, he dipped into a scrapbook that Lugosi had put together himself. It covered the actor's silent film period in the United States, with a mixed bag of stills from such movies as *The Rejected Woman* (1924) and *The Midnight Girl* (1925).

Sifting through the contents, Dick spotted a single photograph from *He Who Gets Slapped*. The still showed two figures, both in clown costumes but both immediately recognizable to the young film addict. Chaney Sr. was on one side of the still, with Bela Lugosi on the other.

Dick never really asked Lugosi about Chaney Sr., the photograph, or the film itself. At that time, his major interests (and thus his questions to the actor) concentrated more on Lugosi's horror films of the thirties and forties. He and Lugosi also spoke of the actor's early years, his adventures and romances, his then-current plans, and his extreme hopes for a comeback; *He Who Gets Slapped* simply never came up.

That image of Lugosi and Chaney Sr., however, burned itself into Dick's mind. Years later, while examining the essay collection *Bela Lugosi* (Midnight Marquee, 1995), he thumbed through the filmography. At that time, it was the most complete such listing of Lugosi's feature-length movies ever compiled in one place.

For some reason as his fingers glided over the twenties, *He Who Gets Slapped* popped into his head. That it had never appeared in any Lugosi filmography never really occurred to him before. In the fifties, it was just another one of hundreds of stills that Lugosi owned; by 1995, any "new" piece of information on Lugosi was avidly sought after by collectors, writers, and fans.

He immediately phoned two Lugosi researchers, Gary D. Rhodes and Charles Heard. "Had anyone ever heard of this?" he quizzed. The response brought a resounding "no." Immediately, those few he spoke with assumed Dick had confused the Chaney film with a 1926 short called *Punchinello*, in which Lugosi did appear in a clown-like costume.

After examining stills from the latter, however, Dick grew more certain that he did remember correctly. After obtaining a print, he, Gary Rhodes, and Bob Shomer—another of Lugosi's old friends—screened the entire film. Eventually, Dick's eyes grew wide. He saw what clearly appears to be Lugosi.

A tall clown, topped with a hat, is visible in at least a few scenes. One medium closeup in particular offers glimpses at facial features that—despite the makeup—definitely looks like Lugosi. Next, Shomer even captured a still of the shot in his computer. All three huddled around the monitor, again scrutinizing what looked to be the Hungarian.

Is it odd that an unknown Lugosi appearance could have eluded film historians and scholars? The answer—without thinking twice—is of course no. Many still believe that there may be as yet uncovered Hungarian and German films with Lugosi. For years, filmographies left off not only early efforts like *Leoni Leo* (1917), but even his Hollywood films like *The Devil's in Love* (1933). Additionally, Lugosi's work in the theater, vaudeville, radio, and television also yield "new" discoveries from time to time.

However, a few problems still remain before embracing *He Who Gets Slapped* into the Lugosi filmography. Unlike the mysteries of *Casanova* (1917) or *Lock Up Your Daughters* (1959), absolutely no known documents, reviews, or paper work of any kind link the actor with the Chaney silent. Even the still photograph of Lugosi from the film is long since missing; initially, the scrapbook went from Dick's collection to that of magazine editor Forrest J Ackerman. By 1995, however, it was no longer in his archives. As a result, no hard evidence can credibly place this in the Lugosi canon. The film itself of course has no on-screen credit for Lugosi, and prints offer only the potentially deceiving proof of an actor under makeup in a clown costume.

Perhaps part of the hesitance to immediately accept the film as a Lugosi appearance stems from the fact it is a Chaney Sr. classic. Rightly or wrongly, Chaney has always been seen as the silent film predecessor to Lugosi and Karloff. If Lugosi — horror's dark prince of the thirties and forties — did appear in one of his films, it becomes a particularly amazing discovery.

Prior to this question, the connections between the two were slight. Comparisons, which Lugosi had quickly downplayed, were made in the 1931 movie fan press. The Hungarian of course worked with Tod Browning, the director so often associated with Chaney Sr., in *The Thirteenth Chair* (1929) and *Dracula* (1931). In the same vein, the duo even collaborated on *Mark of the Vampire* (1935), a remake of Lon Chaney's 1927 hit *London After Midnight*.

Other important questions also arise in the attempt to place Lugosi in the film. For one, the production lasted some 37 days between June 17 and July 28, 1924. MGM shot apparently all scenes in California. Though certainly no "proof" keeps him from Hollywood at that time, it has generally been thought that all of his films of the early to midtwenties had been filmed in the New York area.

This had been the case not just to those numerous films of the period (like *The Silent Command* of 1923) which were made on the East Coast, but also his own quotes from 1928 newspapers. No historical quotes or oral histories should be taken without scrutiny, least of all Lugosi's. However, during a West Coast stage tour of *Dracula*, his comments did seemingly indicate he had not previously been in films made in Hollywood. "I like your California," he told one reporter that year, "And who knows, I may go into pictures here."

For a more critical look at this question, however, an examination of known dates in Lugosi's life during 1924 prove to be a help. Prior to May, he had appeared in one film definitely shot on the East Coast, *The Rejected Woman*. During the fifth month of that year, he appeared in a New York court. The same lawsuit took him back to court on October 1 of the same year.

Interestingly, a gap does occur during those 37 shooting days of *He Who Gets Slapped*. In late May, Béla was in Chicago for rehearsals of the play *The Werewolf*. It had its Adelphi Theater premiere on June 1, though by its second week Lugosi had been replaced by his understudy. The reason was unexplained by newspapers;

reports of Lugosi's performance were mixed, but at least one favorable notice of his work appeared.

Could it be that Béla left for Hollywood at that time, hoping to break into the movie capital at that stage? If he did, the lack of on-screen billing in *He Who Gets Slapped*, a subsequent lack of work in general, old bills and court costs, and a problematic marriage in New York could have drawn him quickly back to the East Coast and its Hungarian community that he loved so much.

The movie itself, which had been copyrighted as LP20745 on November 10, 1924, ran seven reels in length. According to its original registration, it even featured "amber sequences." It was the first film of the fledgling MGM, and received numerous accolades from the critics. Furthermore, almost as interesting as the combination of Lugosi and Chaney is the possible direction of the former by the legendary Victor Seastrom. Regardless, by the time of the film's release, Béla was certainly back in New York, as wife Ilona von Montágh sued for divorce and the two were in court on November 11.

The mystery, however, lives on as so great a puzzle that it is currently impossible to substantiate its inclusion in Lugosi filmographies. Those intriguing scenes within the film itself fan the flames of curiosity all the more. Thus, *He Who Gets Slapped* remains a silent film in more than one way. On the subject of Lugosi, its credits — as well as any known written materials regarding the project — are completely mute.

3. Frankenstein Test Footage, 1931

> *Bela Lugosi*— For Sale: Screen test Bela Lugosi made for the original Frankenstein. 35 mm sound, running time 21 minutes; same scene is shown twice with change in lighting, etc. Between scenes camera was left running and Carl Laemmle, James Whale, Colin Clive and Lugosi can be seen and heard discussing test and wardrobe Lugosi was wearing. Film can be examined and screened *before* purchase is made. Price: $4,000. Don Marlowe. Hollywood, Calif. 90028

The above advertisement appeared in *Classic Film Collector* magazine's Spring/Summer 1970 issue. The same notice appeared in a 1970 edition of the French film publication *Midi Minuit Fantastique* along with the article "Essai Bela Lugosi pour Frankenstein." Startling and wonderful, the notice actually became important news as much as an advertisement. One of the most tremendous events in cinema history, the *Frankenstein* test footage with Lugosi stood as a celluloid record of the Hungarian in the very role that became Karloff's, an event that many cite as *the* crucial decision in his Hollywood career. The film would render a glimpse at another world, one that may have come to pass if Lugosi had merged with the cinematic monster of Shelley's story. Moreover, the footage could act as an oracle, answering questions regarding Lugosi's performance and particularly his makeup. The conversation described in the ad would even present insight into Lugosi's attitude. In short, it was and is the Holy Grail of horror film history.

Marlowe himself had acted as Lugosi's manager during the late forties; the two remained friends until the actor's death. Little doubt exists he labored hard attempting to find work for Lugosi. The manager also spent much time helping forgotten film stars, often taking former headliners like Madge Bellamy to lunch. He also regularly screened old movies at veteran's hospitals. As early as 1963, Marlowe ran ads in *Horror Monsters* magazine, selling duplicates of Lugosi photographs and the bereavement card from his funeral for $2 each.

Immediately after the ads appeared, numerous persons attempted to see the footage, but to no avail. Marlowe told one friend that he sold the film to Carl Laemmle, Jr., for $3,500 on the condition that he guaranteed it had never been duplicated. Laemmle purchased the film not because he himself had been involved in the horror film genre of the thirties, but rather due to the filmed discussion Marlowe described. Along with those named in the ad, Carl Laemmle, Sr.,— the producer's father and founder of Universal Studios — appeared and could be heard briefly. Intrigued, the friend offered Marlowe $500 in cash to make a quick 16 mm dupe prior to completion of the Laemmle sale. "He agreed," the friend recalled recently, "but never produced the film."

Would anyone falsely advertise any one-of-a-kind item in the hopes of making a quick dollar and use their real name, especially if he or she was relatively well-known? Since almost no collector would purchase sight unseen, why should anyone waste money to procure ads knowing from the onset their register would always ring "no sale"? Yet, if someone did honestly advertise such a rarity, why would he or she refuse to show it to buyers with money in hand? Moreover, why would friends of a such a person — again with ready cash — not be allowed the privilege of at least screening the merchandise? Though of course other motivations and actions could impact such a scenario, extreme doubt remains the most likely analysis.

As per Marlowe's "sale" to Carl Laemmle, Jr., could the former studio executive have held a strong desire for the footage? In addition to the "footage" of his father in the test, Junior did retain a fondness for the horror films of Universal. A particularly odd story claims Junior invited director Robert Florey to his home in the late sixties. Out of curiosity, Florey agreed. An Asian servant met the director at the door, with Junior himself emerging from behind a wall of hanging beads. Laemmle's hair touched his shoulders; his eyes grew excited and intense. He had a new idea for another "monster" story and wanted Florey to develop the script. The French filmmaker declined, emphasizing how busy he was directing television programs. Later, in a French article, Florey expressed amusement at the situation.

After the initial shock of reading the footage might exist, Marlowe's ad intrigued collectors at the time in its mention of director James Whale rather than Robert Florey. A tenant of horror film history usually insists that Whale — after taking charge of *Frankenstein* late in the summer of 1931— had nothing to do with Lugosi. Students of film history knew well that Florey directed the test. As early as 1948 in his book *Hollywood d'hier et d'aujourd'hui*, Florey chronicled his memories (translated here by Evelyn Copeland). "I outlined about fifty sketches to illustrate my ideas, and in one of the sets of Dracula, I filmed two reels of tests with Bela Lugosi, specialist in monster roles. The Hungarian actor didn't show himself very enthusiastic for the role and didn't want to play it."

Scholar Brian Taves chronicled the test in his book *Robert Florey: The French*

Expressionist (Scarecrow, 1987). While some historians occasionally doubt the filmmaker's memories, Taves used corroborating oral history from cinematographer Paul Ivano. Both recalled that Lugosi—despite his protests—gave an admirable performance; such is not difficult to imagine, given the actor usually put forth much effort in even the most abysmal of his film projects. Curiously, the two also remembered his interpretation of the role as not too dissimilar to Karloff's.

Taves also discovered cameraman Ivano's notebook, which places the Florey test on June 16 and 17, 1931. Three thousand feet of test footage resulted in some 20 minutes of edited footage, the "two reels" Florey described in his 1948 book. Memories of the director and cinematographer include hints of wide angle lenses, bizarre composition, stark lighting, double exposures, and an elaborate 360° panoramic shot of the laboratory and lifeless monster. Shot on a *Dracula* set, the laboratory more resembled a medieval cave or alchemist's lair suggestive of *Metropolis* (1926) than a more "modern" setting.

Lugosi himself appeared only in the final five minutes of the edited footage, with the director remembering the actor's unhappiness. In one interview, Florey claimed the Hungarian ripped the improvised bolts from his neck. An oft-repeated quote finds Lugosi barking, "I was a star in my country and will not be a scarecrow over here!" Disenchanted with the makeup, the actor also disliked the monster's lack of dialogue; a few years earlier, he almost refused the title role in the 1927 *Dracula* stage production due to the Count's limited lines. After the Hungarian saw the footage, however, he offered Ivano an expensive cigar, proclaiming the cinematographer caught his profile wonderfully.

Both Florey's *Murders in the Rue Morgue* (1932) and Whale's *Frankenstein* (1931) owe much to the brilliant expressionist film *The Cabinet of Dr. Caligari* (1919). Historians have well-covered the German masterpiece, though oral histories of *Caligari*'s production offer skewed and highly contradictory stories covering creative origins. *Frankenstein* brings out equally conflicting memories, with historians left to analyze the extent of Florey's contributions.

With absolutely no photographs or film footage presently available, Lugosi's makeup remains a mystery and the source of perhaps the greatest contradictions. Marlowe told one friend that the test he owned showed Lugosi in a garb resembling the huge, bulky garb of *The Golem* (1920), though without the Star of David that Paul Wegener wore in the German film. The manager went on to say he believed the makeup had not been applied by Jack Pierce, adding that Lugosi said he would have accepted the makeup Karloff wore and played the role. Prior to Marlowe's ads, historian Forrest J Ackerman interviewed actor Edward Van Sloan, who appeared in the test footage. Their talk resulted in Ackerman's belief that Lugosi had in fact resembled the clay statue of *The Golem* (1920). Yet, Marlowe's story relates one major flaw; Paul Ivano's notebook reveals Jack Pierce did apply the makeup, whatever it looked like.

The Golem in its stage and screen appearances was no doubt a creative analogue for the makeup, yet Shelley's own novel and stage versions of *Frankenstein* must have been other possibilities perused. Florey's own memories recall the bolts on either side of Lugosi's neck. Makeup man Jack Pierce remembered for the *New*

York Times that he used medical texts to help understand how such a creation should look. Lugosi himself rarely mentioned the footage, speaking of it once to a British journalist in 1951 as a "costume test," giving no details. Obviously, an investigation of mere oral histories yields little real insight into the design Lugosi wore on those summer afternoons in 1931.

Florey's original director's copy of the script — which by 1996 had never seen publication — offers sketches intended for Lugosi that are basically similar to what Karloff wore in the film. In the Library of Congress, author David J. Skal uncovered designs for Shelley's creature as drawn by Universal artists during 1931. The artwork ranged from a steel and robotic machine with neck bolts to Neanderthal-style beasts. A preliminary movie poster that bears Lugosi's name shows a large titan, with rays of light beaming down upon a frantic crowd. The monster's appearance, which has no bolts or scars, features somewhat curly hair. The result of such archival materials also offer far too many discrepancies to properly indicate Lugosi's makeup in the test. A more conclusive artifact would be the few frames of film that Paul Ivano kept from the raw footage; unfortunately, he discarded them during the forties.

If nothing else, Marlowe's mention of James Whale reveals one very important historical possibility. Admirers of the stylish director sometimes insist he had nothing to do with Lugosi; it is not difficult to assume otherwise. For one, a letter Whale wrote to Colin Clive, which the *New York Times* reprinted on October 11, 1931, mentioned, "I think the cast will be old Frederick Kerr as your father, Baron Frankenstein, John Boles as Victor, Bela Lugosi or Boris Karloff as the Monster, Dwight Frye as the dwarf, Van Sloan as Dr. Waldeman, and I am making a test of Mae Clarke as Elizabeth." No doubt Carl Laemmle, Jr., envisioned Lugosi, Universal's "new Chaney," as the monster to help insure box-office success. Florey once claimed Karloff's appearance in the makeup so convinced Laemmle that he hired the actor on the spot, yet he possibly would have received only second-hand information as he had already been moved to the *Murders in the Rue Morgue* set. Lugosi often mentioned he suggested "his friend Boris" for the role to help keep from becoming the monster himself; his story is almost certainly false.

Whale's 1931 correspondence reveals Lugosi remained a consideration despite the Hungarian's dislike for the role and the fact Florey had already been transferred to the Poe story. Whale opted for Karloff, which could well have been his desire from the start. Any pressure from Universal to use their Dracula might have been allayed from the director and Hungarian's mutual desire that the actor not appear. Yet, obviously Whale chose to shoot numerous tests to insure the appropriateness of his actors and actresses, as can be seen in his letter's mention of Mae Clarke. Even forgetting the Marlowe ad entirely, a second Lugosi test — under Whale's supervision — could have easily been filmed.

Such a test perhaps helped Whale to decide against Lugosi, to help show his inadequacy for the role to the studio, or both. Though there is no real record of it, a second test certainly helps better explain the varied array of memories and descriptions of Lugosi's makeup and the test itself. Moreover, it paves a better understanding of why Whale declined Lugosi's talents and how the actor himself escaped the transformation into Shelley's monster for the released film.

Surveying the many incomplete retellings of the test footage saga, historian Brian Taves once appropriately balked, "Isn't it amazing how much sloppy scholarship has persisted around these questions?" If a deeper investigation of primary sources and survivors like Jack Pierce began while still possible, fewer questions would prevail. More "memories" at this point simply add to the brew of confusion; only the slim chance of extant test footage or stills from the unmade Lugosi version of *Frankenstein* could really shed any important light. Unfortunately, the test footage is not presently for sale, and — unless protected in the hands of a quiet collector — it most likely will always carry the title "lost." The Holy Grail of the horror film remains the missing piece in an important cinematic puzzle.

4. *White Zombie*'s Missing Moments, 1932

Numerous tales exist of footage deleted from Lugosi films, such as Edward Van Sloan's curtain speech in *Dracula* (1931) or Lugosi's dialogue sequences in *Frankenstein Meets the Wolf Man* (1943). Very often such footage lingered for decades in studio vaults, only to be found unusable due to decomposition — in the case of the Van Sloan speech — or for film to actually become "missing/stolen" as with the unused color test footage shot for *Son of Frankenstein* (1939). In the case of Lugosi's classic Universal Studios films, such footage that survived collected dust without any care given it until the company grasped the potential profit. By that late date, a part of film history was sometimes lost.

If scholars and fans reserve a special status for any non–Universal Lugosi film, it is certainly *White Zombie* (1932). The nightmarish, melodramatic chiller continues to fascinate viewers and endures as one of Lugosi's very best sound films of any genre. Pressbooks and initial reviews offered 74 minutes as the original running time, yet through its subsequent releases *White Zombie* prints were cut to 68 minutes and 66 minutes. Others have circulated at under one hour, probably trimmed for early television.

The film has not been seen at 74 minutes in decades, probably since one of its three releases in the thirties. As with some examples of Lugosi's Universal canon, a portion of the cut footage actually managed to escape destruction for some decades. Rather than in the vaults of a major studio, however, the footage rested in the collection of Sherman S. Krellberg. In the late seventies, Storace Films, a distributor of classic movies on 16 mm and Super 8 mm, made arrangements to obtain a print from Krellberg's nitrate negative of *White Zombie*, including any formerly excised footage that still existed.

Frank Storace, president of the Scottsdale, Arizona, based company soon found that only some two or three minutes of cut sequences existed in the Krellberg collection. While not enough to return *White Zombie* to 74 minutes, the footage would restore the film to within a few minutes of that initial length. Visually, the "new" material meant striking shots of zombies lurking over the Haitian countryside, working in sugar cane fields, and other moody images. The footage did not include any dialogue sequences. When discovered, however, the film showed slight deterioration and the final agreement necessitated Krellberg restoring the scenes before turning them over to Storace.

Yet, Krellberg's subsequent death ceased any further activity on the restoration, with Storace left to deal with the attorneys. Among those supportive of his plight was Leonard Kohl, a Lugosi collector and historian with whom Storace corresponded. In 1979, as Kohl offered encouragement, Storace began legal proceedings.

While he waited for the Krellberg estate to follow through, Storace watched numerous other companies duplicate and sell *White Zombie* prints made directly from his own version. Storace Films lost money on their 68 minute version to unscrupulous film duplicators; the company also lost money dealing with the estate's lawyers over the deleted footage. Yet, Storace persisted.

Labs informed him the deleted footage appeared to be deteriorating further, with the Krellberg collection selling to another collector. Attorney fees mounted and Frank Storace's communications to Leonard Kohl illustrate the concern. "It has come to pass that I will probably never get it," he opined in February of 1981. Though he attempted to interest the American Film Institute, they showed little concern. The new owner of the footage apparently cared little of its historical value as well.

Despite his legal right to the footage and his admirable, undying concern for the deleted materials, Storace remained unable to obtain the missing minutes from *White Zombie* (1932). Given 1981 lab reports on the scenes, their fate is easy to guess. Moments of one of Lugosi's most important films — a classic of the cinema — were left to die as decomposed nitrate ... dimly lit images that forever merged with the past.

5. The Strange Death of Yolande Evans, 1940

Though many in the thirties assumed Yolande Evans to be of French birth, she was actually born in New York's East Side around 1913, "a dark child of the tenements, with the angelic face and fear-haunted eyes." At age 17, she married a transportation worker after having known him for only two days. Three weeks later she demanded they both leave town and, when he refused, the penniless Yolande became a stowaway on the *Il de France*. After a short time overseas (including five days in a Havre jail for illegally boarding the luxury liner), she returned to the United States.

In 1935 Yolande (under the name "Iris Fontana") traveled to Asia to study "war conditions for publication and radio broadcasting." In other situations, the young adventuress used pseudonyms, including Yolande Palmer, Iris Johnson, and Iris Patton. By October 1939, she had returned to the United States, remarried, and opened a Broadway office with a branch in Hollywood. Apparently the new marriage found little success, although her business prospered. Among those she knew and attempted to find stories for were Edward Everett Horton, Edmund Lowe, Lenore Ulric, Gladys Cooper, Ruth Chatterton, and Dorothy MacKaill.

Enter Bela Lugosi. Allegedly the most insistent of those attempting to obtain a story from the play broker, the actor offered her $10,000 for a tale that combined horror, romance, and elements of other genres. Perhaps he desired to produce films independently, as he attempted in 1935. Lugosi apparently read or at least heard the treatment and grew excited, but Evans refused to sell.

Shortly thereafter, authorities found the adventuress dead in her lush New York apartment. Gas still rose from three burners on the kitchen stove. Affectionately autographed photos of numerous stars lined the walls. A note on a telephone table began "Call up ...," but trailed off in an unfinished manner. Neighbors later claimed her current husband Harry left the apartment the evening before carrying numerous suitcases.

"There's your story, Mr. Lugosi, and what do you think of it?" journalist Charles Neville asked in his 1940 article "Challenge to the Bogeyman." Neville mentioned Lugosi in suspicious terms throughout his essay, even suggesting the actor would probably develop the story idea without having to pay anyone a dime.

Though few articles appeared on Evans' death, Neville himself strongly attempted to cast a shadow of guilt over Lugosi. His reason remains unknown, as does the extent to which Lugosi actually knew Yolande Evans. In actuality, no evidence connects the actor with the bizarre suicide. The greater mystery perhaps becomes why a journalist so desired to make that connection.

6. *Lock Up Your Daughters*, 1959

Author Ramsey Cambell's fascinating novel *Ancient Images* (Scribner's, 1987) detailed the search for a lost Bela Lugosi film produced in England and titled *The Tower of Evil*. Both *Ancient Images* and its missing movie were a product of Cambell's imagination, resulting in an enjoyable novel. However, the real-life British release called *Lock Up Your Daughters* results in a similar search for the truth.

Biographies and horror film histories occasionally mention this film, with some claiming *Lock Up Your Daughters* is merely a compilation of clips from previous films that starred the actor. Others cite "new," unseen footage of Lugosi that appears along with footage from his Monogram horror films of the forties. Unearthing evidence places much weight for the latter case, though until a print surfaces no final conclusion can be drawn.

Though the British Film Institute's *Monthly Film Bulletin* never reviewed the movie, they did include the following entry in April, 1959:

Lock Up Your Daughters, U.S.A.
Cert: XDist: New RealmD: Phil Rosen
LP: Bela Lugosi, Polly Ann Young, The Bowery Boys.
4,590 feet 50 mins.

A review did appear in *Kinematograph Weekly* on March 26, 1959, mentioning the same vital statistics. Critic John Billings claimed, "The picture, compered by Bela Lugosi, has a slight story about a vampire doctor who experiments on young women in order to bring back to life his lovely young wife and this provides legitimate excuses for the extracts from Lugosi thrillers. Its players range from the Bowery Boys to some of the great favourites of yesteryear."

Obviously, by use of the outdated term "compered," the trade strongly hints Lugosi acted as master of ceremonies of the various clips. Some months later, in January 1960, the British film collector Alan Dodd watched the mysterious movie,

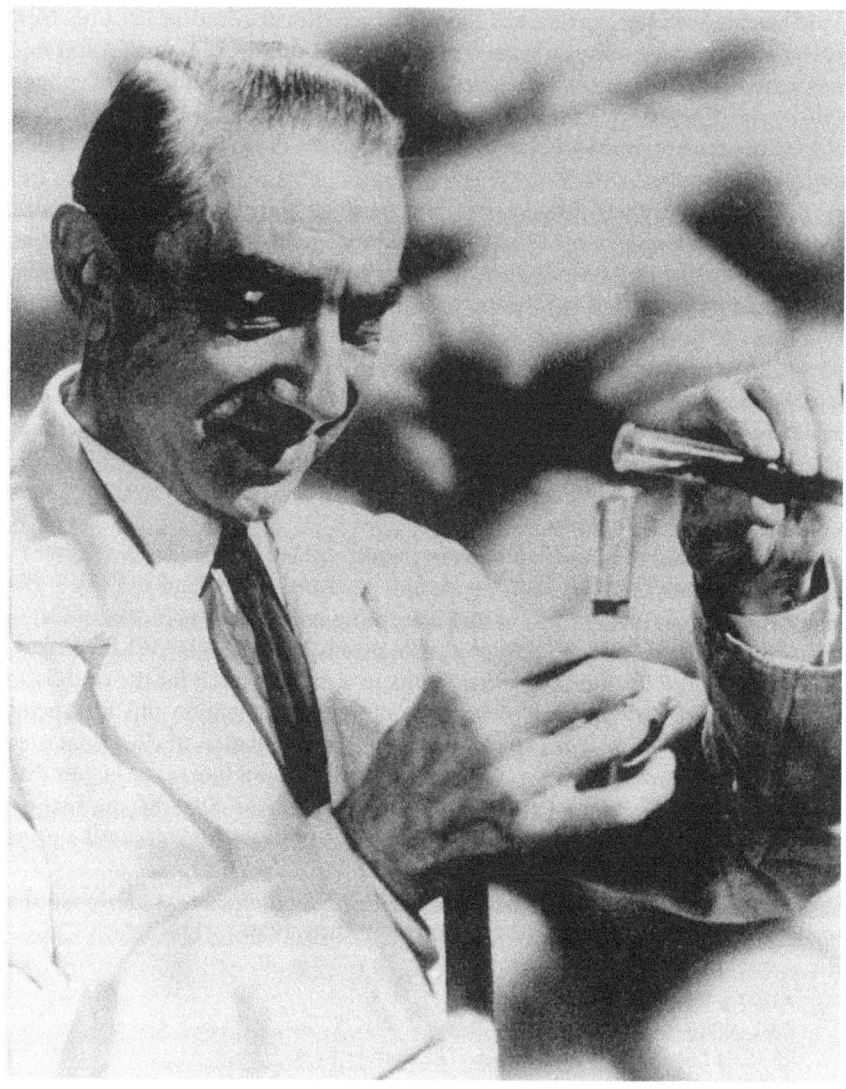

Lugosi in a publicity still for *Bela Lugosi Meets a Brooklyn Gorilla* (1952).

writing his reactions to Forrest J Ackerman on February 1. "Saw an interesting old horror film last week called *Lock Up Your Daughters* which had Bela Lugosi introducing a series of blended excerpts from several of his old horror films — none of which I'd seen before. Sam Katzman was the man concerned," he mentioned to the editor of *Famous Monsters of Filmland* magazine.

Later sources include a 1965 booklet by Harold Jordan called *The Films of Bela Lugosi*, which mentioned the movie featured an "introduction" and "filmed commentary" by the actor. Other fan magazines in the sixties claim an on-camera

Lugosi called the film his "obituary," adding that the footage was filmed in 1956. If New Realm really utilized such clips, they were probably not lengthy given the running time of the overall film.

Though secondary sources should not be considered as reliable evidence, the *Kinematograph* review and the original, preserved account of an audience member become important. The British Film Institute believes these materials clearly suggest the idea of unseen footage, though of course the problem could be solved beyond question by merely viewing the film.

Unfortunately, extreme difficulty exists in finding a copy of the film. Though New Realm released *Lock Up Your Daughters*, they have neither a print or any records concerning the project. The British Film Institute also lacks any print or knowledge of existing copies. Various personal correspondence indicated a copy existed in the personal collection of a British film buff. The collector in question died years ago, with his personal possessions drifting into unknown hands.

As far as the origin of film clips, *Invisible Ghost* (1941), *Voodoo Man* (1944), and either *Spooks Run Wild* (1941) or *Ghosts on the Loose* (1943) definitely contributed scenes to *Lock Up Your Daughters*. An author and film fan, now deceased, that saw the film in the aforementioned private collection also mentioned *The Ape Man* (1943), *Return of the Ape Man* (1944), and *White Zombie* (1932). With this account, however, one must consider that — as it took place during the sixties in a country that had rarely witnessed these films under their original titles — identification of these clips could easily have been incorrect. One rumor, though far from substantiated, also claims out-takes of *Mother Riley Meets the Vampire* (1951) appeared.

Period sources, including British trade magazines, generally list Sam Katzman as producer and Phil Rosen as director, though the latter died in 1951, years before *Lock Up Your Daughters*. New Realm possibly affixed the names of both simply because they were connected with the Monogram films involved. The distributor released numerous Lugosi Monograms under new titles. As to who could have filmed any "new" footage of Lugosi, the question remains. Rather than Sam Katzman, the most likely candidate given the midfifties time period would have been Edward D. Wood, Jr. Yet, no evidence presently affirms Wood's involvement, let alone the secure pronouncement of unseen Lugosi footage. New Realm themselves (being a low-budget firm located an ocean away from Lugosi) probably could not have shot the footage, though some British entity might have while the actor toured England in 1951.

Lock Up Your Daughters remains unusual in even another way, becoming England's "first filmic quiz." Press sheets gave viewers an address to write and gave further details of "over £5,000 in prize money to be won," though Alan Dodd complained that the theater itself made no mention of any method of obtaining the prizes. Audiences needed to identify the film titles from which the extracts were taken. Most viewers had not ever seen the films, and those that had witnessed them under any one of a myriad of title changes. Trades never reported any winners, just as no historians have announced discovering a print of the film.

7. Jean Boullet and the Lugosi Obsession, 1960s

Horror film historiography often tends to be brief and poor, lacking both a theoretical base and original research through primary sources. Perhaps this was most true prior to the eighties, as during that decade David J. Skal, Gregory Mank, and a few others propelled the standards for such work to a much higher level. Yet, despite the difficulties the genre has met in its search for true understanding and documentation, never have facts concerning Lugosi been so oddly and purposely skewed as in the bizarre case of the late Jean Boullet.

Fascination with the cinema in France heightened during the fifties and sixties, yet a stream of misinformation accidentally entered television broadcasts and printed matter on the subject. For example, in approximately 1965, one telecast reported the death of Boris Karloff (who lived until 1969), but claimed Bela Lugosi was alive and well (though he had died in 1956). Into this mix came critic Jean Boullet, a non-professional actor, a painter, and a friend of such noted French artists as Jean Cocteau.

Boullet's interest in Lugosi ignited a fixation that drove the critic to dress completely in black and live in a home with ebony ceilings and red walls. In his numerous essays, the critic claimed Lugosi to be identical to his screen persona. He wrote that the Hungarian lived "in a castle covered with spider webs, without electricity," and slept "in a coffin all night." In giving accounts of Lugosi's death, Boullet asserted that the actor went insane toward the end of his life and died in a hospital at "twelve knocks of midnight." The Hungarian supposedly screamed, "I'm Dracula; I'm immortal!" as the life force left his body. Boullet further contended in his articles that Lugosi's nurse fainted when an enormous bat soared into the room through an open window.

Wildly inaccurate stories of this type became the main biographical data on Lugosi many French cinema fans read during the period. Unfortunately, Boullet's idolatry spurred his imagination to generate tales of what he deeply wanted the actor to have been like in real life. By contrast, the French critic held little regard for Boris Karloff, whose average lifestyle meant the Englishman could never be a "true" horror actor.

In the final weeks of 1970, Boullet committed suicide by hanging. At that time, some accurate information on Lugosi supplanted Boullet's earlier tales; however, it took years for French historians such as Jean-Claude Michel to quell the more ridiculous stories and provide truthful accounts. As for the unfortunate Boullet, he remains evidence of a film buff whose interests grew into a deadly obsession.

Index

Numbers in **boldface** refer to pages with photographs. Numbers *italicized* in parentheses refer to entry numbers on the page given.

Abbott, Bud 31, 32, 136–138 *(88)*, **139**, 206 *(21)*, 208, 261 *(342)*, 334 *(4)*
Abbott and Costello Double Feature 322 *(14)*
Abbott and Costello Meet Frankenstein ix, 31, 55 *(13)*, 57, 64, 136–138 *(88)*, **139**, 140 *(89)*, 181, 196 *(32)*, 206 *(21)*, 209 *(2)*, 214 *(14)*, 223 *(56)*, 261 *(339, 340, 341, 342)*, 298 *(24)*, 307 *(41)*, 324, 326 *(7)*, 330 *(10)*, 334 *(4, 12)*, 349, 354, 363
The Abbott and Costello Show 206–207 *(21)*
Academy of Motion Picture Arts and Sciences 338 *(5)*
Academy of Performing Arts (Hungary) 4
Ackerman, Forrest J x, xi, 37, 199 *(45)*, 211 *(13)*, 266 *(403)*, 269 *(445)*, 272 *(483)*, 273 *(494)*, 276 *(523)*, 283 *(31)*, 287 *(67)*, 307 *(40)*, 321 *(4)*, 327, 330 *(11, 19)*, 335 *(22)*, 337 *(1)*, 356, 363, 365, 369, 374 *(2)*, 377 *(3)*, 382 *(6)*
The Ackerman Archives 337 *(1)*
Action to Liberate Hungary **58**, 193 *(23)*
Actor's Relief Fund 22
Adams, Julie 279 *(7)*
Adams, Marjorie 260 *(333)*
Adler, Nicholas 11
The Admirable Crichton (Egyenlöség) 154 *(16)*
The Adopted Father (A Fogadott Apa) 159 *(97)*
Adrian 79 *(30)*, 104 *(54)*, 113 *(62)*
Aesop (Aesopus) 161 *(119)*, 162 *(144)*
An Affair to Remember 83 *(33)*
Agee, James 259 *(323)*
Ahogy Tetsik see *As You Like It*
Alan, Josh 271 *(471)*, 323 *(20)*, 332 *(3)*, 348
Álarcosbál see *The Masked Ball*
Albertson, Frank 83 *(33)*

Alcohol/Alcoholism x, 34
Alcoholics Anonymous 34
Alexander, Richard 150 *(4)*
All Quiet on the Western Front 87 *(37)*
Allan, Elizabeth 104 *(54)*, 360
Allan, Ted 142 *(92)*
Allen, Fred 201, 204 *(11)*
Allen, Gracie 19, 198 *(39)*
Az Allamtitkam Ur see *The Secretary of State*
Alma, Marian 70 *(13)*
Alraune 68 *(4)*, 70 *(9)*
Alwyn, Kenneth 323 *(18)*
Amazon Women on the Moon 334 *(13)*
The Ambassador's Attaché (Az Attaché) 160 *(109)*
American Film Institute 384 *(4)*
American-Hungarian Defense Federation 26, 61; 1943 bond rally 193 *(22)*
American International Pictures (AIP) 351
American Syrian Society fundraiser 190 *(11)*
Ames, Adrienne 96 *(46)*
Ames, Leon see Waycoff, Leon
Ames, Michael 130 *(81)*, 131 *(82)*
L'Ami des Femmes 161 *(129)*
Amihez Minden Asszony Ert see *What Every Woman Knows*
Amusement Securities Corporation 93 *(43)*
Anatol 158 *(72)*
Ancient Images 285 *(56)*
Anderson, John 232 *(27)*
Anderson, John Murray 82 *(32)*
Anderson, Maxwell 88 *(39)*
Andrew and Joanna (Andre és Johanna) 160 *(102)*
Ankers, Evelyn 121–122 *(71)*, 123–124 *(73)*, 193 *(21)*, 253 *(258)*, 287 *(70)*
Anna Karenina 156 *(41)*, 158 *(72, 78)*

385

386 Index

Anobile, Richard J. 285 *(49)*
The Ape Man 26, 30, 98 *(47)*, 128–129 *(78)*, 131 *(81)*, 132 *(82)*, 198 *(37)*, 255 *(281, 282)*, 325, 327 *(14, 16)*, 354, 383 *(6)*
Apollo Theater (Budapest) 189 *(1)*
Arabesque 11, 167–168 *(176)*, 169 *(177)*, 231 *(20, 21)*, 288
Arabian Nights (Ezeregy Éjszaka) 153 *(6)*
Aranyember see *Golden Man*
Az Aranykakas see *The Golden Rooster*
Az Aranylakodalom see *The Golden Wedding*
Arch, Lillian see Lugosi, Lillian Arch
Archer, John 126 *(76)*
Argyle, John 114 *(63)*
Arkoff, Samuel Z. 283, 300–301
Arlen, Richard 95–96 *(45)*
Armbrister, Cyril 147–148 *(2)*
Armetta, Henry 74 *(22)*, 100 *(50)*, 102 *(51)*
Arsenic and Old Lace (1943) 27, 31, 34, 130 *(80)*, 178–179 *(187)*, 256 *(293)*, 257 *(295, 297)*, 311, 314 *(14, 15, 16)*, 349
Arsenic and Old Lace (1944) 27, 131 *(81)*, 179–180 *(188)*, 258 *(306, 307)*, 314 *(17)*, 315 *(18, 19)*
Arsenic and Old Lace (1954) 186 *(202)*, 263
Arsenic and Old Lace (film) 221–222 *(39)*
Arsenic and Old Lace (radio) 321 *(6)*
Arsenic and Old Lace (summer stock) 152, 182 *(191)*, 183 *(196)*, 184 *(198, 199)*, 185 *(199)*, 193 *(28, 29)*, 208–209 *(1)*, 260 *(336)*, 277 *(533)*, 349
Arsenic and Old Lace (television) 184 *(196)*
Arthur, Robert 137 *(88)*
Árva László Kiraly see *Lonely King Lazlo*
As You Like It (Ahogy Tetsik) 164 *(162)*
Asher, E.M. 86 *(37)*, 91 *(42)*
Atkinson, J. Brooks 232 *(22, 24, 28)*, 242 *(142)*
Atlas, Charles 202 *(6)*
Az Attaché see *The Ambassador's Attaché*
Attack of the Monster Movie Makers: Interviews with 20 Genre Giants 283 *(36)*, 358
Atwill, Lionel 104 *(54)*, 111–112 *(60)*, 112–113 *(61)*, 123–124 *(73)*, 125 *(75)*, 126–127 *(77)*, 135 *(86)*, 136 *(87)*, 148 *(2)*, 201, 222 *(45)*, 255 *(275, 276)*, 309, 360, 361

Aubert, Lenore 136–138 *(88)*
Auer, John 78 *(27)*
Aurora models 366
Austin, Gene 102 *(51)*
Austro-Hungarian Empire 3
Autographs 272, 363, 366
Autry, Gene 36, 226 *(76)*
Ayres, Lew 87 *(37)*

Babbit, Harry 117 *(66)*
Bábjáték see *Puppet Show*
Baccarat 156 *(43)*
Backstage at the Spa Theater 208–209 *(1)*
Baclanova, Olga 175–176 *(184)*
Bacon, Lloyd 88 *(38)*
Bagatelle 165 *(171)*
A Bajusz see *The Mustache*
Baker, Phil 102 *(51)*
Baker, Rick 275 *(517)*
Baker's Broadcast 202 *(5)*
Balázs, Béla 160 *(107)*
Balderston, John 13, 86 *(37)*, 104 *(54)*, 170 *(179)*, 217 *(5)*, 237 *(82)*, 287 *(71)*
A Balga Szüz see *The Foolish Virgin*
The Balkan Princess (A Balkáni Hercegnö) 155 *(37)*
A Balkáni Hercegnö see *The Balkan Princess*
Balla, Ignác 69 *(6)*
The Ban Bank (Bánk Bán) 155 *(35)*
Bánk Bán see *The Ban Bank*
Bankruptcy 17, 49–50 *(8)*
Banky, Vilma 14, 232–233 *(31)*
Banner Productions 76 *(24)*
Bara, Theda 75 *(22)*
Barber, Bobby 136–138 *(88)*, **139**
Barbour, Alan G. 269 *(440)*
Barclay, Joan 122–123 *(72)*, 124–125 *(74)*, 148 *(3)*
Barnes, Binnie **9**, 102 *(51)*
Barnes, Howard 243 *(150)*, 250 *(212)*
Barnett, Buddy 273 *(493)*, 326 *(6)*, 330 *(17)*, 356
Barnett, Vince 124 *(74)*, 126 *(76)*
Baron, Henry 10, 166 *(174)*
Barrymore, John 17, 221 *(33)*
Barrymore, Lionel 104–105 *(54)*, 360
Barta, Irén 69 *(6)*
Barton, Charles 137–138 *(88)*, 279 *(4)*
Barty, Billy 102 *(51)*
Basket Case 3 334 *(14)*

The Bat (A Denevér) 153 *(7)*
Bau, Gordon 143 *(93)*
Bauhaus 322 *(13)*, 368
Baxter, Les 143 *(93)*
Baxter, Warner 81–82 *(31)*, 83–84 *(34)*
Beal, Scotty R. 86 *(37)*, 91 *(42)*, 105 *(55)*
Beath, Warren Newton 286 *(57)*
Beaudine, William 128–129 *(78)*, 129 *(79)*, 130–131 *(81)*, 141 *(90)*, 263 *(362, 363)*
Beaumont, Charles 266 *(401)*, 316 *(26)*
Beck, Calvin T. 281 *(15)*
A Becstelen see *The Ignominious*
Becwar, George 142 *(92)*
Bederski, Henry 141 *(91)*
Bedlam 134 *(84)*
Beebe, Ford 125 *(75)*, 151 *(5)*, 225 *(69)*
Beery, Noah, Jr. 83 *(34)*
Beery, Noah, Sr. 83 *(34)*
Bekeffy, László 68 *(4)*, 69 *(8)*
Bela, Nicholas 86 *(37)*
Bela Lugosi: 1882–1956 272 *(482)*, 357
Bela Lugosi: Behind the Cape 328 *(6)*, 357
"Bela Lugosi: Hollywood's Dark Prince" 329 *(29)*
Bela Lugosi: Then and Now 330 *(17)*, 331 *(24)*, 357
Bela Lugosi: Three Lines 286 *(59)*
Bela Lugosi Benefit 199 *(42)*, 264 *(378)*
Bela Lugosi Bulletin 369
The Bela Lugosi Company 196 *(33, 34)*, 197, 261 *(343, 344)*
Bela Lugosi Hypnotized 215 *(8)*
Bela Lugosi Journal 369
Bela Lugosi Meets a Brooklyn Gorilla 33, 141 *(90)*, 263 *(362, 363, 364)*, 283, 303 *(36)*, 327 *(14)*, 354, 362
Bela Lugosi Meets Alfred Hitchcock (On the Radio) 322–323 *(16)*
The Bela Lugosi Revue 34, 198–199 *(41)*, 263 *(371)*, 264 *(373)*, 280 *(8)*
The Bela Lugosi Show 31, 208, 223 *(56)*
Bela Lugosi Society 272 *(479)*, 369
Bela Lugosi Trophy 29
Bela Lugosi's Dead 322 *(13)*, 368
Bela Lugosi's Horror and Magic Stage Show 196–197 *(37)*, 262 *(353)*
Bela Lugosi's White Christmas 285 *(47)*
Bel-Geddes, Norman 167–168 *(176)*, 169 *(178)*
Bell, Rex 215 *(3)*
Bellamy, Madge 94 *(43)*, 301 *(4)*, 376 *(4)*

Bellamy, Ralph 121–122 *(71)*, 123–124 *(73)*, 253 *(258)*, 287 *(69)*, 330 *(11)*, 361
Belmore, Lionel 111 *(60)*, 123–124 *(73)*
Benedek, Nándor 153 *(1, 2, 3)*
Benedict, Billy 129 *(79)*
Bengal Light (Görgötuz) 165 *(166)*
Benny, Jack 35
Beöthy, László 158 *(73, 74, 75, 76, 77, 78, 79)*
Berle, Milton 32, 210 *(4)*, 261 *(345)*
Berlin, Germany 49 *(7)*, 359
Best Man Wins 75 *(22)*, 102–103 *(52)*, 243 *(157, 158)*, 247, 324
Best of the Monsters 330 *(15)*
Best Years of Our Lives 169 *(178)*
Bevan, Billy 129 *(80)*
The Big Sleep 91 *(41)*
Biggers, Earl Derr 90 *(40)*, 284 *(41)*
Biography 331 *(29)*
The Biography of Dracula: The Life Story of Bram Stoker 280 *(8)*
Bilincsek 155 *(27)*
Billings, John 381 *(6)*
Bird, Chief Justice Rose Elizabeth 56 *(13)*
Birkholz, Gustav 70 *(12, 14)*, 74 *(21)*
Biró, Lajos 156 *(47)*, 158 *(76, 79)*
Birth of a Nation 76 *(25)*
Bishop, Joey 302 *(5)*
Bitzer, G.W. "Billy" 76 *(25)*
Bizánc see *Byzantium*
The Black Camel **8**, 84 *(34)*, 85 *(36)*, 90–91 *(40)*, 208, 238 *(92, 93, 95)*, 284 *(41)*
The Black Cat (1934) **iv**, 19, 41, 44 *(14)*, 98 *(46)*, 100–101 *(50)*, 105 *(54)*, 110 *(58)*, 124 *(73)*, 189 *(5, 6)*, 218 *(10)*, 225 *(73)*, 243 *(149, 150, 151, 152, 153, 154)*, **245**, 271 *(467, 475)*, 273 *(489)*, 189 *(5, 6)*, 215 *(6)*, 274 *(500)*, 281 *(14)*, 292 *(10)*, 293 *(11)*, 309, 311, 326 *(7)*, 334, 337 *(1)*, 354, 359, **360**, 364
The Black Cat (1941) 119–120 *(69)*, 252 *(248, 249)*
Black Dragons 60, 122–123 *(72)*, 125 *(74)*, 126 *(76)*, 131 *(81)*, 253 *(260)*, 254 *(263, 265, 266)*, 274 *(500)*, 325, 326 *(11)*, 327 *(14, 16)*, 368
Black Friday 10, 24, 35, 166, 116–117 *(65)*, 120 *(69)*, 124 *(73)*, **213**, 215 *(8)*, 220 *(27)*, 251 *(232, 234, 235)*, 272 *(479)*, 288, 313 *(12)*, **314**, 322 *(10)*, 326 *(7)*
The Black Sleep x, 36, 64, 100 *(49)*,

143–144 *(93)*, 211 *(13)*, 265 *(389, 390)*, 271 *(466, 470)*, 199 *(44, 45)*, 200 *(46)*, 282 *(21)*, 283 *(36)*, 284 *(39)*, 299 *(28)*, 335 *(18)*, 345, 365
Blake, Judge Samuel R. 52 *(10)*
Blane, Sally 98 *(47)*
Blaskó, István 3, 58
Blaskó, Lajos 3, 39
Blaskó, László 3, 39
Blaskó, Vilma 3, 4, 32, 39
The Blob 334 *(3)*
Bloch, Robert xii, 283 *(31)*, 302 *(6)*
Blood Is the Harvest 322 *(15)*
Bloodletter 286 *(57)*
Bluebeard 220 *(25)*
The Body Snatcher 31, 133–135 *(84)*, 136 *(86)*, 208, 259 *(316, 322, 323, 325, 326, 327)*, 281 *(14)*, 284 *(39)*, 308 *(49)*, 309, 326 *(5)*, 327 *(15)*, 360, 362
Boehm, David 105–107 *(55)*
Bogart, Humphrey 88–90 *(39)*, 221 *(35)*
Bojarski, Richard 268 *(430)*, 279 *(3)*, 281 *(13)*, 356
Boles, John 82 *(32)*, 378 *(3)*
Bolondok Tánca 160 *(105)*
Bondi, Bealuh 109 *(58)*
Bonomo, Joe 91 *(42)*, 95 *(45)*
Boone, Richard 184 *(196)*
Boop, Betty 19, 215 *(3)*, 350
Bordages, Asa 246 *(174)*
Boris Karloff/Bela Lugosi 321 *(6)*
Borland, Carroll 19, 104 *(54)* 105 *(54)*, 189 *(3)*, 268 *(472, 434)*, 269 *(443)*, 270 *(456)*, 272 *(481, 486)*, 274 *(502)*, 275 *(518)*, 279 *(3)*, 284 *(37)*, 286 *(58)*, 288, 302 *(7, 8)*, 312 *(3, 4)*, 316 *(30)*, 330 *(11)*, 331 *(27)*
The Borrowed Residence (A Kölcsonkért Kastély) 161 *(118)*
Borshi, Reverend George 63
Bosko Video 325 *(1)*
Boston University 31, 193 *(27)*, 260 *(334)*
Botrány see *Scandal*
Boullet, Jean 266 *(408)*, 329 *(8)*, 384 *(7)*
Bow, Clara 13–14, 15, 48 *(6)*, 172 *(180)*, 235 *(35)*, 282 *(19)*, 283 *(34)*, 306 *(36)*, 341
Bowery at Midnight 30, 126 *(76)*, 149 *(3)*, 254 *(273, 274)*, 325, 327 *(14, 16)*, 352
The Bowery Boys 145 *(95)*; *see also* The East Side Kids

The Bowery Boys Meet the Monster 224 *(66)*, 264 *(372)*
Boys from Brooklyn 141 *(90)*, 327 *(16)*; see also *Bela Lugosi Meets a Brooklyn Gorilla*
Brackett, Charles 113 *(62)*, 286 *(63)*
Brady, Thomas F. 261 *(339)*
Brecher, Egon 100 *(50)*, 104–105 *(54)*
Breckinridge, John "Bunny" 144 *(94)*
Bredell, Elwood 116 *(65)*, 123 *(73)*
Breese, Edmund 98 *(48)*
Brendel, El 88–90 *(39)*
Brent, Romney **209**, 210 *(3)*, 261 *(346)*
Bressart, Felix 113 *(62)*
Bride of Frankenstein 110 *(58)*, 323 *(18)*
Bride of the Atom 35, 36, 142–143 *(92)*, 199 *(42)*, 225 *(69)*, 226 *(76)*, 264 *(378, 379)*, 268 *(431)*, 272 *(478)*, 282 *(21)*, 283 *(32, 36)*, 323 *(22)*, 325, 326 *(5)*, 327 *(14, 16)*, 334 *(9)*, 335 *(18)*, 355, 362, **382**
Bride of the Monster see *Bride of the Atom*
Bride of the Vampire 130 *(80)*, 222 *(47)*
The Bridge on the River Kwai 121 *(70)*
Bridges, Harry 63
Brigadier General Ocskay (Ocskay Brigadéros) 4, 39, 68, 153 *(1)*
Brix, Herman 148–149 *(3)*
Broadminded 91, 238, 239, 359
Broder, Jack 141 *(90)*
Broderick, Helen 88 *(37)*
Bromfield, Louis 86 *(37)*, 236 *(64)*
Brooks, Conrad 141 *(91)*, 144 *(94)*, 266 *(405)*, 302 *(9)*, 331 *(24)*
Brooks, Mel 112 *(60)*
Brosch, Robert 273 *(491)*, 274 *(504)*, 364
Brosnan, John 281 *(16)*
Brower, Brock 285 *(46)*
Brower, Otto 110 *(59)*, 111 *(59)*
Brown, Barry 267 *(423)*
Brown, Joe E. 91 *(41)*, 238 *(94)*
Brown, Karl 128 *(78)*
Brown, Wally 134 *(85)*, 135 *(85, 86)*, 136 *(86)*
Browning, Tod 14, 19, 79–81 *(30)*, 86–87 *(37)*, 104–105 *(54)*, 188, 236 *(71)*, 237 *(78, 80)*, 238 *(83, 85)*, 244, 263 *(369)*, 283–284 *(37)*, 350, 374 *(2)*
Bruce, Lenny 321 *(5)*, 345
Brunas, John 282 *(28)*
Brunas, Michael 282 *(28)*
Bryan, Dora 138 *(89)*

Budapest, Hungary 4, 5, 20, 370–371 *(1)*
Budapest Kijujsag 63
Buffington, Phyllis and Dale 35
Bull, Clarence Sinclair 104 *(54)*
Bunston, Herbert 86–87 *(37)*, 169–171 *(179)*
Burke, Billie 206 *(18)*, 210 *(4)*
Burke, Kathleen 95–96 *(45)*
Burns, George 19, 98 *(48)*
Burr, Judge William P. 48 *(5)*
Burroughs, Edgar Rice 149 *(3)*
Burton, Tim 274 *(509)*, 275 *(511, 513, 516)*, 276 *(522, 523, 529)*, 287 *(72)*, 311, 323 *(22)*, 328, 335 *(18)*, 345, 369
Bus, László 30
Byrd, Ralph 22, 149 *(4)*, 150 *(4)*
Byzantium (Bizánc) 149 *(95)*, 165 *(168)*

Cabanne, Christy 31, 136 *(87)*, **137**
The Cabinet of Dr. Caligari 8, 77 *(27)*, 92 *(42)*, 219, 377
Caesar and Cleopatra 158–159 *(86)*
Cagliostro 21, 219 *(18)*, 246 *(175)*
Calhern, Louis 36
The Call of Life (Az Élet Szava) 158 *(75)*
Callela, Joseph 112 *(61)*
Calloway, Cab 98–100 *(48)*
Camacho-Romo, Dr. Juan Jose 357
Cambell, Ramsey 285 *(56)*
Candid Microphone 206 *(19)*
Cantor, Eddie 191 *(19)*, 198 *(39)*
Capra, Frank 221 *(39)*
Caravan of Death (Die Todeskarawane) 73 *(17)*, 217 *(1)*
Carney, Alan 134 *(85)*, 135 *(85)*, 135–136 *(86)*
Carr, Thomas 150 *(4)*
Carradine, John x, 36, 55 *(13)*, 100 *(50)*, 130–131 *(81)*, 132 *(82)*, 143 *(93)*, 199 *(44)*, 200 *(46)*, 205 *(16)*, 211 *(10)*, 222 *(45)*, 223 *(54)*, 226 *(76)*, 265 *(389)*, 302–303 *(10, 11)*, 309, 329 *(9)*, 330 *(11)*
Carroll, Earl 174, 175 *(184)*, 218 *(14)*, 309
Carroll, Moon 79 *(30)*, 86 *(37)*
Carroll, Nancy 96 *(45)*
Carruth, Milton 91 *(42)*
Casablanca 68 *(4)*
Casanova 67, 69 *(8)*, 337 *(2)*, 370–372 *(1)*, **372**, 374 *(2)*
"The Cask of the Amontillado" **209**, 210 *(3)*

Cassidy, Hopalong 33, 208
Castle, William 281 *(17)*, 303 *(12)*
The Castle Dracula Quarterly 357
Castle of Frankenstein 267 *(415, 423, 426)*, 268 *(433)*, 356
The Cat and the Canary 133 *(83)*
The Cat People 125 *(74)*, 134 *(84)*
Cawthorn, Joseph *(43)*
The CBS Horror Show 328 *(5)*
Chacon, Mario 357
Chadwick Pictures 76 *(76)*
Chamber of Horrors 222 *(45)*, 256 *(290)*
Chandler, Helen 86–87 *(37)*, 212 *(3)*, 237 *(80)*, 284 *(37)*, 323
Chandu on the Magic Island/Isle 148 *(2)*, 281 *(18)*
Chandu the Magician 75 *(22)*, 94–95 *(44)*, 106 *(54)*, 240–241 *(119, 120, 121, 122, 123, 124)*, 324, 346
Chaney, Lon, Jr. x, 26, 27, 36, 55 *(13)*, 56 *(13)*, 121–122 *(71)*, 123–124 *(73)*, 126–127 *(77)*, 128 *(77)*, 136–138 *(88)*, 143 *(93)*, 191 *(15)*, 200 *(46)*, 201, 206 *(16)*, 207 *(21)*, 211 *(9)*, 222 *(41, 45)*, 223 *(53)*, 226 *(76)*, 261 *(340)*, 268 *(432)*, 271 *(465)*, 311, 361
Chaney, Lon, Sr. 14, 15, 16, 79 *(30)*, 86 *(37)*, 104 *(54)*, 217 *(5)*, 235 *(56)*, 237 *(77)*, 265 *(389)*, 341, 342, 348, 372–375 *(2)*
Chaney, Ron 56 *(13)*, 274 *(508)*, 369
Chaplin, Charlie 15, 63
Charge of the Light Brigade 212 *(8)*
Charlie Chan Carries On 90 *(40)*
Charlotte Kisasszony see *Mademoiselle Charlotte*
Chatterton, Ruth 380 *(5)*
Cheron, Andre 78 *(28)*, 85 *(36)*, 98 *(48)*, 100 *(50)*
Chicago Horror Club 26, 118 *(67)*
The Child-Woman (A Gyere Kasszony) 155 *(39)*
Christmas Dream (Karácsonyi Álom) 160 *(113)*
Christoph, M. Oakley 257 *(304)*
Churchill, Douglas W. 232 *(251)*, 313 *(11)*
Cinema Collectors 356
Citizen Kane 300
Claire, Ina 113 *(62)*, 114 *(62)*
Claire Felho (Felhö Klari) 153 *(3)*
Clarens, Carlos 281 *(10)*
Clark, Colbert 146 *(1)*

Clarke, Betty Ross 91 *(42)*, 165 *(174)*, 172–173 *(182)*, 239 *(107)*
Clarke, Charles 78 *(28)*, 85 *(36)*
Clarke, Mae 378 *(3)*
Clarke, Robert 133 *(84)*, 135 *(86)*, 303 *(13)*
Classics of the Film 280–281 *(9)*
Classics of the Horror Film 281 *(14)*
Clift, Denison 108 *(57)*
Clive, Colin 217 *(5)*, 219 *(19)*, 375 *(3)*, 377 *(3)*
Cloutman, Gerald B. 45 *(10)*
Clyde, Andy 199 *(43)*
Cocteau, Jean 384 *(7)*
Cody, Iron Eyes 148 *(2)*
Coffin, Tristram 124 *(74)*
Cohen, Herman 141 *(90)*, 283 *(36)*, 303 *(14)*
Colgate Comedy Hour 208
Collier, William, Jr. 91 *(41)*
Collier and Flinn, Ltd. 45 *(2)*
Collins, Charles 231 *(17)*
Collyer, June 107 *(56)*
The Colonel (Az Ezredes) 68–69 *(5)*
Colonel Stoopnagle and Bud 98 *(48)*
Colonna, Jerry 279 *(7)*
Colouris, George 133 *(84)*
Columbia Studios 98 *(47)*, 103 *(52)*, 129–130 *(80)*, 204 *(12)*
Columbia University 10
Colvin, Andrew 131 *(81)*
Comic books 225 *(70)*, 250 *(223)*, 367, 274 *(506)*
Coming Soon 328 *(7)*
Command Performance **25**, 206 *(17)*
Communism 26, 33, 57, 58, 59–60, 62–64, 298 *(25)*
Compson, Betty 118 *(68)*
Compton, Joyce 83 *(33)*, 88 *(39)*, 136 *(87)*
Conception 218 *(13)*
Conners, Barry 88 *(39)*, 90 *(40)*, 94 *(44)*
Conrad, Con 83 *(33)*, 102 *(51)*
The Contenders for the Throne (A Trónkövetelök) 161–162 *(132)*
Contested Culture: The Image, Voice, and the Law 283 *(30)*, 352
Conti, Albert 81 *(31)*, 85 *(36)*, 100 *(50)*
The Convention Commissar (A Koventbiztos) 160 *(108)*
Cook, Ethel 346
Cooper, Gladys 119 *(69)*, 380 *(5)*
Cooper, Jackie 215 *(5)*, 317 *(32)*
Cooper, James Fenimore 73 *(18)*

Cooper, Violet Kemble 109 *(58)*
Cooper, Willis 111 *(60)*, 151 *(5)*, 249 *(209)*
Copner, Michael 273 *(493)*, 330 *(17)*, 356, 357
Corbin, John 230 *(9)*
Corday, Rita 133 *(84)*
Cording, Harry 100 *(50)*, 121 *(71)*, 123–124 *(73)*
The Corpse Vanishes 30, 121 *(70)*, 124–125 *(74)*, 126 *(76)*, 129 *(79)*, 132 *(82)*, 149 *(3)*, 254 *(270, 271)*, 325, 327 *(14, 16)*, 349, 354, **355**
Cortez, Ricardo 110–111 *(59)*
Costello, Lou xi, 31, 32, 136–138 *(88)*, **139**, 206 *(21)*, 208, 261 *(342)*, 334 *(4, 16)*
Costello, Maurice 351
Coulter, H. 249 *(204)*
The Count 269 *(447)*, 270 *(455)*, 278 *(1)*, 328 *(3)*, 356, 357
Count Chocula 272 *(480)*, 368
Count Essex (Essex Graf) 160 *(110)*
Countess Dracula 286 *(58)*, 357
Courtenay, William 16, 87 *(37)*
Coward, Noel 115 *(63)*
The Cowboy (A Csikós) 155 *(32)*
Crabbe, Buster 95–96 *(45)*
Craft, William J. 77 *(26)*
Crawford, Broderick 88 *(37)*, 119–120 *(69)*, 198 *(39)*
Crawford, Lester 88 *(37)*
The Creeper 120 *(69)*
Creeps by Night 205 *(15)*
Creepy Classics 323 *(21)*
Cremer, Robert 142, 164, 269 *(450)*, 270 *(455)*, 279 *(2)*, 289, 300 *(2)*, 330 *(12)*, 357
Crewes, Laura Hope 166 *(175)*
Crime Does Not Pay 207 *(23)*
Criswell 144 *(94)*
Crosby, Bing 38, 82 *(32)*
Crosby, Bob 321 *(1)*
Crosland, Alan 84–85 *(35)*
Crouse, Russell 188 *(179)*
Crowley, Aleister 101 *(50)*
Crowther, Bosley 254 *(267)*, 255 *(283)*, 256 *(290)*
A Csikós see *The Cowboy*
Cugat, Xavier 93–94 *(43)*
Currie, Louise 117 *(66)*, 128–129 *(78)*, 130–131 *(81)*, 303 *(15)*
The Curse of Man (Der Fluch der Menschheit) 70–71 *(14)*, 74 *(21)*, 230

Curtiz, Michael (Milhály Kertész) 6–7, 14, 30, 68 *(5)*, 69–70 *(9)* 70 *(10)*, 230 *(3)*, 233 *(31)*
Cushing, Charles Cyprian Strong 286 *(61)*
Cyrano de Bergerac 4, 41, 158 *(82)*, 221 *(29)*, 293 *(11)*

Dade, Frances 86 *(37)*
D'Agostino, Albert 105 *(55)*, 109 *(58)*, 134–135 *(85)*, 135 *(86)*
Dán, Norbert 68 *(2, 3, 4)*, 69 *(8)*, 70 *(11)*, 371 *(1)*
Dance of the Fools (Bolondok Tánca) 160 *(105)*
Dance on the Volcano (Der Tanz auf dem Vulkan) 74 *(21)*, 337 *(3)*
Dane, Karl 146–147 *(1)*
Daniell, Henry 79 *(30)*, 133 *(84)*
Dark Carnival: The Secret World of Tod Browning, Hollywood's Master of the Macabre 283 *(37)*
Dark Continent 223 *(51)*, 258 *(308)*
The Dark Eyes of London 24, 108 *(56)*, 114–115 *(63)*, 151 *(5)*, 190 *(14)*, 221 *(34)*, 251 *(236, 237)*, 252 *(244)*, 324, 325, 327 *(14, 16)*
Dark Romance: Sexuality in the Horror Film 349
Daudet, Alphonse 67 *(1)*, 69 *(7)*
Daughter of the Nabob of Dolova (A Dolovai Nabob Leara) 154 *(24)*
The Daughter of Work 71 *(14)*
Daughters Who Pay 76 *(24)*, 231 *(19)*, 337 *(3)*
Davis, Hubert Henry (Irving) 47 *(3)*, 48 *(4)*, 217 *(2)*
The Day the Earth Stood Still 134 *(88)*
D.C.A. 144 *(94)*
Deane, Hamilton 13, 86 *(37)*, 170 *(179)*, 190 *(14)*, 237, 286 *(62)*, 287 *(71)*
Dear Boris 313 *(8)*
The Death Kiss 96–98 *(46)*, 97, 151 *(5)*, 241 *(130, 131)*, 281 *(18)*, 325, 327 *(14, 16)*
The Death of the Grand Duke 74 *(21)*
Dee, Stephen 369
The Deerslayer 73 *(18)*, 326 *(3)*; see also *Leatherstocking*
Deésy, Alfréd 6, 67 *(1)*, 68 *(2, 3, 4)*, 69 *(6, 7, 8)*, 371 *(1)*
De Gaetano, Al 85 *(36)*, 90 *(40)*
de Grasse, Robert 135 *(86)*

Dehner, John 224 *(66)*
Dekker, Albert 133 *(84)*
De La Motte, Marguerite 76 *(24)*
Delaney, Pat 35
Délibáb see *Fate Morgana*
Dell, Gabriel 321 *(3)*
Dello Stritto, Frank J. xiv, 57, 58, 60, 270 *(455)*, 274 *(505)*, 276 *(525, 526, 531, 532)*, 357
del Olmo, Fred 268 *(439)*
DeMille, Cecil B. 96
"Demons of the Film Colony" 311, 317–320
A Denevér see *The Bat*
Denny, Reginald 85–86 *(36)*
Department of Mental Health 35
de Putti, Lya 14, 233 *(31)*
de Rita, "Curly Joe" 56 *(13)*
The Deserter (A Szökött Katona) 162 *(142)*
Dett, Nathaniel 93 *(43)*
Deva 153 *(4, 5, 6, 7, 8, 9)*
The Devil (Az Ördög) 154–155 *(25)*
The Devil Also Dreams 185 *(200)*, 208, 261 *(348, 349, 350)*, 262 *(351)*
The Devil Bat 26, 118 *(67)*, 252 *(247)*, 283 *(33)*, 313 *(13)*, 324, 325, 326 *(6)*, 327 *(14, 16)*, 334 *(14)*, 349, 367
The Devil Bat's Daughter 118 *(67)*
The Devil in the Cheese 169 *(178)*, 171 *(179)*, 232 *(24, 25)*, 286 *(61)*
The Devil Worshippers (Die Teufelsanbeter) 73–74 *(19)*, 217 *(1)*
The Devil's in Love 84 *(35)*, 98 *(46)*, 100 *(49)*, 242 *(39, 40)*, 374 *(2)*
The Devil's Paradise 36, 186–187, 200, 211
de Vogt, Carl 73 *(17)*, 74 *(74)*, 217 *(1)*
Diamond, David 105 *(55)*
Dieterle, William *(49)*
Dietrich, Marlene 120 *(69)*, 176 *(185)*
Dietz, Jack 122 *(72)*, 124 *(74)*, 126 *(76)*, 128 *(78)*, 129 *(79)*, 130 *(81)*, 131 *(82)*
Dillard, R.H.W. 286 *(59)*
Dillinger 135 *(85)*
Dimensional Designs 367
Discount Video Tape 325 *(2)*
Disney, Walt 213 *(11)*, 303 *(16)*
Distinctive Pictures 75 *(23)*
Dixon, Marion 77 *(26)*
Doak, Virginia 45 *(11)*, 206 *(20)*, 297–298 *(23)*
Dr. Acula 208, 224 *(61)*, 350
Dr. Cadman's Secret 143 *(93)*

392 Index

Dr. Jekyll and Mr. Hyde 71 *(15)*, 169 *(178)*
"The Dr. Prescribed Death" 203 *(10)*
Dr. Robin (Robin Orvos) 156 *(53)*
Dr. Terror's House of Horrors 333–334 *(2)*
Dr. Voodoo 225 *(73)*
Dr. Warren and Mr. O'Connor 72 *(15)*
Dodd, Alan 381–383 *(6)*
Dodd, Claire 120 *(69)*
A Dolovai Nabob Leana see *The Daughter of the Nabob of Dolova*
Don Carlos 162 *(147)*
Don Marlowe Agency 45 *(12)*
Donovan's Brain 116 *(65)*
Douglas, Gordon 134–135 *(85)*
Douglas, Melvyn 113 *(62)*
Dracula (summer stock) 31, 152, 182–183 *(192)*, 184 *(197)*, 260 *(335)*, 349
Dracula (planned, 3-D film version) x, 36, 224 *(62)*
Dracula (radio versions) 202 *(1)*
Dracula (vaudeville) 27, 152, 188, 189 *(3)*, 193 *(24)*, 196 *(33)*, 217 *(4)*, 242–243 *(145)*, 243 *(146)*, 261 *(343, 344)*, 349
Dracula (1927) 12–13, 36, 152, 170–171 *(179)*, 204 *(11)*, 232 *(27, 28, 29, 30)*, 237, 274 *(498)*, 286 *(62)*, 287 *(71)*, 291 *(5, 6)*, 292
Dracula (1928) 13, 14, 42 *(6, 8)*, 78 *(28)*, 171–172 *(180)*, 232–233 *(31)*, 282 *(19)*, 306 *(36)*
Dracula (1929) 13, 172 *(181)*, 234 *(42, 43, 44, 45, 46, 47, 48, 49)*, 235 *(51, 52)*
Dracula (1931 film) xi, 14, 15, 16, 17, 18, 19, 20, 22, 23, 24, 31, 41, 45 *(2, 3)*, 54 *(13)*, 55 *(13)*, 76 *(25)*, 79 *(29, 30)*, 86–88 *(37)*, 92 *(42)*, 93 *(43)*, 98 *(46)*, 105 *(54)*, 111 *(60)*, 112 *(60)*, 127 *(77)*, 130 *(80)*, 138 *(88)*, 169 *(178)*, 181, 182 *(189)*, 190 *(13)*, 191 *(18)*, 236 *(64, 66, 67, 68, 69, 70, 71)*, 237 *(78, 79, 80, 81, 82, 83)*, 238 *(84, 85, 87, 89)*, 248 *(190)*, 249 *(205, 206, 208)*, 258 *(309)*, 260 *(328)*, 266 *(411)*, 270 *(462)*, 271 *(467)*, 274 *(503, 506)*, 277 *(534)*, 283 *(29, 34)*, 284 *(37, 42)*, 285 *(50)*, 287 *(67)*, 291 *(6)*, 292 *(8)*, 293 *(11)*, 294 *(12)*, 296 *(17)*, 300 *(2)*, 307 *(38)*, 309, 315 *(20)*, 316 *(27)*, 317 *(32)*, 319 *(32)*, 324, 325, 326 *(7)*, 328 *(5, 7)*, 331 *(22)*, 334 *(5)*, 335 *(20)*, 341, 343, 346, 348, 350, 353, 354, 359, 362, 363, 364, 367, 368, 374 *(2)*, 379 *(3)*

Dracula (1931 novelization) 284 *(42)*
Dracula (1931, Spanish-language version) 87 *(37)*, 189 *(3)*, 212 *(5)*, 283 *(36)*
Dracula (1932) 173–174 *(183)*, 239–240 *(109)*
Dracula (1943) 27, 177–178 *(186)*, **178**, 255–256 *(284, 285, 286, 287)*, 257 *(298)*, 258 *(306)*, 297 *(36)*
Dracula (1947) 223 *(55)*
Dracula (1951) 32, 140 *(89)*, 185–186 *(201)*, 198 *(37)*, 210 *(6)*, 262 *(354, 355, 356, 357, 358, 359, 360)*
Dracula (1952) 224 *(58)*
Dracula (1954) 224 *(65)*
Dracula: A Cinematic Scrapbook 330 *(21)*
Dracula: The Vampire Play in Three Acts 286 *(61)*
Dracula Has Risen from the Grave 335 *(22)*
Dracula Meets the Wolf Man 222 *(48)*
Dracula's Daughter 20, 21, 27, 54 *(13)*, 55 *(13)*, 76 *(25)*, 218 *(15)*, 219 *(19)*, **220**, 246 *(182)*, 248 *(189)*
Drághy Éva Eskuje see *The Oath of Eva Draghy*
Drake, Frances 108 *(58)*
Dressler, Marie 317 *(32)*
Droop, Marie Louise 73 *(17, 19)*, 74 *(19)*, 217 *(1)*
Drug Abuse/Addiction 34, 36, 53 *(11)*, 264 *(374, 375, 376, 377, 380, 381, 382, 383, 384)*, 298 *(26)*
Dua Film Company 70 *(13)*, 74 *(20)*
Duck Soup 83 *(33)*
Duggan, Tom 211 *(12)*
Dunagan, Donnie 111 *(60)*, 112 *(60)*
Dunne, Harvey 142 *(92)*
Dunne, Irene 198 *(30)*
Dupont, E.A. 73 *(15)*, 218 *(7)*
Durfee, Minta 199 *(43)*
Dwan, Allan 112 *(61)*, 113 *(61)*, 250 *(216)*

Eager, Helen 255 *(286)*
The Eaglet (A Sasfiók) 155 *(36)*
East Side Kids 120–121 *(70)*, 129 *(79)*
The East Side Kids Come Out Fighting 322 *(8)*
Eastman, George 81 *(31)*
Ed Wood 274 *(500)*, 275 *(510, 511, 513, 514, 515, 516, 517, 520, 521)*, 276 *(422, 423, 424, 529)*, 287 *(72)*, 311, 323 *(22)*, 328, 334–335 *(18)*, 345, 369

Index 393

Ed Wood: Look Back in Angora 275 *(512)*, 331 *(28)*
Ed Wood: Original Soundtrack Recording 323 *(22)*
The Ed Wood Story 331 *(26)*
Eddy, Nelson 86 *(36)*
Edington, Harry E. 45 *(10)*
Educational Pictures 215 *(5)*
Edwards, Eustace J. 315 *(20)*
Edwards, J. Gordon 74–75 *(22)*
Egy Karrier Története see *The Story of a Career*
Egy Szegény Ifju Története see *The Story of a Poor Lad*
Egyenlöség see *The Admirable Crichton*
Az Egyszeri Királyfi see *The Prince in the Tale*
Eichberg, Richard 70 *(12)*, 71 *(14)*, 74 *(21)*, 230
Eichberg Films 70 *(12)*, 71 *(14)*, 74 *(21)*
Eilers, Sally 90 *(40)*
Eisener, Lotte 73 *(15)*
The Electric Man 218 *(11)*, 220 *(26)*
Az Élet Királya see *The Royal Life*
Az Élet Szava see *The Call of Life*
"El-Stinko, El-Ropos" x, 30
Ellis, Patricia 110–111 *(59)*
Elnémult Harangok see *Silver Bells*
Elvira 336
Az Ember Tragédiája see *The Tragedy of Man*
Emperor Joseph II (II. József Császár) 164 *(164)*
The Emperor of Atlantis 219–220 *(22)*
The Empty Chair 218 *(11)*
Endore, Guy 104 *(54)*, 105 *(54)*, 106 *(55)*
Endre és Johanna see *Andrew and Joanna*
England 20, 24, 53 *(11)*, 96 *(45)*, 108 *(57)*, 110 *(58)*, 123 *(72)*, 185–186 *(201)*, 246 *(184)*, 262 *(354, 355, 356, 357, 358, 360, 361)*, 266 *(404)*, 295 *(13)*, 316, 383 *(6)*; British ban on horror films 21, 24, 30, 32, 33, 53, 248 *(191)*, 249 *(203)*, 276–277 *(532)*, 346, 348
Ennis, Skinnay 204 *(11)*
Epicurean Reese of California, Inc. Fine Foods 359
Erickson, Leif 125 *(75)*
Erwin, Stuart 98 *(48)*
Essex Graf 160 *(110)*
Etting, Ruth 101 *(51)*
Éva Boszorkány see *Eve, the Witch*
Evans, Madge 176 *(185)*

Evans, Philip R. 357
Evans, Yolande 380 *(5)*
Eve the Witch (Éva Boszorkány) 160 *(115)*
An Evening with Boris Karloff and His Friends 321 *(4)*, 344
Everson, William K. 198, 267 *(426)*, 281 *(14)*, 282 *(24)*, 303 *(303)*, 330 *(12)*
Eyes of the Underworld 222 *(41)*
Expressionism 8
Ezeregy Éjszaka see *Arabian Nights*
Az Ezredes see *The Colonel*

The Faber Book of Movie Verse 286 *(59)*
Factor, Max 190 *(10)*
Fade to Black 334 *(8)*
Fairbanks, Douglas 76 *(24)*, 176 *(185)*
Faith Without Illusion 63
A Fáklyák see *The Torches*
Falk, Richárd 68 *(5)*
Famous Monsters of Filmland x, xi, 253 *(253)*, 266 *(403, 406, 407, 409, 411)*, 267 *(416, 417, 421, 424)*, 268 *(429, 432, 434, 437)*, 269 *(442, 445, 448, 449, 450)*, 270 *(452, 453, 454)*, 271 *(465)*, 276 *(523, 527)*, 321, 331 *(27)*, 351, 352, 354, 363, 365, 369, 370 *(1)*, 382 *(6)*
Famous Monsters of Filmland World Convention 331 *(27)*
Famous Monsters Speak 321 *(3)*
Fantasia 213, 333 *(3)*
Farrell, Tim 141 *(91)*
Fate Morgana (Délibáb) 157 *(61)*
Faust 4, 159 *(101)*, 220 *(28)*
The Favorite (A Kegyenc) 159 *(99)*
Fazenda, Louise 84–85 *(35)*
Fear in the Dark 331 *(25)*
Feature Creature Home Video 326 *(3)*
Federation of American-Hungarian Societies 22
Fedora 153 *(9)*
Fejos, Paul 77–78 *(27)*, 82 *(32)*
Felhö Klári see *Claire Felho*
Fenn az Ernyö Nincsen Kas see *Spending Spree*
Ferenc József Városi Szinház 153 *(10, 11)*, 154 *(12, 13, 14, 15, 16, 17, 18)*
Ferguson, Michael 357
Ferrari 221 *(31)*, 248 *(200)*
Ferrer, Jose 331 *(22)*
Festive Play (Ünnepi Játék) 164 *(151)*

Fetters (Bilincsek) 155 *(27)*
Fiddler, Jimmie 250 *(221)*
Fields, W.C. 19, 98–99 *(48)*
15th Raga for Bela 286 *(59)*
Fifty Million Frenchmen 45 *(1)*, 88 *(38)*, 238 *(86)*
Film Music of Hans J. Salter: The Ghost of Frankenstein, Magnificent Doll, Bend of the River, Against All Flags 322 *(11)*
Film Szemle 370 *(1)*
The Films of Bela Lugosi 268 *(430)*, 279 *(3)*, 356
The Films of Boris Karloff 281 *(13)*, 356
The Final Curtain 36, 226 *(77)*
Fine, Larry 56 *(13)*
Finn, Elsie 256 *(288)*, 257 *(305)*
First National 78–79 *(29)*, 91 *(41)*
Fist, Norman ix, 36
Flemming, Victor 83–84 *(34)*
Florescu, Radu 345
Florey, Robert 17, 18, 91–92 *(42)*, 212 *(4)*, 217 *(5)*, 218 *(7)*, 239 *(98)*, 268 *(436)*, 272 *(477)*, 282 *(26)*, 303 *(18)*, 309, 376–378 *(3)*
Der Fluch der Menschheit see *The Curse of Man*
Flying Saucers Over Hollywood: The Plan 9 Companion 331 *(26)*
The Flying Serpent 118 *(67)*
Flynn, Emmett 78 *(28)*
Flynn, Errol 212 *(8)*
Foch, Nina 129 *(80)*
Fodor, László 30
A Fogadott Apa see *The Adopted Father*
The Foolish Virgin (A Balga Szüz) 155 *(38)*
Foran, Dick 122 *(71)*
Ford, Wallace 98 *(47)*, 103 *(53)*, 128 *(78)*
Foreman, Carl 120–121 *(70)*
Forgotten Horrors 281 *(18)*
Fort, Garrett 76 *(25)*, 86 *(37)*, 218 *(8)*
Fowley, Douglas 132 *(83)*, 136 *(87)*
Fox, Eddie 198–199 *(41)*
Fox, Sidney 92, 359
Fox, Wallace 124 *(74)*, 126 *(76)*, 255 *(274)*
Fox, William 74 *(22)*, 83 *(33, 34)*, 85 *(36)*
Fox Studios 74 *(22)*, 78 *(28)*, 81 *(31)*, 83 *(33, 34)*, 85 *(36)*, 88 *(39)*, 90 *(40)*, 94 *(44)*, 100 *(49)*, 130 *(80)*
Frances, Arlene 91 *(42)*
Francis Rakoczi II in Captivity (II. Rákoczi Ferenc Fogsága) 159 *(91)*
Franken, Jerry 261 *(346)*

Frankenstein (1931) 17, 18, 22, 23, 76 *(25)*, 93 *(43)*, 111–112 *(30)*, 123 *(73)*, 127 *(77)*, 190 *(13)*, 217 *(5)*, 239 *(97)*, 249 *(206, 209)*, 309, 311, 312 *(3, 4, 7)*, 315 *(20)*, 316 *(26, 27)*, 317–319 *(32)*, 325, 343, 367; test footage (1931) 212 *(4)*, 217 *(5)*, 268 *(436)*, 272 *(477)*, 282 *(26)*, 375–379 *(3)*
Frankenstein: A Cinematic Scrapbook 331 *(21)*
Frankenstein Meets the Wolf Man 26, 30, 126–128 *(77)*, 136 *(86)*, 143 *(92)*, 255 *(278, 280, 283)*, 259 *(324)*, 268 *(432)*, 273 *(489)*, 285 *(53)*, 287 *(681)*, 324, 326 *(7)*, 361, 362, 379
"Frankenstein vs. Dracula" 331 *(30)*
Franklin, Joe 207 *(24)*
Die Frau im Delphin see *The Woman in the Dolphin*
Frazer, Robert 94 *(43)*, 122–123 *(72)*
Freaks 79 *(30)*, 81 *(30)*, 94 *(43)*
The Fred Allen Show 27
Free Organization of Theatre Employees 7, 59
French, Philip 286 *(59)*
Freund, Karl 71 *(15)*, 86–88 *(37)*, 91 *(42)*, 102 *(51)*
Friedlander, Louis 105 *(55)*, 111 *(59)*, 130 *(80)*
Friedman, Drew 271 *(471)*
Fright Night 334 *(11)*
Frommer, Ben 142 *(92)*
Frye, Dwight 86 *(37)*, 90 *(40)*, 111–112 *(60)*, 123 *(73)*, 126–127 *(77)*, 169 *(178)*, 212 *(4)*, 237 *(80)*, 266 *(411)*, 274 *(498)*, 378 *(3)*
Fuller, Dolores 141 *(91)*, 142 *(92)*, 199 *(42)*, 225 *(69)*, 275 *(520)*
Fulton, John P. 91 *(42)*, 100 *(50)*, 109 *(58)*, 110 *(59)*, 111 *(60)*, 116 *(65)*, 119 *(69)*, 121 *(71)*, 127 *(77)*
Funeral 37–38
Funt, Allen 206 *(19)*
Furmanek, Bob 208, 286 *(66)*

Gable, Clark 295 *(12)*
Gabor, Zsa Zsa 33
Gaci Film Company 73 *(16)*
Gaines, Jane M. 283 *(30)*
Gal, Gyula 69–70 *(9)*
Gamble, Warburton 166 *(175)*

Games 334 *(5)*
Gamut Club 196 *(36)*, 261 *(347)*
Ganes, Jane M. 352
Garbo, Greta 16, 24, 111 *(59)*, 113–114 *(62)*, 250–251 *(224)*, 286 *(63)*, 317 *(32)*
Gardner, Ava 129 *(79)*, 303 *(19)*
Garland, Judy 198 *(39)*
"Gasoline Cocktail" 207 *(23)*
Gaxton, William 88 *(38)*
The Geisha (A Gésák) 158 *(77)*
Geltzer, George 263 *(369)*, 350
Gemora, Charles 91 *(42)*, 93 *(42)*
General Mills 368
The Genius (A Zseni) 157 *(70)*
Genius at Work 135–136 *(86)*, 260 *(329)*
George, Hazel 172 *(181)*
George Eastman House 337 *(3)*
Gerrard, Charles 86 *(37)*
Gershwin, George 82 *(33)*
Gerstad, Merritt B. 79 *(30)*
A Gésák see *The Geisha*
Ghost Breakers 77 *(25)*
Ghost of Frankenstein 26, 30, 112 *(60)*, 123–124 *(73)*, 125 *(75)*, 127 *(77)*, 136 *(86)*, 192–193 *(21)*, 253 *(261)*, 254 *(262)*, 285 *(54)*, 287 *(69)*, 322 *(12)*, 323 *(19)*, 326 *(7)*, 361
Ghosts on the Loose 121 *(70)*, 129 *(79)*, 132 *(82)*, 256 *(292)*, 325, 327 *(14, 16)*, 383 *(6)*
The Ghoul Goes West 226 *(76)*, 264 *(382)*, 273 *(490)*
Ghouls on the Moon 226 *(79)*
Gibbons, Cedric 79 *(30)*, 104 *(54)*, 113 *(62)*
Gifford, Denis 281 *(12)*
Gift of Gab 75 *(22)*, 101–102 *(51)*, 148 *(2)*, 243 *(490)*
Gilbert, John 114 *(62)*
Gilling, John 139 *(89)*
Gleason, James 20
Glen or Glenda 33, 34, 133 *(83)*, 141–142 *(91)*, 143 *(92)*, 266 *(405)*, 270 *(463)*, 283 *(32)*, 323 *(22)*, 325, 326 *(5)*, 327 *(14, 16)*, 334 *(9)*, 355
G-Man Jitters 332 *(2)*
Goddard, Paulette **25**, 206 *(17)*
Goethe 4, 159 *(101)*
Going My Way 83 *(33)*
The Gold Bug 223 *(52)*
Golden Man (Az Aranyember) 154 *(20)*, 159 *(87)*

The Golden Rooster (Az Aranykakas) 154 *(12)*
The Golden Wedding (Az Aranylakodalom) 156 *(52)*
Golding, Samuel R. 168 *(177)*
Goldstone, Phil 93–94 *(43)*
Goldwyn-Cosmopolitan Company 75 *(23)*
The Golem 377 *(3)*
Gone with the Wind 84 *(34)*, 108 *(56)*
Gooch, Peter 332 *(4)*
Goodkind, Saul A. 151 *(6)*
Goosson, Stephen 81 *(31)*, 83 *(33)*, 85 *(36)*
Gorcey, Bernard 122 *(72)*, 126 *(76)*
Gorcey, David 120 *(70)*
Gorcey, Kay Marvis 129 *(79)*
Gorcey, Leo 120 *(70)*, 129 *(79)*, 224 *(66)*
Gordon, Alex 55 *(13)*, 64, 142 *(92)*, 184 *(198)*, 198 *(39)*, 224 *(63)*, 267 *(413)*, 269 *(442)*, 275 *(521)*, 303–304 *(20, 21)*, 330 *(11)*
Gordon, C. Henry 83–84 *(34)*, 90 *(40)*, 100 *(49)*
Gordon, Richard 32, 184 *(198)*, 279 *(5)*, 282 *(27)*, **301**, 304 *(22)*, 315–16 *(23)*
Görgötuz see *Bengal Light*
The Gorilla 24, 30, 112–113 *(61)*, 133 *(83)*, 250 *(219, 220)*, 325 *(22)*, 326 *(5)*, 327 *(14, 16)*, 331 *(22)*, 360
Gorshin, Frank 328 *(2)*
Gossett, Louis, Jr. 328
Góth, Annie 68 *(2)*, 69 *(7)*, 70 *(11)*, 371 *(1)*
The Government Commissioner (A Kormánybiztos) 155 *(34)*
Graf Tisza Istvan 10, 47 *(2)*, 49 *(7)*
Grainger, Edmund 109 *(58)*
Granach, Alexander 113 *(62)*, 114 *(62)*
The Grandmother (A Nagymama) 164 *(160)*
Grant, Barry Keith 282 *(22)*
Grant, Cary 176 *(185)*
Graven Images 31 *(283)*
Graverobbers from Outer Space 144 *(94)*; see also *Plan 9 from Outer Space*
Gravity's Rainbow 285 *(48)*, 352
Gray, Alexander 84 *(35)*
Gray, Shirley 108 *(57)*
Great, Alexander see Kee, Kim
The Great Radio Horror Shows 322 *(9)*
Green, Carl R. 285 *(54)*
Greenstreet, Sydney 201
Grey, Rudolph 283 *(32)*
Griffin, Merv 198 *(39)*

396 Index

Griffith, Corinne 78–79 *(29)*
Griffith, D.W. 76 *(25)*, 95 *(44)*, 108 *(56)*, 136 *(87)*, 147 *(1)*
Guilty Pleasures of the Horror Film 284 *(38)*
Gunga Din 250 *(217)*
The Guns of the Navarone 121 *(70)*
Gus Arnheim and His Orchestra 102 *(51)*
Guy, Gordon 270 *(456)*, 355, 357
Gwynne, Anne 116 *(65)*, 119 *(69)*
A Gyerekasszony see *The Child-Woman*
Gynt, Greta 114 *(62)*

Hackett, Gabriel D. 32
A Hadifogoly see *The Prisoner of War*
Haines, Jimmy 36
Hale, Wanda 254 *(269)*
Haley, Jack 132–133 *(83)*
Hall, Charles D. 86 *(37)*, 91 *(42)*, 100 *(50)*
Hall, Gladys 229, 235 *(54)*, 237 *(76)*, 253 *(253)*, 266 *(407)*, 269 *(448)*, 272 *(483)*, 289, 347, 348
Hall, Henry 107 *(56)*, 128 *(78)*, 130–131 *(81)*, 148 *(2, 3)*
Hall, Huntz 120 *(70)*, 270 *(452)*, 305 *(24)*
Hall, Manly P. **9**, 29, 34, 35, 117, 219, 220, 251, 273, 313
Hall, Mordaunt 236 *(62)*, 237 *(80, 83)*, 241 *(127)*
Hallmark Cards 368
Halperin, Edward 18, 93–94 *(43)*, 221 *(30)*, 333 *(1)*
Halperin, Victor 18, 93–94 *(43)*, 221, 325, 333 *(1)*
Halsey, Forrest 78 *(29)*
Hamilton, George 270 *(458)*
Hamlet 4, 21, 156–157 *(56)*, 159 *(93)*, 162 *(136, 140, 145)*, 293 *(11)*
Hammond, Percy 231 *(10)*, 232 *(25, 29)*
Hammer Studios 108 *(57)*, 351
Hammerstein II, Oscar 84–85 *(35)*
Hand, Jon 357, 371 *(1)*
The Hand That Rocks the Cradle 334 *(15)*
Hanifin, Ada 234 *(49)*
Hanna, David 257 *(295)*
Hans Salter: Music for Frankenstein 323 *(19)*
Hardwicke, Sir Cedric 123–124 *(73)*, 361
Hare, Lumsden 98 *(48)*
A Harom Testor see *The Three Bodyguards*
Harrigan, Nedda 169–70 *(179)*
Harron, John 93 *(43)*

Hartung, Philip T. 259 *(327)*, 261 *(342)*
Hasbro 365
Hastings, R.W. 264 *(374)*
Hatton, Raymond 279 *(7)*
The Haunting 134 *(84)*
Hawks, Howard 81 *(31)*
Hawks, Kenneth 81 *(31)*
Haynes, "Tommy" 141 *(91)*
Házasodjunk see *We're Married*
He Who Gets Slapped 372–375 *(2)*
Head 334 *(6)*
Head, Cloyd 167 *(176)*
The Head of Janus (Der Januskopf) 8, 71–73 *(15)*, 87 *(37)*
The Headmaster (Az Igazgató Ur) 161 *(123)*
Heard, Charles 357
Heard, Roby 264 *(375)*
Hellzapoppin' 88 *(38)*
Helm, Fay 121–122 *(71)*, 125 *(75)*, 132–133 *(83)*, 176 *(185)*, 253 *(257)*
Henry IV 162 *(143)*
Henry VIII 165 *(170)*
Herbert, Holmes 79 *(30)*, 91 *(41)*, 104 *(54)*, 123–124 *(73)*
Herbert, Hugh 119 *(69)*
Herczeg, Ferenc 68 *(5)*, 153 *(1)*, 154 *(24)*, 157 *(62)*, 160 *(115)*, 163 *(149)*, 164 *(151, 161)*, 165 *(168)*
Herdan-Sherrill Agency 46 *(14)*
Herman, Al 146 *(1)*
Hernani 159 *(98)*
Heroes of the Horror Film 281 *(15)*
Hersholt, Jean **9**, 84–85 *(35)*, 104–105 *(54)*
Hickox, Sid 91 *(41)*
High Noon 121 *(70)*
Hill, Robert S. 148 *(3)*
Hillyer, Lambert 109 *(58)*, 110 *(58)*, 219 *(19)*
Himfy Dalai see *Himfy's Song*
Himfy's Song (Himfy Dalai) 154 *(12)*
Hinds, Samuel S. 105–107 *(55)*
Hintner, Cornelius 371 *(1)*
Hirschfeld, Albert 349
Hitler, Adolph 57, 61, 370
Hively, Jack 115 *(64)*
Hoey, Dennis 108 *(57)*, 126 *(76)*
Hoffman, Jerry 243 *(149)*
Hoffman, John Ivan 86–87 *(37)*
Hogan, David J. 279 *(5)*, 349
Holden, Gloria 219 *(19)*
Hollam Cooley Agency 25, 45 *(6)*

Hollay, Kamilla 69 *(8)*, 70 *(11)*, 371 *(1)*
Holloway, Sterling **25**, 98 *(48)*, 102 *(51)*, 206 *(17)*
Hollywood and the Stars 328 *(1)*, 331 *(23)*
Hollywood Cauldron: Thirteen Classic Horror Films from the Genre's Golden Age 273 *(497)*, 283 *(35)*
Hollywood Ghost Stories 329 *(9)*
Hollywood Gothic: The Tangled Web of Dracula from Novel to Stage to Screen 282 *(29)*
Hollywood Heaven: Tragic Lives, Tragic Deaths 330 *(18)*
The Hollywood Hissables 357
Hollywood Home Theater 326 *(4)*
The Hollywood Movie Parade 215
Hollywood on Parade 215 *(5)*, 365
The Hollywood That Was 268 *(435)*, 281 *(11)*
The Hollywood Walk of Fame 270 *(458)*
Holt, Jack 102 *(52)*
Holy Cross Cemetery 38
Honor of the Sword (A Kard Becsulets) 155 *(31)*
Hooray for Horrorwood! 330 *(19)*
Hope, Bob 88, 206 *(17)*
Hopkins, Charles 169 *(178)*
Hopper, Hedda 16, 81–82 *(31)*, 311, 313 *(10)*
Horrible Horrors 330 *(10)*
The Horror Hall of Fame (1972) 328 *(2)*
The Horror Hall of Fame (1991) 330 *(20)*
The Horror of It All 331 *(22)*
The Horror People 281 *(16)*
Horthy, Miklós 7, 20, 59, 60, 61, 371 *(1)*
Horton, Edward Everett 380 *(5)*
House Committee on Un-American Activities 33, 63
House of a Thousand Candles 212 *(9)*, 220 *(27)*
House of Dracula 138 *(88)*, 222 *(48)*, 223 *(54)*, 348
House of Frankenstein 125 *(75)*, 138 *(88)*, 222 *(45)*, 223 *(54)*, 276 *(530)*, 323 *(19)*
The House of Wax 34, 198 *(39)*, 211 *(7)*, 216 *(10)*, 267 *(413)*
House Party 207 *(22)*
How Green Was My Valley 85 *(35)*
How to Handle Women 77 *(26)*, 233 *(33)*
How to Make a Monster 226 *(78)*
Howard, Leslie 166–167 *(175)*

Howard, Moe 56 *(13)*
Howe, James Wong 94 *(44)*, 104 *(54)*, 305 *(306)*
Hubcaps Afire Over Hollywood: The True Fantasy of Ed Wood Jr. 332 *(4)*
Hudson, Rock 198 *(39)*
Hull, Henry 222 *(45)*
The Human Monster see *The Dark Eyes of London*
The Hunchback of Notre Dame 15, 17, 87 *(37)*, 134 *(84)*, 217–218 *(6)*, 341, 342, 372 *(2)*
Hungarian-American Council for Democracy 26, 62–63, 64, 298 *(25)*
Hungarian Council's Republic 7
Hungarian Film Institute and Film Archive 337 *(2)*, 370 *(1)*
Hungarian State Superior Gymnasium 3
Hungary 3–7, 20, 32, 67, 241 *(132)*, 267 *(424)*, 293 *(11)*, 297 *(20)*
The Hunger 322 *(13)*
Huntley, Raymond 12
Hurst, Brandon 91 *(42)*, 93 *(43)*, 123 *(73)*
Husband in Reserve (Tartalékos Férj) 153 *(11)*
Huston, John 91 *(42)*
Hutchinson, Josephine 111–112 *(60)*
Hyams, Leila 79–81 *(30)*, 95–96 *(45)*

I Changed My Sex 142 *(91)*
I Led Two Lives 142 *(91)*
I Walked with a Zombie 135 *(85)*
Az Igazgató Ur see *The Headmaster*
Ignalits, Sandy 69 *(8)*, 371 *(1)*
The Ignominious (The Becstelen) 157 *(60)*
An Illustrated History of the Horror Film 291 *(10)*
Im Rausche der Milliarden see *In the Ecstasy of Billions*
Image Entertainment 326 *(5)*
The Immigrant (A Kivándorló) 157 *(62)*
Immigration Services (United States) 47 *(2)*
Imperial-Cameo Pictures 39, 107 *(56)*, 202, 269 *(445)*; biographical form 39–42
In Search of Dracula (book) 345
In Search of Dracula (documentary film) 328 *(4)*
In the Sign of the Cross (A Kereszt Jelében) 154 *(14)*

Inescort, Frieda 129 *(80)*, 132 *(80)*
Az Ingyenélök see *The Parasites*
Inner Sanctum 31, 204 *(13)*, 206 *(16)*, 223 *(56)*
Innocent Blood 334 *(16)*, 352
Inspector's Interrogation During Primary Alien Inspection 47 *(2)*
The Insurgents (A Pártüok) 164 *(155)*
International Bela Lugosi Fan Club 357, 369
International House 19, 98–100 *(48)*, 242 *(135, 136, 137)*, **344**
International Museum of Photography at the George Eastman House 337 *(3)*
Interviews of Our Time 321 *(5)*, 345
Interviews with B Science Fiction and Horror Movie Makers 282 *(27)*
Intimate Interviews 215 *(2)*, 328 *(6)*, 330 *(14)*
Into the Night 334 *(12)*
Intolerance 76 *(25)*
Invisible Ghost 26, 118–119 *(68)*, 149 *(3)*, 191 *(18)*, **192**, 222 *(42)*, 253 *(250, 251, 252)*, 327 *(14, 16)*, 361, 383 *(6)*
The Invisible Man 110 *(58)*, 151 *(5)*, 218 *(7)*
The Invisible Man Returns 138, 323 *(23)*
The Invisible Ray 20, 21, 108–110 *(58)*, 125 *(75)*, 135 *(85)*, 151 *(5)*, 212 *(6)*, 246 *(185, 186)*, 247 *(187, 188)*, 271 *(467, 475)*, 309, 323 *(18)*, 326 *(7)*, 337 *(1)*, 360, 363
The Iron Manufacturer (A Vasgyáros) 154 *(17)*, 155 *(30)*, 158 *(80)*, 161 *(127)*
The Island of Dr. Moreau 96 *(45)*
Island of Lost Souls 19, 81 *(30)*, 95–96 *(45)*, 103 *(52)*, 124 *(73)*, 212 *(6)*, 241 *(127, 128, 129)*, 266 *(404, 406)*, 267 *(416)*, 322 *(15)*, 326 *(7)*, 328 *(5)*, 334 *(13)*, 335 *(23)*, 343
Isle of the Dead 133 *(84)*
It Came from Hollywood 334 *(9)*
It Came from Weaver Five: Interviews 20 Zany, Glib, and Earnest Moviemakers in the SF and Horror Traditions of the Forties, Fifties, and Sixties 284 *(39)*
It's Alive 282 *(20)*, 357
Ivano, Paul 377–378 *(3)*

Jaccoma, Richard 332 *(3)*
Jack Oakie's Double Takes 282 *(19)*
Jack the Ripper 221 *(33)*

Jagger, Dean 94 *(43)*, 221 *(30)*
Jailbait 225 *(72)*
James, Alan 149 *(4)*
Der Januskopf see *The Head of Janus*
The Jazz Singer 15, 85 *(35)*
Jefferson, Judge Bernard S. 55 *(13)*, 367
Jeffreys, Anne 134 *(85)*, 135 *(85)*, 135–136 *(86)*
Jessel, George 204 *(11)*
Johann Hopkins III see John Hopkins the Third
John Hopkins the Third *(Johann Hopkins III)* 74 *(20)*
John Zanft Agency 45 *(3)*
Johnson, Fred 15, 233–234 *(48)*, 259 *(317)*
Johnson, Noble 91–93 *(42)*
Johnson, Karl 144 *(94)*
Johnson, Tor x, 142 *(92)*, 143 *(93)*, 144 *(94)*, 199 *(42)*, 200 *(45, 46)*, 226 *(76)*, 268 *(431)*, 335 *(18)*
Jókai, Mór 4, 155 *(33)*, 159 *(87)*
Jolley, I. Stanford 122 *(72)*
A Jómadarak see *The Scoundrels*
Jones, Buck 11, 20
Jones, Darby 134–135 *(85)*
Jordan, Bobby 120 *(70)*, 129 *(79)*, 225 *(69)*
Jordan, Harold 267 *(422)*, 382 *(6)*
Jorgenson, Christine 142 *(91)*
Jory, Victor 83–84 *(34)*, 100 *(49)*
Joyce, Peggy Hopkins 98–99 *(48)*
II. József Császár see *Emperor Joseph II*
Judge, Arline 103 *(52)*
Jukes, Bernard 169 *(179)*, 171 *(180)*
Julius Caesar 161 *(131)*
Just Imagine 90 *(39)*

Kaaren, Suzanne 118 *(67)*
Kabibble, Ish 117 *(66)*
Kaffenberger, Bill 357
Kaiser-Heyl, Willi 70 *(14)*, 71–73 *(15)*
A Kaméliás Hölgy see *Lady of the Camellias*
Kaminsky, Stuart 285 *(52)*
Karácsonyi Álom see *Christmas Dream*
Karaszewski, Larry 287 *(72)*
A Kard Becsulets see *Honor of the Sword*
Karloff, Boris 17, 19, 20, 22, 27, 31, 38, 56, 64, 100–101 *(50)*, 102 *(51)*, 103–104 *(53)*, 105–107 *(55)*, 108–110 *(58)*, 111–112 *(60)*, 116 *(65)*, 118 *(66)*, 121 *(17)*, 123 *(73)*, 127 *(77)*, 133–134 *(84)*, 138 *(88)*, 179 *(187, 188)*, 191 *(17)*, 201, 202 *(5)*,

203 *(8)*, 204 *(13)*, 205 *(15)*, 210 *(2)*, 213 *(12)*, 215 *(4, 6)*, 217 *(5)*, 218 *(6, 7, 10)*, 219 *(18, 19)*, 220 *(23, 25, 26)*, 221 *(33, 35, 39)*, 222 *(40, 45, 46)*, 225 *(73)*, 240 *(111)*, 241 *(126)*, 243 *(148, 149, 152, 153)*, 244 *(167, 168, 169)*, 246 *(185)*, 247 *(186, 187, 188)*, 250 *(212, 214)*, 251 *(230, 233)*, 252 *(246)*, 256 *(293)*, 257 *(295)*, 258 *(306)*, 260 *(333)*, 263 *(368)*, 266 *(412)*, 267 *(425)*, 271 *(465, 469)*, 273 *(488, 494)*, 279 *(4)*, 281 *(13, 16)*, 285 *(56)*, 288, 309–311, 312 *(1, 2, 3, 4, 5, 6, 7)*, 313 *(8, 9, 10, 11, 12, 13)*, 314 *(14, 15, 16, 17)*, 315 *(18, 19, 20, 21, 22, 23)*, 316 *(24, 25, 26, 27, 28, 29, 30, 31)*, 317–320 *(32)*, **310**, 321 *(4, 6)*, 330 *(15)*, 331 *(30)*, 332 *(1)*, 335 *(18)*, 341, 343, 344, 348, 349, 351, 359, 360, 361, 374 *(2)*, 375 *(3)*, 377 *(3)*, 378 *(3)*, 384 *(7)*
Karloff, Sara Jane 56 *(13)*, 274 *(508)*, 331 *(30)*, 369
Karloff: The Life of Boris Karloff, with an Appendix of the Films in Which He Appeared 313 *(12)*
Karloff and Lugosi: The Story of a Haunting Collaboration 273 *(488)*, 279 *(4)*, 357
Károlyi, Michael (Milhály) 59, 60, 63
Katch, Kurt 121 *(71)*
Katzman, David ix, 36
Katzman, Sam 26, 119 *(68)*, 122 *(72)*, 124 *(74)*, 126 *(76)*, 128 *(78)*, 129 *(79)*, 130 *(81)*, 131 *(81, 82)*, 145 *(95)*, 148–149 *(3)*, 223 *(52)*, 382–383 *(6)*
Kay Kyser's Kollege of Musical Knowledge 202–203 *(8)*
Kayser, Kay 117 *(66)*
Keeler, Harry Stephen 103 *(53)*
Keene, Tom 144 *(94)*, 225 *(69)*
Keep Watching the Skies!: Volume One 282 *(21)*
Keep Watching the Skies!: Volume Two 282 *(25)*
A Kegyenc see *The Favorite*
Keith, Ian 16, 31, 78–79 *(29)*, 87 *(37)*, 138 *(88)*, 180 *(189)*, **181**, 182 *(189)*, 259 *(317)*
Kelemen, the Mason (*Kömíves Kelemen*) 164 *(152)*
Kelly, Bert 119 *(69)*
Kelly, Patsy 112 *(61)*, 113 *(61)*, 360

Kemp, Tony ix
Kent, Robert 150 *(5)*
Kenton, Erle C. 95 *(45)*, 96 *(45)*, 103 *(52)*, 123 *(73)*, 124 *(73)*
Kerekjarto, Duci **9**, 29
A Kereszt Jelébem see *In the Sign of the Cross*
Kern, James V. 117 *(66)*
Kerr, Martha 251 *(233)*
Kertész, Milhály see Curtiz, Michael
Kesselring, Joseph 178 *(187)*, 179 *(188)*, 182 *(191)*, 184 *(197)*, 184 *(199)*
Key, Kim 223–224 *(57)*, 270 *(453)*, 304 *(23)*
Kilencvekilenc see *Ninety-Nine*
Killer Bats see *The Devil Bat*
King, Bradley 83 *(33)*
King, Loretta 142 *(92)*, 225 *(69)*
King John 161 *(130)*, 164 *(156)*
King Kong 93 *(42)*, 125 *(75)*, 148 *(2)*
King Lear 160 *(106)*
King of Jazz 67, 77 *(26)*, 82–83 *(32)*
King of Kings 148 *(2)*
King Robot 224 *(63)*
King Sisters 206 *(17)*
The Kingdom of Sancho Panza (*Sancho Panza Királysága*) 165 *(172)*
Kingsford, Walter 108 *(58)*
Kitchen Sink Press 366
A Kivándorló see *The Immigrant*
Klausner, Bertha 45–46 *(13)*
Klay, Andor C. 33
Klein, Philip 85 *(36)*, 90 *(40)*, 94 *(44)*
Kline-Howard Agency 25, 45 *(9)*, 178 *(187)*
Knapp, Evalyn 88 *(38)*
Knowles, Patric 121 *(71)*, 122 *(71)*, 126 *(77)*, 128 *(77)*, 273 *(489)*, 305 *(26)*, 361
Koch, Howard W. 143 *(93)*, 199 *(45)*, 282 *(27)*
Koekler, Margo 70 *(12, 14)*
Kohl, Leonard 357, 380 *(4)*
Kohner, Paul 78 *(27)*, 87 *(37)*
A Kölcsonkért Kastély see *The Borrowed Residence*
Kolosvar, Hungary 4
Kömives Kelemen 164 *(152)*
A Konvertbiztos see *The Convention Commissar*
KOOL Cigarettes 359, **361**
Korda, Alexander 7, 14, 30

Korda, Sándor *see* Korda, Alexander
Korda, Zoltán 30, 37
A Kormánybiztos see *The Government Commissioner*
Kornai, Richárd 68 *(2, 3)*, 69 *(6)*, 70 *(10, 11)*, 371 *(1)*
Kosloff, Theodore 105 *(55)*
Krasner, Milton 123 *(73)*
Krellberg, Sherman S. 379–380 *(4)*
Krecsányi, Ignács 153–154 *(10, 11, 12, 13, 14, 15, 16, 17, 18)*
Kruger, Alma 117 *(66)*
Kun, Béla 7, 33, 59, 60, 63
Kuntz, Thomas 367
Kupfer, Margarete 71–73 *(15)*
Kurd, Viktor 68 *(2, 4)*, 70 *(11)*, 371 *(1)*
Kurucz Féja Dávid see *Stubborn King David*
Küzdelem a Létért see *The Struggle for Life*
Kyser, Kay 117–118 *(66)*, 202–203 *(8)*, 214 *(12)*, 221 *(37)*, 361

LaBelle, Claude A. 248 *(197)*
Ladd, Alan 95–96 *(45)*, 119–120 *(69)*
Lady and the Monster 116 *(65)*
Lady of the Camellias (A Kaméliás Hölgy) 154 *(23)*, 160 *(103)*, 164 *(158)*, 165 *(165)*
Laemmle, Carl, Jr. 82 *(32)*, 86 *(37)*, 91 *(42)*, 100–101 *(50)*, 102 *(51)*, 236 *(67)*, 376 *(3)*, 378 *(3)*
Laemmle, Carl, Sr. 92 *(42)*, 376 *(3)*
Laemmle, Carla 86 *(37)*
Lake Elsinore, California ix, 52 *(10)*, 53 *(12)*
Landau, Martin 274 *(509)*, 275 *(510, 511, 512, 513, 514, 517)*, 276 *(522, 523, 524)*, 305 *(27)*, 331 *(29)*, 335 *(18)*
Landers, Lew 130 *(80)*
Lang, Fritz 73 *(17)*
Langer, Dr. Nicholas 35
Lansbury, Angela 185 *(200)*
La Plante, Laura *(32)*
La Plante, Violet 77 *(26)*
Larson, Randall 282 *(23)*
The Last Day (Az Utolsó Nap) 160 *(107)*
The Last Laugh 70–72 *(15)*, 87 *(37)*
The Last Performance 67, 77–78 *(27)*, 82 *(32)*, 212 *(1)*
Last Will and Testament 53 *(12)*
The Late, Great Creature 285 *(46)*

Late Night with David Letterman 352
Lathjay, Károly 69 *(6)*
Laughton, Charles 95–96 *(45)*, 221 *(29)*
Lawton, Frank 108 *(58)*
Leatherstocking (Lederstrumpf) 73 *(18)*
LeBerthom, Ted 317 *(32)*, 351
Le Borg, Reginald 143 *(93)*, 199 *(45)*, 271 *(472)*, 282 *(27)*
Lebow, Guy 209–210 *(209)*
Lederstrumpf see *Leatherstocking*
Lee, Christopher 55 *(13)*, 267 *(420)*, 305 *(28)*, 312 *(1)*, 328 *(4)*, 334 *(2)*, 335 *(22)*, 351
Lee, Dorothy 103 *(53)*
Lee, Joanna 144 *(94)*
Lee, Lila 10, 76–77 *(25)*
Lee, Rowland V. 23, 111–112 *(60)*
Leifert, Don 279 *(5)*
Lemon, The Reverend Lyn 144 *(94)*
Lengyel, Menyhért 155 *(26)*, 165 *(172)*
Lennig, Arthur 196 *(33)*, 269 *(447)*, 270 *(455)*, 278 *(1)*, 280–281 *(9)*, 327 *(3)*, 371 *(1)*
Leonard, Sheldon 134–135 *(85)*
Leong, James B. 103 *(53)*, 148 *(3)*, 186 *(203)*
Leoni Leo 68 *(3)*, 373 *(2)*
Leontovich, Eugenie 176 *(185)*
A Leopárd see *The Leopard*
The Leopard (A Leopárd) 67–68 *(1)*, 273 *(489)*
Le Picard, Marcel 119 *(68)*, 120 *(70)*, 130 *(81)*, 131 *(82)*, 136 *(87)*
LeRoy, Mervyn 91 *(41)*
Lesser, Sol 135 *(85)*, 148 *(2)*, 219 *(16)*, 293 *(11)*
Levine, Nat 146 *(1)*
Lewis, Jerry 141 *(90)*
Lewis, Joseph H. 119 *(68)*
Lewton, Val 133 *(84)*, 135 *(85)*, 271 *(466)*, 348
Lichello, Bob 266 *(402)*
Lili 70 *(10)*
Liliom 22, 152
Liliomfi 161 *(122, 128)*
Lilley, Jesse 274 *(502)*
Lincoln, Abraham 61
Lincoln Center 337–338 *(4)*
Lindbergh, Charles 81 *(31)*
Lindsay, Howard 179 *(188)*
Lininger, Hope *see* Lugosi, Hope Lininger
Linkletter, Art 207 *(22)*

Lipow Film Company 71 *(15)*
Liquori, Frank 357
Little Caesar 91 *(41)*
Littlefield, Lucien 132–133 *(83)*
Liveright, Horace 170–171 *(179)*, 283 *(34)*, 291 *(6)*
Lock Up Your Daughters 67, 145 *(95)*, 374 *(2)*, 381–383 *(6)*
Lock Your Doors 128 *(78)*
The Lodger 221 *(33)*, 258 *(307)*
London After Midnight 19, 104 *(54)*, 341, 374 *(2)*
Lonely King Lazlo (Árva László Kiraly) 164 *(161)*
Loosz, Béla 36, 44 *(24)*, 53 *(12)*
Lorentz, Pare 345
Loring, Michael 110 *(59)*, 111 *(59)*
Lorre, Peter 24, 38, 112 *(60)*, 113 *(61)*, 117–118 *(66)*, 143 *(93)*, 201, 203 *(8)*, 205 *(15)*, 211 *(9)*, 214 *(12)*, 221 *(37)*, 222 *(45)*, 249 *(207)*, 252 *(246)*, 332 *(2)*, 351, 360, 361
Los Angeles County General Hospital 34
Los Angeles Soccer League 29
Lost Horizon 83 *(33)*
Lóth, Ila 67 *(1)*, 68 *(3)*, 69 *(6, 7)*, 70 *(10, 11)*
Lotti Ezredesei see *Lotti's Colonels*
Lotti's Colonels (Lotti Ezredesei) 156 *(49)*
Louise, Anita 112 *(61)*, 360
Love at First Bite 270 *(458)*, 336
The Love Machine 334 *(7)*
Love the Actor! A Drama in Two Parts 332 *(2)*, 345
Love's Mockery 72 *(15)*
Lowe, Edmund 74–75 *(22)*, 88–90 *(39)*, 94–95 *(44)*, 101 *(51)*, 102 *(52)*, 148 *(2)*, 241 *(121, 124)*, 380 *(5)*
Loy, Myrna 84 *(34)*
Loyola Stadium 29
Lubin, Arthur 10, 116 *(65)*, 166 *(174)*, 220 *(27)*, 251 *(232)*, 272 *(479)*, 305 *(30)*, 313 *(12)*
Lubitsch, Ernst 24, 96 *(45)*, 113–114 *(62)*
Lucan, Arthur 33, 138–139 *(89)*, **140**, 262 *(361)*
Lucanio, Patrick 350
Luce, Clare 185 *(200)*, 217 *(3)*
Luce, Greg 330 *(12)*, 357
Ludlam, Harry 33, 279–280 *(8)*
Lugos, Hungary 3, 39, 47 *(2)*

Lugosi, Bela: naturalization as U.S. citizen 12, 49 *(7)*
Lugosi, Bela G. (Bela Lugosi, Jr.) 22, **27**, 30, 34, 50 *(9)*, 52 *(10)*, 53 *(12)*, 54–56 *(13)*, 199 *(42)*, 250 *(216)*, 251 *(229)*, 268 *(439)*, 269 *(441)*, 274 *(508)*, 275 *(519)*, 279 *(2)*, 305–306 *(22)*, 316–317 *(31)*, 322 *(7)*, 328 *(3)*, 331 *(27, 29)*, 366, 369
Lugosi, Hope Lininger x, 35–36, **37**, 44 *(25)*, 53 *(12)*, 54–56 *(13)*, 264 *(385)*, 265 *(386, 387)*, 266 *(402)*, 269 *(441)*, 275 *(515)*, 306 *(33)*, 335 *(18)*, 366
Lugosi, Lillian Arch 18–19, 20, 21, 22, **23**, **27**, **28**, 29, 30, 32, 33, 34, 44 *(13, 14, 15, 20, 21)*, 50–51 *(9)*, **51**, 52 *(10)*, 53 *(12)*, 108 *(57)*, 186 *(201)*, 188, 196 *(34)*, 221 *(33)*, 241 *(168)*, 244, 256 *(288)*, 258 *(307, 310)*, 262 *(354, 355, 357)*, 263 *(365, 366, 368)*, 269 *(450)*, 279 *(2, 4)*, 288, 300 *(2)*, 304 *(22)*, 328 *(3)*, 370–371 *(1)*
"Lugosi, Stella" 336
Lugosi: The Forgotten King 271 *(473)*, 330 *(11)*, 368
Lugosi: The Man Behind the Cape 57, 142 *(91)*, 164 *(161)*, 269 *(450)*, 270 *(455)*, 279 *(2)*, 289, 300 *(2)*, 330 *(2)*, 356, 357, 371 *(1)*
The Lugosi Files 330 *(13)*
Lugosi vs. Universal Pictures Co. 54–56 *(13)*, 352, 367
Lukas, Paul 7, 32, 35, 102 *(51)*, 348
Lulu 70 *(10)*
Lumivision 326 *(6)*
Luna Film Company 73 *(18)*
Lund, Lucille 100 *(50)*
Lusk, Robert 240 *(115)*
Luxury 217 *(3)*
Lynn, Sharon 83 *(33)*

Macbeth 161 *(117)*, 162 *(137, 141)*
McCarey, Leo 83 *(33)*
McCarthyism 33
McCoy, Donald 142 *(92)*
McCoy, Tony 142–143 *(92)*, 199 *(42)*
McDaniel, Hattie 107–108 *(56)*, 110 *(59)*
McDonald, Frank 132 *(83)*
McDonald, J. Farrell 102 *(52)*, 126 *(76)*, 128 *(78)*
MacDonald, Jeannette 85–86 *(36)*

McDowell, Claire 83 *(33)*, 107–108 *(56)*
McFadden, Hamilton 85 *(36)*, 90 *(40)*
McGuire, John 118 *(68)*
McHugh, Jimmy 117 *(66)*
Mack, Helen 170 *(179)*
Mack, Willard 98 *(47)*
MacKaill, Dorothy 380 *(5)*
McKay, Wanda 126, 130–131 *(81)*
McKinnon, Mona 144 *(94)*
McLaglen, Victor 88–90 *(39)*, 218 *(14)*
McLernon, Harold 84 *(35)*, 93 *(43)*
McMurtry, Larry 286 *(60)*, 352
McNally, Raymond T. 345
McNamee, Graham 102 *(51)*
Madách, Imre 10, 158 *(81)*, 159 *(89)*, 164 *(153)*
Madden, Oden and Olivia 260 *(328)*
Mademoiselle Charlotte (Charlotte Kisasszony) 164 *(163)*
Madison, Bob 279 *(5)*
The Magic Island 93 *(43)*
Magyar Athletic Club 28
Magyar Jovó 18, 289
Magyar Színház 158 *(73, 74, 75, 76, 78, 79)*
Magyarole Vasarpja 63
The Mail Boy and His Sister (A Postás Fiu és Huga) 155 *(28)*
Mail Call 28, 204–205 *(14)*
A Makrancos Hölgy see *The Taming of the Shrew*
Mamoulian, Rouben 96 *(45)*
The Man in the Cab 220 *(26)*
Man-Made Monster 83 *(33)*, 122 *(71)*, 220
The Man Who Is Dracula 332 *(1)*
Mandell, Paul 271 *(469)*
Mander, Miles 129 *(80)*
The Manimals 322 *(15)*
Mank, Gregory xii, 271 *(475)*, 273 *(497)*, 276 *(530)*, 279 *(4, 5)*, 282 *(20)*, 283 *(35)*, 286 *(66)*, 287 *(68, 69, 70)*, 331 *(30)*, 357, 384 *(7)*
Manlove, Dudley 144 *(94)*
Manners, David 86–87 *(37)*, 96–98 *(46)*, 100 *(49, 50)*, 212 *(3)*, 287 *(67)*
Mannix, Edward J. 104 *(54)*
March, Frederic 169 *(178)*, 232, 332
Marco, Paul x, 35, 142 *(92)*, 144 *(94)*, 199 *(42)*, 266 *(402)*, 272 *(478)*, 282 *(27)*, 306 *(34)*
Margaret Herrick Library 338 *(5)*
Mária Antónina see *Marie Antoinette*

Maria Magdalena 164 *(159)*
Maria Stuart 153 *(5)*, 158 *(84)*, 162 *(134)*
Marie, Baby Rose 98 *(48)*
Marie Antoinette (Mária Antónina) 160 *(111)*
Marin, Edward L. 96–98 *(46)*
Maritza, Sari 98 *(48)*
Mark, Michael 123–124 *(73)*
Mark of the Vampire 41, 79 *(30)*, 104–105 *(54)*, **106**, 201, 212 *(5)*, 244 *(161, 166)*, 246 *(176)*, 268 *(434)*, 269 *(443)*, 270 *(456)*, 272 *(481, 486)*, 273 *(497)*, 274 *(502)*, 275 *(518)*, 281 *(14)*, 283 *(35)*, 283–284 *(37)*, 286 *(58)*, 326 *(9)*, 346, 354, 360, 374 *(2)*
Marlowe, Don 31, 34, 38, 45 *(11, 12)*, 138 *(88)*, 184 *(197)*, 194–196 *(31)*, 208, 223 *(56)*, 268 *(435)*, 281 *(11)*, 297–298 *(23)*, 306 *(35)*, 308 *(48)*, 315 *(22)*, 375–378 *(3)*
Marmont, Percy 342
Marshall, Tully 98 *(47)*
Martin, Dean 141 *(90)*
Martinelli, Arthur 93 *(43)*, 118 *(67)*
Martyrs of Szigetvar (Szigetvári Vértanuk) 155 *(33)*
Marx, Groucho 199 *(43)*
Mary Ann 158 *(83)*
Mascot Studios 146–147 *(1)*
The Masked Ball (Álarcosbál) 68 *(2)*
Mason, Tom 144–145 *(94)*, 286 *(65)*
Massey, Ilona 126–128 *(77)*, 361
Massey, Raymond 221 *(39)*
Mathews, Lester 105–107 *(55)*
Matyó Lakodalom see *The Wedding at the Matyo's*
Maur, Mainhart 73 *(17, 19)*, 217 *(1)*
Mauro, John F. 285 *(45)*
May, Karl 73–74 *(19)*, 217 *(1)*
Mayer, Louis B. 114 *(62)*
Maynard, Ken 226 *(76)*
MCA/Universal 326 *(7)*
Media Home Entertainment 326 *(8)*
The Medico (A Medikos) 156 *(48)*
A Medikos see *The Medico*
Medwezcwesky, Judge 47 *(1)*
Meek, Donald 104 *(54)*
Meeker, George 98 *(47)*, 107 *(56)*
Meguntam Margitot see *Tired of Margaret*
Melford, George 87 *(37)*, 92 *(42)*
Melody, Little Jack 332 *(4)*

Meltzer, David 286 *(59)*
Menzies, William Cameron 94 *(44)*
Mercer, Johnny 117 *(66)*
Meredith, Burgess 202 *(7)*
Merrick, Mollie 343
The Merry Widow (A Vig Özvegy) 156 *(55)*
Metropolis 70 *(13)*, 87 *(37)*, 377 *(3)*
Metropolitan State Hospital 35, 44 *(24)*, 53, 211 *(11)*, 226 *(76)*, 264
Meyer, Abe 93 *(43)*, 103 *(53)*, 146 *(1)*
MGM Studios 79 *(30)*, 104 *(54)*, 113 *(62)*, 114 *(62)*, 372, 381 *(2)*
MGM/UA Home Video 326 *(9)*
Michel, Jean-Claude 328–329 *(8)*, 357, 384 *(7)*
Mickey's Gala Premiere 332 *(1)*
Microsoft Scenes: Hollywood Collection 332 *(1)*
Micsey, György 153 *(4–9)*
Midi Minuit Fantastique 375 *(3)*
The Midnight Girl 76–77 *(25)*, 231 *(18)*, 327 *(14, 16)*, 328 *(4)*, 373 *(2)*
Midnight Son 335 *(20)*
A Midsummer Night's Dream (A Szentivánáji Álom) 159 *(88)*, 164 *(57)*
The Mike Douglas Show 328 *(3)*
Miller, Mark A. 279 *(5)*
Miller, Winston 132 *(83)*
Miscey, György 153 *(4–9)*
Mr. Wu 103 *(53)*
Mitchell, Duke 141 *(90)*
Mitchell, Helen *(166)*
Mitchell, Lisa 269–270 *(451)*, 273 *(493)*
Mix, Mrs. Tom 199 *(43)*
Model kits 366–367
Mohr, Hal 77 *(27)*, 82 *(32)*, 100 *(49)*
Mok, Michael 251 *(225)*
Molnár, Ferenc 14, 78–79 *(29)*, 152, 155 *(25)*, 235 *(53)*
Molnár, Dr. István 371 *(1)*
Molnár, László 68 *(5)*, 69 *(9)*
Mondo Lugosi 330 *(14)*
Monna Vanna 70 *(12)*, 160 *(112)*
Monogram Studios 19, 24, 26, 32, 103 *(53)*, 119 *(69)*, 120–121 *(70)*, 122–123 *(72)*, 124–125 *(74)*, 126 *(76)*, 128–129 *(78)*, 129 *(79)*, 130–131 *(81)*, 131–132 *(82)*, 135 *(85)*, 136 *(87)*, 145 *(95)*, 222 *(42, 43, 44, 49)*, 256 *(289)*, 283 *(33)*, 349, 354, 355, 362, 364, 383 *(6)*
The Monster of Zombor 222 *(40)*

The Monster Show: A Cultural History of Horror 283 *(34)*
Monster World 267 *(425)*, 268 *(431)*
Monsters and Maniacs 330 *(16)*
Monsters, Mutants, and Heavenly Creatures: Confessions of 14 Classic Sci-Fi/Horrormeisters 284 *(40)*
The Monster's Warning 223 *(50)*
Monsters We've Known and Loved (1991) 331 *(23)*
"Monsters We've Known and Loved" *(Hollywood and the Stars)* 328 *(1)*
Montgomery, Robert 295 *(12)*
Moore, Clayton 122–123 *(72)*
Moore, Dennis 120–121 *(70)*
Moore, Duke 144 *(94)*
Moore, Pauline 174 *(184)*
Moore, Roger 115 *(64)*
Moore, Victor 102 *(51)*
Moorehead, Agnes 204 *(13)*
Moran, Frank 124–125 *(74)*, 129 *(80)*, 131–132 *(82)*
More Classics of the Horror Film 282 *(24)*
Morgan, Ralph 20, 95 *(44)*, 125 *(75)*
Morosco, Walter 78–79 *(29)*
Morris, Chester 102 *(51)*
Morrison, "Sunshine" Sammy 120 *(70)*, 128 *(78)*, 129 *(129)*
Mosk, Justice Stanley 56 *(13)*
Mother Riley Meets the Vampire (Vampire Over London) 33, 55 *(13)*, 138–140 *(89)*, **139**, 210 *(6)*, 224 *(64)*, 262 *(361)*, 267 *(413)*, **301**, 321 *(2)*, 325, 327 *(14, 16)*, 383 *(6)*
Motion Picture Employee card **40**
Motion Picture Museum and Hall of Fame 365
Mouse, Micky 41, 332 *(1)*
Movie Posters 274 *(501)*, 364
Mozgófénykép Hiradó 370 *(1)*
Mozihét 69 *(7)*, 370 *(1)*
The Mummy 93 *(42)*, 309
The Mummy's Tomb 125 *(75)*
Muni, Paul 16, 87 *(37)*
Murder at the Vanities 39, 174–175 *(184)*, 218 *(14)*, 242 *(141, 142, 143, 144, 145)*
Murder by Television 39, 98 *(47)*, 107–108 *(56)*, 123 *(72)*, 246, 269 *(445)*, 325, 327 *(14, 16)*
Murdered Alive 18, 172–173 *(182)*, 239 *(104, 105, 106, 107, 108)*
Murders in the Rue Morgue 17, 18, 45 *(2)*,

91–93 *(42)*, 119 *(68)*, 173 *(182)*, 212 *(4)*, 217 *(5)*, 218 *(9)*, 239 *(98, 100, 101, 102, 103)*, 249 *(202)*, 271 *(475)*, 272 *(477)*, 273 *(489)*, 282 *(26)*, 283 *(31)*, 284 *(43)*, 285 *(55)*, 292 *(8)*, 300 *(1)*, 317, 326 *(7)*, 336–337 *(1)*, 345, 346, 359, 362, 365, 377–378 *(3)*
Murders in the Rue Morgue and Other Tales of Mystery 284 *(43)*
Murnau, F.W. 8, 72–73 *(15)*, 101 *(50)*, 114 *(62)*, 343
Murphy, Dudley 86 *(37)*
Murray, Ken 202 *(7)*
Muse, Clarence 20, 93 *(43)*, 118–119 *(68)*
Music for Frankenstein, Dracula, the Mummy, the Wolf Man, and Other Old Friends 322 *(10)*
The Music of Hans J. Salter and Frank Skinner 323 *(23)*
Musique Fantastique: A Survey of Film Music in the Fantastic Cinema 282 *(23)*
Muson, Ona 91 *(41)*
Mussolini, Benito 61
The Mustache (A Bajusz) 154 *(18)*
My Son, the Vampire (film) 140 *(89)*
My Son, the Vampire (recording) 321 *(2)*
The Mysterious Abbe 219 *(20)*
The Mysterious Dr. Fu Manchu 90 *(40)*
The Mysterious Mr. Wong 19, 41, 98 *(47)*, 103–104 *(53)*, 123 *(72)*, 244 *(159, 160)*, 281 *(18)*, 325, 327 *(14, 16)*, 335, 354
Mystery House 28, 205–206 *(16)*, 223
The Mystery of the Mary Celeste 20, 108 *(57)*, **109**, 110 *(58)*, 229, 244 *(168)*, 246 *(183)*, 248 *(193, 195)*, 325 *(1)*, 327 *(14, 16)*
Mystery of the Wax Museum 343

Nadja 335 *(21)*
Nagel, Anne 116 *(65)*
Nagel, Conrad 75–76 *(23)*, 79–81 *(30)*, 220 *(28)*
A Nagymama see *The Grandmother*
Naish, J. Carroll 100 *(49)*, 315 *(20)*
Napierska, Violette 8, 70 *(12, 14)*, 71 *(14)*, 74 *(21)*, 230 *(8)*
Narancxvirág see *Orange Blossom*
Naron, Lynn 357
A Nászdal see *The Wedding Song*
Nat Pinkerton 70 *(13)*
National Theater of Budapest 4, **5**, 6, 7, 58, 59, 152, 153 *(4, 5, 6, 7, 8, 9)*, 158 *(80, 81, 85, 86)*, 159 *(87, 88, 89, 90, 91, 92, 93, 94, 95, 96, 97, 98, 99, 100, 101)*, 160 *(102, 103, 104, 105, 106, 107, 108, 109, 110, 111, 112, 113, 114, 115, 116)*, 161 *(117, 118, 119, 120, 121, 122, 123, 124, 125, 126, 127, 128, 129, 130, 131, 132)*, 162 *(133, 134, 136, 137, 138, 139, 140, 141, 142, 143, 144, 145, 146, 147, 148)*, 163 *(149)*, 164 *(150, 151, 152, 153, 154, 155, 156, 157, 158, 159, 160, 161, 162, 163, 164)*, 165 *(165, 166, 167, 168, 169, 170, 171, 172)*
National Trade Union of Actors (Hungary) 7, 20, 59
Neal, Tom 126 *(76)*
Neff, Bill 188, 193–194 *(30)*, 197 *(37)*
Neill, Roy William 127 *(77)*
Nelson, Ozzie and Harriet 202 *(5)*
Nemeskürty, István 68 *(5)*, 69–70 *(9)*, 70 *(10)*
Nemzeti Színeszet see National Theater of Budapest
Neuwald, Alfred 62, 64
New Hope, Pennsylvania, State Fair 193 *(28)*, **195**
New Realm 145 *(95)*
Newsome, Ted 330 *(21)*
Nigh, William 103 *(53)*, 122–123 *(72)*
Night Monster 125 *(75)*, 133 *(83)*, 151 *(5)*, 255 *(275, 276)*, 326 *(7)*
Night of Horror 222 *(43)*
Night of Terror 98 *(47)*, **99**, 242 *(138)*, 324
Night of the Ghouls 143 *(92)*, 225 *(75)*
"A Night on Bald Mountain" 213 *(11)*, 333 *(3)*
Night World 310
Nightmare of Ecstasy: The Life and Art of Edward D. Wood, Jr. 283 *(32)*
A Nightmare of Horror 193 *(26)*
Nimoy, Leonard 328 *(4)*
Ninety-Nine (Kilencvekilenc) 69–70 *(9)*, 71
Ninotchka 24, 113–114 *(62)*, 201, 251 *(226, 227, 228)*, 285 *(49)*, 286 *(63)*
Nissen, Greta 88 *(39)*, **89**
No Traveler Returns 31, 180–182 *(189)*, **181**, 223 *(54)*, 259 *(317, 318, 319)*, 348, 353
Noel, Gerard 269 *(446)*, 272 *(482)*, 273 *(492)*, 357

A Nök Barátja see *The Woman's Friend*
Norris, Edward 112–113 *(61)*
Nosferatu 72–73 *(15)*, 114 *(62)*, 335 *(20)*, 341, 343
The Notary of Peleske (A Peleskei Nótárius) 162 *(133)*
Noy, Wilfred 76 *(25)*
Nugent, Frank S. 251 *(228)*
Nurmi, Maila see Vampira
Nye, Jim 357
Nyiregyhazi, Ervin 29

Oakie, Jack x, 14, 36, 282 *(19)*, 306–307 *(36)*
Oakland, Simon 182 *(192)*
The Oath of Eva Draghy (Drághy Éva Eskuje) 159 *(96)*
Obbaggy, William 357, 369
Obituaries 265 *(391, 392, 393, 394, 395, 396, 397, 398, 399)*, 266 *(401)*
O'Brien, Dave 102 *(51)*, 118 *(67)*
O'Brien, George 215 *(5)*
O'Brien, Margaret 33
Az Obsitos 154 *(22)*
O'Connell, L. William 81 *(31)*, 83 *(33)*, 83–84 *(34)*, 130 *(80)*
Ocskay Brigadéros see *Brigadier General Ocskay*
Of Mice and Men 122 *(71)*
Oh, for a Man 45 *(1)*, 85–86 *(36)*, 237 *(74)*, 324
O'Keefe, Dennis 102 *(51)*, 117–118 *(66)*
O'Keefe, Walter 202 *(6)*, 250 *(224)*
Oklahoma! 85 *(35)*
Oland, Warner 90 *(40)*, 220, 238
The Old Dark House 96 *(45)*, 309
Old Mother Riley Meets the Vampire see *Mother Riley Meets the Vampire*
Old Mother Riley's Ghosts 139 *(89)*
Olsen and Johnson 88 *(38)*, 210 *(4)*, 261 *(345)*
Olson, Gilbert 35
Olt, Arisztid 6, 67 *(1)*, 68 *(2, 3, 4)*, 69 *(6, 7, 8)*, 70 *(11)*, 371 *(1)*
Olt River 3, 6
On the Trail of Ed Wood 331 *(24)*
One Body Too Many 132–133 *(83)*, 136 *(87)*, 258 *(313, 314, 315)*, 307 *(43)*, 325, 327 *(14, 16)*
One Glorious Day 77 *(25)*
One Night of Horror 191 *(18)*, **192**

Open House 168–169 *(177)*, 232 *(22, 23)*
Orange Blossom (Narancxvirág) 156 *(44)*
Az Ördög 154–155 *(25)*
Ormond, Ron 224 *(68)*, 279 *(7)*, 289
Orr, Judge William E. 18
Orrison, Katherine 277 *(533)*
Osborne, Vivienne 100 *(49)*
Ossana, Diana 286 *(60)*
Othello 156 *(50)*, 162 *(138)*
Otterson, Jack 111 *(60)*, 116 *(65)*, 119 *(69)*, 121–122 *(71)*, 123 *(73)*, 125 *(75)*
Ouspenskaya, Maria 121–122 *(71)*, 126–128 *(77)*, 253 *(258)*
Owen, Catherine Dale 81–82 *(31)*

Pagan Fury 218 *(15)*, 243 *(147)*
Pakots, József 68 *(3)*, 69 *(8)*, 70 *(11)*, 161 *(124, 125)*
Pangborn, Franklin 98 *(48)*
Paramount Studios 95–96 *(45)*, 98–99 *(48)*, 132 *(83)*, 342
The Parasites (Az Ingyenélök) 154 *(21)*
Paree, Paree 88 *(38)*
Parker, Albert 75 *(23)*
Parker, Eddie 123 *(73)*, 127 *(77)*, 143 *(92)*
Parker, Jean 132 *(83)*
Parnum, John 276 *(530)*
Parrish, Helen 117–118 *(66)*, 190–191 *(15)*, 252 *(242)*, 361
Parry, Lee 70 *(12, 14)*, 74 *(21)*
Parsons, Louella 22, 249 *(203)*
A Pártütok see *The Insurgents*
The Passion 6, 162 *(135)*, **163**
Passmore, H. Fraser 108 *(57)*
Pasternack, Joe 30, 35, 64
Pavey, Harold 307 *(37)*
Payne, Dennis 357
Pearl Harbor 61
A Peleskei Nótárius see *The Notary of Peleske*
Pembroke, George 118 *(68)*, 120–121 *(70)*, 122 *(72)*, 180–182 *(189)*
Pendleton, Nat 136 *(87)*
Perkins, Osgood 176 *(185)*
Peterdy, Klára 67 *(1)*, 68 *(3)*, 69 *(6, 7)*
Peterson, Dorothy 169 *(179)*
Petrillo, Sammy 141 *(90)*
The Phantom Creeps 24, 98 *(46)*, 125 *(75)*, **150**, 150–151 *(5)*, 250 *(222, 223)*, 326, 327 *(14, 16)*, 365, 367, 368
The Phantom Ghoul 211 *(8)*, 226 *(76)*

The Phantom Killer 119, 222
The Phantom of the Opera 15, 78 *(27)*, 341
Phantom Ship see *The Mystery of the Mary Celeste*
Philbin, Mary 77–78 *(27)*
Philosophical Research Society 35
Phoenix Company 68 *(5)*, 69 *(9)*, 70 *(10)*
Pichel, Irving 212 *(9)*, 219 *(19)*, 220 *(27)*
A Pictorial History of the Horror Film 281 *(12)*
Pidgeon, Walter 84–85 *(35)*
Pierce, Jack 26, 86 *(37)*, 91–92 *(42)*, 100 *(50)*, 111–112 *(60)*, 123 *(73)*, 125 *(75)*, 127 *(77)*, 138 *(88)*, 249 *(211)*, 342, 377–379 *(3)*
Pine, William 132–133 *(83)*
Pinocchio 116 *(64)*, 252 *(238)*
Pirola, Bill 357
Pivar, Maurice 86 *(37)*, 91 *(42)*
Pizor, William M. 107 *(56)*
Plan 9 from Outer Space 144–145 *(94)*, 225 *(69)*, 226 *(79)*, 286 *(68)*, 326 *(5)*, 327 *(12, 14)*, 331 *(26)*, 334 *(9)*, 336, 358, 363, 367
Plan 9 from Outer Space: Original Motion Picture Soundtrack 323 *(17)*
Plan 9 from Outer Space: Thirty Years Later 358, 367
Planks of Reason: Essays on the Horror Film 282 *(22)*
Play Broadcast 203 *(9)*
Poe, Edgar Allan iv, 19, 20, 30, 92 *(52)*, 100–101 *(50)*, 105–106 *(55)*, 119 *(69)*, 210 *(2)*, 218 *(12)*, 223 *(52)*, 243 *(154)*, 244 *(169)*, 260 *(338)*, 284 *(43)*, 359
Pogany, Bella 165 *(173)*
Pollard, Snub 126 *(76)*
Portal Productions 364
Porter, Cole 88 *(37)*
Porter, Don 125 *(75)*
Possessed by the Night 335 *(19)*
Postal Inspector 21, 110–111 *(59)*, 248 *(192)*
A Postás Fiu és Huga see *The Mail Boy and His Sister*
The Postman Always Rings Twice 93 *(42)*
Poverty Row HORRORS! 283 *(33)*, 358
PRC Studios 118 *(67)*, 313 *(13)*, 355
Pretty Boy Floyd: A Novel 286 *(60)*, 352
Prevost, Marie 215 *(3)*
Price, Michael H. 272 *(487)*, 281 *(18)*

Price, Vincent 115 *(64)*, 136–138 *(88)*, 328 *(2)*
The Prince in the Tale (Az Egyszeri Királyfi) 160 *(114)*
Prince of Peanuts 77 *(26)*
Principal Pictures Corporation 148 *(2)*
The Prisoner of War (A Hadifogoly) 164 *(154)*
Prisoners 40, 78–79 *(29)*, 235 *(53, 55)*
Prival, Lucien 147 *(2)*
The Prowler 272 *(487)*
Psycho 83 *(33)*
Punchinello 215 *(1)*, **216**, 232 *(26)*, 373 *(2)*
Puppet Show (Bábjáték) 157 *(65)*
Pursell, June 84 *(35)*
Pymm, Frederick 172 *(181)*
Pynchon, Thomas 285 *(48)*, 352

Quarry, Robert 307 *(38)*
Questel, Mae 215 *(3)*

Rains, Claude 121–122 *(71)*, 218 *(7)*, 221 *(35)*, 222 *(41, 45)*, 253 *(258)*
Rainsford, Ronda 215 *(1)*, **216**
II. Rákoczi Ferenc Fogsága see *Francis Rakoczi in Captivity*
Rákosi, Jenö 160 *(102)*, 161 *(119)*, 162 *(144)*
Randolph, Jane 136 *(88)*
Rang és Mod see *Rank and Style*
Rank and Style (Rang és Mod) 154 *(15)*, 230 *(2)*
The Rape of the Sabine Women (A Sabin Nök Elrablása) 157 *(71)*
Rathbone, Basil x, 23, 111–112 *(60)*, 119–120 *(69)*, 143 *(93)*, 205 *(15)*, 221 *(32)*, 249 *(207)*, 250 *(214)*, 251 *(233)*, 252 *(249)*, 267 *(425)*, 299 *(28)*
Ratoff, Gregory 16
The Raven 20, 105–107 *(55)*, 108 *(57)*, 110 *(58)*, 130 *(80)*, 135 *(85)*, 244 *(169)*, 245 *(172)*, 246 *(173, 177)*, 271 *(467, 471)*, 312 *(6, 7)*, 326 *(7)*, 337–354
Rawlinson, Herbert 149 *(4)*, 225 *(72)*
RCA/Columbia Home Video 326 *(10)*
Realart Pictures 141 *(90)*
Realart Rereleases 274 *(500)*
The Red Poppy 10, 22, 39, 152, 165–166 *(174)*, 168 *(176)*, 230 *(9)*, 231 *(10, 11)*, 235 *(50)*, 293 *(11)*, 296 *(15)*
The Red Skelton Show 32, 208, 211 *(9)*
Rees, Robert 357

Regina Theatre 22, 23, 190 *(13)*, 249 *(205)*
Reicher, Frank 109 *(58)*, 113 *(62)*, 125 *(75)*
Reid, Cliff 115 *(64)*
Reinhardt, Max 70 *(12)*, 220 *(28)*
Reisch, Walter 113 *(62)*, 286 *(63)*
The Rejected Woman 75–76 *(23)*, 231 *(14, 15)*, 373 *(2)*, 374 *(2)*
Remington razors 359
Renaldo, Duncan 215 *(1)*
Renegades 82 *(31)*, 83–84 *(34)*, 236 *(72)*, 237 *(73)*, 324
Renown Pictures 139 *(89)*
Republic Pictures Home Video 326 *(11)*
Republic Studios 149–150 *(4)*, 220 *(27)*
Resin from the Grave 367
Resita, Hungary 4
Retour de Bela Lugosi 357
Return of Chandu 41, 95 *(44)*, 147–148 *(2)*, 219 *(16)*, 243 *(156)*, 244 *(162, 163, 164)*, 273 *(493)*, 285 *(44)*, 293 *(11)*, 326 *(11)*, 327 *(14, 16)*, 328 *(4)*, 333 *(2)*, 346
The Return of Dr. X 221 *(35)*
The Return of Dracula 223 *(56)*
Return of Frankenstein 220 *(23)*
Return of the Ape Man 131–132, 258
The Return of the Ape Man 125 *(74)*, 131–132 *(82)*, 258 *(311, 312)*, 383 *(6)*
Return of the Vampire 27, 55 *(13)*, 129–130 *(80)*, 131 *(81)*, 132 *(82)*, 179 *(187)*, 204 *(12)*, 222 *(47)*, 257 *(299, 300, 301)*, 324, 326 *(5, 10)*
Return of the White Zombie 94 *(43)*, 224 *(59)*
Revenge of the Dead 225–226 *(75)*
Revenge of the Zombies 222–223 *(49)*
Revier, Dorothy 90 *(40)*
Revolt of the Zombies 94 *(43)*, 221 *(30)*, 333 *(1)*
Reynolds, J. Edward 144 *(94)*
Rhapsody of Death 285 *(45)*, 296–297 *(19)*
Rhino Home Video 327 *(12)*
Rhodes, Gary Don 272 *(479, 481, 483, 485)*, 273 *(488, 489, 490)*, 279 *(5)*, 331 *(30)*, 369, 373 *(1)*
Rialto Theatre (New York) 23
Richard III 4, 156 *(42)*, 158 *(85)*, 161 *(126)*, 165 *(169)*
Richman, Helen 277 *(533)*
Ridges, Stanley 116 *(65)*
The Right to Dream 47 *(3)*, 217 *(2)*

Riley, Philip J. 286 *(64, 66)*, 287 *(67, 68, 69, 70)*
Ripley, Robert L. 184 *(196)*, 193 *(29)*, 260 *(337)*
Rittenberg, Louis **60**
The Ritz Brothers 24, 112–113 *(61)*, 360
Rivals 331 *(30)*
RKO Studios 115 *(64)*, 117 *(66)*, 133 *(84)*, 134 *(85)*, 135–136 *(86)*
The Roan Group 327 *(13)*
Robert Florey: The French Expressionist 282 *(26)*
Robert Knowlden Agency 45 *(5)*
Robeson, Paul 63
Robin and the 7 Hoods 135 *(55)*
Robin Orvos see *Dr. Robin*
Robinson, George 111 *(60)*, 127 *(77)*
Robinson, Jackie 210 *(4)*
Robinson, Dr. William J. 346
Roemheld, Heinz 86 *(37)*, 91 *(42)*, 100 *(50)*
Rogell, Albert S. 119–120 *(69)*, 135 *(86)*
Rogers, Ginger 176 *(185)*, 198 *(39)*
Rolla, Marcel 69 *(8)*, 371 *(1)*
Romberg, Sigmund 84–85 *(35)*
Romeo and Juliet (Rómeó és Julia) 154 *(19)*, 165 *(167)*, 230 *(3, 4)*, 242 *(141)*, 293 *(11)*
Romero, Cesare 248 *(190)*
Roosevelt, Franklin D. 57, 61
Rosen, Phil 120 *(70)*, 145 *(95)*, 131 *(82)*
Rosenberg, Max 333–334 *(2)*
Rosse, Herman 86 *(37)*
Rossitto, Angelo 120–121 *(70)*, 124 *(74)*, 136 *(87)*, 220 *(28)*, 271 *(476)*, 307 *(39)*
Rote, Ed W. 119 *(68)*, 120 *(70)*, 122 *(72)*, 124 *(74)*, 149 *(3)*
Roth, Justice Lester William 56 *(13)*
Rotter, Fritz 32
Rowan, Jo 336
Royal Crown cola 359
The Royal Life (Az Élet Királya) 70 *(11)*
Rubens, Alma 75–76 *(23)*
Rudley, Herbert 143 *(93)*, 283
The Rudy Vallee Show 206 *(18)*
Rumann, Sig 113 *(62)*
Rumble Fish 334 *(10)*
The Runestone 334 *(17)*
Ruric, Peter 100–101 *(50)*
Russell, Elizabeth 124–125 *(74)*
Ryan, Tim 141 *(90)*

A Sabin Nök Elrablása see *The Rape of the Sabine Women*
The Sacred Grove (A Szent Liget) 156 *(46)*
St. Cyr, Lili 199 *(41)*
St. Dennis, Madelon 96 *(46)*
The Saint's Double Trouble 115–116 *(64)*, 251 *(231)*, 252 *(238)*, 326 *(8)*
Salkow Agency 45 *(8)*
Salter, Hans J. 121 *(71)*, 123 *(73)*, 125 *(75)*, 127–128 *(77)*, 287 *(68, 69)*, 322 *(10, 11, 12)*
San Diego Exposition 190 *(8)*, 215 *(7)*
Sancho Panza Királysága see *The Kingdom of Sancho Panza*
Sanders, George 115 *(64)*
Sanford, William R. 285 *(54)*
Sanforth, Clifford 107 *(56)*
Sardou, Victorien 153 *(9)*, 157 *(58)*, 159 *(92)*
Sarecky, Barney 128 *(78)*, 131 *(82)*, 146 *(1)*
A Sárga Csikó see *The Yellow Colt*
Sárga Liliom see *The Yellow Lily*
A Sasfiók see *The Eaglet*
Sass, Louis 30
Savada, Elias 283 *(37)*
Scandal (Botrány) 157 *(64)*
Scared to Death 31, 121, 136, **137**, 325, 326, 327, 354
Scarlet Street 274 *(502, 503)*, 276 *(529)*, 356
Scars of Dracula 335 *(22)*
Schallert, Edwin 248 *(198)*, 238 *(86)*, 257 *(296)*
Schary, Dore 106 *(55)*
Schenck, Aubrey 284 *(39)*
Scheuer, Philip K. 235 *(57)*, 238 *(87, 90)*
Schiller, Friedrich 153 *(5)*, 158 *(84)*, 162 *(134)*
Schlegel, Margarete 71 *(15)*, 73 *(15)*
Schnitzer, Gerald 126 *(76)*
Schreck, Max 72 *(15)*
Schrecken 71 *(15)*
Schubert, Bernard 104 *(54)*, 284 *(37)*
Scott, Randolph 95–96 *(45)*
The Scoundrels (A Jómadarak) 156 *(51)*
Screams on Screen: 100 Years of the Horror Film 337
Screen Actor's Guild 20, 60, 270 *(456)*
Screen Classics 141 *(91)*
Screen Guild Productions 136 *(87)*
Screen Snapshots 215 *(4)*, 216 *(9)*, 328 *(5)*
Scully, Vin 208
Sculpting 18, 239 *(106)*

Seabrook, William B. 93 *(43)*
Seastrom, Victor 375 *(2)*
The Secretary of State (Az Allamtit Kam Ur) 157 *(69)*
Segal, Vivienne 84–85 *(35)*
Seiter, William A. 78 *(29)*
Selznick, David O. 219 *(19)*
Senn, Bryan 279 *(5)*
Sennett, Mack x, 36, 199 *(43)*
Sesame Street 345
Seven Keys to Baldpate 133 *(83)*
Shadow of Chinatown 119 *(68)*, 123 *(72)*, 125 *(74)*, 148–149 *(3)*, 272 *(483)*, 326, 327 *(14)*, 334 *(10)*
Shaffer, Rosalind 234 *(50)*
Shakespeare, William 4, 32, 154 *(19)*, 158 *(85)*, 159 *(88, 93)*, 160 *(106)*, 161 *(117, 130, 131)*, 162 *(136, 137, 138, 139, 140, 141, 143, 145)*, 164 *(150, 156, 157, 162)*, 165 *(167, 169, 170)*
Sham Poo the Magician 95 *(44)*
Shearer, Norma 176 *(185)*
Sheffield, Richard ix–x, xiv, 36, 38, 199 *(42)*, 224 *(62)*, 226 *(78)*, 278, 298 *(27)*, 307 *(41)*, 316 *(28)*, 331 *(29, 30)*, 335 *(18)*, 336, 345, 357, 369, 373–374 *(2)*
Shell Chateau 202 *(3)*
Shelley, Mary 17, 26, 348, 375 *(2)*
Sherman, Allen 140 *(89)*, 321 *(2)*
Sherrill, Lou 46 *(14, 15)*
Ship's Reporter 210 *(6)*
The Shock 372 *(2)*
Shock television packages 336–337 *(1, 2)*
Shomer, Bob 373 *(2)*
Shore, Howard 323 *(22)*
Shubert, Lulu 241 *(125)*
Sibiu, Hungary 4
Silent Bells (Elnémult Harangok) 157 *(63)*
The Silent Command 10, 40, 74–75 *(22)*, 231 *(12, 13)*, 273 *(490)*, 293 *(11)*, 324, 374 *(2)*
Silk Stockings 114 *(62)*
Silver Slipper 34, 263, 264
Simms, Ginny 117 *(66)*
Sinatra, Frank 35, 211 *(10)*
Sinclair, John 239 *(99)*
Singin' in the Rain 136 *(87)*
Sinister Cinema (television program) 330 *(12)*
Sinister Cinema (video company) 327 *(14)*, 356
Siodmak, Curt 116 *(116)*, 121–122 *(71)*,

127 *(77)*, 289, 279 *(4)*, 282 *(27)*, 287 *(68, 70)*, 331 *(27)*
Sir Lancelot 134–135 *(85)*
The Six Arms of Siva 224 *(60)*
Skal, David J. 274 *(498)*, 277 *(534)*, 282–283 *(29)*, 283 *(34, 37)*, 286 *(71)*, 331 *(29)*, 384 *(7)*
Skelton, Red 204 *(11)*, 211 *(9)*, 267 *(413)*
Skinner, Frank 121 *(71)*, 137–138 *(88)*
Skinner, Richard Dana 240 *(118)*
Skipworth, Alison 85 *(36)*
Skolsky, Sidney 265 *(388)*
Skrupsky, Julia 369
Slave of a Foreign Will 7, 8, 70 *(12)*, 72, 230 *(8)*
Slaven Fremdes Willens see *Slave of a Foreign Will*
Smith, Alexis 185 *(200)*
Smith, Don G. 274 *(503)*, 279 *(5)*
Smith, H. Allen 250 *(224)*
Soccer 13, 28, 41
Son of Dracula 27, 125 *(75)*, 321 *(4)*
Son of Frankenstein 23, 30, 111–112 *(60)*, 122 *(71)*, 136 *(86)*, 212 *(6)*, 249 *(207, 209, 211)*, 250 *(212, 213, 214, 215, 217, 218)*, 253 *(259)*, 266 *(412)*, 271 *(475)*, 272 *(485)*, 274 *(499)*, 286 *(64)*, 313 *(9)*, 322 *(10)*, 324, 326 *(7)*, 337, 354, 367, 379 *(4)*
Son of Kong 148 *(2)*, 190 *(13)*
Sondergaard, Gale 119–120 *(69)*, 252
Soo, Kim Yen 198 *(38)*
La Sorcière 159 *(100)*
SOS Coastguard 149–150 *(4)*, 248 *(199)*, 254 *(268)*, 284, 326 *(11)*, 327 *(14)*
Sound of Music 134 *(84)*
South Pacific 85 *(35)*
The Spade Cooley Show 211 *(10)*
Sparks, Ned 348
Sparrows 129 *(78)*
Spence, Ralph 112 *(61)*
Spencer, Michael ix, 36, 38, 226 *(78)*
Spending Spree (Fenn az Ernyö Nincsen Kas) 161 *(121)*
The Spider 95 *(44)*
The Spider Woman 120 *(69)*
Spiders 73 *(17)*
Spiegel, Irwin O. 54–55 *(13)*
Spooks Run Wild 26, 55 *(13)*, 120–121 *(70)*, 126 *(76)*, 149 *(3)*, 253 *(254, 255)*, 322 *(8)*, 327 *(14, 16)*, 349, 354
Spring Tempest (Tavaszi Vihar) 68 *(4)*

Stallings, Laurence 88 *(39)*
Stamp Collecting 29, 262 *(354)*
Standing, Joan 86 *(37)*
Stanley, Gabriel 346
Star Film Company 7, 67 *(1)*, 68 *(2, 3, 4)*, 69 *(6, 7, 8)*, 70 *(11)*, 371 *(1)*
Star Strangled Rhythm 222 *(46)*
Stardust Cavalcade 190–191 *(15)*, 252 *(241, 242, 243)*
Starlit Time 210 *(5)*
Starr, Jimmy 248 *(201)*
State Theater (Torrington, Connecticut) 196 *(35)*
Steele, Bob 226 *(76)*
Stein, Michael 276 *(524)*
Step Right Up! I'm Gonna Scare the Pants Off America 281 *(17)*
Stevenson, Robert Louis 71 *(15)*, 133 *(84)*, 218 *(10)*
Stifter, Magnus 71 *(15)*, 73 *(16)*
Stoker, Bram xii, 12, 15, 27, 72 *(15)*, 130 *(80)*, 170–171 *(179)*, 171 *(180)*, 188 *(44)*, 234, 284 *(42)*, 291 *(6)*, 332 *(2)*, 343, 345, 349
Stolen Thunder 85 *(36)*
Stoloff, Benjamin 98 *(47)*, 134 *(85)*
Storace, Frank 379–380 *(4)*
Storm, Olaf 70 *(13)*
The Story of a Career (Egy Karrier Története) 68 *(3)*, 161 *(124, 125)*
The Story of a Poor Lad (Egy Szegény lfju Története) 155–156 *(40)*, 162–163 *(148)*
Strange, Glenn 136–138 *(88)*, 261 *(340)*, 307 *(12)*
Strictly Dishonorable 92 *(42)*
Stritch, Elaine 182 *(190)*, 183 *(193)*
Stromberg, William T. 323 *(23)*
The Struggle for Life (Küzdelem a Létért) 69 *(7)*
Struss, Karl 95 *(45)*
Stuart, Gloria 101 *(51)*
Stubborn King David (Kurucz Féja Dávid) 153 *(4)*
The Student of Prague 70 *(13)*, 341
Stumar, Charles 105 *(55)*
Such Men Are Dangerous 81–82 *(31)*, 236 *(62, 63)*, 288, 324
The Suicide Club 218 *(10)*
Sullivan, Ed 190–191 *(15)*, 252 *(241, 242, 243)*
Sullivan, Frances L. 185 *(200)*, 261 *(349)*

Summers, Walter 114 *(63)*
Sunrise 72 *(15)*
Super Sleuth 135 *(86)*
Susie (Zsuzsi) 162 *(146)*
Suspense 27, 32, 201, 203 *(10)*, 208, **209**, 210 *(3)*, 261 *(345)*, 321 *(6)*, 322 *(7)*, 323 *(16)*
Suspense/Bela Lugosi 322 *(7)*
Sutherland, Eddie 99 *(48)*, 219 *(19)*, 246 *(182)*
Svehla, Gary and Sue 279 *(5)*, 284 *(38)*
Swanson, Gloria 212 *(2)*, 232 *(31)*, 276 *(526)*
Sybil Young 74 *(21)*
Szabadka, Hungary 4
Szegedi Városi Színház (Szeged Repertory Theater) 154 *(19, 20, 21, 22, 23, 24, 25)*, 155 *(26, 27, 28, 29, 30, 31, 32, 33, 34, 35, 36, 37, 38, 39, 40)*, 156 *(41, 42, 43, 44, 45, 46, 47, 48, 49, 50, 51, 52, 53, 54, 55, 56)*, 157 *(57, 58, 59, 60, 61, 62, 63, 64, 65, 66, 67, 68, 69, 70, 71)*, 158 *(72)*
A Szent Liget see The Sacred Grove
A Szentivánáji Álom see A Midsummer Night's Dream
Szigeti, Jozsef 154 *(15)*
Szigetvári Vértanuk see Martyrs of Szigetvar
Szigligeti, Ede 4, 155 *(32)*, 157 *(59)*, 161 *(121, 122, 128)*
Szinészek Lapja 7, 59
Szitja, Willi 30, 36
Szmik, Ilona 6, 14, 47 *(1)*, 59
A Szökött Katona see The Deserter

Tábori, László 332 *(2)*, 345, 371 *(1)*
Taifun see Typhoon
Talbot, Lyle 132–133 *(83)*, 144 *(94)*, 225 *(69)*, 270 *(452)*, 307–308 *(43)*
Taming of the Shrew (A Makrancos Hölgy) 4, 157 *(57)*, 164 *(150)*
Tamiroff, Akim 36, 100 *(49)*, 143 *(93)*
Tanforan Racetrack 22, 190 *(12)*
A Tanitónö see The Teacher
Der Tanz auf dem Vulkan see The Dance on the Volcano
Tartalékos Férj see Husband in Reserve
Tartuffe 159 *(90)*
Tattersall, Viva 146 *(1)*

Taurog, Norman 96 *(45)*
Tavaszi Vihar see Spring Tempest
Taves, Brian 272 *(477)*, 282 *(26)*, 376–377 *(3)*, 379 *(3)*
Taylor, Eric 116 *(65)*, 119–120 *(69)*, 123 *(73)*
Taylor, Forrest 151 *(5)*
Taylor, Henry J. 62
Taylor, Kent 348
Taylor, Ray 148 *(2)*
The Teacher (A Tanitónö) 157 *(68)*
The Tell-Tale Heart 30, 194–196 *(31)*, 206 *(20)*, 260 *(338)*, 281 *(11)*
Telotte, J.P. 271 *(466)*
Temesvar, Hungary 4
Temps X 328 *(8)*, 357
The Tenderfoot 91 *(41)*
Terenzio, Maurice 328 *(6)*, 357
The Terror (1928) 85 *(35)*
The Terror (radio show) 34, 225 *(71)*
Terrytoons 332 *(2)*
Terwilleger, George 76 *(24)*
Die Teufelsanbeter see The Devil Worshippers
Texaco Star Theater 202 *(7)*, 204 *(11)*, 210 *(4)*, 261 *(345)*
That's Right— You're Wrong 117
Them! 135 *(85)*
Them or Us: Archetypal Interpretations of Fifties' Alien Invasion Films 350
Thesiger, Ernest 220 *(23)*
The Thief (A Tolvaj) 156 *(54)*
Thirer, Irene 237 *(78)*, 244 *(168)*
"The Thirsty Death" 205 *(16)*, 322 *(9)*
The Thirteenth Chair 14, 76, 79–81 *(30)*, 105 *(54)*, 235 *(57)*, 236 *(61)*, 272 *(483)*, 282 *(24)*, 283–284 *(37)*, 374
This Gun for Hire 120 *(69)*
Thomas, Bob 263 *(368)*
Thomas, Harry 141–142 *(91)*, 144 *(94)*, 282 *(27)*
Thomas, William 132–133 *(83)*
Thompson, William C. 141–142 *(91)*, 142 *(92)*, 144 *(94)*
Thomson, Kenneth 78 *(28)*, 83 *(33)*
Thorne, Ian 285 *(50, 51, 53)*
The Three Bodyguards (A Harom Testor) 163 *(149)*
Three Indelicate Ladies 31, 182 *(190)*, 193 *(27)*, 260 *(331, 332)*, 273 *(490)*
The Three Stooges 102 *(51)*, 275 *(519)*

Tietjens, Eunice 167–168 *(176)*, 279 *(6)*
Tiffany Studios 97 *(46)*
Tinee, May 238 *(85)*
Tired of Margaret (Meguntam Margitot) 156 *(44)*
Tobacco Road 81 *(30)*
Die Tochter der Arbeit see *The Daughter of Work*
Tod des Grossfuerstens see *The Death of the Grand Duke*
Todd, Mike 197 *(37)*
Todd, Thelma 91 *(41)*
Die Todeskarawane see *The Caravan of Death*
Toland, Mario 358
A Tolvaj see *The Thief*
Tom Duggan Show 211 *(12)*
Toomey, Regis 150 *(5)*
Topps trading cards 365
Tora, Lia 78 *(28)*, **80**
The Torches (A Fáklyák) 159 *(94)*
Torment 222 *(44)*
Tovar, Lupita 87 *(37)*, 283 *(36)*, 308 *(44)*
Tovarich 16, 22, 176–177 *(185)*, 190 *(12)*, 248 *(196, 197, 198)*, 221 *(32)*, 296 *(15)*
Tovarich radio interview 202 *(4)*
Tracy, Lee **9**
Trading cards 365
The Tragedy of Man 10, 158 *(81)*, 159 *(89)*, 164 *(153)*, 165 *(173)*, 166 *(174)*
Treacher, Arthur 190 *(15)*, 252 *(241, 242, 243)*
Tribute to a Star! 210 *(6)*, 330 *(14)*
Trieste, Italy 10, 47 *(2)*, 49 *(7)*
Trilby 4, 153 *(10)*, 157 *(67)*, 230 *(1)*
A Trónkövetelök see *The Contenders for the Throne*
Tryon, Glenn 77 *(26)*, 82 *(32)*
The Tuesday Program with Walter O'Keefe 202 *(6)*
Tully, Jim 106 *(55)*
Turán, Gustav 67 *(1)*, 69 *(8)*, 70 *(10, 11)*, 371
Turner, George 272 *(484)*, 281 *(18)*, 287 *(67)*
Turner Home Entertainment 327 *(15)*
Tuttle, Lureen 205 *(16)*
Tuttle, William 104 *(54)*, 328 *(2)*
Twentieth Century Fox Films 112 *(61)*

Typhoon (Taifun) 155 *(26)*
Tytla, Bill 213 *(11)*, 333 *(3)*

Ullman, S. George 45 *(6)*
Ulmer, Edgar G. 100–101 *(50)*, 271 *(469)*, 308 *(45)*, 325
Ulric, Lenore 380 *(5)*
Undead Masses 226 *(79)*
Underwood, Peter 313 *(12)*
Unger, Gladys 166 *(175)*
The Unholy Three 77 *(35)*
United Artists 36, 93 *(43)*, 143–144 *(93)*, 345
Universal Horrors: The Studio's Classic Films 1931–1946 282 *(28)*
Universal Studios 13, 15, 16, 17, 18, 19, 20, 21, 23, 24, 26, 27, 31, 54–56 *(13)*, 77 *(26, 27)*, 78 *(27)*, 82 *(32)*, 86–87 *(37)*, 91–92 *(42)*, 93 *(43)*, 94, 100–101 *(50)*, 102 *(52)*, 106–107 *(55)*, 109–110 *(58)*, 110–111 *(59)*, 111–112 *(60)*, 119–120 *(69)*, 121–122 *(71)*, 124 *(73)*, 125 *(75)*, 127–128 *(77)*, 130 *(80)*, 133 *(84)*, 141 *(90)*, 151 *(6)*, 196 *(32)*, 206 *(16)*, 215 *(6)*, 217 *(4, 5, 6)*, 218 *(7, 10, 11)*, 219 *(18, 19)*, 220 *(23, 24, 25, 26)*, 222 *(40, 41, 45)*, 236 *(64, 66, 70)*, 239 *(97)*, 243 *(148, 154)*, 249 *(206, 207, 209)*, 254 *(262)*, 256 *(290)*, 273 *(497)*, 282 *(20, 28)*, 286 *(64, 66)*, 291 *(6)*, 309, 316 *(27)*, 317 *(32)*, 326 *(7)*, 336–337 *(1, 2)*, 347, 348, 350, 352, 353, 366, 367, 368, 376 *(3)*, 379 *(3)*
Universal-International 137–138 *(88)*
Ünnepi Játék see *Festive Play*
Urecal, Minerva 124 *(74)*, 128 *(78)*, 129 *(79)*
Ustad Film Company 73 *(17, 19)*
Az Utolsó Nap see *The Last Day*
Utter-McKinley Mortuary 38

A Vagyáros 161 *(127)*
Vajda, Ernest 81 *(31)*
Vajda, László 7
Valentine, Joseph 121 *(71)*
Valentino, Rudolph 77 *(25)*
Vallee, Rudy 19, 98 *(48)*, 206 *(18)*, 211 *(10)*
Vampira (Maila Nurmi) 144 *(94)*, 199 *(42)*, 200 *(45)*, 211, 308 *(46)*

412 Index

The Vampire 221 *(34)*
Vampire of the Skies 219 *(17)*
Vampire Over London 141 *(89)*
The Vampire's Tomb x, 144 *(94)*, 225 *(69)*
Van Enger, Charles 125 *(75)*, 137 *(88)*, 141 *(90)*
Van Horn, Emil 128–129 *(78)*
The Vanishing Body 101 *(50)*
Van Sloan, Edward 36, 86–88 *(37)*, 96–98 *(46)*, 150–151 *(5)*, 169–171 *(179)*, 212 *(3, 4)*, 272 *(484)*, 238 *(85)*, 287 *(67)*, 375–379 *(3)*
Van Trees, James 84 *(35)*
Varconi, Victor 14, 90 *(40)*, 233 *(30)*, 238 *(95)*
Varnel, Marcel 94 *(44)*
A Vasgyáros see *The Iron Manufacturer*
Vaughn, Clifford 105–107 *(55)*
Veidt, Conrad 16, 73 *(17)*, 77–78 *(27)*, 87 *(37)*
The Veiled Woman 78 *(28)*, **80**, 85 *(36)*, 172 *(180)*, 233–234 *(41)*
Veiller, Bayard 79–80 *(30)*
Vernon, Wally 112–113 *(61)*
Viaggio, Vincent 332 *(1)*
Victory Pictures Corporation 148 *(3)*
Video Yesteryear 327 *(16)*
Viola — Az Alföldi Haramia see *Viola, Outlaw of the Lowlands*
Viola, Outlaw of the Lowlands (Viola — Az Alföldi Haramia) 157 *(59)*
Vienna 7
Viennese Nights 237, 324
A Vig Özvegy see *The Merry Widow*
Villarias, Carlos 87 *(37)*
Viola 104 *(104)*
Virginia Doak Agency, Inc. 45 *(11)*
Visaroff, Michael 86 *(37)*, 91 *(42)*, 104–105 *(54)*
Volpe 143 *(93)*
von Montágh, Ilona 10, 48 *(5)*, 375 *(2)*
von Seyffertitz, Gustav 111 *(60)*
von Stroheim, Erich 212 *(2)*, 258 *(306)*
Voodoo Man 26, 30, 126 *(76)*, 129–131 *(81)*, 223 *(50)*, 257 *(302, 303, 304)*, 284 *(38)*, 363, 383

Wachner, Sophie 81 *(31)*, 83, *(33)*, 84 *(34)*, 85 *(36)*
Wadsworth, Henry 104 *(54)*

Waggner, George 121–122 *(71)*, 127 *(77)*, 213 *(73)*, 124 *(73)*, 127 *(77)*
Waite, Edgar 233 *(40)*
Walcott, Gregory 144 *(94)*
Wallace, Edgar 114–115 *(63)*, 218 *(9)*
Wallace, Inez 249 *(202)*
Wallis, Hal 141 *(90)*
Walsh, Raoul 88–90 *(39)*
Walston, Ray 190 *(182)*, 183 *(193)*, 331 *(29)*
Walt Disney Studios 332 *(1)*, 333 *(3)*
Walter, Wilfred 114–115 *(62)*
Walters, Luana 124–125 *(74)*, 148–149 *(3)*
Walthall, Henry B. 94–95 *(44)*, 146–147 *(1)*
Ward, Amelita 129 *(78)*
Ware, Irene 94 *(44)*, 105–107 *(55)*
Ware, Judge Wallace L. 34, 52–53 *(11)*, 264 *(375, 376)*
Warner, H.B. 83 *(33)*
Warner Brothers 83 *(35)*, 88 *(38)*, 111 *(59)*, 343
Warren, Bill 282 *(21, 25)*
Waters, Ethel 102 *(51)*
Watts, Richard, Jr. 237 *(79)*, 241 *(121)*, 345
Waxman, Franz 109–110 *(58)*, 323 *(23)*
Way Down East 76 *(25)*
Waycoff, Leon 92, 173 *(183)*, 270 *(452)*
Weaver, Tom 272 *(478)*, 275 *(520, 521)*, 279 *(5)*, 282 *(27, 28)*, 283 *(33, 36)*, 284 *(39, 40)*, 300 *(3)*, 358
Webb, Kenneth 93 *(43)*
Weber, Harry 45 *(1)*
The Wedding at the Matyo's (Matyó Lakodalom) 160–161 *(116)*
The Wedding Song (A Nászdal) 69 *(6)*
Weeks, Beatrice Woodruff 14–15, 42 *(8)*, 48–49 *(6)*, 172 *(181)*, 234 *(49)*, 235 *(51, 58, 59)*, 276 *(526)*, 308 *(47)*
Wegener, Paul 70 *(12)*, 377 *(3)*
Weird Tales 311, 316, 351
Weiss, George 141–142 *(91)*
Welles, Orson 63, 116 *(65)*
Wells, H.G. 19, 95–96 *(45)*, 218 *(7)*
Wells, Jacqueline 100 *(50)*
We're Married (Hazasodjunk) 153 *(2)*
The Werewolf 11, 166–167 *(175)*, 231 *(16, 17)*, 374–375 *(2)*
Werewolf of London 220 *(24)*
The Werewolf of Paris 105 *(54)*

Index   413

West, Paul 285 *(47)*
West Side Story 134 *(84)*
Westmore, Bud 138 *(88)*
Westmore, Perc 112 *(61)*
Westmore, Wally 95 *(45)*
Weston, Garnett 93 *(43)*
Whale, James 17, 92 *(42)*, 112 *(60)*, 217 *(5)*, 219 *(19)*, 282 *(22)*, 375–378 *(3)*
What Every Woman Knows (Amihez Minden Asszony Ert) 155 *(29)*
Whatever Happened to Baby Jane? 276 *(526)*
What's My Line 208
Wheeler, Bert 199 *(43)*
The Whispering Shadow 146–147 *(1)*, 147, 242 *(134)*, 281 *(18)*, 326 *(11)*, 327 *(14)*
Whitaker, Alma 232 *(31)*, 350
White, Alice 102 *(51)*
White, Marjorie 85 *(36)*, 88 *(38)*, 90 *(40)*, 91 *(41)*
White, Sam 130 *(80)*
White Heat 81, 90, 91 *(41)*
White Zombie xi, 18, 20, 60, 92 *(42)*, 93–94 *(43)*, 98 *(46)*, 119 *(68)*, 123 *(72)*, 126 *(76)*, 191 *(18)*, 208, 221, 224, 240 *(112, 113, 114, 115, 116, 117, 118)*, 271 *(468)*, 272 *(487)*, 279 *(3)*, 281 *(9, 14)*, 282 *(22)*, 285 *(48)*, 301 *(4)*, 322 *(15)*, 324, 325, 326 *(11)*, 327 *(13, 14, 16)*, 331 *(22)*, 333 *(1, 2)*, 334 *(15, 17)*, 335 *(18)*, 345, 362, 364, 367, 379–80 *(4)*, 383
Whiteman, Paul 82 *(32)*
Whitman, Gayne 95 *(44)*, 215 *(3)*
Whitmore, Hazel 171 *(180)*, 172 *(181)*
Whitney, Helen 115 *(64)*
Wild Company 83, 108, 324
Wilde, Oscar 70 *(11)*
Wilder, Billy 113 *(62)*, 286 *(63)*
Wiley, Jo 35
William, Warren 121 *(71)*, 253
William Morris Agency 25, 45 *(7)*
William Stephens Agency, Inc. 25, 45 *(4)*
Willis, Matt 129 *(80)*, 257
Winchell, Walter 308 *(48)*
Windsor, Marie 279 *(7)*
Winkler, Frank 224 *(67)*
Winters, Shelley 198 *(39)*
Winwood, Estelle 10, 39, 165–166 *(174)*, 231 *(10, 11)*, 262 *(355)*

Wise, Robert 133–134 *(84)*, 271 *(460, 470)*, 279 *(14)*, 284 *(39)*, 308 *(49)*, 326 *(5)*
The Witch (A Boszorkány) 157 *(58)*, 159 *(92)*
Witney, William 149 *(4)*, 284 *(40)*
The Wizard of Oz 84 *(34)*, 133 *(83)*
Wlaschin, Ken 286 *(59)*
The Wolf Man xi, 26, 121–122 *(71)*, 124 *(73)*, 127 *(77)*, 253 *(256, 257, 258)*, 258 *(309)*, 285 *(51)*, 287 *(70)*, 323 *(23)*, 326–328 *(7)*
The Wolf Man: A Cinematic Scrapbook 331 *(21)*
Wolfe, Ian 134 *(85)*
The Woman in the Dolphin (Die Frau im Delphin) 73 *(16)*
The Woman's Friend (A Nök Barátja) 161 *(120)*
Women of All Nations 88–90 *(39)*, **89**
Wood, Brett 279 *(5)*
Wood, Edward D., Jr. x, 33, 34, 37, 46 *(15)*, 142 *(91)*, 142–143 *(92)*, 144–145 *(94)*, 198 *(40, 41)*, 199 *(42)*, 211 *(9)*, 224 *(61, 65, 67, 68)*, 225 *(69, 70, 71, 72, 73, 74, 75)*, 226 *(76, 77, 78, 79)*, 270 *(460)*, 274 *(509)*, 275 *(510, 511, 512, 513, 514, 515, 516, 517, 520, 521)*, 276 *(522, 523, 524, 529)*, 283 *(32)*, 289, 304 *(21)*, 308 *(46, 50)*, 323 *(17, 20, 22)*, 331 *(24, 26, 28)*, 332 *(3, 4)*, 334–335 *(18)*, 350, 352, 355, 366, 383 *(6)*
Woodbridge, A.L. 346
Woodward, O.D. 171 *(180)*
Woolcott, Alexander 102 *(51)*
Wooley, John 286 *(65)*, 354, 358, 367
The World at My Shoulder 279 *(6)*
The World of Abbott and Costello 334 *(4)*
The World of Bela Lugosi xi, 272 *(479, 481, 483, 485)*, 273 *(488, 489, 490)*, 356, 357, 369
World War I 5, 6, 7, 33, 57, 64, 371
World War II 26, 30, 31, 33, 57, 60, 122 *(71)*, 349, 371
World Wide Pictures 96 *(46)*
The Worst! 323 *(20)*, 332 *(3)*, 348
Wray, John 87 *(37)*, 96 *(46)*
Wycherly, Margaret 79–81 *(30)*
Wylie, Philip 96 *(45)*

Yankee Products 365
Yarbrough, Jean 118 *(67)*
The Yellow Colt (A Sárga Csikó) 157 *(66)*
The Yellow Lily (Sárga Liliom) 156 *(47)*, 158 *(74, 76, 79)*
You Asked for It ix, 32, 211 *(8)*, 330 *(13)*, 350
You'll Find Out 117–118 *(66)*, 129 *(78)*, 213 *(12)*, 221 *(37)*, 252 *(245, 246)*, 191 *(17)*, 321 *(1)*, 326 *(4, 5)*, 329 *(9)*, 361
Young, Clara Kimball 147 *(2)*
Young, Loretta 100 *(49)*
Young, Polly Ann 91 *(42)*, 118–119 *(68)*, 145 *(95)*
Young Frankenstein 112 *(60)*

Your Career in Hollywood 279 *(7)*
Yurka, Blanche 132 *(83)*

Zacherley 330 *(10)*, 336
Zanuck, Darryl F. 112 *(61)*
Zombie 93 *(43)*
Zombies on Broadway 134–135 *(85)*, 136 *(86)*, 259 *(320, 321, 322)*, 326 *(5)*, 327 *(15)*
A Zseni see *The Genius*
Zsuzsi see *Susie*
Zucco, George 118 *(67)*, 130–131 *(81)*, 132 *(82)*, 136 *(87)*, 201, 222 *(45)*, 257 *(302)*, 309
Zukor, Adolph 115 *(62)*

www.ingramcontent.com/pod-product-compliance
Ingram Content Group UK Ltd.
Pitfield, Milton Keynes, MK11 3LW, UK
UKHW041921140426
5217IPUK00014B/253